KV-140-182

Trademark Acknowledgements

Wrox has endeavored to provide trademark information about all the companies and products mentioned in this book by the appropriate use of capitals. However, Wrox cannot guarantee the accuracy of this information.

Credits

Authors
Andrew Mumford
Mike Cai
Jon Duckett
Paul Wilton

Technical Reviewers
Ian Blackburn
Ian Blackham
Graham Bowden
Robert Chang
Ellen Davidson
Rembrandt Kuipers
Devin Lunsford
Craig McQueen
Sophie McQueen
Douglas Rothaus
Scott Stabbert
Gary Vartanoff

Technical Editors
Dianne Parker
Robin Smith

Managing Editor
Joanna Mason

Development Editor
Sarah Bowers

Project Manager
Chandima Nethisinghe

Design/Layout
Tom Bartlett
Mark Burdett
Jonathan Jones
John McNulty

Figures
William Fallon
Jonathan Jones

Cover
Chris Morris

Index
Martin Brooks

About the Authors

Andrew Mumford

Andrew Mumford is director of a Web and e-Commerce solutions company, Arkenet, based in France. He is responsible for client liaison and product development, and has plenty of hands-on experience managing the technical implementation and development of Internet solutions for client companies.

Andrew grew up in New Zealand, but was born in England, where he lived for the last three years while contracting for many large London based companies and financial institutions. He now lives in France.

Andrew is experienced in developing solutions using Visual Basic, SQL, COM, and ASP technologies. He has used Visual InterDev extensively to develop web-based products for many clients, developing both Internet and intranet based solutions for commercial use. Andrew has Microsoft Certification as a Professional Site Builder, with Certification in Visual InterDev 6, Visual Basic 6 Desktop and Distributed Applications, FrontPage 98, and Access.

With thanks to Karine, for all the help that made this happen.

Mike Cai

Shuofeng (Mike) Cai has worked in the computing industry for more than six years. He is currently a developer support engineer with Microsoft, which involves helping developers to create their web applications using Visual InterDev and ASP.

Prior to joining Microsoft, Mike worked for an international consulting firm and has worked on various commercial software projects as well as in-house applications.

Mike holds a B.S in Computer & Information Science from the Ohio State University.

Outside of programming, Mike enjoys hiking, traveling, playing guitar and Go (an ancient Chinese board game).

I'd like to thank my parents for their endless guidance, support and inspiration.

Jon Duckett

Having graduated from Brunel University, London, with a degree in Psychology, Jon took a change of direction, coming back to his home town to work for Wrox in their Birmingham (UK) offices.

Paul Wilton

After an initial start as a Visual Basic applications programmer Paul found himself pulled into the net, and has spent the last 18 months helping to create Internet and intranet solutions.

Currently he is developing web based systems, primarily using Visual Studio 6 and SQL Server 7 along with numerous other technologies.

Lots of love to my fiancée Catherine who ensures my sanity chip remains plugged in.

Beginning Web Development with Visual InterDev 6.0

Andrew Mumford

with
Mike Cai
Jon Duckett
Paul Wilton

Wrox Press Ltd. ®

Beginning Web Development with Visual InterDev 6

wrox

Published by Wrox Press Ltd,
Arden House, 1102 Warwick Road, Acocks Green, Birmingham B27 6BH, UK.
Printed in Canada

ISBN 1-861002-9-47

Table of Contents

Chapter 3: Visual InterDev Quick Tour   63

Chapter 4: Managing Style and Site Navigation   89

Chapter 7: Writing Active Server Pages   199

Chapter 8: Design Time Controls   233

Chapter 9: Database Access with ADO   263

Chapter 10: XML in Web Applications   293

Chapter 11: Error Handling and Debugging   339

Chapter 12: Creating Code Components   359

Chapter 13: Deployment and Designing for the Bigger Picture   389

Introduction

The explosive growth of the Internet over the past few years has seen an exciting new industry open up for both experienced and new programmers alike. Web sites have evolved from being just a few tacked-together pages into complete applications that link databases, complex business logic, and purchasing capabilities. This extra sophistication has led to increased complexity in the development process of creating a web application, and in the requirements for what is incorporated into a web site.

Because of this rush to build new features into web pages there have been a number of web authoring and development tools released on the market whose purpose is to make the whole process easier. Many of these tools focus on writing web pages, i.e. making them look good and focusing on the appearance. They also often include capabilities for adding advanced features to the web site, such as drawing the contents of a page from a database, or adding script to make the page respond to what the reader does. Visual InterDev 6.0 is one of these tools, and stands out from the crowd by virtue of its completeness, ease of use, and professional features.

Visual InterDev 6.0 is a complete development environment for developing web applications, and offers a surprisingly easy to use Integrated Design Environment (IDE) to facilitate this. It is not only great for straightforward web page design, but it offers many powerful features that make advanced tasks surprisingly simple to perform. In this book, we will be learning how to use Visual InterDev 6.0 to create fully functional web applications.

What is This Book About?

This book is about learning to use the features that Visual InterDev 6.0 offers to develop web applications that can grow with your requirements. Visual InterDev 6.0 is not a programming language - it is a *development environment* for creating web applications. The focus of Visual InterDev 6.0 is on ease of use, powerful features, and integrating database and programming capabilities into your web site. This, then, is what we will be learning about in this book.

In the course of learning to use Visual InterDev 6.0, we will learn how to:

❑ Design web pages and content using its 'What You See Is What You Get' (WYSIWYG) editor.

❑ Use themes and layouts to promote a common appearance and structure to our web applications.

❑ Quickly build navigation toolbars into our web applications to navigate from page to page.

❑ Incorporate data from databases into the web applications, to provide content that is easily updated.

❑ Receive feedback and responses from users and handle it within the web applications.

❑ Make web pages that react to the actions performed by the user.

❑ Make web pages that are dynamically created based on what a user requests, by building the contents of the page every time the page is requested.

❑ Write external programs in Visual Basic to expand the functionality and performance of our web applications.

As we go along, we will learn about and use the major new technologies associated with web development, from DHTML to XML, COM, ASP and ADO.

What isn't This Book About?

This book is primarily focused at creating web applications, using the tools that Visual InterDev 6.0 provides. There are many tools and features available, of which the most flexible are scripting languages such as VBScript and JavaScript. This book will teach you the basics of using these two languages, but will not cover them to an advanced level, and will not cover other scripting languages or methods such as CGI, Perl, and so on.

We will also look at the basics of including database access in the course of the book, using both Microsoft SQL Server 7.0 and Microsoft Access 2000. Once again, we will cover enough information to make use of these products in a web application, but for advanced features of these tools you will need to refer to other resources.

Who is This Book For?

This book is for anyone who wishes to learn how to develop professional, dynamic web applications using Visual InterDev 6.0. The book assumes no previous knowledge of the subjects covered – a reader who is familiar with Windows packages should be able to learn all they need from this book. If you do have some experience in programming, a working knowledge of HTML, or have worked with databases before, but want to now develop your Visual InterDev 6.0 skills, then this book is also for you.

What Knowledge is Assumed?

This book assumes that you have the following:

❑ A working knowledge of the Windows environment.

❑ A basic knowledge of programming would be advantageous, but is not necessary.

❑ A basic knowledge of database concepts and the use of either Microsoft Access of SQL Server would also be of advantage, but again is not necessary.

What Software is Needed?

In order to use this book and perform the examples contained within it, you will need the following software:

❑   Visual InterDev 6.0, Professional or Enterprise Edition, or Visual Studio 6.0 Professional or Enterprise Edition.

❑   Microsoft SQL Server 7.0 (or SQL Server 6.5 which comes with Visual Studio 6.0) or Microsoft Access 2000.

❑   Windows 98 or Windows NT 4.0 or higher.

❑   Microsoft Internet Explorer 4.0 or higher.

❑   Netscape Navigator 4.0 or higher.

❑   NT4 Option Pack (Microsoft Transaction Server and Internet Information Server).

❑   Visual Basic 6.0 would also be useful.

How is This Book Organized?

This book is broken down into the following chapters:

Chapter 1 – Basics of Web Design

This chapter introduces you to Visual InterDev 6.0 and web design in general. Exercises in creating HTML pages teach you the basics of creating simple web pages.

Chapter 2 – Installation of Visual InterDev

This chapter covers installing and configuring Visual InterDev 6.0 and related software on your computer.

Chapter 3 – Visual InterDev - Quick Tour

This is a whirlwind tour through many of the features of Visual InterDev 6.0, designed to introduce you to the Integrated Development Environment and also to build the first few pages of our example site, Wrox Cameras, a web site for promoting cameras online.

Chapter 4 – Managing Style and Site Navigation

This chapter expands on the initial site developed in Chapter 3, and shows you how to easily add navigation features to your site using Visual InterDev 6.0's built in controls. It also covers using themes, layouts and Cascading Style Sheets to quickly add professional graphics and structure to your site.

Chapter 5 – Database Basics

This chapter introduces you to using databases, and how to link them to your web pages. It details building a simple database in either SQL Server or Access, and then uses that database to provide information for the products pages in the Wrox Cameras site.

Chapter 6 – Client Side Scripting

This chapter covers basic VBScript, JavaScript, and DHTML and how to integrate them into your web pages to create web pages that will react to users' interactions.

Chapter 7 – Writing Active Server Pages

Here we cover writing script that is processed on the web server in order to dynamically create a web page that shows information specific to each user. We learn how to receive responses from our users, and how to process them using server side VBScript.

Chapter 8 – Design Time Controls

This chapter covers many of the Design Time Controls (DTCs) that come with Visual InterDev 6.0. DTCs are special controls that you can add to a web page to achieve many different purposes, including representing database information and creating special forms for data entry.

Chapter 9 – Database Access with ADO

This chapter expands on the server side script concepts of Chapter 7, and the database basics of Chapter 5, to show you how to write pages that talk directly to a database using ActiveX Data Objects (ADO). This is an efficient way of using a database that offers very specific control of how information is presented in the finished web page.

Chapter 10 - XML in Web Applications

This chapter shows you how to use XML, an exciting new mark up technology that allows you to exchange data between any platforms, whether the data be a web page, database content, or data in web applications.

Chapter 11 – Error Handling and Debugging

No matter how good your programming, the chances are that a bug will happen at some stage. This chapter talks about how to detect and resolve any bugs that occur in your web applications, using Visual InterDev 6.0's in-built debugging tools.

Chapter 12 – Creating Code Components

This chapter introduces the Component Object Model (COM), and shows how you can create reusable components using Visual Basic or other languages to provide specialized services for your web pages. It also introduces Microsoft Transaction Server (MTS), and uses it to make these components have a minimal effect on your web server's performance.

Chapter 13 –Deployment and Designing for the Bigger Picture

As well as showing how to deploy a web application after development, this chapter offers useful hints and tips for creating a web application that performs well, scales to meet the demands of many users, and is easily maintained. It also covers using Visual SourceSafe to work in teams and how to use the Visual Component Manager.

Chapter 14 – Case Study: Intranet Help Desk

This chapter uses many of the concepts introduced throughout the book to create a Help Desk solution, giving options for logging, monitoring and analyzing support calls.

Appendices

This book also contains seven appendices, which provide useful references to the following areas:

- ❏ A Visual InterDev 6.0 menu reference, which covers the options available in all of its menus
- ❏ The IE5 Object Model
- ❏ The ASP Object Model
- ❏ A comprehensive HTML reference and HTTP error codes
- ❏ A VBScript reference
- ❏ A JScript reference
- ❏ A list of useful resources, many of which are mentioned throughout the book

How to Get the Most Out of This Book

This book is intended to teach you web development in a very hands-on style. Throughout this book we will be developing a web site for a fictitious enterprise - Wrox Cameras, a shop that sells cameras and wants to expand using the Internet. As we learn a new concept or tool, we apply it to this site. This means that the best way to follow the examples is to do them one after the other. This is the way that the book is intended to be used, and following it through in order will give the best insight into how to use Visual InterDev 6.0 to design a complete web application.

Where To Find The Code

We provide the source code and associated files for all the code examples in this book for download from the Wrox web site, together with the SQL and Access databases used in the examples. All the code for the book is contained in one zip file. When you extract the code on your machine, the zip file will create a folder for each chapter containing the relevant code.

To download the code navigate to http://www.wrox.com and click on the Download link on the menu bar at the top of the page. This will take you to a page where you should select Beginning Web Development with Visual InterDev 6.0 from the dropdown list available, and click the Download Source Code button. You can then select to download from our US or our UK site.

The code samples are completely free; you just need to register on the Wrox site. If you have already registered, you will be prompted for your password, otherwise you will be asked to register during the download process – we've tried to make registration as quick and simple as possible.

Conventions

We have used a number of different styles of text and layout in the book to help differentiate between each kind of information. Here are examples of the styles we use and an explanation of what they mean:

Advice, hints, and background information comes indented and italicized, like this.

Important information comes in boxes like this.

Bullets are also indented, and appear with a little box marking each new bullet point, like this:

❏

Important Words are in a bold type font.

Words that appear on the screen, for example in menus like File or Window are in a similar font to the one that you see on screen.

Keys that you press on the keyboard, like *Ctrl* and *Return*, are in italics.

Code has several fonts. If it's a word that we're talking about in the text, for example when discussing the `For...Next` loop, it's in a fixed width font. If it's a block of code that you can type in as a program and run, then it's also in a gray box:

```
Set oCars = CreateObject("WCCCars.Cars")
Set recCars = oCars.GetAll(RegistryRestore("Showroom", "Not Set"))
```

Sometimes you'll see code in a mixture of styles, like this:

```
If IsMissing(ConnectionString) Then
    varConn = RegistryRestore("Showroom", "Not Set")
Else
    varConn = ConnectionString
End If
```

The code with a white background is code we've already looked at and that we don't wish to examine further.

Sometimes you will see an underscore character at the end of a line of code:

```
Window.Alert("An unforseen error has occurred in this application. Error number:" _
            & Err.Number & "Details: " & Err.Description)
```

This indicates that the line was too long for the width of the book and has been continued on the next line. When typing in this code, ignore the underscore, line break and indentation - just type the whole line as one continuous line of code.

Try it Out

How it Works

The chapters in this book are sprinkled with mini-exercises called *Try It Outs*. Each one states an objective and then follows that, where appropriate, with the answer in code and a screen shot. Often, immediately following it is a *How It Works* section that dissects the code line-by line and explains the syntax, choice of techniques, purpose of variables, etc.

These formats are designed to make sure that you know what it is you're looking at. We hope they make life easier.

Tell Us What You Think

We've worked hard on this book to make it useful. We've tried to understand what you're willing to exchange your hard-earned money for, and we've tried to make the book live up to your expectations.

Please let us know what you think about this book. Tell us what we did wrong, and what we did right. This isn't just marketing flannel; we really do huddle around the e-mail to find out what you think. If you don't believe it, then send us a note. We'll answer, and we'll take whatever you say on board for future editions. The easiest way is to use e-mail:

feedback@wrox.com

You can also find more details about Wrox Press on our web site. There, you'll find the code for all of our books, sneak previews of forthcoming titles, and information about the authors and editors. You can order Wrox titles directly from the site, or find out the location of your nearest local bookstore which stocks Wrox titles.

Customer Support

If you find a mistake, please have a look at the errata page for this book on our web site first. If you can't find an answer there, tell us about the problem and we'll do everything we can to answer promptly! Just send us an e-mail (with the title and ISBN of the book, and the page number you're referring to) to:

support@wrox.com

Basics of Web Design

The aim of this book is to teach you how to develop web applications, using Visual InterDev 6 and other tools and technologies. However, before we can launch in to designing a web site with Visual InterDev 6, there are a number of basic concepts that we need to get to grips with. Designing web sites involves many different aspects and steps. For example, you'll need to create the pages that make up a web site, get accustomed to the tools involved, and learn how to develop the code for any programming that may be required.

This chapter will lead you through all that you need to know *before* getting started, so that when you do get going on your first web site you'll already be comfortable with the terminology, ideas and methods behind creating a really successful web site. If you have done any programming or web development before, you may already be familiar with some of the topics covered in this introductory chapter, but other parts may be new to you.

In this chapter we'll look at:

❑ What exactly are web applications and web sites

❑ What web browsers and web servers are, and how they communicate

❑ Basic web pages - introduction to HTML and other markup languages

❑ Introduction to object oriented programming, and scripting languages

❑ What Visual InterDev 6 offers us for web development

Okay, let's get started by finding out the answer to the first question on our list.

What is a Web Application?

A **web application** is a group of files residing on a **web server**. The application's user interface consists of documents, referred to as **web pages**, which are displayed inside a **web browser** (such as Internet Explorer or Netscape Navigator). These web pages are plain text documents containing information indicating how the page should be formatted and displayed. The page may also contain **code** to be executed by the web browser or the web server.

A **web site** is a collection of linked web pages on a web server - there is usually some structure to a web site. For example, there could be a start page with a short introduction, links to other sections on the web site, and maybe even a search facility. The idea is that the web site is easily navigable for your visitors.

The browser gets the web pages from the web server. The web server is a computer that not only stores the pages, but also possibly runs code or does database look-ups, and uses the results to alter pages stored in memory before they are sent to the browser. We'll look at what makes up a web page in more detail soon. First let's take a closer look at web servers and browsers and how they communicate.

All of you reading this should be familiar and comfortable with the concept of a **stand alone application**. Let's take a nice simple example like Windows Notepad. We know where its code is stored – on the *user's computer's hard drive*. We know how to start the application – we just *select its icon* from the Start | Programs | Accessories menu. When we run Notepad we know where the code is being processed – on the *user's computer*. And which resources, such as memory, are being used – the *user's computer's*.

What about a web application? Let's consider an example, say for a books web site. OK, you've opened up your web browser - Internet Explorer 5 perhaps. Now you type the **address** of the website, hit *Return*, and you're looking at the main page. Clearly some processing has been done on your computer, by the browser. We know that the browser sits on your hard drive, but obviously the web pages are stored elsewhere – so, where? And how do they get to you?

Web Page Access

When you type in the web site's address, the browser communicates this request to the server computer that **hosts** the web site. Your computer, the **client** computer, remains idle until the information requested, such as a web page or a file, is passed back by the server computer. On receiving the request, the server computer takes over the processing of the task, and goes away and does a search for the information that you requested.

A web site address is often referred to as a **URL**, which stands for Uniform Resource Locator, and is basically a pathname to the file containing the default page in the web site. Other pages within the site also have a URL. You could in fact access them directly by typing in the relevant URL – however, usually you would use the web site's *navigation* to move from page to page.

OK, before I go on I had better explain the terms 'client' and 'server', which might be new to you. In simple terms the client computer is the computer making the request for information, and the server computer is the one that deals with requests for information, then sends this information back to the client computer. When dealing with web applications, the client computer will be the web site visitor's computer, running a web browser. The user makes requests for information by typing in web site addresses, or clicking on buttons or **hyperlinks** inside web pages. Hyperlinks are text or images which, when clicked by the user, cause the browser to go to another page defined in the link itself.

Any actions, processing or information storage on the client machine is referred to as *client side*. When referring to the server we mean the computer hosting a web server service, such as Microsoft's Internet Information Server. Any actions, processing or information storage on the server machine is referred to as *server side*.

Going back to our books site example, we saw that the server machine processes the request from the client, and then sends the requested information back to the client machine, which displays it, usually in a browser.

Server Side and Client Side Processing

If all that has been requested is a simple page with nothing except text and images, then all that the server does is find the files, package them up and send them to the client for displaying. But what happens when the user wants to do something more involved, such as searching for all of the books by a particular author published between two dates?

Well, first the client machine browses to the book search page. On the search page will most likely be a **form** containing fields into which the user can type their search criteria. When the user is ready, they hit a Go button and submit the search information to the server. However, it's possible to embed some code into the page that checks the validity of the information about to be searched on. Clearly, some of the web application's processing is being done client side. But why not let the information be sent, and then check it when it gets to the server?

Web servers are busy computers. They have to serve up web pages to thousands, maybe hundreds of thousands, of client machines, all demanding information at the same time. Normally, the more we can do to avoid stressing out the server machine the better.

Assuming that information on the search form is valid and that the request has been received by the server computer, what happens next? Well, first the server computer must process the information it's been sent, then do a search, probably of a database, process the results and form them into something readable by the client machine's browser. When it's done all this, the results are packaged and sent back to the browser as a web page, which is displayed by the client computer.

We can see that a lot of processing has gone on at the server side before the results are sent back and displayed by the client machine's browser. We can say that the processing involved in searching for a book title has been shared, or *distributed*, between the client and the server computers. This is another significant difference between a stand alone application, like Notepad, and our web application. With a web application we have some power to decide where processing takes place. We could have done no form checking on the client computer and left it all down to the server to check, hence the processing burden would be shifted to the server. But is this a good idea? Well it's another consideration that must be taken into account when developing applications for the Web, and we'll see more on this later in the book.

We have talked a lot about the client and server computers communicating with each other, the client passing requests for web pages, information or files, and the server going away and getting the information together and passing it back to the client. But how do they communicate? Is this a permanent link between client and server?

Server-Client Communication

Well, they communicate over a network using a **network protocol**. The computers might be connected via cables and network cards or it can be via a modem and phone lines. Web pages and requests are packaged in a common format so that both the client and server computers know what to expect and how to unpack it. This common format, or protocol, is called **HyperText Transfer Protocol** (**HTTP**). However, although we refer to the client and server computers as being connected, this is not totally true. Although they do temporarily make a connection with each other, they usually close the connection once they have finished that particular request. Each time the client computer makes a request to the server it's as if they have never communicated before, and neither has any prior knowledge of the other. So why is this important to us as web developers?

Firstly, when developing web pages and web components we must think in terms of a series of independent relationships – the client computer makes a request, the server answers that request, and then all is forgotten. Once finished, all resources used in the request must be freed up for future use - this is much more important for the server computer than for the client. Secondly, every time we make a request, such as searching for a book title, we must submit all of the information again, as the server computer won't remember our last request. This is why web applications are referred to as being **stateless** - they never hold a particular state, but have all the information destroyed once processing is finished.

The following diagram summarizes the overall process of how a user gets to see a web page.

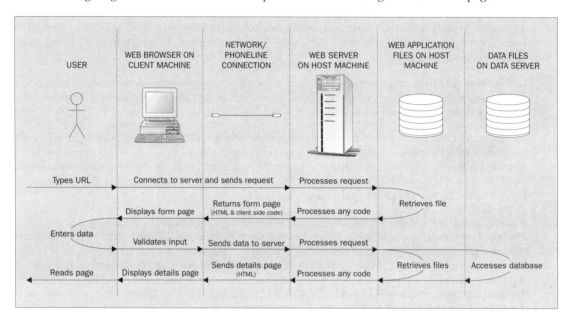

Browser Compatibility

Web applications are designed to be viewed in programs capable of displaying web pages, which we term browsers. Unfortunately, browsers are not all created equal. There are different creators of browsers, such as Microsoft and Netscape, and their products are different in the way that they operate and react to web pages and any code that they contain. To compound matters, each browser family, such as Microsoft's Internet Explorer, has different versions and sub versions, which again all have slightly (or sometimes more than slightly) different features, ways of displaying web pages, and level of code support. So, while Internet Explorer 4 might allow code to change a page's background color after the page has been loaded, just try that on Internet Explorer 3, which will look blankly at you and display lots of error messages. If all of this was not bad enough, the same browser and version may act differently depending on which operating system it's running on. It's therefore very important to make sure, at all phases of development, that your application will work with all of the browsers that you expect your web site visitors to be using. This issue of **browser compatibility** will crop up throughout the book.

Markup Languages

The World Wide Web is made up of millions of pages of information. The "information super highway", as it is called, is all about making sense of those pages, and that's where markup languages come in.

There are three main markup languages, **SGML**, **HTML** and **XML**. The term markup is a carry over from the old days of publishing when editors used to write markup instructions on text submitted by an author. These markups would tell typesetters how to make the printed document look, e.g. "italicize this word, underline this one, start a new paragraph here". Essentially, that is what XML and HTML do today.

Standardized Generalized Markup Language (SGML)

SGML is a complex markup language that has been used as a basis from which to create other markup languages. The most famous language written in SGML is HTML, which is widely used on the Web. HTML is known as an **application** of SGML. The problem with SGML is that it is very complicated, and HTML and XML are simplified versions of SGML, retaining some of SGML's functionality, yet designed for use on the Web.

Back in 1986, Standardized Generalized Markup Language became an international standard (ISO 8879) for defining markup languages, long before the Web was even thought of (although SGML had been in existence since the late 1960's). Its purpose was to describe markup languages, by allowing the author to provide formal definitions for each of the elements and attributes in the language, thus allowing authors to create their own markup "tags" that relate to their content.

As a language, SGML is very powerful, but with its power came complexity, and many of the features are rarely used. It is very difficult to interpret an SGML document without the definition of the markup language, kept in a **Document Type Definition** (DTD). The DTD is where all the rules for the language are kept - after all, you cannot make up your own markup language without specifying how it should be used. The DTD has to be sent with, or included in, the SGML document so that the custom-created tags can be understood.

Hypertext Markup Language (HTML)

Being far simpler, and a fraction of the size of SGML, HTML is very easy to learn, a factor which quickly made it popular and widely adopted by all sorts of people. HTML is a cut back version of SGML that is used to format content for the World Wide Web. We've just said that markup languages contain **tags** that tell your browser how to make the page look. HTML is used in the Web because it is lighter than SGML, which contains lots of tags that are not needed in a web environment.

HTML was created by Tim Berners-Lee in 1991 as a way of marking up technical papers so that they could easily be organized and transferred across *different platforms* for the scientific community. The idea was to create a set of tags that could be transferred between computers so that others could render the document in a useful format. For example:

```
<H1> This is a primary heading</H1>
<H2>This is a secondary heading</H2>
<PRE>This is text whose formatting should be preserved</PRE>
<P>The text between these two tags is a paragraph</P>
```

Back then, the scientific community had little concern over the appearance of their documents. What mattered to them was that the meaning was preserved. They weren't worried about the color of their fonts or the exact size of their primary heading!

However, as HTML usage exploded and web browsers started to become readily available, lots of non-scientific users soon started to create their own pages. These non-scientific users became increasingly concerned with the presentation of their material. Manufacturers of browsers used to view web sites were all too ready to offer different tags that would allow the web page authors to display their documents with more creativity than just using ASCII text. Netscape were the first, adding the familiar <FONT> tag, which allowed users to change the fonts themselves, as well as their size and weighting. This triggered a rapid expansion in the number of tags that browsers would support.

With the new tags came new problems. Different browsers' implementations of the new tags were inconsistent. Today we have sites that display signs saying that they are Best Viewed Through Netscape Navigator or Designed For Internet Explorer, and we expect to be able to produce web pages that resemble documents created on the most sophisticated Desk Top Publishing systems.

Extensible Markup Language (XML)

While the widespread adoption of HTML propelled the rise in numbers of people on the Web, users wanted to do an ever-increasing variety of new and more complex things, and weaknesses with HTML became apparent. Two problems in particular are that HTML is fixed and that it tells the browser nothing about the information, only how to display it.

For most documents to be useful in a business situation, there is a need to know about the document's content. If a document does contain details about its own contents, then it is possible to perform generalized processing and retrieval upon that file. This means that it is no longer just suitable for one purpose - in HTML's case the language is only used for display on the Web. So, marking up data in a way that tells us about its content, in other words making it **self-describing**, means that the data can be re-used in different situations. While SGML made this possible, it is now also possible with XML, which is far simpler and rapidly gaining in popularity.

The major players in the browser market made it clear that they had no intention of fully supporting SGML and its complexity prevented many people from learning it. So, moves were made to create a simplified version for use on the Web, signaling a return to documents being marked up according to their content. These moves have resulted in XML being created, which retains some of the simplicity and ease of use of HTML, but which enables you to define your own tags, and to add tags describing the content and what it means. Essentially it is a lean alternative to SGML and is far more accessible, its specification running to around a fifth of the size of the specification that defined SGML.

XML got the name *Extensible* Markup Language because it is not a fixed format like HTML. While HTML has a fixed set of tags that the author can use, XML users can create their own tags (or use those created by others if applicable) so that the tags actually describe the content of the element.

Although we mostly concentrate on HTML in this book, Chapter 10 covers XML and how you can use it to create high-level, cutting-edge applications.

Basic Web Pages

The actual file that your browser downloads when you request a page does not look anything like what you see as the end result. Underneath it all is HTML, basically just plain text surrounded by the special formatting markups (tags) that we have just discussed, in a file. This file normally resides on the server that your browser is talking to. The file is downloaded to your browser, which reads it, interprets what it's read and then renders it on your screen. The act of reading and interpreting a file is referred to as **parsing** it.

HTML Introduction

So what exactly do these HTML files contain? Let's take the following extremely basic web page as an example:

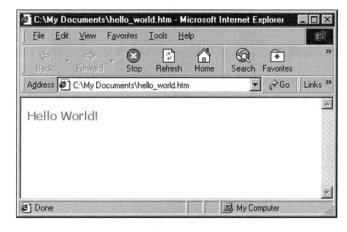

I'm hearing all those groans of "not another Hello World!" but aside from that, we see the browser displaying bold gray text saying Hello World!.

In actual fact, what the browser sees underneath that, in the file `hello_world.htm`, is quite different. Here are the contents of `hello_world.htm`:

```
<HTML>
<B><FONT COLOR="gray" FACE="Tahoma">Hello World!</FONT></B>
</HTML>
```

This is an example of HTML. Looking at it you can see how HTML consists of **tags** – markups surrounded by angle brackets (< >). In the above example we have the following tags:

`<HTML>`	specifies that this is HTML.
`<B>`	sets the text to bold.
`<FONT>`	specifies the font style, in this case `Tahoma`.

Each of the above tags has a matching closing tag, denoted by a /, so we have in fact the following *pairs* of tags, each surrounding the text that they are meant to format:

```
<HTML> </HTML>
<B> </B>
<FONT> </FONT>
```

The `<FONT>` tag also contains further instructions called **attributes** detailing the color and font face, and in the middle of it all we have the actual wording, "`Hello World!`". The text takes its formatting from the collection of tags around it. This is basically the way HTML works, it just has a lot more tags to it!

In most cases a tag, such as `<P>` for paragraph, has a closing tag as mentioned above, e.g. `</P>`. There are quite a few exceptions to this rule, in other words tags which stand alone, such as `<BR>` for a carriage return, and `<IMG SRC="filename">` for placing an image on the page. There are also codes for certain special characters. These begin with an ampersand (&). Examples of these are:

` `	adds a space.
`&gt;`	adds a greater than (>) character.
`&lt;`	adds a less than (<) character.

Enough of the theory, let's see how to create a very basic web page and view it in your browser.

Try it Out –Basic HTML Web Page to Display Data

In order to create a web page, you need to create a file that contains the text and formatting tags to present your document. Whenever a client's web browser requests a page, your web server will send this file. The client's web browser then has the task of presenting it. We are now going to create this file, but because it is a simple HTML file we will be able to view it in our browser without the need for a web server.

1. Open up Notepad, which we will use to create the file. Type into it the following text:

```
<HTML>

<HEAD>
<TITLE>Jo Bloggs Resume</TITLE>
</HEAD>

<BODY>

<H1><FONT COLOR="Blue"><B>Resume for Jo Bloggs</B></FONT></H1>
<H3>Personal Information</H3>
<TABLE BORDER="0" WIDTH="100%">
  <TR>
    <TD WIDTH="40%">Date of Birth</TD>
    <TD WIDTH="60%">28/03/1974</TD>
  </TR>
  <TR>
    <TD WIDTH="40%">Place of Birth</TD>
    <TD WIDTH="60%">London, UK</TD>
  </TR>
  <TR>
    <TD WIDTH="40%">Drivers License</TD>
    <TD WIDTH="60%">Current</TD>
  </TR>
  <TR>
    <TD WIDTH="40%">Email</TD>
    <TD WIDTH="60%">jobloggs@bloggsemail.co.uk</TD>
  </TR>
  <TR>
```

```
    <TD WIDTH="40%"> </TD>
    <TD WIDTH="60%"> </TD>
  </TR>
  <TR>
    <TD WIDTH="40%"><B>Qualifications</B></TD>
    <TD WIDTH="60%"> </TD>
  </TR>
  <TR>
    <TD WIDTH="40%">Bachelor of Computer Science</TD>
    <TD WIDTH="60%">Cambridge, 1998</TD>
  </TR>
</TABLE>

<H3>Work Experience</H3>
<P><B>June 1997 - Aug 1997</B></P>
<P>Work placement at ABC Net Developments Ltd, where I was responsible for developing
a Web Site using Visual InterDev 6</P>

</BODY>

</HTML>
```

2. Save the file as `jo_bloggs_resume.htm` somewhere on your hard drive (the **My Documents** folder is as good a place as any). You will see that, when saved with an `.htm` extension, the icon for the file changes from the normal Notepad icon to an Internet Explorer icon:

jo_bloggs_resu me.htm

3. Double click on this file in Windows Explorer and it should open your web browser and display a page looking something like this:

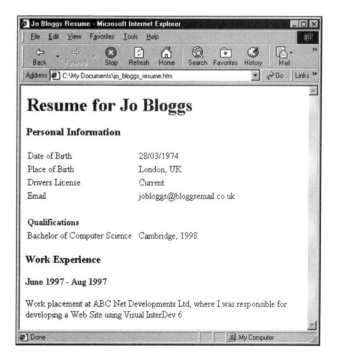

How it Works – Basic HTML Web Page to Display Data

What can we see from this, apart from the fact that our friend Jo Bloggs needs to seriously get to work on his resume?

One thing of importance that this example shows is that to position items precisely, we use a **table**. The table tag, <TABLE>, along with its rows <TR> and columns <TD>, is often used in HTML to control the position of the items on a page. In our example, we used the following HTML as part of our table definition:

```
<TABLE BORDER="0" WIDTH="100%">
  <TR>
    <TD WIDTH="40%">Date of Birth</TD>
    <TD WIDTH="60%">28/03/1974</TD>
  </TR>
```

❑ The first line states that the table will have a border that is of width 0, meaning that the user cannot see it. Numbers such as 1 and higher *will* be visible and progressively thicker.

❑ Also in the first line we see that the WIDTH attribute of the table is set to 100%, meaning that it will take up the full width of the client's browser.

❑ The <TR> tag starts a row.

❑ The <TD> tags are for each column – the first one is set to 40% of the width of the table, the second is set to 60%.

❑ Within the <TD> tags are the text items, Date of Birth and 28/03/1974.

❑ The table is closed further on in the code with </TABLE>.

You will also notice two other tags, <H1> and <H3>. These tags represent Header Level 1 and Header Level 3. Not surprisingly, there are other tags available such as <H2> for Header Level 2, and the <P> that we have already discussed for normal paragraph text. These tags provide information that the browser uses to decide how to display the content.

Try it Out – Basic HTML Web Page With Response to User Action

Let's take a look at a slightly more detailed piece of HTML. This one contains a button that when clicked on, opens up a message box that says, once again, "Hello World!".

1. Open up a new page in Notepad and type in the following:

```
<HTML>

<HEAD>
<TITLE>Hello World</TITLE>
</HEAD>

<BODY>
```

```
<P>
<B><FONT FACE="tahoma" COLOR="gray">Yet another Hello World sample</FONT></B>
</P>
Click here for a surprise result:
<INPUT TYPE="button" VALUE="Click Me" onclick="alert('Hello World!');">

</BODY>

</HTML>
```

2. Save the file as `helloworldagain.htm`.

If we look at this in the browser (by double clicking on the file in Explorer), we see the following screen:

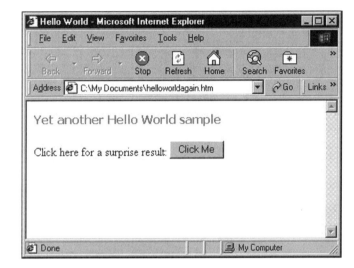

And the surprise result is:

How it Works – Basic HTML Web Page with Response to User Action

So, let's pull this masterpiece of design apart and see what makes it tick. The first part of the HTML specifies the title of the document, **Hello World**, which as you can see in the screenshot is displayed in the title bar of the browser.

Within the `<BODY>` tags we find the majority of the text that makes up the page. We started with some red text similar to our first example, then another line containing the text Click here for a surprise result: . This is the next line:

```
<INPUT TYPE="button" VALUE="Click Me" onclick="alert('Hello World!');">
```

This line does some interesting things – not all of it is just HTML:

❑   First off, the INPUT TYPE="button" is the tag for drawing a button on the screen.

❑   The VALUE attribute wrote the words Click Me in the button.

❑   The onclick="alert('Hello World');" is a bit of JavaScript that makes the message appear when the user clicks on the button. This is an example of code that runs on the client's browser, in other words when you look at this page in your browser and click on the button, it is your browser that has to decide what to do with this bit of code.

Finally, we ended the <BODY> and <HTML> tags by using matching closing tags of </BODY> and </HTML>, to finish off the document.

This example showed more of how an HTML document is formatted, and also showed you a small snippet of JavaScript, which will be used frequently in this book and covered in detail in Chapter 6. JavaScript and VBScript are scripting languages that enable you to make HTML interactive, among other things. These are not actually parts of the HTML language - they are ways of coding a page to do things beyond simple formatting, in a similar way to writing code in a more traditional environment such as Visual Basic.

HTML contains many additional tags that enable the browser to render text into pages containing formatted text, images, sound, video, and tables of information. Throughout this book you will see examples of HTML pages that contain tags in addition to those found here. On these occasions, I will explain the concepts behind the code that is displayed. There is also an extensive HTML reference in Appendix D and a list of further useful resources in Appendix G.

Forms and Controls

HTML also supports some of the standard controls, such as buttons, text input boxes and list boxes that you would find in a Windows program. These are usually embedded inside an HTML form. An HTML form is a tag defining a group of controls, which allow the user to enter information. The form can be sent (posted) to the web server, and the information within its controls is accessed and processed. We'll come across more controls as we progress through the book, but let's take a look at a simple example.

Try it Out – Creating an HTML Form

This form allows you to enter your name and select which country you are from. I realize that this is not the most useful of pages, but it's a good grounding for later chapters where you'll learn how to develop more complex examples, and how to manipulate the information sent to the server. This form does not send the information to the server as would normally be the case, but simply shows a message box telling you what you just entered, (as if you didn't know that already)!

1. Open up Notepad, which we will use to create the file. Type into it the following text:

```
<HTML>
<BODY>
<H3>Enter your details</H3>
<FORM NAME="frmUserDetails">
  <INPUT TYPE="text" NAME=txtName><BR>
  <SELECT NAME=selCountry SIZE=1>
    <OPTION VALUE=USA>United States</OPTION>
    <OPTION VALUE=Can>Canada</OPTION>
    <OPTION VALUE=UK>United Kingdom</OPTION>
    <OPTION VALUE=Aus>Australia</OPTION>
    <OPTION VALUE=Ger>Germany</OPTION>
    <OPTION VALUE=Fra>France</OPTION>
    <OPTION VALUE=Spa>Spain</OPTION>
    <OPTION VALUE=Rus>Russia</OPTION>
  </SELECT><BR>
  <INPUT TYPE="submit" VALUE="Submit" NAME=sub1
        onclick="alert('Hello ' + txtName.value + ' from ' + selCountry.value)">
</FORM>
</BODY>
</HTML>
```

2. Save the file as `form.htm` in a convenient directory on your hard drive.

3. Double click on this file in Windows Explorer, it should open your web browser and display a page for you to enter your details into, something like this:

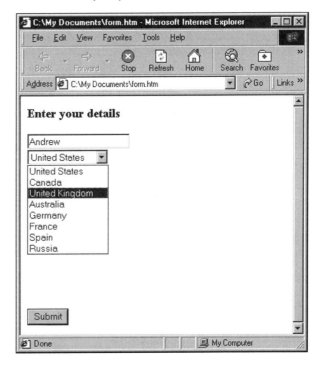

4. Click the button and you should see a message box similar to:

How it Works – Creating an HTML Form

The first three tags defining the document type, where the body starts, and a heading, should be fairly familiar now:

```
<HTML>
<BODY>
<H3>Enter your details</H3>
```

The next tag, `<FORM>`, is new to us and defines the start of a collection of controls which make up the HTML form. If this form were to be posted to the server, then the contents of the textbox and the select control, also known as a drop down list, would be sent. The end of the form is marked by the use of the form's closing tag, `</FORM>`.

In the line `<INPUT TYPE="text" NAME=txtName>` we define a text input box control. We give it a name so that we can manipulate it in code and can access its information when it's sent server side. Whatever the user enters into the textbox will be sent, along with its name, to the server. The `<BR>` tag tells the browser to start another line.

We define the start of our select box using `<SELECT NAME=selCountry SIZE=1>`. Again we give it a name so that we can access it – the `SIZE` determines how many lines it displays. If `SIZE` is set to one, it acts like a drop down listbox. If we set `SIZE` to two or more then it will look like a listbox but will no longer drop down. The drop down option is good for saving space.

Although the `<SELECT>` tag defines the start of a select control, it does not determine what is in the list – that is determined by the `<OPTION>` tags.

For example, in the first `<OPTION>` tag, the value property actually determines what information is sent to the server when the form is posted. Although we have a number of `<OPTION>` tags, only the value of the tag that the user selected will be sent to the server. The others are inaccessible once the form is posted.

What is actually displayed to the user in the drop down list is whatever text is between the end of the option start tag (`<OPTION>`) and the beginning of the option end tag (`</OPTION>`). In our case, `United States` is displayed.

The remainder of the option tags follow the same principles – you can have as few or as many option tags as you want, so if your country is not listed then feel free to add it.

Finally, we indicate the end of the `<SELECT>` tag by using its closing tag: `</SELECT>`.

In the next line we have a submit button:

```
<INPUT TYPE="submit" VALUE="Submit" NAME=sub1
        onclick="alert('Hello ' + txtName.value + ' from ' + selCountry.value)">
```

The submit button would normally cause the information in the form's controls to be sent to a page on the server. We have not defined a page for it to be posted to so that won't happen here – you'll see how to submit forms in a later chapter. `TYPE="submit"` determines that this is a submit control. `VALUE="Submit"` decides what is shown on the button.

As we did in the "Hello World" example, some JavaScript code has been defined to fire whenever the user clicks the submit button:

```
onclick="alert('Hello ' + txtName.value + ' from ' + selCountry.value)"
```

This causes a message box to be displayed, which shows the value entered in our text input box (`txtName.value`) and the value of the item that the user has selected in the `selCountry` select drop down list.

Finally, we need to tell the browser where our form ends. It's possible to have more than one form on a page, each with its own submit button and page to which it posts. The `</FORM>` tag sets the form's end. We also need to end the `<BODY>` tag and the document using `</BODY>` and `</HTML>`.

Don't panic if you still feel unsure of how you actually use forms, as we'll be looking much more fully at this in a later chapter.

In closing our small review of HTML, I'd like to mention that HTML is, like the Web itself, evolving. The standard changes, and with each new version of browsers that are introduced, more features are added to the language and capabilities of the browsers themselves. The sad thing about this is that older browsers, and in fact different browsers such as Netscape Navigator or Microsoft Internet Explorer, are not always compatible with all of the features that a page includes. This is perhaps the biggest headache facing web developers today, since it means that if they use the latest features in their web applications, they can cut out people using older browsers that do not support the enhancements. There are means and ways around this, and we will discuss a few in later chapters.

Object Oriented Programming

Object oriented programming (OOP) is a slightly scarier way of saying "programming using objects". But what are these objects that we will be programming with? Where are they, and how and why would we want to program with them?

Well, think of what is meant by an object in the 'real world' outside of computing. The world is composed of things, or **objects**, such as tables, chairs and cars (to name just a few!!!). In the real world we manipulate objects such as a car. For example, if I want to make the car start I must find a **method** of doing so. In the case of a `Car` object I would use its `StartCar` method to make it start. In response to me turning the ignition key an **event** occurs, the electronics come on, the engine fires and the car is ready to move off. A car also has **properties** associated with it. For example, the bodywork has a certain color and the car has a speed property, which changes depending on what methods we use to act on the car. If we hit the accelerator then the speed property increases, but if we hit the brakes it decreases.

In OOP the idea is to model real world situations by defining objects, giving them methods, properties and events.

We've already defined our car as an object. We have said that our Car object has a StartCar method. It would have lots of other methods such as BeepHorn, ChangeGear and so on. But, taking the change gear method as an example, we can see that we need to tell the Car object which gear we want. How can we do that using a method? Well, when we use our ChangeGear method we can also pass information along with the method, in this case the gear required, which the Car object uses to decide which gear we want. We refer in OOP to information passed to methods as **parameters**. We might have a whole load of information or parameters that we want to pass or, as in the CarStart method, no parameters at all. We'll see later in the book that methods can also pass information back.

Our Car object, as mentioned, will also have a number of properties, such as its color, current speed, current gear selected, to name just a few. Sometimes in OOP we refer to the particular values of an object's properties as a whole as its current state. For example, our Car object may be red (color property), moving at 55mph (speed property) and be in fourth gear (gear property). A property can be changed directly, by telling it to be a certain value, or it may change as a result of us using methods. For example the StartCar method used with the ChangeGear method would make the Car object's speed property change. However you'll find that some properties can't be changed, for example, the Car object's bodyshape property (well not unless you hit a brick wall with the speed property set at 100mph!!!).

We often want our objects to tell us that something important is happening. Events are an object's way of catching our attention and informing us of something, such as a change of speed. For example, going downhill will cause our Car object's speed property to increase. It would be nice if the car fired off a notification (event) of this change so that we could react accordingly, such as using the ApplyBrakes method.

Okay, so this OOP stuff is all very well and good, but why do we need to know about it and how does it help us as web developers?

Well, browsers such as Internet Explorer (IE) and Netscape Navigator (NN) let you to add code inside your web page allowing you to change your web page, interact with the user and access databases, and many other things. The languages available in those browsers are referred to as **scripting languages**. The two most common scripting languages are JavaScript and VBScript. JavaScript is available in both Internet Explorer and Netscape Navigator. The "Hello World" page you saw above contained an example of JavaScript, admittedly very simple JavaScript, in action. In addition Internet Explorer also includes VBScript, which can be used as an alternative to JavaScript. We'll learn more about these scripting languages and how to use them later in the book.

However, the important thing is that both these scripting languages are object based, that is they both rely on the manipulation of objects to perform useful tasks. Both Internet Explorer and Netscape Navigator make a large number of objects available to the scripting languages, to enable you to manipulate the web page and interact with the user. Just like our car example, these objects reflect the real world as it relates to a browser. So for example, there's a Screen object. This will give you information about the screen resolution of the machine that the browser is running on. Unfortunately, although IE and NN have a similar set of objects there are differences – the screen object being one of them. The Screen object only works with IE4 and above.

Try it Out – Using the Screen Object

Let's take a quick look at a simple example of accessing the width property of the browser's Screen object. Note that this example will only work under IE4 and above. (You can freely download this browser from www.microsoft.com and many other sources.)

1. Open up Notepad and type in the following text:

```
<HTML>
<BODY>
<INPUT TYPE="button" VALUE="Show Width" NAME=button1
    onclick="alert('Screen width is ' + Screen.width + ' pixels');">
</BODY>
</HTML>
```

2. Save the file as screen_test.htm somewhere on your hard drive (again, the My Documents folder is a good place).

3. Double click on this file in Windows Explorer, it should open your web browser and display a page looking something like this:

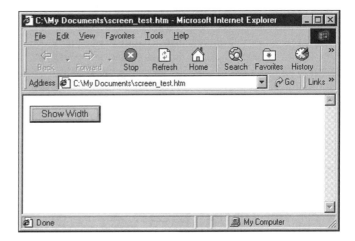

4. Click the Show Width button and you'll see the following dialog pop up (the width value will change depending on what your screen settings are under Windows):

You can try changing your computer's screen resolution using the Window's Control Panel and see how this affects the page.

How it Works – Using Objects in a Browser

This example works very much like our previous "Hello World" example, except here our JavaScript inside the `onclick` event uses the `Screen` object's width property to find out how many pixels across the computer's screen there is, and then displays this in a message box.

As before, the `<HTML>` tag tells the browser what sort of document it's dealing with, here a document defined using Hyper Text Markup Language.

Then in the next line we define our button:

```
<INPUT TYPE="button" VALUE="Show Width" NAME=button1
       onclick="alert('Screen width is ' + Screen.width + ' pixels');">
```

❑ `TYPE=button` defines what we want to create.

❑ `VALUE="Show Width"` displays "**Show Width**" on the button.

❑ `NAME=button1` gives our button a name so that we can reference it in our code.

Now for where the action is at:

```
onclick="alert('Screen width is ' + screen.width + ' pixels');"
```

We are saying here that when the button is clicked we want to fire the code (JavaScript) `alert('Screen width is ' + screen.width + ' pixels');`.

We saw this before but here, instead of displaying a message "Hello World", we are obtaining the width of the screen by using the `Screen` object's width property, and then displaying that. The results are wrapped up in a nice sentence telling the user what the magic number represented by `screen.width` means. JavaScript is clever enough to know that in this context the + sign means "join all the words and the information given to us by the `Screen` object's width property into a nice text sentence that we can display".

The `Screen` object is built into the browser so we don't need to create it ourselves. However, it is possible to create your own objects. You'll learn all about the browser's built in objects and how to create your own as you progress through the book.

What is Visual InterDev 6 and Why Use it for Web Development?

Visual InterDev 6 is, curiously, the successor to Visual InterDev 1 – but the product is definitely worth the missing 4 releases! (From now on, whenever we refer to Visual InterDev we'll be talking about Version 6, unless stated otherwise.) It offers tools to create, edit, and manage your web pages. It has features that assist you in writing code, linking to databases, and managing how users navigate your site. With these and other features comes the main strength of Visual InterDev – it moves the developer away from focusing on creating web pages and instead into designing solutions. This then is what we shall be using it for, to design a web solution. The solution I have in mind is a fictional camera shop, Wrox Cameras, which wants to set up business on the Web. Throughout this book, we will be developing this 'real-life' solution and seeing how Visual InterDev can be used to do it.

Visual InterDev is Microsoft's premier web application development tool. There are a lot of web design tools out there, and indeed you could design your web site using just Windows Notepad. Before you rush back to the shop to return your copy of Visual InterDev, let's look at some of the excellent features that it has to make your life as a web application developer that much easier.

First off, you have probably noticed that I keep referring to Visual InterDev as a *web application tool* rather than a web page creator, this is because Visual InterDev goes much further than simply creating a web page – it's a sophisticated development tool to create whole web sites. To tell the truth, Visual InterDev's page composition tools are not the best and are unlikely to be the key attraction for many web designers. So, what are Visual InterDev's main benefits? We'll be looking at all of these in more detail later in the book.

- ❑ It has a number of design time tools which make tasks such as creating HTML forms and linking pages together very easy, and possible with little or no code.

- ❑ Visual InterDev is an integrated tool that works closely with the operating system and Microsoft's web server software. It enables you to easily debug code in server and client side pages, and root out difficult bugs.

- ❑ If you have any components installed on your machine, written in Visual Basic, C++ or Java, then Visual InterDev makes it easy to insert them into your web pages and write code that interacts with them. Components are just pre-written chunks of code to carry out specific tasks. We'll be using and creating components later in the book. Visual InterDev will even help you out by giving you a list of properties and methods associated with each component.

- ❑ Visual InterDev has been very much written with programmers in mind and includes syntax highlighting, code completion and easy scripting of HTML events. Syntax highlighting means that keywords in script or HTML are color coded. Code completion gives you a list of properties and methods associated with any code that you type.

- ❑ To help you with your web design and site consistency, Visual InterDev includes a number of pre-defined themes and templates that you can use if you so desire. A site layout view lets you look at a bird's eye view of pages in your website and how they link together. If you want to see what your pages will actually look like in a browser, then with Visual InterDev this means simply clicking to another view.

- ❑ If you're working in a team on a particular web application, then you'll find a combination of Visual InterDev and Visual SourceSafe will allow you to work together without the risk of someone overwriting another person's changes, and allows you to see who's working on which page.

- ❑ Visual InterDev has tools to ease integration of database applications, such as Microsoft Access and SQL Server, into your web application.

A web application is a *complete* solution for a business or activity. With Visual InterDev and the various technologies it supports, a web application can be as complex and involved as any of the traditional client-server applications that you might have worked on before.

Summary

We have seen in this chapter that a web application can be much more than just the sum of its pages! We discovered what makes up a web application, and discussed the difference between processing that takes place on the server and that which takes place on the client computer. We also saw that communication between client and server machines is stateless, when in the context of web servers and client browsers.

We went on to look at the three most important markup languages for web development, including HTML, which is currently very commonly used, and XML, whose use is rapidly increasing. In essence we found that markup languages have been around for a long time, providing ways of defining a document's properties, how it's displayed, and what information it contains. HTML and XML have brought markup languages into the limelight with the growth of the Internet.

We took a look at how to create some basic web pages, what HTML forms and controls are, and how we might use them to pass information from client computer to server computer.

You were also introduced to object oriented programming (OOP) and it's central idea – that of having objects with methods, properties and events. We saw how using scripting language enables us to manipulate things in our web pages, and found out information using built-in browser objects such as the Screen object.

Finally, we looked at what Visual InterDev is and how it can help you as a web developer.

In the next chapter we'll go through the installation all of the necessary software required, both to work through the examples in this book, and to enable you to develop your own web applications.

Installing Visual InterDev

Gone are the days when the only thing that you needed to create a web site was your trusty old Notepad. It is still possible to do everything by hand, but the face of the Web has grown, and the tools to develop it have matched pace. Today, web professionals need a solution that enables them to not only develop web pages, but to also manage complete sites, and integrate them tightly into their development process and backend databases. This is obviously a task that requires a fairly comprehensive piece of software, and that is where Visual InterDev 6 enters the fray.

In the previous chapter we discussed what a web application is, and introduced the role played by web browsers and servers. We briefly saw why Visual InterDev is an ideal tool for developing web applications. But before we can get stuck in to using it ourselves, we need to install some software. In this chapter we'll go through the installation of all of the necessary software, which will include:

- ❑ Visual InterDev
- ❑ Visual Basic
- ❑ Help files
- ❑ Web server components, such as Personal Web Server, ADO database components, SQL Server, and the FrontPage 98 Extensions

Installing Visual InterDev

Well, we've talked about it enough so far - now it's time to break open your Visual Studio CDs and install Visual InterDev. I'm installing using Visual Studio Enterprise Edition, but the options should be very similar if you're using the Professional version of Visual Studio or Professional Visual InterDev. The installation of Visual InterDev should be identical for all versions of Windows; here I'm installing on NT 4 Workstation. If you find that your screens are not exactly identical to the screenshots shown, don't worry – the installation routines do vary very slightly. Here I'm using the latest version as of September 1999.

1.   Close down all currently open applications, then insert the first Visual Studio disk. When you insert Visual Studio disk one you should find that it automatically starts the set up routine. If not, run `setup.exe` on disk one, then click Next:

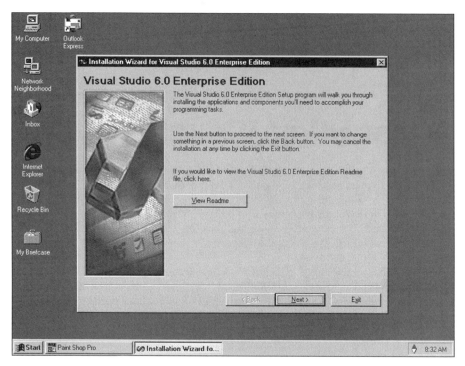

2.   Read the license agreement, then select the I accept the agreement radio button and click Next:

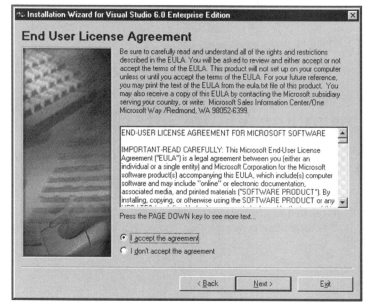

3. The next screen requires you to enter the CD key, which you'll find on the CD case, and your name and company. Click Next when you're ready:

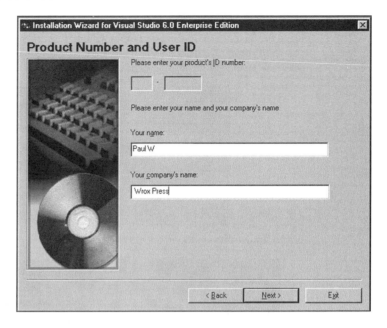

4. The next screen you'll see asks if you want to install an updated Java Virtual Machine. If you want to install Visual InterDev then you *must* check the Update checkbox and click Next. (You may not get this screen if you have previously updated your Java Virtual Machine or if you're using Windows 98, as it will already be installed.)

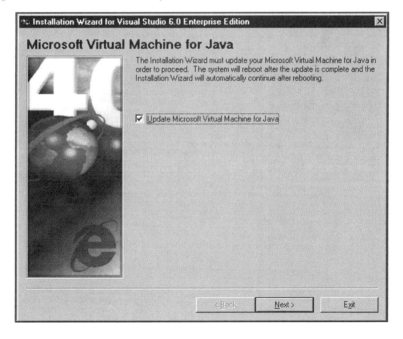

5. If all goes well then the next message will be the one shown below - click OK. Make sure you leave the Visual Studio disk one in the CD drive, as installation of Visual InterDev will continue automatically once the machine has re-booted. (If it doesn't then run `setup.exe` on disk one, using Run from the Windows Start menu.)

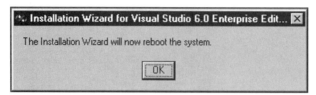

6. Once your computer has restarted you should see the Visual Studio setup dialog box appear. The easiest way to install Visual InterDev is to select the Products option. If you're an experienced user you may find the extra available customization under the Custom option useful. I have chosen the Products option as I like an easy life! Click Next when you're ready:

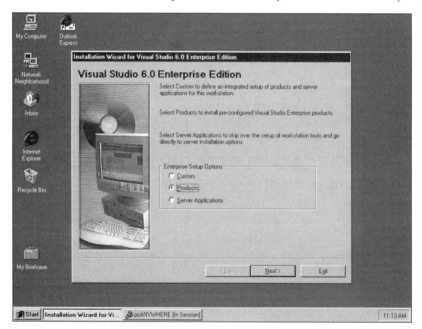

7. The next screen gives you the choice of where you want Visual Studio's common or shared files to go on your hard drive. The default setting is fine unless you're very short of hard drive space. Click Next to continue:

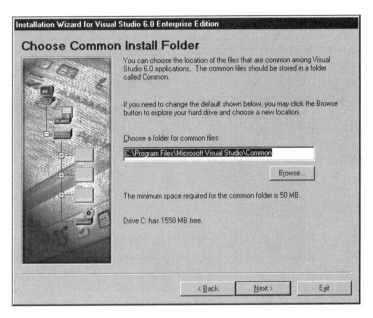

8. In the next screen you get to choose which products you want to install, check as a minimum Visual InterDev and Visual Basic, which we use later in the book, and any others you require, then click Next. (It is possible to come back later and install the other components.)

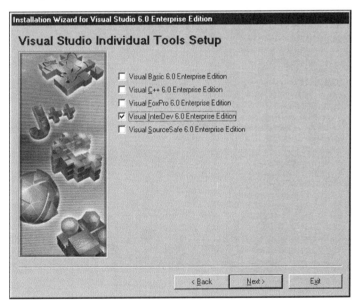

9. At the next screen click Continue:

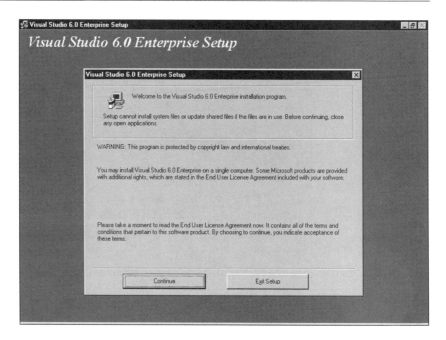

10. Make a note of your Product ID displayed on the next screen, although if you forget you can get this number from the Help | About menu in Visual InterDev once it's installed.

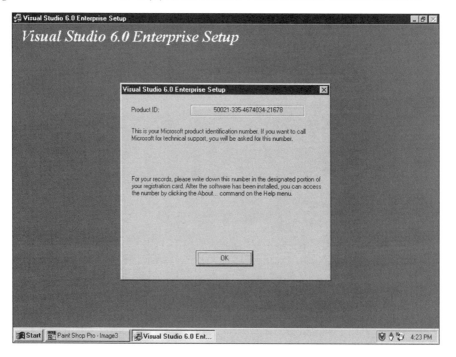

11. In the next screen you can customize which components are installed. The typical installation options for the products you chose a couple of screen ago are checked automatically.

The typical options are usually correct for most users and certainly are for us. Component installation defaults to your C *drive - you can change that to another drive and path from here for most of the components, although some can only go in the Windows* System32 *directory. If at a later date you want to install new components or remove some of the ones you selected, you can easily do so from the Windows Control Panel's* **Add/Remove programs** *option.*

Investigate the options to see if there's anything you think might be handy. One possibly useful addition is the range of extended web themes available. You can add these by selecting Visual InterDev in the list box, then clicking the Change Option button, clicking Themes and then checking the Extended Themes box.

12. Click Continue when you're ready:

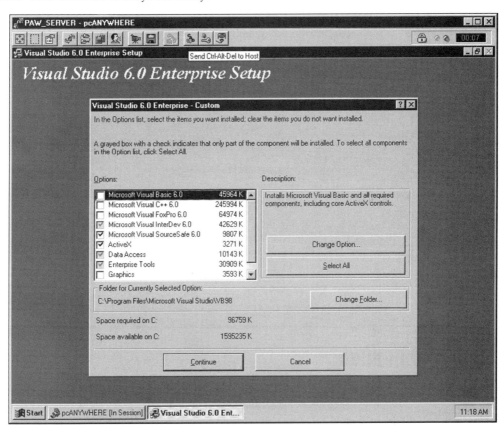

13. The next dialog box asks if you want to upgrade to the latest version of Visual SourceSafe's database format. Visual SourceSafe comes with Visual Studio and is Microsoft's team working tool, enabling team members to work on the same project without the risk of destroying each other's work. This will be discussed later in the book. Unless you or someone else in your team use Visual Studio 97, then I suggest you go for the latest file format and click the Yes button:

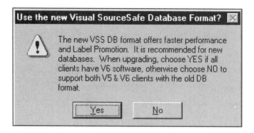

14. OK, it's time to make coffee, chomp a doughnut or two and wait while Visual Studio's installer does its stuff. When it's finished, you need to restart your computer - click the Restart Windows button to do so. Make sure that you leave the installation CD-ROM in the drive as, once your computer has rebooted, the installation will continue. (Again, if it fails to do so, run `setup.exe` on disk one.)

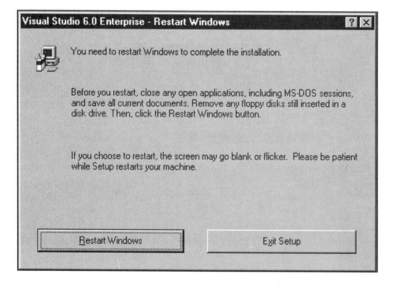

Installing Help Files

OK, the installation of Visual InterDev itself is complete, but there's still more to install if we want to make the best use of it. Next, the set-up wizard asks us if we want to install MSDN, which acts as the help for Visual InterDev and is a tremendous source of information regarding almost everything about developing with Microsoft technologies. Without the MSDN files, the help for Visual InterDev is extremely limited.

1. You need to insert the first CD of the two MSDN CDs that come with Visual Studio, then click Next. If you decide not to install MSDN, then click Exit and skip the next few pages of this book, until you get to the *Installing Server Components* section.

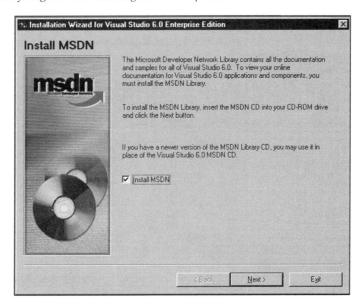

2. At the next screen, once you have studied every legal nuance of the license agreement, click Continue:

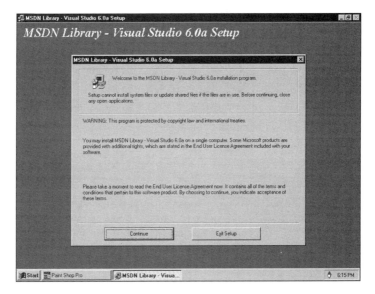

3. At the next screen note your MSDN Product ID then click OK:

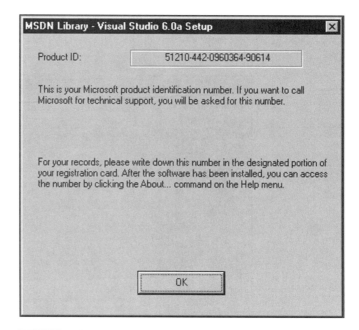

4. Will these license agreements never end?! Click I Agree if you want to continue:

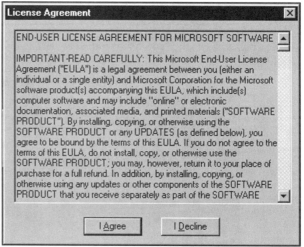

5. Your selection at the next screen depends much on which Visual Studio products you will be using and how much hard drive space you have. If you use a range of Microsoft technologies and are short of hard drive space then click the Typical button as this only takes up 60MB on your hard drive. This gives you access to most of the information on the MSDN CDs, but you will have to have the CD in the drive whenever you want to use it.

If you have acres of hard drive space then go for the Full install, though you may find some of the information irrelevent and confusing. It takes a fair chunk of hard drive, currently about 800MB, but you'll have access to all of the information on the CDs and won't need to always have the CD in the drive. It also means that access to the help files, when you hit *F1*, will be much faster.

If you only use a couple of the Microsoft products, for example Visual InterDev and Visual Basic, then go for Custom and just choose information for the products you use.

I chose the Custom *option from the following screen. The sort of things you'll find useful are the* Full Text Search Index, *and the* Visual InterDev Documentation. *The* Platform SDK *also comes in useful as it has information on web related stuff. I've also included the* VB Documentation *because I use Visual Basic. We'll be using Visual Basic later in the book so you also might want to include this.*

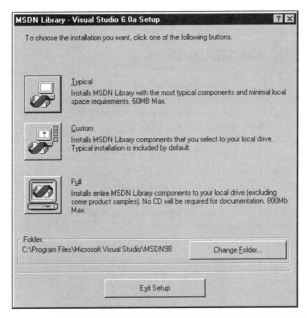

6. Click Continue when you're ready and the MSDN will start installing. Again, it's time to open a fresh pack of doughnuts, or if you went for the full install then you've plenty of time to order in pizza.

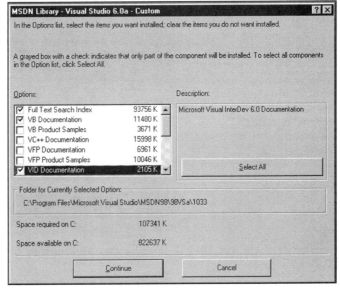

41

7. Finally, when the MSDN install is complete you'll be rewarded with a "completed successfully" dialog box:

Installing Server Components

Well, the installation of Visual InterDev and its help files is complete. You could exit the installation wizard now as all of the Visual InterDev components are installed. However, to really make use of all the great features that Visual InterDev provides to make web application development easier, you need to have access to an Internet Information Server (IIS) web server with FrontPage 98 Extensions installed, and preferably a database such as Microsoft SQL Server. If on your network you already have such a machine set up then you can use that - you have all you need to start using Visual InterDev and to follow the examples in this book. You can exit the wizard, though you may find having the server components on your client machine very useful for initial development prior to deploying to a full NT server machine.

If you don't currently have access to an Internet Information Service (IIS) web server then you will find that Visual Studio comes with developer versions of IIS and FrontPage Server Extensions that we will install shortly.

Before we come to install the server components, the installation wizard offers the option to install InstallShield. Although a good program, it's not so useful if you're just doing web development as it's designed to create setup programs for non web based standalone deployment. If you do decide to install it, you'll find after installation that you'll be returned to this dialog. You should click Next to continue.

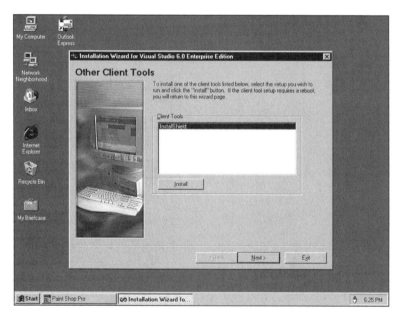

Before we install the server components let's look at what they are and how they help you as a web developer.

Windows NT Option Pack 4

Also known as Personal Web Server (PWS) on Windows 9x and Windows NT Workstation, this is the web services component. Installing this enables your machine to process requests for web pages, and allows you to emulate the sort of system that web applications will be installed on when you're ready to go live. The Windows NT version also includes a mail service and a file transfer service (FTP).

Using the World Wide Web server component in the Option Pack you, and any computers on the same network as yours, will be able to browse to your web sites. Without access to a web server it's impossible to properly test pages containing code that executes on a server, such as Active Server Pages (ASP), which we will be making great use of later in the book.

FrontPage Server Extensions

These need to be installed to enable Visual InterDev projects to be created. They allow a much closer integration between Visual InterDev and the web server you are developing with, and simplify things for you. For example, if you move a web file from one directory to another, then all pages linking to that file will have their links updated automatically.

FrontPage Server Extensions on Windows NT Workstation and MS Office 2000

Once the installation of the server components is complete there is a little gotcha that it's important to be aware of. If you install MS Office 2000 onto your development machine later, Office 2000 updates the FrontPage98 Server Extensions but, unfortunately, can also disable them in the process. This only applies to Windows NT Workstation machines – you should be OK if you're running Windows 9x.

The solution is fairly easy. From the Windows Start menu you need to select Programs | Administrative tools (Common) | Server Extensions Administrator. You should see the screen below:

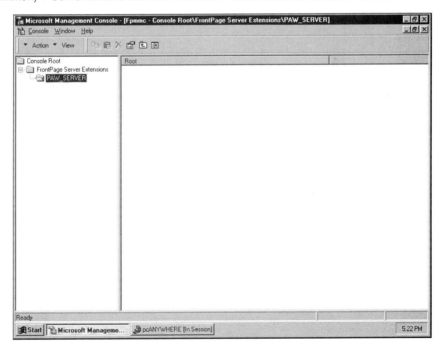

Under the Console Root should be the name of your machine, but nothing else. Right click your machine name and choose New | Web. The Server Extensions Configuration wizard should appear:

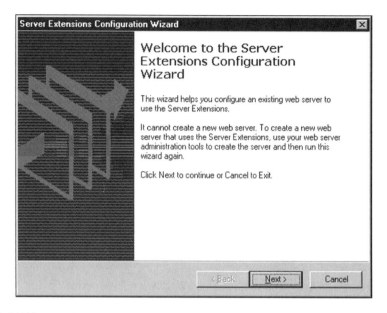

After this you need to just click OK/Next at all the screens and accept the default settings. When asked if you want to install a mail server, choose No, as we don't need it for this book.

Microsoft Data Access Components 2.0

Often shortened to MDAC, this consists of a number of components that enable your web application to link to data sources, such as SQL Server databases. You'll see later in this book how to link your web pages to a database.

At this point we temporarily need to split off depending on which operating system you're using. The installation of the server components differs from Windows 9x to Windows NT 4.0 and 2000.

Installing the Visual Studio Server Components on Windows NT and Windows 2000

The install of the server components for Windows NT and 2000 is much more integrated and is combined under the product name Microsoft BackOffice. BackOffice is a Microsoft marketing term for a number of separate products, such as NT Option Pack and SQL Server database. These have in common their purpose as server side services and applications, providing the functionality needed in web based applications, such as a web server, a mail server, a database and so on.

On the next page there are three items but we are only installing the first, BackOffice, and once that's done our Visual InterDev installation is complete.

1. Put the second Visual Studio CD into your drive, select Launch BackOffice Installation Wizard from the list, and then click the Install button:

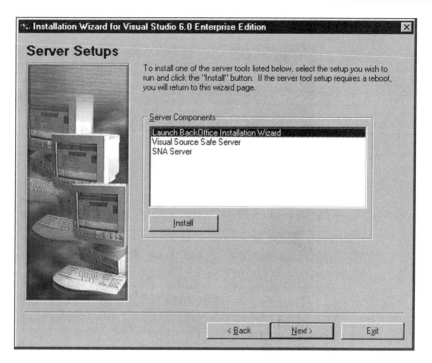

At the next screen we get to choose which combination of BackOffice applications we want to install. As we're using Visual InterDev, we'll select the Visual InterDev Developer option.

If you're an advanced user or have particular needs, and lots of hard drive space, then the full or custom installs might be more suitable. However, for this book, and for most of your needs, the best choice is the Visual InterDev Developer option.

In addition to the components we mentioned earlier we will also be installing SQL Server, SQL Server Debugger and the Remote Machine Debugger. Before we move on let's quickly look at what's about to be installed. These are:

SQL Server 6.5
This is Microsoft's enterprise level database. Whilst databases like Microsoft Access are fine for standalone computer use, for sophisticated web based applications, which must handle many simultaneous user requests, then a powerful database is required. SQL Server integrates well with the Windows Operating System and with the web services provided by Option Pack 4.

SQL Server Debugging
This enables you to execute database code and step through it line by line, making it a whole lot easier to stamp on any pesky bugs that might occur.

Remote Machine Debugging
This installs the components necessary for debugging any code executing in pages on a remote server machine. You'll find this particularly useful once you have deployed your web application, then find that it no longer works on the computer that it's been deployed to.

Well that's enough talking, let's continue with our installation of BackOffice.

2. Make sure that you have selected the Visual InterDev Developer option then click **Next** to continue:

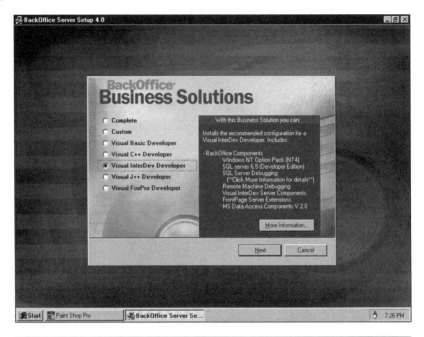

3. The next screen just confirms which parts of BackOffice will be installed, click **Next** to continue:

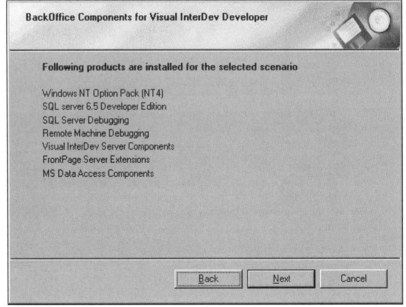

4. Again, the next screen confirms, in slightly more detail, what we will be installing. If you want to ensure that you have sufficient disk space, click the Customize/Check Space button, otherwise just click Next to continue. As I know I have enough space I have just clicked Next:

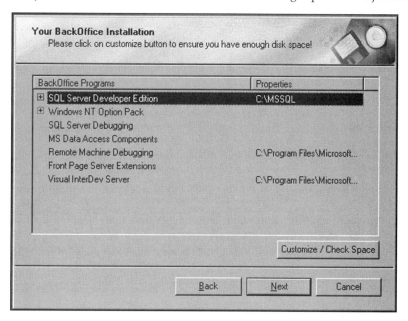

5. You're given one last chance to check that the correct components will be installed. If you need to, click Back to change your preferences, else click Next and installation will start:

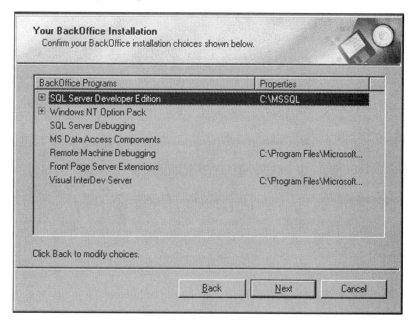

6. Congratulations! Hopefully all has gone well and you should be looking at the screen below:

7. You must reboot before we can continue with the set up, so click Finish and then Yes:

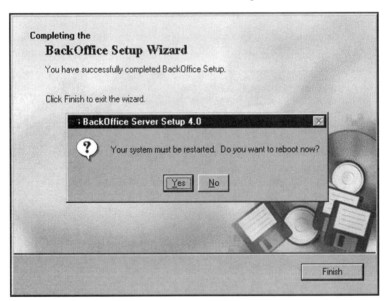

8. That completes the installation of Visual InterDev and its associated components. Click Next to continue and optionally register Visual Studio. If you don't want to register over the Internet then just click Finish and send in your registration card to entitle you to support from Microsoft.

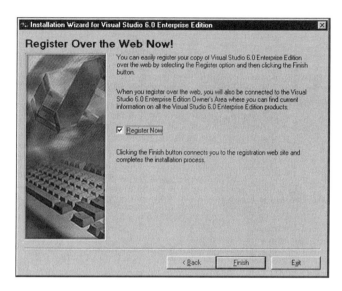

Installing the Visual Studio Server Components on Windows 9x

The first thing we need to install is the NT Option Pack (for Windows 9x). This will install Personal Web Server (PWS) which is a cut down version of a fully fledged web server like NT 4.0 Server. It's great for doing development but it's not a secure, high performance web server for real world situations and it simply won't cope with a large number of people trying to access web pages.

1. You'll need to put Visual Studio disk two in your CD drive, then select NT Option Pack (for Windows 9x) in the list and click Install:

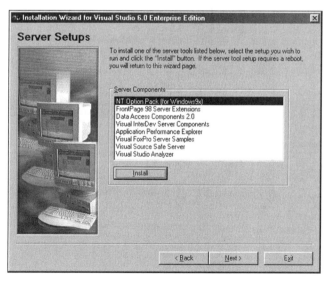

2. At the following screen click Next:

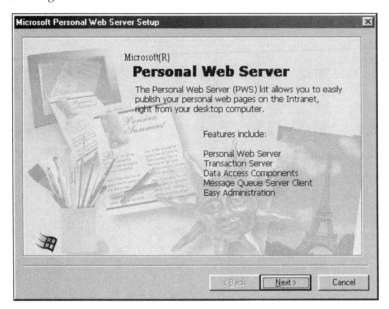

3. To continue click Accept:

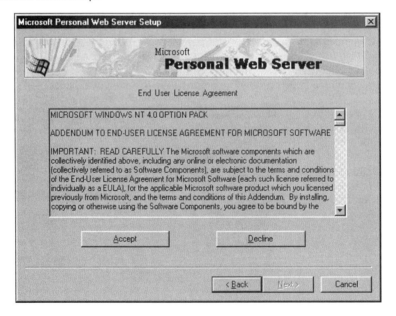

4. To install the components that you'll generally need for web development click the **Typical** button. If you're short of drive space, **Minimum** will give you enough to develop with but some useful components will be missing, as will the documentation. The **Custom** option is for fine-tuning your install when you have special purposes in mind and if you are an advanced user.

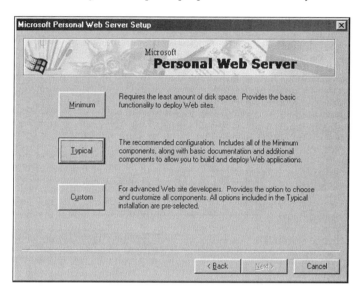

5. Personal Web Server requires a directory to act as the default directory for web files. When you publish web projects it will usually be to new sub directories under this default directory.

You can install to any drive or directory but the default option is the best choice. Click **Next** to continue:

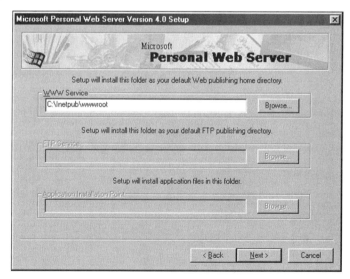

6. It'll take a few
minutes, plenty of
time for some
exercise to burn
off the doughnuts
you ate earlier, but
when it's ready
you should see the
next screen. Click
Finish to continue:

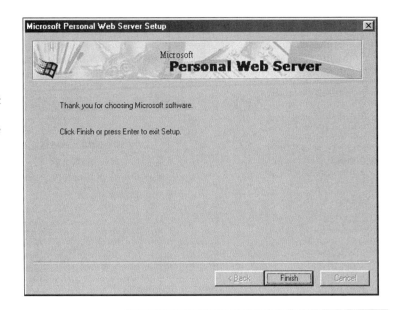

7. Yet another re-start, click Yes to restart and continue the installation.
Once your computer is re-booted,
it'll return to the installation wizard
screen, as long as you leave the
Visual Studio CD in the drive.

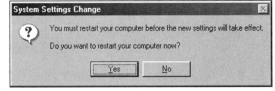

8. Next on our install
shopping list is
the FrontPage 98
Server
Extensions. Select
them from the list
then click Install:

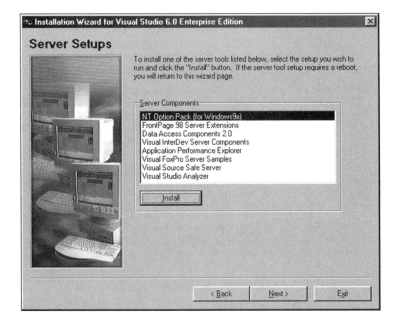

9. Click Next at the Welcome dialog box:

10. You may find the next dialog box a little surprising, after all, when did you previously install FrontPage Server Extensions and if you did why are we doing it again? Well, when we installed Personal Web Server it also installed FrontPage Server Extensions, however what we are doing here is updating them to FrontPage *98* Server Extensions.

Click Next to continue and install the FrontPage Server Extensions:

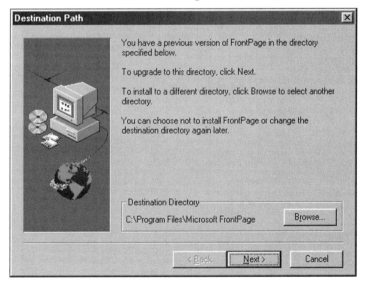

11. Click Finish at the next dialog box to resume our installation wizard:

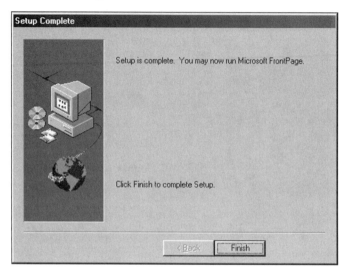

You should find yourself back at the Visual Studio installation wizard screen. Our next task is to install the Data Access Components 2.0. These components enable us to access various data sources, such as OLE DB and ADO, from our web pages.

12. Select Data Access Components 2.0 from the menu and click the Install button.

13. At the yet another license agreement screen click Yes if you want to continue:

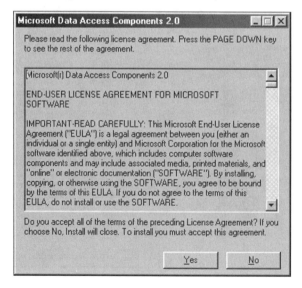

14. At the next screen click Continue:

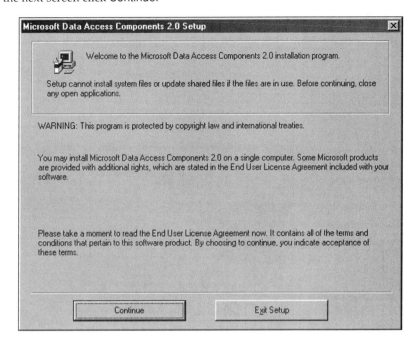

15. We will be using most of the components in this book so, unless your disk space is very limited, go for a Complete installation:

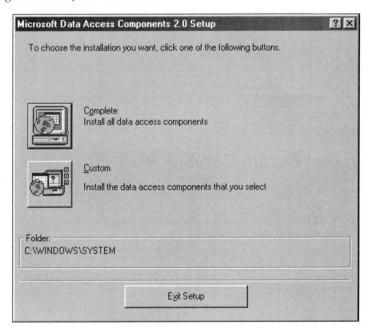

16. Once the components have been installed you should see the screen opposite. Click OK and it'll return you to the Visual Studio installation screen.

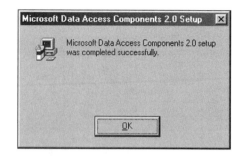

17. That completes the installation of Visual InterDev and its associated components. Click Next to continue and optionally register Visual Studio. If you don't want to register over the Internet then just click Finish:

18. It's worth doing one more reboot of your system just to ensure that all the components register successfully.

Installing Visual Studio Service Pack 3

Microsoft has released three updates, also known as Service Packs, to Visual Studio, which add new features and fix any issues and bugs found with the initial release of Visual Studio 6. In particular they address problems with Internet Explorer 5, released after Visual Studio, and Visual Studio 6 itself. The latest Service Pack is version 3, this includes all the updates of services packs one and two so there is no need to install them first.

There are two parts to updating Visual Studio: first you must install the Service Pack for the ADO database access components, then we can install the Service Pack for the Visual InterDev and Visual Basic programs.

You can obtain Service Pack 3 from a number of places. A copy may have been included with your copy of Visual Studio when you bought it. Or you can often obtain it from the free CDs on the front of computer magazines. Also, if you subscribe to Microsoft's TechNet or MSDN Universal subscription services then you'll get a copy sent to you. Failing that, you can download it from the Microsoft website, though be warned - it's a very big download.

Let's start by installing the ADO Service Pack.

Installing MS ADO Service Pack 1

1. You'll need to run the file `mdac_typ.exe` on your CD, it should be in the CD's root directory:

2. Check the license agreement then click Yes to continue:

3. At the next screen click Continue:

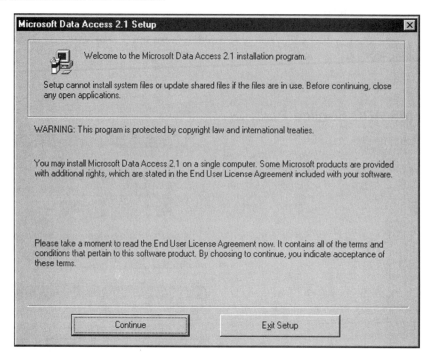

4. At the next screen click the Install Complete button and the installation will commence. The install directory is fixed as your Windows System directory.

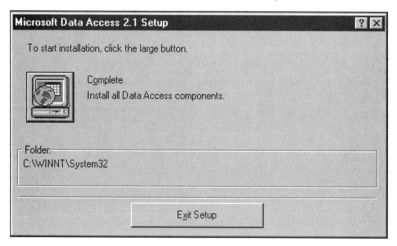

5. Finally the Microsoft Data Access Service Pack install is complete. You must re-boot your system before we install the update to Visual Studio - do so by clicking the **Restart Windows** button. When the computer re-starts, the install will finalize its setup and then we are ready to install Visual Studio Service Pack 3.

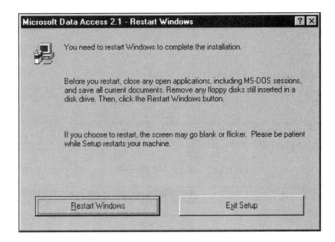

Installing Visual Studio Service Pack 3

1. First run the file setupsp3.exe contained on your CD, it should be in the same place as the Data Access Component Service Pack that we installed previously.

2. Click the Continue button in the dialog box that appears, making sure you have closed down all other programs.

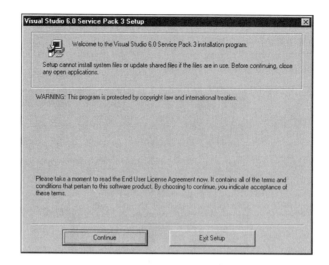

3. Next the set up will check to see what parts of Visual Studio are installed on your computer, then the license agreement screen will appear. Read it then click I Agree to continue, and the installation will start:

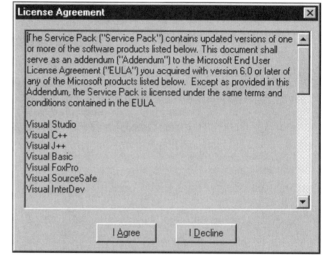

4. Once it's complete you should see the screen opposite - click OK to continue:

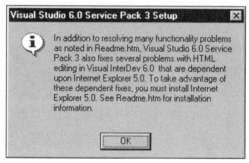

5. Finally the installation is complete and you need to just re-start your computer before you use Visual Studio:

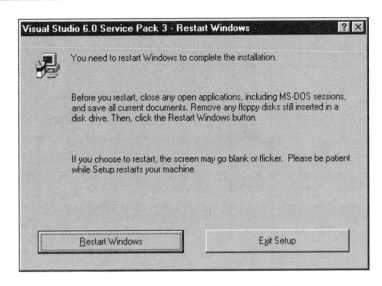

Visual Studio 6.0 Service Pack 3 - Restart Windows

You need to restart Windows to complete the installation.

Before you restart, close any open applications, including MS-DOS sessions, and save all current documents. Remove any floppy disks still inserted in a disk drive. Then, click the Restart Windows button.

If you choose to restart, the screen may go blank or flicker. Please be patient while Setup restarts your machine.

Restart Windows | Exit Setup

6. It's a good idea to re-boot your system to allow all of the changes to take effect.

Summary

In this chapter, we have installed Visual InterDev and all the necessary server components to enable us to start creating web applications.

In the next chapter we will start using Visual InterDev to create web sites. We will make use of many of its features to speed up web site development, as we begin to create an example web site, which we will develop further throughout the book.

Visual InterDev Quick Tour

In the previous two chapters we introduced and installed Visual InterDev, and explained its purpose – that of providing all of the necessary tools for developing web applications. We learned that it has lots of features that speed up development, and that change the focus of web development from creating *pages* to creating *applications*. We also should know that a web application is more than just a few web pages tacked together – it is a dynamic collection of pages, information, and programs that has, among others, maintainability and extensibility as strong goals.

We were told that Visual InterDev is great for developing these web applications, but we didn't go into too much detail on the tools that make this true. The goal of this chapter is to introduce you to many of these tools, and to give you an understanding of what can be achieved with the Integrated Development Environment that is such a strong feature of Visual InterDev. As the chapter heading suggests, this will only be a *brief* introduction to the key features, as the rest of the book covers these topics in much greater detail.

We are going to create a basic web site that makes use of many of the time saving features available in Visual InterDev. The site is for a fictional camera shop, Wrox Cameras. Throughout the book we will expand on this site so that it eventually includes a full electronic catalogue of all the products that the shop offers.

In creating the initial site, this chapter will cover:

- ❑ Connecting to your web server and creating a project.
- ❑ Working with modes, and understanding how changes to your files affect those on the web server.
- ❑ Applying a theme and a layout to a project.
- ❑ Adding pages and a navigation system using a site diagram.
- ❑ Adding content to web pages, and designing a basic home page using the What You See is What You Get (WYSIWYG) editor.
- ❑ Using the editor to create an HTML form for receiving customer queries.
- ❑ Adding code to a web page to provide feedback to the user.
- ❑ Adding a task to the task list to remind you of outstanding work.
- ❑ Other features of the Integrated Development Environment (IDE).

Since it normally works best, we'll start at the beginning – by creating our project.

Creating a Project

As we have mentioned, Visual InterDev is focused on creating web applications. By its very nature, a web application can contain many different types of files and information. This could easily create a nightmare scenario for managing those files if it weren't for **web projects**. Visual InterDev groups all of the files that make up your web application into a web project.

A web project contains all of the information necessary to *create* and *publish* your web application. The project can contain many sorts of files, including HTML pages, images, database connection information, and so on. By giving a web project an easy to remember name, it becomes less complicated to work with multiple projects at once, and to keep track of where everything is.

When you create a web project, you will need to connect to the web server that you set up in Chapter 2. The web server will be used to store the master copies of all of the files in your project.

Try it Out – Creating a Project

We are going to create a web project for Wrox Cameras. This will eventually contain all of the files that we will work on throughout this chapter and this book.

1. Start Visual InterDev. You should automatically see the New Project dialog, which looks like this:

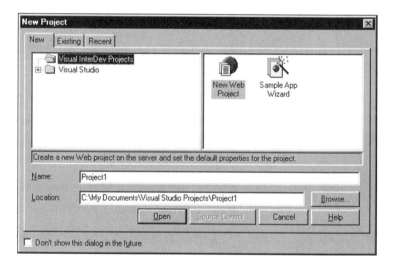

If you want to re-open a project later, the **Existing** *and* **Recent** *tabs show any existing or recently opened projects that you have worked with. You would simply need to browse to the required project folder, double click on the folder, and select a web project to open – identified by the web project icon as seen in the above screenshot.*

2. We are going to create a new project, so we're in the right place, on the **New** tab. In the **Name** box, enter the name of our project, which is **Wrox Cameras**. Note that Visual InterDev is *not* case sensitive.

3. The Location box is where the project files will be stored on your computer; change it if you want to, otherwise accept the default. You will notice that Project1 at the end of the path name will have changed to Wrox Cameras. Clicking Open brings up the Web Project Wizard:

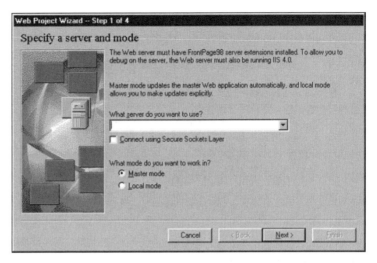

4. Type in the name of the web server that you are working with, as discussed in Chapter 2. If it is a local server residing on the same machine that you are working on, such as Personal Web Server (PWS), you can type in localhost. If you are on a network, then type in the name of the server that you will work on. Unless you have been told otherwise by an administrator, leave the Connect using Secure Sockets Layer checkbox blank, and leave Master mode selected. Both local and master modes will be explained later. Click on Next to proceed to the next step of the Wizard.

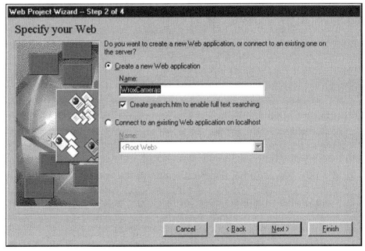

One useful point to mention here is that sometimes, when first using Visual InterDev, you might get an error at this point about not being able to connect to the web server. This happens often, and the best way to resolve it is to first off make sure that the URL you entered is correct (for example, if you've named your computer, you may need to type its name instead of localhost), that the web server is running, that you have the correct security if running NT4, and if all else fails, reinstall the web server! This is a quirk that has been addressed in many MSDN knowledge base articles, available at www.microsoft.com. Perseverence will win through the day!

5. We are creating a new web application, so the default shown above is correct. Note that the **Name** has had the spaces removed, so that **Wrox Cameras** becomes **WroxCameras**. This is because spaces generally don't work well in file names on some web servers. Clicking **Next** again will take you to the next step, which is all about applying a layout.

6. Press **Next** to avoid this as we'll discuss it in a little while.

7. The last step is about applying a theme. Once again, we will not do this yet, so press **Finish** and your project will be created! You should be taken into Visual InterDev, and in the top right hand corner of the screen you should see the following window:

If it doesn't appear, select **View | Project Explorer** from the main menu. This is the **Project Explorer** window, and it shows the directories (folders) and files on the web server that make up your web application. The first line specifies the **solution**, which can contain one or more complete projects. A solution is in fact a file with the extension ".sln". Beneath that you will see all of the **projects** within the solution, for which there is currently only one. A project is a file with the extension ".vip" (as in **V**isual InterDev **P**roject) which contains a list of the files within the project. The **Project Explorer** window simply reads the ".sln" and ".vip" files to display the list that you see.

You can add projects to the solution by selecting **File | Add Project**, and specifying which project is to be added to the current solution. We will do this later in the book. You can remove a project from the solution by selecting it in the **Project Explorer** window, and then choosing **File | Remove Project**. This will simply remove the project from the solution, but it will not delete the project.

Let's now look at what the **Project Explorer** window contains for a selected project, for example the Wrox Cameras project. You will see three directories and two files; the purpose of each of these is as follows:

_private   This folder contains any files that you do not want people using the final application to be able to see. This could come in useful later on, for example when you write web applications that store feedback from users in files. A common practice is to create those files in this directory.

_ScriptLibrary This folder contains special files used by Visual InterDev – it will be described later. **Do not touch these files!**

images	This folder is where you can store all of your image files. This is the suggested location only – you can actually put them anywhere you want. There is, however, a big advantage to putting images in one directory if your design allows it – namely that when a picture is loaded once by a client browser, it will normally be cached and reused. This means that by reusing the exact same picture and path to it within all of your web pages, your application might work that little bit faster, because the client's browser will already have downloaded it in prior pages.
global.asa	This file stores information about your web application. It actually does a whole lot more than this, which we will cover in Chapter 7 when we start writing server side script, and begin using ASP pages.
search.htm	This is a search form generated automatically by Visual InterDev, if the checkbox Create search.htm to enable full text searching was left checked in step 5 above. This is the first page in our web application and we'll be using this file very soon.

All of these folders and files will be described in greater detail later. What is important to see here is that the web project that you have created *automatically* includes some folders and files. When other files are added, such as web pages and pictures, they will all be saved into this structure, and will be viewable in the Project Explorer window.

Any folders that you add will, by default, appear as part of the structure of your web site. For example, if the Wrox Cameras site had a URL of http://www.wroxshop.com/wroxcameras, and it had a folder called products that contained a web page new_cameras.htm, then you could access this page from the finished site by typing in http://www.wroxshop.com/wroxcameras/products/new_cameras.htm.

If you do not want a user to be able to view files in one of your folders, then you need to change the permissions on your web server. You should use the documentation of your web server to do this.

Working with Modes

So, what exactly have we just done? Visual InterDev has created your web project for you not just once, but twice! It has created two sets of files – a *master copy* on the web server, and a *local copy* on your hard disk.

First off, it talked to the web server and created the master copy of the files, then it copied all of these files into the local directory that you specified in the Location field of the New Project dialog. What is the purpose of this? There are two reasons for this way of working with projects:

- ❑ The first is performance. By having files local to your PC, they are a lot faster to access than grabbing them off a network web server.

- ❑ The second reason is to assist teams of developers in working together. By controlling who has which files out for editing, it becomes easier for multiple developers to work on a project.

Visual InterDev maintains both versions of your project – the local copy on your hard disk, and the master copy on the web server. Initially the local files exist on your PC as read-only copies – not the best idea when you want to edit them. When you work on a file, you must first retrieve it from the web server. This process overwrites the local file with a write-enabled copy from the server. When you have finished working on it, you put it back on the server.

> **When you retrieve a file, you are** *getting a working copy* **of that file.**
>
> **When you have finished working with a file, and update the file back to the master copy, you set your local file back to read-only, and you are** *releasing the working copy.*

To support this process of working with files, Visual InterDev has project **modes**. A project mode can be one of two options – either **local** or **master**. When we built this project, we accepted (in step 1 of the Web Project Wizard) the default mode of Master. The two modes work like this:

❑ *Master* mode means that when you save changes to a file on your local copy, the changes are immediately updated to the master copy on the web server. This means that you only need to choose Release Working Copy when you want to tell the web server that you have finished editing the page. This is important when working in a team of developers.

❑ *Local* mode means that changes to the local copies are not updated to the master copy until you explicitly update them. Local mode can be very useful when you are working in teams, as long as only one person is working on each file. In this case, everyone can work in local mode and make changes to their local copies. When they want to update their changes back into the master copy, they simply specify which files to update. It is also useful when making changes to a "live" site, because you can test your changes locally without risking a blow-out on the live site.

It is possible to change the working mode of your web project at any time. To do this, open the project, go to the Project | Web Project | Working Mode menu and choose the mode that you want.

> **One last note about modes and working in teams: for situations where team work is important and it is necessary to keep track of changes, Visual InterDev integrates strongly with Visual SourceSafe to provide excellent source control. This is covered in detail in Chapter 13.**

Try it Out – Modifying a File

When we created our Wrox Cameras web project, Visual InterDev automatically created a search page. This page is a simple search utility that allows users to search the content of your web site. We are going to modify the search page to make it a little bit more specific to Wrox Cameras.

1. In the Project Explorer window, double click on the file search.htm. The following dialog opens:

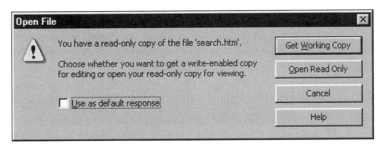

2. Select Get Working Copy. This will copy the master file to your local files area, and you will be able to modify it. (Selecting Open Read Only will copy a non-editable version of this file to your local files area.)

3. The file will open in the Design view of the HTML Editor window (a WYSIWYG editor), showing you roughly what a user browsing your page might see, plus various items to help you in designing the page.

4. Type directly into this window as you would in a word processor. As mentioned, this is the page Design view of the search.htm file – there are other views available at the bottom of the window that will be explained later. Using the editor as you would use a word processor, simply select the text that you want to change, and type in what you want to replace it with. Change the top part of the page from its initial appearance so that the bit above the first box (the one containing the '0') looks like this:

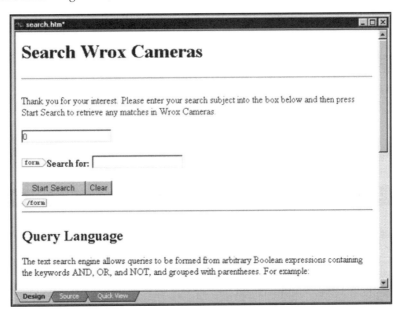

5. Hardly the most exciting of search pages, but it will do for our purposes! Select File | Save search.htm from the menu to save the changes to your local copy. Since, when you created this project, you specified to work in master mode, this save will automatically update your changes to the master copy as well. If you had been working in local mode, you would have had to right mouse click on the file search.htm in the Project Explorer window and select Release Working Copy to update your changes to the server. Do this anyway, as it is good practice for when you are working in a large team.

6. Close the search.htm file, using File | Close from the menu.

It's as simple as that! You have now learned how to create a project and open a file for modifications, but as you saw, the page is not looking particularly inviting. This is where themes and layouts can come to your rescue.

Themes and Layouts

The purpose of most web sites is to attract customers and readers. Four or five years ago, plain text pages with the odd picture or table would have been quite acceptable, but nowadays the average reader wants more. Today's web applications have many pages of content that require sophisticated menu systems for users to navigate. Maintaining these menus can quickly become a difficult task, and making them appear attractive at the same time makes for a complete job in itself.

Visual InterDev is targeted at exactly this sort of web site – the difficult ones with lots of dynamic menus, and requirements for a good interface for the user. Not surprisingly, it provides some excellent tools to help you to build a consistent menu system with an attractive presentation. These tools are called **themes** and **layouts**, and are covered in detail in the next chapter.

In brief:

❑ a *theme* is a template that you apply to your page or site, which makes it look consistent. It can include a background image, text styles, buttons, and so on. It specifies the general look and feel of your page.

❑ a *layout* is a way of formatting the structure of your page or site – it controls where the various navigation links and buttons appear. It might, for example, state that a menu bar for the site goes down the left hand side of the page, a title appears at the top, and the content appears beneath the title.

Try it Out – Applying a Theme and Layout to the Project

We are going to spruce up the Wrox Cameras site a little bit by applying a theme and a layout.

1. In the Project Explorer window, right mouse click on the project folder, i.e. localhost/WroxCameras, and choose Properties.

2. Select the Appearance tab, then press the Change button to open the Apply Theme and Layout dialog.

3. In the Apply Theme and Layout dialog, select the Theme tab and choose Apply theme. Select Raygun – the following preview window of the theme appears:

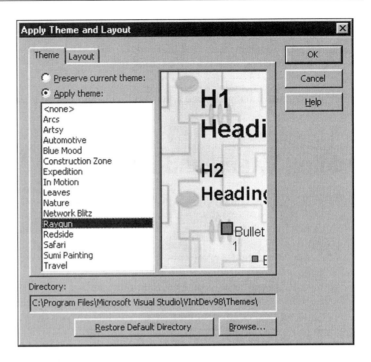

4. Switch to the Layout tab and click Apply layout and theme, then Top 1. This layout adds a banner to the top of the page, and beneath that a menu item for each main page of the site.

5. Press OK to close the Apply Theme and Layout dialog, then OK to close the Properties page. Since we chose to work in master mode when creating this project, Visual InterDev will apply the theme and layout to both your local and master copies of any *new* files which you add to your site. It will also add two new folders to your Project Explorer window: _Themes and _Layouts. These folders contain the various graphics and control files necessary to present the theme and layout on your site.

One important thing to note here is that if you now open up the search.htm file, either by double clicking on it in the Project Explorer window or by right clicking on it and selecting View in Browser, you'll notice that it has *not* assumed the look and style of the Raygun theme or the Top 1 layout, as were previewed in the Apply Theme and Layout dialog. We need to also apply the theme and layout to our *existing* pages (which in our case is just search.htm).

6. In the Project Explorer window, right mouse click on the project folder, i.e. localhost/WroxCameras, and choose Apply Theme and Layout. The same window appears as shown above.

7. Click on the Theme tab, then choose Apply theme, and select Raygun.

8. Click on the Layout tab, choose Apply layout and theme, and select the Top 1 layout.

9. Click OK, and then save all of your work.

> There are two ways of applying a theme and layout to the pages in a project, as described above. The first method only affects new pages. The second method applies the theme and layout to all existing ones.

A similar method is used for applying a theme and layout to individual pages – we'll see how to do this in the next chapter.

Adding Pages and Navigation

We've now defined a layout and added a snazzy theme to our fledgling site, but there's still not much content there. The next thing we need to do is to add a page, and then we're going to need to design a way of navigating between that page and any others we add, including the existing `search.htm` page.

Managing **navigation** is a very important part of your site, since it is how your users will jump from page to page. If it is not intuitive and consistent, then users will not stick around. To promote a consistent *interface* for navigation, we use the theme and layout that we have already chosen. To add pages to the site and to control its navigation, we use a **site diagram**. As with themes and layouts, this is covered in more detail in the next chapter, but for now we will show you the basics.

A theme defines *how* a menu will *look*, while a layout defines *where* the menu will *be*. The next item in Visual InterDev's bag of tricks is a site diagram. A site diagram is a place where you can create new pages and manage navigation by dragging **links** between those pages. Once you've got your pages onto the site diagram and made a few links, the diagram can then be used as the basis for a **navigation bar**.

A navigation bar is a special item that you can add to a page, known as a **control**. This particular group of controls – Design Time Controls or DTCs – is covered in detail in Chapter 8. The navigation bar is a DTC that comes with Visual InterDev, and is called the **PageNavBar DTC**. It is a control that you put on a page to build a menu from the information contained in the site diagram. It creates menus at various levels of a hierarchy from the site diagram, but for now we are just interested in two of its uses: the ability to create a *banner* (title) for our site, and the ability to provide a *global navigation bar* that enables us to jump between our pages. This functionality could be implemented by using hyperlinks (as mentioned in our HTML introduction in Chapter 1), but this method does it with more style and maintainability, as will be demonstrated more fully in the next chapter.

Try it Out – Using a Site Diagram to Add Pages and Navigation

We are going to create a site diagram for our Wrox Cameras project, and use it to add two new pages – a default home page, and a Contact Us page. We are then going to make a navigation bar that jumps between all three pages in our site.

1. You should already have open in Visual InterDev the Wrox Cameras project. Select Project | Add Item from the menu. In the following screen, select Site Diagram and press Open. This will create a site diagram with the file name `Site Diagram1.wdm`:

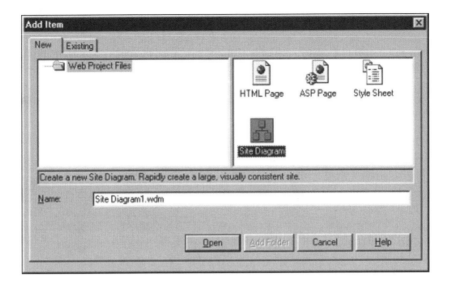

2. The following Site Diagram opens, showing a new home page:

3. The box containing the text Home represents a page – in this case the home page for the site. Overwrite Home with Wrox Cameras.

4. Right mouse click on an area outside of the Wrox Cameras box. The following menu should appear:

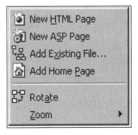

73

5. Select New HTML Page. In the box that opens, overwrite the text with Contact Us.

6. Right mouse click again as in step 4 above. Select Add Existing File. In the dialog that opens, select the search.htm page and click OK.

7. You should be left with a site diagram showing the three pages: Wrox Cameras, Contact Us, and search.

8. Drag the Contact Us page beneath the Wrox Cameras page until a link appears between the two. Repeat this with the search page. You should end up with something like this:

9. Press the save button on the toolbar or select File | Save Site Diagram1.wdm from the menu. This will save the site diagram file and create two new files in your Project Explorer window: ContactUs.htm and Default.htm. The Wrox Cameras page became Default.htm because it had been set as the home page, and Visual InterDev knows to name that Default.htm. The Contact Us page became ContactUs.htm because when a new file that is not a home page is added, Visual InterDev simply removes the spaces to make the file name. Close the site diagram.

10. We now need to make the PageNavBar controls on each page include the correct pages for displaying in the menus. If you open the home page, i.e. Default.htm, you will see the following:

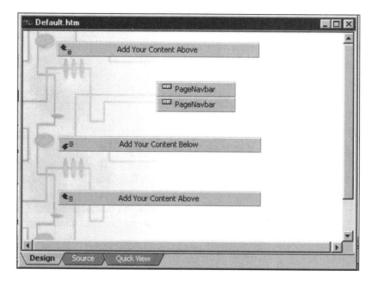

11. The gray rectangles saying Add Your Content… are **layout place holders** with arrows pointing to where you should write text for displaying on the page. These rectangles do not appear in a web browser, and are there just to help you design the page. The two boxes labelled PageNavBar are what we are concerned with here. The first one is for the banner, i.e. the title of the page. Leave this one alone. The second one is the navigation bar – this is what displays the menu on the finished page. If you right click on this control and select Properties, you will see a Properties dialog box which gives you various options for specifying what pages the control will display. In the Type section, select Children pages and press OK. This specifies that the current page (the home page) will show any children pages in its navigation bar. As you can see in step 8 above, the children pages are the other two pages, as they sit below the home page in the site hierarchy. We'll look more closely at hierarchy in the next chapter.

12. Close the home page, `Default.htm`, saving changes when prompted.

13. Open the Contact Us page and select the second PageNavBar control. In the Properties page, accessed by right mouse clicking on the control and clicking on Properties, place a check in the Home box in the Additional pages section. This will create a link to the home page from the Contact Us page. Press OK, save and close the page.

14. Open the search page (if not already open) and select the second PageNavBar control. In the Properties page, accessed by right mouse clicking on the control and clicking on Properties, place a check in the Home box in the Additional pages section. This will create a link to the home page from the search page. Press OK, save and close the page.

15. You have now created the navigation for the site! If you right mouse click on Default.htm in the Project Explorer window and select View in Browser, you will see the page in your browser. It should look similar to this:

As you can see, it certainly looks a lot better in the browser! The big Wrox Cameras title is a banner that displays the name of the page, as entered in the site diagram. This is the first PageNavBar control on the page. The navigation bar beneath it displays the two children pages – Contact Us and search. These buttons have derived their appearance from the theme. The actual names and links to the two pages were derived from the site diagram – the names were what appeared in each box on the site diagram, and the link is to the relevant page. If you click on either of these buttons, you will be taken to the relevant page, where you will also see an additional button: Home. The Home button takes you back to the `Default.htm` page above.

We've just created a fully functioning site, albeit one that has very sparse content! As you can see, it is very easy to add new pages and link them in to the navigation structure using the Site Diagram. So far we haven't got our hands dirty writing code, yet in the pre-Visual InterDev days this sort of navigation could only have been achieved at the cost of repetitive code and graphic design. A wide range of themes for providing a friendly user interface supplements this ease of use, and gives you an idea of the strengths of Visual InterDev for rapid application development.

If your company has a defined theme that a graphic artist has created especially, you can create a custom theme and layout based on these custom graphics and styles, which can then be applied quickly and easily across an entire site, and managed using Visual InterDev. This drastically eases the burden of creating pages that need to conform to a particular corporate standard.

Adding Content to Web Pages

So far we've got three pages in our site, and at least two of them are badly in need of some content. Let's now take a look at another strong feature of Visual InterDev – its **HTML editor**. When you open an HTML page you are taken to an HTML editor that works in a way very similar to a word processor. If you want to add text to a page, you can just type it in. Many of the shortcut keys that you use in Microsoft Word, such as *Ctrl+B* for bold and *Ctrl+I* for italicize, will work in the editor.

At the bottom of the editor are three tabs: Design, Source, and Quick View. They switch the views as follows:

❑ **Design** view is used to type documents in a manner similar to a word processor. It also enables special controls to be positioned and manipulated.

❑ **Source** view enables you to modify the HTML of a web page directly, and to write script, which we'll do later.

❑ **Quick View** gives a close approximation of what the page should look like in a browser. No editing is possible in this view.

Since this is, after all, the quick tour, we are not going to go into exhaustive detail on the capabilities of the editor, we're just going to jump in and use the Design view to quickly write some information into our home page.

Try it Out – Adding Content to a Web Page

The people at Wrox Cameras are just beginning to experience web design, so with this excuse in mind let's add some awe-inspiring content to their home page.

1. The first thing that we need to do is to add a camera graphic to the site. You can download all of the graphic files from the Wrox web site at http://www.wrox.com. Once you've downloaded and saved the Cam1.jpg file onto your hard drive, you are ready to use this image on your web site.

2. In Visual InterDev, if you look at the Project Explorer window for our Wrox Cameras project, you will see a folder conveniently named images. We will add our image to this directory before placing it on the home page. To add the file, right mouse click on the images folder in the Project Explorer window and select Add | Add Item. In the dialog box, select the Existing tab.

3. In the Files of type drop down box, select Image Files and then browse to find the picture Cam1.jpg. Clicking Open adds this file to the master copy of your project on the web server, and copies it to your local copy of the project.

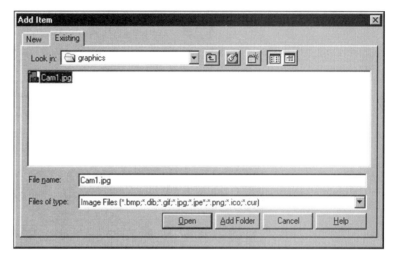

It is also possible to drag image files from Windows Explorer and drop them into the images directory. Whichever method you choose, the graphic will then appear under the images directory, visible in the Project Explorer window.

4. Double click on the Default.htm file in the Project Explorer window to open it in the editor. If prompted, get a working copy for editing.

5. We are now ready to insert the camera image onto the page. Position your cursor below the box labelled Add Your Content Below. As mentioned before, this is a helper for you to know where you should place your text.

6. From the HTML menu, select Image. In the box that appears, enter the following:

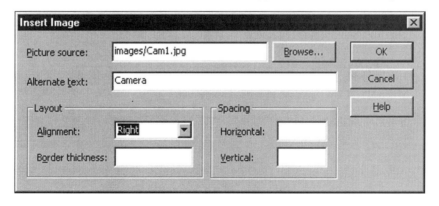

The Browse button can be used to look for images on your web site. The alternate text entry of Camera is what appears if your visitor's browser does not download images – it is a very good idea to always fill this in. It also sometimes appears when a user moves their mouse over the image. Finally we have specified a Right alignment to force the image to the right hand side of the page. Press OK to insert the image onto the page.

7. Now that we have a colorful image on the page, we can write some eye-catching text. The inspired crew decided for a minimalistic approach, so here it is. Position your cursor on the left hand side of the page just below the Add Your Content Below layout reminder. Type in the following text:

Thank you for visiting us. Should you require information about any products on this site, please contact us

8. So far so good. The last task at hand is to link the text contact us to one of our other web pages – ContactUs.htm. To do this, select the text and choose Link from the HTML menu. The following Hyperlink dialog appears:

Entering ContactUs.htm and pressing OK creates a hyperlink to the web page, which you can see because the text turns blue and is underlined. You could also choose Browse to look for other pages on the site.

9. Save and close your work, then right mouse click on the file Default.htm in the Project Explorer window. Select View in Browser. Your browser will launch showing you a slightly more attractive home page similar to this:

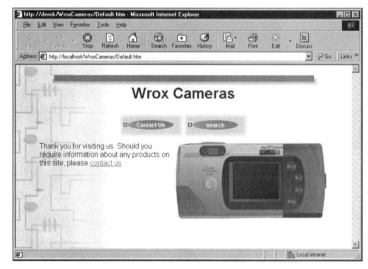

As you can see, using the editor is a fast and painless process. Practice with it – you'll quickly discover some useful features. You can easily insert HTML tables, change font types, resize graphics – the HTML editor will generally make your life a whole lot easier than if you were using something like Notepad to achieve the same goals.

Creating an HTML Form

Next on the list is to change our Contact Us page, which is sadly still a blank page. We are going to create an **HTML form**, which we will use to gather information from the user. An HTML form is a tried and proven way of getting information from a user, and it has long been used in web applications.

In Chapter 1, we looked at examples of simple HTML pages, and were introduced to some of the tags that HTML uses to *present* information on a page. We also saw that a form is slightly different, in that it also provides a means to *collect* information input by the viewer. Historically, developers would write the various tags in HTML that represent the controls that make up a form. These controls consist of familiar items such as textboxes, checkboxes, option groups, list boxes, and so on. Building a detailed form in this manner can easily become a daunting task, which is where Visual InterDev comes to the rescue again.

The editor, as mentioned above, can insert, format, and present many items onto a web page. It includes a handy Toolbox, normally visible on the left hand side of the editor window, from which you can easily drag and drop any HTML form control that you require. In conjunction with a Properties window that enables you to modify the various aspects of a component quickly and easily, this aspect of Visual InterDev makes it an invaluable tool for developing forms.

Try it Out – Creating an HTML Form

The Contact Us page is an ideal candidate for an HTML form, as it would be very useful for a user to be able to type in a few comments and have them automatically sent to the owner of the web site. We are going to create this form, but for now we will not actually make it send responses, as that will be covered in a later chapter.

1. Double click on the file ContactUs.htm in the Project Explorer window. The file should open and a Toolbox should appear to the left of it. If it doesn't, select View | Toolbox from the menu. The Toolbox is split into categories, of which HTML is the first. The other categories are groups of various types of components that can be placed on a page. These will be covered in later chapters. The HTML tab contains many of the HTML fields that you should be familiar with, either from Chapter 1 or simply from your own exploration of the WWW. This is the tab that we will be using now, so make sure that it is selected.

2. The first thing that we need to do is to create a form on the page. To do this, in Design view, position your cursor below the Add Your Content Below layout control, then select HTML | Form from the menu. Two little images should appear entitled form and /form. These are placeholders to assist you in placing controls on the form – you must place all items that are to be part of the form between pairs of these images. If you don't – things might not appear where you want them to.

3. Let's add a bit of text to explain to the user how they should use the form. Write the following text just after the first form placeholder:

Thank you for visiting us. Should you require information about any products on this site, please contact us

4. We are now going to add fields for the user to enter their email address and subject line. For each new line which we will create, you will first need to drag and drop a Line Break control from the HTML tab of the Toolbox, to make the page look more attractive. Do this now, positioning the control after the text that you have just typed in.

5. Type in a descriptive label, Your Email Address:. Then, select the Textbox item from the Toolbox and drag it to the right of the label that you just wrote. Releasing the mouse will create the textbox.

6. Click on the Textbox that you just added. Next to (or beneath) the Project Explorer window you will see a Properties dialog like this:

Every item on a page can have a variety of **attributes** that define its look and behaviour. When you click on an item, those attributes, known as **properties**, are displayed in the item's Properties dialog. We have just created a textbox that has the fairly uninformative name of text1. In the Properties dialog, change the (Id) and name properties to txtEmailAddress. (You may need to scroll down through the properties to find the required property.) The name field is used by the web server to retrieve the contents of the field when the user submits the form. The (Id) field is used by any code to uniquely identify the control. Both of these aspects will be covered later.

7. We are now going to add a new textbox for the subject field. Drag and drop a Line Break control to the right of the txtEmailAddress textbox, to create a new line, and then type in the label for your second textbox, Subject:. Once again, drag and drop a Textbox control after this text, then change its (Id) and name properties to be txtSubject.

80

8. The txtSubject textbox is a little on the short side if the customer has a big chip on their shoulder, so we need to expand it a bit. Click on the txtSubject textbox. You will notice that little white boxes appear around it like this:

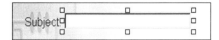

These are **handles** for repositioning and resizing the textbox. Move your mouse over the middle handle on the right hand side until your mousepointer changes into a two-headed arrow pointing to the left and right. Clicking the handle at this time will enable you to drag the size of the textbox. Make it about twice as wide to give our customers space to type. Then, stretch the txtEmailAddress box so that its right hand border is at the same point.

9. Next up, we want to give our customer a larger box into which they can type the body of their comment. Add a new line after the txtSubject box. Type in a new label, Body:, then select the Text Area control in the Toolbox. The Text Area control is similar to the Textbox control, it's just a bit bigger and capable of multi-line entries. Drag and drop the control onto your page, then set its (Id) and name properties to txtBody. Finally, drag its size to be as wide as the txtSubject box and about four lines deep.

10. We are now going to add a checkbox, which is a control that the user can click on to toggle between it having a check mark or not. Add a new line after the txtbody text area control, with the label Do you want to be added to our mailing list?. Select the Checkbox control from the Toolbox and add it to the right of the label. Change its (Id) and name properties to be chkMailingList.

11. Last on the list, the user needs a button to press when they want to send the finished message. This is called a submit button, and is on the HTML Toolbox along with the other fields we have added. Drag and drop the Submit Button control onto the form on a new line just below the chkMailingList checkbox control and above the /form placeholder.

At the end of all this, if you save and view the ContactUs.htm page in your browser, you should see something like the following:

81

We've now got one form created in a hurry, without writing any HTML by hand. OK, so the page is not going to win any awards for innovation and excellence, but you can see how easy it is to create forms using the advanced editor that Visual InterDev provides.

As well as using the Toolbox as shown, Visual InterDev offers an HTML menu in the main menu. This enables you to insert familiar HTML items such as hyperlinks, images, bookmarks, and so on, by using the menu. This facility saves you having to remember and type in by hand the various tags and paths required in your page. For example, if you use the HTML | Image menu option, a dialog box appears that prompts you to select an image. This then writes the necessary tag and file path into your web page – much easier than doing it the old-fashioned way!

The HTML menu works based on the current cursor position and selected items within the Design window so that, for example, if you select a word and then choose HTML | Link, you will in fact change the selected word into a hyperlink.

Adding Code to a Web Page

Visual InterDev is all about developing web applications – and a very important part of any application is **code**. Visual InterDev is not a programming language, such as Visual Basic or C++, but it has been built from the beginning as a development environment that utilizes two of the most popular web scripting languages available – JScript and VBScript. (JScript is Microsoft's version of Sun's JavaScript – for our purposes there are no major differences, but this will be discussed further in Chapter 6.) Both of these are object oriented programming languages, as discussed in Chapter 1, so they each have objects, methods, events and properties which we use to build our code.

The editor includes a Source view that we mentioned before, drag and drop functionality in the Toolbox, and numerous other tools that make it the premier environment for coding web applications.

We're going to start by showing you a very basic bit of code, but code that nevertheless introduces a few important concepts, at the same time as promoting the ease of use of the Visual InterDev Integrated Development Environment (IDE).

Try it Out – Adding Code to a Web Page

We have just created a form on the Contact Us page, but have not yet finished it by making it send responses. If you view the page in a browser and press the Submit button, you actually get an HTML error – 405 Method not allowed. Eventually, we will make this page work correctly, but for now we want to stop this message appearing.

What we are going to do is to write some code that tells the user that the submit functionality is not working at this time. This will happen whenever they click on the Submit button, after which they should not see the error page. This sort of code is called an **event handler**, because every time the user clicks on the Submit button an *event* occurs, which is *handled* by the piece of code that we are going to write. The code itself will form part of the HTML that makes up the web page, and will be contained within <SCRIPT> tags. Every time a user views this page in their browser, their browser will interpret this code and carry out the instructions.

We will write this script using JavaScript, a popular programming language that has the advantage of being understood by a lot of client browsers. Note that JavaScript is case sensitive, so be careful with your typing!

1. Open the `ContactUs.htm` file, if it is not already open.

2. Position your cursor at the very top of the page. This is an easy way of selecting the document that is the web page. In the **Properties** window, ensure that the **defaultClientScript** property is **JavaScript**.

3. Click on the **Source** tab at the bottom of the editor. This will take you to the HTML **Source** view of the web page, which shows the raw HTML contents of the `ContactUs.htm` file.

4. At the bottom of the **Toolbox** to the left of the editor, select the **Script Outline** tab. This opens a hierarchical, explorer-like view of the structure of the document. This view is based on the HTML tags that make up the document, and the ID fields of each element. It is used both to view the outline, and to automatically build basic event handlers – the use to which we will put it.

5. Under **Client Objects & Events**, expand **FORM1**, which is the ID of the form that contains the various contact fields. You will see a list of events for which you can write code that applies to FORM1. You will also, towards the bottom of the list, see the names of the various text fields and objects that we added to the form. Expand the **submit1** object, which is the submit button.

6. You will now see another list of events for which you can write event handlers. Double click on the event called **onclick**. The following code will automatically appear in the editor window:

```
<SCRIPT ID=clientEventHandlersJS LANGUAGE=javascript>
<!--

function submit1_onclick() {

}

//-->
</SCRIPT>
```

7. This is a skeleton event handler, to which you add code. We are going to write code between the { } that make up the `submit1_onclick` function. Every time a user presses the submit button, an `onclick` event is fired. If you scroll down and look at the HTML definition for the `submit1` button, you will notice it to be the following:

```
<INPUT ID="submit1" NAME="submit1" TYPE="submit" VALUE="Submit" LANGUAGE=javascript
onclick="return submit1_onclick()">
```

Double clicking on the event in the **Script Outline** also changed the definition of the submit button to include this link to the skeleton event handler. This says that when someone clicks on the submit button and an onclick event occurs, return (i.e. go off and do) the code in `submit1_onclick`, which contains the rest of the code. All we need to do now is to write the function.

8. Here is the function that you should write:

```
<SCRIPT ID=clientEventHandlersJS LANGUAGE=javascript>
<!--

function submit1_onclick() {
  window.alert("This functionality is not yet implemented.");
  return false;
}

//-->
</SCRIPT>
```

This function firstly displays a message box to the user stating This functionality is not yet implemented, then it causes the event handler to return a false value. This effectively cancels the event, meaning that the browser behaves as if the user did not click the submit button. Save your work and view it in your browser to test this. You will see that the http 405 error no longer occurs.

This has only lightly touched on the subject of code – later chapters of this book are dedicated to writing script for web applications in Visual InterDev. You will have noticed the ease with which you can add script to your document, the coloring of different code elements, and also the way in which Visual InterDev provides handy auto-complete menus and syntax reminders as you type in your code. This last feature is known as the **IntelliSense** and it can be a great help when you are dealing with complex controls, and objects with lots of properties and methods. After typing a period, you can double click on code in the drop down list, and it will be written for you in the editor. Not only does this save time and aid your memory, but it avoids typos too.

Adding a Task

The last stop on our tour is **tasks**. We have just left a glaring hole in our ContactUs.htm file – namely, it doesn't work! We're obviously going to need to go back and fix this at a later stage, but luckily we don't need to remember this ourselves. Because human beings are fallible, especially in larger projects with scores of pages to keep track of, Visual InterDev includes a **task management system** that can be used to jog your memory.

The task management system can be used to add quick *notes* manually, to add *shortcuts* to places within a file, and to manage the *priority* of these tasks and their *status*. It can be an invaluable tool when used properly, as tasks can be *sorted* based on file, priority, category, and so on.

The two main types of tasks are general comments/reminders, and shortcuts. A general comment or reminder is simply a note to yourself. You can specify its priority and use that to sort later. A shortcut is more useful in that it is attached to a specific line of text within a file. It can be used to open that file from the Task List window, and return you directly to the specified line – invaluable when you have a large project!

Try it Out – Adding a Task

We are going to use the Task List to add a reminder to complete the `ContactUs.htm` file. We want this reminder to automatically take us to the Contact Us page; so we will make it a shortcut. The Task List appears by default beneath the editor at the bottom of the IDE. If it does not appear, select View | Other Windows | Task List from the menu. The Task List looks like this:

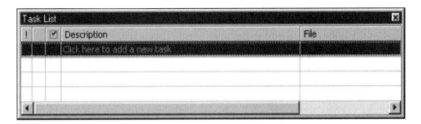

1. Open the `ContactUs.htm` file by double clicking on it in the Project Explorer window.

2. Select the Source tab and position your cursor in the function for `submit1_onClick()`.

3. Right mouse click and select Add Shortcut. A blue arrow will appear to the left of the line of text. This indicates that there is a shortcut. A task will also have been created in the Task List. The description will be the line of code you had selected, the file name will include the full path of `ContactUs.htm`, and the line number will also appear.

4. You can change the description to be more useful. Select the description and change it to Make Contact Us page submit details. Save the changes and close the Contact Us page.

5. If you now double click on the task that we have just added, the `ContactUs.htm` file will be automatically opened and your cursor taken to the specified line of text!

Fairly simple isn't it?! Here are a few other things that you can do with the Task List:

❑   To change the priority of a task, simply click in the first column of the Task List and choose from Low, Normal, or High.

❑   To mark a task as completed, simply check the third column with the check mark.

❑   To add your own general comment, just click on the first line that says Click here to add a new task. You can then immediately type in your description and set the priority.

❑   To delete a task, right mouse click on it and select Delete Task.

❑   You can select from various sort orders and filters by right mouse clicking on any task and selecting Sort By or Show Tasks.

The Task List in Visual InterDev, while not a fully blown project management system by a long shot, is ideal for developers needing to keep track of difficult projects. It is quick, easy to use, and can be just the thing when you are working with long files and want to return to a specific place.

Other Features of the IDE

We have only touched on a few of the capabilities of Visual InterDev, yet you can see that as a package it is both powerful and easy to use. There are many features that are shared with other Windows packages, for example you can cut and paste items, undo actions, insert tables, format text, arrange windows, and much more. The environment itself will be immediately familiar to those who have used Visual Basic or other members of the Visual Studio 6 family. It is a complete development environment that offers a surprising degree of flexibility and customization. Appendix A offers a description of the menu options, and you'll also come across many of them throughout the book.

If you feel like experimenting more, here is a list of some handy ways that you can customize the IDE (Integrated Development Environment) to make it look the way you want it to:

❑ Various windows can be docked to appear as toolbars on any corners of the development environment, or made to float where you wish. There is an extensive collection of useful windows for assisting in various activities, many of which we will cover as the book progresses.

❑ On the right hand side of the standard toolbar is a drop down box with the text Design selected. Selecting other options will apply various different layouts to your development environment. You can also save your own layout by arranging the various windows as you like them, then simply typing a name for your layout into this box.

❑ You can drag fragments of HTML from your editor directly onto the Toolbox for later reuse. If you have a piece of code or text, or a favorite group of fields, simply dragging them to the Toolbox means that, at any stage, you can insert them into another page as you would any other HTML object in the Toolbox. This feature is great as it means that you can effectively build your own toolbar of commonly used code snippets – a great time saver as you start to build a collection of useful code.

❑ The menu system is fully customizable, just right mouse click on a blank place by the toolbars and choose Customize.

❑ The View menu contains two useful options, which you might like to add. View Details will show visible markers for various HTML formatting, such as paragraph breaks, that do not normally appear. Visible Borders shows borders for items such as HTML tables, greatly simplifying precise positioning of text and objects.

The full list of features of the IDE is very comprehensive, and it is in fact impossible to keep up to date with because the environment is *extensible* – people can write add-ins that enhance it. Later chapters will give you more exposure to the IDE, but you should now have a basic familiarity with it and a healthy appetite for more.

Summary

In this chapter we've taken a whirlwind tour of Visual InterDev, without going into too much detail. We've looked at some of the features that make Visual InterDev so useful, and put it to work, creating a basic site with very little coding. We have seen how Visual InterDev manages projects, how to make menus in web pages, and how to apply a consistent theme to our site using some handy development tools. To recap, we've learned that:

❑ Visual InterDev organises your files into web projects, and maintains two copies – one on the web server and one on your local machine.

❑ Themes and layouts can be used to quickly add a professional look and feel to your site.

❑ A site diagram, in conjuction with a navigation bar, can be used to quickly create menus that make navigating your site easy.

❑ Visual InterDev includes an easy to use editor and toolbox for quickly creating HTML pages and writing script.

❑ You are no longer limited by your memory – the task list can help you to keep track of outstanding tasks.

Visual InterDev is capable of a lot more than we have covered, but we have seen that it can be used to quickly create working web sites with minimal effort.

In the next chapter, we are going to look more closely at the tools that Visual InterDev provides for defining the *appearance* of a site. We have touched lightly on themes, layouts, and site diagrams already, now we're going to put them to the test, and introduce a few other tools to make your life easier.

Managing Style and Site Navigation

The last few years have been heady times for the growth of the Internet. Once upon a time it was solely the domain of tech-heads and universities, but now it seems that every man and his dog uses the Internet for some aspect of their lives. This growth has seen the requirements for what makes a good web site change almost as fast, and with it the tools that we use to make those sites.

Originally, the Internet contained mainly textual information, loosely formatted and heavily focused on delivering written content to its users. Images and graphics were present but rare, because of the prohibitive download times required to view them. With the advent of faster modems, ISDN lines, and millions more users, the face of the Internet has changed into the familiar beast that we see today.

Your average web site these days will normally contain a mixture of graphics and text, along with hyperlinks to connect the various pages that make up the site. This works fine, but sadly does not always offer the kind of finished product that most companies demand. When the purpose of a web site is to make money for a company, or present a positive image to its customers, then it is important that the site maintains the interest of its audience. This is where customers expect to see an attractive layout, easy to navigate menus, and a consistent style in a web site. If any one of these elements is missing, then the impression that the reader has of the site is diminished, and they might not return.

So now we have this modern Internet, where appearance and ease of use are a holy grail to which we must all aspire. As web developers, we are expected to be able to quickly produce sites like this without flinching. Thankfully, we need not all be expert designers and graphic artists to do this – Visual InterDev contains those wonderful tools of themes and layouts that we met in the last chapter.

During this chapter, we are going to look at how to use the various tools that Visual InterDev provides, to design and manage the *appearance*, *navigation*, and *style* of our site. By the end of this chapter, you will be familiar with:

- ❑ Why site navigation is so important.
- ❑ Applying themes and layouts, to your whole application and to individual pages.
- ❑ How to use site diagrams.
- ❑ How to use the various types of navigation bars.
- ❑ Creating and applying styles using cascading style sheets (CSS).

So without further ado, let's get started.

Why are Style and Site Navigation so Important?

First impressions count. It's true in person, and it's just as true on the Internet. If the purpose of your site is to inspire confidence in the quality of your goods and the professionalism of your company, then those qualities must be evident in your web site. In many cases, your web site can be the first point of contact between your company and your customers, so it is important that they are not scared away.

Here are some of the features that a user might expect in the interface of a large web site:

❑ Attractive presentation.

❑ Quick download times in most situations.

❑ Easy to use menus that are consistent on every page of the site. This can often be used to help define the site as an entity, with its own distinctive look and feel.

❑ Similar layout, i.e. positioning of information, from page to page. Users don't want to be looking all over the place to find the required information.

Creating such a web site can be a fairly ambitious task, but it is crucial if you want to make a site that's worth the time it takes to put it on the server. As we have seen, Visual InterDev comes with some tools to help you achieve these goals.

Themes and Layouts

As we mentioned in the last chapter, a **theme** is a collection of graphics and fonts that you can use to apply a colorful and persistent look to your web site. A **layout** is used to control how the content is presented on your page, as we saw when we applied a layout that gave us a menu at the top of every page.

We are going to look at how these tools work their magic, and at the sorts of things that you can do with them.

Layouts

Layouts are an invaluable tool for creating the consistent menus and interfaces that are required of so many sites today. A quick browse through the list of available layouts (accessed by right mouse clicking on the project in the Project Explorer window, selecting Apply Theme and Layout and choosing the Layout tab) will reveal that there are seventeen layouts to choose from. You have the choice to apply a layout as simple as previous/next buttons on the bottom of the page (Bottom 1) up to fairly complex layouts. For example, Top, Left and Bottom 1 displays a banner at the top, a list of child pages on the left hand side, and a list of first level pages along the bottom.

How a Layout Works

A layout determines where content is positioned on your page. To do this, it divides a page into **regions**, of which there are five available. The layout defines which of those available regions will be used. The regions are shown in the following diagram:

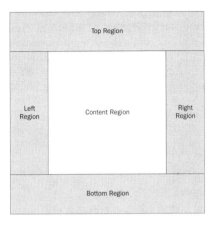

In general, a layout will use one, two or three of the above regions. Visual InterDev divides the page into regions by writing HTML tables within which the various content, menus, and graphics are written. This is a very simple, straightforward approach that web developers have in fact been using for a long time. Visual InterDev has just simplified the process into a nice wizard!

When you use a layout, a folder called _Layouts is added to the Project Explorer window, and all of the necessary files, which Visual InterDev uses to know how to apply the layout, are added to the project. This is shown in the screenshot opposite:

As we will see shortly, it is possible to have many different layouts in a project (in fact you can have one for every page). If this is the case, then there will be a different folder under _Layouts for each layout in the project.

When a page uses a particular layout, Visual InterDev automatically adds a reference to the necessary files in the HTML source of the document. It also writes the table formatting necessary to present the regions that the layout requires.

How it Works – Looking at the HTML Source Code that Visual InterDev Generates

To tie this in to the Chapter 3 *Applying a Theme and Layout* example, remember that we chose the Top 1 layout. This in effect used the top region and the content region. The *top* region displayed the banner for the page, and the menu bar, while the *content* region displayed any information that we wanted to present to the reader.

Let's examine the source code of the `Default.htm` file to see what makes this layout tick. Here it is (you can access it for yourself by viewing the **Source** tab of the editor for `Default.htm`):

```
<HTML>
<HEAD>
<META NAME="GENERATOR" CONTENT="Microsoft Visual Studio 6.0">
<TITLE></TITLE>


<LINK REL="stylesheet" TYPE="text/css" HREF="_Themes/raygun/THEME.CSS"
      VI6.0THEME="Raygun">
<LINK REL="stylesheet" TYPE="text/css" HREF="_Themes/raygun/GRAPH0.CSS"
      VI6.0THEME="Raygun">
<LINK REL="stylesheet" TYPE="text/css" HREF="_Themes/raygun/COLOR0.CSS"
      VI6.0THEME="Raygun">
<LINK REL="stylesheet" TYPE="text/css" HREF="_Themes/raygun/CUSTOM.CSS"
      VI6.0THEME="Raygun"></HEAD>
<BODY>
```

```
                Add Your Content Above
```

```
<TABLE BORDER="0" WIDTH="100%" HEIGHT="100%">
  <TR>
    <TD WIDTH="100%" HEIGHT="110" ALIGN="middle">
```

```
   PageNavbar
```

```
<BR>
```

```
   PageNavbar
```

```
    </TD>
  </TR>
  <TR>
    <TD WIDTH="100%" VALIGN="top">
<!-- VI6.0LAYOUT = "Top 1"-->
```

```
                Add Your Content Below
```

```
<P><IMG ALIGN="right" ALT="Camera" SRC="images/Cam1.jpg" WIDTH="248" HEIGHT="237"
    STYLE="LEFT: 337px; TOP: 42px"></P>
    <P> </P>
    <P>Thank you for visiting us. Should you require information about any products
    on this site, please <A HREF="ContactUs.htm">contact us</A></P>
</TD>
```

> Add Your Content Above

```
</TR>
</TABLE>
```

> Add Your Content Below

```
</BODY>
</HTML>
```

Here is what is happening:

- ❑ The <LINK> lines have nothing to do with the layout; they in fact point to the files that make up the **Raygun** theme of the page. Ignore them for now, as they will be explained later in the chapter.

- ❑ There is a table, with a border set to 0 so that it is not displayed, that is split into two rows. Each row is one of the two regions in the selected layout – namely the top region, and the content region.

- ❑ The various layout controls, that say **Add your Content Below**, or **Above**, assist you in positioning your text within the boundaries of the rows of the table. This in effect keeps your content in the correct region of the layout, since that is all that the table rows are. If you recall from the *Quick Tour* of Chapter 3, these layout controls are for your assistance, and are not actually visible on the final web page.

- ❑ The first row contains two PageNavbar controls. These will be explained later, but what they do is present the page banner, and the menu structure, as reflected in the site diagram that we created in the *Quick Tour*.

- ❑ The second row contains the content; in this case the camera picture and some text. You will also notice this line, which is a reference to the layout applied:

```
<!-- VI6.0LAYOUT = "Top 1"-->
```

So there you go. It's not rocket science, but it works. We can see that, in reality, a layout is just a fancy name for a table that has a few whizzy extras. Those extras are the PageNavbar controls for menus and banners, and the layout controls to assist you in positioning your content.

Applying Layouts to Your Project

You have the option of defining a *default layout* for your *project*, which will be the initial layout of each page, or you can add layouts *individually* to each *page*.

You might want to apply a layout that is different to the rest of the project when you have a group of pages that are somehow distinct from the others. A good example might be a company that publishes a catalogue of products on their web site. The normal pages, containing the contact details, about us information, and marketing blurb, might use a standard layout such as Top 1, where a general menu appears at the top. When the user jumps into the catalogue, each page might have a specific layout such as Top and Bottom 3. This template is similar to the other, but includes previous and next buttons along the bottom of the page, which the user could use to jump between the available products.

Using layouts like this can add a logical structure to your web site that actually promotes the goals of each page. As long as you don't choose layouts that are radically different (without good reason that is), then the users should be able to happily find their way around your site.

Try it Out – Applying a Layout to an Individual Page

Our Wrox Cameras site, when last we saw it, had a default layout of Top 1 applied to the whole site. You will recall that we applied this as the project default for *new pages* by right mouse clicking on the project in the Project Explorer window, selecting Properties, and then changing the default theme and layout in the Appearance tab. You will also remember that we had to apply the theme and layout to all *existing files* by right clicking on the project in the Project Explorer window, selecting Apply Theme and Layout, and changing the theme and layout on the relevant tab. Now we want to change the layout of just the search page, to have a different look from the rest of the site. Here's how to do this:

1.   In the Project Explorer window, right mouse click on the file search.htm.

2.   Select Apply Theme and Layout. This will apply a theme and layout directly to just the one page.

3.   In the Layout tab, select Apply layout and theme and then choose Top and Left 3. Applying this layout will put the menu on the left hand side of the page. Press OK.

4.   The files that make up the new template will be copied to the _Layouts folder, and the layout will be applied to the page. If you look at the Design view of search.htm in the editor, you will see that the layout helpers have moved to reflect the new layout.

5. Save the `search.htm` page, then right mouse click on it in the Project Explorer window, and select View in Browser to view the page in your browser. It should now look like this:

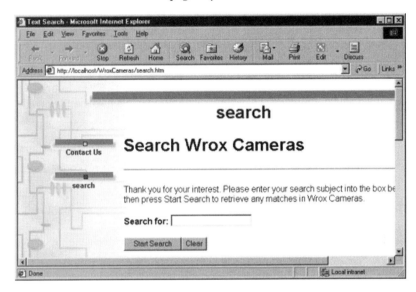

That's all there is to it. You can see that the page has taken on the new layout, where the buttons appear down the left hand side. If you click on one of these, you will see that the other pages remain as they were.

Removing a Layout from a Page or Project

Just as you can *add* layouts to your project, you can easily *remove* them, either from an individual page or a complete project. You might want to do this if you have applied a layout in error, do not want a layout on a particular page, or don't want to use layouts at all. Whatever the reason, it's a very simple task, as shown below.

To Remove a Layout from One Page

1. Right mouse click on the file in the Project Explorer window and select Apply Theme and Layout.

2. Select the Layout tab.

3. Select the Apply layout and theme option and then <none> from the list.

4. Click OK.

To Remove the Default Layout of a Project

There are two ways of removing the default layout from a project, the first of which only affects the layout of *new* pages created afterwards (the pages already created keep the old layout):

1.   In the Project Explorer window, select the project name.

2.   Select View | Property Pages from the main menu.

3.   Select the Appearance tab in the dialog box.

4.   Press the Change button.

5.   Choose the Layout tab, then select Apply layout and theme, select <none> and press OK.

The second way of removing the default layout of the project affects all new *and* existing pages in the project:

1.   In the Project Explorer window, right click on the project name.

2.   From the menu that appears select Apply Theme and Layout.

3.   In the Layout tab check Apply layout and theme: and select <none>.

4.   Press OK.

This will remove the default layout for the whole project, so that any pages that used the default layout will now have no layout at all. This will result in your items not appearing as they would have under the layout – with items that were in a sidebar now being included above or below the main contents. It will not, however, remove the files that made up the layout from the _Layouts folder of the Project Explorer window. If you want to actually delete these files, then simply select the folder of the layout that you want to delete, right mouse click on it, and select Delete.

Themes

The flip side of a layout is a theme, which provides all of the necessary graphics and style to pull it off with a bit of panache. A theme is used to apply a professional look to your page, incorporating the following visual elements:

❑   Background images for your web site.

❑   Images for buttons, banners and menu options.

❑   Graphical bullet points.

❑   Pre-defined styles for all of the text on the page, such as headers, normal text, and so on.

Themes can be a great aid when you don't have the time to put together your own consistent set of professional graphics for your site. They are easy to apply, fast, and when used with your audience in mind, can make the final product look visually appealing.

How Themes Work

When you add a theme to your project, the first action that Visual InterDev performs is to create a folder called _Themes in your project and copy a pile of files into it. One folder will be created within the _Themes folder for each theme in your project. This folder contains all of the necessary graphics and control files that Visual InterDev needs to use a particular theme. As with layouts, you can have many different themes in your project, but only one per page.

The **control files** are called **cascading style sheets** (CSS), which we will be covering in more detail shortly. What these do is contain a list of formatting instructions for applying various styles to the elements of a web page. This is very similar to a template in a modern word processor. You define styles, such as Header 1, Bullet, Normal, and so on. Each style contains instructions on the type of font, size, etc to use when presenting that style. This is basically what the CSS files in a theme do. When you write your HTML page, using the editor to format your text with these styles, the actual styling comes from the theme's style sheets.

Visual InterDev will write some links to these style sheets into each page that uses a theme. When a client browser renders a page that uses a theme, it reads the style sheets to determine how to display the information.

How it Works – Looking at the HTML Code that Applying a Theme Generates

Let's look at our `Default.htm` page for the Wrox Cameras site. You will recall that, in Chapter 3, we applied the Raygun theme to this site. Opening this file in the editor and viewing its source reveals the following fragment of HTML at the beginning:

```
<HTML>
<HEAD>
<META NAME="GENERATOR" CONTENT="Microsoft Visual Studio 6.0">
<TITLE></TITLE>


<LINK REL="stylesheet" TYPE="text/css" HREF="_Themes/raygun/THEME.CSS"
     VI6.0THEME="Raygun">
<LINK REL="stylesheet" TYPE="text/css" HREF="_Themes/raygun/GRAPH0.CSS"
     VI6.0THEME="Raygun">
<LINK REL="stylesheet" TYPE="text/css" HREF="_Themes/raygun/COLOR0.CSS"
     VI6.0THEME="Raygun">
<LINK REL="stylesheet" TYPE="text/css" HREF="_Themes/raygun/CUSTOM.CSS"
     VI6.0THEME="Raygun"></HEAD>
<BODY>
```

The `<LINK REL>` lines are special links automatically inserted by Visual InterDev when a theme is applied to a page. They point to the cascading style sheets in the folder of the theme, and tell the client browser to look there to determine how to present information.

When a page has a layout and a theme applied, the PageNavbar controls assume their appearance from the theme. These controls will then present the graphics that the cascading style sheet defines. All of this has the result of changing the slightly bizarre looking page displayed in the Design tab into a finished page with buttons and menus, when viewed in the browser.

Applying Themes to Your Project

As with layouts, themes can either be added as the *default* for an entire *project*, or applied on a *page-by-page* basis. The reasons for having individual themes are also similar for layouts – to give a special accent to a page, to make it stand out from the rest of the site, and to group pages together.

Try it Out – Adding a Theme to Your Project

Let's apply a theme to the search page, so that it is a little different from the rest of the site.

1. Right mouse click on the file search.htm in the Project Explorer window and select Apply Theme and Layout.

2. Select Apply theme on the Theme tab, and choose the Expedition theme, then press OK to apply it.

3. That's it! Visual InterDev will add the necessary files for the theme to the _Themes folder, and your page will now use the Expedition theme. Save your work and view it in the browser. It should look like this:

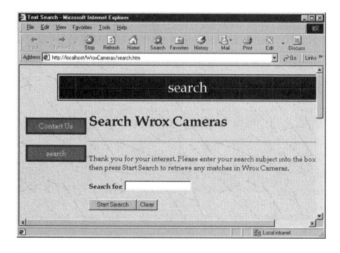

As you can see, it has quite a different look and feel from the Raygun theme.

Let's try and maintain a bit of consistency in our site by changing the theme of the search.htm page back to Raygun. Perform the above steps to do this, except at the end apply the Raygun theme, so that the search page once again has the same look as the rest of the site.

Removing a Theme From a Project

You can remove a theme either from an *individual page* or from being the *default* for a *project*. This is done in basically the same manner as removing layouts, and in fact uses the same dialog.

To Remove a Theme from One Page

1. Right mouse click on the file in the Project Explorer window and select Apply Theme and Layout.

2. In the Theme tab, choose the Apply theme option and then select <none> from the list.

3. Press OK.

To Remove the Default Theme of a Project

As with layouts, there are two ways of removing a theme from a project, the first of which only affects the theme of *new* pages created afterwards (the theme remains the same in any pages which have already been created):

1. In the Project Explorer window, select the project name.

2. Select View | Property Pages from the main menu.

3. Select the Appearance tab in the dialog box.

4. Press the Change button.

5. In the Apply Theme and Layout dialog, select Apply theme, then select <none> and press OK.

The second way of removing the default theme from a project affects *all* of the project (i.e. all existing pages in the project as well as any new pages created afterwards):

1. In the Project Explorer window, right click on the project name.

2. From the menu that appears select Apply Theme and Layout.

3. In the Theme tab check Apply theme and select <none>.

4. Press OK.

This will remove the default theme from the project, so that any pages that used the default theme will now have no theme. It will not, however, remove the files that made up the theme from the _Themes folder of the Project Explorer window. If you want to actually delete these files, then simply select the folder of the theme that you want to delete, right mouse click on it and select Delete.

Site Diagrams

Managing a large site or web application with lots of pages can be tricky. Such a site can have many pages that are constantly changing, and a deep hierarchy for navigating to specific pages. To assist in managing this, and to create a working navigation system for such a site, Visual InterDev uses **site diagrams**.

A site diagram is a graphical way of viewing the pages that make up a site, managing the relationships between those pages, and managing the pages themselves. With a site diagram, the tasks of managing and developing large sites are greatly simplified, which is after all one of the goals of Visual InterDev.

Here are some of the tasks that you can accomplish using a site diagram:

- ❑   Add new or existing pages and give them banners.
- ❑   Define the relationship between pages for use in navigation bars.
- ❑   Remove pages from the navigation structure or even from the project.
- ❑   Apply themes and layouts to pages directly from within the site diagram.

If your site uses themes and layouts, or has many pages and a deep navigation structure, then a site diagram is an invaluable tool that can save you many hours of effort. Let's take a look at how they work.

Creating a Site Diagram

The first thing that you need to do is to create a site diagram. A site diagram is a file that is saved in your project along with the other files, such as HTML pages, graphics, etc.

To Create a Site Diagram

This process is exactly the same as we carried out in the *Quick Tour* in the previous chapter:

1.   In the Project menu choose Add Item.

2.   Select the Web Project Files folder of the New tab, and select Site Diagram from the list on the right.

3.   In the Name box, type the name for the site diagram, e.g. MySiteDiagram.wdm, and click Open.

This will create a new site diagram. If it is the first site diagram for the web application, a home page will automatically be added. If you then choose File | Save, the home page will be created for you if one does not exist already.

Adding Pages to Your Site Diagram

Once you have a site diagram in your project, you need to add some pages to it. Depending on what you want to achieve, you have a few options for adding pages to your site diagram.

❑ If the page does not exist, you can create it directly in the site diagram.

❑ If the page exists, you can drag it from the Project Explorer window and drop it directly onto the site diagram.

❑ You can right mouse click on a blank part of the diagram and select Add Existing File to add an existing page to the site, or New HTML Page to add a new page. These options are also available in the Diagram menu.

As you can see, there is no shortage of ways to add a page to your diagram – so let's jump in and do it ourselves.

Try it Out – Adding a New Page to a Site Diagram

Okay, so back to Wrox Cameras. The first thing that we should have all realized by now is that we're getting a bit limited with just the three pages, so we're going to add a new page to the site. This page is eventually going to contain information for prospective buyers, and will give instructions on how to purchase goods, as well as mentioning a money-back warranty. We are going to call the page buyinginfo.htm.

To add the page:

1. Open the SiteDiagram1.wdm file from the Project Explorer window.

2. In the Diagram menu, choose New HTML Page. A page labeled Page1 will appear in the diagram.

3. Change Page1 to read Buying Info, which is the title of the page as it will appear in any banners.

4. Drag the new page on the site diagram until it is just to the right of the search page. A link should appear to the home page, looking something like this:

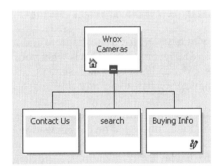

5. This is the link that the layout and PageNavbar controls discussed earlier will use for determining site navigation. The pen icon at the bottom of Buying Info means that the page is new and does not exist in the project yet. Save your site diagram and close it. This will automatically create the new page, `BuyingInfo.htm`.

6. Our last tasks are necessary to make the new page appear happily in our existing menus. Open the BuyingInfo.htm file by double clicking on it in the Project Explorer window.

7. In the editor, write the words Buying Information to go here between the content layout controls that say Add Your Content Below and Add Your Content Above.

8. Right mouse click on the second PageNavbar control and select Properties to bring up its Properties page. Under Additional pages, check the Home box and click OK. This will make the menu bar for the page display the home page. Save your work.

That's it! We have created a new page and tied it in with the existing navigation structure of the site. If you view `BuyingInfo.htm` in the browser, you should see the following page, where the menu buttons will work in connecting you with the rest of the site:

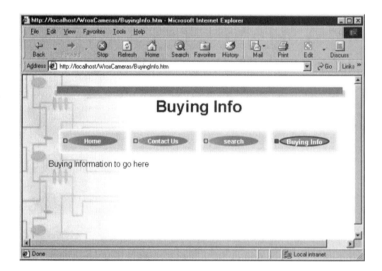

Using a Site Diagram to Manage Your Navigation

After you have created a site diagram and made some pages with it, you can start building a **navigation structure** for your project. This is what your users will use to move, or navigate, from page to page of your site. As mentioned, this should be easy to use, consistent, and suitably attractive in its presentation. Visual InterDev uses navigation bars to achieve this, as we saw earlier in the Wrox Cameras site.

So what have we learned already about this? We know that the pages that we link together on a site diagram are eventually displayed on the navigation bars of our finished site, and we know that a control called the PageNavbar helps make this happen. We are now going to look at what a PageNavbar control is, and how it is used to display information from a site diagram as a navigation bar.

What is a PageNavbar Control?

A PageNavbar control is a special object provided by Visual InterDev, which is used in layouts and themes. When you apply a layout and theme to a page or project, it uses a PageNavbar control to display banners and navigation bars.

A PageNavbar control:

❑ is positioned by the layout.

❑ is told what sort of information to display by the layout.

❑ derives its graphical look from the theme.

❑ gets the structure of a site from its site diagram.

❑ wraps it all up into a tidy navigation bar or banner.

Each PageNavbar control can display one type of information – either a banner for the page, or a level from the structural hierarchy of the site. When a layout is applied, the PageNavbar control is automatically created and set to display the correct information. This tightly coupled relationship all comes together to build a professional solution where the user can navigate the site in a consistent manner.

How Do You Define Relationships Using a Site Diagram?

To successfully create a page with a menu from a layout and theme, we need to ensure that the relationships between all pages are correctly defined in the site diagram. A site diagram is very easy to maintain, enabling us to quickly add pages and drag them around to form links to other pages.

To make a link between two pages, simply drag them close to each other and a link will be automatically created. To break the link, just drag them further apart.

With a site diagram, you can define the following types of relationships:

❑ **Parent-Child relationships** where one page is lower than the other in the hierarchy:

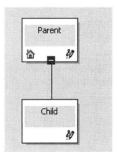

- ❏ **Sibling relationships** where children of one page are all at the same level:

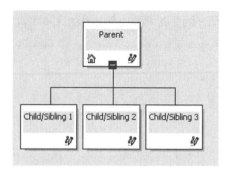

- ❏ Separate groups of pages, called **Trees**:

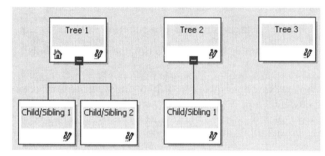

- ❏ A **Global Navigation bar**, which is a list of pages (typically the top level pages of a site) that will appear in a specified PageNavbar.

Generally, you will have one **Global Navigation bar** that contains all of the major categories of your site. The Global Navigation bar shows links to pages that should be available from *all* the pages in your site, such as contact us pages, disclaimer pages, the home page, and so on. You can position this navigation bar wherever you want, depending on the layout that you select. Along with the Global Navigation bar, you will probably have other trees of pages to do with various topics.

In the following example, the top-level pages would be in the Global Navigation bar, and the other pages would form separate trees off each page that is in the Global Navigation bar:

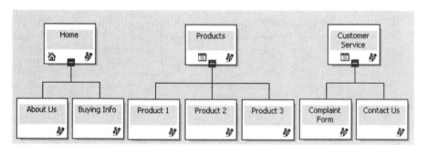

If you then applied a layout such as Top and Left 1, you would have two navigation bars on your page: along the top you would see the Global Navigation bar containing Home, Products, and Customer Service, while on the left you would see the children pages of the currently selected page. For example, the Home page would show you About Us and Buying Info.

Working with the Global Navigation Bar

The Global Navigation bar is displayed by a PageNavbar control as part of a layout, such as Top and Left 1. You can modify the content of the Global Navigation bar in a site diagram by the following methods:

❑ You can add pages to your Global Navigation bar by selecting them in the site diagram and selecting Add to Global Navigation Bar from the Diagram menu.

❑ To reorder the pages on the Global Navigation bar, select Reorder Global Navigation Bar from the Diagram menu.

❑ To remove a page from the Global Navigation bar, select it in the site diagram and select Remove from Global Navigation Bar from the Diagram menu.

Putting it Together – How the PageNavbar Knows What to Display

Once you have created your site diagram and added any pages you want to your Global Navigation bar, any pages that use a layout will automatically reflect the new site structure in their navigation bars. How does Visual InterDev perform this magic?

A layout places one or more PageNavbar controls onto a page in order to display the necessary navigation bars and banners. When a layout is applied to a page, the necessary PageNavbar controls are automatically created. Each PageNavbar control will also have been configured by the layout to automatically display a specific sort of link. This selection is made from the following available options:

❑ **Global Navigation bar** – all pages that are part of the Global Navigation bar in the site diagram.

❑ **First Level Pages** – all pages one level below the home page for the site.

❑ **Parent Level Pages** – all pages one level above the current page.

❑ **Sibling Pages** – all pages at the same level as the current page.

❑ **Back and Next Pages** – will display back and next buttons that jump to pages of the same level as the current page, based on the order in the site diagram.

❑ **Child Pages** – will display all pages one level lower than the current page.

❑ **Banner** – displays the title of the page as entered in the site diagram, or the file name if no title has been assigned.

Each PageNavbar can also optionally display a link to the home page for the site, and the immediate parent page of the currently selected page.

If you are not happy with the navigation bar of a particular page as applied by a theme, it is a simple matter to change what is displayed.

Try it Out – Manually Changing a PageNavbar Control's Display Settings

Earlier, we changed the layout of the search page from Top 1 to Top and Bottom 3. By doing this, we no longer have a link to the home page from our search page. To fix this, we have to manually change the properties of the PageNavbar control.

1. Open the search.htm file in the editor.

2. The first PageNavbar control displays the banner, and the second control is responsible for the navigation. Right mouse click on the second PageNavbar control and select Properties to bring up the following dialog, which displays all of the options for the control:

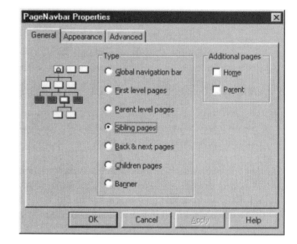

3. You can see that the Type and Additional pages lists correspond exactly to the options described above. We want to add an additional page, so check the Home checkbox and press OK.

4. Save your work.

Viewing the search page in the browser will now show a link to whichever page was specified as the home page in the site diagram.

Cascading Style Sheets

We have already seen that when you apply a theme to a page, a browser automatically displays the images, fonts and styles that make up the theme. Now we're going to look at what makes this happen – cascading style sheets (CSSs).

With the development of the web in recent years, style sheets have become more and more popular with web designers for three main reasons. Firstly, a single style sheet can be developed and applied to many web pages, rather than writing the layout and theme details into each individual page. This saves a lot of time when creating web pages. Secondly, it also means that it is easy to change a particular detail of the layout of many web pages in one easy swoop, rather than opening up all of the web pages and changing them one by one. Finally, it means that the site you create will have a constant feel and look to it, without any discrepancies in its layout.

You will remember that when you look at the source HTML of a page that has had a theme applied, there are lines of code inserted, such as this:

```
<LINK REL="stylesheet" TYPE="text/css" HREF="_Themes/raygun/THEME.CSS"
      VI6.0THEME="Raygun">
<LINK REL="stylesheet" TYPE="text/css" HREF="_Themes/raygun/GRAPH0.CSS"
      VI6.0THEME="Raygun">
<LINK REL="stylesheet" TYPE="text/css" HREF="_Themes/raygun/COLOR0.CSS"
      VI6.0THEME="Raygun">
<LINK REL="stylesheet" TYPE="text/css" HREF="_Themes/raygun/CUSTOM.CSS"
      VI6.0THEME="Raygun">
```

These are links to cascading style sheets that reside in the _Themes folder. When the client browser reads the page, it looks in the specified folder and reads the contents of the CSS file. This file contains instructions on how to present all of the fonts and graphics that make up the theme for the web page.

So that is basically what a cascading style sheet is: a set of instructions on what makes up a style. These instructions are in a standardized language similar to HTML, and contain information on how to present the elements of the HTML page.

The cascading style sheets that make up the various themes available with Visual InterDev are all ready-made. All themes work by using these files, but it is also possible to use CSS files outside of a theme. This enables you to create your own styles that can be every bit as in-depth as a theme. To assist in making your own CSS files, Visual InterDev provides an easy to use CSS editor.

Using the CSS Editor

The CSS editor is used to edit CSS files. These files are then referenced in documents by a line such as this:

```
<LINK REL="stylesheet" TYPE="text/css" HREF="mystyles.CSS">
```

To Create a Style Sheet

1. From the Project menu, choose Add Web Item | Style Sheet.

2. In the dialog that opens, type in a Name for your style sheet, e.g. mystyles.css, and click Open.

3. The style sheet will be created, and the CSS editor will open, as shown overleaf:

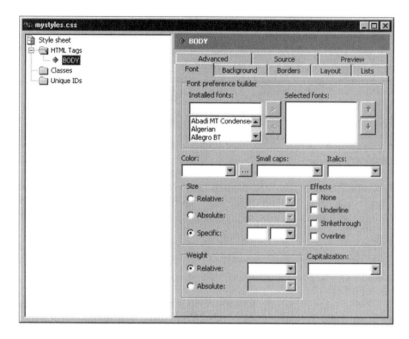

To Edit Styles in a Style Sheet

The CSS editor is an easy way to edit style sheets in your project. For example, if you want to add, or change, a background color for your web pages you could follow these steps:

1. Open the CSS editor, by double clicking on an existing CSS file in the Project Explorer window.

2. Highlight the BODY tag in the left hand pane.

3. Select the Background tab in the right hand pane.

4. To choose a color you can either select one in the drop down listbox, or click the ... button to bring up the Color Picker and choose one from there (we'll cover the Color Picker in more detail below).

5. To see the result of your choice, select the Preview tab. The window in the Preview tab displays a default page. If you want to view one of your own pages as the preview, you can simple type its address in the HTML page to preview the style sheet with: textbox, or browse for it using the ... button.

6. When finished, close the editor and this will prompt you to save the changes.

Another feature of the Background tab allows you to place an image as the background for your pages. Simply type the location of the image that you wish to use in the Use background image: textbox, or browse for an image. If the image is smaller than the page, the CSS editor will automatically tile the image so that it will fill the page.

As well as background colors, the CSS editor can change font type, font size, border size, layout, and so on, in the corresponding tabs.

The Color Picker

The Color Picker has three tabs: Named Colors, Safety Palette and Custom Color.

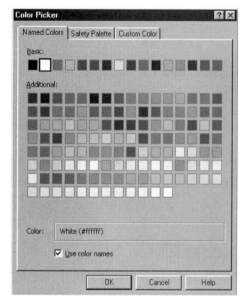

The Named Colors tab allows you to select one of 140 colors, and at the bottom of this tab the color is displayed as a **hex value**. All browsers recognize a basic set of 16 colors and some browsers, such as Internet Explorer, recognize all 140 colors. If you don't know which browser your page will be viewed on then it's best to use the hex value of the color, so that if the browser does not recognize the color name, it will be able to process the hex value. To do this all you have to do is uncheck the Use color names checkbox.

The Safety Palette is a collection of 216 colors that are optimized for cross platform use. If you select a color from this palette then you minimize the chance that a browser viewing your page will encounter a color that it cannot display, and therefore substitute another color, with unexpected results.

Finally, the Custom Color tab allows you to create your own color by mixing red, green and blue, and displays the results as a hex value.

Inserting New Tabs into the CSS Editor

The CSS editor also allows you to add HTML tabs and classes, so that you can apply a style to every tab in your pages.

1. Open the CSS editor.

2. In the list on the left are the tags currently available. Right mouse click on a folder and choose Insert HTML Tag to edit the style of a new item.

3. In the Insert New HTML Tag dialog that appears you can choose a tag from the list in the drop down listbox.

4. Press OK.

5. The inserted tag will now appear in the left hand pane and, when highlighted, the style of the tag can be edited as before.

To Apply a Style Sheet Manually

If you have written your own style sheet, you need to apply it to any page that should use it. This involves writing a `<LINK REL="stylesheet">` line to the page. You could do this manually, but there is an easier way:

1. Open the page to which you want to apply the CSS.

2. Switch to Source view and scroll until you reach the area where the reference is to be written.

3. Drag the CSS file from the Project Explorer window and drop it into the page at the desired location. The necessary link will be written and the page will now use the cascading style sheet.

Once a page references a style sheet, any HTML tags that are in the page will assume the style that was defined in the CSS editor.

> **If you apply a theme and layout to a whole project, the theme and layout will take priority over any style sheet that you link to an individual page. To apply a style sheet to a page in a project with a default theme and layout, you first have to turn off the theme and layout for that page.**

There is, however, something that you should be aware of when using CSSs, and it is something that will be a bane of your existence for a while to come: browser incompatibility.

Cascading Style Sheets and Browser Compatibility

The Cascading Style Sheets Level 1 specification was released by the WWW Consortium in late 1996. It was supported to a large degree in both Netscape Communicator 4 and Internet Explorer 4. Since then a Level 2 specification was released in May 1998, some of which has been incorporated into Internet Explorer 5. In addition, at the time of writing, a third level is under progress. In an ideal world CSSs would work in every browser that attempted to render the page. Sadly, we do not live in such a world, and the world of web design is fraught with problems of browser compatibility. This is something that we will hit on quite often in this book, as it is an important consideration for all web developers. Here is the problem in a nutshell.

HTML is a published standard, one that is constantly evolving. Web browsers are designed to render HTML into something useful for the reader to view. These browsers are written by companies with the aim of attracting customers and, to grab customers, a tried and tested marketing technique is to provide extra features, so that is what they've done. Each browser handles HTML slightly differently, and while the browser of one company might be able to handle a particular tag, that of another might fail, or display it differently. Add to this the fact that the HTML standard is changing, and that each new version of a browser has evolved to meet this standard, and you begin to see the big picture in all its glorious chaos.

This is the Internet that we have inherited and have to work with, one where the more features of a particular browser you decide to use, the less capable a different browser might be at handling those features. You guessed it – cascading style sheets is one of these features.

In general, Microsoft Internet Explorer versions 4.0 and above, as well as Netscape Navigator versions 4.0 and above, will support most of the features of CSSs. Internet Explorer 3.0 supports a subset of it that will possibly not look quite how you expected it to. Anything older than these versions will basically not be able to render the styles as defined in the style sheet. In this situation, the page will still be readable, it just won't be quite as pretty as you wanted it to be.

If you are wondering how to get around this, the basic answer is (at least for CSSs) that it is pretty difficult. If you want to use style sheets, then you must ensure that your intended audience will be able to support them. If they can't, then you need to design alternate means for displaying the appearance you want. This could mean not using CSSs at all in your project, or using script techniques (which we will cover later in this book) to make certain that the page that a browser receives is one that it is capable of using.

Generally, if you can specify browsers of version 4.0 and above, you will have a good set of features. One of the most important parts of developing a site that will be used in multiple browsers is testing it against those browsers. For this reason, it is useful to create test machines that run specific browsers and view the functionality of your web page in each of those browsers.

We will cover the issue of browser compatibility again later in this book, as it is a subject that comes up regularly. This is one of the challenging aspects of web design that gives design a stronger meaning than just drawing graphics and creating attractive pages.

Changing Layouts of Individual Pages

Another aspect of page design that we will briefly look at is changing the layout of an individual page. You may have a page that contains important information that you wish to stand out to catch the eye of the reader. To do this you could increase the size of the font, display it in a different color or with a different colored background. Obviously, you don't want to change the style sheet which may be linked to the page, as this will change the layout for all pages linked to that style sheet. Writing a separate style sheet just for this page is one solution, but the easiest way is to change the properties of the area in question. With Visual InterDev this is very easy. Let's have a go at making some text stand out in a page.

Try it Out – Changing Layouts of Individual Pages

1. Open any page in Design view.

2. Place your cursor in the block of text that you want to change (or highlight more than one block of text if you want to change more than one piece of text at the same time).

3. In the Properties window select .backgroundColor and click on the ... button.

4. In the Color Picker that appears, select a color of your choice.

5. Press OK.

The area of the page that was highlighted is now a different color from the surrounding page. If you now view the code for the page in Source view you will see that the `<P>` element for the block of text that you changed has been modified to include the style you chose, e.g. `<P STYLE="BACKGROUND-COLOR: violet">`.

Using the Properties window you can achieve many changes in the style of your page, including changing the font color and size, adding background graphics and changing the margin sizes. Feel free to experiment.

Summary

In this chapter we have looked at some of the tools that you can use to apply a professional look and feel to your site. We saw that these tools all work together to create a working site navigation bar that matches the look you selected. You use these tools in a manner similar to this:

❑ Apply a theme to give professional graphics and styling to your site. A theme works by writing links to a collection of cascading style sheet (CSS) files, automatically copied to your project by applying the theme.

❑ A layout divides your page into regions, which are in fact cells of a large table. When you select a layout, you also select what type of navigation bar(s) you want to use.

❑ Navigation bars are in fact PageNavbar controls, which are automatically inserted and configured by the layout. They determine what information to display by reading the structure of a site diagram.

❑ A site diagram is used to build the navigation structure of your site, and to quickly add new pages as part of this structure. You can also use it to maintain a Global Navigation bar, which is a "top level" navigation bar for the main categories of your site.

❑ Cascading style sheets contain instructions on how elements of a page should be rendered. They are used in themes, or you can create your own.

We have used these tools to modify the Wrox Cameras site, which now has a consistent look and feel based on the **Raygun** theme. The purpose of this site, as we mentioned earlier, is to eventually serve as an online catalogue. Currently, the site is a little bit light on content, a problem that we will rectify in the next chapter.

The next chapter is all about making your web pages talk to databases. This moves your page away from a *static* model, where you have to manually change the contents of a file to change the content of the web page, into a *dynamic* model, where web pages display information from a database and do not require manual changes.

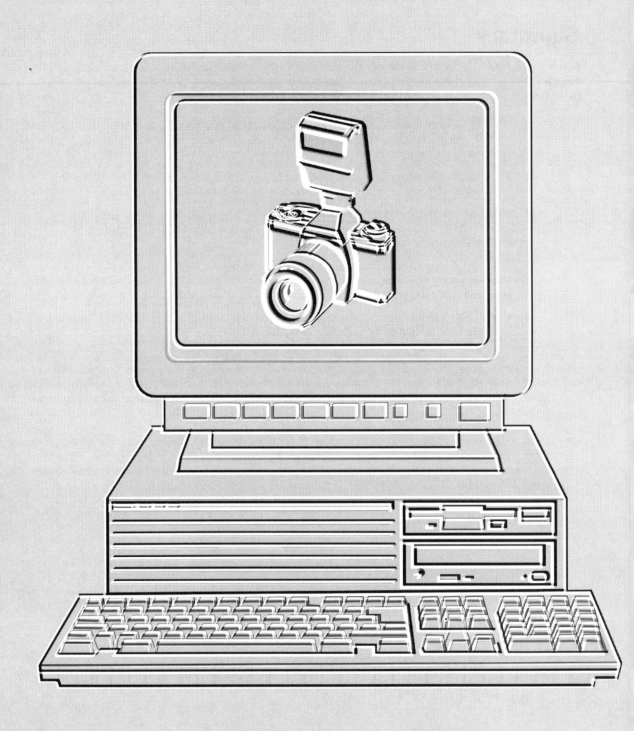

Database Basics

Something that has often been said about web applications is that they are "work in progress". This can be taken in many ways, but one aspect close to the hearts of most developers is the fact that web sites are constantly changing. Take our Wrox Cameras site as an example. When it grows beyond its current state into a site that will present a complete catalogue of products, what happens when those products change? Or maybe the price of a product changes?

When you are dealing with changing information such as lists of products, statistical reports, sales figures, and the like, there is no way that you want to get your hands dirty and rewrite every page whenever a change happens. This would quickly become both unmanageable and highly expensive. The solution to this sort of requirement is to link your web project to a **database**. The database can then provide the information that your various web pages portray to the users. Updating the database involves less work and disruption than updating all of your web pages.

In this chapter, we will take a look at what a database is, what you can use it for in a web application, and how Visual InterDev makes it easy to do so. By the end of this chapter, you will be familiar with:

- ❑ What a database is and how it can help you.
- ❑ How to create your database, add tables, and add data.
- ❑ How to configure Visual InterDev to talk to your database.
- ❑ Working with database projects and data environments.
- ❑ Using data bound controls – getting to grips with some of the controls that Visual InterDev offers to work with a database, specifically the Recordset and Grid controls to display data.
- ❑ Queries and SQL basics – understanding how to get information out of your database.
- ❑ Using the SQL Query Builder.

We will use these concepts and tools to begin to build a basic product catalogue for Wrox Cameras. Before we can do this, however, we should look at what a database can do for us.

Why Use a Database?

Databases are designed to *store* information and *deliver* it on demand. When you link your web project to a database, you add to the flexibility and maintainability of your project. If you are developing a site that will have lots of changing content, or information specific to each user, then you really don't have much choice in the matter – you either use a database or prepare yourself for a never-ending task of updating your web pages.

Here is a simple idea for a site that will show you where a database might be required. The Wrox Cameras site will offer a catalogue of cameras that the shop will sell. Let's take a step back, and look at how you would actually portray the cameras themselves. It is quite possible that for each camera you would want a separate page, with maybe a picture, some textual information, and a price. Without a database, you would have to create a separate page for every camera! We have already mentioned that without a database, every time the information about a camera changes, you would have to change the page for that product. Even if you have only got 8 cameras, this is quickly going to become a big task. Now, think about a stationary supplier with a catalogue of maybe 5000 products …

So, we can see that there are cases when plain HTML web pages are not enough, and seeing as we are reading a chapter about databases, it's a safe bet that using one is the answer. There are now two questions that we need to ask – what is a database, and what can it do for your web site?

What is a Database?

❑ A database is an application that *manages* information (or **data**), and provides that information on demand to other applications, known as clients.

❑ When you use a database application, your data is stored in **files** that the database application manages.

❑ Databases are used to store all sorts of information, such as financial details, catalogue information, timetables, and so on. When you create a database, you specify what data will be stored, and design **tables** to store it in.

❑ Client applications talk to the database using standard communication tools (which will be explained more fully in Chapter 9), and receive the information requested.

❑ In a web environment, your web server typically talks to the computer that runs the database application, called the **database server**, to request information. In this case, your web server is the *client* of the database server.

Both can in fact exist on the same machine if you want, but if a very fast network is available, it can often be advantageous to keep them on separate servers.

What Can a Database Do for Your Web Site?

❑ In our catalogue example, you can create *one* page that talks to the database to retrieve information on *all* products, instead of having one page for *each* product.

❑ Web pages can be made that will actually put data directly *into* the database, giving you a useful way of receiving feedback from your users.

❑ Changes made to the data in a database can be immediately reflected the next time the web server displays a page that uses the data. This means that if we have a large catalogue of products, we can change all of the pages from one central place, instead of opening every page and changing each one separately.

❑ The data that makes up the page can be accessed by other programs, giving rise to a host of reporting options, maintenance possibilities, sharing of information with your marketing and accounting software, and so on.

❑ Changes to the structure of a page, such as the way a product appears on the page, or the navigation structure of a site, can be made without worrying about the data, since it is stored elsewhere.

❑ You can make certain information available only to specific users, by creating a login screen and cross-referencing the user name with information in the database.

As you can see, a database can do some pretty impressive things for your site. The good news, which should by now come as no shock to you, is that Visual InterDev comes with some very sophisticated tools to make life easier for you when working with databases. Before we get into looking at these tools, we are going to need to create a database to use.

Basics of Database Design

The first task in using a database with your project is to decide which database application you are going to use. Visual InterDev will work with any number of databases, such as Microsoft Access, Oracle, Sybase, or SQL Server. Every database application has its own particular strengths and weaknesses that should be taken into account when deciding which to use.

For our database solution, we are going to use Microsoft SQL Server Version 7.0, because Visual InterDev has been designed to work very closely with this product. If you would prefer to use another database system, as long as it has ODBC drivers available for it, then there should be no problems. In fact, we will also take a quick look at using Microsoft Access in place of SQL Server, and Chapter 14 gives a more complete example of building an application that uses Microsoft Access as the database. However, if you have it available, you should use SQL Server 7.0 for the Wrox Cameras database, since this is what the majority of the examples in this book will be based on.

If you have installed Visual InterDev as part of Visual Studio 6, then you will already have a Developer edition of Microsoft SQL Server 6.5 to use. Although this has a different user interface to version 7.0, which we're using here, it does pretty much the same thing. The choice of database application is up to you but, as stated above, for this initial coverage we will use SQL Server version 7.0.

We need to understand a few concepts before we can jump into using SQL Server or Access. One of these concepts is how our pages get to talk to the database. We know that a web server, such as Microsoft Personal Web Server (PWS) or Microsoft Internet Information Server (IIS), hosts a web page. If a client browses to a web page that utilizes a database, then the web server will request information from the database server. This interaction looks like this:

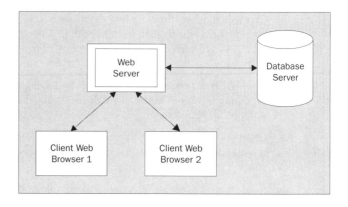

This is the most common architecture used for communicating with a database. Whenever a client browser requests a web page that requires information from the database, it just communicates this request to the web server. The web server then retrieves information from the database server, creates the web page, and sends it to the client browser. In this model, the web server and database server can be on the same machine, but in most live instances the poor performance of loading all your work onto one machine will dictate that two or more machines be used.

Creating Your Database in SQL Server

In order for us to use a database in our web application, we need a database server. For development purposes it can be quite acceptable to use a copy of SQL Server running on your local machine. SQL Server 7.0 comes with a Desktop version that will run under Windows 98 or Windows NT, and this is quite suitable for developing the Wrox Cameras site. At a later stage, this database can be copied onto a separate server running a full-blown version of SQL Server 7.0.

SQL Server 7.0 is a database application that is responsible for managing data. It is what is known as a **relational** database, meaning that it stores information in tables that model groups of related information. For example, we might have a database comprising tables called *customers*, *products*, *orders*, and so on. You can imagine how these tables are related, because an entry in the *orders* table will have a reference to the *customer* who placed the order, and one or more references to the *products* that they want to buy. When you need to extract information from the database that involves combining data from two or more of these tables, for example to show all *orders* for a particular *customer*, you write a **query** to retrieve the information, and the query forms a temporary relationship between the tables concerned. In SQL Server, this query is written in a language called Transact-SQL. We will firstly see how to create a SQL Server database, and later on how to retrieve information from it and use it in our application.

We now need to create a place to store the data that will be accessed by our Wrox Cameras web site.

Even if you've chosen to use Access instead, read through the next few pages for information. We'll be showing how to create the database in Access in a while, but some of the important theory discussed in the next few pages will not be repeated in the Access section.

Try it Out – Creating the Wrox Cameras Database in SQL Server

The database that we have decided to use is a local copy of SQL Server 7.0 Desktop edition, or else the full version on a different server, depending on your setup. We are going to create a database for Wrox Cameras, which we will eventually expand to be able to serve all of the data requirements for the Wrox Cameras site.

1. Start the SQL Server Enterprise Manager, which is normally found on the Windows Start menu under Programs | Microsoft SQL Server 7.0 | Enterprise Manager.

2. On the left of the Console screen, you will see an explorer-like interface, which you use to drill down into the various databases that you have configured. Select your machine name under SQL Server Group. (You may need to first expand this node.) You should see a taskpad such as this:

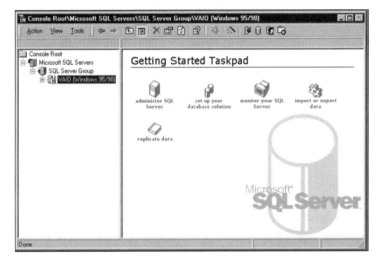

If your server does not appear, then right mouse click on the SQL Server Group line and choose New SQL Server Registration to register a new server. This will launch a wizard, which will take you through the process of adding the server to the list of available servers.

3. The above taskpad contains various choices that launch wizards to assist you in performing particular tasks. We want to create a database, so click on set up your database solution to bring up the following taskpad:

119

4. Click on the create a database option to choose the Create Database wizard. Press Next to start the wizard.

5. In the wizard, specify WroxCameras as the database name, and optionally change the location of where the actual database file will be created. Press Next.

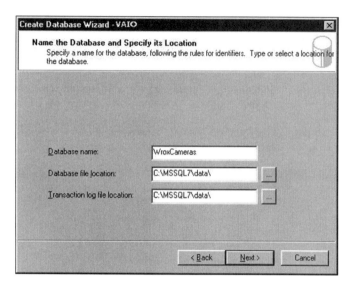

6. This step is where you define the initial size of your database. This file is where all the data will be stored, and should be big enough to store whatever data you want to place in it. Analyzing the size of a database can be a huge task in itself – thankfully, SQL Server 7.0 can dynamically grow a database that is too small. If you are creating a database with a few tables and a few thousand rows of data that is mainly numbers, a small size such as 15-25MB should suffice initially. If your table has lots of tables, tens of thousands of rows, and contains images and large amounts of text, you should consider 100MB, 200MB, and so on. For now, specify 25 as the file size, and then press Next.

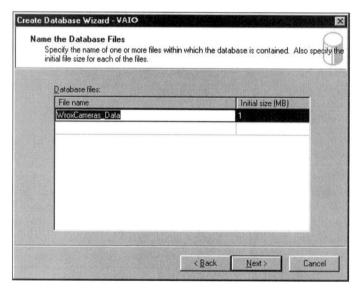

7. This step is where you tell SQL Server how to handle database growth, as we mentioned above. You will notice that the default is to automatically grow the files. This is what we want, so leave the default and press Next.

8. The next step is where we define the size of the log file. A log file is where SQL Server automatically writes information about events such as errors, clients requesting information, and so on. This can be set to automatically grow in the same manner as the database file above. A very general guideline for determining the size of the log file would be to take the database file size and either specify half of that size or the same size. Enter 10 and then press Next.

9. This step is for defining log file growth, which works in the same way as for databases. Accept the default and press Next.

10. You will be given a brief report on the actions that the wizard is about to perform, summarizing database name, file locations and sizes, and so on. Press Finish to complete the wizard and to create your database.

11. You will be prompted to create a maintenance plan – select No. You should now see a "The database was successfully created" message box, so click OK again.

12. If you drill down using the Console into the database server and then the Databases folder, you will see a database named WroxCameras. Double clicking on it will bring up a maintenance screen which should look like this:

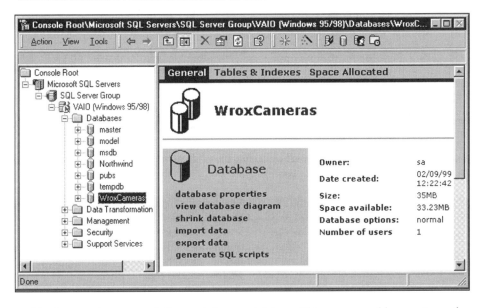

If you see this, then you've successfully created your database. This screen enables you to perform all sorts of wonderful maintenance tasks on your database, such as creating tables, creating stored procedures, etc. However, we are more interested in doing this from within Visual InterDev, so that's the next task that we'll look at. For now, you can close the Enterprise Manager.

Connecting to Your SQL Server Database

Visual InterDev is designed to be able to manage databases directly, and it works seamlessly with SQL Server 7.0 to enable you to perform many administrative and data manipulation tasks directly within the IDE. There are two ways of using Visual InterDev to interact with SQL Server:

❑ If you want to do some pretty serious database maintenance work, it can often be useful to create a **database project**. This is similar to a web project with the exception that, instead of working with web pages and images, it works with databases. A database project does not help your web site talk to the database, it just enables you to maintain your database.

❑ It is also possible to communicate with a database directly from within your Visual InterDev web project, by simply adding a **connection** to the database. This gives you limited capabilities for maintaining the database, but its main purpose is to enable your web pages to display information from the database.

The main advantage of using a database project is that you get a clean project solely concerned with the database – without any clutter of the web site itself.

If you want to actually display data from a database in your web pages, you only need use the second method – adding a connection in your web project. This also gives you some capabilities to maintain the database as well.

In this chapter, we will show you how to achieve *both* methods, beginning with creating a database project to maintain the database. Later, we use the second method to get the data from the database into your web pages. This is covered in the section entitled *Using Data Environments*.

The first part of creating a database project is actually connecting to your database. This is achieved using a standard database access method such as ODBC or OLE DB. Both of these terms, and other methods of accessing databases, will be covered in detail in Chapter 9 – *Database Access with ADO*. For now, we just need to know that in order to connect to a database, Visual InterDev requires various connection settings.

Try it Out – Creating a Database Project and Connecting to Your Database

Now that we have created our SQL Server 7.0 database, we need to connect to it in Visual InterDev. To do this, we add a database project to our solution, and point it at the new database.

In Visual InterDev, when you open the WroxCameras project and look at the top of the Project Explorer window, you will see the line Solution 'Wrox Cameras' (1 project). A *solution* is a collection of projects joined to create one application. In this case, the solution is the Wrox Cameras site. Currently, the solution consists of just one project - the *web project* that contains all of the web pages that make up the Wrox Cameras site. We are going to add a new project to the solution, namely a *database project*, to enable us to work with the Wrox Cameras SQL Server database that we have just created.

1. In Visual InterDev, open the WroxCameras project.

2. Select File | New Project. In the New tab of the dialog, expand the Visual Studio node, select Database Projects, then select New Database Project in the right hand pane. Enter WroxCamerasDB into the Name field - this will be the name of the new project. The New Project dialog should look like this:

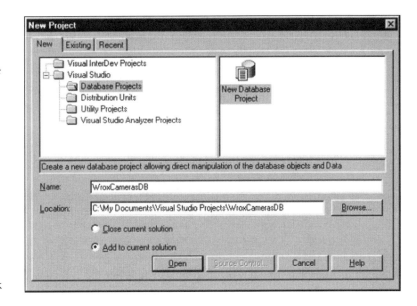

3. Select Add to current solution at the bottom of the New Project dialog. This will add the new database project WroxCamerasDB to the currently open solution. Press Open.

4. The Data Link Properties wizard will be opened. This wizard helps you to actually connect your database project to a database. In the first dialog box, select Microsoft OLE DB Provider for SQL Server. This is a method of connecting to SQL Server, which will be explained in Chapter 9. Basically, it is one the better methods currently available, which is why we are using it here.

5. Press Next to bring up the next step of the wizard. This is where you specify the database server, login name, password, and database to which you want to connect. The server name will be your machine name, or else the name of another server if you are using a different one. The User name and Password will default to "sa" and blank respectively, so you only need to type sa. If you have defined security for your SQL Server, then use a correct user name and password at this stage. The database that we want to connect to is the one that we recently created – WroxCameras, which should be visible in the drop down list. The completed dialog should look something like this:

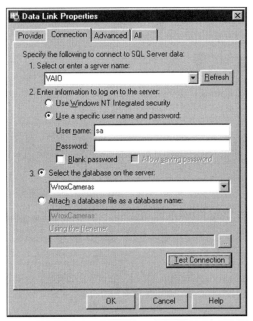

If you have not defined security, it is advisable to do so – using the system administrator account, sa, is not a good idea! Security is configured in the SQL Enterprise Manager, under the **Security** *tab for the SQL Server that you want to administer. You create logins using the logins icon, where you can easily manage the databases that a login can control. You should at least change the password for the sa account, to tighten security. Once security is configured, it is a simple matter of connecting using the login name and password created.*

6. Once entered correctly, these settings should be enough to talk to the database. Press the Test Connection button to ensure that you can connect to the database. It should respond with a message - Test connection succeeded.

If you do have problems connecting, refer to the MSDN Knowledge Base that comes with Visual Studio and is available at the Microsoft web site, www.microsoft.com. *By typing in the error code at the search page, you should be able to find some excellent articles to help you to overcome any problems in connecting to your database.*

7. Click OK to accept the message and then OK again to close the above window. This will create the database project and add it to your new solution.

If you now look at your Project Explorer window, you will notice that it looks something like this:

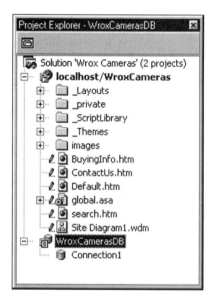

The new project, WroxCamerasDB, contains a connection object, Connection1. This is a connection to our Wrox Cameras database in SQL Server.

You will also notice that the Properties window contains a new tab, **Data View**. Clicking on this tab displays a list of the database objects that are in the Wrox Cameras database:

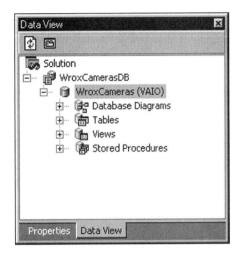

We have now managed to create a database and get Visual InterDev to connect to it successfully. However, we still haven't managed to use it for anything, which is what we're going to look at next. To do this, we are going to learn what some of those items in the **Data View** are for, and how we can use them to make developing with a database an easy task.

Creating Tables in a SQL Server Database

One of the many strengths of Visual InterDev, when it comes to working with databases, is that it enables you to create objects in those databases without stepping out of the IDE. (This feature is only available in the Enterprise edition of Visual InterDev – the Pro edition is limited to enabling you to browse the database structure.) In most other development environments, actually manipulating the structure of a database had to be performed directly in the database itself. Visual InterDev, as part of its integrated approach to web development, incorporates database manipulation nicely into its repertoire of friendly features.

Using Visual InterDev, you can quickly and easily add tables to your database, fill them with data, and run queries on those tables. What does all this mean?

Structure of Database Tables

The purpose of using a database is invariably to store data. The way in which data is stored in SQL Server 7.0, and in most other database programs out there, is in user-defined **tables**. A table is a collection of information that is normally to do with one precise subject or entity. An example might be a table to store customer details, or product details.

Each table can contain many **fields**, which are aspects of the data that the table is concerned with. If we took the example of a table that stored customer data, then we would expect to find fields such as customer name, address, telephone number, and so on. These fields can store many different types of data, such as free-format text, numeric data, and dates. When you create a table, you need to define its fields and **data types**.

Each table consists of zero or more rows of data. A **row** of data is one instance of the information that the table is concerned with. A row of data is referred to as a **record**, and in our customer table example this is especially easy to see since each row represents one customer record.

A customer table within a database might look something like this:

customer_number	first_name	last_name	telephone	fax
1	Jane	Brighton	4445555	4445556
2	Andrew	Smith	3336666	3336667
3	Greg	Bloggs	3332121	

Each row (record) represents one customer. There are five fields in the table. The first customer is Jane Brighton, and her telephone number is 444 5555. This is all fairly simple and easy to understand.

The same database might also store a table called orders, which might contain a reference to the customer_number field of our customer table above. A simple orders table might be:

order_number	customer_number	order_date	amount
1	3	20 June 1999	432.05
2	1	26 June 1999	300.00

Using SQL Queries to Talk to the Database

It is possible to **join** the contents of two tables like this by using **SQL queries**. SQL stands for Structured Query Language, and it is pretty much a widely used standard in relational databases today. As with HTML, there are quite a few standards of SQL, of which Microsoft SQL Server 7.0 uses Transact-SQL. Most of these standards are fairly similar and achieve the same results through slightly different syntax. You could use SQL to join the customer and orders tables using a simple query, looking something like this:

```
SELECT order_number, first_name, last_name, amount
FROM customer, order
WHERE order.customer_number = customer.customer_number
ORDER BY order_number
```

SQL is very similar to the English language, and the query above is fairly self explanatory – we can see that it will *select* data in the four listed fields *from* the two specified tables, but only *where* there is a match between the data in the two fields named in the WHERE clause. The results will be sorted by the order number (ascending is the default). The results of this query would then be:

order_number	first_name	last_name	amount
1	Gregg	Bloggs	432.05
2	Jane	Brighton	300.00

This is basically how databases work. They store all the information in tables, and you write queries to retrieve subsets of that information to meet your requirements, from the data in the various database tables.

Visual InterDev includes a **SQL Query Builder** to help you build SQL queries like that shown above. Further information about how to use this, and more SQL syntax, is given at the end of this chapter.

Keys in Database Tables

Now for one more important point about tables. As mentioned, they are comprised of rows of information. In many instances it is important to specify that each row of data is unique, and not repeated. It also is important to be able to quickly search for a record within a table, and to be able to identify what it relates to. In a database table, this is achieved by adding what is known as a **key**. A key is simply a field that the database keeps track of – it can either be unique within the table, or there can be duplicates – all of this is configurable. Any field, or indeed a combination of fields, can form a key, which offers great performance increases when searching for data. A key does this at the expense of speed when adding and updating records – this occurs because the database needs to modify the index for the key to incorporate the changes.

For each table it is possible to also specify one key as the **primary key**, which must always be *unique* within the table. The primary key is used to identify a record - for example, in our customer table above, the customer_number field would be a good candidate for the primary key.

In summary, keys are useful for joining records, performing searches, and enforcing uniqueness. A primary key specifies that the record is unique across the entire table, and is the identifier field for that record.

This book is not going to look too deeply at how to design great databases or write SQL queries, as there are many books dedicated to that topic. We are going to look at how Visual InterDev can be used to manage a database and use the data stored in one. The tools that we'll see include facilities for creating tables, entering data, running queries, and creating stored procedures for use in your applications.

Try it Out – Creating a Database Table Using Visual InterDev

Now that you know what a table is, and what it is for, it is time to make one for our Wrox Cameras site. We are eventually going to build web pages that will display the various cameras that the site sells. There will be two pages: a *preview* page that lists the cameras and provides a basic thumbnail image, and a *detailed* page, which displays full information and a large picture of the chosen camera.

Our requirement is to store the underlying information for these two pages in the Wrox Cameras database. This will be in a table called product, since it is conceivable that at some stage the shop might sell items other than cameras, such as film, printers, scanners, etc. This is the structure of the table that we will create:

Field Name	Description	Type of Data
product_id	ID of the product.	Alphanumeric, up to 50 characters, e.g. WCSLR23456.
name	Name of the product.	Alphanumeric, up to 50 characters.

Table Continued on Following Page

Field Name	Description	Type of Data
type_id	ID of type of product, link to product_type table.	Numeric.
description	Description of the product.	Alphanumeric, up to 50 characters.
price	Price of the product.	Money.
thumbnail	Name of the file that makes up the thumbnail image.	Alphanumeric, up to 50 characters.
picture	Name of the file that makes up the full image of the product.	Alphanumeric, up to 50 characters.

The product_id field will be the primary key for this table. The field called type_id will contain a number that relates to the product_type field in another table, product_type. We can later do joins between the two tables using SQL, when we retrieve information to display products of a particular type. Joins like this are discussed in the section on *The SQL Query Builder* at the end of this chapter.

The product_type table looks like this:

Field Name	Description	Type of Data
product_type	ID of the product type.	Numeric.
type_description	Description of the product type, e.g. "35mm compact", "35mm SLR", "Digital".	Alphanumeric, up to 50 characters.

The product_type field is the primary key for this table.

In order to create these tables, we will use the Data View to directly create them in SQL Server from within Visual InterDev. Let's go…

1. In the Data View window, click on the WroxCameras database to expand it, if it is not already expanded.

2. Right mouse click on the Tables item and select New Table from the menu that appears.

3. Type in the name of the new table, product, and then press OK.

4. You will now see the table designer window. This is where you type in the details of the fields that you want in the table. Enter the details shown below, noticing how the Datatype and Length columns approximate what we specified above for the table (varchar represents alphanumeric). Datatypes can either be selected from the drop down list or, if you begin to type them, Visual InterDev will auto-complete them for you.

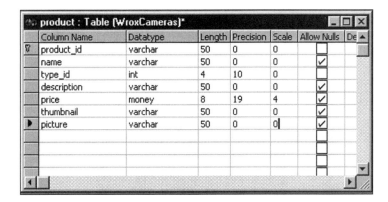

	Column Name	Datatype	Length	Precision	Scale	Allow Nulls	De
🔑	product_id	varchar	50	0	0	☐	
	name	varchar	50	0	0	☑	
	type_id	int	4	10	0	☐	
	description	varchar	50	0	0	☑	
	price	money	8	19	4	☑	
	thumbnail	varchar	50	0	0	☑	
▶	picture	varchar	50	0	0	☑	

5. Note the Allow Nulls column. A **null** value is a special value that means "Nothing has been entered here", and occurs when the field has not been modified, or if it has been set purposely to null. If a field should be allowed to be empty like this, then the Allow Nulls column should be checked. The minimum information we require to define a product is its ID and type, which is why the Allow Nulls boxes for the product_id and type_id fields are unchecked.

6. Also, notice the key to the left of the product_id column. This means that it is the primary key of the table. A primary key must always be unique, as discussed earlier, i.e. the data in the field must be different for each record. A primary key can also never be null. To define the primary key, right mouse click on the gray column to the left of the product_id row, and select Set Primary Key.

7. The last points to notice in this table are the columns Precision and Scale, which are relevant for the numeric data types, such as int and money. Precision is the number of digits in a number, while Scale is the number of digits to the right of the decimal point in a number. For example, the number 123.45 has a precision of 5 and a scale of 2.

8. Select File | Save product. This will create the table.

9. In the Data View window you will now see an icon for the product table. If you expand this icon, you will see icons for each field that you added above:

10. If you right mouse click on any of these fields, you can switch the Data View window to the Properties window and display the properties of that field, such as data type and size.

11. That's it! You have created a table. Let's quickly create the product_type table by repeating steps 1-4 above and using the table name of product_type. The table designer for the product_type table should be completed with the primary key set to product_type, to look like this:

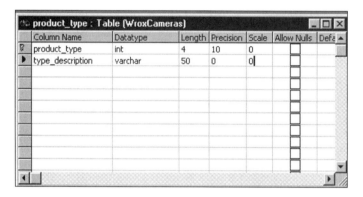

12. Save the product_type table. You should now see the two new tables in the Data View window:

That's all there is to it. As you can see, it is a very easy process to create tables from within Visual InterDev. For those of you who have used older versions of SQL Server, you will be particularly appreciative of the table designer – it's a giant leap above writing the scripts by hand! If you need to edit a table at any later stage, you can open it in the table designer by right mouse clicking on the table in the Data View window and selecting Design.

Using Microsoft Access Instead of SQL Server

Before jumping in and entering data into our tables, we are going to have a quick look at using Access in place of SQL Server.

If you do not have access to SQL Server, then you can easily use Microsoft Access in its place and achieve fairly similar functionality. The trade offs in using Access instead of SQL Server are many, but for learning purposes or small projects, they are not too severe. The main trade offs are:

❑   Access is not as fast or as robust as SQL Server.

❑   Access does not cope well with large numbers of users. If you are going to have above 20 users in a web environment, it would be very hard pushed into cope, and the whole web site would suffer as a result.

❑   Database projects can only be used to enter information into existing tables, they cannot be used to create new tables.

All this said, however, Access is a lot cheaper and more easily available. We are going to quickly look at how to use Access 2000 with Visual InterDev. There is another more in-depth example in Chapter 14 that covers using Access 2000 for a different solution.

The first difference that we will encounter is that we not only have to create the *database* within Access, we also have to create the *tables* in there as well. This is because the Visual InterDev database projects do not work as comprehensively with Access as they do with SQL Server.

> **If you have chosen to use SQL Server, then ignore the examples in this section and go on to *Entering Data into a Table Using Visual InterDev.***

Try it Out - Creating an Access Database

Here are the steps necessary to create your database in Access 2000. If you have an older version of Access, the steps shown below should be quite similar to those required in older versions.

1.   Start Access 2000.

2.   In the dialog that appears, choose to Create a new database using a Blank Access database, and press OK.

3. You need to specify a filename and location for your database. This is important, because to connect to your database, Visual InterDev will need to know this information. The location should also be the same in both your development environment and on the server to which you will eventually publish your web application. For this reason, it is probably best to place it in a simple directory such as `c:\databases`. Save the file as c:\databases\wroxcameras.mdb and press OK.

4. The database window will now appear. This window contains tabs to various lists of items within the database, and will default to the list of all tables in the database. The database is, in fact, now created.

Try it Out - Creating Tables in an Access Database

Having created the database, we can now continue by creating the tables. These tables are the exact same tables as we created in the previous example for SQL Server.

1. In the Database window, double click on the Create table in Design view item in the Tables tab:

2. We are going to create the first of the tables, product, which is the same as in our SQL Server example. The Table editor will have appeared in design view, looking like a grid. Fill in the Field Names and Data Types as shown:

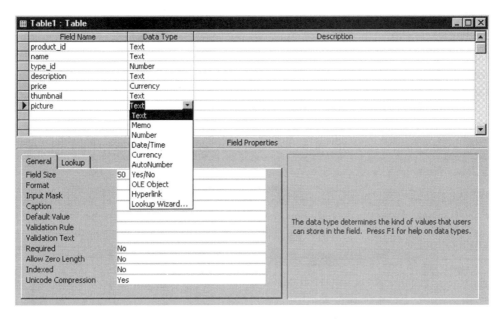

There are a few steps here that are similar to those for creating a table in SQL Server 7. Firstly, you need to make the product_id field a primary key. To do this, select the product_id row and right mouse click on it. Select Primary Key from the menu that appears.

You can also specify further details about a field by clicking on its row and then editing the details that appear in the Field Properties pane beneath. This can include details such as Field Size, Format, and so on.

3. Close the Table editor. You will be prompted for the name of the table, which is product. Press OK to save the table.

4. Now, repeat the above steps to create the product_type table. This has two fields, as shown here:

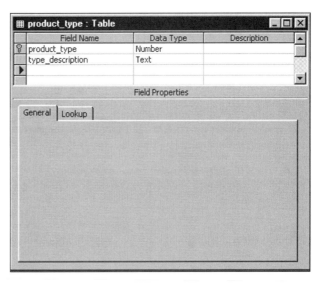

We have finished creating the tables. We could happily enter the data directly into the Access tables immediately, but we will bring this example back in line with the main SQL Server example by connecting our Access database into a Visual InterDev database project and entering the data from there.

Try it Out – Connecting a Database Project to an Access Database

Once we have connected an Access database to a Visual InterDev database project, we can use it in a similar manner to a connected SQL Server database, with the limitation that we cannot create new tables. Seeing as we don't need to do this, let's connect our Access database to Visual InterDev.

1. In Visual InterDev, open the WroxCameras project.

2. Select File | New Project. In the dialog, select Database Projects in the New tab, then New Database Project in the right hand pane. Enter WroxCamerasDB into the Name field, this will be the name of the new project. The New Project dialog should look like this:

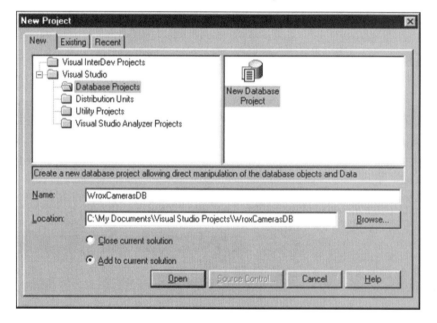

3. Select Add to current solution at the bottom of the New Project dialog. This will add the new database project, WroxCamerasDB, to the currently open solution, which is WroxCameras. Press Open.

4. The Data Link Properties wizard will be opened. This wizard helps you to actually connect your database project to a database. In the first dialog box select Microsoft Jet 4.0 OLE DB Provider.

5. Press Next to bring up the next step of the wizard. This is where you specify the details of the database to connect to. Enter the full name and path of the database c:\databases\wroxcameras.mdb into the first textbox. In the second textbox, leave the default User name of Admin. If you later secure the database within Access, a valid user name should be entered here.

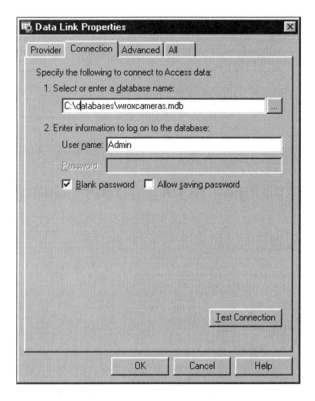

6. Press Test Connection to determine if the details that you entered are correct for accessing the database. If the test is successful, press OK and the connection will be created in your database project!

We have now created our database, made some empty tables, and connected our database into a Visual InterDev database project. We are now ready to populate the tables with data, which will be done using the exact same steps that we mention soon for SQL Server in the section *Entering Data into a Table Using Visual InterDev*. Once you have done that, you can continue using the examples in this book without any problems **except for the following**.

Access Connection Strings

> **If you come across any of the later examples that include a reference to a connection string in code, then you need to change the connection string to a different one from that shown. A connection string contains all of the necessary information to connect to a database, and the ones detailed in the examples in this book assume that you will be using SQL Server, so will not work with Access. Any connection strings that you encounter should be replaced with the following string:**
>
> **Provider=Microsoft.Jet.OLE DB.4.0;Data Source=C:\Databases\wroxcameras.mdb;User ID=Admin;Password=""**

This specifies the type of connection as **Microsoft.Jet**, i.e. Access. It then specifies the path and filename of the database as the **Data Source**, followed by **Admin** as the **User** and a blank string as the **Password**. This string will enable you to connect to your Access database when following the other examples in this book.

> Also, when creating data connections, you should use the **Microsoft Jet 4.0 OLE DB Provider** as we did in the example above.

We will see an example dedicated solely to Access, which in fact includes all of the steps that we have just gone through as well as more, in the case study in Chapter 14.

Entering Data into a Table Using Visual InterDev

Now that we have made a few tables either in SQL Server or Access, we need to get the product information into them. For both Access and SQL Server 7.0, it is possible to enter information into tables from within their own environments, but seeing as this is a book about Visual InterDev, we are going to use the database project that we have created to do this from within Visual InterDev.

You will recall that each table stores information in the form of rows, and that each row is one record. Therefore, a product table would have one row of data for each product. So what we need is a way of typing these rows of data into our tables.

Visual InterDev provides a very easy way to enter information into a table, reminiscent of the ease of use offered by products such as Microsoft Access, or filling in a spreadsheet. Let's take a look at this.

Try it Out – Entering Data into a Table Using Visual InterDev

We are going to put some information into both our product and product_type tables. You will recall that a product has a field called **type_id**, which relates to the product_type table. This means that when we create a product and define its type, that type must have a corresponding record in the product_type table. We must therefore enter our product types before entering the products.

We are going to have four product types, as shown below:

product_type	type_description
1	35mm Compact
2	35mm SLR
3	APS
4	Digital

This means that if we wanted to define a camera as being "Digital", we would give it a **type_id** value of 4 in the product table.

We now need to decide on some information to enter into the product table. Let's start with six models of camera. We are going to leave the thumbnail and picture fields empty for now, since we are only going to be creating a basic web page at first, and will expand on it later. Here is the product data that we need to enter:

product_id	name	type_id	price	description
WRC00001	WRC Supra 70	1	100.00	35mm Compact with 70mm lens
WRC00002	WRC Supra 90	1	130.00	35mm Compact with autofocus and zoom lens
WRC00003	WRC Mini 70	3	190.00	APS with autofocus
WRC00004	WRC Focus 210	2	220.00	35mm SLR
WRC00005	WRC Focus 300	2	310.00	35mm SLR with autofocus
WRC00006	WRC Digi 35	4	420.00	Digital camera with high resolution and color LCD

This will be the basic catalogue that Wrox Cameras has to offer. We are going to want this information to appear on a web page, and every time the price changes or new models are added, then that web page will change automatically. Great. Let's put the data into the tables so that we can start using it:

1. We'll start with the product types. With the Wrox Cameras project open in Visual InterDev, in the **Data View** window, expand the **Tables** icon until you see the two tables. Double click on the product_type table icon.

2. The table will be opened in data entry mode, with the two column headers representing the fields of the table: product_type and type_description. All you need to do is enter the data directly into each row. Enter the information from our first table above, until the table looks like this:

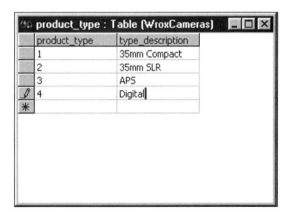

3. Close the table. If you then reopen it by double clicking on the product_type table in the **Data View** window, you will see that the information that you entered is still in the table.

4. Now, we enter the product information. This is done in exactly the same way. Double click on the product table in the Data View window then, in the window that opens, enter the following information from our second table above (the <NULL> will be automatically entered if you leave the field blank):

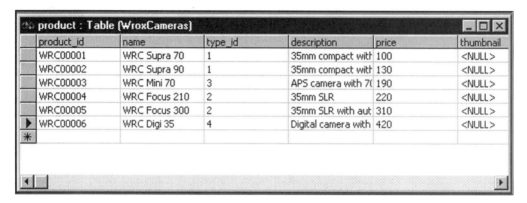

product_id	name	type_id	description	price	thumbnail
WRC00001	WRC Supra 70	1	35mm compact with	100	<NULL>
WRC00002	WRC Supra 90	1	35mm compact with	130	<NULL>
WRC00003	WRC Mini 70	3	APS camera with 7(	190	<NULL>
WRC00004	WRC Focus 210	2	35mm SLR	220	<NULL>
WRC00005	WRC Focus 300	2	35mm SLR with aut	310	<NULL>
WRC00006	WRC Digi 35	4	Digital camera with	420	<NULL>

5. Close the tables – this automatically saves them.

Having created our tables and entered data into them, we are now ready to start using them.

Using Data Environments

We have now built up our Wrox Cameras solution so that it contains two projects, one a web project, and the other a database project. The web project is used to create the actual web site, while the database project is used to maintain the database and data that the web site will use. So far, so good. The next step is getting our web project to talk to the database, and for that Visual InterDev offers a great feature called the **data environment**. It is also possible to get information by writing code the old-fashioned way – by hand. Chapter 9 tells you more about this. For now, we are going to look at using data environments.

A data environment represents the information necessary for your web project to connect to and manipulate any databases you might require. It consists of a variety of items that assist you in talking to those databases. The primary item is a **data connection**.

A data connection object represents the information necessary to connect to one specific database. When you establish a data environment, it automatically configures a data connection to one database. If you have further databases that you wish to access, you can add more connections to your data environment. Therefore, you can have one data environment in your web project, which can have many data connections to different databases.

The purpose of all of these environments and objects is to integrate a database with a web site with a minimum amount of work. The tools are very powerful, and can enable you to create web pages that retrieve information from a database with a few simple clicks and drags of the mouse.

The easiest way to understand it all is to wade in, so let's begin by creating a data environment.

Creating a Data Environment

As we've just seen, the first step in getting your web project to talk with your database is to create a data environment. This is a simple matter of telling Visual InterDev how to find the database, and providing it with the necessary login name and password to connect to it. This information is stored in a data connection, which can be re-used by your web site to actually access the information when required.

Let's take a look at how to do this.

Try it Out – Creating the Data Environment

As we have said, to create a data environment you need to create a data connection to the database you want to talk to. In the case of Wrox Cameras, we need to build a data connection to the Wrox Cameras SQL Server database. You will notice that this procedure is very similar to setting up the connection for your database project. Let's take a look at how to do this:

1. Right click on the WroxCameras web project in the Project Explorer window and select Add Data Connection.

2. In the Data Link Properties dialog, select Microsoft OLE DB Provider for SQL Server (unless you're using Access) and press Next. (Note that if you are not using Visual InterDev Service Pack 3 or higher, the Connection Properties dialog of step 7 below appears before this step).

3. Type the server name of your SQL Server.

4. Type the User name and Password to connect to the database. The default to use will be sa as the user name and a blank password, if you have not configured any security.

5. In the textbox for selecting the database, type or select WroxCameras.

6. Press Test Connection. A message box saying Test connection succeeded should appear if your connection details are correct. If not, repeat steps 3 to 6 until the test is successful.

7. Press OK and then OK again. Visual InterDev will chug away and present a Connection Properties dialog like this:

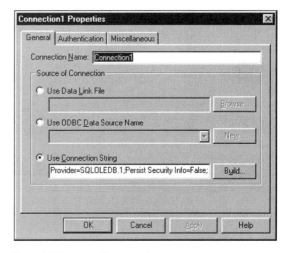

8. This dialog shows the result of the previous **Data Link Properties** dialog. The result is the **Connection String** displayed in the lowermost textbox. This is the actual information that the data connection will store. Change the **Connection Name** to WroxCameras and press OK.

9. The data connection string has been created.

If you have a look in the **Project Explorer** window you will see that, beneath the file called `global.asa`, there is now an icon for a data environment, beneath which is an icon for the connection that you just created. If you were to create more data connections to other databases, they would all appear here.

The `global.asa` is a file that contains important configuration information for your web server. It can be very useful in large web applications for performing tasks when a user starts or finishes browsing your site, and as we can see, it stores information about the data environment for when we use it in our application. We'll see what else this file does in Chapter 7.

Creating Data Commands

A data environment consists of one or more data connections. Each data connection can have one or more **data commands**. A data command is a collection of information from a database. It can be a complete table, the result of a SQL query, data from a stored procedure, a view, and so on. This flexibility means that you can build commands that represent the specific information you require. For example, if you wanted to know the best selling product for the last month, you would write a query that returned this information, and then create a data command to represent that query.

By adding a data command to your data environment, the data that it represents can then be easily and quickly added to any web pages in your project.

Try it Out – Creating a Data Command

We are going to create a data command that shows all of the products from the product table, along with the description of their type. To do this, we will need to base the command on a simple query that joins the product and product_type tables. We will shortly have a quick look at how to write SQL queries, as well as introducing the SQL Query Builder, a tool that Visual InterDev provides to simplify query creation. For now, we will just blindly write the query without looking at how it works.

This query will be:

```
SELECT product.*, product_type.type_description
FROM product, product_type
WHERE product.type_id = product_type.product_type
ORDER BY product.type_id, description
```

This will display all products and the description of their type, sorted by the product type and description of the product. Let's now turn this into a data command.

1. Right mouse click on the WroxCameras data connection in the Project Explorer window and select Add Data Command. The following dialog opens:

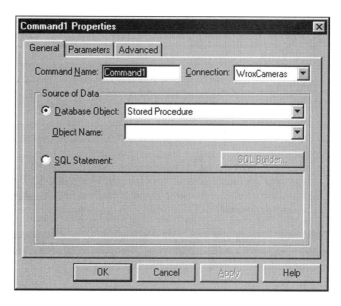

2. This dialog is where you configure the command. Type in the name of the command, which will be products.

3. In the Source of Data frame, select SQL Statement, and type in the SQL query from above.

4. Press OK to create the data command.

You will see that the data command has been added beneath the WroxCameras data connection in the Project Explorer window. Beneath it, you will see icons representing each of the fields that the data command returns. All of these objects can be used to add data quickly and easily to your page. Now we're going to look at how to do this.

Using Data Commands to Add Database Access

We have now built our data environment and set up the necessary connection and command objects to talk to the database and return some data. Now we need to do something with this data.

An important feature of the data environment is that it is drag and drop enabled. When you select a data command object and drag it onto a web page, a **Recordset control** is automatically added to the page. A Recordset control uses a data command object to retrieve data from a database. Other controls then bind to the Recordset control in order to present the data that the object contains. These controls are called **bound controls,** and are made up out of a library of script commands that are automatically included in the _ScriptLibrary folder of your project when Visual InterDev creates a new project.

There are many sorts of bound controls, and they are dealt with in more detail in Chapter 8. For now, all you need to know is that these controls present the information from a Recordset control. These controls include textbox controls, grids, listboxes, drop down boxes, combo boxes, and so on. In fact, most of the common controls that you would use in an HTML form have a data bound version in Visual InterDev. You can very easily add a data bound textbox by just dragging a database field from a command object in the Project Explorer window, onto a selected form. The textbox will then automatically display

141

information from the specified field. This sort of drag and drop functionality gives Visual InterDev a very easy interface to use for adding database access to web pages.

One last point about data command objects – they are reusable. This means that you can add one data command to multiple pages, and you can then automatically change what those pages display by changing the data command object.

This re-use is a strength, but you should be aware that when you change a data command object that is in use, you might unwittingly change what another part of your site is displaying.

We are shortly going to create a page that shows a table of product information, taken directly from the database and displayed in our web site. Before we do this however, we will learn just how easy it is to work with a database using Visual InterDev, by literally throwing together a page in a few quick drag and drop operations.

Try it Out – Displaying Database Information on a Web Page

We are going to create a page that introduces you to the power offered by the Visual InterDev design time controls. After developing this page we will not use it again, instead we will develop a more advanced page better suited to the Wrox Cameras site. This example simply serves to reassure you that database access is actually very easy with Visual InterDev.

1. Create a new .htm page by right mouse clicking on the Wrox Cameras project in the Project Explorer window and selecting Add | HTML Page from the menu that appears. In the dialog, enter the page name as products_example.htm and press Open to create the page.

2. We are not going to bother linking this page into the site diagram for the site, as it is just an example of how to use the data commands. Drag the products data command that we just created and drop it into our new web page, in the content area specified by the PageLayout DTCs. A Recordset DTC will appear that is automatically linked to the products command object:

3. The Recordset DTC that we have just added specifies the command from which to display information. We will now add data bound DTCs to specify the fields within the command which we want to display. To do this, expand the products data command in the Project Explorer window until you can see the fields that the command returns. To add fields to our page, simply drag them from the Project Explorer window and drop them on the web page. Drag the following fields to just beneath the Recordset control: name, description, price. You will now have three textboxes that are linked to the database, looking like this:

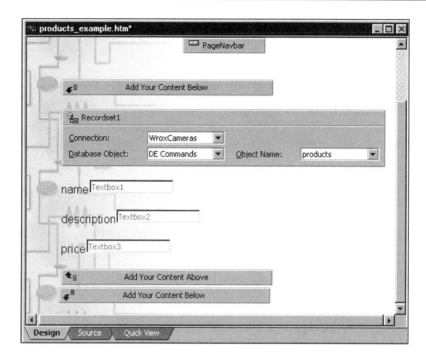

4. The last thing that we need is a way to navigate within the records that the data command contains. To do this we add a RecordsetNavBar control, which simply provides video-like controls to navigate through the records of the Recordset DTC. You will find this on the Design Time Controls tab of the Toolbox. Drag the RecordsetNavBar control from the Toolbox and drop it just beneath the price textbox.

5. We need to link the RecordsetNavBar DTC to the Recordset DTC. To do this, right mouse click on the RecordsetNavBar DTC and select Properties. In the dialog that appears, select the Recordset dropbox and within it specify Recordset1, which is the name of our Recordset DTC that we added before. Press OK to link the two controls together.

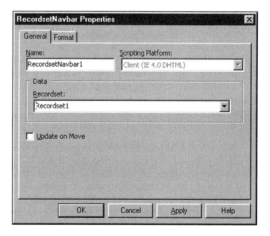

6. That's all there is to it! Save your page and view it in the browser, by right mouse clicking on the page within the Project Explorer window and selecting View in Browser. You will see the following page:

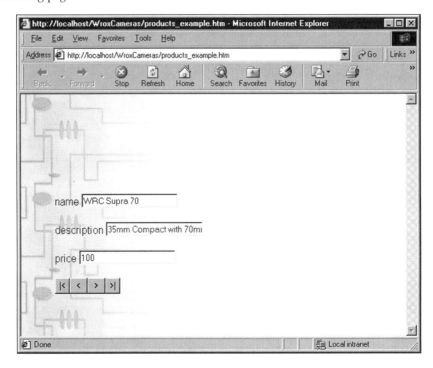

Okay, so we haven't added any nice embellishments such as a title bar, some explanatory text, and so on, but you can see how very easy it is to add database access to your web site. By using the buttons on the RecordsetNavBar, it is very easy to change the current record. As you switch records, the fields automatically reflect the correct contents of the new record! This is the magic of data-bound DTCs at work, and it is one of the easiest methods available for adding data access.

Behind the scenes, this page pivots on the Recordset DTC that we added. This Recordset control is linked to the product data command, and reflects the contents of the current record within the data command. Every field on the page is linked to this Recordset, and as the record changes, the contents displayed in the fields are changed. The RecordsetNavBar simply changes the current record of the Recordset DTC. The end result is a very quick and effective manner of displaying the contents of your database.

We are not going to return to this example page or link it into our site navigation at all. What we are now going to do is to build a better page that displays all of the records in the products table at once.

Try it Out – Using the Grid DTC to Add Database Access to Your Web Page

We are now going to create a products page that will sit nicely in our existing structure, and then we are going to make it show the data represented by the data command that we recently created. Unlike the previous example, this page will display *all* the records within the data command at once, and to do this we will be using a different design time control, called the Grid DTC.

1. Open the site diagram by double clicking on Site Diagram1.wdm in the Project Explorer window.

2. Add a new page to the site diagram by right mouse clicking and selecting New HTML Page. Type in the title of the page as Products, and make it a child of the home page (by dragging it to beneath the home page). Organize the children pages of the home page so that the site diagram looks like this:

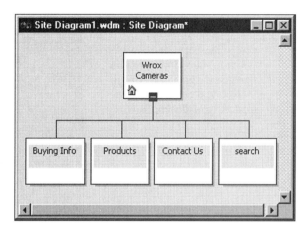

3. Save the site diagram to create the page.

4. Open the Products.htm page from the Project Explorer window.

5. Select the second PageNavBar control, right mouse click on it and open the Properties page, and place a check mark in the Home checkbox. Press OK. This will allow a user to return to the home page from the Products page.

6. In the main content area of the page, write the text:

   We currently have the following products available for you:

7. From the Project Explorer window, drag the products data command and drop it just beneath the text written in step 6. A Recordset control will automatically be added to the page:

8. We want to display a table of the products available in the database. To do this, we are going to use the Grid control, which can be found in the Design Time Controls tab of the Toolbox window. Simply drag the Grid control from the Toolbox and position it beneath the Recordset control on the Products.htm page. This will create the Grid control, which is currently unbound, i.e. it does not know which Recordset control to present data from.

9. Right mouse click on the Grid control and choose Properties. This brings up the Properties page for the Grid control, which allows us to configure how it appears and displays information.

10. Switch to the Data tab. This is where you configure the data that will be displayed. In the Recordset drop box, select Recordset1, which is the name of the Recordset control that we added to represent the products data command.

11. A list of available fields appears. Place check marks next to the following fields which we want the table to display: product_id, name, price, type_description:

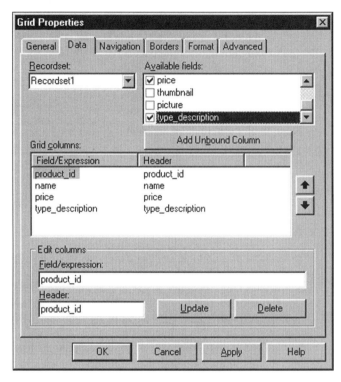

12. This is enough to display the table of products, but now we'll add a few touches to make its appearance a bit better. The grid will display a header row, and the default header for each field will be the field name. This means that the user will see column headers such as product_id and type_description – hardly the most user-friendly titles. To edit the titles that are displayed, click on the field in the Grid columns table of the Properties sheet. Once you have selected the field, in the Edit columns frame beneath it, change the contents of the Header text box and then press the Update button. Repeat this for each of the following:

product_id should read Product

name and price should both have their first letters capitalized

type_description should read Type

13. The last little touch is to switch to the Format tab and uncheck the Fixed column width box. If checked, all columns have the same width, which doesn't look too nice in this example.

14. Press OK. The grid should now contain the column headings and representations of the type of data that each column portrays:

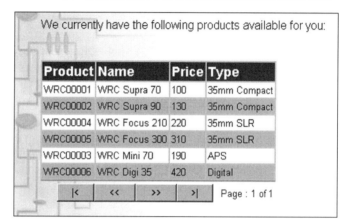

Product	Name	Price	Type
Xxxx[0,0]	Xxxx[0,1]	Xxxx[0,2]	Xxxx[0,3]
Xxxx[1,0]	Xxxx[1,1]	Xxxx[1,2]	Xxxx[1,3]
Xxxx[2,0]	Xxxx[2,1]	Xxxx[2,2]	Xxxx[2,3]
Xxxx[3,0]	Xxxx[3,1]	Xxxx[3,2]	Xxxx[3,3]
Xxxx[4,0]	Xxxx[4,1]	Xxxx[4,2]	Xxxx[4,3]
Xxxx[5,0]	Xxxx[5,1]	Xxxx[5,2]	Xxxx[5,3]
Xxxx[6,0]	Xxxx[6,1]	Xxxx[6,2]	Xxxx[6,3]
Xxxx[7,0]	Xxxx[7,1]	Xxxx[7,2]	Xxxx[7,3]

15. Save your work and view the home page in the browser. Click on the link to the Products page - you will see a page which displays the products from the Wrox Cameras database. The table will look like this in its finished format:

We currently have the following products available for you:

Product	Name	Price	Type
WRC00001	WRC Supra 70	100	35mm Compact
WRC00002	WRC Supra 90	130	35mm Compact
WRC00004	WRC Focus 210	220	35mm SLR
WRC00005	WRC Focus 300	310	35mm SLR
WRC00003	WRC Mini 70	190	APS
WRC00006	WRC Digi 35	420	Digital

|< << >> >| Page : 1 of 1

Using Other Data Bound DTCs

We have looked briefly at the Grid design time control (DTC) and have seen that it can display multiple records from a database at once. This is very useful when we want to show lots of records together, but this might not always be what we want to do.

Once you have added a Recordset control to a page, either manually or by dragging a command object from the Project Explorer window, you can then add a variety of data bound controls to present the information from the recordset. These controls include:

❑ RecordsetNavBar – a control that changes the current record of the Recordset control. If you are not using a DTC such as the Grid, which displays multiple records at once, then this is an easy way of changing which record is displayed. This typically creates video-like controls for navigating forwards and backwards through the recordset. Any control bound to the same Recordset control will change to reflect the current record. It is also worth noting that if you add a Grid control to a page, it automatically places a RecordsetNavBar control on the page as well.

❑ Textbox – similar to the textbox control of a normal HTML form, except that it automatically displays the contents of a field from the recordset. If you drag a database field from under a command in the Project Explorer window onto a page, then a Textbox control will automatically be created.

- ❏ Listbox – Creates a listbox that is automatically populated with all records from one field of a recordset. In our example above, you could create a data command bound to the type_description field of the product_type table, and then bind a listbox to a recordset of this command object. The result would be a list of all product types.

- ❏ Checkbox/Option box – creates checkboxes and option boxes that normally reflect the value of a byte field in the database.

The use of these controls, and other more sophisticated ones, will be explained in Chapter 8 – *Design Time Controls*.

Working with SQL

SQL, which as we have seen, stands for **Structured Query Language**, is a language for writing queries against databases to retrieve specific data. In the examples that we have used in this chapter, we have seen basic queries designed to retrieve data for presenting on the web pages of Wrox Cameras. SQL Server is a very powerful database, and SQL itself is a sophisticated language for data retrieval. The capabilities offered by using Visual InterDev and SQL Server together can be quite daunting, which is why for those with slightly less SQL experience, Visual InterDev offers an easy to use **SQL Query Builder** to create queries.

If you are working with a SQL Server database and need to retrieve information from it, Visual InterDev gives you two options:

- ❏ You can write the SQL query for yourself, as we did in the previous examples.

- ❏ You can use the SQL Query Builder to automatically generate the necessary SQL syntax.

Let's start by having a quick look at the types of queries that you will commonly use:

- ❏ A SELECT query is used to retrieve data from one or more tables or views.

- ❏ An INSERT query is used to insert rows of data into a table.

- ❏ An UPDATE query is used to change the contents of existing data in a table.

- ❏ A DELETE query is used to delete rows of data from a table.

- ❏ A MAKE TABLE query is used to create new tables in a database. However, this functionality is easier to accomplish using the table designer that we introduced earlier in this chapter.

Basic SQL Syntax

The SQL language is very much like the English language, in that statements are made up of a series of **clauses**. Each clause has a SQL **keyword** and various **arguments**, and may also include the use of **operators**. Let's take our earlier SQL statement as an example:

```
SELECT order_number, first_name, last_name, amount
FROM customer, order
WHERE order.customer_number = customer.customer_number
ORDER BY order_number
```

- ❑ We used the keywords SELECT, FROM, WHERE and ORDER BY, and our arguments were field names and table names.

- ❑ In the SELECT statement we listed several field names, separating each with a comma. The order in which we listed them is the order in which they will be displayed, but does not have to be the same as the order in which they are stored in the database table.

- ❑ The WHERE clause consists of a field name, a comparison operator (in this case the "is equal to" operator), and a value (in this case another field name). More complex clauses can be built using logical operators AND, OR, and NOT.

- ❑ The field names used in the WHERE and ORDER BY clauses do not have to be included in the SELECT clause.

- ❑ Where the same field name is used in multiple tables we need to specify tablename.fieldname.

- ❑ The ORDER BY clause defaults to ascending order (A to Z, 1 to 100...), unless we specify DESC for descending order. In this example we sorted on a unique field but if we hadn't, we could have specified a second field to sort on once the first sort was complete.

- ❑ If we wanted to select *all* of the fields we could use the wildcard character * (which means "everything"). It is much better to specify only the *required* fields, as it wastes resources to retrieve *all* data from the database unneccessarily.

If you want to learn more about SQL, Wrox Press publish *Instant SQL Programming* (ISBN 1-874416-50-8). However, all of the above types of query can be designed without writing any SQL yourself, using the SQL Query Builder.

The SQL Query Builder

The SQL Query Builder is a graphical query design tool that enables you to quickly create SQL syntax for a query. It includes all of the time saving interface features that the rest of Visual InterDev offers, such as drag and drop, visual representation of the query, and so on. If you are not too experienced with writing SQL statements, using this tool can be a lifesaver, and examining the results it creates should quickly improve your familiarity with the language.

Try it Out – Using the SQL Query Builder

We are going to use the SQL Query Builder to create a query for a new data command in the Wrox Cameras database. The query will show each product type, and the number of products that are of that type. This could eventually be used as the source for a drop down box for selecting products based on type, or for management reporting.

1. Right mouse click on the WroxCameras data connection in the Project Explorer window and select Add Data Command.

2. This dialog is where you configure the command. Type in the name of command, which will be product_types_count.

3. In the Source of Data frame, select SQL Statement, then click on the SQL Builder button. The SQL Query Builder will open, containing four panes as shown:

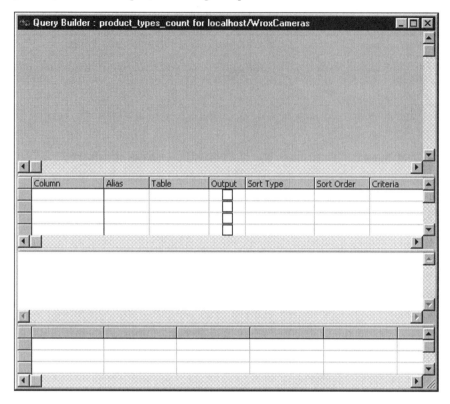

4. In the Data View window, expand the tree until the tables in the Wrox Cameras database appear. Drag and drop each of the two tables individually into the top gray area of the Query Builder. The two tables will appear in the Query Builder looking something like this:

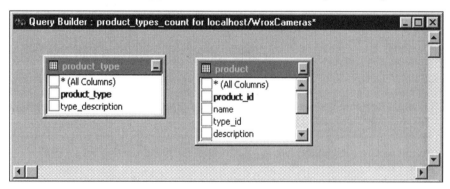

5. Drag the product_type field from the product_type table and drop it over type_id in the product table. This action will create a join between the two tables on those fields:

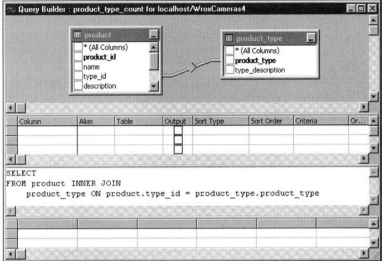

6. The Query Builder will display the SQL syntax of this basic join in the third pane, as follows:

```
SELECT
FROM product INNER JOIN
    product_type ON product.type_id = product_type.product_type
```

7. Place a check mark in the checkbox of type_description in the product_type table. This will add the field to the selected fields list in the second pane.

8. Place a check mark in the checkbox of product_id in the product table.

9. In the Query menu, select Group By. This will add a Group By column to the second pane.

10. In the second pane, find the row for product_id. Go to the Group By column and change it to Count. This will make this field be counted – which should tell us how many items exist for each product type:

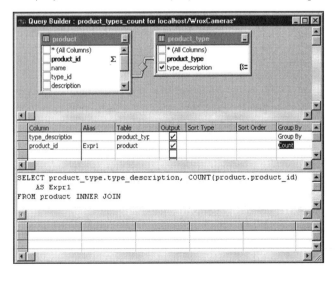

151

11. Change the Alias column for product_id from Expr1 to num_products. This is the name of the field that the count of product_ids will be called.

12. In the Query menu, choose Run. This will run the query and display the results in the bottom pane. As you can see, there are two columns: type_description and num_products, the first containing the description of the type, and the second containing the number of products of that type:

type_description	num_products
35mm Compact	2
35mm SLR	2
APS	1
Digital	1

13. The third pane, containing the SQL statement, will now contain the complete syntax of the query that we have built. This will be:

```
SELECT product_type.type_description, COUNT(product.product_id)
    AS num_products
FROM product INNER JOIN
    product_type ON
    product.type_id = product_type.product_type
GROUP BY product_type.type_description
```

14. Save the product_types_count query. The data command will be built and will automatically appear in the Project Explorer window under the WroxCameras data connection.

If we were to now create a table on a page based on this command, using the same method as we did before for the Products.htm page, we would see a table containing the count of every product type.

You can see that all the SQL Query Builder has done is to create the SQL syntax for us. As you get more experienced with writing SQL queries, you might find it faster to write them directly by hand. In any case, it is always nice to have the SQL Query Builder there if you forget a tricky bit of syntax. Let's take a look at some of the other things that you can achieve with the SQL Query Builder:

❑ To change the type of query, from the Query menu select Change Type, and then choose the type of query, such as Insert, Delete, Update.

❑ To change the type of join between two tables, right mouse click on the center of the join line. You will be given options to always include rows from either table of the join, and by selecting Property Pages you can change the join operator. For our example, the options are to Select All Rows from product, or to Select All Rows from product_type. In the query we designed in the example above, if a product type had no products, then that type would not be shown if we used the normal join. If this was not what you wanted, then you could modify the join by choosing Select All Rows from product. This would then show all rows from the product table, and blank results in fields from the product_type table.

❏ You can add criteria to a field in the field selector (second) pane. There is a Criteria column where you can directly enter the expression that the data must meet in order for it to be included, for example >100, or between 10 and 20. In our query above, if you only wanted to display product types that had two or more products, you would enter >1 in the Criteria column.

❏ You can directly enter SQL into the SQL pane. To verify that it is correct, right mouse click and choose Verify SQL Syntax. If there are any errors, you will be advised of them.

❏ You can easily sort results on a particular field by right mouse clicking on the field within the table, in the top pane, and selecting Sort Ascending or Sort Descending.

❏ You can modify the query of an existing data command object using the SQL Query Builder, by right mouse clicking on the data command object in the Project Explorer window and selecting SQL Builder.

The SQL Query Builder is very useful for creating the most common queries, and presents an easy to use interface in common with the rest of Visual InterDev.

Summary

Here is a quick recap of what we have learned about database access in this chapter:

❏ A database can store data that is used throughout a web site.

❏ By changing the data in a database, the web site is automatically updated.

❏ SQL Server is a powerful database application that works well with Visual InterDev and the requirements of a web site. Microsoft Access is suitable for development purposes, where the volume of data and users will be small.

❏ Once a database has been created in SQL Server, it can be administered directly in Visual InterDev.

❏ To administer a database, you can add a database project to your solution, which enables you to create tables and enter data into your database for use in your project.

❏ For your web project to talk to the database, you need to create a data connection.

❏ A data environment contains data connection objects, which connect to databases, and command objects, which represent queries and tables within a database connection.

❏ The SQL Query Builder is a powerful and easy to use tool for writing SQL queries, which can be used in a data command.

❏ You can drag data commands directly onto a web page to connect the page to the data that the command represents. This creates a Recordset control on the page, which stores the data from the command object.

❏ Various data bound controls can be bound to a Recordset control to display information from the recordset.

The tools that Visual InterDev offers for working with databases are all very powerful, yet also intuitive to use. They enable you to very quickly create a web page or project that is fully integrated with a database, and do so without requiring any coding on your behalf.

This speed of development is great when you are starting out or wanting to prototype a web site. There are, however, other ways of talking to databases, which we will look at shortly. These methods involve writing code to handle the interaction between our web page and the database. Such code enables a greater range of flexibility in how we handle the data, and how we present it. This code can also be used to make the web site both easier to manage, and more alive to the user by providing interface enhancements, such as rollover effects. (For example, which change the appearance of text when a user moves their mouse over the text.)

In the next chapter, we are going to look at writing code that will run on the client's browser. This code can be used to perform calculations, validate that all information is completed, and provide dynamic changes to the page itself in response to user actions. It is a big step towards making your web site really come alive.

Client Side Script

The web has developed beyond being simply a reservoir of static information. Today's web sites can be made to respond to what a reader does, hopefully making the site a more rewarding place to visit. A very common example of reacting to a user's actions are **rollovers**, a term used to explain the pervasive practice of using text that changes its appearance when a user moves their mouse cursor over it. This is a relatively common use of a powerful tool – **client side script**.

Script, as we have lightly touched on in the *Quick Tour* of Chapter 3, is code written into the HTML of a page. In the case of client side script, the code is actually interpreted by the client browser when it reads the page. Using client side script gives a web designer a powerful tool for creating actual applications that deliver functionality as well as content across the web.

In this chapter, we will be looking at what client side script is, and what you can use it for. We will cover the following areas in this discussion:

- ❏ Why use script? What it is and what it can offer us.
- ❏ When to use client side script.
- ❏ Basics of VBScript and JavaScript.
- ❏ Client side script and browser compatibility.
- ❏ Introduction to DHTML.
- ❏ The document object model.
- ❏ Writing event handlers to respond to user events.
- ❏ Using ActiveX controls.

We'll begin by taking a look at what script is.

Introduction to Client Side Script

Web pages are simply files of plain text written in HTML. We know that within HTML you can have various sorts of tags that serve different purposes – one of those is a <SCRIPT> tag. The script tag encloses a block of code that is referred to as script. When the client's browser encounters a script tag, it attempts to understand the code therein and action it. This is how script is contained within HTML. This much we knew already - but what exactly is script, and what can it do for us?

What is Script?

Script is code written in a programming language specifically designed for working with web pages. There are two main script languages: **VBScript**, and **JavaScript**, which were developed by Microsoft and Sun Microsystems respectively. (Microsoft also developed a version of JavaScript, which they call JScript, just to add to the confusion.) Script also comes in two distinct flavors: **client** side and **server** side, both of which have different purposes:

❑ *Client side script*, the subject of this chapter, is used to make a page react to the user's actions. This script is interpreted by the client's web browser, so the script is actually sent with the HTML file to the client browser.

❑ *Server side script*, the subject of the next chapter, is used to change the contents of a page prior to the client receiving it. The client never sees the server side script – the web server actions it and then removes it from the HTML that it sends out.

Script strongly resembles more traditional programming languages that you might have already used: VBScript is based on Microsoft Visual Basic, and JavaScript uses a very similar syntax to C++. In both cases, the script language is generally cut back and easier to use.

❑ For VBScript, one of the big differences when compared to Visual Basic is that variables are all **variants** (they can hold any type of data). There are no variable type declarations – so for example, where in Visual Basic you might define a variable as an integer if it was to store someone's age, in VBScript you would not define its type at all.

❑ In JavaScript, one of the main differences when compared to C++ is that there are no pointers. Pointers are used heavily in C++ to refer to various objects used in programming, and their omission in JavaScript greatly simplifies the language as a whole.

Another major difference between script and a normal programming language is that the script cannot run by itself – it always requires another program to interpret it – such as a web server or web browser. If you write client side script, it will be processed by the client's web browser, whereas if you write server side script as covered in the next chapter, it will be processed on the server before being sent to the client's browser.

Scripting is designed to improve the capabilities of a web server or client browser, and to meet the requirements of designing interactive, dynamic web pages.

What Can You Do with Client Side Script?

As we have said, the purpose of client side script is to improve what a web page looks like and offers in terms of functionality. There are many ways in which script can do this, and you are bound to have come across examples of them in your own browsing of the Internet. Let's take a look at some of the things that you can do:

❑ Include the ever-present *mouse rollovers*; these are so common now that it's almost hard to find a site that doesn't use them! A mouse rollover is a bit of script designed to make the appearance of a web page change when you move your cursor over a part of the page. For example, this could change the color of some text, make some hidden text appear, change the source file of an image, and so on.

❏ Add *dynamic effects*; not only can you do mouse rollovers, you can also create dynamic effects such as drop down menus, simple animations, add drag and drop capabilities, and so on.

❏ Change the target URL of an *anchor*; based on user selections in a form, you could write some code that changed the URL of an anchor to reflect those changes. For example, you could have a selection list of categories, and a GO button that was an anchor to a URL. As the user selects a different option, the URL could be changed using script so that the GO button takes the user to the correct page.

❏ *Validate* a form; if you have a large form with lots of data entry fields, you can use script to ensure that all of the information has been entered correctly before letting the user submit the form. You could also display helpful messages about any errors that they may have entered.

❏ Perform *calculations*; you could create a form where the user enters figures and the results are automatically calculated and displayed in a results field. This can be useful in creating forms for insurance premium calculations, loan amortizations, and so on. You could even create your own fully functional calculator using client side script.

There are many ways to use client side script, as you can see. Basically, if you want to change the appearance of a page in response to a user event, or perform calculations where you don't need to get information from the server, then client side script is the tool for you.

Browser Compatibility – Choosing a Scripting Language

There's a reason why this all sounds too good to be true – it's not as straightforward as it seems. You will recall that when we covered cascading style sheets in Chapter 4, we talked about browser compatibility and how it throws a spanner in the works. Well, with scripting, that spanner is a large obstacle that you need to take into account right from day one.

To recap on browser compatibility; each of the major browsers supports HTML in a slightly different way. This differentiation is for many reasons – marketing, adding functionality to attract users, timing of release, and so on. The differences carry through into the level of support offered by each browser for a given scripting language. The result of it is that you, as a developer, need to be aware of how a particular browser will react to your script. A good caveat might be: not always as you'd expect!

Generally, browsers come in different versions, which are sometimes referred to as generations. Here is a rough genealogy of browsers and scripting support:

❏ Scripting became widespread around generation 3, for example Netscape Navigator 3.0, and Internet Explorer 3.0. The problem was that Netscape did not support VBScript, and Internet Explorer 3.0 supported JavaScript in a different manner from Netscape Navigator.

❏ Generation 4 saw better support for JavaScript in both browsers, but the support was still different in each browser. Additionally, if you wanted to take advantage of the newer features, then generation 3 browsers were not guaranteed to be able to handle them. VBScript in Internet Explorer 4.0 became much enhanced in the same manner.

❏ Generation 5 continued in the same vein, with backwards compatibility not being seen as a holy grail in the rush to add new features.

For you as a developer, all of this means that you need to keep on your toes. You basically have two options when it comes to using scripting in your web project: either enforce a minimum client browser, or try to target multiple browser types.

By far the easiest option is the first; specifying which browser a client will use. Sadly, on the Internet, this will result in people who are using older browsers not being able to read your pages as you intended. On an intranet, however, this option becomes much more feasible, because the clients can hopefully be standardized as a matter of company procedure.

In developing an Internet web site, you will probably take the last option of targeting multiple browsers. This is normally termed 'downgrading nicely', and means that you try to develop a site that will still work on older browsers. There are many ways to do this, ranging from simply writing two versions of the same page (a beefed up version with client side code for up-to-date browsers and a plain vanilla HTML version for the underprivileged), through to detecting the type of browser a client is using and writing your script to match. This last approach is normally the best thing to do, if you have the time!

We are going to teach you a bit of both, since in the real world you'll need to keep your options open. Generally speaking, JavaScript is used more often for Internet sites because VBScript does not work in Netscape Navigator. If you are working on intranet sites – where it is often possible to specify a specific browser – it is quite common to make use of VBScript to take advantage of certain advanced features of the browser. There are gaps twice the width of this book in what we'll teach you about each language in this chapter – we will give you an introduction and an understanding of some techniques, and leave the rest up to a dedicated book on the language (such as *Instant JavaScript*, ISBN 1-861001-27-4, and *VBScript Programmers Reference*, ISBN 1-861002-71-8, both by Wrox Press).

With that in mind, let's look at how it's done.

How to Add Script to Your Page

Once you have decided on a scripting language and target browser, you're ready to start writing some script. This raises the question: just how do you do that?

For each web page in your project, it is possible to specify the default scripting language that will be used on the client side (and also, separately, on the server side). Once this is done, whenever you use the editor to create a script block automatically, as we will cover shortly, it will default to being written in the specified default language.

❑ To set the default scripting language for an individual page, simply open the page in Source view, and in the Properties window set the defaultClientScript and defaultServerScript properties to the language preferred.

❑ It is also possible to specify the default languages for an entire project, which can be overwritten at the page level using the above method. To set the default, right mouse click on the project in the Project Explorer window and select Properties. In the Default script language pane of the Editor Defaults tab, set the correct script language as shown below:

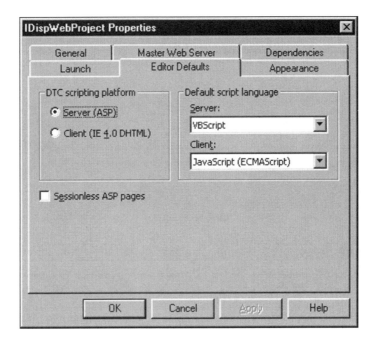

The next step is to add the script to your page.

Placing Script in a Web Page

The general idea is to just write the script into the page as you would any other HTML. The script should be contained within a `<SCRIPT></SCRIPT>` tag pair, which should specify the script language. For example, if you were using VBScript the tag would become:

```
<SCRIPT LANGUAGE=VBScript>

'enter some code here

</SCRIPT>
```

For JavaScript it would become:

```
<SCRIPT LANGUAGE=JavaScript>

//enter some code here

</SCRIPT>
```

The script can be anywhere in the page, but it is good practice to place your main script blocks in the `<HEAD>` section of the page, as shown on the next page. This is because it is then easy to find the script, which otherwise might be all over the place. It also ensures that the script is loaded before the other elements of the page, which can sometimes be an issue with slower or older browsers.

```
<HTML>
<HEAD>
<TITLE>Example of Script Positioning</TITLE>

<SCRIPT LANGUAGE=VBScript>

'enter some code here

</SCRIPT>

</HEAD>
<BODY>
<H1>Page Heading</H1>
<P>content</P>
</BODY>
</HTML>
```

What the Client Sees

When a page includes client side script, the server sends the actual script to any client browser. This means that by simply selecting View Source, the user can see all of your code. This is not only a strong reason to write good code, it is also something that you should be aware of if your code reveals anything that it shouldn't – such as passwords, confidential figures used in a calculation, etc. If you don't want people to view your code, then the safest option is to do all the calculations on the server, which is the subject of the next chapter.

Assuming that you are happy to send your script to browsers like this, then Visual InterDev has some pretty good tools to assist you in writing code. Before we start writing some code of our own, let's take a look at the basics of scripting for both languages.

Controlling the Flow of Code

When you write code into a page, it is normally executed in a top to bottom manner – i.e. the first line of code is executed, then the next, and so on, until the bottom of the code is reached. This flow can be changed by the use of certain code structures.

Making Decisions Using If

Often you will need to write code that can make decisions about what to do next. For example, you might perform some calculations and then need your code to perform action A if the result is above a certain value, or else action B if it is below. In these circumstances you use an **If** statement that checks the value of an expression, then branches off to code that you specify based on whether that statement is true or false.

For Statements

A **For** statement enables you to repeat a block of code for a specified number of times. This can be very useful for calculations, or when dealing with a finite number of items, such as the rows contained within a listbox.

While Statements

A **While** statement is used to repeat a statement or block of code while an expression evaluates to true. As soon as the expression is false, the loop stops. This is very handy when you are not certain how many times the code should repeat, as it means that you can check every time through the loop whether it should continue or not.

Structuring Your Code

Another way to remove code from the normal top to bottom flow of execution is to write it in a **subprocedure** or **function**. These are blocks of code that are only executed when they are specifically called in a line of code, which not only makes them useful for removing code from the normal flow of things, but makes them excellent when you have blocks of code that are used in many places on your page. By writing this code into a function, it can be called again and again without having to type it in repeatedly.

Sub procedures and functions can also accept **parameters**, which are variables that are passed into the sub procedure or function when it is called. These parameters can then be used in the procedure code. For example, there might be two parameters to accept two numbers into a function, which then adds the two parameters together and returns the result.

Basics of VBScript

The good thing about VBScript is that it is very similar to its parent language, Visual Basic. Those of you who are familiar with programming in Visual Basic will be right at home with VBScript. Client side VBScript is, as we have mentioned, designed to be written directly into the web page and then interpreted by a web browser. Apart from the different environment, and lack of variable types, VBScript is essentially the same old beast as its parent. Let's look at the basics of VBScript:

To try out any of the following script code, all you have to do is add the script in a `.htm` *page in the* `HEAD` *section as shown above, save it, and view it in a web browser. Many of the examples output the results of the script with* `Window.Alert`*, which produces a dialog box, or write the results directly to the page using* `Document.Write`*.*

Comments

Comments are ignored by the web browser and should be added to improve the readability of your code. A comment is added by using a single apostrophe, for example:

```
'some examples of
'using comments
'in your VBScript code

Dim Cost, Quantity, Price        'define variables

Quantity = 3         'set quantity bought
Cost = 40          'cost of 1 item
Price = Cost * Quantity         'calculate Price
MsgBox("The Price is: " & Price)        'display price to user
```

Sub Procedures

VBScript offers both sub procedures and functions. Sub procedures are blocks of code that perform an action and do not return a result. A function is similar to a sub procedure, except that it returns a result, and is therefore normally used either to perform calculations, or else perform actions and then return a true or false value to say whether it was successful or not.

Within the `<SCRIPT>` tags, code can be broken down into sub procedures, using a Sub and End Sub structure like this:

```
Sub name (parameter1, parameter2, parameter3,...)
  Code goes here
End Sub

'to call the sub procedure
name parameter1, parameter2, parameter3,...
```

> VBScript is case insensitive, meaning that if you were to name the above sub procedure `SayTime`, you could refer to it as `SayTIme`, `saytime`, `SAYTime`, and so on, without any problems.

If code is written outside of a sub procedure, it is executed as soon as the web browser reads it. Code in a sub procedure has to be *called* before it is executed, with a statement.

Sub procedures can have variables passed as parameters, which can then be used within the sub procedure. These parameters are passed **by reference**, meaning that if you make changes to them within the sub procedure, those changes will not affect their values outside of the procedure. For example:

```
<HTML>
<HEAD>
<TITLE>Example of Script Positioning</TITLE>

<SCRIPT LANGUAGE=VBScript>
Dim x,y

x=3
y=4
AddTogether x,y          'calls the AddTogether procedure, passing it x and y

Sub AddTogether(variable1,variable2)
  Window.Alert(variable1 + variable2)
End Sub
</SCRIPT>

</HEAD>
<BODY>
<H1>Page Heading</H1>
<P>content</P>
</BODY>
</HTML>
```

Functions

Functions are similar to sub procedures, but as already mentioned, return a value. The syntax for a `function` is:

```
Function name (parameter1, parameter2, parameter3,…)
  code goes here
  name = return value         'assign a result to the function's name to return
                              'to the calling line
End Function

'to call the function
result=name(parameter1,parameter2,parameter3,…)

'or if it returns true or false only, you could use
If name(parameter1,parameter2,parameter3,…)= true then
  …
```

For example, you could have a function called `ConcatenateStrings` that accepted two strings as parameters and returned the concatenated results, as shown below:

```
FirstName = "Jo"
Surname = "Bloggs"

'display full name to user by adding strings together using function
Window.Alert("The full name is " & ConcatenateStrings(FirstName,Surname))

Function ConcatenateStrings(string1,string2)
  ConcatenateStrings = string1 & " " & string2        'adds strings, separated by space
End Function
```

Variables

Variables are used as placeholders for information to be used later. As stated before, variables do not have defined types such as *date, number, string*, and so on. A variable is of variant data type, meaning it can hold pretty much any sort of data. To declare a variable, use the `Dim` statement:

```
Dim CurrentDate
Dim LowValue, HighValue
```

You can assign and read from variables in the standard Visual Basic manner, for example:

```
'to assign a string
strName = "Your Name"

'to assign a date
datDate = #12-21-96#

'to assign a number
lngLowValue =20

LowValue = 3
HighValue = 7
HighValue = LowValue + HighValue
Window.Alert("The High Value is: " & HighValue)
```

Loops

You can use traditional loop constructs such as For...Next, Do...Loop, and so on. The syntax of a For statement (commonly known as a For...Next statement) is:

```
For counter = StartValue To EndValue (Step StepValue)
   Statement or block of code
Next (counter)
```

Counter is a variable which will be used to count from StartValue to EndValue. This defaults to counting in steps of 1, but it is possible to specify a different step value by including the optional Step keyword followed by your chosen StepValue. You could, for example, specify 2 to increment by 2 each loop, or -1 to decrement by 1 each loop.

So, if you wanted to count from 1 to 10 using a For...Next loop, you could write:

```
Dim intCounter

For intCounter = 1 to 10        'could add Step 1, but not necessary
   Window.Alert(intCounter)
Next
```

The syntax for using If in VBScript is:

```
If condition Then statement or block of code if value is true

'Or, alternatively

If condition Then
   Statement or block of code if value is true
Else
   Statement or block of code if value is false
End If
```

So, for example, if you wanted to add 1 to a value if it was above 5, else subtract 1 from it if it was below five, you might write:

```
If intValue >= 5 then
   intValue = intValue + 1
Else
   intValue = intValue - 1
End If
```

In VBScript, the syntax for a Do While loop is as follows:

```
'if you want to test the expression at the beginning of the loop, meaning you might
'not enter the loop at all if the expression is initially false, then use:
```

```
Do While expression
  Statement or block of code
Loop

'if you want to test the expression at the end and thus ensure that at least one loop
'occurs, use:

Do
  Statement or block of code
Loop While expression
```

VBScript also offers a derivative of the `While` loop, which is the `Until` loop. This is similar, except it continues until the expression evaluates to `true` (which is subtly different from continuing *while* the expression is `true`.). The syntax for the `Do Until` loop is similar to that above, and is:

```
'if you want to test the expression at the beginning of the loop, meaning you might
'not enter the loop at all if the expression is initially false, then use:

Do Until expression
  Statement or block of code
Loop

'if you want to test the expression at the end and thus ensure that at least one loop
'occurs, use:

Do
  Statement or block of code
Loop Until expression
```

The following example shows you how to count to 10 using both the `Do While` and `Do Until` methods:

```
Dim intCounter

intCounter=1

'using Do While
Do While intCounter <= 10
  Window.Alert(intCounter)
  intCounter = intCounter + 1
Loop

'using Do Until

intCounter = 1
Do Until intCounter  > 10
  Document.Write(intCounter)
  intCounter = intCounter+1
Loop
```

For obvious reasons, this example would be a lot shorter using the `For` statement shown above!

In general, you should find writing VBScript to be a snap if you are experienced in Visual Basic or other programming languages. One very useful feature of Visual InterDev is context sensitive help in the source window. If you can't recall the syntax for a particular statement, type in the keyword and press *F1* for help. You can also refer to Appendix E of this book.

Basics of JavaScript

JavaScript is a very fashionable language to use in the Internet world. It is more popular than VBScript because, as long as you don't use the more demanding features of the language, more browsers support it. JavaScript is, like VBScript, an easy to use scripting language for adding interactive features to a web browser. It has been around for longer than VBScript, and because of that it comes in different flavors. Netscape supports JavaScript, in various versions, while Microsoft supports JScript, its own version of the language. Both are subsets of ECMAScript, which is a published standard that was introduced to try to stop the divergence of features that lead to browser incompatibility issues.

❑ JScript, from Microsoft, as implemented in Internet Explorer 4.0 and above, is fully ECMAScript compliant.

❑ Netscape's JavaScript is not fully ECMAScript compliant.

Looking at all of these versions of the language would be too space consuming for this chapter. We are going to write code that will work on browsers of version 3.0 and above, which tends to cover the largest chunk of users out there, and is a typical benchmark used in the real world.

Let's take a look at the basics of JavaScript:

With JavaScript, it is common to use inline scripts to tie functions in a main script block with the events of a particular page element. **Inline script** is code that is written directly into the declaration of the element. The inline script is then executed immediately upon a certain **event** occurring. Events will be explained shortly, but basically if a user interacts with a page element, for example moving their mouse over it, an event occurs and the programmer has an opportunity to react to it using script. In JavaScript, this is when inline script gets executed – usually to branch off to another function (which can even be in a different script language such as VBScript). This code could also be complete within itself, maybe simply displaying a message to the user.

If you wanted to trap the `onmouseover` event for a hyperlink, you would write something like this:

```
<SCRIPT LANGUAGE=JavaScript>

function change_appearance() {
  //some code here to change the appearance of the image
}

</SCRIPT>

<A HREF="anypage.htm" onmouseover="return change_appearance();">visit any page<A>
```

When a `mouseover` event occurs for the hyperlink above, it knows to execute the code in the `change_appearance` function.

Comments

Comments are ignored by the web browser and should be added to improve the readability of your code. A single line comment is added by using two forward slashes (//), while multiple line comments are enclosed in /*...*/, for example:

```
//Define variables
var cost = 40;
var quantity = 3;
var price;

/* multiply cost by quantity
to determine price */

price = cost * quantity;        //calculate Price
window.alert('The Price is: ' + price)       //display price to user
```

Statements

A **statement** of code is an action that is to be performed. Normally, this is on one line, as in:

```
return SayHello;
```

A statement should end in a semi-colon (;).

Functions

Code can be broken down into functions, which are delimited by { }, as shown below:

```
function SayHello() {
  window.alert('Hello');
}
```

Code is broken down into **blocks** of code. Each block is a statement that will be executed, as in the `window.alert('Hello');` above. Blocks should be delimitated with a semi-colon (;).

In JavaScript you can only write functions, which execute a statement or block of code, and then might or might not return a value to the calling line. If you want to return a value, you simple add a return statement.

The syntax for a function in JavaScript is:

```
function name(parameters)
{
  statement or block of code, possibly including a 'return' statement
}

//to call the function, use:

name(parameters);

//if it returns a value, use:

result=name(parameters);
```

169

So, if you wanted to write a function that added two numbers together in JavaScript, you could write:

```
var number_one=5;
var number_two=3;

alert(add_numbers(number_one,number_two));

function add_numbers(num1,num2)
{
  var result=num1+num2;
  return result;
}
```

If code is written outside of a function, it is executed as soon as the web browser reads it. Code in a function has to be called before it is executed, with a statement such as (for the example above):

```
return SayHello;
```

> JavaScript is case sensitive, meaning that if you wrote the above function, SayHello and tried to reference it with sayhello, it would fail. For this reason, it is probably a good idea to make all functions use only lower case letters, and separate them with underscores, for example say_hello.

Variables

Variables are used as placeholders for information to be used later. In JavaScript, a variable automatically assumes a type from the information stored within it. Basically, if you store text, it will be a *String* data type, if you store true/false, it will be *Boolean*, numbers will be *Number*, and so on. Declare a variable using the following syntax:

```
var current_date;
var low_value;
var high_value = 30.10;        //this declares a variable and assigns a value in one line
var result = true;
```

You can assign variables using various **operators**, as shown below:

```
var low_value;
var high_value=20;

low_value=10;
high_value += low_value;       //same as high_value = high_value + low_value;
window.alert ('The High Value is: ' + high_value);
```

```
//examples of assigning various types of data
var myresult1=true;
var mystring1="hello";
var mystring2='hello';
var mynumber=10;
var myresult2=1.08e+23;
var myresult3=10.24;

//create a date
dt=new Date(1999,11,21,8,30,0) //November 21, 1999 at 08:30AM
```

Functions can have variables passed as **parameters**, which can then be used within the function.

```
var x = 3;
var y = 4;

add_together (x,y );        //calls the add_together procedure, passing it x and y

function add_together(variable1,variable2) {
  window.alert(variable1 + variable2);        //displays 7
}
```

Loops

You can use traditional C++ constructs such as `if`...`else`, `while`... and `for`. The syntax for using `if` in JavaScript is:

```
if (condition)
  statement or block of code if value is true


//or, alternatively


if (condition)
  statement or block of code if value is true
else
  statement of block of code if value is false
```

So, to use the same example, if you want to add 1 to a value if it was above 5, else subtract 1 from it if it was below five, you can write:

```
if (intValue >= 5)
  intValue++;
else
  intValue--;
```

If a block of code covers more than one line of code, surround it in braces { }:

```
//example of using if...else
y=2

if (y > 1)          //this will be true, since y = 2
  document.write('finished, y = ' + y);
else
  document.write('not finished');
```

Initially, the `for` statement in JavaScript looks a bit more scary then in VBScript, but it works in essentially the same manner. The syntax for this statement in JavaScript is:

```
for(setup; condition; change)
  statement or block of code
```

`setup` is a JavaScript statement that occurs before the `for` loop begins. `condition` is a JavaScript expression or condition that is evaluated before the repeated bit begins – if this condition is `true`, then the `for` loop is exited. `change` is a JavaScript statement that occurs just before the loop is re-started, prior to the condition being re-evaluated.

So, in JavaScript, our counting from 1 to 10 example would be:

```
var count;

for (count=1; count <=10; count++) {

  window.alert(count);
}
```

In this example, `intCounter` starts at 1, the condition upon which it will exit the loop is when `intCounter` reaches 10, and every time through the loop, `intCounter` is incremented by 1.

In JavaScript, the `while` statement has the following syntax:

```
while (condition)
  statement or block of code
```

So, while the condition evaluates to true, the code will continue to loop. Counting to 10 using the `while` statement would look like this:

```
var intCounter=1;

while(intCounter<=10)
{
  alert(intCounter);
  intCounter++;
}
```

In general, you should find writing JavaScript easy if you are experienced in C, C++ or other similar programming languages. As before, if you are stuck, and can't recall the syntax for a particular statement, type in the keyword and press *F1* for help, or check out Appendix F of this book.

Handling Events

The main use of client side script is to write script that will perform an action in response to a user doing something. When a user performs an action, such as clicking on a picture or hyperlink, pressing a submit button, or moving their mouse over certain page elements, an **event** occurs.

There are many different events that can occur on a web page – far too many to discuss here. Visual InterDev offers strong tools to assist you in remembering these events, which we will explain shortly. It is possible to write code that happens when an event occurs – this sort of code is called an **event handler**.

An event handler is therefore a chunk of code that the client browser interprets and actions whenever the event on which it is based is triggered. Using event handlers it is possible to change many aspects of a web page – it is also possible to *cancel* the event if certain conditions are not met. This can be useful if you are writing validation code for a large form, and the user has not completed all of the necessary information.

Basically, an event handler is one of the main purposes of client side script. Let's now take a look at how they work, and how to write them.

Writing Event Handlers

The first thing that you need when writing an event handler is an event to base it on. This is comprised of the object that the event is for, such as an image, and the event for which it is to occur, such as when the mouse moves over it. Obviously, with all the different objects and events supported, it would be a bit of a nightmare trying to remember all but the most common events. Visual InterDev comes to the rescue with a great tool called the Script Outline view.

Try it Out – Writing an Event Handler in VBScript using the Script Outline View

We are going to create a basic event handler for a button. Whenever the user clicks on a button, we want to display a message saying "Hello World!".

1. First off, we're going to create a new project. Create a new web project called Client Script Test. Do not apply any themes or layouts.

2. We need to specify the default scripting language for our project – which will be VBScript. As we saw earlier in the chapter, in the Project Explorer window, right mouse click on the project and select Properties. In the dialog box that appears, select the Editor Default tab:

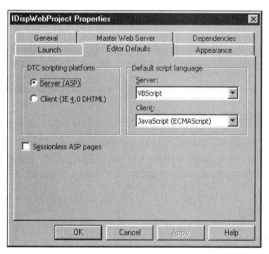

3. In the Default script language pane, change the Client drop box from JavaScript to VBScript. Press OK. From now on, every page that we create will by default use VBScript for both client and server side script.

4. Create a new HTML page, `HelloWorld.htm` by choosing Project | Add Web Item | HTML page. In the dialog that appears, type HelloWorld.htm in the Name text box, then press Open.

5. From the Toolbox, drag and drop a Button control onto the page.

6. Click on the button that you have just added, select the text Button and replace it with Click on me.

7. Switch the editor to the Source view.

8. At the bottom of the Toolbox, you will find a Script Outline tab – switch to it. The Script Outline view will appear:

The Script Outline is useful in both client side and server side scripting, as you can see from the tree shown. The Client Objects & Events view currently displays all objects in the selected page – namely button1 (which we just added), the document object, and the window object.

9. Click on button1 in the Script Outline to expand it. You will see all of the various events for which you can write event handlers. As you can see, it's quite a list! We want to write an event handler for when the user clicks on the button – so for us, the one we want is onclick. Double click on the onclick line of events shown. Code will be added to the editor as follows:

```
<HTML>

<HEAD>
<META name=VI60_defaultClientScript content=VBScript>
<META NAME="GENERATOR" Content="Microsoft Visual Studio 6.0">
<TITLE></TITLE>
```

```
<SCRIPT ID=clientEventHandlersVBS LANGUAGE=VBScript>
<!--

Sub button1_onclick

End Sub

-->
</SCRIPT>
</HEAD>
<BODY>

<P><INPUT ID=button1 NAME=button1 TYPE=button VALUE="Click on me"></P>

</BODY>
</HTML>
```

This has created the necessary skeleton code for us to quickly write a function in our event handler. We will shortly explain what exactly all this code that has been added means, but for now, let's get the function working.

10. Beneath the line of code `Sub button1_onclick`, add a line of code that says `Alert ("Hello World!")`. This uses the `Alert` method of the `Window` object of the client's browser to display a message. It is the same as using `Window.Alert`, or `msgbox` in VBScript.

11. Save your work and switch to the **Quick View** tab of the editor. The **Quick View** is useful for seeing the effects of your client side code quickly – it does not run any server side script and might not look exactly the same as the final output, but for our purposes it will serve just fine.

12. Click on the button, a message box will appear saying **Hello World!**

The **Script Outline** view is a great tool for automatically building the skeletons for your event handlers. Let's take a look at the code that it added to your HTML.

How it Works – Writing an Event Handler Using the Script Outline

The button had an ID attribute added, with the VALUE of button1. This is what the browser uses to determine which control has just had an event fired. When a user causes on event on the button, such as clicking it, then the browser knows to automatically look for an event handler named button1_onclick(). This is obviously comprised of the ID, and underscore, and the event.

The Script Outline also added the basic skeleton of your event handler, as follows:

```
<SCRIPT ID=clientEventHandlersVBS LANGUAGE=VBScript>
<!--

Sub button1_onclick

End Sub

-->
</SCRIPT>
```

The SCRIPT tag defines its language, which is VBScript, and then within the tag it includes comment tags (<!-- and -->) so that any browser that does not understand VBScript will ignore it. This is because the <!--and --> marks are recognized by most browsers as comments, and all that is contained within is ignored. If, however, it is within a script block, then the code parser of a browser which is capable of understanding script blocks will understand this and action the code.

The last thing it does is to write the button1_onclick function. As you saw, any code entered in this function is executed whenever the event is fired.

Try it Out – Writing an Event Handler in JavaScript

We are now going to look at how to do the same thing in JavaScript.

1. Create a new page in the Client Script Test project, HelloWorldJS.htm.

2. Write the following script into the Source view of the page:

```
<HTML>
<HEAD>
<SCRIPT Language=JavaScript>
<!--

function say_hello(){
   window.alert("Hello World!");
}

-->
</SCRIPT>
</HEAD>
<BODY>
```

```
<FORM NAME="Hello World">
<INPUT TYPE="button" VALUE="Click on me" onclick="return say_hello();" NAME=button1>
</FORM>

</BODY>
</HTML>
```

3.   Save your file and view it in Netscape Navigator. The page will look the same as in Internet Explorer 4.0, and when the user clicks on the button, a message saying Hello World! will appear.

How it Works – Writing an Event Handler in JavaScript

This example uses inline script to tie the `onclick` event of the button to the `say_hello()` function. This is seen in the line:

```
<INPUT TYPE="button" VALUE="Click on me" onclick="return say_hello();" NAME=button1>
```

This is the definition for the Click on me button. When the user clicks on the button, the browser will read the `onclick` statement included in the definition, and branch off to the `say_hello` function defined above.

As you can see, we have achieved the same functionality in both languages. There are differences in what each language is capable of, especially as you start using the more advanced features of each, but it is normally possible to achieve a similar effect using either one, it just takes more work in some cases.

Canceling an Event in an Event Handler

There might be times when you want an event to *not* occur. A good example of this is a form with lots of fields that the user has to complete. If the user has not completed all of the necessary fields, you might not want a submit button to work. You could achieve this by adding code to the control's `onclick` event to ensure that the necessary fields are filled in. If they are not, then you can easily alert the user with a message box, and then cancel the event.

To do this in Internet Explorer 4.0 or above, you would enter the following line of code in VBScript:

```
Window.Event.returnValue = False
```

In JavaScript, you would use:

```
return false;
```

This makes the event return a false value, which makes the browser act as if it did not occur.

Let's look at this in action, using a VBScript example.

Try it Out – Canceling an Event

We are going to use a relatively simple case of canceling a hyperlink. Normally, whenever a user clicks on a hyperlink it takes them somewhere. We are going to write some code to prevent this from happening. The same code could happily be applied to cancel most events in VBScript.

1. Create a new HTML page, `CancelledEvent.htm` by choosing Project | Add Web Item | HTML page. In the dialog that appears, type CancelledEvent.htm in the Name text box, then press Open.

2. In Design mode, type in Link to Hello World at the top of the page.

3. Select the text that you have just entered, and then from the HTML menu select Link to create a link.

4. In the dialog box that opens, replace http:// in the URL box with HelloWorld.htm. This will create a hyperlink to the page that we created in the previous example. If you test this page in Quick View you will see that the link works.

5. Switch the editor to Source mode and the Toolbox to the Script Outline view.

6. You will notice that you cannot find the hyperlink under the Client Objects & Events node of the Script Outline. When this occurs, we need to manually add an ID to an element to make it appear in the Script Outline (more on this soon). Find the hyperlink in the Source view of the editor, then change the line from:

```
<P><A HREF="HelloWorld.htm">Link to Hello World</A> </P>
```

to:

```
<P><A ID=LINKA HREF="HelloWorld.htm">Link to Hello World</A> </P>
```

7. You will now see the hyperlink appear in the Script Outline as linka. Expand this, and then double click on the onclick event.

8. Within the `linka_onclick` code that the Script Outline added, write a line of code that says:

```
Window.Event.returnValue = False
```

9. The full source of the document should now be:

```
<HTML>
<HEAD>
<META name="VI60_DefaultClientScript" Content="VBScript">

<META NAME="GENERATOR" Content="Microsoft Visual Studio 6.0">
<TITLE></TITLE>
<SCRIPT ID=clientEventHandlersVBS LANGUAGE=VBScript>
<!--
```

```
Sub linka_onclick

  Window.Event.returnValue = False

End Sub

-->
</SCRIPT>
</HEAD>
<BODY>

<P><A ID=LINKA HREF="HelloWorld.htm">Link to Hello World</A> </P>

</BODY>
</HTML>
```

10. Save your page and view it in the Quick View tab of the editor. If you click on the link, you will see that it does not work.

This example has shown you how to cancel an event. If you comment out (by placing a single apostrophe mark in front of the line of code) the `Window.Event.returnValue = False` statement, you will see that the hyperlink works again.

Dynamic HTML (DHTML)

If you've used HTML for a while, you might be asking yourself, what's all this stuff about an **ID attribute**? The ID attribute is part of **DHTML** – a technology that enables web pages to really come alive. Using DHTML you have the capability to make a web page much more interactive than is easily achievable in plain HTML. By providing an ID attribute, DHTML permits you to manipulate any element on a page, and change its colors, positions, and styles, on the fly. This enables any element of a page to react to what a user does – you could move your mouse over a paragraph and it would change color, grow, be replaced by a picture, and so on. Just how does DHTML provide this wonderful interactivity?

DHTML enables a programmer to change elements after a page is downloaded to a client browser. It lets client side script take control– enabling it to change any element on a page. In order to do this, every element needs to be identifiable – hence the ID attribute. By adding an ID attribute to an element, you can all of a sudden write code for it in either VBScript or JavaScript. In fact, in the example above for canceling an event, the event only appeared in the script outline when we added an ID attribute. What we actually wrote was an example of DHTML – as you can see, it's not too hard.

Once an element has an ID attribute, it becomes recognizable by the browser, which then knows that "This piece of code refers to this element", or in the example above it knows that the `linka_onclick` code refers to the element with an ID of `linka` – the hyperlink. The object then has various events exposed as we saw in the script outline. These events are provided by the **document object model**, which is part of DHTML. The document object model states what events, properties and methods are available for every element on a document. The Script Outline view uses the document object model to determine what to display.

179

So once an element has an ID attribute, DHTML gives you control of it. That is basically what it is all about – control! Using this control you can provide a richer experience to the readers of a page, but there is one big factor that you should be aware of – you guessed it, compatibility!

Like most good things in the Internet development arena, DHTML comes with a cost – it is incompatible with older browsers. DHTML became available with Internet Explorer 4.0, and any older browser simply won't cut it. Netscape Navigator does not correctly support the DHTML standard, so you have to be careful which features you include if you are targeting these browsers.

Now that we have an idea of what DHTML is, we should plunge into some more examples and use it.

Using DHTML to Respond to Events

Once you have given an ID attribute to your page elements, you all of a sudden have a lot of control over the web page. You can write script that will make a web page function as fluidly and dynamically as any traditional program that you might have written in other languages, with the added advantage of *reach* that a web page intrinsically offers. (In other words it can be accessed by many more users, via the Internet.)

Using the events offered by the DHTML document object model, which are conveniently accessible in the Script Outline view, it is possible to add intelligent functionality to a web page. This functionality is not just limited to pretty effects and style changes – it can make your web page function as a true application. Let's take a look at a simple example of how to write a price calculator.

Try it Out – Writing an Event Handler with DHTML

We are going to use DHTML and VBScript to create a product price calculator for the Wrox Cameras site. We are going to put this on the Buying Info page, and allow users to enter a product price, select a few payment and delivery options, and have the final payment price automatically displayed for them. All of this will take place on the client browser, meaning that the calculation will be quick, as there is no need to ask the web server for an answer.

1. Open the WroxCameras project.

2. Double click on the BuyingInfo.htm file in the Project Explorer window.

3. Replace the text Buying Info to go here with Please enter the price of the product you want as shown, then select the payment and delivery details to see the final price to you.

4. Switch to the Source view. Instead of dragging and dropping from the Toolbox the controls necessary to make our form, this time we are going to enter the HTML directly to ensure that everything is the same. Beneath the message that you just wrote in step 3, enter the following:

```
<P>Price: <INPUT ID=txtPrice NAME=txtPrice></P>
<P>Payment type:</P>
<P>
<INPUT ID=btnCheque NAME=btnCheque STYLE="WIDTH: 100px" TYPE=button VALUE=Cheque>
<INPUT ID=btnWroxstorecard NAME=btnWroxstorecard STYLE="WIDTH: 100px" TYPE=button
VALUE=Wroxstorecard>
```

```
<INPUT ID=btnPlanetbank NAME=btnPlanetbank STYLE="WIDTH: 100px" TYPE=button
VALUE=Planetbank>
<INPUT ID=btnBranchcard NAME=btnBranchcard STYLE="WIDTH: 100px" TYPE=button
VALUE=Branchcard>
</P>
<P>Delivery Type:
  <SELECT ID=selDelivery NAME=selDelivery>
    <OPTION SELECTED VALUE=25>Courier</OPTION>
    <OPTION VALUE=12>First Class, Insured</OPTION>
    <OPTION VALUE=4>First Class</OPTION>
  </SELECT>
</P>
<P><STRONG><LABEL ID=lblResult></LABEL></STRONG></P>
```

5. If you switch to Quick View, you will see that entering the HTML above has created a basic form for selecting the payment options:

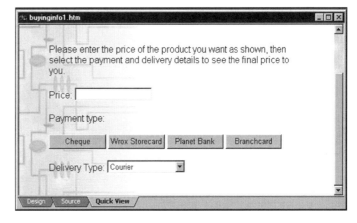

6. The way we want this form to work is fairly simple; the user enters a price, hits a button that corresponds to their payment manner, and then selects a delivery type. We will then write some code that determines any fees for the payment and delivery type, calculates the final cost and then displays it to the user. We are going to write all this in VBScript using DHTML. Switch the Toolbox to Script Outline view.

7. Switch the editor to Source view.

8. You will see that the Script Outline contains entries for all of our controls – this is because we wrote an ID attribute for each, which is how they are identified in the Script Outline:

181

9. In the Script Outline, expand the btnBranchcard node and double click on the onclick event. The following script will be added:

```
<SCRIPT ID=clientEventHandlersVBS LANGUAGE=VBScript>
<!--

Sub btnBranchcard_onclick

End Sub

-->
</SCRIPT>
```

10. This is the area where we will write all of our script. Above the line Sub btnBranchcard_onclick, write the following:

```
<SCRIPT ID=clientEventHandlersVBS LANGUAGE=VBScript>
<!--

Dim PaymentCharge

Sub btnBranchcard_onclick

End Sub

-->
</SCRIPT>
```

11. PaymentCharge is a variable that we will use to store the payment charge based on the user's selections. This will be explained shortly. We now need to write some code to set the payment charge for using 'Branchcard' into the onclick event handler that we have just created. In btnBranchcard_onclick, write the following code:

```
<SCRIPT ID=clientEventHandlersVBS LANGUAGE=VBScript>
<!--

Dim PaymentCharge

Sub btnBranchcard_onclick
  PaymentCharge = 1.90
  CalculateCost
End Sub

-->
</SCRIPT>
```

12. This code assigns a value to the PaymentCharge variable, and then calls a sub procedure that we have not yet written, called CalculateCost. We have three other payment options to enter, all of which work in the same way. For each of these payment options, find the buttons in the Script Outline and double click on the onclick event to add the code for the sub procedures. Within each sub procedure we need to now set the payment charge, as shown below:

```
<SCRIPT ID=clientEventHandlersVBS LANGUAGE=VBScript>
<!--

Dim PaymentCharge

Sub btnBranchcard_onclick
  PaymentCharge = 1.90
  CalculateCost
End Sub

Sub btnCheque_onclick
  PaymentCharge = 2.50
  CalculateCost
End Sub

Sub btnPlanetbank_onclick
  PaymentCharge = 1.65
  CalculateCost
End Sub

Sub btnWroxstorecard_onclick
  PaymentCharge = 1.50
  CalculateCost
End Sub

-->
</SCRIPT>
```

13. As you can see, the four different methods of payment have different costs involved. The next bit of code that we need to add is an event handler for the Delivery type selection box. You will find it in the Script Outline as selDelivery. Add an event for onchange. This event occurs after the user has changed the selection.

14. In the selDelivery_onchange sub procedure, add one line of code, as follows:

```
Sub selDelivery_onchange
  CalculateCost
End Sub
```

15. We have now created event handlers that handle the actions we are concerned with. We now need to write code for CalculateCost that does exactly that – calculates the total cost based on fees and delivery types, and then displays it. Write the following code beneath the last End Sub of the script section:

```
<SCRIPT ID=clientEventHandlersVBS LANGUAGE=VBScript>
<!--

Dim PaymentCharge

Sub btnBranchcard_onclick
  PaymentCharge = 1.90
  CalculateCost
End Sub
```

```
Sub btnCheque_onclick
  PaymentCharge = 2.50
  CalculateCost
End Sub

Sub btnPlanetbank_onclick
  PaymentCharge = 1.65
  CalculateCost
End Sub

Sub btnWroxstorecard_onclick
  PaymentCharge = 1.50
  CalculateCost
End Sub

Sub selDelivery_onchange
  CalculateCost
End Sub

Sub CalculateCost
  Dim Cost
  If not isnumeric(txtPrice.Value) Then
    Window.Alert("Please enter the product price in the Price field")
  Else
    'only display results if a payment type has been entered
    If PaymentCharge <> "" Then
      Cost = txtPrice.value + PaymentCharge + selDelivery.value
      lblResult.innerText = "The Total Cost is " & Cost
    End if
  End if
End Sub
-->
</SCRIPT>
```

If you save your work and view the page in your browser, you will be able to enter a price in the price field. If you then click on a payment type and select your delivery type, the total price will automatically be displayed in bold at the bottom of the form.

How it Works – Event Handler with DHTML

So how does it do this?

❑ Every time the user clicks on one of the payment options, the PaymentCharge variable stores the charge associated with that type, then attempts to display the answer by calling CalculateCost.

❑ When the user selects a different delivery type, it attempts to display the answer by calling CalculateCost.

❑ The CalculateCost sub procedure first off determines whether a price value has been entered into the txtPrice field. If it has not, an error message is generated by the following code:

```
Window.Alert("Please enter the product price in the Price field")
```

❏ If a valid numeric price has been entered, then the procedure adds together the price, the value of the `PaymentCharge` variable, and the value of the selected option of the `selDelivery` selection box, using the following code:

```
If PaymentCharge <> "" Then
    Cost = txtPrice.value + PaymentCharge + selDelivery.Value
    lblResult.innerText = "The Total Cost is " & Cost
  End if
```

❏ The result is displayed in `lblResult` by modifying the `innerText` property of the control. `lblResult` is a label that initially contains no text. The `innerText` property modifies the text between an element's tags, so that if the tag was `<LABEL></LABEL>`, and the `innerText` property was changed to `Hello`, the tag would then read `<LABEL>Hello</LABEL>`. When using DHTML, this is a convenient way of displaying simple results to the user.

This code introduced the concept of **variable scope** when we declared the variables `PaymentCharge` and `Cost`. Let's now look at what the scope of a variable is and how it works in VBScript.

Variable Scope

The concept of a variable is a standard one in modern computer languages – a variable is a place to store data that can be referred to by the rest of your code. In VBScript, as in Visual Basic, a variable is defined by using the `Dim` statement. Since all variables are variants in VBScript, meaning that they can be a date, string, number, and so on, then a simple line such as `Dim PaymentCharge` is enough to create a variable for use in our code.

The scope of a variable defines where it can be accessed by other code. Scope is determined by where the variable is declared:

❏ If the variable is declared within a sub procedure, then its scope is local to that sub procedure. This means that you can use it within the sub procedure where it was declared, but not in other sub procedures. In our example above, the `Cost` variable defined within the `CalculateCost` procedure has local scope.

❏ If the variable is defined outside of a sub procedure, then it can be used in all sub procedures on your page. An example of this above is the `PaymentCharge` variable. You can see that this variable is modified and referenced in most of the sub procedures on the page.

❏ If a sub procedure contains a declaration for a variable that already exists with page scope, then a separate local variable will be created within the sub procedure that has no effect on the page variable.

It is good practice to always declare your variables with the minimum scope necessary, as this minimizes the memory requirements of the client browser while it interprets your code. It also makes your code easier to maintain, and avoids bugs creeping into your code when you adjust variables in various sub routines.

Scope in JavaScript works in the same manner, provided that you declare the variables with the `var` keyword. If not, the variable will always have a global scope.

Using DHTML to Change Images

Of course, DHTML is ideally suited to making a web page look and feel better to a user. A good web page offers an experience to the user that will hopefully keep their interest, make them want to explore the site in more detail, and then draw them back again later. To have this effect, a web site needs to be well ordered, intuitive, and attractive. The odd 'bell and whistle' doesn't do any harm either.

We have discussed how DHTML gives developers control over the elements of a page. We are now going to look at how to exercise that control to change a web page in response to a user's actions.

Try it Out – Changing the Source of an Image

We are going to enhance the Buying Info page by adding thumbnail graphics of the various payment types. Initially, no image will be displayed, but when the user clicks on one of the buttons relating to a payment option, a thumbnail of that option will be displayed on the page.

1. The graphics for this are available at `http://www.wrox.com`, and should be added to your project by right mouse clicking on the **Images** folder in the **Project Explorer** window and selecting **Add | Add Item**. Switch to the **Existing** tab, and then locate the files that you have downloaded. The files are `cheque.jpg`, `branchcard.jpg`, `planetbank.jpg`, `storecard.jpg`, and `blank.jpg`.

2. Open the file `BuyingInfo.htm` by right mouse clicking on it in the **Project Explorer** window.

3. Switch to the **Source** view of the editor.

4. Add the following code just before `lblResult`:

```
<P><IMG ID=imgPayment SRC="images/blank.jpg">
    <STRONG><LABEL ID="lblResult"></LABEL></STRONG></P>
    <P></P>
```

5. The above HTML adds `blank.jpg` to the page. This is an image that is transparent, so nothing will be displayed on the web page. Because this image has an `id` of `imgPayment`, we can modify its attributes using client side script. The attribute that we are interested in changing is the `src` attribute. The `src` attribute specifies the source of the graphic file, which is displayed in the image, so by changing the `src` attribute you change the picture. Find the code for `btnBranchcard_onclick`, and add the following code:

```
Sub btnBranchcard_onclick
  imgPayment.Src = "images/branchcard.jpg"
  PaymentCharge = 1.90
  CalculateCost
End Sub
```

6. The line of code that we just entered changes the image when the user clicks on the Branchcard button. We have three more buttons and, luckily enough, three more jpg files, so change the rest of the onclick events to display the correct image. The script should look like this at the end:

```
<SCRIPT ID="clientEventHandlersVBS" LANGUAGE="VBScript">
<!--

Dim PaymentCharge, DeliveryFee

Sub btnBranchcard_onclick
  imgPayment.Src = "images/branchcard.jpg"
  PaymentCharge = 1.90
  CalculateCost
End Sub

Sub btnCheque_onclick
  imgPayment.Src = "images/cheque.jpg"
  PaymentCharge = 2.50
  CalculateCost
End Sub

Sub btnPlanetbank_onclick
  imgPayment.Src = "images/planetbank.jpg"
  PaymentCharge = 1.65
  CalculateCost
End Sub

Sub btnWroxstorecard_onclick
  imgPayment.Src = "images/storecard.jpg"
  PaymentCharge = 1.50
  CalculateCost
End Sub

Sub selDelivery_onchange
  CalculateCost
End Sub

Sub CalculateCost
  Dim Cost
  If not isnumeric(txtPrice.Value) Then
    Window.Alert("Please enter the product price in the Price field")
  Else
    'only display results if a payment type has been entered
    If PaymentCharge <> "" Then
      Cost = txtPrice.Value + PaymentCharge + selDelivery.Value
      lblResult.InnerText = "The Total Cost is " & Cost
    End if
End if
End Sub
-->
</SCRIPT>
```

7. Save your work, and view the results in the browser. You should see the following form, and every time you click on a different button, the image will change to represent the payment type:

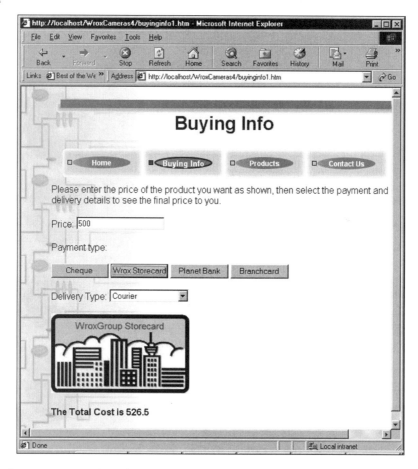

There are in fact many ways of changing the source of an image, some of which are a lot more browser-independent than the one shown here. This particular method is based on DHTML, as are most others in this chapter, and as such will work best in Microsoft Internet Explorer versions 4.0 and above. Let's have a quick look at a method for changing images using JavaScript, which is more suitable for older browsers.

Try it Out – Changing Images Using JavaScript

If you intend to target older browsers that do not support DHTML and VBScript, then you are still able to achieve similar effects by using JavaScript. Let's create a simple page that contains our WroxGroup Storecard image, and make it change to the Planetbank image whenever the user rolls their mouse over the image.

1. Open the project, Client Script Test.

2. Add the images to the Images folder of the project by right mouse clicking on the Images folder in the Project Explorer window and selecting Add | Add Item. Switch to the Existing tab, and then locate the files `planetbank.jpg` and `storecard.jpg`. Press Open to add the files to the project.

3. Create a new HTML page, `ImageSwap.htm` and open it in the editor.

4. In the Source view enter the following code:

```
<HTML>
<HEAD>

<META NAME="GENERATOR" Content="Microsoft Visual Studio 6.0">
<TITLE></TITLE>
</HEAD>
<BODY>

<P>
<A HREF="HelloWorldJS.htm"
onmouseover="Window.Document.images[0].src='images/planetbank.jpg';"
onmouseout="Window.Document.images[0].src='images/storecard.jpg'">
<IMG SRC="images/storecard.jpg">
</A>
</P>
</BODY>
</HTML>
```

5. Save your file and view it in Netscape Navigator.

You will see a picture of the WroxGroup Storecard logo, and when the mouse moves over it, the logo changes to that of the Planetbank. Moving your mouse off the image changes it back to WroxGroup Storecard. Why, however, did we include a hyperlink and write code for the hyperlink element instead of the image?

The problem with using JavaScript to support various browsers is that sometimes not all events are supported. In the case of Netscape, images do not have `onmouseover` or `onmouseout` events. The way to get around this is to wrap the image in another element, such as the hyperlink anchor we used in this example. By trapping the events of the anchor, we know that the user has moved over and out of the image.

One other problem we faced is that without using DHTML it becomes hard to pinpoint which element we want to change. There is no handy `IMAGE` tag, so we had to rely on the `Window.Document.images` collection, which is an array of all the images on the page. `Window.Document.images[0]` is the first image on the page, `[1]` is the second, and so on. This is not as nice as using a DHTML `id` tag, and can easily become unwieldy on pages with a large number of pictures. If it were easy, they never would have invented DHTML!

189

So, to achieve our simple rollover image change effect, we used the following method:

❑ We trapped the onmouseover and onmouseout events of the `<A>` hyperlink tag surrounding the images.

❑ The onmouseover event occurs when the mouse moves over the image. The code `Window.Document.images[0].src='images/planetbank.jpg` changes the source of the first image on the page (which is our WroxGroup Storecard image) to the Planetbank image.

❑ The onmouseout event occurs when the mouse moves off the image. We used the same code, but switched the image back to the original WroxGroup Storecard picture.

As you can see, applying dynamic effects is certainly a lot easier with DHTML!

Changing Text Styles

Another area in which DHTML is commonly used to help web developers is in giving control over the styles used in a web page. By changing the styles of a web page you can draw a user's attention to certain areas, or provide an interactive experience that enhances the page as a whole.

Affecting the style of an image is very easy in DHTML. Most elements on a page have a style attribute, which can be used to control the aspects that govern the element's appearance. By modifying the style attribute you can make text larger, smaller, bold, change the font, color, and so on. All you need is an element with an id tag, and a few lines of code. The good thing is that because Visual InterDev uses IntelliSense, you don't even need to remember all of the many attributes – by simply typing in an element, adding .style, and then entering another period, you will be given a handy list of all the style attributes that you can modify! This is shown in the example below.

Try it Out – Changing Text Styles Using a Rollover

We are going to write a simple web page that contains a line of text. When the user moves their mouse over the text, it gets bigger. When they move it away, it returns to normal. This is a basic rollover effect.

1. Open the Client Script Test project and create a new page, ChangeText.htm.

2. Open the new page in the editor, and in Design view write the following line of text: Move your mouse over me.

3. Switch to Source view. Find the `<P>` tag before the line of text and add an ID attribute of pText, the tag definition therefore becomes `<P ID=pText>`.

4. In the Script Outline, expand the pText node and double click on the onmouseover event.

5. In the sub procedure that has been automatically created in the editor, type the following code:

```
<SCRIPT ID=clientEventHandlersVBS LANGUAGE=VBScript>
<!--

Sub pText_onmouseover
  pText.style.fontSize = "large"
End Sub

-->
</SCRIPT>
```

6. Now, double click on the onmouseout event for the pText object in the Script Outline.

7. In the onmouseout sub procedure that has been added, type the following code:

```
<SCRIPT ID=clientEventHandlersVBS LANGUAGE=VBScript>
<!--

Sub pText_onmouseover
  pText.style.fontSize = "large"
End Sub

Sub pText_onmouseout
  pText.style.fontSize = "small"
End Sub

-->
</SCRIPT>
```

8. Save your work and view it in a browser or by selecting the Quick View tab of the editor. When you move the mouse over the text, it gets bigger, and it shrinks when you move the mouse away. Just as advertised!

How it Works – Changing Text Styles Using a Rollover

This example uses two events – onmouseover and onmouseout. The code simply changes the text size in each event. Rollovers like this can also be used with images to provide a much more pleasing look. Typically, pages like this have attractive text images that have a highlight effect when the mouse is over them. This sort of rollover is easy to implement and very effective – the main difference is that they are changing the image's *src* attribute instead of the *style* of text.

When you typed in this example (as in others), you will have noticed that after typing each period, a list of properties and methods appeared in a drop down box. If you double click on a line or select a line and press *Tab*, that line is automatically added to your code. This is a great feature of Visual InterDev that really speeds up coding, and makes your life easier. Just look at the options available in the drop down box after typing style. – you will see that there are quite a few! All of those options can be modified in code to make big changes to the appearance of an element, and therefore the way the user interacts with your web page.

ActiveX Controls

Using client side script, you can achieve some impressive results in a web page. DHTML, as we have seen, gives you the necessary control over a page to make it respond to a user in a truly interactive manner. This works well when you want to respond to a user, but when you want to present a very complex structure to the user, it normally would be quite a task in script.

Let's take an example of writing a calendar in client side script. This fairly simple requirement would actually be quite a time consuming task using script. Here are some of the things you would need to consider:

❑ You would need to write a small, concise table structure to align all the days.

❑ You would need to write code to determine how many days are in each month, and take into account whether the year is a leap year or not.

❑ There would be code to position the days in the table.

❑ There must be a way of moving between months and years.

❑ Each day would need an ID and must respond to the user clicking on it.

❑ You would need a variable to keep track of the selected date.

❑ It would need a nice style sheet to make it attractive.

This partial list of the requirements of a calendar is enough to put off all but the most desperate or dedicated programmers. This is where yet another technology comes to save the day – **ActiveX controls**. An ActiveX control is basically a compact, precise program for achieving one purpose. An ActiveX control normally displays a visual aspect in your web page, and provides a programming interface to enable you to make it do things. How does this help us?

One example of an ActiveX control is a calendar control. The visual aspect of this is a nice looking calendar, and the programming interface it exposes lets you easily write script to change its appearance, select the date, and determine the data a user has selected. It's a lot easier than writing your own calendar in script, as all you have to do is put the calendar control into your web page.

ActiveX controls come in a variety of shapes and sizes to meet your programming needs. There are a host of controls designed to connect to databases, add drawing support, display short movies, produce fancy tables, and so on. Visual InterDev comes with a few ActiveX Controls, and you can find many more for sale on the Internet. If you can't find a control to do what you need, you can even write your own using Visual Basic or another language such as C++.

Issues with ActiveX Controls

Once you have a control, it needs to be added to the Visual InterDev Toolbox where it is easily accessible, after which you can easily place it in your web page and start using it. Before we look at how this is done, however, there are as always costs involved in using advanced technologies in a web page. First off there is the browser incompatibility issue, as ActiveX controls only work with Internet Explorer. Other big issues are download times and security.

An ActiveX control is a packaged program, and as such it is a bit bigger than a few lines of script in a page. Adding an ActiveX control means that a client browser that does not have the control must download it. This might be a time consuming process, depending on the size of the control and speed of the client's modem. This needs to be taken into account when using an ActiveX control, but in environments like a corporate intranet it need not be a problem.

The biggest issue with ActiveX controls is the **security** settings of a client browser. In many cases, a web browser might be configured to not download an ActiveX control for security reasons. This is because of the fear of letting malicious programs attack a computer from within a downloaded control. A common tactic employed by the more security conscious is to prevent these controls from downloading in the first place, which makes a page that uses them have problems. If you expect a page to include a control and code it accordingly, then all sorts of errors in your code and the appearance of the page can occur if the control is not downloaded.

A common approach to making people trust an ActiveX control enough to download it is to digitally sign it. The creator of the control obtains a **digital signature** from a reputable third party, such as Verisign. (You can find out more about them at `www.verisign.com`.) The third party creates a security certificate for that control, which verifies that company XYZ has created the control, and that it has not been modified. When a modern web browser attempts to read a page with a digitally signed ActiveX Control, a message box displaying the security certificate will appear and prompt the user whether to download the control or not. Using this approach, if a malicious party in any way modifies a control, then the digital signature will be invalid, and the message box will state this.

Digital signatures can help to make people trust a control, but they don't help if the person still refuses to download the control. In these cases, your page is probably not going to work as expected. This is an issue that you need to be aware of when using ActiveX controls, which is why you should probably only use them when they are absolutely necessary.

Using ActiveX Controls

Once you have made the decision to use an ActiveX control in your page, Visual InterDev makes the task easy for you. The Toolbox includes a handy tab from which you can simply drag and drop a control onto your page, and the editor will automatically assist you when writing script to interact with it.

Try it Out – Using the Calendar ActiveX Control

We mentioned how difficult and time consuming writing your own calendar in script would be, so let's have a look at how easy using a calendar control can be. We are going to use the standard calendar control that Visual InterDev supplies from Microsoft. Our goal is to create a simple page that includes a calendar. When a user clicks on a date, the full date will appear on the page along with a message to say whether it is a weekend or not.

1.   Open the Client Script Test project and create a new page, SimpleCalendar.htm. Open this page in the editor.

2. In the Toolbox, click on the ActiveX Controls tab. A list of the ActiveX controls that your copy of Visual InterDev is currently aware of appears:

3. Drag the Calendar control icon and drop it onto the page. This will add a calendar control to your page:

4. You can set the ID of the calendar by selecting it and changing the ID property in the Properties window. It will initially be Calendar1 – change it to calMyExample.

5. To view and change other properties for the calendar, right mouse click on it and select Properties. You will see a Properties window that enables you to easily control the appearance of the calendar. To give us something to do in this step, switch to the Color tab and change the color for the DayFontColor property to Dark Red. It is also possible to change these attributes in the normal Properties window, but sometimes it can be hard to find the required property amongst all the other default ones. The choice is yours.

6. Switch to the Source tab of the editor. You will see that the calendar still appears as a picture. If you find it easier, you can view the calendar as a textual list of its parameters by right mouse clicking on it and selecting Always view as text. I personally find this a little verbose, and so normally don't bother.

7. After the </P> tag and beneath the calendar, add the following HTML for a label control that we will use to display messages to the user:

```
<LABEL ID=lblDateDisplay></LABEL>
```

8. Switch the Toolbox to the Script Outline view.

9. Expand the node for calMyExample and double click on the Click event to create an event handler for the calendar.

10. In the calMyExample_Click procedure, write the following code:

```
<SCRIPT ID=clientEventHandlersVBS LANGUAGE=VBScript>
<!--

Sub calMyExample_Click
    lblDateDisplay.InnerText = formatdatetime(calMyExample.Value,vbLongDate)
End Sub

-->
</SCRIPT>
```

11. Save your work and view it in your browser. When you click on a date, the label should display the full date beneath the calendar.

Using the calendar control saved us quite a bit of work in coding our own control. The code we have written in this example is very simple, but you could enhance it by querying a database when a user clicks on the calendar and pulling in a list of meetings that they need to attend on that day. This sort of task is made easy when you use other ActiveX controls to automatically display data from the database, or use the data bound DTCs (design time controls) that we used in the previous chapter.

As you can see, once an ActiveX control has been given an ID, you can modify its properties in script by typing in the ID, a period, and the property or method that you require. You will have seen that the full list of properties and methods is displayed in the auto complete drop box that appears after you type in the period, as shown here:

The auto complete feature is a great help when using ActiveX controls as it saves you having to remember the individual properties of every ActiveX control.

Adding ActiveX Controls to the Toolbox

The Visual InterDev Toolbox comes pre-configured with certain ActiveX controls already in it. This list is by no means a complete list of all the available controls, and it probably isn't even a complete list of the controls on your computer. You can easily add new controls to the Toolbox after you have put them on your computer; here's how.

Try it Out – Adding an ActiveX Control to the Toolbox

Before you add a control, it needs to be registered on your computer. You will find that there is a large selection of controls available, especially if you have Visual Studio Enterprise edition installed. If you need more controls, there are many third parties who create controls and distribute them over the Internet. A quick search in your favorite search engine will probably pull up a control or two that matches your requirements. Once you have installed the control on the computer using the control's setup program, it is very easy to get Visual InterDev to display it in the Toolbox.

1. Right mouse click on the Toolbox and select Customize Toolbox.

2. The dialog that appears enables you to add DTCs (covered in more detail in Chapter 8) and ActiveX controls to the Toolbox. Switch to the ActiveX Controls tab:

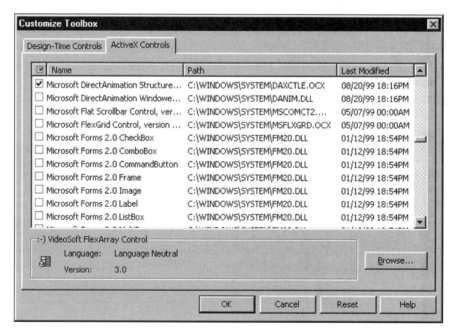

3. Place a check mark next to any controls that you want to appear in the Toolbox. If you want to remove an existing control, simply uncheck it. If the control that you want is not in the list, use the Browse button to find the .DLL or .OCX file that represents the control. Be aware that not all ActiveX controls are designed for working on web pages – some are for use in other environments such as Visual Basic. Be careful of what controls you select.

4. Press OK.

The changes you made will be reflected in the **Toolbox**. You can now add any controls from the **Toolbox** to a web page simply by dragging and dropping as normal.

Summary

In this chapter we have looked at various ways of making a web page respond to its readers using client side script. We have learned that script comes in many flavors, of which VBScript and JavaScript are the most common. We covered the following key points:

❑ Deciding on a script language and the features you use should be determined by the type of browser that your intended audience uses.

❑ VBScript is good for Internet Explorer 3.0 and above.

❑ JavaScript is supported to varying levels within most modern browsers, but the features you use can limit your target audience.

❑ Both VBScript and JavaScript are based on other languages, and are easy to learn and use.

❑ DHTML is an extension to HTML that enables all the elements of a page to be changed on the fly by client side script. This results in pages that can offer a more interactive feel to the reader.

❑ With DHTML, each element of a page has an ID attribute that can be used to identify that element in code.

❑ Using script and DHTML you can easily write code that responds to a user's actions, such as clicking on a button or a piece of text.

❑ Changing the appearance of elements dynamically using older browser relies on using JavaScript, and is typically harder than using DHTML (available with version 4.0 and above browsers).

❑ ActiveX controls can be used to quickly add advanced functionality.

Adding client side script to your page offers many advantages to web developers. It is fast, it can add to the attractiveness of a page, and it cuts down on requests to the server for information. It does, however, have some problems:

❑ All of the source code is sent with the page, meaning that readers can view your code.

❑ It is heavily dependent on a browser understanding the scripting language and features that we have used.

The way to get around these and other problems is to write script that runs on the web server, known as server side script. In the next chapter, we are going to look at Active Server Pages (ASP), a platform for writing server side script that greatly extends the reach and power of a web project.

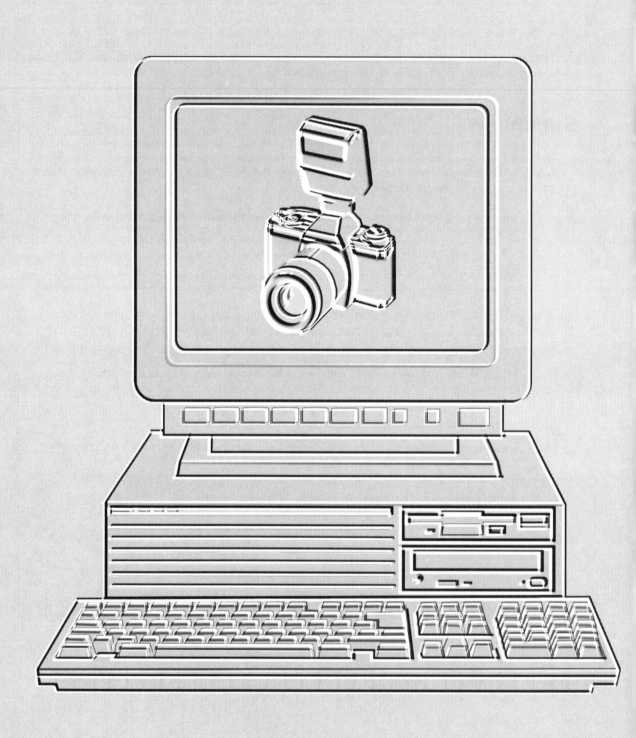

Writing Active Server Pages

In the last chapter we saw how to write script that runs on the client's browser. We discovered that the main purpose of client side script is to create pages that respond to the user's actions. Adding these capabilities to a web page can both speed up the user's interaction with a site, and improve their appreciation of it.

In this chapter we are going to look at the flip side of writing client side script, that is, writing script that runs on the *server*. This is achieved using a technology known as **Active Server Pages** (**ASP**). Adding "Active" to "Server" gives away the game – it's all about making the server do a bit more work. With an Active Server Page, the web server processes the script in the page, and then sends the finished results out to the user as HTML.

ASP is a huge topic, one for which many books have been written. Visual InterDev offers excellent support for ASP, which we will look at in this chapter. We will not by a long shot cover the entirety of ASP, but we will introduce you to what it is, what it can be used for, and how to use it. In this chapter we'll be covering:

❑ What ASP is.

❑ Using the ASP object model.

❑ Processing submitted forms.

❑ Sending responses to the user.

❑ Maintaining state.

❑ Targetting specific browsers using ASP.

❑ Writing reusable include files.

We will begin by looking at what ASP is.

What is ASP?

ASP is a technology that is designed to allow web pages to be dynamically generated. This means that for each request of a page that the server handles, the code that is run on the server might in fact reply with different page contents. So, we now have two capabilities that we can use – client side script to provide rich interaction for the user, and server side script to ensure that the right content is sent to the user in response to their request – the two work very well hand in hand. Unlike client side script, ASP works its magic on the *server*, to give you different capabilities.

To include ASP in your project, you write ASP files. An ASP file is very similar to a normal web page, and even contains plain vanilla HTML. The two main differences are that it uses .asp as an extension, as opposed to .htm, and that it contains server side script that the server processes before sending a page to the client.

When the web server is asked to serve up a page, it checks the extension of the file. If the file ends in .asp, it will interpret any server side script in the file before sending the page. This server side script can be written in many languages, including VBScript, JavaScript, and others such as PERL, in fact any languages that have an Active Scripting component written for them. It offers very powerful capabilities for interacting with the server and the web page that is being created. ASP works in Internet Information Server versions 3.0 and higher, and Personal Web Server (PWS).

What is ASP Used For?

The end result of processing an ASP page is normally a web page that is similar to the others that you have written so far in this book. The final page can contain client side script, data bound controls, pictures, CSSs, and so on. The one thing that it will not contain is the server side script that generated it.

ASP is used for many purposes, among them are:

❑ Sending specific information in a web page to each user.

❑ Processing HTML forms that are submitted to the server.

❑ Sending responses to a user's query.

❑ Talking to other applications, such as databases, and including information in a page.

❑ Sending the results of a detailed calculation to a user, such as a mortgage amortization table.

❑ Writing web pages that will work in specific browsers. This is a good way of working around browser compatibility issues.

ASP is designed to enhance HTML by creating *dynamic* web pages. By creating an ASP page, you are writing code that will actually write HTML dynamically in response to a user's request. Just one note – don't confuse this with dynamic HTML (DHTML), where the actual content stays the same, but the appearance is modified as the user interacts with a page. ASP actually sends different source HTML – quite a different result. Because of the power offered by ASP, pages can be targeted at each individual user, creating a more interactive experience.

What Advantages Does ASP Offer Over Client Side Script?

One of the biggest disadvantages of using client side script is that it is dependent on the capabilities of the client's browser, meaning that the script language and features that you choose can have a major effect on which browsers can make sense of your page. ASP does not suffer from this limitation, since all of the script is processed on the web server, after which it sends out a normal HTML file.

ASP can in fact be used to overcome browser compatibility issues in client side script. There are capabilities built into ASP for determining which browser is requesting a page. You can then write ASP code that interprets the browser type, and writes client side script specifically for that client browser. This can be a lot of work, but it produces a web site that works well no matter who looks at it. We will look at how to do this towards the end of this chapter.

When ASP is processed on the server, the server side script is actually removed from the code. This is a lot more private than when you use client side script, where anybody can view your source code. It also results in smaller files to download, since large chunks of code have been automatically removed.

ASP is also great for receiving forms that contain feedback from users. It is possible to write a page that receives an HTML form containing feedback, processes it into a file or database, and then writes out a friendly "thank you" message to the user.

At the end of the day, ASP script *complements* client side script. If you just want to perform a mouse rollover effect, or a simple calculation or style change, it would be pointless to make a round trip to the server to grab a new page for every request. Both client and server side script have their place - it is a case of choosing which is the best for a particular task, taking into account issues of browser incompatibility.

Writing ASP Code

Writing ASP code is very similar to writing client side script. As with client side script, you write code directly into the web page concerned, the main difference is that the tags are not quite the same.

In client side script, code is written in a `<SCRIPT></SCRIPT>` block. For ASP code, you have two main choices:

❑ Using `<% ... %>` server script delimiters. Everything within these two delimiters is script that will be run on the server, as shown below.

❑ Adding a `RUNAT=server` attribute to the `<SCRIPT></SCRIPT>` tag.

Let's look at these two methods; firstly, the `<% ... %>` delimiters. Code added using these delimiters looks something like this:

```
...
<%

  'add some ASP script here

%>
...
```

ASP script, like client side script, can be written in many supported languages, such as JavaScript or VBScript. The default language, and the language most commonly used for ASP pages, is VBScript, which we will be using here. VBScript is commonly used because it has good error handling capabilities, and has been designed to make good use of the ASP object model. In addition, there are many developers out there who are familiar with the language, making it a good choice for maintenance and familiarity reasons.

You will recall that for client side script, the language being used is written inside the `<SCRIPT>` tags. When using the `<% ... %>` delimiters for server side script, there is no mention of which language is to be used, so how does the server know which is applicable? This is taken care of by a special language directive, which must be set at the top of each page. If it is not at the top of the page, an error will occur. It looks like this:

```
<% @ LANGUAGE = VBScript  %>
```

201

That's how to use the first option, which is often referred to as inline script, because it is possible to write single lines of code directly into your HTML without requiring huge script blocks – not that this is always advisable!

Alternatively, we have the other option of adding an attribute to our existing <SCRIPT> tag. The <SCRIPT> tag is a catchall for adding script to a page. It defaults to client side script unless it specifically states that the script should be run on the server. Code added using the <SCRIPT> tag to run on the server would look like this:

```
...
<SCRIPT LANGUAGE=VBScript RUNAT=server>

  'add some ASP script here

</SCRIPT>
...
```

With this method, there is no need for an @ LANGUAGE line, since the tag already specifies the language to use. If you do not set the @LANGUAGE directive, the page will default to using VBScript for server side script.

The choice of method is yours to make, and you can even use both in the same page. One thing to be aware of if you do use both methods – sometimes the server will process script within <SCRIPT RUNAT=server> blocks before script within <%...%> delimiters. This is a situation that can be very painful, so it is probably best that you stick to a method that you know. I tend to use the <%...%> inline script delimiters to call functions that are contained within <SCRIPT RUNAT=server> blocks. This tends to avoid issues concerning order of execution.

Let's try an example of creating a simple ASP script.

Try it Out – Writing a Simple ASP Page

We are going to create, once again and for the last time, a "Hello World" example. This time, the Hello World message will be written by the server to the HTML directly. We will use the <% ... %> server side script delimiters in this example.

1. First off, we're going to create a new project for writing simple ASP test pages in. Create a new web project called **ASP Test**. Do not apply any themes or layouts.

2. Create a new ASP page, HelloWorld.asp by choosing **Project | Add web item | Active Server Page**. In the dialog that appears, type **HelloWorld.asp** in the **Name** text box, then press **Open**. A plain ASP page will be created and opened in the editor in **Source** mode. The following HTML will exist in the page initially:

```
<%@ LANGUAGE=VBScript %>
<HTML>
<HEAD>
<META NAME="GENERATOR" Content="Microsoft Visual Studio 6.0">
```

```
</HEAD>
<BODY>

<P> </P>

</BODY>
</HTML>
```

3. As you can see, it has automatically set the default scripting language for server side script to be VBScript, which is the language of choice for server side ASP script. Add the following code to the page:

```
<% @ LANGUAGE = VBScript %>
<HTML>
<HEAD>
<META NAME="GENERATOR" Content="Microsoft Visual Studio 6.0">
<TITLE>Hello World in ASP</TITLE>
</HEAD>
<BODY>
<P>Here is our ever present Hello World example, this time in ASP: <P>
<%

  Response.Write "Hello World"

%>
<P> </P>

</BODY>
</HTML>
```

4. Save your work and view the page in your browser, by selecting View | View in Browser. You will see the following page:

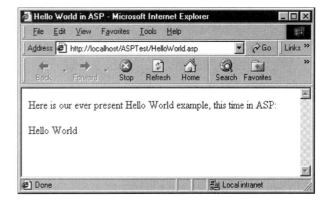

As you can see, the server has changed the `Response.Write "Hello World"` statement into a line of text saying Hello World. If you view the source of this document in your browser, you will see that it is just plain HTML as shown below, with no server side script remaining:

```
<HTML>
<HEAD>
<META NAME="GENERATOR" Content="Microsoft Visual Studio 6.0">
<TITLE>Hello World in ASP</TITLE>
```

```
</HEAD>
<BODY>
<P>Here is our ever present Hello World example, this time in ASP:</P>
Hello World
<P>   </P>

</BODY>
</HTML>
```

As I said earlier, the server has stripped out the ASP code from the document and sent a plain page of HTML text to the user. The statement Response.Write is used to write a string of text to the finished document, in this case Hello World.

So, there you have it – you have written an ASP page that sends plain HTML minus server side script to the user!

Introduction to the ASP Object Model

So far we've seen that ASP is a technology which enables you to write script that makes the server process a page prior to sending it out. To do this, you write script that interacts with the server, in the same way that when you are writing client side script, you are interacting with the browser.

To enable ASP script to be painless to write, Internet Information Server provides an easy to use **object model**, which manages the interaction between the client and server. The phrase "object model" sounds daunting, but it's not. In fact, you have been using various object models in your scripting to date:

❑   When we wrote Response.Write above, we were using the Write method of the ASP Response object.

❑   In client side script, Window.Alert uses the Alert method of the Window object to display a message box to the user.

❑   When we added the calendar control to our test page in the last chapter, the code that we used to retrieve the date, calMyExample.value, was using the value property of the calendar control's object model. All ActiveX controls expose an object model which you program.

❑   Whenever you see a drop down auto-complete box after typing a period in script, you are seeing the properties and methods of the object model in the list.

In fact, object models are so much a part of modern programming, that it's almost impossible to write script without using one. As we saw in Chapter 1, each object can have many properties and methods. To recap, properties are attributes of the object, such as the text property, which is the text within a textbox. A method is an action that the object can perform, such as a Save method which saves the information in the object to a file. There can also be collections of other objects contained within an object, such as a Wheel object having a collection of Spoke objects. The total picture of the properties, methods, and collections of an object is referred to as an object model.

The ASP object model is covered in more detail in Appendix C, but for now I would like to mention two of the more common objects that are used in ASP:

❑ The **Response** object is used whenever the server wants to send output to the client. In script, you can use the various properties, collections, and methods of this object to control what is sent to the client and how. An example of this was our `Response.Write` statement above, which writes to the outputted page as a string of text.

❑ The **Request** object is the flip side of the `Response` object, and is concerned with the information being sent from the client to the server. This object contains information about what the user is requesting and, for example, enables you to read the contents of a form that is being submitted, or find out what they are searching for.

These two objects are perhaps the most central part of the ASP object model. In the examples to come, we will be using them extensively to build ASP pages. These objects, and the four or five others that make up the ASP object model, give you a powerful level of control over what the server does and what the client receives. Let's start looking at how we can use them.

Controlling How ASP Returns Information

We have seen that the `Response` object's `Write` method is used to write information to the web page that is transmitted. It is actually possible to control not just *what* is written, but *how* and *when*.

Generally, the web server processes all of your ASP script and combines it with HTML into something known as the output stream. Once all of the ASP script has been processed, it sends the HTML and the script to the client in one fell swoop. This is great in most cases, but sometimes we might write script that takes a long time to process. In this case, it might not be the best of ideas to make the client wait until it is all processed.

Using the `Response` object it is possible to send some information to the client, and then send more as it is ready. This sort of control would allow us to send, for example, the top of a page showing menus, and then send the main body of the page once it is prepared. The user then does not sit around waiting with a blank screen.

The `Response` object has one property and three methods to manually control when information is sent to the client, they are `buffer`, `Flush`, `Clear`, and `End`.

Buffer

The `Buffer` property is used to tell the server that we will be manually controlling *when* we want to send information. By default, it is set to `False`. To turn it on, we need to write the following:

```
<%@ Language=VBScript %>
<% Response.buffer = True %>
<HTML>
```

This statement should always be located at the top of your page as shown, before the `<HTML>` tag and after the language declaration.

Flush

The Flush method is used to send information to the client immediately. The script will continue processing after this statement, making it useful to send partial results, such as from within a loop that is writing data from a file or database. If Response.buffer has not been set to True, an error occurs. If buffering is set to True, and you do not call Response.Flush or Response.End, then the buffer will flush automatically when the page completes processing.

Utilize this statement to use the Flush method:

```
<% Response.Flush %>
```

Clear

This is used to erase any information that has been added by your ASP since the last Flush statement. This is useful in some cases where you have written information to a page that your script later determines should not be shown. If the Flush statement has not been called, then it will erase from the beginning of the page. Once again, if Response.buffer has not been set to True, an error occurs.

Utilize this statement to use the Clear method:

```
<% Response.Clear %>
```

End

If Response.buffer has been set to True, the End statement flushes all output to the client and then stops processing any further ASP script. This is often used in response to an error occurring, to stop the processing of ASP script.

The End method is called in the following way:

```
<% Response.End %>
```

Processing Submitted Forms

A big part of making a web site interactive is letting the user send you feedback. This feedback might be in the form of completed questionnaires, customer comments, requests for information, purchase orders, and so on. By giving users the capability to interact with your site in this manner, your web site moves from being a simple use of space into being a valuable sales and customer relations tool.

Using Visual InterDev's drag and drop editor, it is possible to quickly and easily create HTML forms for customers to fill in. These forms can be quite sophisticated, and can contain DHTML or other script, that provides a high level of responsiveness and intelligence. When the HTML form is submitted to an ASP page by a user pressing a submit button, it is possible to process that form in a number of useful ways. This capability is one of the great strengths that ASP offers your site, and we're now going to look at how it's done.

Try it Out – Processing a Submitted Form

Remember how, in the *Quick Tour* of Chapter 3, we created a Contact Us form? We made a basic HTML form that contained three boxes: the sender's email address, the subject of the message, and the body of the message. We also added a submit button, and then wrote some basic client side JavaScript that stopped the submit button from working.

We are now going to change this page so that when the user presses the submit button, a page appears displaying the information that they submitted. Later, we are going to write this information into a file on the server, and later still in Chapter 9, we will write it into the database. For now, we are just going to look at how to read the submitted form and write a message back to the user.

1. Open the ContactUs.htm file by double clicking on it in the Project Explorer window.

2. Switch the editor to Source view.

3. Find the following line of code:

```
<FORM ACTION ID="FORM1" METHOD="post" NAME="FORM1">
```

4. Change it to:

```
<FORM ACTION ="save_contact.asp" ID="FORM1" METHOD="post" NAME="FORM1">
```

5. We need to get rid of the client side script that is stopping the submit button from working. Find the following code:

```
<SCRIPT ID="clientEventHandlersJS" LANGUAGE="javascript">
<!--

function submit1_onclick() {
  window.alert("This functionality is not yet implemented.");
  return false;
}

//-->
</SCRIPT>
```

6. Comment out the bits that mean business:

```
<SCRIPT ID="clientEventHandlersJS" LANGUAGE="javascript">
<!--

function submit1_onclick() {
  //window.alert("This functionality is not yet implemented.");
  //return false;
}

//-->
</SCRIPT>
```

7. Save and close the `ContactUs.htm` page.

8. Right mouse click on the project in the **Project Explorer** window and select **Add | Active Server Page**. In the dialog that appears, type the name of the page, which is **save_contact.asp**, and press **Open** to create it.

9. We need to add this page into the site diagram, so that it has the correct title in the navigation bar that is added by the layout of the project. Open **Site Diagram1.wdm** by double clicking on it in the **Project Explorer** window.

10. Right mouse click on a blank area of the site diagram and choose **Add Existing File**. Select **save_contact.asp** and click **OK** to add the page.

11. Change the title of the page as displayed in the site diagram to **Details Sent**, then save and close the site diagram. Note that we have not linked this page to any others on the site diagram. This is because doing so would make it appear in the navigation bars, which is no good because we don't want to allow users to browse directly to this page – it should only work when the `ContactUs.htm` page is submitted to it.

12. The new page, `save_contact.asp`, will be open in the editor in **Source** view. We need to ensure that the navigation bar it displays will be meaningful, so that when information is submitted, the user will have a useful list of pages to browse to. Locate the second **PageNavBar** control, right mouse click on it and then select **Properties**. In the dialog that appears, specify that it should display **First level pages**, then press **OK**.

In our `save_contact.asp` page the default server script language will be set to VBScript by the first line: `<% @ LANGUAGE = VBScript %>`. We now need to write some code to process the `ContactUs.htm` page, and display the results to the user. Locate the main content area of the page, below the **Add your Content Below** layout control. Write the following code:

```
<P> </P>
<%

Response.Write "The information you submitted was:<BR>"
Response.Write "Email Address: " & Request.Form("txtEmailAddress") & "<BR>"
Response.Write "Subject: " & Request.Form("txtSubject") & "<BR>"
Response.Write "Body: " & Request.Form("txtBody") & "<BR>"
Response.Write "Add to Mailing List: " & Request.Form("chkMailingList") & "<BR>"

%>
```

13. Save and close your work. Using the **Project Explorer** window, view the original Contact Us page in your browser, by right mouse clicking on **ContactUs.htm** and selecting **View in Browser**.

14. In the Contact Us form, enter some information and press the Submit button. You will be taken to the new page, which will look something like this (note that if the mailing list box was checked, it has a value of "on"):

How it Works – Processing a Submitted Form

So, what is happening behind the scenes to get all of this working? First off, we made a few changes to the first page, ContactUs.htm:

- ❑ We changed the ACTION method of the form to save_contact.asp. The ACTION method of a form specifies the name of the file that the form will be submitted to when the submit button is pressed. This can be, among other technologies, an ASP page. So, by writing save_contact.asp in the ACTION method, the server will automatically load that ASP page to process the Contact Us form.

- ❑ We also removed the JavaScript that was stopping the submit button from working. When a submit button in a form is pressed, it will automatically submit the information to the page specified by the ACTION method, in this case save_contact.asp.

Secondly, we wrote the save_contact.asp page:

- ❑ We added it to the site diagram and changed the PageNavBar control so that, when viewed, the page would provide meaningful information. This is not part of the task at hand, but certainly makes for a better page!

❑ In script, we used `Request.Form(field name)` to retrieve values. The `Request` object deals with information submitted by the client. When a form has been submitted to a page with the `POST` method, the `Form` object specifies the submitted form, and the names in brackets represent the names of form elements on the submitted form. So when we wrote `Request.Form("txtBody")"`, we were referring to the control named `txtBody` on the submitted Contact Us form. This would return what the user had typed into the Body text area.

❑ We then wrote each value to the page that the server sends in response, by using `Response.Write`. You will also notice that the strings of information which we wrote to the browser also included HTML formatting codes, namely a line break `<BR>`. `Response.Write` simply writes what you tell it as HTML, so if the string that you are writing contains HTML tags, they will be faithfully reproduced in the finished HTML document.

The end result of all this was a simple form confirming the details that had been sent.

Using ASP offers a high level of control over what actually happens with information that is submitted to a server. We have seen the basics of submitting a form, processing it, and sending a response. Let's now look at doing something more interesting with the message, namely saving it to a file.

Try it Out – Saving a Submitted Form to a File

We are now going to build on the last example to make it write the user's message automatically to a file. This information could just as easily be written directly to a database, and eventually will be when we get around to Chapter 9. For now, we are going to simply write the contents to a file in the following format:

```
<MESSAGE>
Email Address: anaddress@anydomain.com
Subject: your subject goes here
Body: your message body goes here
Add to Mailing List: on
</MESSAGE>
<MESSAGE>
...and so on...
```

We can write this information in any format, but this simple one will do for our purposes. We are going to write some code that saves the submitted information into a file called `messages.txt`. To do this, we are going to use something called the **FileSystemObject** object. The `FileSystemObject` object is a special object that you can use to talk to the file system of the server. It is used to create files, read files, and so on. For those of you who have used programming languages before and are used to being able to communicate with the filing system directly, it might seem a little strange to use an object to do this. The reason is security – script is not allowed to modify the filing system, it runs in what is known as a **sandbox**. You can do what you want in the sandbox but not anywhere else. To get over this, objects are used, which are not script and therefore are not subject to these security limitations.

To use the `FileSystemObject` object, or any other object that sits on the server for that matter, we first need to create an instance of it. This is a simple procedure, which uses the following syntax:

```
Dim objAnyObject
Set objAnyObject = Server.CreateObject("ObjectName.ObjectClass")
```

Think of an object provided in an object model as a kind of template. When you want to use that object, you make a copy of it based on the template – you don't use the actual master copy. You can then use and modify the copy of the object as much as you like. This copying process is what is known as instantiation, as you create an instance of the object and then use that in your code.

For our `FileSystemObject` object, the code to create an instance of the object would be:

```
Dim objFS          'file system object
Set objFS = Server.CreateObject("Scripting.FileSystemObject")
```

Once the object is created, you can use it in the standard `Object.property` or `Object.Method` syntax, for example:

```
objFS.OpenTextFile("filename.txt")
```

Forewarned with this knowledge, let's write some code that will make our `save_contact.asp` page actually do what its name suggests it will:

1. In the My Documents folder on your `c:` drive, create a new text document called `messages.txt`.

2. In Visual InterDev, open the page **save_contact.asp** by double clicking on it in the Project Explorer window.

3. In the Source tab, locate the following code:

```
<%

Response.Write "The information you submitted was:<BR>"
Response.Write "Email Address: " & Request.Form("txtEmailAddress") & "<BR>"
Response.Write "Subject: " & Request.Form("txtSubject") & "<BR>"
Response.Write "Body: " & Request.Form("txtBody") & "<BR>"
Response.Write "Add to Mailing List: " & Request.Form("chkMailingList") & "<BR>"

%>
```

4. Replace this code with:

```
<%

Dim objFS          'file system object
Dim objSaveFile         'file to save message to
'dim variables to store form contents
Dim strEmailAddress,strSubject,strBody,strMailingList

'read form and save in variables to save reading again later
strEmailAddress = Request.Form("txtEmailAddress")
strSubject = Request.Form("txtSubject")
strBody = Request.Form("txtBody")
strMailingList = Request.Form("chkMailingList")
```

```
'create filesystemobject and open file
Set objFS = Server.CreateObject("Scripting.FileSystemObject")
Set objSaveFile = objFS.OpenTextFile("c:\My Documents\messages.txt",8,True)

'write message to file
objSaveFile.Write "<MESSAGE>" & vbcrlf    'vbcrlf is a constant representing a newline
objSaveFile.Write "Email Address: " & strEmailAddress & vbcrlf
objSaveFile.Write "Subject: " & strSubject & vbcrlf
objSaveFile.Write "Body: " & strBody & vbcrlf
objSaveFile.Write "Add to Mailing List: " & strMailingList & vbcrlf
objSaveFile.Write "</MESSAGE>" & vbcrlf

objSaveFile.Close                  'close the file
set objSaveFile = nothing          'remove references to objects
set objFS = nothing
'now, write response to user showing what was submitted
Response.Write _
  "Thank you, the message shown below has been successfully submitted:<BR><BR>"
Response.Write "Email Address: " & strEmailAddress & "<BR>"
Response.Write "Subject: " & strSubject & "<BR>"
Response.Write "Body: " & strBody & "<BR>"
Response.Write "Add to Mailing List: " & strMailingList & "<BR>"

%>
```

To clarify things a little, the `OpenTextFile` method accepts four parameters, of which all except the first are optional. They are `filename`, `create`, `iomode`, and `format`. The `filename` is the full path to the file to be opened, `create` specifies whether to create the file if it doesn't exist (true or false), the `iomode` specifies the input output mode of the file (`ForReading=1`, `ForWriting=2`, `ForAppending=8`), and the last parameter, `format`, specifies what type of file to create. We did not specify the last parameter, meaning that it defaults to ASCII.

5. Save your work. Using the **Project Explorer** window, view the original Contact Us page in your browser, by right mouse clicking on **ContactUs.htm** and selecting **View in Browser**.

6. In the Contact Us form, enter some information and press the **Submit** button. You will be taken to the new page, which will look pretty much the same as it did in the last example.

7. Use Notepad to open the file that you specified in code, in this example `c:\My Documents\messages.txt`. You will see that it contains your message, for example:

```
<MESSAGE>
Email Address: anaddress@anydomain.com
Subject: your subject goes here
Body: your message body goes here
Add to Mailing List: on
</MESSAGE>
```

8. Submit a few more messages. You will see that every message is appended to the end of the last message in the `messages.txt` file.

This example went quite a bit more in depth than the last, but it has produced a much more rounded solution.

It would now be possible to write a page that was viewable on an intranet but not published to the Internet, to display the contents of this file. This would be a fairly similar exercise to the one above. All you would need to do would be to create an ASP page that used the `FileSystemObject` object to read the contents of the `messages.txt` file. By using `Response.Write`, you could then present this in any format you wanted to, by including HTML formatting commands in the string.

The example above uses some good tips that you can apply to any code that you write:

❑ Put comments in your code to make it easier to read. This is not just to help others - a good enough reason in itself – but to help you understand your own code when you come back to it after a long absence. This is a good practice to get into that pays big dividends when you write very large scripts.

❑ If you are going to refer to the values on a form more than once, it pays to load them into variables as we did in the beginning of our code. This achieves two goals:

   ❑ It is much easier to read.

   ❑ It makes your page work faster, since it does not need to constantly refer back to the object model and the submitted form.

❑ When writing parameters for methods, Visual InterDev automatically displays the known parameters for a method to help your memory, for example:

```
'create filesystemobject and open file
set objFS = Server.CreateObject ("Scripting.FileSystemObject")
set objSaveFile = objFS.OpenTextFile (
                       OpenTextFile (FileName, [IOMode], [Create], [Format])
                       Open a file as a TextStream
'write message to file
objSaveFile.Write "<message>" & vbcrlf   'vbcrlf is a constant repre
objSaveFile.Write "Email Address: " & strEmailAddress & vbcrlf
objSaveFile.Write "Subject: " & strSubject & vbcrlf
objSaveFile.Write "Body: " & strBody & vbcrlf
objSaveFile.Write "Add to Mailing List: " & strMailingList & vbcrlf
objSaveFile.Write "</message>" & vbcrlf
```

Maintaining State Between Pages

One of the big problems with HTML historically has been that it doesn't have much of a memory. We have looked at how to get information from the client to the server, and from the server to the client, but this is quite different from keeping track of what happened a few pages ago.

To get around this, developers used various tricks such as hidden fields, storing temporary information in a database or file, and so on. All of these approaches work, but are sometimes either clumsy, time-consuming, over-designed, or just plain difficult to write.

ASP comes to the rescue by using various objects to keep track of important information. The objects become the memory for your web application, enabling you to pass information from one page to another without any of the clumsy constructs that were used in the past.

ASP offers two places to store data: an **Application** object and a **Session** object.

Using the Application Object

The `Application` object stores information that is accessible by all users of your web application. Your web application consists of all of the files that exist within your web project and all of its sub directories.

Using the `Application` object, it is possible to create variables and objects that can be used in any ASP page that is part of the application. These are then referred to as application variables, or `Application` objects.

Application variables are great when you have fairly static information that you don't want to put into a database, but is subject to change. It is also possible to load information from a database into these variables when your application starts. For example, you might want to store contact e-mail addresses and phone numbers in application variables, so that they can quickly and easily be accessed when needed.

To use application variables, you need a place to store them and a place to initialize them. This can be any page in your application, but it is often a good idea to initialize them in the `global.asa` file, so that you can find them easily later.

Using the global.asa File

The `global.asa` file is a place to store global information about your application. We have seen that this is used to store database environment information, we are now going to learn what else it's capable of.

Firstly, whenever certain events happen, the web server looks in the `global.asa` file to see if there is an event handler for that event. If there is, the code in that event handler is executed. There are four possible events:

❑   `Application_OnStart`: occurs when the first visitor opens a page in your application.

❑   `Application_OnEnd`: occurs when the server is stopped.

❑   `Session_OnStart`: occurs whenever a new user begins a session on the web site.

❑   `Session_OnEnd`: occurs whenever a session terminates, normally due to a timeout occuring after about 20 minutes.

The two session-related events will be discussed when we get around to the `Session` object. For now, we are concerned with the `Application_OnStart` and `Application_OnEnd` events.

Application_OnStart

This event happens when the first visitor to your application browses the first `.asp` page. It occurs once, after which it will not occur again until the application has terminated and starts again, which occurs when the server is stopped and restarted.

The `Application_OnStart` event should be used to initialize any variables that you want to be available to all pages of your application. The event handler can either explicitly define the value of a variable, or it can retrieve it from a file or database.

To create an application variable, you would write the following code into the global.asa:

```
Sub Application_OnStart
  Application("VariableName") = "Value"
End Sub
```

Once initialized in this manner, the variable will be usable in any ASP page by writing:

```
Application("VariableName")
```

Application_OnEnd

The Application_OnEnd event occurs when the web server is stopped. If this is because of a power failure or any other severely terminal events, the chances are that it probably won't work, of course. The idea of this event is to perform any clean-up operations. The most typical examples might be to save any information that is important to a database or file, and to delete any unnecessary temporary records from a database.

Try it Out – Using Application Variables

We are going to create a simple web page that demonstrates how to use application variables. To do this, we are going to initialize an application variable in the Application_OnStart event of the global.asa file. We are then going to create a page that displays the value of this variable, and enables us to easily change it. By changing the variable, closing our web page, and opening it again, we can prove that the application variable remains the same beyond the length of our browsing session.

1. Open the project **ASP Test**.

2. Open the **global.asa** file by double clicking on it in the **Project Explorer** window. (Get a working copy if you are prompted.)

3. The global.asa file contains one server side <SCRIPT> block and some commented information on how to use it. Basically, we write a sub procedure for the event we wish to handle, then put our code in it. Write the following code:

```
<SCRIPT LANGUAGE=VBScript RUNAT=Server>

'You can add special event handlers in this file that will get run automatically when
'special Active Server Pages events occur. To create these handlers, just create a
'subroutine with a name from the list below that corresponds to the event you want to
'use. For example, to create an event handler for Session_OnStart, you would put the
'following code into this file (without the comments):

'Sub Session_OnStart
'**Put your code here **
'End Sub

'EventName                 Description
'Session_OnStart           Runs the first time a user runs any page in your application
'Session_OnEnd             Runs when a user's session times out or quits your application
'Application_OnStart       Runs once when the first page of your application is run
                           'for the first time by any user
'Application_OnEnd         Runs once when the web server shuts down
```

```
Sub Application_OnStart
  Application("ContactName")="Bob"
End Sub
```

```
</SCRIPT>
```

4. Save the `global.asa` and close it. The code we just wrote will initalize an application variable named `ContactName` with the initial value of `Bob`.

5. Add a new ASP page by right mouse clicking on the project in the Project Explorer window and selecting Add | Active Server Page. Name the page ApplicationVariables.asp. Click Open.

6. Type the following into the editor (we shall look at what the code means shortly):

```
<%@ LANGUAGE=VBScript %>
<HTML>
<HEAD>
<META NAME="GENERATOR" Content="Microsoft Visual Studio 6.0">
<%
If Request.Form("txtContactName") <> "" Then
  Application("ContactName")=Request.Form("txtContactName")
End if
%>
</HEAD>
<BODY>

<FORM ID=Form1 ACTION="ApplicationVariables.asp" METHOD="post">

<P>Contact Name: <INPUT NAME=txtContactName
VALUE="<%=Application("ContactName")%>"></P>
<INPUT TYPE="submit" VALUE="Change" ID=submit1 NAME=submit1>
</FORM>
</BODY>
</HTML>
```

7. Save the file, and view it in the browser. You should see this web page:

8. The Contact Name box displays the value contained in the application variable. If you change it and then press the Change button, this will update the value of the application variable and reload the form. Change the Contact Name from Bob to Mary, then press Change.

9. The page will reload and display Mary. This means that the value of the application variable has been updated. Now, close your web browser.

10. Reload the web page by selecting View in Browser from Visual InterDev. The Contact Name will be Mary. This shows that the application variable has stayed the same.

11. Stop and restart your web server. Now view the page again and you should see the same screen as shown above – the variable has been re-initialized in the global.asa to Bob. (Sadly, if you are using PWS, the best way to do this is to shut down and restart your computer.)

How it Works – Using Application Variables

Let's take a look at how this code works. First off, we'll examine the second chunk of code that we added, line by line:

```
<FORM ID=Form1 ACTION="ApplicationVariables.asp" METHOD="post">

<P>Contact Name: <INPUT NAME=txtContactName
VALUE="<%=Application("ContactName")%>"></P>
<INPUT TYPE="submit" VALUE="Change" ID=submit1 NAME=submit1>
</FORM>
```

❑ The first line creates a form and sets the ACTION method to the same page. This means that the form will post to itself.

❑ The second line creates a text box called txtContactName, and sets the value property, which is the content of the text box, to the value of the application variable. Notice the way that this was done. By writing an = sign at the beginning of an ASP statement, it actually performs a Response.Write, in this case writing the value of the ContactName variable. The positioning of this piece of server code, actually within a tag, effectively enables us to have control over the HTML that is written. Initially, the textbox's value property would be Bob.

❑ The third line is a submit button, and the fourth line finished the form.

❑ When the user hits the submit button, the form is submitted to itself. This is where the first bit of code we wrote comes in:

```
If Request.Form("txtContactName") <> "" Then
  Application("ContactName")=Request.Form("txtContactName")
End if
```

❑ The first time our ASP page is loaded, no form is submitted. This only occurs after the user has pressed the Change button to submit a form. If no form has been submitted, then the value of any variables on that form will be "". By checking to see if this field is empty, we can ensure that the second line of code is only actioned when the user has pressed the Change button. One thing this method does do however, is that it forces somebody to actually write a name. This is, in this example, a good point because if they entered a blank, then the name would not change.

❑ The second line of code sets the application variable ContactName to the value of the txtContactName field on the submitted form.

So the flow of things is this. The first time the page is loaded the form displays the initial value of the application variable. When the user changes it and presses **Change**, the txtContactName field of the submitted form will contain a new value, readable using Request.Form("txtContactName"). This causes our first block of code to change the application variable, which is displayed in the text box by the second block of code.

Using the Session Object

We have seen how the Application object is used to store variables that are available to all users of the web application, and that these variables remain alive until the web server is stopped or the application is unloaded. This is a great tool for managing shared information – the Session object is similar, except that it stores separate information for every user.

A **session** occurs when a user first browses an ASP page in a web application, and ends when the session times out, which occurs if the user does not request or refresh a page before a specified time period ends. Therefore, every time a user visits your application, the server creates and manages a session for them, and one way or another, the session will eventually terminate.

Sessions work by storing information in **cookies**. Cookies are little packets of information that are sent between the client and server with each request. To maintain a session, cookies store information about the current session for the user. The server then knows which set of session variables belong to the user. In most cases this works fine, but it is possible for users to configure their browser to *not accept* cookies. Also, certain older browsers will not understand them. If either of these scenarios occurs, then the session variables will not be accessible. In circumstances where this is likely to occur, your best option is to use a database to store any information that you would otherwise store in session variables.

The Session object is like a limited Application object. It works in the same way – it's just personal to each user. This makes it a very powerful tool to the web developer, as it enables information to be carried from page to page, and stored for retrieval throughout the user's stay on the site.

There are many examples in which this ability to store information for each user on a temporary basis comes in handy. Paramount among them is a **login** feature. You could for example, have a web page where the user enters information into a form. This form would submit to an ASP page that checks to see if a user is valid, and if so, stores their name and the fact they have logged in successfully into a session variable. On every page that needs security, you could simply check to see if these session variables are correct, and if not, kick the user out. The session timeout feature then becomes an added bonus in the case of a user forgetting to log out and walking away from their desk – after a set time the session expires, and the user needs to log in again.

Let's take a look at how to use the Session object.

Try it Out – Using Session Variables

We are going to write a simple login page that is just an HTML form with user name and password boxes, and a login button. This form submits to an ASP page that simply checks to see that the password entered is "password". If it is, then the login is successful, otherwise it is not. The ASP page will store the result in some session variables and display those variables to the user.

1. Open the project **ASP Test**.

2. Create a new HTML page by right mouse clicking on the project in the **Project Explorer** window and selecting **Add | HTML Page**. The name of the file is `login.htm`.

3. Click **Open** and the `login.htm` file should automatically appear in the editor. Switch to **Source** mode, and key in the following:

```
<HTML>
<HEAD>
<META NAME="GENERATOR" Content="Microsoft Visual Studio 6.0">
<TITLE></TITLE>
</HEAD>
<BODY>

<FORM ID=frmLogin ACTION="login_check.asp" METHOD="post">

<P>Please Enter your Login Details below:</P>
<P>User Name: <INPUT ID=txtUsername NAME=txtUserName></P>
<P>Password: <INPUT ID=txtPassword NAME=txtPassword TYPE=password></P>
<P><INPUT ID=btnLogin NAME=btnLogin TYPE=submit VALUE=Login></P>

</FORM>

</BODY>
</HTML>
```

4. This is a very basic HTML form with no surprises although, if you haven't used one before, the password text box needs explaining – it will automatically put asterisks into the text box in place of every character typed. The form will submit to an ASP page called `login_check.asp`. Save and close the `login.htm` file.

5. Create a new ASP page, `login_check.asp`, by right mouse clicking on the project in the **Project Explorer** window and selecting **Add | Active Server Page**.

6. Write the following code into the new ASP page:

```
<%@ LANGUAGE=VBScript %>
<HTML>

<HEAD>
<META NAME="GENERATOR" Content="Microsoft Visual Studio 6.0">

</HEAD>
<BODY>
<%
Dim LoginOK

'check login details of login.htm
If Request.Form("txtUserName") = "" or Request.Form("txtPassword") = "" Then
  'missed something
  Response.Write _
    "<STRONG>Please ensure that you enter both a UserName and Password</STRONG>"
```

219

```
  'save login failure to session variables
  Session("ValidUser") = False
  Session("UserName") = "Not Logged In"
Else
  'check that password entered is "password"
  'this could be replaced by any sort of check, such as to a database
  If Request.Form("txtPassword") = "password" Then
    LoginOK = True
  Else
    Response.Write "<STRONG>Invalid Password</STRONG>"
    LoginOK = False
  End if

  'save login results to session variables
  Session("ValidUser") = LoginOK
  Session("UserName") = Request.Form("txtUserName")

End if

%>


<P> </P>
<%
  If Session("ValidUser") = False Then
    Response.Write _
      "You must <A HREF='login.htm'>login</A> before you can view this page."
  Else
    Response.Write "<P>Welcome, " & Session("UserName") & _
      ", you have successfully logged in.</P>"
  End if
%>

</BODY>
</HTML>
```

7. We will look at how this code works shortly. What it does, however, is check that all the fields are filled in on the login page, and that the password is "password". If this is the case, the login is successful, otherwise it is a failure, and offers a link back to the login page. Save this file.

8. Right-click on the file login.htm in the Project Explorer window and select View in Browser. A simple login page like this should appear:

9. Press the Login button without filling in the User Name or Password fields. You will be taken to the login_check.asp page which will report a login failure, as shown below:

10. The second piece of code in our page determined that the user had not successfully logged in and provided a link back to the login page. Click on this link to return to the login page.

11. If you now type in your name, and a password of "password", the login should work:

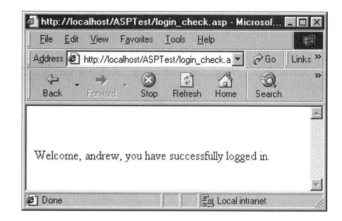

If you then close the page and re-enter it, you will again be asked for your login details – they have not been remembered because they were stored only as *session* variables.

How it Works – Using Session Variables

There's quite a lot we can learn from this example, even with its slightly rudimentary login credentials check. Let's take a look at how it all works. First off, let's look at the first of our blocks of code:

```
<%
Dim LoginOK

'check login details of login.htm
If Request.Form("txtUserName") = "" or Request.Form("txtPassword") = "" Then
  'missed something
  Response.Write _
    "<STRONG>Please ensure that you enter both a UserName and Password</STRONG>"

  'save login failure to session variables
  Session("ValidUser") = False
  Session("UserName") = "Not Logged In"
Else
  'check that password entered is "password"
  'this could be replaced by any sort of check, such as to a database
  If Request.Form("txtPassword") = "password" Then
    LoginOK = True
  Else
    Response.Write "<STRONG>Invalid Password</STRONG>"
    LoginOK = False
  End if

  'save login results to session variables
  Session("ValidUser") = LoginOK
  Session("UserName") = Request.Form("txtUserName")

End if

%>
```

The purpose of this code block is to read the `login.htm` form and check that the login is successful. Here's how it works:

❑ We firstly check to see if the fields were completed, if they were not, their values will be "". In this case, we write a message asking the user to fill in the fields, then assign a `False` value to the `ValidUser` session variable. We also specify that the `UserName` session variable is `Not Logged In`.

❑ If all the information is provided, we perform a very stringent security check to ensure that the `password` field contains the value `password`. If this is the case, we set a local variable named `LoginOK` to be `True`. Otherwise, we specify that it is `False`. We then set the `ValidUser` session variable to the value of the `LoginOK` variable, and the `UserName` to that supplied on the form.

So, at the end of this section of code, we will have set our two session variables to contain the login status. `ValidUser` will be `True` if the login was successful, else it will be `False`. The `UserName` variable will either store the name of a successfully logged in user, else it will contain `Not Logged In`.

Let's move onto our second block of code:

```
<%
  If Session("ValidUser") = False Then
    Response.Write _
      "You must <A HREF='login.htm'>login</A> before you can view this page."
  Else
      Response.Write _
      "<P>Welcome, " & Session("UserName") & ", you have successfully logged in.</P>"
  End if
%>
```

This is a piece of code that reads our session variables and displays a meaningful message to the user based on the success of their login. We could have incorporated this into the first block of code but, by separating it, we can easily copy this code to other pages that need to know if a user is logged in.

❑ If the value contained in the session variable `ValidUser` is `False`, then a message is displayed stating that the user needs to login, and a link to the login page is provided.

❑ If the value is `True`, then a welcome message is displayed.

This last snippet of code could be added to any ASP page that requires a user to be logged in. In the second part of the `If...Else` block that currently just displays a welcome message, ASP code could be written that displays the content for a successful login.

Session Timeout

The example above shows how easy it is to assign and read session variables. Assigning a variable is simply:

```
Session("variable name") = variable value
```

Then, in any other page of your application you can retrieve the value, for the duration of the session, with a simple line of code such as:

```
local_variable = Session("variable name")
```

Once a session has been started by a user visiting your application, it will last until a **timeout** occurs. A timeout happens after a set time period, which you can specify. Normally, this value is set to 20 minutes within IIS, but at any time during a session you can specifically set a timeout period for that specific session by simply writing:

```
<% Session.Timeout = 15 %>
```

This above example will set the timeout value to 15 minutes. You can also retrieve the value of the timeout property with this line of code:

```
<% Session.Timeout %>
```

You should try to take care when changing the timeout values. If it is too short, a user will get upset about constantly having to login every time the session times out, or losing their information all the time. If you set it too long, then the server will maintain all the session information in memory for long periods of time. This can slow your computer down, especially if there are a lot of users and therefore a lot of session variables.

If you want to specifically end a session, which might occur if you wanted the user to press a logout button for example, then you can use the following line of code:

```
<% Session.End %>
```

This will end the current session immediately.

Fighting Browser Incompatibility

Up until now, we've told you to live with issues of browser incompatibility and work around it. Now we're going to look at using ASP to fight back.

Browser incompatibility, as we have mentioned, occurs when script or even plain HTML is written to take advantage of the features available in a specific browser. Typically, the newer the browser, the more advantages there are to writing code specifically for it. Sadly, the more use you make of such features, the less the page will work with older browsers.

This is a major pain when writing client side script into a web page, because the chances are that over the Internet you stand to lose potential readers, if their browsers are older than the version for which you coded. ASP is a great technology because all of the work it does is performed on the server. This means that there are no incompatibility problems when using ASP. Still, there are many cases when ASP code won't cut the cake – it would be pointless, for example, to do a round trip to the server to completely rewrite a page every time the user moved their mouse over a button with a rollover effect. For these and other situations, client side script is the answer. So how can you work around the incompatibility issues?

The Browser Capabilities Component

ASP offers a server side object that detects what sort of client browser a request has come from. This object is called the **Browser Capabilities component**, and not only does it detect the type of browser, it also detects what capabilities it has. This means that you can detect if a browser supports a version of JavaScript, Frames, and so on. Using the Browser Capabilities component enables you to know just what your client is capable of, which means that you can write a web page for them using Response.Write that works on their browser. This can even extend to writing specific sections of client script for each browser type.

The Browser Capabilities component is in fact an easy interface for another method of detecting what a client can do, called the **HTTP_USER_AGENT**. This is information sent to the server and stored in a variable accessible through the Request object. It is a much harder method of determining what a client can do, but it does work. We are going to look at the Browser Capabilities component because it is easier and offers the same result.

The Browser Capabilities component works by reading information about the capabilities of various browsers in a file called browscap.ini, which is automatically installed on your system along with Visual InterDev.

When a client browser connects to the web server, it automatically sends an **HTTP User Agent header** to the server. This header is an ASCII string that identifies the client browser and its version number. The Browser Capabilities component then compares the header to the various entries contained within the browscap.ini file.

❏ If it finds a match, then the properties of the Browser Capabilities component will be defined by the contents of the browscap.ini file for the matched browser.

❏ If it does not find a match for the header in the browscap.ini file, it searches for the closest match using wildcards. If a match cannot be found using wildcards, then the Browser Capabilities component will use the default browser settings, if they have been specified in the browscap.ini file. If the object does not find a match, and default browser settings have not been specified in the browscap.ini file, then every property of the Browser Capabilities component will be set to the string "UNKNOWN".

To define what a specific browser is capable of, you simply need to create or edit an entry for it within the browscap.ini file. A sample part of a browscap.ini file entry might look like this:

```
;;;;;;;;;;;;;;;;;;;;;;;;;;;;;;;;;;;;;;;;;;;;; IE 4.x
[IE 4.0]
browser=IE
Version=4.0
majorver=4
minorver=0
frames=TRUE
tables=TRUE
cookies=TRUE
backgroundsounds=TRUE
vbscript=TRUE
```

225

```
javascript=TRUE
javaapplets=TRUE
ActiveXControls=TRUE
Win16=False
beta=False
AK=False
SK=False
AOL=False
crawler=False
cdf=True
```

By creating and editing these entries, it is a very simple matter to make the `Browser Capabilities` component understand the capabilities of specific browsers.

> *If you want to support the most recent browser, an easy way to update your* `browscap.ini` *file is to download a more current version from the following site:*
>
> `http://www.cyscape.com/asp/browscap/`

We will now have a look at how to use the `Browser Capabilities` component.

Try it Out – Using the Browser Capabilities Component

We are going to create a simple web page that changes an image when a mouse moves over it. This will be a simple effect, similar to what is found in many web sites. We are going to use the `Browser Capabilities` component to detect if the web page supports VBScript, and if it does, we will write a DHTML version of the page. If it does not support VBScript, we will instead output a JavaScript version of the page.

Obviously, this example is fairly trivial, so in real life you could probably get away with using just the JavaScript method. But it serves to outline the process that you need to use, without cluttering the scene with too much other code.

Let's begin:

1. Open the project **ASP Test**.

2. Add two images, `home_nml.gif` and `home_mo.gif`, to the images folder; they are available as part of the download from `http://www.wrox.com`, or you can create any two graphics you want with the same names. The `home_nml.gif` is the normal image state, while `home_mo.gif` is the mouse over image.

3. Create a new ASP page, `bctest.asp`.

4. Write the following code into the editor window. (Note that `chr(34)` is a VBScript function to represent `"`. Using this function ensures that the quotes will appear in the resulting string, whereas if we used `"`, it would cause confusion in the `Response.Write` statement.)

```
<%@ LANGUAGE=VBScript %>
<HTML>
<HEAD>
<META NAME=VI60_defaultClientScript CONTENT=JavaScript>
<TITLE>Browser Capabilities Test</TITLE>
<META NAME="GENERATOR" Content="Microsoft Visual Studio 6.0">
<%
  Dim objBrowserCap
  Dim blnUseVBScript            'will be True if OK to use VBScript, else False

  'create Browser Capabilities Component
  Set objBrowserCap = Server.CreateObject("MSWC.BrowserType")
  'determine if VBScript is usable, store in variable
  blnUseVBScript = objBrowserCap.vbscript
  Set objBrowserCap = nothing 'release object reference

  If blnUseVBScript Then
    'write a VBScript Event Handler using DHTML
    Response.Write "<SCRIPT ID=clientEventHandlersVBS LANGUAGE=VBScript>" & vbcrlf
    Response.Write "<!-- " & vbcrlf
    Response.Write "Sub imgHome_onmouseover" & vbcrlf
    Response.Write "imgHome.src = " & chr(34) & "images\home_mo.gif" & chr(34) & _
                   vbcrlf
    Response.Write "End Sub" & vbcrlf & vbcrlf
    Response.Write "Sub imgHome_onmouseout" & vbcrlf
    Response.Write "imgHome.src = " & chr(34) & "images\home_nml.gif" & chr(34) & _
                   vbcrlf
    Response.Write "End Sub" & vbcrlf
    Response.Write "-->" & vbcrlf
    Response.Write "</SCRIPT>" & vbcrlf
  Else
    'Javascript will be written inline with the image
  End if

%>
</HEAD>
<BODY>
<P>
<IMG ID=imgHome SRC="images/home_nml.gif"
<% If not blnUseVBScript Then
    Response.Write "onmouseover=" & chr(34) & _
         "Window.Document.Images[0].Src='images/home_mo.gif'" & chr(34)
    Response.Write " onmouseout=" & chr(34) & _
         "Window.Document.Images[0].Src='images/home_nml.gif'" & chr(34)
  End if
%>
>

</P>
</BODY>
</HTML>
```

5. Save your file, and view it in Internet
    Explorer 4.0. You will see a simple home
    page image that changes colour when the
    mouse moves over it:

6. If you view the source code for this page, you will see that it only contains the VBScript code,
    since the Browser Capabilities component successfully detected that Internet Explorer 4.0
    supports VBScript:

```
<HTML>
<HEAD>
<META NAME=VI60_defaultClientScript content=JavaScript>
<TITLE>Browser Capabilities Test</TITLE>
<META NAME="GENERATOR" Content="Microsoft Visual Studio 6.0">
<SCRIPT ID=clientEventHandlersVBS LANGUAGE=VBScript>
<!--
Sub imgHome_onmouseover
  imgHome.src = "images\home_mo.gif"
End Sub

Sub imgHome_onmouseout
  imgHome.src = "images\home_nml.gif"
End Sub
-->
</SCRIPT>

</HEAD>
<BODY>
<P>
<IMG ID=imgHome SRC="images/home_nml.gif"

>
</P>

</BODY>
</HTML>
```

7. Now, view the same page in Netscape Navigator 4.0. Netscape Navigator 4.0 does not support
    VBScript, but the mouse over effects will still work. If you view the source, you will see that it
    contains just the JavaScript code:

```
<HTML>
<HEAD>
<META NAME=VI60_defaultClientScript CONTENT=JavaScript>
<TITLE>Browser Capabilities Test</TITLE>
<META NAME="GENERATOR" Content="Microsoft Visual Studio 6.0">

</HEAD>
<BODY>
<P>
<IMG ID=imgHome SRC="images/home_nml.gif"
onmouseover="Window.Document.Images[0].Src='images/home_mo.gif'"
onmouseout="Window.Document.Images[0].Src='images/home_nml.gif'">
</P>

</BODY>
</HTML>
```

This example was very simple, yet it showed you how to detect the capabilities of a browser and write code specific to its requirements. You can see how easy it is to use the Browser Capabilities component – simply create an object, and then read its properties to see if a particular language or feature is available.

To stop us from having to constantly refer to the Browser Capabilities component, we used the blnVBScript variable to store whether the browser is VBScript capable or not. Then, later in our code, we only needed to refer to this variable to know what to write.

After that, the rest of the code simply used Response.Write to write client side script that was suitable for the specific browser. This capability of writing client side script from server side script is very powerful, and means that if you spend the time and effort, browser incompatibility issues can be severely minimized.

Using Include Files

The last part of our whirlwind tour of ASP is to mention **include files**. When you start writing large applications, you can often find bits of code that are reusable. To save yourself having to write this code over and over again each time you need it, it is possible to save just the required code into an include file and reuse it later. This is great when it comes to maintaining your site, since the maintenance only needs to be done in one place.

An include file is a simple text file that contains your code, or fragments of HTML. When a web page includes a line such as:

```
<!-- #include file = "mycode.inc" -->
```

it automatically inserts the contents of that file into the web page when the server processes the file. The contents of that file are then processed as if the code from the include file was actually in the same file.

> One very important point to realize here is that an include file is applied *before* the web server processes any ASP. This means that it is not possible to use ASP code to decide which include file you want to use.

Apart from this limitation, include files can be used to insert chunks of HTML, client side script, and server side ASP script. They are great in larger applications and for heavily reused code. A good example would be to create an include file that contained various database connection information, or a login checker such as we created in the section about *Sessions*.

If we look at the code we wrote for checking our logins, it looks like this:

```
<%
  If Session("ValidUser") = False Then
    Response.Write _
       "You must <A HREF='login.htm'>login</A> before you can view this page."
  Else
    Response.Write _
       " <P>Welcome, " & Session("UserName") & ", you have successfully logged in.</P>"
  End if
%>
```

This is probably close to, but not quite, what we want to include every time. This is because the above code expects you to write the response you need into the If...Else statement. A better example for an include file would be:

```
<%
  If Session("ValidUser") = False Then
    Response.Redirect "login.htm"
  End if
%>
```

If you save this code to a text file named login_check.inc, then you could reference it in any page that needed to check security by simply writing the line:

```
<!-- #include file = "login_check.inc"  -->
```

If the user had not logged in, they would automatically be redirected to the login page and be forced to login. One important factor to realize when using a Response.Redirect statement is that you must have the Response buffer turned on. The Response.buffer statement was covered earlier in this chapter in the section entitled *Controlling How ASP Returns Information*. You should also ensure that the Response.buffer statement is at the top of your page, just after the language directive. If you do not have a Response.buffer=True statement at the top of your ASP page, then calling Response.Redirect will fail.

Summary

In this chapter, we have looked at various methods of using Active Server Pages to add a level of dynamism to your web site. Using ASP can free you up from laboriously creating hundreds of pages to meet the demands of your clients, and it can help you to battle browser issues – thereby expanding the reach of your site.

We have only lightly dived into ASP, which is the topic of many books in itself. Two excellent books by Wrox Press are Beginning Active Server Pages 2.0 (ISBN 1-861001-34-7), and Professional Active Server Pages 2.0 (ISBN 1-861001-26-6), which will give you a thorough understanding of how to use this great technology. (Also Beginning and Professional ASP 3.0 are available, ISBN 1-861003-38-2 and 1-861002-61-0 respectively.)

We have seen how Visual InterDev provides some great user-friendly features to assist us in coding ASP, and you should hopefully have an appreciation of what the technology can do for your web projects. In summary, ASP offers features that can:

- ❑ Target information at specific users.
- ❑ Process feedback from users.
- ❑ Control when information is sent to the user.
- ❑ Amalgamate information from outside sources into a web page, such as files and databases.
- ❑ Store information and share it between pages and users of a web application.
- ❑ Overcome browser incompatibility issues, by detecting client browser features and writing code specific to those features.

In the next chapter, we are going to look at some of the advanced design time controls (DTCs) that Visual InterDev offers to speed up the development process. These controls, which we lightly touched on in Chapter 5 - *Database Basics*, offer an easy way to build advanced features into your web project.

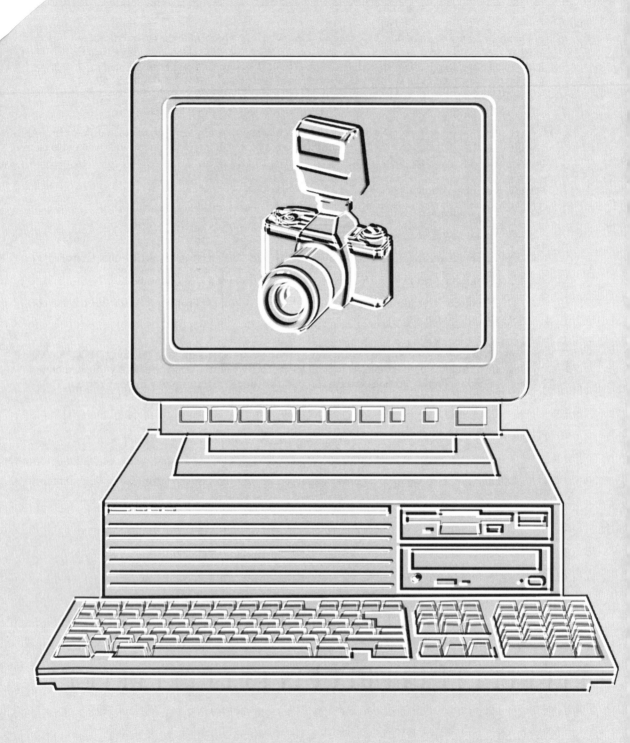

Design Time Controls

In the previous two chapters, we've seen how we can use client side and sever side script to enhance our web pages. Design time controls (DTCs) are an exciting new feature of Visual InterDev 6.0 that do not require much, if any, scripting on your part, but which offer an easy way to add functionality to your web pages. Using design time controls you can, for example, easily create data bound HTML forms. Simply drag and drop a few controls to the page, bind them to specific fields in the database, and you've got yourself a data access web page! The way you work with Visual InterDev DTCs is much like how you would work with controls to create data bound forms in Visual Basic: lots of dragging and dropping controls, setting properties for the controls, and writing code for your event handlers.

DTCs are not a whole new concept to Visual InterDev. If you have used Visual InterDev 1.0, you may have already worked with a few DTCs, such as the data range header control, data range footer control, and the data command control. Visual InterDev 6.0 greatly enhances the usability of DTCs by introducing a *new* group of design time controls that are more powerful and easier to use. We will be focusing on these *new* controls in this chapter.

In previous chapters you have already had some exposure to DTCs, and created web pages that use them. In this chapter we will explain DTCs in greater detail, and continue to expand our Wrox Cameras site by adding new web pages incorporating DTCs. By the end of the chapter you will be familiar with:

- ❏ What are design time controls?
- ❏ What is the scripting object model?
- ❏ Selecting a scripting platform for design time controls.
- ❏ Recordset DTC and data binding.
- ❏ PageObject DTC and how it enables object oriented programming across web pages.
- ❏ FormManager DTC and defining modes for your web pages.

We will first see what DTCs are, and then start working with DTCs for the Wrox Cameras application, so here we go.

What are Design Time Controls?

Design time controls (DTCs) are ActiveX controls, but of a special type. Unlike most ActiveX controls, which usually participate at *run-time*, design time controls, as their name implies, serve their purpose at the time a developer *designs* or develops his web application. Most DTCs, but not all, are concerned with the display of input/output controls such as textboxes.

A DTC generates code, **run-time text**, based on the properties that you set in its Properties window. So rather than writing the code yourself, you can have the design time control do it for you based on the properties that you specified. The controls do not need to be installed on the client machine, because the run-time text is all that is required for them to work.

> *The run-time text that Visual InterDev generates is JavaScript — there is no way to set it to use VBScript instead. This is because the DTCs use the scripting object model, which we will discuss soon – and the scripting object model uses JavaScript.*

DTCs are displayed in the Visual InterDev IDE with a graphical user interface. You can also see what specific code a DTC generates: once you've placed your control on the page, right click on the DTC in Source view and select Show Run-time Text. Visual InterDev also gives you the option to remove the DTC altogether, and only keep the run-time text it has generated. (However, if you choose to do this you will lose the ability to use the graphical interface to the control.) You remove the DTC by right clicking on the DTC and selecting Convert to Run-time Text. The following screenshot shows both of these options:

Because DTCs do not participate at run-time, the only thing that matters at that moment is the run-time text that the DTC has generated.

> After you have used a DTC to generate some run-time text, if you decide to delete the DTC but keep the run-time text, your page will *function* no differently than if you had kept the DTC on the page, but you will lose the graphical interface.

Understanding this aspect is important, as you may modify the run-time text for your needs if the text that a DTC generates does not serve your purposes well enough. Using a DTC in this way is great for generating the initial code, which you can then modify to suit your requirements.

DTCs are not a new concept, but the difference between Visual InterDev 6.0 DTCs and the earlier Visual InterDev 1.0 DTCs is that the latest versions center round a new programming model called the Scripting Object Model.

What is the Scripting Object Model?

To make web development less complex, Visual InterDev 6.0 introduces the **Scripting Object Model** (SOM). SOM is a programming model which provides the web developer with a set of objects, each having events, properties, and methods. SOM allows the programmer to do web development in an object-oriented and event-driven way, as discussed in Chapter 1, and much like how Visual Basic programmers work with forms in VB.

SOM allows the web developer to think of web development as programming against a set of **script objects**. The script objects are JavaScript objects that are defined in the **script library**, and just like any objects they have a certain number of methods, events and properties associated to them. SOM handles the construction, initialization, and destruction of these script objects, maintaining states and events transparently to the user.

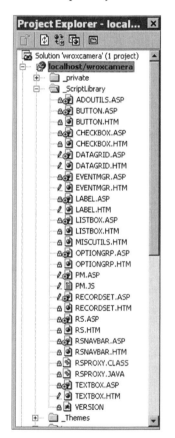

As we said, the scripting object model is implemented by the script library, which is a collection of JavaScript files. When you create a new Visual InterDev project, you will notice about two dozen script library files being copied to your project. These files are placed in the _scriptlibrary directory under your project directory, as shown below. With these files in your project, you can use all of the objects provided in the SOM:

How DTCs and SOM Work Together

DTCs work with SOM by calling functions in the script library to create and initialize script objects. Usually, a DTC will create a script object with the same name as itself. For example, a Textbox DTC named `Textbox1` will create a script object called `Textbox1`. At run-time, the DTC itself is gone, and we program against the script object that it created.

To see how DTCs work with the SOM, let's examine the run-time text shown below, which is for a client side Textbox DTC that has not been bound to a database field. (Remember, to view this text we would right click on the DTC and select **Show Run-time Text**):

```
<SCRIPT LANGUAGE="JavaScript" SRC="_ScriptLibrary/EventMgr.HTM"></SCRIPT>
<SCRIPT LANGUAGE="JavaScript" SRC="_ScriptLibrary/TextBox.HTM"></SCRIPT>
<SCRIPT LANGUAGE=JavaScript>
function _initTextbox1()
{
  Textbox1.setStyle(TXT_TEXTBOX);
  Textbox1.setMaxLength(20);
  Textbox1.setColumnCount(20);
}
createTextbox('Textbox1', _initTextbox1, null);
</SCRIPT>
```

At the beginning of the run-time text created by the `Textbox1` DTC, there are two `<SCRIPT>` tags that include two HTML files: `EventMgr.HTM` and `TextBox.HTM`. These are script library files and they are cached (temporarily saved) on the client side machine, for reference by the Textbox DTC. `EventMgr.HTM` manages client side events for all of your client side DTCs, while `TextBox.HTM` contains methods and properties specific to the Textbox DTC.

When the page is processed, method `createTextbox()` is called to create the `Textbox1` script object, and `_initTextbox1()` is called to initialize it. There are three methods in the `_initTextbox1()` function – `setStyle()`, `setMaxLength()` and `setColumnCount()` – and they are all defined in the `Textbox.HTM` file. As you can see, the `Textbox1` DTC doesn't do much by itself – it simply generates code that makes function calls to the script library.

Now that we know what DTCs and SOM are, and how they interact with each other, let's take a look at the DTCs that come with Visual InterDev.

Visual InterDev DTCs

Visual InterDev comes with the following group of DTCs that use the script library. Most of these DTCs have a certain user interface at run-time, such as a textbox, label, checkbox, listbox, button, or optiongroup. You can use them either to bind to a `Recordset` object or to respond to certain user inputs. Some DTCs do not provide a user interface at run-time, but play an even greater role in many cases, such as the FormManager, PageObject and Recordset controls. We will go through these DTCs in more detail later in this chapter.

❑ **Textbox DTC** – A simple DTC used to show a textbox on the page. Textbox DTC can be data-bound (i.e. linked to a data field as was discussed in Chapter 5) or unbound. You may select one of three styles for the Textbox DTC: Textbox, Text Area, or Password.

❑ **Label DTC** – Like the Textbox DTC, the Label DTC can be data-bound or unbound. Unlike the Textbox DTC, it's read-only and not updateable.

❑ **Checkbox DTC** – The Checkbox DTC can be bound or unbound. Since a checkbox can only show up as being checked or unchecked, it is only useful when bounded to fields with Boolean values.

❑ **Grid DTC** – This is used frequently for data display purposes. Grid DTC can only be data-bound. The Grid DTC is also read-only and not updateable.

❑ **Listbox DTC** – The Listbox DTC has two parts that can each be data-bound or unbounded: the data value and a valid list of values. You may choose to bind it to a recordset or to set its value to a static list of values. You may select one of two styles for the Listbox DTC: Dropdown or Listbox.

❑ **Button DTC** – The Button DTC cannot be data-bound. It's mainly used to trigger an event by having the user click on it.

❑ **OptionGroup DTC** – OptionGroup DTC can be data-bound or unbound. In a similar way to the Listbox DTC, you may choose to bind it to a recordset or to set its values to a static list of items.

❑ **RecordsetNavbar DTC** – The RecordsetNavbar DTC is used to navigate through your recordset. A user may click on one of its four "video-like" buttons to move backwards or forwards in the recordset. If Update on Move is checked, changes in data-bound controls are written back to the database.

❑ **Recordset DTC** – The Recordset DTC specifies a data connection, a database object or SQL statement, and other properties that determine how data is read from and written to a database. A Recordset DTC acts as a data source when binding data-bound DTCs at design time. It creates the `Recordset` script object that exposes a rich set of methods and properties for sophisticated data manipulation.

❑ **PageObject DTC** – The PageObject DTC lets you treat a web page as an object; you may call functions across web pages as if they were defined on the same page. It also provides the means for you to carry values across pages.

❑ **FormManager DTC** – Instead of creating a corresponding script object like all of the above DTCs, FormManager DTC manipulates the script objects of *other* DTCs on the form. You can use FormManager DTC to define different modes for a single web page, for example: browse, edit, and insert modes for a data entry form.

Each of the above DTCs, with the exception of FormManager, creates a corresponding script object. When we work with these script objects, we work with their events, methods and properties. The following table shows the methods, events, and properties for Visual InterDev DTCs. Strictly speaking these are for the corresponding *script objects* that each DTC creates:

Control	Properties	Methods	Events
Button	id, name, disabled, value, src, alt, maintainState	isVisible, show, hide, advise, unadvise, display, getStyle, setStyle	onclick
Label	id, name, maintainState	isVisible, show, hide, getCaption, setCaption, getDataFormatAs, setDataFormatAs, getDataSource, setDataSource, getDataField, setDataField, advise, unadvise, display	N/A

Table Continued on Following Page

237

Control	Properties	Methods	Events
Textbox	id, name, disabled, value, maintainState	isVisible, show, hide, getColumnCount, setColumnCount, getRowCount, setRowCount, getMaxLength, setMaxLength, advise, unadvise, display, getDataField, setDataField, getDataSource, setDataSource, getStyle, setStyle	onchange
Listbox	id, name, disabled, size, selectedIndex, maintainState	isVisible, show, hide, addItem, removeItem, clear, getCount, getValue, setValue, getText, setText, selectByValue, selectByText, getRowSource, setRowSource, getDataSource, setDataSource, getDataField, setDataField, advise, unadvise, display	onchange
Checkbox	id, name, disabled, value, maintainState	isVisible, show, hide, getChecked, setChecked, getCaption, setCaption, getDataSource, setDataSource, getDataField, setDataField, advise, unadvise, display	onclick
OptionGroup	id, name, maintainState	isVisible, show, hide, getBorder, setBorder, getAlignment, setAlignment, getButton, addItem, removeItem, clear, getCount, getValue, setValue, getCaption, setCaption, selectByValue, selectByCaption, selectByIndex, getSelectedIndex, getRowSource, setRowSource, getDataSource, setDataSource, getDataField, setDataField, advise, unadvise, display	onchange
Grid	N/A	isVisible, show, hide, getPagingNavbar, bindAllColumns, getRecordsetNavbar	N/A

Control	Properties	Methods	Events
Recordset	id, name, fields, absolutePosition, BOF, EOF	getCount, moveNext, moveFirst, movePrevious, moveLast, moveAbsolute, move, updateRecord, cancelUpdate, addRecord, deleteRecord, addImmediate, requery, advise, unadvise, getRecordSource, setRecordSource, open, isOpen, close, getConnectString, getSQLText, setSQLText, setBookmark, getBookmark, isDHTMLAware, getDHTMLDataSourceID, getParameter, setParameter	onrowenter, onrowexit, ondatasetcomplete, ondatasetchanged, onbeforeupdate, onafterupdate, onbeforeopen
RecordsetNavBar	id, name, updateOnMove, pageSize, maintainState	isVisible, show, hide, getAlignment, setAlignment, cancelOperation, isOperationCancelled, getButton, getDataSource, setDataSource, advise, unadvise, display, getButtonStyles, setButtonStyles	onfirstclick, onprevclick, onnextclick, onlastclick
PageObject	cancelEvent, firstEntered	advise, createDE, endPageContent, getproperty, getState, navigateURL, setproperty, setState, startPageContent, unadvise	onbeforeserverevent, onenter, onshow
FormManager	N/A	N/A	N/A

You don't have to memorize all these, as IntelliSense will show you all of the available methods and properties for a certain script object, while the **Script Outline** window will list all of the available event handlers for each DTC that you add to the page. Generally, it's good practice to always use the **Script Outline** to add event handlers to your web page, as this avoids typos, which can cause errors and may be difficult to spot at a later date.

> *There is also a growing market for third party DTCs, and you can even create your own using Visual Basic or other programming languages. This is covered in greater detail in Professional Visual InterDev 6.0 Programming (ISBN 1-861002-64-5).*

Now that we've learned the basics of DTCs and SOM, let's write a simple event handler, to give us some practice.

In this example, we will use the `thisPage` object (part of the PageObject DTC) and a simple event handler, `thisPage_onenter`, to tell the user if this is the first time that they have entered the page. We will make use of both the Script Outline window as well as the IntelliSense features. Here are the steps:

1. Open Visual InterDev and create a new project, without a theme and layout, and call it DTCTest. Right click on your project and select Add | Active Server Page. Name this page dtc_eventhandler.asp and click Open.

2. In Source view, drag a PageObject DTC from the Design-Time Controls tab of the Toolbox, and place it between the <BODY> tags of your page. (You may also do this by simply clicking on the page and then double clicking on the PageObject DTC – the DTC will be placed in the location that you clicked on the page.)

3. As you add the PageObject DTC to the page, you will be asked if you want to enable SOM – click Yes to accept.

4. Click on the HTML tab in the Toolbox and drag a Submit Button to the page, again placing it within the <BODY> tags. This will simply add an HTML intrinsic submit button to the page. We will use this button to submit the page. The following code will appear in the Source view:

```
<INPUT TYPE="submit" VALUE="Submit" ID=submit1 NAME=submit1>
```

5. Now switch to the Script Outline window and expand Server Objects & Events, then thisPage, and double click on onenter. The `thisPage_onenter()` event handler will be added to the page.

6. Add the following code to the `thisPage_onenter()` event handler. Here we use the `firstEntered` property of `thisPage` to determine if this is the first time that this page has been loaded. If the page is sent to the browser for the first time, `firstEntered` will return `true`; if a round trip to the server has occurred after the page is loaded, `firstEntered` returns `false`.

```
Sub thisPage_onenter()
  If thisPage.firstEntered=true then
    Response.Write "Hello, this is a test"
  Else
    Response.Write "This page has been loaded"
  End if
End Sub
```

7. That's all, and we will now save the page and view it in the browser. You will see that the page loads with the text Hello, this is a test, but once you click on the Submit button, the page is sent to the server and is refreshed in the browser with the text This page has been loaded.

DTCs do many things nicely without requiring a lot of code, because numerous scripts are pre-written for you in the script library. Whether you want the scripts to be executed on the server or on the client's machine is specified by a DTC property called the **scripting platform**. The scripting platform determines where the scripts are created and where the event handling occurs.

Selecting the Scripting Platform for DTCs

By default, when you drag and drop a DTC to the page, it inherits the scripting platform from the page. If you set the scripting platform of a page to Server (available for .htm files), DTCs on the page will by default be server side DTCs. Similarly, if you set the scripting platform of the page to Client (available for .asp and .htm files), all DTCs on the page will, by default, be client side DTCs.

You may set the scripting platform at the *project* level, at the *page* level, or for an *individual* DTC. We'll see in a later example how to set the scripting platform for an individual DTC.

To Set the DTC Scripting Platform at Page Level

1. Right click on your file in Source view and select Properties. This displays the Properties window.

2. Switch to the General tab and select Server (ASP) or Client (IE 4.0 DHTML) under the DTC scripting platform section.

It's important to keep in mind that setting the DTC scripting platform for the page does not affect DTCs already on the page, unless you have specified that they should inherit the scripting platform from the page. So, if you change the DTC scripting platform for a page where you have not specified this, and want it to apply to all of the DTCs on that page, you will need to manually change the scripting platform of the DTCs already there.

To Set the DTC Scripting Platform at Project Level

Setting the scripting platform at the project level sets the default scripting platform for all pages in the project, and the procedure is similar to setting the scripting platform at the page level. To do this:

1. Right click on your project name in the Project Explorer window and select Properties.

2. Click on the Editor Defaults tab.

3. Select either Server (ASP) or Client (IE 4.0 DHTML) in the DTC scripting platform section.

Selecting Server (ASP) defaults to using server side DTCs in all ASP pages in the web project; selecting Client (IE 4.0 DHTML) defaults to using client side DTCs in all ASP and HTML pages in the web project.

Server Versus Client

When you specify that the scripting platform is to be server, your DTC generates server side ASP script code, and script objects and all of your event handlers run on the server. As a result, you may use ASP intrinsic objects and ADO objects. However, you may not call VBScript or JavaScript functions that have a user interface. For example, if you try to call the VBScript function `msgbox()` from server side ASP code, errors may occur.

If your scripting platform is set to be client, your event handlers will be executing on the client's machine and you can write client side code which utilizes the DHTML intrinsic objects. When working with design time controls, you are also prompted if you want to enable the SOM. It is not necessary to enable this if all of your design time controls have client as their scripting platforms, because all the script objects will be created and maintained on the client's machine.

When data binding is involved, a server side Recordset DTC uses **Active Data Objects** (ADO) for data accessing, while a client side Recordset DTC uses a part of ADO called **Remote Data Services** (RDS). You don't need to specify the scripting platform for your data-bound controls, as they will inherit the scripting platform from the Recordset design time control to which they are bound.

The following table summarizes the differences of using server side DTCs as opposed to client side DTCs.

Server Side DTCs	Client Side DTCs
DTC generates server side run-time text.	DTC generates client side run-time text.
DTCs' script objects are created and maintained on the server (until the page has been processed and then they disappear).	DTCs' script objects are created and maintained on the client's machine.
Event handlers run on the server (ASP, ADO intrinsic objects available).	Event handlers run on the client's machine (DHTML intrinsic objects available).
Roundtrip to the server for event handling.	No roundtrip necessary for event handling.
Must enable SOM.	Not required to enable SOM, although it is still used.
Data binding uses ADO.	Data binding uses RDS.

Selecting the Desired Scripting Platform

Before you develop web pages using DTCs, you would need to decide which scripting platform to use. As a web developer, you would generally make this decision based on the following factors:

❑ **Browser Compatibility** – Most browsers support server side DTCs, because this generates server side run-time text and all of the event handling occurs on the server, thus relying less on the client. Still, the scripting object model generates some client side text that is not supported by all browsers.

The following table shows the compatibility of different browsers with DTCs:

Server Side DTCs	Client Side DTCs
Most Netscape 3.x and 4.x versions, Internet Explorer 3.02 or above (except PageObject DTC because this puts some client side code on the page which fails in browsers of version 3 and below).	Browsers that support Dynamic HTML (DHTML). Internet Explorer 4.0 or 5.0.

❏ **Performance Concern** – When no data binding is involved, your page will run faster when all DTCs are client side. This is because, for client side DTCs, event handling occurs on the client's machine, thus avoiding unnecessary roundtrips to the server.

❏ **Data Access Concern** – Server side recordsets use ADO, which does all the data operations on the server. Client side recordsets use RDS, where you can perform certain operations on the recordset without going to the server. Naturally, if it's critical to keep the data on the server up to date, then a server side recordset will make sense. On the other hand, if you don't mind caching the data on the client side, you may choose a client side recordset. Be aware that this might expose security details, such as user name and password, in the HTML source of the page.

Now that we know what scripting platforms are, and the pros and cons of server versus client, let's try a simple data binding example, and have a go at setting the scripting platform for DTCs.

Try it Out – Simple Data Binding and Setting Scripting Platforms for DTCs

In this example, we will change the scripting platform of a Recordset DTC from server to client.

1. Add a new ASP page to your DTCTest project, by right clicking on the project in the **Project Explorer** window and selecting **Add | Active Server Page**. Name the page `dtc_platform` and click **Open**.

2. From the **Toolbox** window, under the **Design-Time Controls** tab, drag-drop a **Recordset** DTC between the <BODY></BODY> tags, and enable SOM when prompted.

3. Drag-drop a **Textbox** DTC to the page, also between the <BODY> tags.

4. The **Recordset** DTC will have its scripting platform set as **Inherit from page** by default – we will change this to **Client (IE 4.0 DHTML)**. Right click on the **Recordset** DTC, and select **Properties**.

5. Switch to the **Implementation** tab of the **Properties** page of the **Recordset** DTC, and select **Client (IE 4.0 DHTML)** as the **Scripting platform** from the drop down list, as shown opposite. Close the window.

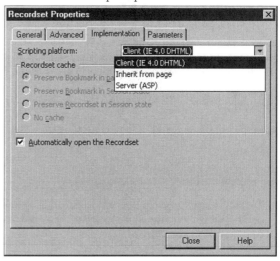

6. After we have set the scripting platform of the Recordset DTC, let's bind the textbox to the recordset. Right click on the Textbox DTC and select Properties.

7. In the Recordset field of the Data pane, specify the Textbox DTC to be bound to Recordset1. Notice that as soon as you specify Recordset1 for the Recordset field, the Scripting Platform field automatically changes, from Inherit from page to Client (IE 4.0 DHTML). Click OK.

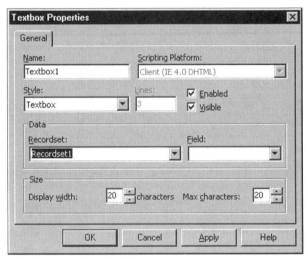

8. Save the page. There's not much to see in the browser, but this example has taught you how to change the scripting platform of an object both explicitly and implicitly (i.e. by binding one DTC to another).

So far we have learned what DTCs and the SOM are. We will now start learning more about DTCs by creating real life samples. As we mentioned earlier, Recordset, FormManager, and PageObject DTCs do not provide a user interface at run-time, but they serve a greater purpose in general than DTCs that are used simply for data display purposes. In the following sections of this chapter, we will create examples for the Wrox Cameras web site, and demonstrate these three particularly useful DTCs. We will start with the Recordset DTC.

Recordset DTC and Data Binding

This is similar to the data control in Visual Basic – the Recordset DTC enables data access by acting as a data source and allowing other DTCs, such as the Listbox, Textbox, and Grid controls, to bind to it. The Recordset DTC defines a set of records that you can access from your web pages.

For each Recordset DTC that you use on the page, you would need to specify, among other properties, a *connection*, a *database object* and an *object name*. These concepts were introduced in Chapter 5 when we looked at *Database Basics*.

❑ **Connection** – specifies the data connection to use for the recordset.

❑ **Database Object** – you can choose whether the data source will be a data command, a stored procedure, a SQL statement, a table, or a view.

❑ **Object Name** – you can select the name of a database object (of the type you selected for the database object).

There are two ways to add a Recordset DTC to a page. Usually, you drag-drop the control from the **Toolbox** and specify its properties. If you have created a data command under your data connection, you may also directly drag-drop the data command from the **Project Explorer** window to the **Source** view or **Design** view window. Visual InterDev will automatically create a Recordset DTC that uses the data command.

We have seen some simple examples using the Recordset DTC in earlier chapters, now we will create a more complex one by building a page for the Wrox Cameras web site, using a Recordset DTC.

Try it Out – Retrieving Data Using the Recordset DTC

In this example, we will build an ASP page that will change the products displayed, based on the product type that a user selects.

1.   Open the **WroxCameras** project. In the Project Explorer window, right click on the project and select **Add | Active Server Page**. Name the new ASP page products_dtc.asp. Click **Open**.

2.   In Source view, from the Design-Time Controls tab of the **Toolbox** window drag-drop a Recordset DTC between the `<BODY>` `</BODY>` tags. When you are prompted if you want to enable SOM, click **Yes** to accept.

3.   Right click on the Recordset DTC and choose **Properties**. Specify the properties of the recordset: **Name** as product, **Connection** as WroxCameras, **Database object** as Tables, and **Object name** as product. (You may do this by clicking on the drop down arrow and selecting from the available choices, which we set up in Chapter 5.) Your Recordset DTC will look like the following:

4.   On the Implementation tab, select the radio button **Preserve Recordset in Session state**. We will be changing the data source for this Recordset based on the user's selection in this example, and setting this property will allow the **product** Recordset to 'remember' the data source when we change it. Close the **Properties** sheet by clicking OK.

5.   Now add another Recordset DTC below the first and change its name and other properties as shown below. Again, close the **Properties** window.

Chapter 8

6. We now add a listbox, which we will
use to accept user input. Drag-drop a
Listbox DTC to the page, right click on
the Listbox DTC and select Properties.
Specify product_type for the Recordset
and Field properties, in the Data pane
of the General tab:

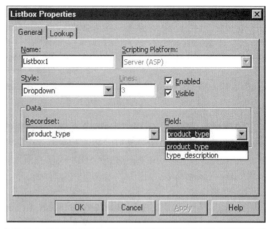

7. Click on the Lookup tab, and specify the
properties of the Listbox DTC as
follows, then click OK:

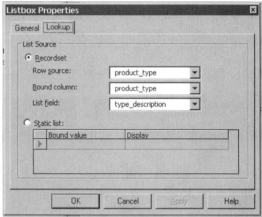

8. Beneath the listbox, add about a half
dozen line breaks from the HTML tab of
the Toolbox, then add a Grid DTC to the
page to display the results. Open the
Properties window, switch to the Data
tab and, after specifying the Recordset
as product, select name, type_id,
description, and price fields for
displaying, from the Available fields list:

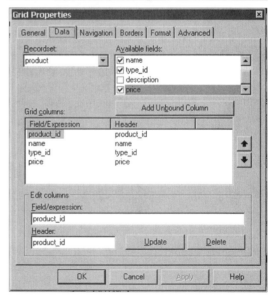

9. Click OK. We have completed adding DTCs to the page, now let's add an event handler to the page. Switch to the Script Outline window, expand Server Objects & Events and Listbox1, double click on onchange, and add the following code to the event handler:

```
Sub Listbox1_onchange()
  If product.isOpen() then product.close
  product.setSQLText "SELECT * FROM product WHERE type_id = " & Listbox1.getValue()
  product.open
End Sub
```

10. Save the page, right click on the page, and select View in Browser to view it. We will have a page that looks like the following:

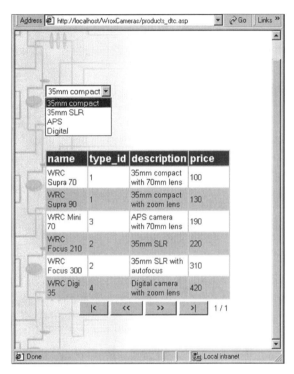

11. Click on any of the listbox items and you will see that the grid displays the cameras matching the type that you selected.

Calling Stored Procedures Using a Recordset DTC

We have just demonstrated retrieving data from the database. In some cases, you may want to store the queries as stored procedures and call them from your web pages using a Recordset DTC. The following example shows how we could implement the above example differently, by using this method.

Try it Out – Calling SQL Stored Procedures Using the Recordset DTC

We will first create a parameterized SQL stored procedure for Wrox Cameras, and then use it to retrieve products of a certain product type. A parameterized stored procedure is one that has parameters passed to it, whereas in our earlier look at stored procedures in Chapter 5, all of the information required by the stored procedure was written in the procedure itself.

1. To create a new stored procedure, switch to the **Data View** window, expand the WroxCamerasDM node until you can right click on **Stored Procedures**, and select **New Stored Procedure**.

2. Visual InterDev will create a page with text similar to the following:

```
Create Procedure StoredProcedure2
/*
(
@parameter1 datatype =default value,
@parameter2 datatype OUTPUT
)
*/
As
/* set nocount on */
return
```

3. Replace the above text with the following text; this will create a stored procedure with a parameter called `prod_type`.

```
CREATE PROCEDURE byproducttype @prod_type int
AS
select * from product
where type_id = @prod_type
return
```

4. Now save your work and you will see that a new stored procedure, **byproducttype**, appears under the **Stored Procedures** node in the **Data View** window. Close the stored procedure window.

5. We will modify the `products_dtc.asp` page to call this stored procedure instead. Open `products_dtc.asp` and save it as `products_dtc1.asp`.

6. In `products_dtc1.asp`, modify the Recordset DTC named **product** to use the stored procedure **byproducttype** that we just created, as follows:

7. Modify the existing event handler `Listbox1_onchange` to look like the following. Notice that this time we are using the `setParameter` method of the `Recordset`, instead of `setSQLText`.

```
Listbox1_onchange()
If product.isOpen() then product.close
product.setparameter 1, Listbox1.getValue()
product.open
End Sub
```

8. Similarly, we will need to modify the `product_onbeforeopen` event handler for our changes. This ensures that the page will load with the grid displaying cameras with type_id = 1, which is the default selection of the listbox. Using the Script Outline, double click on the onbeforeopen event for the product item under Server Objects & Events, and type in the following:

```
Sub product_onbeforeopen()
  If thisPage.firstentered=true then
    product.setParameter 1,1
  End if
End Sub
```

9. That was it! Now we have modified `products_dtc.asp` to call a SQL stored procedure when the user selects a product type, and to display the results in the grid. Save the page and try it out in your browser. You should get a similar result to the previous example, except the page opens displaying only cameras with type_id = 1.

As you can see in the two examples above, it's quite convenient to write data access pages with DTCs, requiring very little code to achieve basic functionality.

PageObject DTC – Working Across Pages

While the Recordset DTC helps to simplify data access by enabling data binding, the PageObject DTC helps to simplify things when working across web pages. Using the PageObject DTC, you can identify and treat your pages as objects – instead of referencing each page using URLs, you can now reference them with an ID. In addition, you can expose methods or properties on existing web pages to other pages, and you can call these methods and properties from other pages.

The PageObject DTC introduces some quite neat features, including:

- ❑ **Page navigation** – instead of having to use URLs to track pages, you can now identify a page with an object ID, and navigate to it by calling the show function.

- ❑ **Exposing functions across web pages** – you can expose a function on a page to make it accessible from other pages.

- ❑ **Maintaining state** – you can define properties that can persist their value over the lifetime of a page, session or application.

- ❑ **Remote scripting** – you can call a server side function from the client side and have it return a string or an array.

Defining Methods

There are two kinds of methods you can define on each page using the PageObject DTC.

❑ **Navigate** methods – when you call a `navigate` method defined on a target page from a calling page, the function is invoked on the target page and the target page loads in the browser.

❑ **Execute** methods – when you call an `execute` method defined on a target page from a calling page, you simply call that function, but your current web page stays in the browser.

To define a method on a page:

1. Drag-drop a PageObject DTC to the page.

2. Right click the PageObject DTC and select Properties.

3. Switch to the Methods tab.

4. Use the drop down arrow to select from the existing methods. You can define a method to be a Navigate method or an Execute method. It is OK to have a method being both navigate and execute.

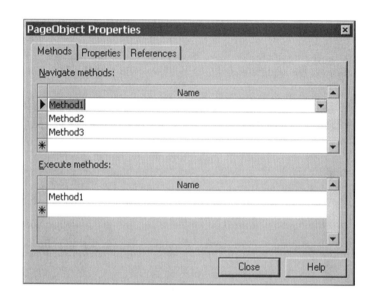

Defining Properties

In addition to allowing you to invoke methods across pages, the PageObject DTC allows you to set application level, session level, or page level properties, thus allowing you to persist values between web pages. Think of the properties as variables that you can define with different lifetimes. (Applications and sessions were defined in Chapter 7.)

To set properties for a PageObject DTC:

1. Right click on the PageObject DTC and select Properties.

2. Switch to the Properties tab of the Properties page.

3. Name a few properties, and select the Lifetime accordingly:

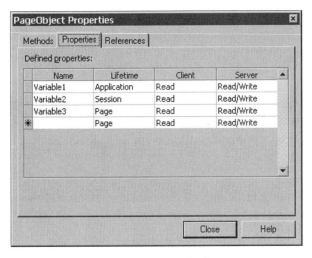

4. After you have defined the properties, you may use the following methods to set or retrieve the values of these properties:

❏ setxxxx allows you to set a value for a property, xxxx being the name of the property.

❏ getxxxx allows you to get the value stored in a property.

Creating References Across Pages

To utilize methods and properties on a page, we will need to create **references**. For example, imagine we have a page called page2.asp, with a few methods and properties defined on it. We would like to use these methods or properties from another page, page1.asp. We will need to create a reference from page1.asp to page2.asp, so that page1.asp is aware of the existence of page2.asp and the methods and the properties defined on it.

To create a reference from page1 to page2:

1. Drag-drop a PageObject DTC onto page1.asp.

2. Right click on the PageObject DTC and select Properties.

3. Switch to the References window, click on the ... button.

4. Select page2.asp in the Create URL window.

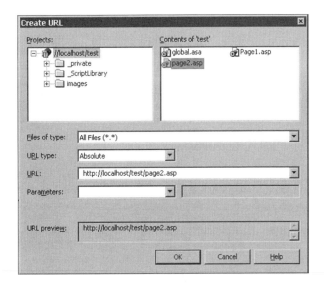

5. Click OK, and `page2.asp` is now added to the references of `page1.asp`. If you have multiple pages, you may define multiple references by repeating the above steps.

Now that we know how to define methods and properties, and set references, let's try an example using the PageObject DTC.

Try it Out – Using the PageObject DTC

Going back to our Wrox Cameras project, on the `products_dtc.asp` page that we created earlier, a user can make a selection of a certain type of camera and we then retrieve the data from the database, based on the user's input. In some cases, you may want to create two pages to do this: one for *user input* and one to display the final *results*. This is especially necessary when you have a crowded input page. Typically, web developers use a *form* page for input and then submit the form to an *action handling* page (otherwise known as a report or response page) for processing. With the PageObject DTC, you can simply call a `navigate` function on the report page from the user input page to achieve the same task. Let's modify the `products_dtc.asp` page to create an input page and a report page.

1. Double click on products_dtc.asp in the Project Explorer window, go to the menu bar and select File | Save products_dtc.asp As. Save the file as products_response.asp, we now have a copy of `products_dtc.asp` that we will modify to create the report page.

2. Remove the product_type Recordset DTC and the Listbox1 DTC, leaving only the Grid DTC and the product Recordset DTC.

3. Modify the `listbox_onchange` event handler that was already on the page to add the following method. This will be used to re-query the database, based on the product type selected by the user in the form page that we'll soon be creating. This method will accept a parameter, `prodtype`, which we will supply when calling this function from the form page.

```
Sub showProducts(prodtype)
  If product.isOpen() then product.close
  product.setSQLText "SELECT * FROM Product WHERE type_id = " & prodtype
  product.open
End Sub
```

4. Add a PageObject DTC to the page beneath the other controls. We now expose the showProducts method by going into the Methods tab of the Properties window of the PageObject DTC, and setting the method showProducts as a Navigate method:

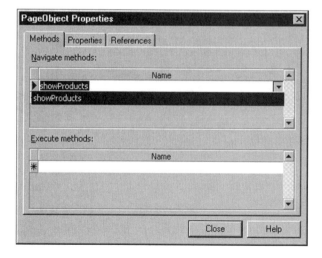

5. Save the page. We will now create the form page. Make another copy of `products_dtc.asp`, and save it as `products_form.asp`.

6. This time we want to remove the Grid DTC and product Recordset DTC, so that we are left with a Listbox DTC and the product_type Recordset DTC.

7. Again add a PageObject DTC to the page; it will by default be given the name products_form, the same as the name of the page.

8. We now need to set a reference to the response page, so that we can call the `showProducts` method from the form page. Right click on the PageObject DTC and select Properties. In the References window, click on the ... button and select products_response.asp. Click OK and close the window.

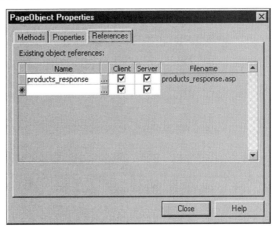

9. Now add a Button DTC to the page. Right click on it and select Properties. Change the Caption to be Click here.

10. Use the Script Outline to add the following code for the button. (Double click on the onclick event of the Button1 under Server Object & Events.) Here we call our `navigate` method, `showProducts`, and pass the currently selected value to the `navigate` function.

```
Sub Button1_onclick()
  Dim temp
  temp=Listbox1.getvalue()
  products_response.navigate.showProducts(temp)
End Sub
```

11. Save the page, and then view it in your browser. You should see the following:

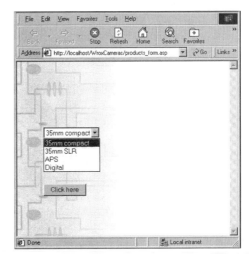

12. Select any type of camera and click on the Click here button – you will notice that `products_response.asp`, instead of `products_form.asp`, is now loaded, with the results showing the products of the selected type:

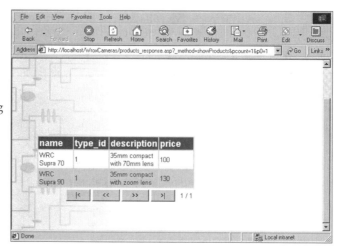

In the above example, we have demonstrated calling a `navigate` function on a separate page using the PageObject DTC. Similarly, you may call an `execute` method from a client side page to a server side page. To the developer, this is almost identical to the above example, except that the target page does not show up in the browser – only the function is utilized by the calling page.

FormManager DTC

The last of the three DTCs we will introduce is the FormManager DTC. This allows you to create multipurpose pages that would otherwise require separate pages to accomplish the same task. With FormManager, you may design different **modes** for your page. At each specific mode, you may decide whether to show or hide your controls, and enable or disable them. FormManager is frequently used for data entry pages.

FormManager differs from other DTCs in that it does not create any script objects. You work with it mostly through setting its properties at design time.

> **Since FormManager is used to manage the other controls on your page, you should always place this control towards the end of the page, after all the other DTCs, so it will be aware of their existence.**

The following properties need to be defined for a FormManager DTC:

❑ **Form modes and a default mode** – a form typically has two or more modes: the default mode is the mode that the form is in when the page is first displayed.

❑ **Actions performed for a specific mode** – for any specific mode, you may want to hide or show specific controls, or populate a listbox with a certain set of values. The settings here determine how your controls will appear.

❑ **Form mode transitions** – the form mode is changed when a specific event is triggered, for example, when a certain button is clicked. These settings define what events you will use to trigger a form mode change.

❑   **Actions performed before transition** – you may invoke methods here before a form mode transition actually takes place. For example, you may want to update the data before the mode changes.

Back to Wrox Cameras; let's create a data entry page using the FormManager DTC.

Try it Out – Using the FormManager DTC

In this example, we will create a three-mode page that allows the user to enter data into the product_type table. Users will be able to browse the table in a read-only page, edit it by switching to the edit mode, and then commit the changes in insert mode. This would normally require two pages, but with the FormManager DTC, we can do it by setting form modes.

1.   In the Wrox Cameras project, add a new ASP page and name it prodtype_entry.asp. We start by adding two Button DTCs to the page, with the names Display and Edit and the captions Display Mode and Edit Mode, in the order that they appear on the page. (These can be changed in the General tab of the Properties window for each DTC.) We will have the page start in display mode, and use these two buttons to switch between the modes.

2.   Add a couple of line breaks and then add Insert, Update, Delete and Cancel Button DTCs to the page, naming and captioning them accordingly. These buttons won't be shown until the user switches to Edit Mode.

3.   Add two more line breaks then drag-drop a Recordset DTC to the page, and specify the product_type table as the Source of data Object name in the Properties window.

4.   Add some more line breaks then drag-drop two Textbox DTCs to the page, and bind them to the two fields of the product_type table: product_type and type_description. (You can do this in the General tab of the Properties window for each textbox; in the Data Recordset field choose Recordset1 and then select the required Field.) Add some text above the first textbox; Product Type, and add some above the second textbox; Type Description. Use more line breaks to give the page a pleasing appearance.

5.   Drag-drop a RecordsetNavbar DTC to the page, and bind it to the Recordset DTC, in a similar way as described above for the Textbox DTCs.

6.   After all the other controls are in place on the page, drag-drop a FormManager DTC to the page, placing it after all the other controls.

7.   Right click on the FormManager control and select Properties. Now we will specify the properties of the FormManager DTC by creating three modes: *Display, Edit* and *Insert*. In the Form Mode tab, create these modes by typing their names into the New Mode box and clicking on the > button.

8.   For each of these modes, specify the Actions Performed for Mode as follows, using the drop down boxes:

Form Mode	Object	Member	Value
Display	Display	disabled	true
	Delete	hide	()
	Insert	hide	()
	Update	hide	()
	Cancel	hide	()
	Textbox1	disabled	true
	Textbox2	disabled	true
	RecordsetNavBar1	show	()
	Edit	disabled	false
Edit	Textbox1	disabled	false
	Textbox2	disabled	false
	RecordsetNavbar1	hide	()
	Edit	disabled	true
	Insert	show	()
	Insert	disabled	false
	Delete	show	()
	Delete	disabled	false
	Update	show	()
	Cancel	show	()
	Display	disabled	false
Insert	Insert	disabled	true
	Display	disabled	true
	Delete	disabled	true

These property settings simply specify what controls are shown or hidden, enabled or disabled, in a certain mode. The FormManager Properties window will look like this after we have completed inputting these settings:

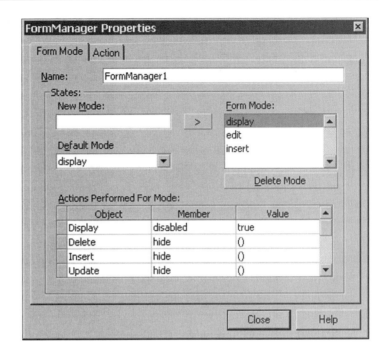

9. Now we will switch to the **Action** tab and specify what will trigger a *form mode transfer*, and what are the *actions performed*, if any, before a mode transition. First we specify the form mode transitions, and for each form mode transition, we specify the actions which need to be performed before the transition takes place. We specify these properties (which are all for the `onclick` event) as follows:

Form Mode Transitions			Actions Performed Before Transitions		
Current Mode	Object	Next Mode	Object	Member	Value
Edit	Update	Edit	Recordset1	updateRecord	()
Edit	Delete	Edit	Recordset1	deleteRecord	()
Edit	Insert	Insert	Recordset1	addRecord	()
Edit	Display	Display			
Insert	Cancel	Edit	Recordset1	cancelUpdate	()
Insert	Update	Edit	Recordset1	updateRecord	()
Display	Edit	Edit			

The following screenshot shows what the **Action** tab will look like when we have almost finished entering the above details:

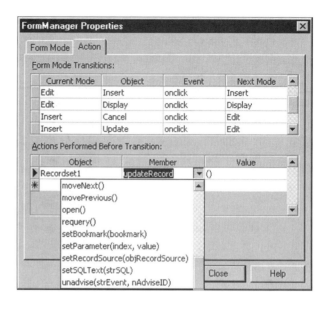

10. Close the window, save the page, and select View in Browser. You should have a page similar to the following. Try navigating through the recordset, entering a few values, and switching between the **Display Mode** and the **Edit Mode**. Note how the buttons change from being enabled to disabled, and what actions are performed, when a form transition takes place – as defined in the above table.

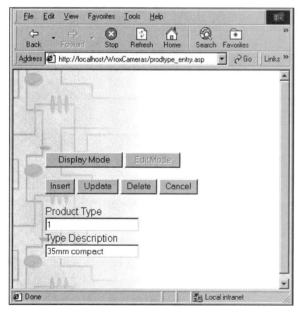

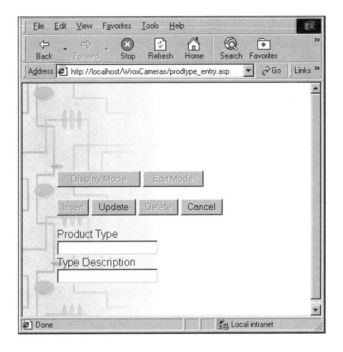

Summary

Here is a quick recap on what we have learned about DTCs in this chapter:

❑ DTCs are a special kind of ActiveX control that help to simplify web development.

❑ The Scripting Object Model (SOM) is the model that enables object-oriented and event-driven programming when using DTCs.

❑ Always use the Script Outline window to have Visual InterDev automatically create the event handlers for you. This reduces the chance of introducing typos and case sensitivity errors into your code.

❑ Setting the scripting platform of DTCs determines where the script objects will be created and where the event handlers will be executed. Server side DTCs have a wider range of browser support than client side DTCs.

❑ You may use Recordset DTCs and data-bound controls to rapidly develop data access pages.

❑ The PageObject DTC further extends the object-oriented programming model by allowing you to identify each web page as an object.

❑ The FormManager DTC allows you to define different modes for a single page. This is useful for data entry pages.

So, DTCs are great, but should you use DTCs in all your web applications? The answer is - not in all cases. While DTCs are powerful and easy to use, they don't always yield the fastest pages. Because the script library is written in JavaScript, instead of being compiled code, it tends to be slower than pages that do not use DTCs. And, generally, the more DTCs you have on a page, the slower it gets. Nevertheless, DTCs are great for prototyping, Intranet applications, and mid or low traffic web sites.

While DTCs allow you to develop data access applications rapidly, additional overhead is introduced due to the large number of lines of script, which need to be executed in the script library. This disadvantage of slightly poorer performance needs to be traded off against the savings in development time and cost. In the next chapter, we will learn an alternative way to access data that's faster and more efficient than using DTCs.

Database Access with ADO

Compared with DTCs, creating data access web pages with ActiveX Data Objects (ADO) yields faster and more efficient web pages. Since ADO can be used directly from ASP, as well as other development tools such as Visual Basic or Visual C++, you also have the flexibility of wrapping your data access code in a COM Dynamic Link Library (DLL) file for even better performance. We'll see more on that in a later chapter.

ADO is efficient, yet easy to use. It has a fairly simple object model, with reduced objects and layers compared to some of the earlier data access technologies, such as DAO (Data Access Objects) or RDO (Remote Data Objects). Because it has reduced hierarchical layers, it is quite easy to learn and use.

In this chapter, we will study the ADO Object Model, how to retrieve data using ADO, how to enter data, as well as how to handle data access related errors. By the end of this chapter, you will be familiar with:

- ❑ ADO and other data accessing technologies.
- ❑ The reasons for using ADO.
- ❑ The ADO Object Model.
- ❑ Entering information into a database using ADO.
- ❑ Presenting information from a database using ADO.
- ❑ ADO error handling.
- ❑ The Data Environment (DE) Object Model and how it compares with ADO.

We will use ADO to build pages for our Wrox Cameras web site, creating reporting pages as well as data entry pages. Before we do that, let's first examine the ADO technology.

ODBC, OLEDB and ADO

You may already be familiar with **Open Database Connectivity (ODBC)**, which was the technology first introduced to create a standard to simplify data access across relational databases. ODBC provides programmers with a consistent programming syntax and hides the implementation details of different database and database drivers. Instead of writing different code against different backend databases, now the programmer can write the same code regardless of what relational databases he will be using, and program against different types of databases consistently. The ODBC driver manager handles the dirty work, and translates the standard data access commands into appropriate syntaxes understandable by each specific database driver. ODBC was a great success and quickly became an industrial standard by greatly simplifying data access across different data sources.

OLE DB can be considered to be an improvement over ODBC. Like ODBC, OLE DB was introduced to provide consistent data access across different data sources. OLE DB allows data access not only to relational databases, but also to non-relational data sources (text, mail, and so on) as long as an OLE DB provider is written for the data source. If no OLE DB provider is written for a data source, OLE DB allows you to use the ODBC driver, if one exists.

ActiveX Data Objects (ADO) is a thin layer on top of OLE DB. ADO provides a standard COM interface to OLE DB, which is easily understandable by programmers. ADO can be used directly from Active Server Pages, as well as other development tools such as Visual Basic and Visual C++.

OLE DB, ODBC, ADO and RDO together comprise the **Microsoft Data Access Components (MDAC)**, a product produced to facilitate data access to different data sources. MDAC is included in both Windows NT Option Pack as well as Microsoft Visual Studio. Microsoft constantly updates the MDAC to fix existing bugs and add new features. The current version is 2.1 Service Pack 2, which you may freely download from `http://www.microsoft.com/data`.

Why Use ADO?

RDO and DAO are the two other commonly used data access technologies. **Data Access Objects (DAO)** was one of the first data access technologies developed. DAO was designed mostly for Jet (which is the driver used by Microsoft Access). It can connect to other databases via ODBC but is performance tuned for Access databases. DAO was intended for local applications and was not tested or intended for a multi-threaded, web development environment.

Similar to DAO, **Remote Data Objects (RDO)** is one of the earlier technologies designed for ODBC, but RDO was not designed with any single database type in mind. Since it provides a rich feature set and exposes many of the low level functionalities of ODBC, it attracts SQL and Oracle database developers. Both RDO and DAO have more hierarchical layers and objects than ADO, making them both more complex to learn and use.

ADO was developed *after* DAO and RDO and integrates lessons learned in developing those technologies. ADO is greatly simplified compared to DAO and RDO, yet still retains most of the features necessary for creating complex data access applications. ADO is more flexible and allows you create its objects regardless of their hierarchical orders. Unlike DAO and RDO, ADO was developed for OLE DB rather than ODBC, a newer and improved standard. ADO was designed and tested to work with a multi-threaded environment, which makes it a perfect choice for web developers.

This diagram shows how these data access technologies fit together.

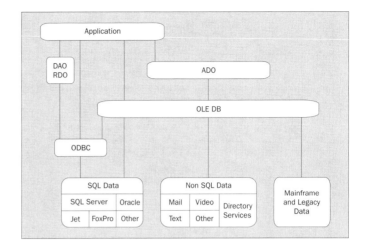

The ADO Object Model

ADO has seven main objects: Connection, Command, Recordset, Field, Error, Parameter, and Property. The ones you will be working with the most are Connection, Command and Recordset. The diagram opposite shows how they fit within the ADO object model.

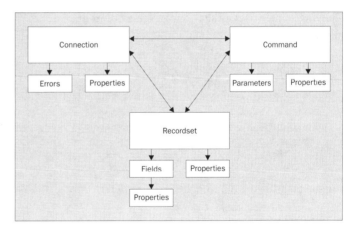

The ADO Connection Object

An ADO Connection object represents a unique session with a data source. The Connection object has a few key properties which specify the detailed information of the connection: ConnectionString, ConnectionTimeout, CommandTimeout and CursorLocation. When you add a data connection to your project in Visual InterDev, it adds the following information to your global.asa file. These application variables are later used to specify connection information when you open connections on data accessing pages.

```
Sub Application_OnStart
  '==Visual InterDev Generated - startspan==
  '--Project Data Connection
    Application("Connection1_ConnectionString") = "DSN=advworks;DBQ=C:\Program _
                 Files\Common Files\System\msadc\Samples\advworks.mdb;DriverId=25; _
                 FIL=MS Access;MaxBufferSize=512;PageTimeout=5;"
    Application("Connection1_ConnectionTimeout") = 15
    Application("Connection1_CommandTimeout") = 30
    Application("Connection1_CursorLocation") = 3
    Application("Connection1_RuntimeUserName") = ""
    Application("Connection1_RuntimePassword") = ""
  '-- Project Data Environment
    'Set DE = Server.CreateObject("DERuntime.DERuntime")
    'Application("DE") = DE.Load(Server.MapPath("Global.ASA"), _
                 "_private/DataEnvironment/DataEnvironment.asa")
  '==Visual InterDev Generated - endspan==
End Sub
```

ConnectionString Property

ConnectionString is the property used to specify information necessary to establish a connection to your database. ConnectionString varies slightly depending on whether you are using ODBC or OLE DB. The following sample uses a Data Source Name ConnectionString for ODBC:

```
<%@ Language=VBScript %>
<%
  ConnectionString = "DSN=pubs;SERVER=(local);UID=sa;APP=Microsoft Development _
                 Environment;DATABASE=pubs"

  Set objRS=Server.CreateObject ("ADODB.Recordset")
  Set objConn=Server.CreateObject("ADODB.Connection")
  objConn.Open ConnectionString
  Set objRS= objConn.Execute ("SELECT * FROM authors")
  While not objRS.EOF
    Response.Write objRS.Fields(0)
    Response.Write "<BR>"
    objRS.MoveNext
  Wend
>
```

Here we specify a data source name and a user ID. The password is omitted because no password is required for the user 'sa' in our project. (Remember though, that it is bad practice not to set a password for data access in real life situations!)

A connection string using OLE DB provider for SQL looks like the following:

```
<%
  ConnectionString ="Provider=SQLOLEDB;Data Source=(local);User _
                 ID=sa;Password='';Initial Catalog=pubs"

  Set objRS=server.CreateObject ("ADODB.Recordset")
  Set objConn=server.CreateObject("ADODB.Connection")
  objConn.Open ConnectionString
  Set objRS= objConn.Execute ("SELECT * FROM authors")
```

```
  While not objRS.EOF
    Response.Write objRS.Fields(0)
    Response.Write "<BR>"
    rs.MoveNext
  Wend
%>
```

Here we specify the OLE DB provider, a user name, and the database we will be using.

ConnectionTimeout and CommandTimeout Properties

The `ConnectionTimeout` property defines the wait time for establishing a connection before an error is generated. The default timeout value is 15 seconds.

The syntax of the `ConnectionTimeout` property is as follows:

```
Conn.ConnectionTimeout [=integer in seconds]
```

The `CommandTimeout` property defines how long a command will execute before it terminates and generates an error. The `CommandTimeout` value needs to be increased appropriately, especially for queries that may take a long time to complete. The syntax of setting the `CommandTimeout` is similar to `ConnectionTimeout`, and also has a default timeout value of 15 seconds:

```
Conn.CommandTimeout [=integer in seconds]
```

`CommandTimeout` is also a property of the ADO `Command` object. The `CommandTimeout` property of the ADO connection does not overwrite the `CommandTimeout` value of its commands.

CursorLocation Property

Another important property of the ADO `Connection` object is the `CursorLocation` property. You may specify to use server-side cursors (`adUseServer`) or client side cursors (`adUseClient`). If you don't specify its value, it defaults to using server side cursors. Client side cursors use cursors provided by the local cursor library while server side cursors uses data provider or driver supplied cursors. The latter tend to be more flexible, but with fewer features. Below is a sample that specifies a client side cursor:

```
<%
  ConnectionString ="Provider=SQLOLEDB;Data Source=(local);User _
            ID=sa;Password='';Initial Catalog=pubs"

  Set conn=Server.CreateObject("ADODB.Connection")

  ' specifies connection timeout value
  conn.ConnectionTimeout=15

  ' use client-side cursor
  conn.CursorLocation=adUseClient

  ' Open the connection to pubs sample database
  ' specifying data source name, userid, and password.
  objConn.Open ConnectionString
  conn.Close
%>
```

You may also specify a `CursorLocation` for the `Recordset` object. If not specified, it will inherit the `CursorLocation` property from its connection.

> In order to use constants such as **adUserClient**, it is necessary to incorporate a reference to an **INCLUDE** file at the top of your code:
>
> `<!--#INCLUDE FILE="ADOvbs.inc" -->`
>
> This file contains all of the constants that may be used by ADO and makes them available to your project. If you don't have this file on your system it can be downloaded with the rest of the code for this book and it should be placed in the **WroxCameras** project folder.

The ADO Recordset Object

The `Recordset` object can be used to store records from a table or the results of executing a query or stored procedure. The `Recordset` object refers to only one record at a time, but with methods available to it such as `movefirst` or `movenext`, you can traverse through all the records associated to it. Here is a simple sample that uses the `Recordset` object to move through a set of records:

```
<%@ Language=VBScript %>
<%
  ConnectionString ="Provider=SQLOLEDB;Data Source=(local);User _
                ID=sa;Password='';Initial Catalog=pubs"
  Set conn=Server.CreateObject("ADODB.Connection")

  'constructs the ado recordset
  Set rs=Server.CreateObject ("ADODB.Recordset")
  objConn.Open ConnectionString
  Set rs= conn.Execute ("SELECT * FROM authors")

  ' this loop moves through the recordset
  While not rs.EOF
    Response.Write rs.Fields(0) & "<BR>"
    rs.MoveNext
  Wend
%>
```

CursorType Property

`CursorType` is an important property of the `Recordset` object. You specify the `Recordset CursorType` using the following syntax:

```
rs.CursorType= [CursorType]
```

You may specify one of the following cursors (adOpenForwardOnly-0, adOpenKeyset-1, adOpenDynamic-2 or adOpenStatic-3):

❑ **Forward-only cursor** (adOpenForwardOnly-0). This is the default cursor if you do not specify one. As the name suggests, you can only scroll forward through the records. This improves performance when you only need to move through the records once.

❑ **Static cursor** (adOpenStatic-3). With a static cursor, you can generate reports based on a static copy of records. You cannot see additions, changes, or deletions made by other users.

❑ **Dynamic cursor** (adOpenDynamic-2). This is the most flexible cursor. Additions, changes, and deletions by other users are visible, and all types of movement through the recordset are supported. Dynamic cursor supports bookmarks, but doesn't rely on them.

❑ **Keyset cursor** (adOpenKeyset-1). This is similar to the dynamic cursor, but you can't see records that other users add. You can still see data changed by other users.

In web applications it is possible to open a recordset on the client machine using ProdID ADOR. These recordsets may then be cached locally. When using a client-side Recordset object, you may only use a static cursor (adOpenStatic).

LockType Property

Another important property of the Recordset object is the LockType property. The default LockType of a recordset is read-only (adLockReadOnly). This prevents you from updating the data, and if you need to write to the database, the LockType would need to be altered depending on your needs. There are four available choices:

❑ adLockReadOnly. This is the default setting. You cannot alter the data with this setting.

❑ adLockPessimistic. This locks records using a method known as 'pessimistic' locking; it locks data as soon as you start to edit it, which makes the record inaccessible to other users for the entire editing process.

❑ adLockOptimistic. This locks records using 'optimistic' locking, which only locks the record when you call the Update method of the ADO Recordset object.

❑ adLockBatchOptimistic. This is similar to 'optimistic' locking and is required for batch update modes.

The ADO Command Object

The ADO Command object can be used to define a specific command that you intend to execute against a data source. You define the executable text of the command (for example, a SQL statement) with the CommandText property. The CommandType property is used to define what specific type of command is contained in the CommandText. Let's examine the following sample, in which we use the ADO Command object to execute a query and return the resultset to an ADO recordset:

```
<%@ Language=VBScript %>
<!--#INCLUDE FILE="ADOvbs.inc" -->
<%
```

```
ConnectionString = "Provider=SQLOLEDB;Data Source=(local);User ID=sa; _
                    Password='';Initial Catalog=pubs"

Set conn=Server.CreateObject ("ADODB.Connection")
Set cmd=Server.CreateObject ("ADODB.Command")
Set rs=Server.CreateObject("ADODB.Recordset")
Conn.Open ConnectionString
cmd.ActiveConnection=conn
cmd.CommandText="SELECT * FROM authors"
cmd.CommandTimeout =30
cmd.CommandType=adCmdText

Set rs=cmd.Execute

While not rs.EOF
  Response.Write rs(0)& "<BR>"
  rs.MoveNext
Wend

rs.Close
Set rs=nothing
conn.Close
Set conn=nothing
%>
```

You can create the command object using the following syntax:

```
Set cmd=Server.CreateObject ("ADODB.Command")
```

In the above example, we specified the CommandText to be executed as "SELECT * FROM authors" which, after executing, will return all records in the authors table. CommandType is defined in this example as adCmdText (1). The commonly used CommandTypes are as follows:

❑ adCmdUnknown (0). This is the default CommandType if unspecified.

❑ adCmdText (1). This is used when you are specifying a SQL statement as the CommandText.

❑ adCmdTable (2). This is used when you are specifying the name of a table as the CommandText.

❑ adCmdStoredProc (4). This should be specified if you are using the name of a stored procedure or query directly as the CommandText.

While it is not necessary to specify a CommandType value, it helps to improve performance when you do so, because it saves processing time that would be spent determining the command type.

So far we have covered all the major objects of ADO and have seen a few basic examples of how we can use them to retrieve data. Let's put them into use by creating a few pages to retrieve products for Wrox Cameras.

In the following example, we will create a new products page (`products.asp`) to replace our products pages in the last chapter that used DTCs. This new page will display all the available cameras and once the user selects a specific camera, another page (`products_detail.asp`) is shown to display the details of the selected camera. Let's begin by creating the `products.asp` page.

1. Right click on your project and select **Add | Active Server Page**, name it `products.asp`.

2. At the top of the page add the following reference to the `ADOvbs.inc` include file:

```
<%@ Language=VBScript %>
<!--#INCLUDE FILE="ADOvbs.inc" -->
<HTML>
<HEAD>
```

3. Add the following code in the body of the page to create an HTML table as well as the headings for each of the columns. We will display the product, name, cost and type of each of the cameras:

```
<P>We currently have the following products available
    for you. Please click on an image to view details of
    the product:</P>
    <P> 
    <TABLE BORDER="0" CELLPADDING="1" CELLSPACING="1" WIDTH="590">

      <TR BGCOLOR="blue">
        <TD WIDTH="130"><STRONG>Product</STRONG></TD>
        <TD WIDTH="200"><STRONG>Name</STRONG></TD>
        <TD WIDTH="130"><STRONG>Cost</STRONG></TD>
        <TD WIDTH="130"><STRONG>Type</STRONG></TD>
      </TR>
```

4. Add the following code to create an ADO connection, an ADO command, and a recordset:

```
<%
  'retrieve catalogue of products from DB and write to table
  Dim adoConn
  Dim adoCmd
  Dim adoRS
  Dim strConnectionString

  'create ADO Objects
  Set adoConn = Server.CreateObject("ADODB.Connection")
  Set adoCmd = Server.CreateObject("ADODB.Command")
  Set adoRS = Server.CreateObject("ADODB.Recordset")
```

5. Now define a connection string. You may simply copy this from your `global.asa` file. Mine looks like the following; yours will vary slightly (note that my machine is called `VAIO`):

```
strConnectionString="Provider=SQLOLEDB.1;Persist Security Info=False;User ID=sa; _
            Initial Catalog=WroxCameras;Data Source=VAIO;Locale Identifier=2057; _
            Connect Timeout=15;Use Procedure for Prepare=1;Auto Translate=True; _
            Packet Size=4096;Workstation ID=VAIO"
```

6. We will use the following query to retrieve all the products from the product table and the resulting recordset will be ordered by the name of the cameras. `CommandType` is set to `adCmdText (1)`:

```
'set ADO Command Properties
adoCmd.CommandType = adCmdText
adoCmd.CommandText = "SELECT product.product_id, product.name, product.price, _
      product.thumbnail, product_type.type_description FROM product, _
      product_type WHERE product.type_id = product_type.product_type ORDER BY _
      name"
```

7. Add the following code to open the ADO connection and execute the command. The result of the command `adoCmd` is sent to recordset `adoRS`:

```
'Open the Connection
adoConn.Open strConnectionString

'associate the Command with the Open Connection
adoCmd.ActiveConnection = adoConn

'retrieve recordset
Set adoRS = adoCmd.Execute
```

8. Add the following code to loop through the resulting recordset and display each of the products in a table format. Notice the thumbnails are linked to the `product_details.asp` page which we will be creating in a while. This allows the user to click on an image and bring up the details of the individual product.

```
Do While not adoRS.EOF
   'process results to create table
   Response.Write "<TR>" & vbcrlf
   Response.Write "<TD><A HREF=" & chr(34) & "product_details.asp?product_ID=" & _
            adoRS("product_id").value & chr(34) & "><IMG SRC=" & chr(34) & _
            "images/" & adoRS("thumbnail").value & chr(34) & "></A></TD>" & vbcrlf
   Response.Write "<TD>" & adoRS ("name").value & "</TD>" & vbcrlf
   Response.Write "<TD>" & adoRS("price").value & "</TD>" & vbcrlf
   Response.Write "<TD>" & adoRS("type_description").value & "</TD></TR>" & vbcrlf
   adoRS.MoveNext
Loop
```

9. We close the connections and release resources after data is displayed successfully:

```
adoConn.Close
Set adoConn = nothing
Set adoCmd = nothing
Set adoRS = nothing

%>
</TABLE>
```

10. Now that we have written all the code for the page, we have to link the images into the database. The images that we are using can be downloaded from the Wrox web site and consist of six thumbnails (thm_WRC00001.jpg to thm_WRC00006.jpg) and six larger pictures (WRC00001.jpg to WRC00006.jpg). Once you have downloaded them, right click on the images folder in the Project Explorer window.

11. Select Add | Add Item and in the following dialog click on the Existing tab. Simply browse to where you have the images stored on your computer, select them and press Open. You can actually select more than one image at a time, by holding down the *Shift* button as you select them with your mouse and then import all 12 files at once. This saves you from having to import each image one at a time.

12. We now have to enter the file names of the images into the database. In the Data View expand the node for the WroxCameras database then the node for Tables. Double click in the product table and the table will be opened in the Editor window.

13. Enter the file names of the images under the appropriate headings as shown below:

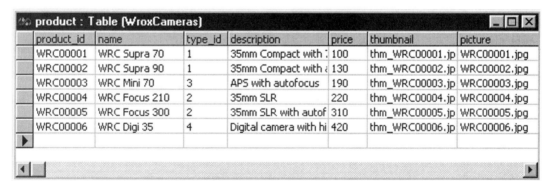

product_id	name	type_id	description	price	thumbnail	picture
WRC00001	WRC Supra 70	1	35mm Compact with	100	thm_WRC00001.jp	WRC00001.jpg
WRC00002	WRC Supra 90	1	35mm Compact with	130	thm_WRC00002.jp	WRC00002.jpg
WRC00003	WRC Mini 70	3	APS with autofocus	190	thm_WRC00003.jp	WRC00003.jpg
WRC00004	WRC Focus 210	2	35mm SLR	220	thm_WRC00004.jp	WRC00004.jpg
WRC00005	WRC Focus 300	2	35mm SLR with autof	310	thm_WRC00005.jp	WRC00005.jpg
WRC00006	WRC Digi 35	4	Digital camera with hi	420	thm_WRC00006.jp	WRC00006.jpg

14. We have now all the information in our database and can view it in our page. One final touch is to link this page with the rest of the project. This is simply done in the site diagram, by adding the page and then making sure that the lower PageNavbar of the page in Design view has been set up to show siblings and home pages, as before.

15. View `products.asp` in your browser and you will have the products page:

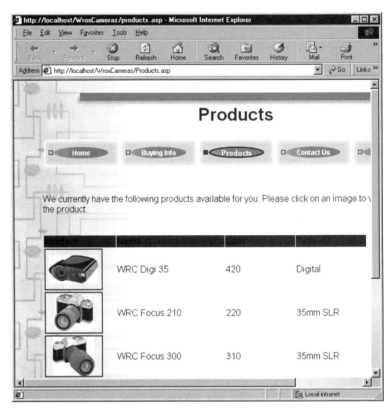

We now create the `product_details.asp` page, which is referenced in `products.asp`. As mentioned earlier, we will use this page to display the details of each individual camera.

1. Create a new ASP page and name it `product_details.asp`.

2. Add the following code to create the ADO objects:

```
<%
  'retrieve product details from database and write in HTML
  Dim adoConn
  Dim adoCmd
  Dim adoRS
  Dim strConnectionString
  Set adoConn = Server.CreateObject("ADODB.Connection")
  Set adoCmd = Server.CreateObject("ADODB.Command")
  Set adoRS = Server.CreateObject("ADODB.Recordset")
```

3. Add the connection string. You may simply copy this from the global.asa file of your Wrox Cameras project (again remember that VAIO is my machine's name):

```
strConnectionString="Provider=SQLOLEDB.1;Persist Security Info=False;User ID=sa; _
            Initial Catalog=WroxCameras;Data Source=VAIO;Locale Identifier=2057; _
            Connect Timeout=15;Use Procedure for Prepare=1;Auto Translate=True; _
            Packet Size=4096;Workstation ID=VAIO"
```

4. Add the following lines to define CommandType and CommandText for your ADO command:

```
adoCmd.CommandType = 1
adoCmd.CommandText = "SELECT product.*, product_type.type_description FROM product, _
            product_type WHERE product.type_id = product_type.product_type AND _
            product.product_id = '" & Request.QueryString("product_id") & "'"
```

5. Open the connection and associate the command with the connection:

```
adoConn.Open strConnectionString
adoCmd.ActiveConnection = adoConn
```

6. Add the following lines for displaying the record:

```
Set adoRS = adoCmd.Execute

Do While not adoRS.EOF
    'process results to create table
    Response.Write "<STRONG><FONT COLOR='orange'>" & adoRS("name").value & _
            "</FONT></STRONG><BR><BR>" & vbcrlf
    Response.write "  <TR><TD WIDTH='50%' ROWSPAN='4'><IMG SRC=" & chr(34) & _
            "images/" & adoRS("picture").value & chr(34) & "></td<" & vbcrlf
    Response.Write "  <TR><TD WIDTH='50%'><STRONG>Name:</STRONG> " & _
            adoRS("name").value & " </TD> </TR>"
    Response.Write "  <TR><TD WIDTH='50%'><STRONG>Description:</STRONG> _
             " & adoRS("description").value & "</TD> </TR>"
    Response.Write "  <TR><TD WIDTH='50%'><STRONG>Price:</STRONG> " & _
            adoRS("price").value & " </TD> </TR>"
    Response.Write "  <TR><TD WIDTH='50%'><STRONG>Type:</STRONG> " _
            & adoRS("type_description").value & "</TD> </TR>"
    adoRS.MoveNext
Loop
```

7. Add the following lines to close the connection and set the ADO objects to nothing:

```
adoConn.Close
Set adoConn = nothing
Set adoCmd = nothing
Set adoRS = nothing

%>
```

Now if you open the products.asp page in your browser and click on any of the pictures, the product_details.asp page will be shown like this:

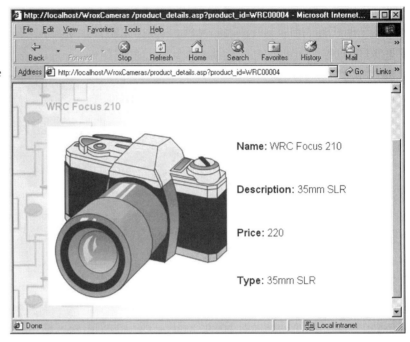

So far we have shown how you may present data to the user using ADO. Similarly, we may enter data into the database using ADO methods. We will demonstrate this in the following example.

Try it Out – Entering Data Using ADO

In this example, we will create a page (new_products.asp) which will allow users to enter new types of cameras. Then we will capture the user input and update the database using ADO in addrecords.asp. Let's start by creating new_products.asp:

1. Right click on your WroxCameras project and select Add | Active Server Page, name it new_products.asp.

2. Add a form to the page below the Add Your Content Below layout guide, using the following code. The Action attribute specifies that the form action handler will be the addrecords.asp file:

```
<FORM NAME=thisForm METHOD=POST ACTION="addrecords.asp">

</FORM>
```

3. Below the `<FORM NAME=thisForm METHOD=POST ACTION="addrecords.asp">` tag add the following code to create an input field for the product id field and the name field, which we will be using to enter data:

```
< FORM NAME=thisForm METHOD=POST ACTION="addrecords.asp">
<P>Please add a new product:</P>
<BR>
<TABLE>
<TR>
      <TD><STRONG>PRODUCT ID</STRONG></TD>
      <TD><INPUT TYPE="text" ID=prod_id NAME=prod_id></TD>
</TR>
<TR>
      <TD><STRONG>Name</STRONG></TD>
      <TD><INPUT TYPE="text" ID ="name" NAME="name"></TD>
</TR>
```

4. Assuming we will only be adding cameras of existing types, we can have the user select an existing type, by adding this code below:

```
<TR>
      <TD><STRONG>Type</STRONG></TD>
      <TD><SELECT  ID=type_id NAME=type_id>
        <OPTION VALUE="1" SELECTED>35mm Compact
        <OPTION VALUE="2">35mmSLR
        <OPTION VALUE="3">APS
        <OPTION VALUE="4">Digital
        </SELECT>
      </TD>
</TR>
```

5. We will repeat this process to add the remaining fields: description, price, thumbnail, and picture. For demo purposes, we will simply use one of the existing pictures for this new product:

```
<TR>
      <TD><STRONG>Description</STRONG></TD>
      <TD> <INPUT TYPE="text" ID=description NAME=description></TD>
</TR>
      <TD><STRONG>Price</STRONG></TD>
      <TD> <INPUT TYPE="text" ID=price NAME=price><BR></TD>
</TR>
<TR>
      <TD><STRONG>Thumbnail</STRONG></TD>
      <TD><SELECT ID=thumbnail NAME=thumbnail>
      <OPTION   VALUE ="thm_WRC00001.jpg" SELECTED >WRC00001.jpg
      <OPTION   VALUE ="thm_WRC00002.jpg">WRC00002.jpg
      <OPTION   VALUE ="thm_WRC00003.jpg">WRC00003.jpg
      <OPTION   VALUE ="thm_WRC00004.jpg">WRC00004.jpg
      <OPTION   VALUE ="thm_WRC00005.jpg">WRC00005.jpg
      <OPTION   VALUE ="thm_WRC00006.jpg">WRC00006.jpg
      </SELECT> <BR>
      </TD>
```

277

```
</TR>
<TR>
      <TD><STRONG>Picture</STRONG></TD>
      <TD><SELECT ID=picture NAME=picture>
      <OPTION   VALUE ="WRC00001.jpg" SELECTED >WRC00001.jpg
      <OPTION   VALUE ="WRC00002.jpg">WRC00002.jpg
      <OPTION   VALUE ="WRC00003.jpg">WRC00003.jpg
      <OPTION   VALUE ="WRC00004.jpg">WRC00004.jpg
      <OPTION   VALUE ="WRC00005.jpg">WRC00005.jpg
      <OPTION   VALUE ="WRC00006.jpg">WRC00006.jpg
      </SELECT>
      </TD>
</TR>
</TABLE>
<BR>
<INPUT TYPE="submit" value="submit" ID=submit1 NAME=submit1 >
</FORM>
```

6. Save new_products.asp and then right click on the icon in the **Project Explorer** and select **View in Browser**:

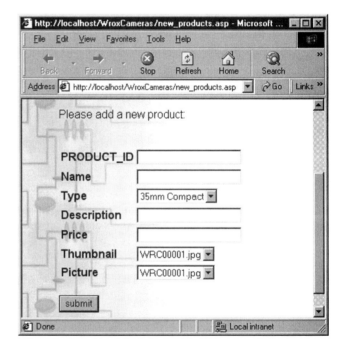

7. We will now add another page by right clicking on your project, and selecting **Add | Active Server Page**. We will name this page addrecords.asp.

8. At the top of the page add the following code to create the ADO connection and recordset and open the connection (remember to change VAIO to the name of your machine):

```
<%@ Language=VBScript %>
<!--#INCLUDE FILE="ADOvbs.inc" -->
<%

  'creating the connection and recordset
  Set conn=Server.CreateObject("ADODB.Connection")
  Set rs=Server.CreateObject("ADODB.Recordset")

  'open ADO connection
  strConnectionString="Provider=SQLOLEDB.1;Persist Security Info=False;User ID=sa; _
               Initial Catalog=WroxCameras;Data Source=VAIO;Locale Identifier=2057; _
               Connect Timeout=15;Use Procedure for Prepare=1;Auto Translate=True; _
               Packet Size=4096;Workstation ID=VAIO"
  conn.Open strConnectionString
```

9. Since the ADO LockType default is read only, we will need to change it to allow updating. The following line changes the LockType to adLockOptimistic and opens the recordset:

```
  rs.LockType =adLockOptimistic

  'sets the recordset rs to records in the table "product"
  rs.Open "product", conn
```

10. The following code will create a new record and populate its fields based on the user input in new_products.asp:

```
'Adding a record based on the user input on "new_products.asp" page
     rs.AddNew
     rs("product_id")=Request.Form("prod_id")
     rs("name")=Request.Form("name")
     rs("type_id")=request.Form("type_id")
     rs("description")=Request.Form("description")
     rs("price")=Request.Form("price")
     rs("thumbnail")=Request.Form("thumbnail")
     rs("picture")=Request.Form("picture")
     rs.Update
```

11. As always, we close the recordset and connection to release system resources:

```
  rs.Close
  Set rs=nothing
  conn.Close
  Set conn=nothing
  'Go back to "new_products.asp" if user wants to enter any additional records
  Response.Redirect "new_products.asp"

%>
```

12. Now let's try to enter a new record into the database. Save `addrecords.asp` and then open `new_products.asp` in the browser and enter information as follows:

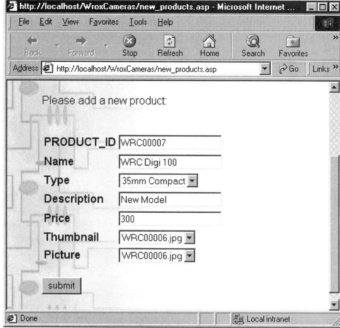

13. Click on the submit button and the data is now saved to the database. In the meantime, `new_products.asp` is refreshed and ready for new data entry again.

14. To verify that the data is entered correctly, enter the following into the address box of your browser: http://localhost/WroxCameras/product_details.asp?product_ID=WRC00007 and you will see the information of the camera we just entered:

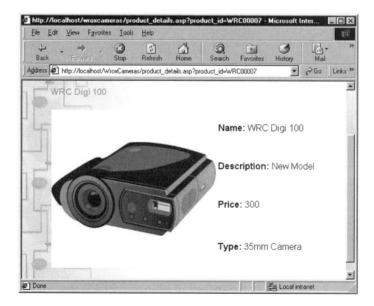

Additionally, you can open up the **product** table within Visual InterDev to check that the entry has been added. Here you can edit any of the entries made or delete them altogether if, for example, a product has been discontinued. To delete an entire row just highlight the row by clicking on the corresponding gray box on the left hand side, and press *Delete*:

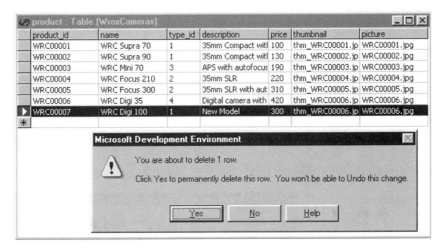

Error Handling

When you work with databases, errors do sometimes occur: the database may not be located successfully or opened properly, or the table might be read only when you try to edit it. Additionally, users may not enter valid data into the form. It's important to pick up these errors, otherwise your database will soon be filled with many spurious entries.

ADO Error Handling

In the example above, if you didn't enter a valid price or simply didn't specify one, the following error would be generated:

```
Provider error '80020005'
Type mismatch.
/WroxCameras/addrecords.asp, line 24
```

It is never a good idea to have the error go to the browser un-handled. ADO provides an `Errors` collection that allows you to identify errors pertaining to your database operations. The ADO `Error` object has 3 key properties: the `Description` property, the `Number` property and the `Source` property. The `Description` property contains the text of the error; the `Number` property contains the long integer value of the error number; and the `Source` property identifies the object that raised the error.

The ADO `Errors` collection allows you to track multiple errors that occurred relating to your data access operations. To see how this can be done, let's add a few lines in the `addrecords.asp` file we just created.

Try it Out – Adding ADO Error Handling

1. Add the following line at the top of the page just below the `<%` tag:

```
<%
on error resume next
```

2. Add the following after the line `rs.update`.

```
If conn.Errors.Count>0 then
  Response.Write "The following ADO errors are detected: <BR>"
  For i=0 to conn.Errors.Count-1
    Response.Write "Error Description: " & conn.Errors(i).Description &"<BR>"
    Response.Write "Error Number: " & conn.Errors(i).Number &"<BR>"
    Response.Write "Error Source: " & conn.Errors(i).Source &"<BR> <BR>"
  Next
End if
```

3. Now if we view `addrecords.asp` directly, we will have the following error. These errors are generated because we view `addrecords.asp` directly with no data posted to it from the `new_records.asp` page.

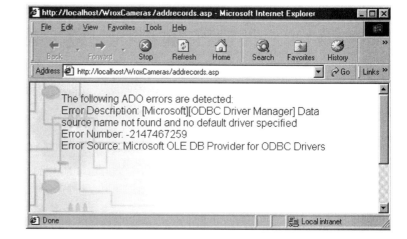

4. Rather than dump the error message to the screen, you can modify the `addrecords.asp` file as follows, to send meaningful messages to the users:

```
<%@ Language=VBScript %>
<!--#INCLUDE FILE="ADOvbs.inc" -->
<%
  ' This following line allows the error handling code to take over instead of dumping
  ' the error messages directly to the browser.
  on error resume next
  'creating the connection and recordset
  Set conn=Server.CreateObject("ADODB.Connection")
  Set rs=Server.CreateObject("ADODB.Recordset")

  'open ADO connection
```

```
strConnectionString="Provider=SQLOLEDB.1;Persist Security Info=False;User _
             ID=sa;Initial _
             Catalog=WroxCameras;Data Source=VAIO;Locale Identifier=2057; _
             Connect Timeout=15;Use Procedure for Prepare=1;Auto Translate=True; _
             Packet Size=4096;Workstation ID=VAIO"


conn.Open strConnectionString

'set locktype to adLockOptimistic for editing
rs.LockType =adLockOptimistic

'sets the recordset rs to records in the table "product"

rs.Open "product", conn
conn.BeginTrans
'Adding a record based on the user input on "new_products.asp" page
    rs.AddNew
    rs("product_id")=Request.Form("prod_id")
    rs("name")=Request.Form("name")
    rs("type_id")=Request.Form("type_id")
    rs("description")=Request.Form("description")
    rs("price")=Request.Form("price")
    rs("thumbnail")=Request.Form("thumbnail")
    rs("picture")=Request.Form("picture")
    rs.Update

  'Error handling code here

errornum=conn.Errors.Count

If conn.Errors.Count>0 then

  For i=0 to conn.Errors.Count-1

    If conn.Errors(i).Number=-2147352571 then
      Response.Write "You have entered an invalid price. Please go back to the _
             data entry page and enter a valid price for the camera"
      Exit for

    Elseif  conn.Errors(i).Number=-2147217887 then
      Response.Write "Please use new_products.asp to enter data first, you _
             cannot view this page directly"
      Exit for
    End if
  Next

  conn.RollbackTrans
Else

  conn.CommitTrans

End if
```

```
'release resources
rs.Close
Set rs=nothing
conn.Close
Set conn=nothing

'use if statement to check if there has been no errors
If errornum =0 then
   Response.Redirect "new_products.asp"      'if no errors redirect to new_products.asp
End if

%>
```

How it Works – Adding ADO Error Handling

This is a simple solution that uses ADO error numbers to print out specific problems that may have arisen in the data entry stage. First we implement a transaction using `conn.BeginTrans`, so we can use `conn.RollbackTrans` if there are any problems.

A **transaction** provides *atomicity* to a series of data changes to a recordset within a connection, allowing all of the changes to take place at once, or not at all. Once a transaction has been started, any changes to a recordset attached to the connection are cached until the transaction is either completed or abandoned. At this stage, all of the changes will either be written to the database (if the transaction is committed with `conn.CommitTrans`) or discarded (if the transaction is aborted with `conn.RollbackTrans`). For more information on transactions read the MSDN article *Microsoft SQL Server: An Overview of Processing Concepts and the MS DTC*, available at:

`http://msdn.microsoft.com/library/backgrnd/HTML/msdn_dtcwp.htm`

Then it's a simple matter of using `If` statements to check any ADO error numbers produced, with set replies. The error numbers -2147352571 and -2147217887 are ADO error codes that specify the error types. If one of these error codes occurs, the `conn.RollbackTrans` is called and no changes to the database are made. If there aren't any problems with the submitted data, `conn.CommitTrans` kicks in and the data is sent to the database.

Now if the user forgets to enter a valid price, rather than dumping the meaningless '80020005' Type Mismatch error directly to the browser, your user is told that he did not enter a valid price and is prompted to re-enter it:

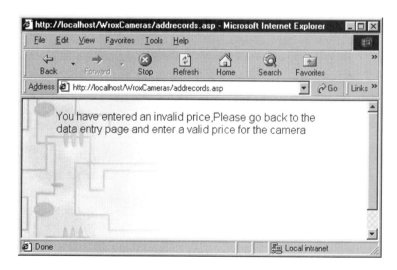

We only used two error codes in this example, but you could use this technique to check for a whole list of potential error codes. There are too many ADO error numbers to include here, but for a full list check out http://msdn.microsoft.com/library/psdk/dasdk/mdae4dv1.htm. To make things even more transparent to the user, you may also modify the error handling routine to redirect the user back to new_records.asp after displaying the message. To build a professional looking web site, it is necessary to have error handling routines to avoid sending users unsightly and confusing error messages directly.

Error Handling Using Scripts

There is another way to check for errors during data input and that is by using scripts. Instead of writing error handling code to addrecords.asp we can write code to handle errors directly in new_products.asp. This has the advantage that it checks for errors *before* the data is submitted. To demonstrate this we are going to add some script to our new_products.asp page to check that a price has been entered into the price field. If you added the ADO error handling code in the previous example to your addrecords.asp file, then comment out that code using apostrophes, so that you can see script error handling code in action.

Try it Out - Adding Scripts to Check Data Entry

1. Open up new_products.asp and in Source view scroll down to find this line:

```
<BR>
<INPUT TYPE="submit" VALUE="submit" ID="submit1" NAME="submit1">
</FORM>
```

and change it to:

```
<INPUT TYPE="button" VALUE="submit" ID="submit1" NAME="submit1">
```

2. Then scroll down past the </FORM> tag and add the following script:

```
<SCRIPT LANGUAGE="VBscript">
  Sub submit1_OnClick()
    If Len(thisForm.price.value) = 0 Then      'Verify price has been entered
      Alert (" Please enter a valid price")
      Exit Sub
    End if

    call thisForm.submit()
  End Sub
</SCRIPT>
```

That's it! Now if you view `new_products.asp` in a browser and forget to put in a price into the price field, you will be confronted with the following:

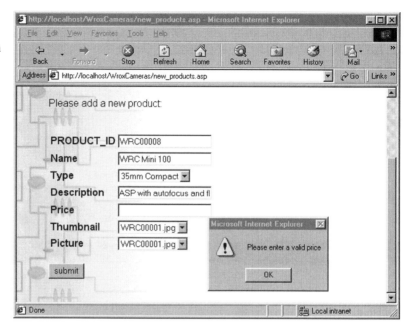

When you click OK, the details are not sent and the page waits for you to add the missing details.

How it Works - Adding Scripts to Check Data Entry

We changed `"submit"` to `"button"` in the line at the bottom of the form, so that when the submit button is clicked the details aren't automatically submitted to the database straight away. Instead we will now have to submit the form ourselves, which allows us to check the contents of the form first in the button's `OnClick()` event.

We then write a sub procedure that checks to see if a price has been entered when the submit button is clicked. The line:

```
Sub submit1_OnClick()
```

executes the sub procedure when the button `submit1` is clicked. Then the lines:

```
If Len(thisForm.price.value) = 0 Then      'Verify price has been entered
Alert (" Please enter a valid price")
```

simply uses `If Then` to check whether the length of the `value` in the `price` field is equal to 0. If it is, `Alert` is used to bring up a dialog warning the user that the price needs to be filled in. If a value has been entered into the price field (i.e. the length of the input is not 0), the `Then` part of the `If` statement doesn't execute and the data is submitted using the line:

```
call thisForm.Submit()
```

Using scripts like this you can test all of the fields in the table to check that they contain relevant data.

Data Environment (DE) Objects

Visual InterDev allows you to script against existing Data Environment (DE) objects directly. Rather than having to specify SQL text directly in your code or introducing additional ADO objects, you may simply use data connection or data command objects already defined in your project. This gives you the advantage of using Visual InterDev to graphically build the connection and the command, and still be able to use them in your ADO code.

For example, if you have already created a few DE Commands for your project as follows:

you may simply use these DE commands (products, product_type, command1, and so on) in your scripts.

Suppose product_type specifies the table "product_type", you may use the following line to set the ADO recordset rs to the results of executing the DE command "product_type":

```
Set rs=Server.CreateObject ("ADODB.Recordset")
rs=DE.Recordsets("product_type")
```

Similarly, you can use an existing DE command for an ADO command rather than having to define the properties in code:

```
Set cmd=Server.CreateObject("ADODB.Command")
Cmd=DE.Commands ("Command1")
```

Like ADO objects, the DE object needs to be initialized before we can make use of it. The following code is the proper syntax of initializing a DE object:

```
<%
  Set DE=Server.CreateObject("DERuntime.DERuntime")
  DE.Init(Application("DE"))
%>
```

This may not sound like a big deal, but using DE can simplify coding quite a bit in some cases. For the products.asp page we created earlier, we had the following ADO code:

```
<%
  'retrieve catalogue of products from DB and write to table
  Dim adoConn
  Dim adoCmd
  Dim adoRS
  Dim strConnectionString

  'create ADO Objects
  Set adoConn = Server.CreateObject("ADODB.Connection")
  Set adoCmd = Server.CreateObject("ADODB.Command")
  Set adoRS = Server.CreateObject("ADODB.Recordset")

  'define connection string
  strConnectionString="Provider=SQLOLEDB.1;Persist Security Info=False;User ID=sa;_
              Initial Catalog=WroxCameras;Data Source=VAIO;Locale Identifier=2057; _
              Connect Timeout=15;Use Procedure for Prepare=1;Auto Translate=True; _
              Packet Size=4096;Workstation ID=VAIO"

  'set ADO Command Properties
  adoCmd.CommandType = 1
  adoCmd.CommandText = "SELECT product.product_id, product.name, product.price, _
              product.thumbnail, product_type.type_description FROM product, _
              product_type WHERE product.type_id =product_type.product_type _
              ORDER BY name"

  'Open the Connection
  adoConn.Open strConnectionString

  'associate the Command with the Open Connection
  adoCmd.ActiveConnection = adoConn

  'retrieve recordset
  Set adoRS = adoCmd.Execute
  Do While not adoRS.EOF
    'process results to create table
    Response.Write "<TR>" & vbcrlf
    Response.Write "<TD><A HREF=" & chr(34) & "product_details.asp?product_ID=" & _
              adoRS("product_id").value & chr(34) & "><IMG src=" & chr(34) & _
              "images/" & adoRS("thumbnail").value & chr(34) & "></a></TD>" & vbcrlf
    Response.Write "<TD>" & adoRS("name").value & "</TD>" & vbcrlf
    Response.Write "<TD>" & adoRS("price").value & "</TD>" & vbcrlf
    Response.Write "<TD>" & adoRS("type_description").value & "</TD></TR>" & vbcrlf
    adoRS.MoveNext
  Loop
  'close connection and set ADO objects to nothing
  adoConn.Close
  Set adoConn = nothing
  Set adoCmd = nothing
  Set adoRS = nothing

%>
```

In the next example, we will use the DE object to rewrite `products.asp`. You will see that it requires much less code compared with using ADO alone.

1. Make a copy of `products.asp` and name it `products2.asp` and remove everything between the `<% %>` tags.

2. Rather than specifying the SQL text directly in the scripts, we will create a DE command and specify the query in its **Properties** window as follows. In the **Project Explorer** window expand the node under **global.asa** and the **DataEnvironment** node and then right click on the data connection **WroxCameras**. Select **Add Data Command** and name the DE command **products**:

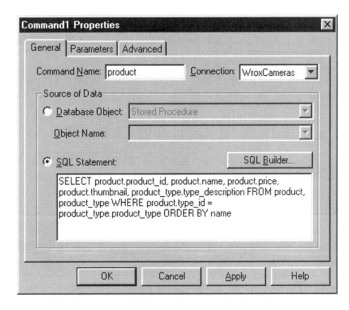

3. Now we can do away with the ADO connection and command objects we had earlier and simply use the DE command we just created. Add the following code to instantiate and initialize the DE object:

```
<%
   Set DE = Server.CreateObject("DERuntime.DERuntime")
      DE.init Application("DE")
```

4. Add the following code to the page. Here we simply use the existing DE command to populate the recordset `adoRS` rather than programmatically specifying it:

```
Set adoRS=Server.CreateObject("ADODB.Recordset")
   Set adoRS=DE.Recordsets("products")


   adoRS.Open
```

5. Since we set the results of the DE command to an ADO recordset adoRS, you can manipulate it using all methods and properties available to the ADO recordset. The following will be the same as for products.asp, and you can simply copy it from products.asp:

```
Do While not adoRS.EOF
  'process results to create table
  Response.Write "<TR>" & vbcrlf
  Response.Write "<TD><A HREF=" & chr(34) & "product_details.asp?product_ID=" &
            adoRS("product_id").value & chr(34) & "><IMG src=" & chr(34) &
            "images/" &
            adoRS("thumbnail").value & chr(34) & "></a></TD>" & vbcrlf
  Response.Write "<TD>" & adoRS("name").value & "</TD>" & vbcrlf
  Response.Write "<TD>" & adoRS("price").value & "</TD>" & vbcrlf
  Response.Write "<TD>" & adoRS("type_description").value & "</TD></TR>" & vbcrlf
  adoRS.MoveNext
Loop
```

6. Add the following lines to close the ADO recordset:

```
'close connection and set ADO objects to nothing
adoRS.close
Set adoRS = nothing

%>
```

7. Now save and view the page in your browser, and notice that we have the same products page.

Using DE in this case has simplified our programming task. Since DE is simply a wrapper on top of ADO, the DE commands are equivalent to ADO commands, and DE recordsets are equivalent to ADO recordsets. Without sacrificing on performance, DE gives you more flexibility by allowing you to script against the DE objects already defined, reuse them in different pages, while saving you time by requiring less coding in general.

Summary

Here is a quick recap on what we have learned about ADO in this chapter:

- ❑ ADO is one of the latest data access technologies and a key element of the Microsoft Data Access Components (MDAC).

- ❑ ADO is the data access technology of choice for ASP development, compared with RDO and DAO.

- ❑ ADO allows fast and efficient data access and can be used directly from ASP as well as other development tools such as Visual Basic and Visual C++.

- ❑ The key objects of ADO are connection, command and recordset.

- ❑ Using the ADO errors collection allows you to capture errors and create more professional looking web pages.

- ❑ You can use ADO to *present* data as well as *entering* data.

- ❑ You can script against the existing Data Environment objects by using the DE object. Using the DE object can simplify coding without sacrificing performance.

The neat thing about ADO is that it is easy to use, fast, and may be used from different development tools. ADO has been developed as a user-friendly interface over OLE DB, while RDO and DAO were designed as interfaces over ODBC, an earlier standard. As OLE DB gradually gains wider acceptance, ADO will become increasingly important as a data access technology.

Although Visual InterDev 6.0 has introduced a set of data binding DTCs that allow you to create data access pages without any coding, the ability to write data access pages using ADO gives you additional flexibility and choices. For professional web development, it is almost always necessary to write your own ADO code for different purposes. To achieve even higher performance, you may wrap your ADO code in COM components. This gives you fast running compiled code rather than interpreted scripts. In Chapter 12, we will see how we can create COM components that access data using ADO. First we'll have a look at another exciting new technology for enhancing our web applications – XML.

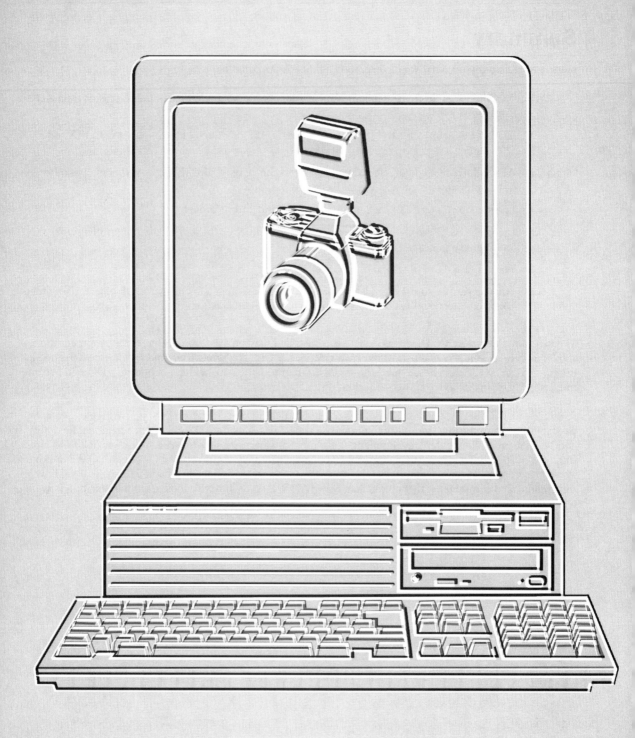

XML in Web Applications

We have already briefly come across XML in Chapter 1. In this chapter we will learn more about this exciting new technology that is causing such a stir in almost every area of programming. It is a common misconception that XML is just a replacement for HTML. This is most certainly not the case. While it *is* having a strong impact on web development, there are a number of other areas of programming where XML is gaining popularity, not just for displaying data, but also for transporting data, merging disparate data sources, e-commerce and even describing interfaces of components (such as in Windows Script Components).

We have already mentioned that XML is a way of marking up your data in tags that actually describe their contents, so this chapter will focus on the syntax of XML documents, whether you are writing XML by hand or using it programmatically. We will also see a number of related technologies that help build up the XML programmer's toolkit.

Of course, as XML is just a way of marking up your data so that it is self describing, there is no way in an XML document of specifying how the data should be displayed, so we will need bring in our old friend cascading style sheets (CSSs), which we met in Chapter 4. We will also see various ways that we can store our XML. With a lot of data already residing in relational databases we will see how we can create XML from this content. In addition, we need a way to access the values of elements and attributes programmatically, as one of the important reasons for marking up your data in XML is that you can then perform processing and retrieval upon the file rather than just displaying it for use on the Web. This is where we introduce the W3C Document Object Model, which is an Application Programming Interface that allows you to work with XML documents in a standard way.

Overall, in this chapter we will introduce:

❑   XML as a way of marking up data.

❑   Displaying XML using CSSs.

❑   Creating XML from relational contents of a relational database using ASP and ADO.

❑   Accessing XML documents using the W3C Document Object Model.

Using Visual InterDev as an XML Editor

Visual InterDev does not offer many special features dedicated to writing XML. However, as it is an integrated web development environment, there are still advantages in using it over, say, Notepad or some other simple text editors. As it is likely that you will be using other techniques along with XML in your web development, it still makes a lot of sense to use Visual InterDev when writing applications that make use of XML. For example, you will be able to use the CSS editor and will often be writing projects that use HTML forms, ASP, and require database access. In addition, Visual InterDev helps us read our code by coloring it in a similar vein to other HTML pages, so our comments are seen in green, and unrecognized elements are in pink. (I say unrecognized because there are some tags that are used with XML that Visual InterDev does not understand, such as the `<XML>` tag, which is in fact HTML.)

When you start Visual InterDev to create your first XML file, you need to select an HTML page if you want the advantages of colored text. A simple text file will only give you black text. You can then save the file as an XML file (rather than HTML) by giving it a `.xml` extension. In fact it is useful to create a simple document that you can use as a starter, which we shall do when creating our first XML document. You then open this as if it were a template file.

Unfortunately you cannot use the Quick View option to display your XML file in the same way that you can open up an XML file in Internet Explorer 5. IE5 allows you to display the file with its default Extensible Stylesheet Language (XSL) style sheet that usually reports problems, so you might like to keep an instance of Internet Explorer open at the same time to test your XML files.

Internet Explorer 5 was the first of the major browsers to implement XML, so we shall be using it throughout the chapter. If you do not have a copy, you can download it from `http://www.microsoft.com/windows/ie/default.htm`.

Although XML looks like HTML, it has a different format. HTML components such as forms are not relevant to XML, because there is no default way of styling the document. So your Toolbox window is of little use when writing a simple XML file, although it would be useful for other parts of projects that use XML. In fact, using the Toolbox with your XML document makes Visual InterDev add default HTML, which will cause a browser to attempt to interpret your XML file as HTML. Needless to say, it probably will not be successful. Nor is the Properties window of any help to us, as the environment has no knowledge of the XML vocabulary we are using, so it cannot offer us a list of available properties, which would have to be retrieved from a file that defines what content elements it can have (which is described in a file called a Document Type Definition or schema).

In this chapter we will not only introduce you to XML, so that you can consider using it further in your web development, we will also be showing you a couple of ways in which it can be used in our Wrox Cameras example that we've been developing throughout the book so far. We will start by introducing you to writing XML, and then create a catalogue of cameras in XML. There are two ways that we will cover to do this. Firstly we shall create the catalogue in XML manually so that you can get to grips with the syntax and structure of XML documents. We will also style the XML catalogue in a different way to the one seen in the rest of the book, to see how we prepare our XML documents for use on the Web. One of the great advantages of XML is that it allows us to exchange data in a platform independent manner, as it is just plain text. So we will then go on to look at how we can create the XML version of the catalogue on the fly from the content of our SQL Server database, using ASP. This will illustrate one of the ways in which other people would be able to use our catalogue if we were to make it available as XML. We will also briefly look at ways in which we can manipulate our XML documents once we have created them.

Shortfalls of HTML

When we were looking at markup in Chapter 1 we noted some problems with HTML. While HTML is the great language that made the Web popular with the masses, it is not suitable for the type of applications that many are trying to build on the Web these days. The core problem lies in it being used to mark up documents for viewing on the Web. This means that there are all sorts of tags in HTML that are used to say how the document should appear; they say nothing about what the markup is actually holding. Just to re-cap from Chapter 1:

❑ **HTML has a fixed tag set.** You cannot create your own tags that can be interpreted by others.

❑ **HTML is used for presentation.** It doesn't carry information about the meaning of the content held within its tags.

❑ **HTML is 'flat'.** You cannot specify the importance of tags, so a hierarchy of data cannot be represented.

❑ **HTML is not suited to exchanging data in web applications.** HTML does not provide the power needed for creating advanced web applications at a level that developers are currently aiming for. For example, it does not readily offer the ability for advanced processing and retrieval upon documents (you cannot select information that could be held within an element without knowing what each element's content is, because the data is just marked up for presentation purposes).

❑ **High traffic volumes.** Existing HTML documents that are used as applications clog up the Internet with high volumes of client-server traffic, for example sending large general results of data across a network when only small amounts are required. With XML it will be possible to request only a relevant part of the document, rather than a document as a whole.

While HTML has proven to be very useful as a way of marking up documents for display in a web browser, a document marked up in HTML tells us very little about its actual content. For most documents to be useful in a business situation, there is a need to know about the document's content. If a document does contain details about its contents then it is possible to work with the data held within that file, manipulating its content and retrieving specified sections of it. This means that XML is no longer just suitable for one purpose. While HTML is a language that is only used for display on the Web, XML can also be used as a way of holding and exchanging data within applications. Marking up data in a way that tells us about its content, making it **self-describing**, also means that the data can be re-used in different situations. For example, the same set of data marked up in XML may be used on the Web, as well as in other applications. While SGML made this possible, it was only widely used for marking up documents and was considered too complex for the Web. Its offspring, XML, is not only far more popular, but is also being used in a wider range of situations.

What is XML?

While HTML has a fixed set of tags that the author can use to mark up data for display on the Web, XML users can create their own tags (or use those created by others if applicable). Thus it is **extensible**, so that the tags actually describe the content of the element. So, let's dive straight in and look at an example.

At its simplest level XML is just a way of marking up data so that it is self-describing. What do we mean by this? Well, in Chapter 9 we had a page called `products.asp` that generated details about the cameras and displayed them in a page called `product_details.asp`. If you have `product_details.asp` displayed in your browser, you can then view the source code by selecting View | Source in the main menu of the browser. The source code will be displayed in Notepad and will contain the following code for displaying the product details:

```
<strong><font color='orange'>WRC Digi 35</font></strong><br><br>
   <tr>
      <td width='50%' rowspan='4'><img src="images/WRC00006.jpg"></td>
   </tr>
   <tr>
      <td width='50%'><strong>Name:</strong> WRC Digi 35</td>
   </tr>
   <tr>
      <td width='50%'><strong>Description:</strong> Digital camera with
                     high resolution and colour LCD</td>
   </tr>
   <tr>
      <td width='50%'><strong>Price:</strong> 420</td>
   </tr>
   <tr>
      <td width='50%'><strong>Type:</strong> Digital</td>
   </tr>
```

That's all we need to do if we just want to put information about a camera on a web page. It looked something like this:

So, when we are building our web pages we have a lot of this data in HTML. As an ASP developer you can use script and databases to generate content dynamically. However, you still have a lot of information marked up just for display on the Web, and a lot of information stored in a proprietary format, such as a SQL Server database, that is not available to everyone.

The tags (or markup) don't tell you what you are talking about, and there is no way of telling from the tags that you are displaying information about cameras; it could be anything. With XML you can create your own tags, so that they actually describe the content that they are marking up, hence the term self-describing data. And because it is plain text, it is platform independent and can be shared and easily sent over the Internet for anyone who wants to use it.

So, how could we mark up the information in a more logical way using XML, so that we know what we have in the file?

Try it Out – My First XML Document

We are going to mark up some data so that it will hold the same sort of information as the ASP page that we have just looked at.

1. Open up Visual InterDev, and in the WroxCameras project choose to add a new HTML file. Name the file cameraList1.xml.

2. Remove all of the HTML that Visual InterDev generates automatically for you, and enter the following code in the Source view:

```
<?xml version="1.0"?>
<cameraList>
    <camera>
        <name>WRC Supra 70</name>
        <product_id>WRC00001</product_id>
        <type_id>1</type_id>
    <price currency="US$">100</price>
    </camera>

    <camera>
        <name>WRC Supra 90</name>
        <product_id>WRC00002</product_id>
        <type_id>1</type_id>
    <price currency="US$">130</price>
    </camera>

    <camera>
        <name>WRC Mini 70</name>
        <product_id>WRC00003</product_id>
        <type_id>3</type_id>
    <price currency="US$">190</price>
    </camera>
</cameraList>
```

3. Save the file.

And that is it; you have created your first XML document. From this file, you can see that you are dealing with a list of cameras. You can tell what type of information each tag contains because we have used tags that explain the type of data they are marking up. We will see what it looks like in a browser in a moment, but for now let's see what we have done in that file.

How it Works – My First XML Document

We started with the following line:

```
<?xml version="1.0"?>
```

This is called the **XML declaration**. It tells the receiving application that it is getting an XML document compatible with version one of the XML specification. (This was the only version out at the time of writing, October 1999, and is likely to stay so for a while – to keep up to date you can visit `http://www.w3.org/xml/`). Note that the `xml` is in lowercase and that there are no whitespaces between the question mark and the opening `xml`. While the XML declaration is not strictly necessary in an XML document, it is good practice to include it in XML files, so that the application using the file knows that it is receiving an XML file.

Since we are describing data about cameras, the whole file (apart from the XML declaration) is included in the following tags:

```
<cameraList>
</cameraList>
```

This is known as the **root** element. All XML tags *must* have a corresponding closing tag; unlike HTML you cannot leave out end tags and expect your application to accept it. The only exception to this is called an **empty** element, one in which there is no element content. An example of this in HTML would be an `<IMG>` tag. In XML, if you have an empty element, you must add a slash before the closing delimiter, such as `<tag attribute="value" />`. Empty elements are only used when you do not have any content between the elements, in the way that the HTML `<IMG>` tag only uses attributes.

> Note that XML, unlike HTML, is case sensitive, so `<cameraList>` and `<CAMERAlist>` would be treated as two different tags.

In the same way that we made sensible opening and closing tags for the document using the `<cameraList>` element, we use similarly descriptive tags to mark up some more details. This time we will use a `<camera>` tag to include the details about each camera. Inside the tags are the details about each camera.

```
<camera>
    <name>WRC Supra 70</name>
    <product_id>WRC00001</product_id>
    <type_id>1</type_id>
    <price currency="US$">100</price>
</camera>
```

Here we have `<name>` holding the name of the camera, followed by `<product_id>` and `<type_id>`. The opening `<price>` tag contains an attribute to stipulate the currency that the price has been quoted in. In this case we have chosen US dollars.

> Note that all XML attribute values must be enclosed in quotes. While Internet Explorer is forgiving of this omission in HTML code, it follows the XML standard and does not accept them in XML.

As there are several cameras in the list we put the list of details about the camera in **nested** elements. We start with an opening `<camera>` tag and then nest inside this a `<name>` tag for each name or model of camera. Notice how each element actually describes its content.

The ability to nest tags is a very important aspect of XML with data, because it allows us to create **hierarchical** data records that would not easily fit in the row and table model of relational databases without the use of linked tables. This counters the problem that HTML has of being a 'flat' way of describing data.

And that's all there is to your first XML document. It is plain text, its tags describe their content and it is easily readable by a human being.

From this alone, you can tell that we are now talking about a catalogue; the tags that meant little, such as `<td>` and `<tr>` are gone. Here when we markup the data about cameras using XML, the product's identification number is in tags that are called `<product_id>`. Now, this seems a lot more logical than the previous example – it is simple to see what we are talking about.

Displaying our First XML Document in a Browser

How will this look in a web browser? Browsers understand tags such as `<H3>`, referring to a category 3 heading, but we are making up these tags, so we cannot expect a browser to understand all of the ones that everyone creates. As XML is such a new technology, browsers are only just starting to support it. We saw earlier that Internet Explorer 5 was the first browser to offer full support for the XML specification and therefore a lot of the examples in this chapter will use it. It is likely that the next version 5 offering from Netscape will offer similar support for XML. However at the time of writing the nearest thing available was a beta download from an open source site at `http://www.mozilla.org` (which is for a community of developers involved in creating the browser) under the name Gecko.

To open your XML file in Internet Explorer just select View in Browser from the View menu. Alternatively fire up IE5 and use Open from the file menu and browse to the file, or you can type in the URL. Here is how our XML version of the camera details page is displayed when we open it in IE5.

Once open in Internet Explorer it should look something like this:

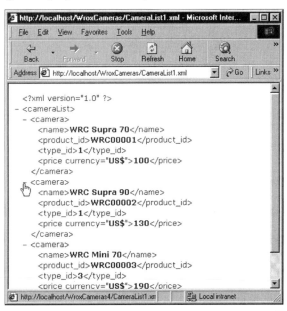

Note that you can expand and collapse the elements that have children. You can see this on the `<cameraList>` and `<camera>` elements. Internet Explorer 5 actually uses a default style sheet to display XML files like this that do not have a style sheet associated with them. To display the file it uses a language called XSL (Extensible Stylesheet Language) for the style sheet. Unfortunately there is not space to discuss XSL in depth in this chapter, but it is something well worth learning if you start to use XML a lot.

As it is, this is not as attractive to look at as the HTML version, but as we said HTML is a language for displaying data on the Web. XML is just a way of marking up your data. It is still possible to make our XML documents more attractive by using a style sheet. In fact there are several reasons why you might want to keep your data separate from styling rules and we shall look at these in a moment.

The Data Revolution

As computers have found their way into more areas of our work and home life, we are storing ever-increasing amounts of information electronically. While we may think of our business data mainly residing in relational databases, such as SQL Server, Oracle or DB2, the reality is that we probably have more data in other formats:

- ❑ Quotes and reports in word processor formats, such as Word or Word Perfect.
- ❑ Web pages in HTML.
- ❑ Presentations in PowerPoint.
- ❑ Mail and memos in mail servers such as Exchange and Notes.

Some of this data is replicated and some of it is as good as lost, because not everyone knows how to access it. In addition, the ubiquity of the Internet has meant that we are trying to share more and more data with people in other physical places.

But what has all this got to do with XML? Going back to our camera example, Wrox Cameras might use this type of catalogue information we have just seen for many purposes in different ways: web pages, trade catalogues, public catalogues, information for retail purchasers (camera shops), many of whom require it in different formats etc.

If we mark up our camera details just once in XML, we can re-purpose it. So, if we were to create an XML file containing all of our camera catalogue we would not need to put it in HTML for the Web, individually mail the retailers with new camera details, etc. We could just re-format the one XML source for each purpose.

Furthermore, if people wanted to find out about some of our cameras, they could just collect information about those that they are interested in, rather than wasting bandwidth having to download a large file with a lot of irrelevant data.

In fact, in the same way that we see Save As HTML options in many office applications, we are likely to see an option such as Save As XML appearing in the near future. In addition, many database vendors have already released or are working on technologies that will allow you to save data as XML or to create XML from data stored in standard relational databases.

Breaking Beyond Data Display

Up to now, it may seem as though we have been concentrating on how XML can be an alternative to HTML. Let's quickly expand this view a little and see the other effects of marking up our data as XML, before we take a look at some of the associated specifications and techniques that you need to learn.

As XML is just stored and transferred as plain text it has a strong advantage over most other data formats. Firstly, because it is pure text it is not a proprietary format that can only be used on certain platforms or with limited applications (any application could be written to accept pure text). Secondly, (disregarding the small matter of character encoding schemes) as opposed to binary formats, the pure text data that is transmitted does not have to be translated from 8-bit bytes into the 7-bit format that is required with HTTP. Finally, the data can easily be validated. If you remember that we said in Chapter 1 that SGML uses a Document Type Definition (DTD) to define the use of any markup language written in SGML, so does XML. This means that applications can verify whether the structure and content of an XML file is correct as laid down in the DTD – with everyone creating their own tags, a DTD is a file which you can write to say what tags you can use in your XML document and how your set of tags should be used.

This universality is one of the main reasons why XML is an ideal format for applications as well as displaying data on the Web. It can transcend different operating systems and is ideal for distributed computing environments.

So we are not only seeing XML being used as a way of presenting data that is marked up as HTML, it is also being used for many other purposes, including:

❑ Data transfer; we can use XML as a language for passing data between client browsers and servers, and between servers and servers. This is very helpful in areas such as e-commerce where the ability to speak a language that is platform independent is a great bonus.

❑ Data storage in plain text files rather than pre-purposed formats such as HTML and proprietary word processor files.

❑ Interface descriptors for components, as is done in Windows Script Components (see `http://msdn.microsoft.com/scripting/` for more on Windows Script Components)

Of course, we cannot cover all of them in this chapter. But what we will do is teach you enough to get you started using XML. From this point you will be able to see how it can help you in your programming activities.

A Closer Look at Creating XML Documents

The XML 1.0 specification lays out two types of XML document: either **well-formed** or **valid**. The distinction between the two is simple. Well-formed documents comply with the rules of XML syntax, such as: all elements must have a corresponding end tag, or else have a closing slash in the empty elements, every document must have a unique opening and closing tag, etc. Valid documents, on the other hand, are not only well-formed, but they must also comply with a DTD.

Well-Formed Documents

The XML 1.0 specification defines the syntax for XML. If you understand the specification properly, you can construct a program that will be able to 'look' at a document which is supposed to be XML, and if the document conforms to the specification for XML, then the program can do further processing on it. The idea underlying the XML specification is therefore that XML documents should be intelligible as such, either to humans or processing applications.

Well-formedness is the minimum set of requirements (defined in the specification) that a document needs to satisfy in order for it to be considered an XML document. These requirements are a mixture of ensuring that the correct language terms are employed and that the document is logically ordered and coherent in the manner defined by the specification (in other words that the terms of the language are used in the right way). You can see the XML specification at `http://www.w3.org/tr/xml/`. There is also a helpful annotated version of the specification available at `http://www.xml.com/axml/testaxml.htm` and some helpful tutorials at `http://msdn.microsoft.com/xml/`.

So, what are these rules? Well, nearly everything we need to know about well-formed documents can be summed up in three rules:

❑ The document must contain one or more elements.

❑ It must contain a uniquely named element, no part of which appears in the content of any other element. This is known as the root element.

❑ All other elements must be nested correctly within the root element.

So, let's look at how we construct a well-formed document.

The XML Declaration

This is actually optional, although you are strongly advised to use it so that the receiving application knows that it is an XML document and also the version used (at the time of writing version 1.0 was the only one).

```
<?xml version="1.0">
```

Note that the `xml` should be in lowercase, and when it is used, the XML declaration must not be preceded by any other characters (not even white space).

You can also define the character set, or language in which you have written your XML data, in the XML declaration. This is particularly important if your data contains characters that aren't part of the English ASCII character set. You can specify the language encoding using the optional `encoding` attribute:

```
<?xml version="1.0" encoding="iso-8859-1" ?>
```

The most common ones are shown in the following table:

Language	Character set
Unicode (8 bit)	UTF-8
Latin 1 (Western Europe, Latin America)	ISO-8859-1
Latin 2 (Central/Eastern Europe)	ISO-8859-2
Latin 3 (SE Europe)	ISO-8859-3
Latin 4 (Scandinavia/Baltic)	ISO-8859-4
Latin/Cyrillic	ISO-8859-5
Latin/Arabic	ISO-8859-6
Latin/Greek	ISO-8859-7
Latin/Hebrew	ISO-8859-8
Latin/Turkish	ISO-8859-9
Latin/Lappish/Nordic/Eskimo	ISO-8859-10
Japanese	EUC-JP or Shift_JIS

If you want to read more about internationalization, check out the W3C's page on this topic at `http://www.w3.org/International/`.

Elements

As we have already seen, the XML document essentially consists of data marked up using tags. Each start-tag/end-tag pair, along with the data that lies between them, is an **element**.

```
<mytag>Here we have some data</mytag>
```

The start and end tags must be exactly the same, except for the closing slash in the end-tag. Remember that they must be in the same case: `<mytag>` and `<MyTag>` would be considered to be different tags.

In this example, the section that says `Here we have some data` between the tags is called **character data**, while the tags either side are the **markup**. The character data can consist of any sequence of legal characters (conforming to the Unicode standard) except the start element character `<`. This is not allowed in case a processing application (we say this as it might not only be a browser that uses XML) treats it as the start of a new tag.

The tags can start with a letter, an underscore _, or a colon character :, followed by any combination of letters, digits, hyphens, underscores, colons, or periods. The only exception is that you cannot start a tag with the letters `XML` in any combination of upper or lowercase letters. In addition, you are also advised not to start a tag with a colon, in case it gets treated as something called a namespace.

Here is another example, marking up some details for a hardware store:

```
<inventory>
    <buckets>
        <bucket>
            <make>Addis</make>
            <capacity>3 litres</capacity>
        </bucket>
        <bucket>
            <make>Metro</make>
            <capacity>2.5 litres</capacity>
        </bucket>
    </buckets>
</inventory>
```

If you remember back to the three rules at the beginning of this section, you will be able to work out that this is a well-formed XML document:

❑ We have more than our one required element.

❑ We have a unique opening and closing tag: `<inventory>`, which is the root element.

❑ The elements are nested properly.

Let's have a look at some more examples to help us get the idea of well-formed XML.

At the simplest level we could have either:

```
<my_document></my_document>
```

or even:

```
<my_document />
```

Remember that this is known as an empty element. To make sure that tags nest properly, there must be no overlap. So this is correct:

```
<parent>
   <child>Some character data</child>
</parent>
```

while this would be incorrect:

```
<bad_parent>
    <naughty_child>
        Some character data
</bad_parent>
    </naughty child>
```

because the closing `</naughty_child>` element is after the closing `</bad_parent>` element.

Attributes

Elements can have attributes. These are values that are passed to the application, but do not constitute part of the content of the element. Attributes are included as part of the element's start tag, as in HTML. In XML all attributes must be enclosed in quote marks. For example:

```
<food healthy="yes">spinach</food>
```

Elements can have as many attributes as you want. So you could have:

```
<food healthy="no" tasty="yes" high_in_cholesterol="yes">fries</food>
```

For well-formedness, however, you cannot repeat the attribute within an instance of the element. So you could not have:

```
<food tasty="yes" tasty="no">spinach</food>
```

Also, the string values between the quote marks should not contain the characters <, &, ' or ".

Other Features

There are also a number of other features of the XML specification that you need to learn if you progress to using XML frequently. Unfortunately there is not space to cover them all here. We will, however, briefly describe a few.

Entities

There are two categories of entity: **general entities** and **parameter entities**. Entities are usually used within a document as a way of avoiding having to type out long pieces of text several times within a document. They provide a way of associating a name with the long piece of text so that wherever you need to mention the text you just mention the name instead. As a result, if you have to modify the text, you only have to do it once (rather like the benefits that ASP server side include files offer).

CDATA Sections

CDATA sections can be used wherever character data can appear within a document. They are used to escape blocks of text that would otherwise be considered as markup. So if we wanted to include the whole of the following line, including the tags:

```
<to_be_seen>Always wear light clothing when walking in the dark</to_be_seen>
```

we could use a CDATA section like so:

```
<element>
<! [CDATA[ <to_be_seen>Always wear light clothing when walking in the
dark</to_be_seen> ]]>
</element>
```

And the line including the `<to_be_seen>` tags would be recognized.

305

Comments

It is always good programming practice to comment your code, in a manner that would explain, remind you about, or simply point out salient sections of code. It is surprising how code that seemed perfectly clear when you wrote it can soon become a jumble when you come back to it. While the descriptive XML tags often help you understand your own markup, there are times when the tags alone are not enough.

The good news is that comments in XML use exactly the same syntax as those in HTML, as shown below:

```
<!--I add a comment here to remind me how the code works -->
```

However, you should not include either the - or -- character in the characters that delimit your comments (i.e. inside the <!-- and --> characters) to avoid confusing the receiving application.

Processing Instructions

These allow documents to contain instructions for applications using the XML data. They take the form:

```
<?NameOfTargetApplication     Instructions for Application ?>
```

The target name cannot contain the letters xml in any combination of upper or lower case.

Try it Out – Badly formed XML

We can tell a lot about whether our XML is well-formed by simply loading it into Internet Explorer 5. It has the ability to tell us about a lot of errors. When you are first writing XML, it is very helpful to do this quick check so that you know your XML is well-formed.

1. Open up your cameraList1.xml file.

2. Remove the opening <cameraList> element.

3. Save the file as bad_cameraList1.xml.

4. Load it into Internet Explorer 5.
Here is the result:

As you can see, while it doesn't tell you that you have omitted an opening tag, it can tell that you have more than one element at the same level, in this case there are several `<camera>` elements. So, IE5 flags this up for us.

5. Put the opening `<cameraList>` tag back in again and change the line:

```
<name>WRC Supra 70</name>
```

to:

```
<name>WRC Supra 70<name>
```

by removing the closing slash.

6. Save the file again, and open it up in IE5. You should get a result like this:

Again, we are not given the exact error, but IE was expecting a closing `<name>` tag, which it did not receive.

7. Finally, correct the closing `</name>` tag, and remove the opening quote from the `currency` attribute for the `price` element. Save the file and refresh your browser. This time you get the exact error:

While it is not the most elegant way to test code, it certainly does help to quickly find errors. If you have made more than one error, just correct your mistakes one at a time and watch the error messages change.

Valid Documents

As we mentioned earlier, valid documents are well-formed documents that conform to a DTD. When we read a book, manual, or magazine article, we rarely notice its structure; if it is well written then the structure will be transparent. Yet, we need structure in order to communicate. We may notice headings and paragraphs, but many other aspects pass us by. For one thing, this structuring makes the information in the document intelligible, either to us or to an application using it. But it also means that when a document is **parsed**, by an application for example, the presence of required portions can be checked for.

There are many programs known as **parsers** available for XML, and some are able to validate a document against its DTD - these are known as **validating parsers**. If the document does not follow the structure of the DTD then the parser will raise an error. (We will come back to look at parsers later in the chapter when we talk about the Document Object Model.)

Assuming that we have planned well the appropriate structure for a type of document in the first instance, then the resulting document instances should be logically complete with respect to the predefined structure laid out in its DTD. So, in our cameras example earlier we had:

❑ The unique opening and closing tags of `<cameraList>`.

❑ Followed by details of each camera, with each camera having its own `<camera>` element.

❑ The details of the camera nested in tags that described the aspects of the camera they were marking up, nested within each `camera` element.

If we had to exchange a lot of information about cameras in this format with different people, there would be many advantages to writing a DTD. Such a camera DTD would lay out the structure of how we expect camera details following the camera DTD to be marked up. While we do not need one to write an XML document, it would mean that anyone following the DTD would be able to write an XML file about cameras that would be valid according to our DTD. So, we could guarantee that any application using the camera information marked up according to our DTD could understand the document. It could even check that the document followed the DTD to prevent the application showing errors if we passed in the wrong data. After all, if it were looking for the third element under the `<camera>` element, and someone had added another tag in its place, the processing application would not know what to do. You could think of this as like form validation for incoming and outgoing data to make sure that it would conform to the DTD, without the need for writing complex script to check the document.

So, if we had written any applications to process information according to our camera DTD, then we would be able to process any files that were valid according to the camera DTD, and indeed check that they were valid before trying to do so. So, if the camera company had different members of staff all writing XML documents about the cameras, then they could all follow the DTD to make sure that they were valid. Then, should other camera retailers adopt the same DTD, then others who might make use of our XML files would be able to use the same applications to process the files sent from several different camera suppliers.

Writing DTDs

DTDs are an example of what is known as a **schema**, and are part of the original core XML 1.0 specification. In order to learn about DTDs we will develop one for our sample `cameraList1.xml` file that we built earlier. DTDs use a language called **Extended Backus-Naur Form**, or EBNF for short. The DTD needs to declare the rules of the markup language, which as we said at the beginning of this chapter:

❑ Declare what exactly constitutes markup.

❑ Declare exactly what our markup means.

Practically speaking, this means that we have to give details of each of the elements, their order, and say what attributes (and other types of markup) they can take. They can either be an external file, or declared internally, actually in the XML document within a **Document Type Declaration**, which is used to determine the schema to which the XML document is written.

Referencing a DTD from an XML Document

The DTD for our cameras example would be external, so that many documents could be written according to it. So we need to add a document type declaration for the `cameraList1.xml` example to say that it is written according to a DTD. The document type declaration would look like this (and would live in the `cameraList1.xml` file):

```
<!DOCTYPE cameraList SYSTEM "cameraList.dtd">
```

Here `cameraList` is the name of the root element and the name of the DTD. In this case we have followed it with the keyword `SYSTEM` and the URI of the DTD. (A URL is a subset of a URI; URIs can just be any sort of unique identifier.) The URI is a value that a processing application could use to validate the document against the DTD, which means that there must be an instance of it available from that location. As we are just trying this out as a test we can just keep the DTD in the same folder as the XML document. However, if we were to make it available to all we would have to give a location for it that would be available to any application, so we might choose:

```
<!DOCTYPE cameraList SYSTEM "http://www.wrox.com/DTDlibrary/cameraList.dtd">
```

While we have just said that it is possible to include the DTD in this declaration, in most cases you will want to reference an external file, so we will look at how to do this. After all, there is no point copying the DTD into several files, if you can just have it in one place. To do this we also add the `standalone` attribute to the XML declaration of the XML document (which comes directly before the document type declaration – remember that nothing is allowed to come before the XML declaration, not even white space).

```
<?xml version="1.0" standalone="no" ?>
<!DOCTYPE cameraList SYSTEM "cameraList.dtd">
```

If the value of the `standalone` attribute is `no`, this indicates that there may be an external DTD (or internally declared external parameter entities - but do not worry about this second option until you get more involved in creating complex XML documents). If the value is `yes`, then there are no other dependencies and the file can truly stand on its own.

Why not add this line to the `cameraList1.xml` file we created earlier, as we will be creating a DTD for our cameras example next?

It is very easy to get confused between Document Type Definitions and Document Type Declarations. To clarify, just remember that a Document Type Declaration either refers to an external Document Type Definition, or else contains one in the form of markup declarations, as in the example we are about to see.

Try it Out - Writing a DTD for the Camera Example

Creating your own markup language using a DTD need not be excessively complicated. Here is the external DTD for our cameras example. You can write it in Visual InterDev, or in a simple text editor like Notepad (note that this does not include word processors, which will add characters that are not understood), although there are some special tools available especially for writing them (for more details on these check out `http://www.schema.net/`). As you can see, it is very simple:

```
<!DOCTYPE cameraList [
<!ELEMENT cameraList (camera+)>
<!ELEMENT camera (name, product_id, type_id?, price+)>
<!ELEMENT name (#PCDATA)>
<!ELEMENT product_id (#PCDATA)>
<!ELEMENT type_id (#PCDATA)>
<!ELEMENT price (#PCDATA)>
<!ATTLIST price
        currency      CDATA      #REQUIRED
>
]>
```

How it Works – Writing a DTD for the Camera Example

Let's take a closer look at this. The opening line:

```
<!DOCTYPE cameraList
```

gives the same name as the root element of the document. `<!Element` is used to declare elements in the format:

```
<!ELEMENT name (contents)>
```

Where `name` gives the name of the element, while `contents` describes what type of data can be included and which elements can be nested inside that element. The `cameraList` element must include the element `camera` at least once, denoted by the use of the + symbol, which indicates one or more:

```
<!ELEMENT cameraList (camera+)>
```

While the `camera` element declared in this line:

```
<!ELEMENT camera (name, product_id, type_id?, price+)>
```

must include exactly one instance of each of the `name` and `product_id` elements. The `type_id` is optional, indicated by the question mark, and there must be at least one `price` element. These elements must appear in the given particular order. We then have to define each of these elements individually. Here is a brief summary of the operators we can use to describe element content:

Symbol	Usage
,	Strict ordering
|	Selection, in any order (can be used in conjunction with +, * and ?
+	Repetition (minimum of 1)
*	Repetition
?	Optional
( )	Grouping

Next we see the line:

```
<!ELEMENT name (#PCDATA)>
```

This indicates that the title element can contain **character data**, indicated by #PCDATA. The # symbol prevents PCDATA from being interpreted as an element name.

When we came to the price element in our `cameraList1.xml` file, there was an attribute to indicate its currency. This was how it looked in our `cameraList1.xml` example:

```
<price currency="US$">100</price>
```

So we need to declare the attribute as well. First we will use this line:

```
<!ELEMENT price (#PCDATA)>
```

to indicate that the element's name is `price`, and that it can take character data. Then we have to declare the attribute using the `<!ATTLIST` instruction, the data types or possible values, and the default values for the attributes:

```
<!ATTLIST price
        currency        CDATA       #REQUIRED
>
```

Each attribute has three components: a name (e.g. currency), the type of information to be passed (in this case character data), and the default value (in this case there is not one, but we are required to provide a value).

Then we just have to close the opening DOCTYPE declaration:

```
]>
```

311

That covers the example camera DTD called `cameraList.dtd` for the `cameraList1.xml` example. You will find it with the rest of the code in the download for this chapter. If you want to create one yourself, you can simply use Visual InterDev or a text editor, such as Notepad; just save the file (which will have the same name as your root element) with the extension `.dtd`. If your program tries to save it with a `.txt` or `.htm` extension after the `.dtd` you have added, just put the whole name of the file in quotes.

Obviously, if you have a well-formed instance of an element in a document, but do not declare it in the DTD, then it cannot be validated. An element is only valid if:

❑ There is a declaration for the element type in the DTD which has a name matching that of the element itself.

❑ There are declarations for all of the element types, attributes and their value types in the DTD.

❑ The data type of the content matches that of the content schema defined in the declaration (e.g. `PCDATA`).

So, we have just created our own XML application - our own markup language for exchanging data about cameras. However, it is worth noting that there are other types of schema on the horizon. The W3C (the standards body responsible for the HTML and XML standards – amongst others) is working on a version of schemas written in XML rather than Extended Backus-Naur Form, to be called XML Schemas.

XML Schemas

XML Schemas have several advantages over their DTD counterparts. The group working on the specification has looked at several proposals that you can see if you want to get an idea of what XML Schemas are going to be like. The main ones are XML-Data and Document Content Description. Links to both can be found with all of the submissions and specifications in progress on the W3C site at `http://www.w3.org/tr/`. They also have a Working Draft available for public view, which has been split into two parts, which are accessible from `http://www.w3.org/tr/xmlschema-1/` and `http://www.w3.org/tr/xmlschema-2/`.

There are a number of reasons why these XML Schemas will be an advantage over DTDs. Firstly, they use XML syntax rather than Extended Backus-Naur Form, which many people find difficult to learn. Secondly, if you needed to parse the schema (we will look at parsers shortly), it will be possible to do so using an existing XML parser, rather than having to use a special parser. Another strong advantage is the ability to specify data types in XML Schemas for the content of elements and attributes, which means that applications using the content will not have to convert it into the appropriate data type from a string. If you think about an application that has to add two numbers together, or perform a calculation on a date, it would not have to be converted into the appropriate type of data from a string. While this will still have to be performed with XML Schemas, the job could be done by a standard parser, and the basic validation will be done before handing it on to the application. There will be other advantages too, such as support for namespaces, and they are extensible themselves (whereas now you need to include all of your markup in your DTD, you cannot just extend them when you want to add new elements).

Even HTML Has Schemas

Being an SGML application, HTML has several SGML DTDs (at least a strict and loose one for each version), and the coming XHTML specification has an XML DTD. XHTML is a new version of HTML that is designed as an XML application, as opposed to an SGML application, so XHTML documents will be able to be parsed by XML parsers. You can view an HTML DTD at `http://www.w3.org/TR/REC-html40/loose.dtd`. According to the HTML standard you should include the following line:

```
<!DOCTYPE HTML PUBLIC "-//W3C//DTD HTML 4.0 //EN">
```

It tells the user agent the location of HTML's DTD. However, it is often left out because, practically speaking it is not necessary, and if you are using browser specific tags which deviate from the specification it may cause unpredictable results.

Styling XML

So far we have created our first application of XML, a language for exchanging data about cameras, and we have created an XML document in our `cameraList1.xml` file. This is great for defining data, as our tags clearly explain their content and it is written in plain text which is easy to transfer, but if we are putting things up on the Web we want our pages to look good. As our earlier example showed, even in an XML aware browser, such as IE5, a plain XML file did not look that impressive. This is because the tags that we have proposed for our camera example don't say anything about how the tags should appear, whereas HTML tells the browser how the data should look.

So, to make it look attractive we must supply another file; a style sheet. In case this sounds like a lot of extra effort, having to write a style sheet as well, let's just have a look at what it means for us.

Why Use Style Sheets?

Unfortunately using style sheets means that we have to use a completely separate language in a separate file to declare how we want our document to be presented.

We can, however, use cascading style sheets (CSSs) to do this (which you met in Chapter 4). In any case HTML 4.0 deprecated many of the style elements in HTML in favor of using CSS. (Deprecated is a term which means that a feature will be supported for backwards compatibility only.) So what are the real advantages of using style sheets?

❑ Improved clarity of the document.

❑ Can help reduce download time, network traffic and server load.

❑ Allows you to change the presentation of several files, just by altering one style sheet.

❑ Allows you to present the same data in different ways for different purposes.

If we do not need to have a lot of rules that tell us how we should display our document included in with the data, then the core content of the file will be easier to read. It is not cluttered up with styling directives like `<font>` tags, which are not important to the content of, say, our `cameraList1.xml` file. With a style sheet, all of the style rules are kept in one file that is just linked to the source document. This means that if several pages use the same type of display, which is often the case as we display an ever-increasing amount of data on web pages, we do not need to repeat the style rules in each page. The browser can download the style sheet and cache it on the client. All other pages can then use the same styling rules. This also means that, should you need to change the style of your site – perhaps if your company changes its corporate colors – then you do not need to laboriously change every file individually by hand, you just change one style sheet and the changes are propagated across the pages. Indeed, on the other hand, it also means that you can use the same data, and display it in different ways for different purposes.

Cascading Style Sheets

We were introduced briefly to cascading style sheets in Chapter 4, when we looked at defining the style of a web site. We saw that Visual InterDev allows you to create and modify CSSs to your own specification.

Cascading style sheets are already popular with HTML developers for the reasons we have just expanded upon here. Here we will look at them in more depth, and see how to use them with XML.

How CSS Works

CSS is a rule-based language comprising of two sections:

❏ A **pattern matching section**, which expresses the association between an element and some action.

❏ An **action section**, which specifies the action to be taken upon the specified section.

For CSS, this means that we have to specify an element and then specify how it has to be displayed. So, if we were to develop a cascading style sheet for our `cameraList1.xml` file, we would have to specify a style for each of the elements that contains markup that we want to display.

CSS separates up the browser screen into areas. As shown in the following diagram, the browser is split up into areas that take a tree-like form. You can think of this much like the tree that Windows Explorer exposes:

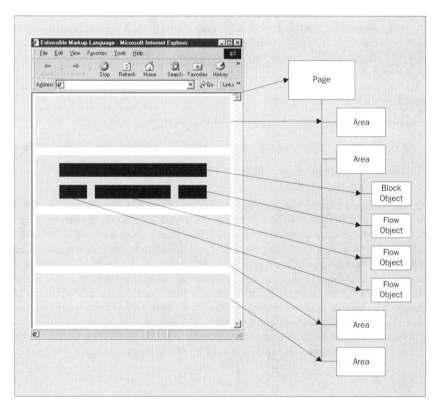

Here we have a page with several **areas**. Inside the second area are a **block object** and a number of **flow objects**. So, using CSS we can specify a style for each of these objects, page, area and flow. Note that we have two types of objects: one looks as though it is taking up the whole line, while the others look to be on the same line (although in practice they are all actually on the same line). The one that is taking up the whole line need not contain text or an image that will take up the whole line, it may just be a short title that needs to be displayed in a line of its own.

It is important to decide whether the values are to be displayed in-line or as a block. The difference being that if they are in-line, the next element will be displayed as if it were on the same line as the previous one, whereas if it is displayed as a block, each will be treated separately. To see the difference, look at the following screen shot. You can see that the product_id and type_id numbers, despite being in separate elements in the cameraList1.xml file, are displayed on the same line. We need to make this decision for each object in CSS.

Let's try it out and write a style sheet for our cameraList1.xml file. While we cannot cover a full reference to CSS here, it will be easy to catch on, and you can always check the specification at http://www.w3.org/tr/css1/if you need to find out a special implementation.

Here is what our cameraList1.xml file will look like once we have written a style sheet for it. As you can see from the URL, it really is the same XML file we wrote earlier in the chapter.

Try it Out – Displaying XML with CSS

You might be tempted to start by opening up the Visual InterDev CSS editor. But this is not the option we will take. The problem is not that it only lets us add HTML elements to which the style is associated, rather that the CSS editor only allows us to make *uppercase* elements. While this does not matter for HTML, we have to remember that XML is case sensitive. To be perfectly honest, this will still work in IE5, however, we should not allow ourselves to get into bad habits, and there is no way of telling that it will work in future versions of Internet Explorer or other browsers. In any case, hand coding the style sheet will teach us more. In fact, if you go on to learn XSL, a more advanced language that can be used to style XML documents, you have to be case sensitive.

1. Fire up Notepad, or some other text editor. Cascading style sheets do not require any kind of heading or opening elements, so we can get straight on to selecting the elements we want to style. In this case we will just be adding styling for the <name>, <product_id>, <type_id>, and <price> elements. So we can just add them to the file like so:

```
name
product_id
type_id
price
```

This specifies the pattern matching section.

2. Having declared the elements that we want to display, we must associate some action with them. So, let's see how to display the content of the <name> element. We want it to be displayed as a block, so we add the opening and closing curly brackets { }. Inside the brackets we add the directive to display the element as a block:

```
name {
display:block;
}
```

This simply specifies that we want to make the title a block level element. We still need to specify the style that the title should be displayed in.

> **All properties are specified with a colon delimiting the attribute, and values have a semi-colon after them.**

3. Add a font to display the content of the <name> element in. In the screen shot you have just seen the browser is using Arial. However, in case the machine using the file does not have Arial, we have allowed it to use Helvetica instead. In addition, we want it to appear in the center of the screen, in a size 20pt, bold font, and in a lilac color. So, we add some more action rules, or style elements. As you can see, these are very similar to those used for HTML:

```
name {
     display:block;
     font-family: Arial, Helvetica;
     font-weight: bold;
     font-size: 20pt;
     color: #9370db;
     text-align: center;
     }
```

4. We can then add some similar rules for the other element content we want to display, like so:

```
product_id {
     display:inline;
     font-family: Arial, Helvetica;
     font-weight: bold;
```

```
      font-size: 12pt;
      color: #c71585;
      text-align: left;
      }

type_id {
      display:inline;
      font-family: Arial, Helvetica;
      font-style: italic;
      font-size: 10pt;
      color: #9370db;
      }

price {
      display:block;
      font-family: Arial, Helvetica;
      font-size: 12pt;
      color: #ff1010;
      text-align: left;
      }
```

5. Having added the styles to the selectors, simply save the file as `cameraList` with a `.css` extension. We have now finished creating our first style sheet for XML. The only problem is that our `cameraList1.xml` file has no way of telling how it should be associated with this style sheet, so we will have to add a link to this style sheet into our original XML file.

Remember, if the program tries to save the file with an extension other than `.css`*, save it again, but this time put the name and extension in quotes.*

6. To add the link to the style sheet, open up your `cameraList1.xml` file again, and add the following line between the XML declaration and the opening `<cameraList>` element:

```
<?xml version="1.0"?>
<?xml:stylesheet href="cameraList.css" type="text/css" ?>
<cameraList>
```

Save the file. The `href` attribute acts just like it would in HTML, while the `type` attribute specifies the type of style sheet that is being attached. This is an example of a processing instruction, which we mentioned earlier in the chapter when we were discussing XML syntax.

> **Remember that, because the style sheet link is still in the XML file, the values of the attributes need to be kept in quotation marks for the XML to be well-formed.**

7. Open the `cameraList.xml` file in your browser. Since it is not an ASP file, you can open it by simply browsing to the file in Windows Explorer, as the web server does not need to do any processing on the file.

Obviously, there is a lot more to CSS than we can describe here, such as all of the appropriate styling tags. To find our more, check out the specification at `http://www.w3.org/style/css/` or pick up a copy of a dedicated book, such as *Professional Style Sheets for HTML and XML* by Wrox Press (ISBN 1-861001-65-7). Note that due to the rapid advancement of XML technologies the XSL section of this book only covers the older XSL specification.

Data as Data

You may still be thinking that this is a lot to learn, just to have data in a self-describing format that you, as a programmer, can read a bit more clearly. After all, we are still getting similar results to what we can already achieve with HTML. Well, let's stop looking at our XML file as just being used for display on the Web, and let's take a look at the different ways that we use the same data that is currently used in HTML-based applications.

If we are keeping our data separate from the rules by which it can be displayed, we can easily use it in other applications for two reasons:

❑ It is not cluttered with style rules.

❑ The tags are describing their content, not presentation just for the Web.

Taking our camera example further, imagine we own a camera store. As we are interested in cameras, our small store does more than display details of cameras on the Web. We use it for the following:

❑ A browser-based application for staff to monitor stock.

❑ To send out details of our catalogue of cameras in stock to customers.

Rather than keeping several versions of the same information in different places, we decided to re-use the same data in different ways. In order to do this, we can add a quantity tag into our XML document to show the numbers of each camera we have in stock.

```
<camera>
    <name>WRC Supra 70</name>
    <product_id>WRC00001</product_id>
    <type_id>1</type_id>
    <price currency="US$">100</price>
    <quantity>3</quantity>
</camera>
```

In fact, why don't you add the `<quantity>` elements to your `cameraList1.xml` file now, as we will be using them later in the chapter. You can enter any value you like, depending on how well you think your store would be stocked.

You may be wondering how a text file like this could actually be used in a practical situation. There are, in fact, a number of ways:

❑ Expose the elements and their values using the W3C Document Object Model.

❑ Use a specialized component that can read XML data, and use it to interact with the application or data store directly.

❑ Use text string manipulation techniques, which look for matching text in the tags and then retrieve their values.

❑ Data Binding in IE4/5.

We shall not look at each of these in detail in this chapter, although we will see how to access the data stored in our XML file.

XML Parsers

For a system to use XML, it requires two components:

❑ The XML processor

❑ The application

The first part, known as the XML processor, checks that the XML file is well-formed (or that it follows the XML specification). Then, so that the computer can interpret the file, the XML processor creates a document tree, which we shall see in a moment. It is the parser, which we have already mentioned, that takes up the role of the XML processor. The application is the part that then uses the data in the tree.

> As we mentioned earlier, some parsers can also check that the syntax of your document instance, such as the `cameraList1.xml` file, is written in accordance with the markup language that defined it, which would be specified in the DTD or other schema, such as our `cameraList.dtd` schema.

Parsers expose the document as a tree, or structured set of objects and properties, implementing the methods that allow you to work with them. Several do this in accordance with the Document Object Model specification from the W3C, which we shall meet in a moment.

This is, in fact, what happens when Internet Explorer 5 opens an XML document; it loads it using a parser called **MSXML**, which is a COM component housed in a file called `msxml.dll`. It can be used like any other COM component in both client and server applications and web pages.

There are many implementations of parsers available, written in a number of languages for different uses. MSXML is also available as a standalone parser for those who need to re-distribute it, and for use on servers that do not have IE5 installed. If you do not have IE5 installed on the machine you are using as your web server, you should either install it to get the XML support, or download the standalone parser from Microsoft at `http://msdn.microsoft.com/xml/`. You just register it like any other COM component, which we'll be seeing more of in Chapter 12. Go to the Start menu, and choose Run. Then type:

```
Regsvr32 c:\foldername\msxml.dll
```

To use the MSXML parser on the client, the client machine must have IE5 installed, or the standalone component registered. Then we can create an instance of it, as we do any other client side component, using:

```
CreateObject("microsoft.xmldom")
```

On the server, in our ASP pages, we use:

```
Server.CreateObject("microsoft.xmldom")
```

For information on other parsers visit http://www.xmlsoftware.com/parsers/.

In order to manipulate the XML document, MSXML implements the W3C XML Document Object Model, so let's turn our attention to that for a moment.

The W3C Document Object Model

The W3C Document Object Model is a set of object-oriented **Application Programming Interfaces** (APIs) for HTML and XML documents. These define how our documents can be structured, setting out objects, properties and methods that allow us to access parts of any XML document (such as their elements, attributes, and their values), and manipulate their structure with programming languages (such as adding elements, attributes, changing their values, and order).

> *Note that Document Object Model is a term that has been applied to browsers for some time, with intrinsic objects such as* window, document *and* history *being considered part of the browser object model. The W3C DOM is an attempt to standardize the different implementations of browsers.*

Here we are not particularly interested in the part of the model that holds information about the browser environment or the HTML pages that it loads. Rather we are interested in the area that contains information about an XML document when loaded in a browser or on a server. On the client this may be done by loading the document directly, but it is often likely to be through the <XML> element in IE5, which we shall meet shortly. This area that we are interested in is also known as the DOM Level 1 and can be seen at http://www.w3.org/tr/rec-dom-level1/. At the time of writing, this was at version 1.0. The W3C recommendation does not actually use the term objects, it uses the term **interfaces** instead. However, objects can be an easier way of thinking about them for web developers.

If we look at our cameraList1.xml file, we can see that its structure is hierarchical. As we have already seen, we have a **root** element, which is <cameraList>, under which there are a number of other elements, known as **child** elements.

```
<?xml version="1.0" ?>
<!DOCTYPE cameraList SYSTEM "cameraList.dtd">
<cameraList>
    <camera>
        <name>WRC Supra 70</name>
        <product_id>WRC00001</product_id>
        <type_id>1</type_id>
        <price currecny="US$">100</price>
    </camera>

</cameraList>
```

We could actually show this in terms of a diagram, like so:

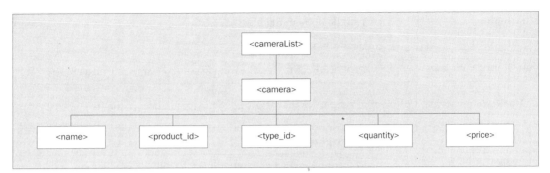

You can think of this as a tree, similar to a family tree in the way that it can be represented. You can see that the root `<cameraList>` element is where the root of the tree grows from, branching out with child elements. The more child elements there are, the more the tree would branch out. So, we would have a new `<camera>` element for each camera in the list, and the tree would get wider. If there were more elements under each `<name>` or `<quantity>` element, the tree would become deeper.

Each of the elements is referred to as a **node** in the W3C XML DOM, and there is an important reason for this. The DOM for HTML is actually quite different from the XML DOM, mainly because we are using XML to create our own languages whose structures are unknown. You can contrast this with HTML, which is a fixed language.

In HTML you always have an `images` collection, whether or not your HTML page includes images. In addition, in HTML you always have one `forms` collection, no matter how many form elements there may be in an HTML document instance. Each form is accessed using the `document.forms` collection, with its own `elements` collection. However, when we are creating our own markup languages in XML, we do not have this previous knowledge. We can be certain that there is a root element, but we cannot be sure of what is underneath it, and we do not know what name it has.

Because of the problem with us creating our own elements, each item within the tree is referred to as a generic **node**. Earlier we said that you could think of the tree in terms of a family tree. If a node has a node underneath it, the node underneath is called a **child**, and the node that sprouts the child is known as a **parent**. So, camera is a parent of name, quantity, product_id etc., and they are children of camera. If a child has no other children it is known as a **leaf** node (borrowing again from the tree metaphor because leaves do not branch off into other branches). If a node is at the same level as another in the hierarchy, they are known as **sibling** nodes; in our example name, quantity, and product_id are siblings.

In this section, we will see how we can use the DOM to retrieve elements from the DOM tree and how to add elements to the tree. But, before we can look at how to retrieve them, we should have a look at the node object and its properties that make nodes available.

The Base Objects

As we have said, the DOM provides a set of objects, methods and properties that allow us to access and manipulate the DOM, which represent the hierarchical nature of the tree. We will not be covering all of the DOM objects here, however we have been referring to nodes, so we should look at the base objects:

Object	Description
Node	A single node in the hierarchy.
NodeList	A collection of nodes.
NamedNodeMap	A collection of nodes allowing access by name as well as index.

The Node object has a number of properties that allow us to navigate through the tree.

Property	Description
childNodes	Returns a NodeList containing the children of the node.
firstChild	Returns a Node that is a reference to the first child.
lastChild	Returns a Node that is a reference to the last child.
parentNode	Returns a Node that is a reference to the parent node.
previousSibling	Returns a Node that is a reference to the previous sibling, i.e. the previous node at the same level in the hierarchy.
nextSibling	Returns a Node that is a reference to the next sibling, i.e. the next node at the same level in the hierarchy.
nodeName	The name of the node.
nodeValue	The value of the node.

This isn't a complete list, but gives you an idea of what's possible. If we refer back to our diagram, and add in some of the relationships, we will be able to see how these work:

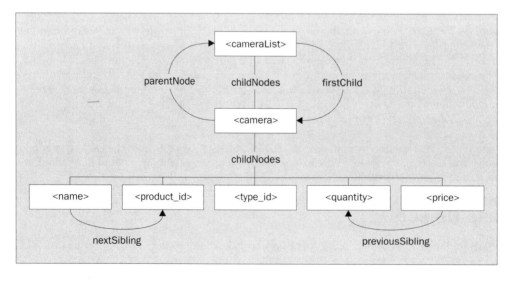

Specific DOM Objects

Because XML is designed to be extensible, as opposed to the fixed structure of HTML, there are also specific objects for different types of node. Most inherit the properties and methods of the Node object, as well as adding specific methods and properties relevant to the particular node type.

Object	Description
Document	The root object for an XML document.
Element	An XML element.
Attr	An XML attribute.
CharacterData	The base object for text information in a document.
CDATASection	Unparsed character data. Equivalent to !CDATA.
Text	The text contents of an element or attribute node.
Comment	An XML comment element.
ProcessingInstruction	A processing instruction, as held in the <? ?> section.

So, having seen some of the objects and properties of the DOM, let's use them to discover values of an XML document programmatically.

To do this we will use the MSXML parser, provided by Microsoft, which as we said exposes the W3C XML DOM.

Retrieving Values from an XML Document

Having said that MSXML exposes the W3C DOM, let's see how our tree would look in terms of nodes in a parser. This particular implementation adds an Error object of the Document object to help us troubleshoot any problems in our application.

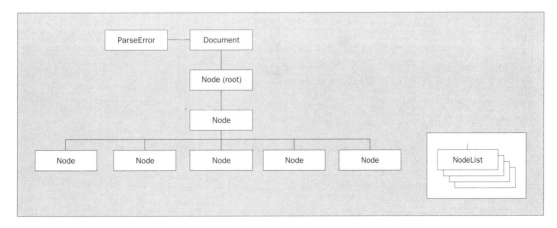

So, the root node represents the <cameraList> element, and its child node is the <camera> element. Underneath that we have the elements <name>, <product_id>, <type_id>, <quantity>, and <price>. The <camera> element could also be seen to expose a set of child nodes, which can be referred to as a nodeList as shown in the extra box on the side.

In addition, MSXML exposes an Error object called parseError, which contains information about the last parsing error. The parseError object exposes a lot of useful information, which can be very helpful for debugging and error handling within pages. It exposes the following information:

Property	Description
errorCode	The error code.
filepos	The absolute position of the error in the XML document.
line	The line number of the line that caused the error.
linepos	The character position of the line containing the error.
reason	The cause of the error.
srcText	The data where the error occurred.
url	The URL of the XML document containing the error.

Using the MSXML parser, we can get to the values of any of these nodes, navigating the tree using the DOM. We shall do precisely this; however, to demonstrate using ASP, we shall use the parser on the server in an ASP page, and write the values of the name, product_id and price to the client.

Try it Out – Walking the DOM

1. Fire up Visual InterDev and enter the following code into a new ASP page called dom_example1.asp in the Wrox Cameras project, replacing *filepath* with the location of cameraList1.xml:

```
<%@LANGUAGE="VBScript"%>

<%
'create an instance of MSXML to retrieve the report
set objXML = Server.CreateObject("microsoft.XMLDOM")

'load the XML document that we want to add to the database
objXML.load("C:\filepath\cameraList1.xml")

'see if it loaded OK, i.e. is a well-formed XML file
If objXML.parseError.errorCode = 0 Then
```

```
strName = objXML.documentElement.firstChild.firstChild.text
strProduct_ID = objXML.documentElement.firstChild.ChildNodes(1).text
strPrice = objXML.documentElement.firstChild.ChildNodes(3).text

Response.Write ("Name:" & strName & "<BR>")
Response.Write ("Product ID:" & strProduct_ID  & "<BR>")
Response.Write ("Price$:" & strPrice & "<BR>")

'write out if an error occurred
Else
Response.Write ("An error occurred loading information, please contact _
              your system administrator.")

End If
%>
```

2. Type in the URL of the file into your browser, and watch the values appear.

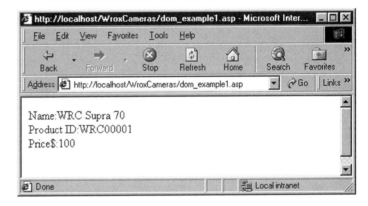

How It Works – Walking the DOM

We start the page with some simple ASP, setting the language that we will be using, and creating an instance of the XML DOM using the MSXML component:

```
<%@LANGUAGE="VBScript"%>


<%
' create an instance of MSXML to hold the xml
set objXML = Server.CreateObject("microsoft.XMLDOM")
```

Next we have to load in the XML file into the DOM, so we use the load() method of MSXML. This is done by referencing the object and the load() method using the traditional dot notation as with any other component. The value of the load method is the URL of the file that is holding the XML.

```
'load the XML document that we want to add to the database
objXML.load("c:\filepath\cameraList1.xml")
```

Next we use MSXML's special parseError object to check that the file loaded properly. We do this by checking to see if the error code of the parseError object is 0. Zero indicates that there is no reported error. Using an If... Then statement, providing everything went well we continue processing. If not, we will raise an error as you will see soon.

```
'see if it loaded OK, i.e. is a well-formed XML file
If objXML.parseError.errorCode = 0 Then
```

Providing that no error occurs we set a variable `strName` to the value of the first child node of the `camera` element, exposed by the `text` property of the node.

```
strName = objXML.documentElement.firstChild.firstChild.text
```

This string will now be holding the value `WRC Supra 70`.

We then use the `nodeList` object, which exposes collections of nodes, to obtain the product id and the price into strings. Note that this is a zero based index, so the `<name>` would be 0. We, however, want the `product_id`, and then the `price` elements, which are 1 and 3 respectively in the index.

```
strProduct_ID = objXML.documentElement.firstChild.ChildNodes(1).text
strPrice = objXML.documentElement.firstChild.ChildNodes(3).text
```

Next we use a simple `response.write` to write out the value of the strings.

```
response.write ("Name:" & strName & "<BR>")
response.write ("Product ID:" & strProduct_ID  & "<BR>")
response.write ("Price$:" & strPrice & "<BR>")
```

To cover ourselves in case an error occurred, we have to finish our `If... Then` statement with an `Else`. If it fails we will write a simple message back to the client.

```
'write out if an error occurred
Else
Response.Write ("An error occurred loading information, please contact your system _
                administrator.")
End If
```

Finally we clean up our resources by setting our XML parser to `nothing`.

```
Set objXML = nothing
%>
```

Of course the presentation leaves something to be desired, but this shows you how you can access the values of the XML elements using the DOM.

This is fine for displaying selected nodes of an XML document. However, in order for it to be truly useful programmatically, we not only need to retrieve nodes, we also need to change the structure of a document. This is done using the `Node` object's methods.

Node Object Methods

In order to change the content of a loaded XML document using the XML DOM we use the read/write methods exposed by the properties. The `Node` object offers us a set of methods for use when editing an XML document. For example the `cloneNode()` method creates a new `Node` object and copies an existing node. You can also set a value to copy all of its descendant nodes as well:

Method	Description
`cloneNode(recurse_children)`	Creates a new node object that is an exact clone of this node; if you include the Boolean parameter `deep` within the parentheses, it will copy all child objects.

There are also four methods that allow us to add, replace or remove existing nodes:

Method	Description
`appendChild(new_node)`	Appends a new object `new_node` to the end of the list of child nodes for this node
`replaceChild(new_node, old_node)`	Replaces the child node `old_node` with the new child node `new_child`, and returns the old child node
`insertBefore(new_node, this_node)`	Inserts a new node object `new_node` into the list of child nodes before `this_node` or at the end of the list if no `this_node` is specified
`removeChild(this_node)`	Removes the child node `this_node` from the list of child nodes for this node, and returns it

Do not let the use of child nodes confuse you; it is not a limitation, as it is expected that you would not need to alter a root element.

We can also check to see if the current node has any child nodes by calling the `hasChildNodes()` method, which returns `true` if the selected node has any child nodes.

Data Binding

In IE5 we are able to create an **XML data island** within a web page. This uses the **XML Data Source Object** (DSO), which is made available to IE5 using the `<XML>` tag. Using the XML DSO we can bind HTML elements to an XML data set. So, we can use a table to display the data and move between the records in the XML file.

Let's use the XML DSO to create a table that allows users to scroll through cameras, their catalogue number and the quantity available.

These are the steps we shall take:

❑ Embed a data island into an HTML page

❑ Link the data island to a source of XML data

❑ Link HTML `<INPUT>` tags into the DSO

❑ Provide buttons for navigating through the XML

First we should say a quick word about the XML DSO.

Data Source Objects

Microsoft Data Access Components (also referred to as Universal Data Access) are a set of COM interfaces, designed to replace ODBC. Rather than merely putting a component wrapper around relational data access, a new layer of abstraction was introduced. Their aim is to provide one single approach to accessing any body of persistent data that can be expressed in terms of rows and columns (comma delimited text, XML, Excel Spreadsheets, relational databases, etc.). This family of interfaces collectively take the name Microsoft Data Access Components (MDAC), providing robust data access services to COM-aware applications.

Although comparatively new, MDAC is the designated successor to ODBC. Although MDAC provides a driver for ODBC sources, database vendors are beginning to provide native COM drivers in order to support MDAC. We have already met ADO (ActiveX Data Objects) earlier in the book. They provide the client side of MDAC. Data binding, which has been used in Microsoft Foundation Classes for a long time, and more recently a feature of Microsoft's implementation of DHTML, is a popular technique now built on top of MDAC.

One of the ideas behind Microsoft's Uniform Data Access strategy is the ability to provide access to data without respect to the underlying native storage format. The XML Data Source Object is an ideal demonstration of this. Although the XML DSO was a Java applet in the earliest implementation of XML support in Windows, in the latest version the DSO is a COM object closely integrated with Internet Explorer. The DSO exposes XML encoded text as both data rowsets (as if they were from a relational database), and also as XML DOM parse trees. The choice of which to use is ours; we are able to use whichever model best suits our programming needs. We shall start off by embedding an XML data island into our page, because XML data islands actually expose the XML DSO.

Try It Out - Creating a Data Island

1. In Visual InterDev create a new HTML page called Databind.htm to incorporate a data island.

2. By selecting Table | Insert Table from the main menu bar, add a table to the page with three rows and two columns.

3. In Design View add the title 'Camera List' to the page and then three titles in each row of the first column of the table: Name, Product ID and Quantity.

4. Add a textbox in each of the rows in the second column using the HTML tab of the Toolbox.

5. Add four buttons below the table as shown in the following screen shot.

6. Change the names of the buttons to First, <, >, and Last. This will be used to go to the first, previous, next, and last records in the XML file.

7. Now if you go to the Source view, you should have the following code:

```
<HTML>
<HEAD>
<META NAME="GENERATOR" Content="Microsoft Visual Studio 6.0">
<TITLE></TITLE>
</HEAD>
<BODY>

<P>Camera List</P>
<P>
<TABLE border=1 cellPadding=1 cellSpacing=1 width="75%">

  <TR>
    <TD>Name</TD>
    <TD><INPUT id=text1 name=text1></TD></TR>
  <TR>
    <TD>Product ID</TD>
    <TD><INPUT id=text2 name=text2></TD></TR>
  <TR>
    <TD>Type_id</TD>
    <TD><INPUT id=text3 name=text3></TD></TR></TABLE></P>

<P><INPUT id=button1 name=button1 style="LEFT: 237px; TOP: 139px" type=button
value=First>
```

```
<INPUT id=button2 name=button2 type=button value="<">
<INPUT id=button3 name=button3 type=button value=">">
<INPUT id=button4 name=button4 type=button value=Last></P>

</BODY>
</HTML>
```

8. We need to add the <XML> element to create the data island. We can put this after the opening <BODY> tag:

```
<BODY>
<XML id=xmlData src = "cameraList1.xml"></XML>
<P>Camera List</P>
```

The `src` attribute must point to the XML file that you have created.

9. We don't need to add new values for the `id` and `name` attributes of the `INPUT` elements. In fact we don't need them at all. However, we do need to add two new attributes to each input element in the table.

❑ `dataFld`

❑ `dataSrc`

They should look like this:

```
<TD><INPUT id=text1 name=text1 dataFld=name dataSrc=#xmlData></TD></TR>
<TD><INPUT id=text2 name=text2 dataFld=product_id dataSrc=#xmlData></TD></TR>
<TD><INPUT id=text3 name=text3 dataFld=type_id dataSrc=#xmlData></TD></TR>
```

10. Add the following to the buttons so that we can move between the records:

```
<INPUT id=button1 name=button1 onclick=xmlData.recordset.moveFirst() type=button
        value=First>
<INPUT id=button2 name=button2 type=button value=&lt; onClick="if
        (xmlData.recordset.absoluteposition > 1) xmlData.recordset.movePrevious()">
<INPUT id=button3 name=button3 type=button value=&gt; onClick="if
        (xmlData.recordset.absoluteposition < xmlData.recordset.recordcount)
        xmlData.recordset.moveNext()">
<INPUT id=button4 name=button4 type=button value=Last
        onClick="xmlData.recordset.moveLast()"> </P>
```

11. Save the file in the same folder as `cameraList1.xml`.

When you load it up the result should look like this:

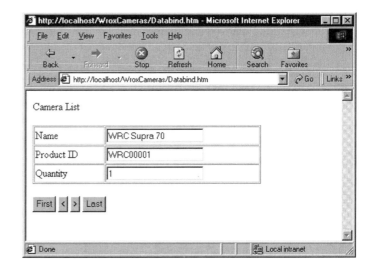

How It Works – Creating a Data Island

We embedded an XML data island into the HTML with the <XML> element. The id attribute gives us a name to refer to the XML that is held within the data island, while the src is the source. Note that this need not be an XML document, it can be any source that generates XML, such as an ASP page.

```
<XML id="xmlData" src="cameraList1.xml"></XML>
```

We can now refer to the XML throughout the document using the id XMLdata. It is actually a COM object, but we do not need to use the CreateObject method, because of this new <XML> tag.

Note that this is an HTML element and not an XML element, so it must have a separate closing tag - you can't use <XML ID="xmlData" />.

There are actually two ways of providing the XML content. If we did not want to specify an external source we could have simply placed the XML content within the boundaries of the <XML> tags:

```
<XML id="xmlData"></XML>
<cameraList>
<camera>
   <name>WRC Supra 70</name>
   <product_id>WRC00001</product_id>
   <type_id>1</type_id>
   <price currency="US$">100</price>
</camera>

...

<camera>
   <name>WRC Mini 70</name>
   <product_id>WRC00003</product_id>
   <type_id>3</type_id>
   <price currency="US$">190</price>
</camera>
</cameraList>
```

When the page is loaded, Internet Explorer will read the data from `cameraList1.xml` file. When a data island is loaded with a page, Internet Explorer transparently loads the data into a parse tree and offers several COM interfaces for our use. The standard DSO interfaces allow XML elements to participate in data binding as if the data were coming from a database. In addition, the familiar XML DOM interfaces are available as well. This is not surprising, as MSXML is the component that implements the XML DSO. The DSO parses the XML content and keeps bound elements synchronized with the content. As the user navigates through the data, the DSO will navigate through the parse tree, exposing each top-level child in turn as a 'row' of data.

We already have our XML data island, which exposes the XML DSO. When the page is loaded we can either use the XML file through the standard DOM interfaces or through the COM interfaces supplied by the XML DSO.

Displaying the Data

We display the camera data by binding the XML DSO to HTML `<INPUT>` elements, allowing us to navigate the data as if it were coming from a relational database.

We simply linked the `<INPUT>` elements in our page to the XML DSO by adding two attributes:

- ❑   `dataSrc`
- ❑   `dataFld`

The `dataSrc` attribute value is the name of the DSO with the prefix #. Remember, in this example, we called our data island `XMLData`, so we use `dataSrc="#XMLData"`.

The `dataFld` attribute specifies which column of the rowset provided by the DSO should be bound to the page element. In this example, our first `<INPUT>` element displays the name of the camera, so we need to link to the `<name>` element of our XML file.

```
<INPUT dataFld="name" dataSrc="#xmlData" style="HEIGHT: 22px; WIDTH:
          286px">
```

That will bind the user interface elements to the XML data. But, when we first view the page it will display the first `<name>` element from our XML file. So, we need to give the users some way of looking at the details of the other cameras.

Navigating through the Data Island

There are a number of ways we could move between the data in the XML file. In this example we will use the `recordset` property. All the properties and methods of an ADO recordset are accessible through the data island's `recordset` property. In our example, we would move the internal cursor of the DSO to the next row of the recordset like so:

```
XMLdata.recordset.moveNext()
```

This is what we will be using to allow the users to move between the cameras in stock on our page. This is just how we can manipulate data from a database using the ADO recordset property.

The key is in the inline JavaScript fragments we provide to handle the `onClick` event. For example, look at the handler for moving ahead one row:

```
if (xmlData.recordset.absoluteposition < xmlData.recordset.recordcount)
                                   xmlData.recordset.moveNext()
```

The ADO `recordset` object is a child of the data island, and the `absoluteposition` property tells us what row the cursor is on. In this handler, if the cursor isn't on the last row of the recordset, we tell it to advance to the next row. When this happens, the DSO keeps the `<INPUT>` elements synchronized with the recordset, and the user sees the values for the next `<camera>` element.

It's as simple as that. We don't need manipulation scripts and we have the data exposed by the XML DSO as if it were coming from a relational database. Which, in fact, it could be, as we will see in the next section.

Creating XML from a Relational Database

Many networks already have a lot of information held in relational databases. If we are writing systems that are based on XML, we need a way of generating XML from the data stored in relational databases. Luckily we can do this quite easily with ASP.

So, let's have a look at the way we can create XML from a database, using ASP.

We will be using the Wrox Cameras database, which we met in Chapter 5 and which is holding details of the cameras. The product table holds the product_id, name, type_id, price, thumbnail and full size picture. From this, we want to create the following XML file from the database:

```
<?xml version="1.0" ?>
<cameraList>

<camera>
<product_id>WRC00006</product_id>
<name>WRC Digi 35</name>
<price>420</price>
<product_type>Digital</product_type>
</camera>

<camera>
<product_id>WRC00004</product_id>
<name>WRC Focus 210</name>
<price>220</price>
<product_type>35mm SLR</product_type>

<camera>
<product_id>WRC00005</product_id>
<name>WRC Focus 300</name>
<price>310</price>
<product_type>35mm SLR</product_type>
</camera>
```

So, let's see how we create the XML using ASP.

Try it Out – Creating XML from a Database

1. Fire up Visual InterDev with a new HTML page, and remove all of the HTML. Save the file as `createXML.asp`.

2. Enter the following code:

```
<%@ Language=VBScript %>
<% Response.ContentType = "text/xml" %>
<?xml version="1.0" ?>
<cameraList>
```

3. Copy the database connections from your `Products.asp` file. Your code will differ slightly to this below, in that the name of your machine in the connection string will be different (my machine is called `Vaio`):

```
<%
'retrieve catalogue of products from DB and write to table
dim adoConn
dim adoCmd
dim adoRS
dim strConnectionString

'create ADO Objects
set adoConn = server.CreateObject("ADODB.Connection")
set adoCmd = server.CreateObject("ADODB.Command")
set adoRS = server.CreateObject("ADODB.Recordset")

'define connection string
strConnectionString="Provider=SQLOLEDB.1;Persist Security Info=False;User _
            ID=sa;Initial Catalog=WroxCameras;Data Source=Vaio;Locale _
            Identifier=2057;Connect Timeout=15;Use Procedure for Prepare=1; _
            Auto Translate=True;Packet Size=4096;Workstation ID=Vaio"

'set ADO Command Properties
adoCmd.CommandType = 1
adoCmd.CommandText = "SELECT product.product_id, product.name, product.price, _
            product_type.type_description FROM product, product_type WHERE _
            product.type_id = product_type.product_type ORDER BY name"

'Open the Connection
adoConn.Open strConnectionString

'associate the Command with the Open Connection
adoCmd.ActiveConnection = adoConn

'retrieve recordset
set adoRS = adoCmd.Execute
```

4. Then add this following code yourself:

```
    do while not adoRS.EOF
      strProduct_id = adoRs("product_id")
      strName = adoRs("name")
      strPrice = adoRs("price")
      strProduct_type = adoRs("type_description")
%>
<camera>
<product_id><% = strProduct_id %></product_id>
<name><% = strName %></name>
<price><% = strPrice %></price>
<product_type><% = strProduct_type %></product_type>
</camera>

<%
    adoRS.MoveNext
    loop

'close connection and set ADO objects to nothing
adoConn.Close
set adoConn = nothing
set adoCmd = nothing
set adoRS = nothing

%>

</cameraList>
```

5. Type in the URL for the page into your browser and the result should look like this:

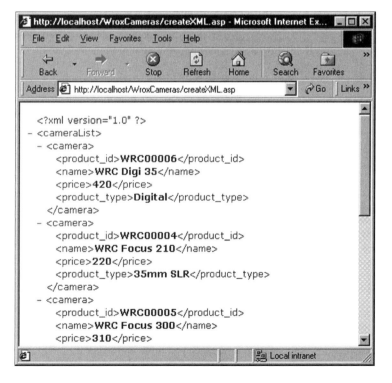

How it Works – Creating XML from a Database

`createXML.asp` starts by setting the language that we are using, and the `ContentType` property of the `Response` object to ensure that we have the correct headers written back to the client. As we will be sending back XML, the value is `"text/xml"`, and this allows us to simply write XML back to the client rather than HTML outside of the ASP delimiters.

```
<%@LANGUAGE="VBScript"%>
<% Response.ContentType = "text/xml" %>
```

We then write out the XML declaration and the opening `<cameraList>` element:

```
<?xml version="1.0" ?>
<cameraList>
```

Having already set the content type to XML the receiving application should know what it is going to receive, and anything outside the ASP delimiters will be treated as XML.

Next we use exactly the same database technique used in the *Presenting Data Using ADO* example of Chapter 9 to select the data we need from the database, and put it into a recordset object.

Next comes the interesting part. This is where we start a loop to go through the content of the recordset and set a variable to the value of the data we want from the recordset:

```
do while not adoRS.EOF
    strProduct_id = adoRs("product_id")
    strName = adoRs("name")
    strPrice = adoRs("price")
    strProduct_type = adoRs("type_description")
%>
```

Here we will have the variable `strName` holding the name of the product from the first record in the recordset. In turn the variables `strProduct_id`, `strProduct_type` and `strPrice` hold the `product_id`, `type_description` and the `price` respectively from the database.

So, having gathered this information from the recordset we can start writing the XML out. This is done with some simple string manipulation. We write an opening element for each, then open the ASP delimiters, write out the value of the appropriate string for each element, close the delimiters, and add a closing tag. Like so:

```
<camera>
<name><% = strName %></name>
<product_id><% = strProduct_id %></product_id>
<price><% = strPrice %></price>
<product_type><% = strProduct_type %></product_type>
</camera>
```

Having done this, we can loop through to the next record; the loop will continue until the end of the file is found.

```
<%
    adoRS.MoveNext
    loop
```

We then clean up our resources:

```
'close connection and set ADO objects to nothing
adoConn.Close
set adoConn = nothing
set adoCmd = nothing
set adoRS = nothing

%>
```

and add one final closing root element:

```
</cameraList>
```

And that's all there is to fetching the content from the database and writing it out as XML.

Summary

In this chapter we have learnt a lot about the exciting new technology XML. We have seen how it is very similar in appearance to HTML. However, it is very different in what it allows us to do. The contents of the elements are described in the tag name, that we can create ourselves.

Because XML is plain text, it is easy to transport between different applications on different platforms, and it is a truly open standard for exchanging all sorts of data. It also has some advantages over relational data in that we can express hierarchies.

We have seen how to write our own XML files, even create them from relational database content. We have seen how to render XML documents using CSS, and how we can access values in our XML documents. So you should be able to see where it may help you out in your programming tasks. Should you want to learn more about it, check out *Professional XML* from Wrox Press (ISBN 1-861003-11-0).

Specifically, we have seen:

- ❑ An introduction to the new topic of XML
- ❑ How to write XML documents
- ❑ How to write a schema for new languages that you create
- ❑ How to display your XML using CSS for the Web
- ❑ How to access values of XML documents using the W3C DOM
- ❑ How to bind XML element content to HTML elements
- ❑ How to create XML from a database

Hopefully you will have seen some of the advantages of this exciting new technology and will be able to make use of it in your web applications.

Error Handling and Debugging

If you have successfully copied every exercise in this book to date without one HTML error occurring, then well done! You are a better typist than I ammm! For the rest of us mere mortals, errors are a part of life, and learning ways to detect and correct them is a necessity.

There are three main types of error that can creep into your code:

- ❑ **Syntax** errors occur when you have written code incorrectly in your page. This might be a genuine typing mistake, or not having written a statement correctly.

- ❑ **Run-time** errors occur when an unexpected or invalid result happens, as a result of your code. For example, if you try to divide a number by zero, you will get a run-time error.

- ❑ **Logic** errors occur when the code that you wrote works correctly, but it just doesn't do what you intended it to. This sort of error is the hardest to detect, because often no error messages appear and everything seems to be okay, but possibly the results of a calculation might be incorrect. If you notice something like this, then you either need to look at your code again manually, or else use the debugging tools outlined in this chapter to single step through your code and find out where the error is.

As well as these three main types of errors, you might also have problems due to incorrect setup of your programs, for which the solution is often to reinstall the software, or reconfigure it. This chapter will not cover this sort of error, but is instead concerned with errors in the script that you write.

Errors can occur in both your client side script and server side script, so it is important to know how to detect and remove them (**debugging**), and how to cope with them gracefully (**error handling**). Luckily, Visual InterDev includes some excellent features for assisting you in tracking down bugs in your code.

In this chapter, we are going to cover the following topics:

- ❑ Why use error handling?
- ❑ Writing error handlers.
- ❑ Enabling and using client side script debugging.
- ❑ Enabling and using server side script debugging.

So let's jump in by learning why we should bother with error handling in the first place.

Why Use Error Handling?

There is nothing more embarrassing than writing a wonderful application that falls over the first time a user presses the OK button. Error handling might not stop the error creeping into your code, but it can definitely help your application to fail in a graceful manner. If we are going to try to understand why error handling is important, we need to look at just how easy it is to introduce errors into your code.

Let's take a look at this simple snippet of code:

```
Dim x,y

x=Request.Form("txtStartingNumber")
y=Request.Form("txtDivideBy")

Response.Write x/y
```

This code at first glance looks pretty solid, but in fact it is a hive of potential errors just waiting to occur. What this code attempts to do is to read a form submitted by the user. That form contains two textboxes, one in which the user has entered a number, and the other in which they have entered a second number to divide the first number by. The user expects to receive the answer.

This will all work fine as long as the user is fairly careful. However:

❏   If the user enters text instead of a number, you will have difficulty trying to divide it.

❏   If the user enters 0 in the Divide By box, you will be trying to divide a number by zero, which is not allowed.

Both of these circumstances will result in an error. An easy way to handle this particular error would be to put some *validation* on the client web page (the form which requests the user to enter the two numbers), that attempts to detect potential errors before they occur. However, sometimes this might not be possible because of client compatibility issues and the browser not understanding script. Also, what happens if an error occurs in the client side script?

Error handling enables us to trap these errors when they occur. By writing an error handler around your code, when an error occurs it can be handled gracefully, with a message appearing such as A number cannot be divided by zero. Please enter a number greater than zero in the Divide By text box. Obviously, this is a lot nicer than a big hash of HTTP server script error codes appearing all over a web page.

In Appendix D you will find a list of the various error codes that you might come across, because even with error handling, you as the programmer will still need to know what the error codes represent.

Error handling gives you the chance to look good when you can't think of all the potential problems. It makes an application much more robust, and in cases where an error is not too severe, can enable the script to keep running without stopping immediately.

Because error handling is so important, it is a good idea to implement error handling at the *beginning* of the development of your web applications. This can save time by helping you to iron out bugs during development, and can make testing much easier. It is a good idea to include error handling in all of your critical code, as a little time spent at the beginning protecting against unforeseen events can make a big difference later on when a bug occurs. The bottom line is: use error handling – it promotes a professional product that works.

Let's have a look at how to write error handlers into your code.

Writing Error Handlers

Writing an error handler is easy – so easy, in fact, that it's a shame more people don't do it all the time. The number of un-handled errors that I have encountered in arguably professional web applications is huge – and I've been guilty of more than a few myself in the past. It's all been good experience, as they say, and now I am a firm believer in writing error handlers into my code.

It is possible to write error handlers for both *server side* and *client side* script. Let's first look at how to handle errors in VBScript – this uses the same method for both client side and server side scripting.

Error Handling in VBScript

Of the two main scripting languages VBScript has, until recently, been by far the easiest for error handling purposes. VBScript uses a similar syntax to Visual Basic for handling errors, but be warned – it offers only a limited subset of Visual Basic's capabilities.

For those of you who are familiar with error handling in Visual Basic, the biggest difference is that you cannot use an `On Error Goto Errorhandler` statement. With VBScript you are limited to `On Error Resume Next` and `On Error Resume`.

`On Error Resume Next` causes execution to continue to the line immediately after an error occurs. This means that your code does not stop executing immediately, it simply moves on to the next line, effectively ignoring the error. You can use the **Error object** (`Err`) to handle the error, as shown in the example on the next page.

`On Error Resume` causes execution to try again at the line where the error occurred. This could potentially get you into a bit of a loop, so use it carefully and keep track of what is happening.

The `Error` object contains details of the most recent error. Its properties are:

❑ `Number`, which contains the error number.

❑ `Description`, which contains a textual description of the error.

❑ `Source`, which contains the source of the error (the file path and line number).

The `Clear` method is used to clear the `Err` object of all errors, and should be used once you have finished handling the error.

There is also a Raise method, which you can use to generate your own errors if you want to. This can be useful in client side script if you want to handle custom errors alongside real errors.

This means that you can use the On Error Resume Next statement to continue processing, and write code such as:

```
On Error Resume Next

intResult = intNumber/intDividedBy

If Err<>0 Then          'an error occurred

  Select Case Err.Number
  Case 11          'divide by zero
    Response.Write "You cannot divide by Zero"
  Case Else
    Response.Write "An error occurred. Number: " & Err.Number & ", Description: " _
                & Err.Description
  End Select

  Err.Clear          'clear the error object

End if

'continue code
```

If an error occurs, then the Err object will not be equal to zero, meaning that we can try and handle the error. If Err is equal to zero, then the error handling code within the If statement is not executed.

Once the error has occurred, the above code checks the Err.Number – if it is 11 (division by zero), then a message about dividing by zero is written. Any other error will write the details of the error.

Here is a list of some of the more common error codes that you might encounter in VBScript (there is a full list in Appendix E):

Error Code	Message
5	Invalid procedure call or argument
11	Division by zero
13	Type mismatch
35	Sub or Function not defined
53	File not found
58	File already exists
70	Permission denied
75	Path/File access error

Error Code	Message
76	Path not found
91	Object variable or With block variable not set
92	For loop not initialized
94	Invalid use of Null
424	Object required
429	ActiveX component can't create object
438	Object doesn't support this property or method
445	Object doesn't support this action
446	Object doesn't support named arguments
448	Named argument not found
449	Argument not optional
450	Wrong number of arguments or invalid property assignment

Displaying Error Messages to the User

In *client side* script, it is common to use `Window.Alert` to display to the user an error message in a box, such as:

Another idea is to modify the `innerHtml` or `innerText` properties of a label control, to display well-formatted error messages actually within the page.

When you use *server side* script, the `Window.Alert` method is useless. For server side script errors, any error messages should be written into the HTML that is output to the user. To do this, use the standard `Response.Write` statement.

Try it Out – Handling an Error in Client Side VBScript

We are going to create a very basic calculator and then trap possible errors in it – such as our friendly division by zero error. We will be using client side VBScript and DHTML to create our calculator.

1. Open the project Client Script Test.

2. Create a new HTML page, `Calculator2.htm` and open it in the editor.

3. In the Source view, type the following details:

```
<HTML>
<HEAD>
<META NAME="VI60_DefaultClientScript" CONTENT="VBScript">

<META NAME="GENERATOR" CONTENT="Microsoft Visual Studio 6.0">
<TITLE>Calculator</TITLE>
</HEAD>
<BODY>
<P>Simple Calculator:</P>
<P>
<INPUT ID=txtNumber1 NAME=txtNumber1>
<SELECT ID=selOperator NAME=selOperator>
<OPTION SELECTED VALUE=+>+</OPTION>
<OPTION VALUE=->-</OPTION>
<OPTION VALUE=*>*</OPTION>
<OPTION VALUE=/>/</OPTION>
</SELECT>
<INPUT ID=txtNumber2 NAME=txtNumber2>
</P>
<P><INPUT TYPE="button" VALUE="=" ID=cmdEquals NAME=cmdEquals>
<STRONG><LABEL ID=lblAnswer></LABEL></STRONG></P>

</BODY>
</HTML>
```

4. This has created a basic form, we now need to add some script to the "=" button. Open the Script Outline view.

5. Locate the entry under **Client Objects & Events** for **cmdEquals**, expand it and double click on the onclick event to create our basic event handler.

6. Type the following code into the cmdEquals_onclick event:

```
<SCRIPT ID=clientEventHandlersVBS LANGUAGE=vbscript>
<!--

Sub cmdEquals_onclick
  Dim strResult
  If txtNumber1.Value="" or txtNumber2.Value="" Then
    Window.Alert("Please complete all information")
  Elseif Not(isnumeric(txtNumber1.Value) and isnumeric(txtNumber1.Value)) Then
    Window.Alert("Please enter only numbers")
  Else

    'okay to calculate
    On Error Resume Next
    Select Case selOperator.Value
    Case "+"
      strResult = CDBl(txtNumber1.Value) + CDbl(txtNumber2.Value)
    Case "-"
      strResult = CDBl(txtNumber1.Value) - CDbl(txtNumber2.Value)
    Case "*"
      strResult = CDBl(txtNumber1.Value) * CDbl(txtNumber2.Value)
    Case "/"
```

344

```
      strResult = CDBl(txtNumber1.Value) / CDbl(txtNumber2.Value)
   End Select

   'CDbl is a VBScript conversion function which returns
   'the argument value converted to a variant type of double

   'detect any errors
   If Err <> 0 Then
     If Err=11 Then          'division by 0
     Window.Alert("You cannot divide by zero")
       strResult = "Division by zero error"
     Else
       Window.Alert("An Error occurred. Error Number: " & Err.Number & " Details: " _
                   & Err.Description)
       strResult = "Err " & Err.Number
     End if
     Err.Clear
   End if
   lblAnswer.InnerText = strResult
 End if
End Sub

-->
</SCRIPT>
```

You will notice that in the code above, Err was sometimes used in place of Err.Number. This is because Number is the default property of the Err object.

7. Save your file and view it in your browser. You should see a very basic calculator form like the following:

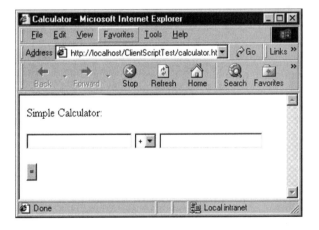

8. The idea here is to enter a number in the first box, select an operator from the drop down box, and then enter a number in the second box. Pressing the '=' button displays the result in a label. Use it to add 10 and 20 together. It should successfully display the answer of 30. If you press the '=' button without entering any information, it should prompt you to enter information. If you do not enter numbers but instead enter text, you should be told to just enter numbers.

9. Try to divide 10 by 0. The error handling code that we added should successfully detect that an error has occurred, and the following error message should appear:

10. Pressing OK in the error dialog should enable us to correct our mistakes and continue calculating.

That's all there is to it. Using VBScript, it is quite easy to trap errors and handle them in a tidy manner. The same methods work in both server side script and client side script, making for a pretty nice time of things if you have the luxury of coding this way.

Handling Errors in Server Side VBScript

As we've said, error handlers in server side VBScript are the same as in client side VBScript. We will see this with the following quick example. About the only real difference with errors in server side script is that they occur *before* the page is sent to the user, meaning that the user sees something like this when they try to browse a page with errors:

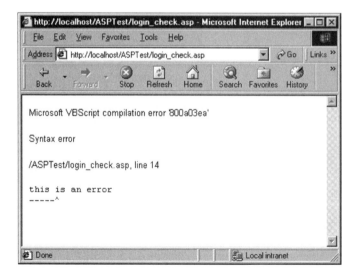

When you handle an error in server side script, you can display error messages to the user using `Response.Write`. This means that the user will see a more user-friendly error message, such as:

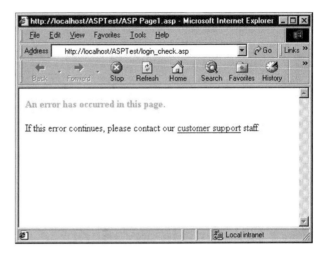

A more user-friendly error message has been achieved by simply using `Response.Write` in our handler. With this in mind, an error handler for server side VBScript would look like:

```
On Error Resume Next

If Err<>0 Then
  Response.Write "An error has occurred in this page.<BR>If this continues, _
      Please contact our <A HREF="support.htm">customer support</A> staff."
End if
```

Looks familiar? As advertised, it's the same code as for client side script. Just remember to use `Response.Write` as opposed to `Window.Alert`.

Handling Data Access Errors in ADO

If you are using ADO to access your database with server side script as we saw in Chapter 9, it is possible to trap and handle various data errors, such as problems connecting to the database, errors in any SQL statements passed, and so on. The ADO `Connection` object provides an **Errors collection** to make this easy. In fact, apart from having to use this to get at the errors, the only unusual aspect of trapping data access errors is the fact that there can often be more than one error. What this means is that you should use a loop to ensure that you get *all* of the errors.

Here is an example of error handling script for dealing with ADO errors:

```
Dim cnnMyConnection
Dim strErrorMessage

Set cnnMyConnection = Server.CreateObject("ADODB.Connection")

cnnMyConnection.Open strConnectionString          'connection string to DB

If cnnMyConnection.Errors <> 0 then

  'errors have occurred, so loop through errors collection for more information
  strErrorMessage = "An error occurred while accessing data. Details were: " & vbcrlf
```

```
  For Each Error in cnnMyConnection.Errors
    StrErrorMessage = strErrorMessage & Error.Description & vbcrlf
  Next

  Response.Write strErrorMessage         'write error message to user

End If
```

To use the `Errors` collection you need to have explicitly created a `Connection` object as in the example above. After that, after any database action you just need to check that the errors count is not equal to zero. If the errors count is not equal to zero, an error has occurred and you should write out an error message to the user, using code similar to that above.

Let's now have a look at how to handle errors in JavaScript.

Error Handling in JavaScript

If you are writing JavaScript for Internet Explorer 4.0 and above, or Netscape Navigator 3.x or above, then it is possible to trap errors using the `window.onerror` event.

The `window.onerror` event occurs whenever an error happens in a document, and it enables programmers to write code to respond to the error. When the `onerror` event fires, it passes information to a function that is defined as an error handler for the whole document. The following example explains this:

```
<SCRIPT Language=JavaScript>

function doc_error_handler(message,url,line)
{
  /* The parameters are passed by the error event automatically, and are:
  message: - a description of the error message
  url: - the url where the error was generated
  line: - the line number at which the error occurred
  */

  //add some code to handle the error

  //specify that the error has been handled successfully
  return true;
}

//tell the browser which function handles errors on this document, i.e. the above one
window.onerror = doc_error_handler;
</SCRIPT>
```

So, if your clients are using one of the fairly recent browsers mentioned above, it is quite a simple manner to trap errors in JavaScript.

Let's take a look at handling JavaScript errors in practice.

Try it Out – Handling an Error in Client Side JavaScript

We are going to write a simple form with a button on it. When the user clicks on the button, it will attempt to execute a nonsensical JavaScript function, which should trigger our event handler using `window.onerror`.

1. Open the Client Script Test project.

2. Create a new HTML page, `jserror.htm`, and open it in the editor.

3. In the Source view, enter the following information:

```html
<HTML>
<HEAD>
<META NAME="VI60_DefaultClientScript" content=JavaScript>

<META NAME="GENERATOR" Content="Microsoft Visual Studio 6.0">
<TITLE></TITLE>
<SCRIPT ID=clientEventHandlersJS LANGUAGE=javascript>
<!--

function button1_onclick() {
  this.has.many.errors = 50
}

function error_handler(message, url, line)
{
  alert("An error has occurred." + "\n" +
    "The error was: " + message + "\n" + "in URL: " + url + "\n" +
    "Line: " + line);

  return true;
}

window.onerror = error_handler;

//-->
</SCRIPT>
</HEAD>
<BODY>
<FORM>
<P><INPUT ID=button1 NAME=button1 TYPE=button VALUE="Click Me" LANGUAGE=javascript
onclick="return button1_onclick()"></P>
</FORM>
</BODY>
</HTML>
```

349

4. Save the file, and view it in Netscape Navigator 4.x. When you click on the Click Me button, an error will occur as the browser tries to understand the code in the function `button1_onclick`:

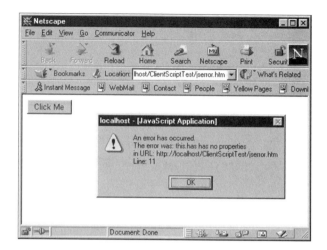

So there you have it – using `window.onerror` enables you to create a global error handler for your page that will intercept and handle any errors that occur in your JavaScript.

Debugging

Now that we understand how to write error handlers, let's put things in perspective – an error handler will help your application handle errors that you cannot easily prevent – such as division by zero, but it does not mean that your code will work.

If your code has wonderful error handlers that trap for all sorts of errors, a simple mistake in your code will cause those error handlers to be continually called – and the work that you want your code to achieve will never get done. In these cases, you will want to locate the incorrect code in your script and fix it. This process is known as debugging, and Visual InterDev includes a full debugging environment that you can use to great effect.

Errors can creep into your code both in server side script, and in client side script, so Visual InterDev gives you tools to debug in both environments. Let's take a look first at how to debug client side script.

Debugging Client Side Script

When you are searching for errors in your code, there are many tried and tested techniques that apply equally well in a web environment as in a traditional environment. Foremost among these is the judicious use of **messages** to gauge the progress of your code.

Messages can be written to keep track of what your script is doing. For example, if you have a loop of code that has a bug happening somewhere in it, you could write an `Alert` statement every time the loop occurs, and display the various values of the variables being used. In server side script, you could write lots of messages to the `Response` object and see what was happening that way. This sort of debugging works, but has some big disadvantages:

❑   It is tiresome and laborious.

❑   You constantly have to stop and start to widen the scope of your search, by adding more alerts.

❑   It is intrusive, i.e. you are changing the code that you are trying to debug, which might possibly add some other errors into the code.

❑   You can often forget to remove all the alerts, leaving weird messages popping out at users of the finished application.

This is not to say don't use alerts – often they are great for quick one-off checks, but Visual InterDev provides some much better tools.

The Visual InterDev editor doubles as a fully featured script debugging environment, enabling you to debug both client side and server side script. For those of you familiar with debugging in Visual Basic, you should be right at home in the Visual InterDev debugging environment. Let's take a look at how it works.

Enabling Client Side Script Debugging

If you are only going to be debugging client script in .htm files, Visual InterDev is ready to go without any extra work. If you want to debug script from Active Server Pages however, you need to be running Internet Information Server 4.0 (or PWS 4.0 for NT Workstations, which is essentially IIS 4.0) or later versions – PWS on Win 9x will not do it. Assuming that you have the correct web server, you need to do a little groundwork to get things started.

Before you can actually start debugging ASP pages, which might contain both client side and server side script, you need to *enable* debugging. Debugging has to be enabled on your server, but to save you the effort of switching out of the IDE, Visual InterDev offers a handy option to automatically switch on debugging on the server from within the IDE.

Try it Out – Automatically Enabling Client Side Script Debugging in ASP Pages

Here are the steps necessary to enable client side script debugging in ASP pages. Open the project ASP Test and do the following:

1.   In the Project Explorer window, right mouse click on the project and choose Properties.

2.   Choose the Launch tab.

3.   In the Server Script frame, ensure that Automatically enable ASP server-side debugging on launch is checked.

4.   Press OK.

Each time you start debugging in Visual InterDev, this ensures that the server is configured for debugging. When you stop debugging by selecting End in the Debug menu, Visual InterDev will automatically reset the server settings to their previous values.

How to Debug Client Side Script

Now that we are ready for it, let's look at how to actually debug client side script. The first thing to realize is that script in a web page, as in all programming environments, is executed in a *top to bottom* manner. The browser will interpret statements at the beginning of the page and continue until it reaches the bottom. The exceptions to this are sub procedures, functions, and event handlers, all of which change the flow of execution, as we discussed in Chapter 6.

Code inside a sub procedure or function is not executed until it is *called* in another line of code. If the code is called in the normal flow of code, then eventually your browser will execute it. However, code in event handlers is only executed when the event is fired. This means that if you want to debug code in the `onclick` event of a button, or in a sub procedure that is called from that event, you must first trigger the event by clicking on the button, in order to debug the code.

With this in mind, debugging is simply a matter of setting a **breakpoint** in your code, ensuring that the flow of execution gets to your breakpoint by triggering any necessary events, and then sitting back and looking at the results. Let's try it.

Try it Out – Debugging Client Side Script

We are going to debug the `calculator.htm` file that we created back in Chapter 6. We are going to use debugging to step through the execution of code and find an error that we will purposely introduce.

1. Open the Client Script Test project.

2. Open the file calculator.htm by double clicking on it in the **Project Explorer** window.

3. Let's quickly introduce an error. We're not going to be imaginative here - we just want to show how things work. Find the comment line `'detect any errors`, and insert a new line above it as shown:

```
End Select
strResult = 10          'this is an error - all calculations will equal 10
'detect any errors
```

4. So now we've got a highly sophisticated and difficult to locate error. Now we'll use the debugging tools to track it down. In order for debugging to happen, we need to make the page the start page for the project. This tells the debugger that we will start debugging on this page. In the **Project Explorer** window, right mouse click on calculator.htm and choose **Set as Start Page**.

5. We now need to set a breakpoint, which is the place where we want the editor to stop and let us control afterwards. Let's add a breakpoint to the first line of the event handler. To do this, click in the gray area to the left of the line, and a big brown circle will appear to symbolize a breakpoint:

```
Sub cmdEquals_onclick
    dim strResult

    if txtNumber1.value="" or txtNumber2.value="" then
```

You can remove a breakpoint by clicking on it in the gray sidebar.

6. Let's also stick a **watch** on the `strResult` variable, since we are fairly certain that the error is going to happen in that variable. When debugging, a Watch window is displayed that shows the values of any watches that we have defined. So, by setting a watch on the `strResult` variable, we can easily see its value at any time. Using the watch, you can also change the value of a watch variable to help you continue processing. To add a watch, double click on the variable name, strResult, so that it is selected. Then, right mouse click on the selection and choose Add Watch from the menu. The Watch window will appear to show you that a watch has been added:

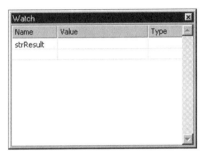

7. Right then, we're ready to start debugging. To do this, select Start from the Debug menu, or else press *F5*. Visual InterDev will launch Internet Explorer and the page will be displayed looking just fine. If we had added a breakpoint in code outside of a function, chances are it would have stopped processing by now and thrown up the debugging environment. We added code into an event handler, so we need to trigger it. Use the calculator to add 20 + 25, then press the '=' button. Our introduced bug would display the answer of 10, but we have added our breakpoint at the beginning of the function, so something else happens instead – we see the debugging environment:

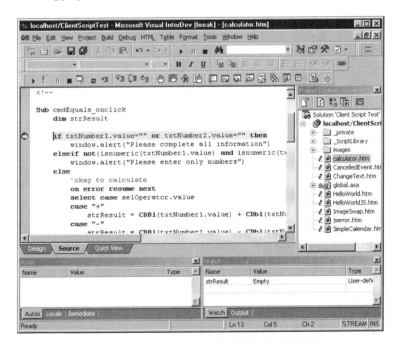

8. As you can see, execution has stopped at the line after our breakpoint. Why is this? We actually selected a Dim statement for our breakpoint. Dim statements are not valid breakpoints, so the debugger automatically moved on to the next line. The Watch window at the bottom right shows us that, at the current time, the value of strResult is empty. Since we know that the bug we are trying to find always forces the result to be 10, no matter what, we are looking for strResult to be 10. Once you are in debug mode, you **step** through (**into**) lines of code which the browser executes as you do so. It is also possible to step **over** lines of code if you do not want to execute them, or to step **out** of the current sub procedure or function without finishing the rest of the code. The toolbar contains three buttons to quickly assist you in these options:

9. These are Step Into, Step Over, and Step Out, in that order.

10. Use the Step Into button to step through your code, keeping an eye on the strResult value in the Watch window. You will notice that when you get to the calculations code, the correct value of 45 will appear in the watch. However, when you get to our purposely introduced bug, the value switches to 10. There you have it – bug located.

11. Now, we can remove the bug. For this bug, simply delete the line of code that we added in step 3.

12. Save the changed file to update our copy, then press Step Into to finish processing. The answer will still be 10 this time round, because we had already executed the error, but next time through, you should get the correct answer.

13. Switching back to Visual InterDev by clicking on End or closing the browser, you will see that the line of code containing the error has been removed.

So there you have it. Debugging client side script in Visual InterDev is every bit as easy as in other environments that you might have used, such as Visual Basic.

Debugging Server Side Script

The good news is, now that you know how to debug client side script, you can also debug server side script – they basically use the same process, and the same debugging environment.

The first requirement is that your web server is Internet Information Server 4 or above - if it's something else then you are not able to debug ASP pages. This means that if you are using Personal Web Server (PWS), you will not be able to debug your server side script at all. If you absolutely have to stick with PWS, then your best option at this stage is probably going to be the intrusive method of sticking Response.Write progress messages to yourself to pinpoint the error, and then removing them afterwards.

Assuming that you have the correct web server, then you need to ensure that server side script debugging is enabled. This is exactly the same process as outlined in the section on *Debugging Client Side Script* above.

Debugging in a Team Environment

Before continuing and showing you how to debug server side script, there is one issue you should be aware of if you are working in a team: if you are working in master mode, only one person can debug at a time. The way around this is to work in local mode, in which case more than one person can debug at a time. The better way of working in a team, for a number of reasons, is local mode anyway, so this should not be a problem.

How to Debug Server Side Script

Once you have debugging enabled, then the actions you take to debug an ASP page in your project are the same as for debugging client side script:

1.   Set the page you wish to debug as the start page for the project.

2.   Set one or more watches if you want. These can be added at design or debug time by right mouse clicking on a selected variable and choosing **Add Watch** from the menu.

3.   Add a breakpoint to your code, this time in a section of server side script.

4.   From the **Debug** menu, choose **Start** to launch the project, or else press *F5*.

5.   The browser will open, and when execution hits the breakpoint, you will be taken to the Visual InterDev debugging environment.

6.   Locate the bug using the **Step Into** control and the **Watch** window, then fix the bug and save the file.

7.   From the **Debug** menu, choose **Restart** to run the page again and see if the error is fixed. Initially do this without debugging anything – if the error is still there, welcome to the reiterative world of bug fixing – back to step 1!

As you can see, there is effectively no difference between debugging client side script and debugging server side script. The differences are simply in the nature of the code.

Summary

Large web applications can be complicated beasts that make use of server side and client side code. It is very easy for errors to slip into such applications, and in this chapter, we have looked at the debugging environment that Visual InterDev includes to combat errors in web projects. In addition we have covered the following:

❑   Using the debugging environment, we have seen how easy it is to single step through code and fix errors. We have also seen that there is little noticeable difference between debugging for client side script and server side ASP code.

❑   We also looked at methods of adding error handling to our script, so that in those cases where we fail to catch an error, or the generation of an error is outside of our control, we can make our application recover, or at least fail gracefully.

❑ Adding strong error handling is part and parcel of creating a web site that users will feel comfortable using. An error free web site promotes a feeling of professionalism to the users of the site that will hopefully make them trust it.

So far in this book we have looked at adding functionality to our web site through the use of design time controls, client side script, server side script, and XML. In the next chapter, we are going to look at wrapping up large chunks of our server side code into little reusable programs, known as COM objects, which can help to increase the performance of a web server and promote a faster web site to its users.

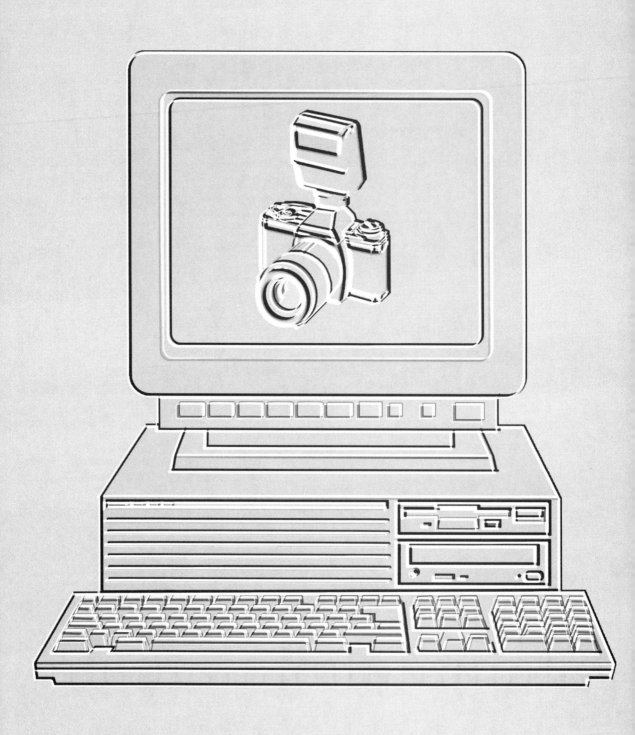

Creating Code Components

In the last chapter, we looked at how to improve the reliability of your web application by looking at debugging techniques and methods of handling errors. Good use of these techniques can be pivotal in creating a site that works. Now we're going to look at one way of making the site work *faster*.

Throughout this book, we have used various reusable objects to add functionality to our site. Examples of these have included the data bound DTCs, ActiveX controls such as the calendar control, built in script objects such as the `FileSystemObject` object to access the file system, and so on. We also used a set of objects called ADO to talk to SQL Server in our advanced database chapter. All of these are examples of reusable objects.

In this chapter, we are going to look at making our own reusable components that will run on the server. The type of reusable component that we will create is known as a **COM component**, which can be used to replace large chunks of server side ASP script with a tidy package that is both fast and reusable.

We will cover the following topics in this chapter:

- ❑ What is COM and what does it offer?
- ❑ Basics of creating a component in Visual Basic 6.
- ❑ What is MTS?
- ❑ Hosting your component in MTS.
- ❑ Talking to your component with Visual InterDev.
- ❑ Guidelines for creating COM components for use with MTS.
- ❑ Application architecture.

This chapter is not about teaching you how to do something in Visual InterDev, it is about using a *technology* to get the most out of the web sites that you create. Let's begin by finding out just what COM is.

What is COM?

As mentioned above, we have seen many sorts of reusable components in our exploration of Visual InterDev, now we're going to look at making our own. We are going to create a special sort of component, using a technology based on a definition known as the **Component Object Model** (COM). This brings to mind the million dollar question - what exactly is COM?

First off, let's set a goal. This chapter will not turn you into a COM expert, but what it *will* do is give you a basic understanding of what COM is, and take you through making a basic COM component and using it in your site. Now that we know what we are going to do, let's learn about what it is.

COM is all about creating reusable components that reveal enough information about themselves for other programs to be easily able to utilize them. These reusable components are known as COM **objects**, and the information exposed is known as the **interface** of an object. Before we go into explaining this, let's understand the purpose of such an object – it has to be easily used by external programs, and can be upgraded without needing to change the manner in how those programs talk to it.

Lofty goals! Here's how it works.

❏ A COM object is written in a popular language such as Visual Basic, Visual C++, Delphi, and so on. It is written to meet the definition laid down by COM – which means that it must have an interface that it exposes in a standard manner.

❏ This interface tells other programs what functionality is available – in other words it exposes the properties and methods of the object. For example, an object for calculating loan amortizations might have properties for loan amount, interest rate, period, and payment frequency. It might then have a method called Amortize to actually perform the calculations. These properties, events and methods are defined in the interface of a COM object.

❏ An interface, once created, should not be changed. To change an interface means that any programs that use older versions of an object might not work with the new one. An example might be if you changed the Amortize method to Calculate_all and Calculate_one methods. All of a sudden, any program designed to take advantage of the Amortize method will not be able to find the method.

❏ Any COM compliant program can use a COM object and communicate with it by reading the exposed interface. The COM object is a complete program in itself and, by manipulating the properties, events and methods exposed in its interface, the COM object will perform an action, return some information, and so on.

By enforcing a strict standard, COM objects are designed to be reusable. When writing a COM object, it therefore pays to spend a bit of time designing its interface and getting it right first time. Contrary to what is said above, it is actually possible to change the interface later, but only to *add* new properties, events, and methods. You cannot change the existing ones. So, for our example above, if the interface still supported the Amortize method, it would in fact be acceptable to add the two other methods, which of course an existing program would not use.

As part of this chapter, we will be writing a simple COM object to replace the catalogue that we wrote in previous chapters. To do this, we will be using Visual Basic 6 – which is a very powerful and easy language in which to create COM components. It also has one big advantage – it automatically writes the interface for a COM object, meaning that we don't need to know how to make such an interface. The other big advantage is that it comes with Visual Studio 6.0, which you probably have if you are using Visual InterDev.

Before we get into writing a COM object, we still don't know how it can benefit us as web developers. Let's look at the advantages that COM offers us.

What Does COM Offer a Web Project?

COM objects are especially advantageous to web applications for many reasons. The most readily apparent advantage is that once you have written a COM object, it can be used again and again without having to recode it. If you were writing lengthy calculations, database access logic, and so on, that was used a lot throughout your site, then wrapping it up in a COM object would save you having to retype that code all the time.

This is a good advantage, but one that could arguably be achieved in a web project by using an **include file**. However, COM objects offer us a lot more advantages:

❑   When designing a project, you can specify that all of the business logic will be incorporated into COM objects, which are essentially "black boxes" of functionality. These can then be developed by other people if necessary, who just need to know the required interface and what the object should do. This enables a project to effectively use multiple programmers at the same time, and possibly reduce overall cost and development time.

❑   Sometimes you can buy ready made COM objects that have the functionality you require. There are a large collection of objects for handling payment details, security, custom grids, financial calculations, and so on.

❑   Confidential information and logic can be hidden from programmers and others who can read the raw pages of your site. This could protect your confidential database's access passwords, internal rates, and so on.

❑   When a web server handles plain ASP pages, it has to interpret the script of every page whenever it sends information to a user. This can significantly degrade performance. Using COM objects, the code can run a lot faster and more efficiently than similar code in an ASP environment.

❑   The more users there are of a web site, the more work the server needs to do. If the programming logic is encapsulated into COM objects, it is possible to distribute the work so that the objects do not provide such a drain on the resources of the server. With COM objects, it is possible to use **Microsoft Transaction Server** (MTS) to make components run on different machines, and to make them handle multiple requests at the same time. This greatly improves the scalability of your web application – in other words the number of users who can access your site at once. We will cover MTS later in this chapter.

❑   When the logic encapsulated in a COM object changes, you only need to change it in one place, as opposed to all of the places that make use of it.

❑   You can use COM objects to extend the functionality of VBScript by writing objects that do things the language cannot do natively. A good example of this is the `FileSystemObject` that we used in Chapter 7 to save results to a file.

❑   If the calculations or actions performed by a COM object fail or are incorrect, it is easy to recognize that the error is in the object. It is then possible to upgrade or repair the object in one place, resulting in a much more stable environment.

This list shows you just what a great idea using components really is. We are now going to look at how you can write your own COM components.

Creating COM Components in Visual Basic 6

We are going to create a component that wraps up the catalogue for Wrox Cameras. In Chapter 9 - *Database Access with ADO*, we wrote some ASP script that linked to our SQL Server database using ADO. For our introduction to COM, we are going to rip most of that code out of ASP script and put it into a COM object. That's the task and now we learn how to do it.

Deciding What the Component Will Do

The first thing that you need to know is what the purpose of the component is, and how it will fit into your application. Is your component going to present some information from a database? Will it perform a calculation? You need to decide the purpose of your component, and you should take into account the fact that it should be reusable.

Here is what the component that we will create will do:

❑   The purpose is to replace the ASP script that draws the catalogue for Wrox Cameras.

❑   The component will need to talk to the database to do this and should return information in the form of a string of HTML.

❑   This HTML will include the necessary formatting information to present the catalogue in the final web page.

❑   We will also require that the component returns either a single product when given its ID, or else a table of all products.

This is as good a time as any to give the component a name as well. We will call our component `WroxCamerasCatalogue`.

Deciding which Language to Create the Component in

Secondly, we need to decide which language to write the component in. When writing COM objects, you have quite a choice of languages, among them are Visual Basic, C++, and Delphi. All have various strengths and weaknesses, but for our example we will be using Visual Basic 6. The reasons for this are:

❑   The interface in Visual Basic 6 is very similar to that of Visual InterDev.

❑   Visual Basic is very similar to VBScript, minimizing the changes that are necessary when taking our ASP script and rewriting it in Visual Basic. There are a few changes that need to be made to switch the code from one environment to the other, but generally it is a fairly easy process that helps sell Visual Basic as a good solution when migrating to COM.

❑   Visual Basic takes care of writing the interface of a COM object and makes the process fast and painless.

Having decided upon our language, we can look at designing the interface to match the functionality we want the component to have.

Designing the Interface

Once you have decided what your component will do, it is time to expand on it to define its interface.

As we mentioned above, the interface of a component is a listing of the properties, events, and methods it exposes, along with the parameters that should be passed as arguments. These are all used in exactly the same way as all the other objects that we have dealt with throughout this book.

For our `WroxCamerasCatalogue` component, we will have the following interface methods.

Method	Type	Parameters	Description
ShowProduct	method	ProductID	Returns details of one product in HTML.
ShowCatalogue	method	none	Returns details of all products in the catalogue in an HTML table.

The idea, therefore, of this object is that it will be used in ASP code in a manner similar to this:

```
<%

Dim objWroxCatalogue          'dim object

Set objWroxCatalogue = Server.CreateObject("WroxCamerasCatalogue.Catalogue")

Response.Write objWroxCatalogue.ShowCatalogue          'displays table of products

%>
```

If you wanted to display the details of just one product, you could use:

```
<%

Dim objWroxCatalogue          'dim object

Set objWroxCatalogue = Server.CreateObject("WroxCamerasCatalogue.Catalogue")

Response.Write objWroxCatalogue.ShowProduct "WRC00001"          'displays details of one
                                                                'product

%>
```

This is a very simple interface for a basic component. As you can see, in comparison with the code written in Chapter 9 and reproduced below, it is a lot easier to write our product catalogue using the object than by writing the HTML by hand:

```
<P> 
<TABLE BORDER="0" CELLPADDING="1" CELLSPACING="1" WIDTH="590">

<TR BGCOLOR="blue">
<TD WIDTH="130"><STRONG>Product</STRONG></TD>
<TD WIDTH="200"><STRONG>Name</STRONG></TD>
<TD WIDTH="130"><STRONG>Cost</STRONG></TD>
<TD WIDTH="130"><STRONG>Type</STRONG></TD>
</TR>
<%
'retrieve catalogue of products from DB and write to table
Dim adoConn
Dim adoCmd
Dim adoRS
Dim strConnectionString

'create ADO Objects
Set adoConn = Server.CreateObject("ADODB.Connection")
Set adoCmd = Server.CreateObject("ADODB.Command")
Set adoRS = Server.CreateObject("ADODB.Recordset")

'define connection string
strConnectionString = "Provider=SQLOLEDB.1;Persist Security Info=False;UserID=sa;" _
                    & "Initial Catalog=WroxCameras;Data Source=VAIO;Locale" _
                    & "Identifier=2057;Connect Timeout=15;" _
                    & "Use Procedure for Prepare=1;Auto Translate=True;" _
                    & "Packet Size=4096;Workstation ID=VAIO"

'set ADO Command Properties
adoCmd.CommandType = 1
adoCmd.CommandText = "SELECT product.product_id, product.name, product.price, " _
                & "product.thumbnail, product_type.type_description FROM product, " _
                & "product_type WHERE product.type_id = product_type.product_type " _
                & "ORDER BY name"

'Open the Connection
adoConn.Open strConnectionString

'associate the Command with the Open Connection
adoCmd.ActiveConnection = adoConn

'retrieve recordset
Set adoRS = adoCmd.Execute

If adoRS.Eof Then
  'write nothing -no results
Else
  Do while not adoRS.EOF
    'process results to create table
    Response.Write "<TR>" & vbcrlf
    Response.Write "<TD><A HREF=" & chr(34) & "product_details.asp?product_id=" _
             & adoRS("product_id").Value & chr(34) & "><IMG SRC=" & chr(34) _
             & "images/" & adoRS("thumbnail").Value & chr(34) & "></A></TD>" & vbcrlf
    Response.Write "<TD>" & adoRS("name").Value & "</TD>" & vbcrlf
```

```
      Response.Write "<TD>" & adoRS("price").Value & "</TD>" & vbcrlf
      Response.Write "<TD>" & adoRS("type_description").Value & "</TD></TR>" & vbcrlf
      adoRS.MoveNext
   Loop
End if

'close connection and set ADO objects to nothing
adoConn.Close
Set adoConn = nothing
Set adoCmd = nothing
Set adoRS = nothing

%>
</TABLE>
</P>
```

Building a Component in Visual Basic

Once you have designed the interface, you are ready to build the component. As discussed, we will be using Microsoft Visual Basic 6 to create the component, primarily because it is an easy environment to develop in, it strongly resembles Visual InterDev, and our script from Chapter 9 will only need minor changes to work in the new environment.

This is not a tutorial in how to program in Visual Basic 6, so we'll just cover what we need as we go along. We will be taking a step by step approach to creating our COM object, without trying to become experienced Visual Basic 6 programmers along the way.

With these general conditions in mind, let's take a quick look at how to make our object in Visual Basic 6.

Try it Out – Building a Component in Visual Basic 6.0

1. Open Visual Basic 6, and in the dialog that appears, choose to create a new ActiveX DLL project:

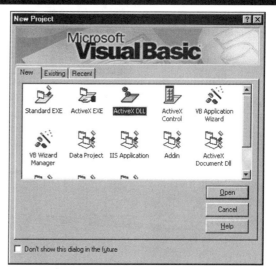

2. Press Open to create the project. The environment is immediately recognizable as being in the same family as Visual InterDev, including a Toolbar on the left, Project Explorer window on the right, and a Properties window beneath it. You will see that a window has been opened with the title Project 1 – Class1 (Code). This is a new **class module**, which has been automatically created for us. A class module is a place for us to write the properties and methods that will be used in our finished component. In the Properties window, select the (Name) property and change it to Catalogue.

3. We now need to name our project and set some necessary information to make the project create the component correctly. In the Project menu, select Project1 Properties. In the dialog that appears, set the Project Name to WroxCamerasCatalogue, and the Project Description to Wrox Cameras Catalogue. Place a check mark in the Unattended Execution checkbox – this tells Visual Basic that there is no need to draw any forms or visual interface in the finished product. This is what we require, as the component will only be used from code. The Upgrade ActiveX Controls checkbox will make Visual Basic inform you if any of the ActiveX Controls used within your project have been upgraded since you last saved the project. If this is the case, then you are prompted to upgrade them if this checkbox is checked. Press OK to commit your changes.

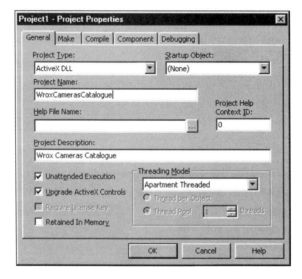

4. One last step before writing our code is telling Visual Basic how to deal with other objects required by our project. We will be using ADO to talk to the SQL Server database, just as we did in Visual InterDev. In order to tell Visual Basic how to use ADO, we need to add a **reference** to it in our project. To do this, select Project | References. In the window that appears, place a check mark in the box before Microsoft ActiveX Data Object 2.1 Library (or whichever is the highest number that will be available on the server), and press OK:

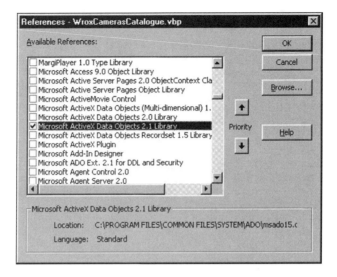

5. We are now ready to actually start writing our code. You will recall that the interface we want for our component is to include two methods: ShowProduct and ShowCatalogue. This makes things easy for us, because we have two chunks of code in ASP that do just about exactly what we are after: the products.asp page contains the code for ShowCatalogue, and the product_details.asp page covers the other method. This means that generally we could just cut and paste our code and make a few changes. Let's begin with ShowCatalogue. In the code window in Visual Basic, type in the following and press *Return*:

```
Function ShowCatalogue() As String
```

6. Visual Basic will have automatically created the corresponding End Function for you, as shown below:

```
Function ShowCatalogue() As String

End Function
```

7. Whatever we write in here is the code that will be executed whenever the ShowCatalogue method of the object is called. Because we have defined the function As String, it will return a string value. This is where we will write the information that will be written to the web page using Response.Write. Type the following code into the function, again remembering to change VAIO (the name of my machine) to the name of your machine:

```
Function ShowCatalogue() As String

'retrieve catalogue of products from DB and write to table

Dim adoConn As New ADODB.Connection
Dim adoCmd As New ADODB.Command
Dim adoRS As New ADODB.Recordset
Dim strConnectionString As String
Dim strCatalogue As String   'string to hold the catalogue's HTML
```

```
'define connection string

strConnectionString = "Provider=SQLOLEDB.1;Persist Security Info=False;User ID=sa;" _
                    & "Initial Catalog=WroxCameras;Data Source=VAIO;" _
                    & "Locale Identifier=2057;Connect Timeout=15;" _
                    & "Use Procedure for Prepare=1;Auto Translate=True;" _
                    & "Packet Size=4096;Workstation ID=VAIO"

'set ADO Command Properties

adoCmd.CommandType = 1
adoCmd.CommandText = "SELECT product.product_id, product.name, product.price, " _
                   & "product.thumbnail, product_type.type_description FROM product, " _
                   & "product_type WHERE product.type_id = product_type.product_type " _
                   & "ORDER BY name"

'Open the Connection

adoConn.Open strConnectionString

'associate the Command with the Open Connection

adoCmd.ActiveConnection = adoConn

'retrieve recordset

Set adoRS = adoCmd.Execute

If adoRS.EOF Then
    strCatalogue=""         'write nothing -no results
Else
    Do While Not adoRS.EOF
        'process results to create table
        strCatalogue = strCatalogue & "<TR>" & vbCrLf
        strCatalogue = strCatalogue & "<TD><A HREF=" & Chr(34) _
                     & "product_details.asp?product_id=" & adoRS("product_id").Value _
                     & Chr(34) & "><IMG SRC=" & Chr(34) & "images/" _
                     & adoRS("thumbnail").Value & Chr(34) & "></A></TD>" & vbCrLf
        strCatalogue = strCatalogue & "<TD>" & adoRS("name").Value & "</TD>" & vbCrLf
        strCatalogue = strCatalogue & "<TD>" & adoRS("price").Value & "</TD>" & vbCrLf
        strCatalogue = strCatalogue & "<TD>" & adoRS("type_description").Value _
                     & "</TD></TR>" & vbCrLf
        adoRS.MoveNext
    Loop
End If

'close connection and set ADO objects to nothing

adoConn.Close
Set adoConn = Nothing
Set adoCmd = Nothing
Set adoRS = Nothing
```

```
'return contents of strCatalogue to user

ShowCatalogue = strCatalogue

End Function
```

8. You will notice that the code is very similar to that contained in `products.htm` – there are effectively only two changes. The first change is that when dimensioning our ADO variables, we use the `As New` keywords to create the object there and then – saving us from having to later use `CreateObject`. The other change was that instead of outputting our results directly to `Response.Write`, we put them into a string, `strCatalogue`, and then output the whole string as the result of the function. This means that when this function is called, the result will be a string containing the HTML necessary for our catalogue table. In ASP, you could then use something like:

```
<TABLE BORDER="0" CELLPADDING="1" CELLSPACING="1" WIDTH="590">

<TR BGCOLOR="blue">
<TD WIDTH="130"><STRONG>Product</STRONG></TD>
<TD WIDTH="200"><STRONG>Name</STRONG></TD>
<TD WIDTH="130"><STRONG>Cost</STRONG></TD>
<TD WIDTH="130"><STRONG>Type</STRONG></TD>
</TR>
<%
Dim objWroxCamerasCatalogue

Set objWroxCamerasCatalogue = Server.CreateObject("WroxCamerasCatalogue.Catalogue")

Response.Write objWroxCamerasCatalogue.ShowCatalogue
%>
</TABLE>
```

9. We now need to create our last function for the component: `ShowProduct`. This function will display the details for one specific product, so it needs a way of being told what product to return. This is performed by specifying a parameter of `product_id`. By calling this function and passing it a product, it will then know to return the information for that product. At the top right of the code window in Visual Basic, you will find the Procedure Selection window, click on (Declarations) as shown below:

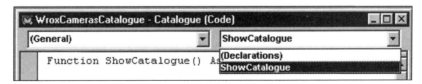

10. On the new blank line, type in the declaration for our new function as shown below, and press *Return*:

```
Function ShowProduct(ProductId as string) As String
```

11. Once again, this will have created the shell for our function:

```
Function ShowProduct(ProductID As String) As String

End Function
```

12. Either type in the following code for the new function, or copy and paste it from
product_details.asp and modify it to be the same as below. If you type it in, remember to
change VAIO to the name of your machine:

```
Function ShowProduct(ProductID As String) As String

'retrieve product details from database and write in HTML

Dim adoConn As New ADODB.Connection
Dim adoCmd As New ADODB.Command
Dim adoRS As New ADODB.Recordset
Dim strConnectionString As String
Dim strProduct As String  'string to hold the product's HTML

'define connection string

strConnectionString = "Provider=SQLOLEDB.1;Persist Security Info=False;User ID=sa;" _
                    & "Initial Catalog=WroxCameras;Data Source=VAIO;" _
                    & "Locale Identifier=2057;Connect Timeout=15;" _
                    & "Use Procedure for Prepare=1;Auto Translate=True;" _
                    & "Packet Size=4096;Workstation ID=VAIO"

'set ADO Command Properties

adoCmd.CommandType = 1
'build query string using ProductId parameter
adoCmd.CommandText = "SELECT product.*, product_type.type_description FROM product," _
                & " product_type WHERE product.type_id = product_type.product_type" _
                & " AND product.product_id = '" & ProductID & "'"

'Open the Connection

adoConn.Open strConnectionString

'associate the Command with the Open Connection

adoCmd.ActiveConnection = adoConn

'retrieve recordset

Set adoRS = adoCmd.Execute

If adoRS.EOF Then
    strProduct = ""   'write nothing -no results
```

```
Else
    Do While Not adoRS.EOF
        'process results to create table
        strProduct = "<STRONG><FONT COLOR='orange'>" & adoRS("name").Value _
                & "</FONT></STRONG><BR><BR>" & vbCrLf
        strProduct = strProduct & "  <TR><TD WIDTH='50%' rowspan='4'><IMG SRC=" _
                & Chr(34) & "images/" & adoRS("picture").Value & Chr(34) _
                & "></TD<" & vbCrLf
    strProduct = strProduct & "  <TR><TD WIDTH='50%'><STRONG>Name:</STRONG> " _
                & adoRS("name").Value & "</TD> </TR>"
        strProduct = strProduct _
                & "  <TR><TD WIDTH='50%'><STRONG>Description:</STRONG> " _
                & adoRS("description").Value & "</TD></TR>"
        strProduct = strProduct & "  <TR><TD
                WIDTH='50%'><STRONG>Price:</STRONG> " _
                & adoRS("price").Value & "</TD></TR>"
    strProduct = strProduct & "  <TR><TD WIDTH='50%'><STRONG>Type:</STRONG> " _
                & adoRS("type_description").Value & "</TD></TR>"
        adoRS.MoveNext
    Loop
End If

'close connection and set ADO objects to nothing

adoConn.Close
Set adoConn = Nothing
Set adoCmd = Nothing
Set adoRS = Nothing

'return product details

ShowProduct = strProduct

End Function
```

13. We have finished writing our component, all we need to do now is to wrap it up into a nice package – in this case it will be what is known as a **Dynamic Link Library** (DLL). A DLL is an object which can be used by other programs – exactly what we are after! In the File menu, select Make WroxCamerasCatalogue.DLL. In the dialog that opens, you will be prompted with a name for the DLL – keep it as it is, and specify a suitable location on your computer. This might be either a folder in which you contain all DLL components you have created, or maybe the WINDOWS\SYSTEM folder – the choice is yours. Pressing OK creates the DLL.

14. Save your project.

Well done! You have just created a component in Visual Basic that is now ready for use in Visual InterDev. Before we actually use the component, let's take a look at some other points for writing objects in Visual Basic 6.

> *Suppose that you had managed to buy a pre-made component that was exactly the same as above – all you would have to do is install it using the install program that it came with, and then use it from here on in using the same code as we are about to use.*

Object Methods

The component that we just wrote exposed two methods for its interface. To recap, a method is an *action* that the object can perform, that can return a *response*. In our example, we asked the object to provide us with a list of catalogues, or to provide us with specific details of one product. What we actually wrote was a normal function, which just so happens to be how a method is written for an object in Visual Basic.

So, to summarize what we wrote above, a method is written as a function in code, for example:

```
Public Sub DoSomething()
  'do something here
End Sub

Public Function DoSomethingElse(Paramater as integer) As String
  'do something here
  'return a value
  DoSomethingElse = strSomeString
End Function
```

You will notice that the above examples use the Public keyword. This defines the scope of the procedure, with the following options:

- **Public** procedures are visible outside the object, meaning that they are part of the interface that other programs can use.

- **Private** procedures are only usable within the class that they are written in, and are not visible outside of the object. This means they are not part of the interface. They are used to perform internal functions of the object, such as a common function for connecting to a database or manipulating data.

- **Friend** procedures are usable by any class within the object, but are not visible outside the object. This means they are not part of the interface. Friend procedures are used for sharing common code and information between the various internal parts of an object.

Once the object is created, any method of that object which was created with the Public keyword can be called using one of the following:

```
Object.Method

Object.DoSomething

Response.Write Object.DoSomethingElse(3)
```

Object Properties

Objects have properties, as we have seen. A property of an object is a value, and when referenced, you can normally assign a value to it, or read the value. An example might be a car. One of its properties would be color, which might default to orange. When you paint it, you can change its color to green. In code, you could do this by writing something like:

```
Dim strColor As String
Dim objCar As New Car.Sportscar

strColor = objCar.Color        'reads car's color into strColor

'change color of case
objCar.Color = "Green"
```

To create a property in Visual Basic, you use the `Property` keyword. The definition for the color property of a car might then be:

```
Public Property Get Color() as String
  'code here to retrieve the color, ie
  Color = strCarColor
End Property

Public Property Let Color(strNewColor as string)
  'code here to assign the color
  strCarColor = strNewColor
End Property
```

For this example, the `strCarColor` string would have been declared in the declaration sections of the class, giving it a module wide scope so that it was accessible in all procedures within the class.

- ❑ If you have a `Property Get`, then you can retrieve the value.

- ❑ If you have a `Property Let`, then you can change the value of the property

- ❑ If you have both a `Property Let` and a `Property Get`, then the property is read/write enabled.

- ❑ If you are missing the `Property Get`, then it is impossible to retrieve a value (i.e. it is a *write-only* property

- ❑ If you are missing the `Property Let`, then it is impossible to change a value (i.e. it is a *read-only* property).

Class_Initialize and Class_Terminate Events

It is possible to write code that happens whenever an object is created or ended. This occurs in the `Class_Initialize` and `Class_Terminate` events. These two events have a similar analogy in ASP, namely the `Application_OnStart` and `Application_OnEnd` events of the `global.asa` file, which we saw in Chapter 7.

- ❑ The `Class_Initialize` event is often used to set internal settings of the object, such as retrieving database connection strings, and sometimes restoring the initial values of properties.

❑ The `Class_Terminate` event is used to tidy up an object when it is no longer needed. This might involve housekeeping such as closing database connections, writing results to a file, and so on.

To write code for these events select the Class object in the Object drop box at the top of the Code window, then in the Procedure drop box to the right of it, select the event for which you wish to write code. This will automatically place your cursor in the correct event handler where you can then type your code.

Using Your Component in Visual InterDev

Now that we know how to make a component, and have made our first one, let's look at how we can use it in our web application. A web server can create an instance of our component for use in our ASP page. There are better ways of doing this than getting the server to directly create the object, which we will look at shortly.

Creating an Install Program for Your Component

The first part of using your component is to install it on the server. Your component is a DLL file, which means that you have two main ways of installing it:

❑ DLLs made using Visual Basic require VB runtime files to be present on a computer that uses the DLL. These are automatically installed by the Visual Basic Setup program, or with any other VB program that is installed. If your computer already has the VB runtime files, then you can run `regsvr32` to install it. This is a command line utility that registers DLLs.

❑ You can create a setup program to install the necessary VB runtime files, install the component, and register it.

Using `regsvr32.exe` is a straightforward process that uses the Run option of the Start menu. Simply select Run, then type in regsvr32 dllname.dll, where dllname.dll is replaced by the full name and path of the DLL.

If you need to create a setup program, you will need to use the Package & Deployment wizard that comes with Visual Basic. This is found under the Visual Studio 6.0 Tools directory of your Visual Studio group in the Start menu. The Package & Deployment wizard is used to create a setup program that you can use to install a Visual Basic program – such as your DLL. Once run, the setup program will automatically install your DLL for the server to use.

Using Your Component

Once the DLL is successfully set up on the web server, be it a proper server on a network, or your desktop PC running PWS, it is possible to use the DLL in your web pages.

Let's now take a look at how to do this.

Try it Out – Using Your Component in Visual InterDev

We are going to edit the code in our pages `products.asp` and `product_details.asp` so that they now use the component that we have just created.

1. In Visual InterDev, open the project WroxCameras.

2. Open the page products.asp.

3. In the Source view, locate the main block of ASP code that displays the product table and replace it with the following:

```
<%

Dim objWroxCamerasCatalogue

Set objWroxCamerasCatalogue = Server.CreateObject("WroxCamerasCatalogue.Catalogue")

Response.Write objWroxCamerasCatalogue.ShowCatalogue

%>
```

4. Save the page and view it in the browser, you should see the catalogue successfully displayed from the database:

5. As you can see, we have replaced numerous lines of code with just three! This is much easier to write if we want to display our catalogue elsewhere. We now need to change the `product_details.asp` page. Open it in the editor by double clicking on it in the Project Explorer window.

6. In the Source view, locate the main block of ASP script and replace it with the following:

```
<%

Dim objWroxCamerasCatalogue

Set objWroxCamerasCatalogue = Server.CreateObject("WroxCamerasCatalogue.Catalogue")

Response.Write objWroxCamerasCatalogue.ShowProduct (Request.QueryString("product_id"))

%>
```

7. Save your work and view the products.asp page in the browser. Selecting an individual product and clicking on its image should take you to the product_details.asp page and successfully display the correct product details.

The actual workings of this are really quite simple. In the case of our product_details.asp page, we are simply passing the product_id query string parameter to our component's productID parameter to display the relevant product. For both pages, the object simply returns a string of HTML that is written to the page using Response.Write.

Microsoft Transaction Server

We have now looked at how to create a component and use it on our web server. This offers many advantages over running plain ASP script, mainly in the areas of speed, reusability, and application robustness.

By creating a DLL and registering it on the server, we have created a little program that we can use in our web pages to offer an enhanced application. There are, however, a few issues that could be improved upon, namely:

❑ When the server creates an object based on a DLL registered in the normal manner on a server, it creates that object in-process on the web server. This means that the DLL shares the memory and resources of the web server, meaning that it still needs to perform a lot of work.

❑ If an in-process DLL needs updating or repairing, the whole web server needs to be shut down to change the DLL, resulting in down time.

❑ There is the possibility of a corrupt or badly written DLL causing problems, which can slow down, halt, or cause major damage to the web server application – not a good idea when it's trying to serve up web pages to hundreds or thousands of users.

To combat these and other issues, Microsoft provides a program called **Microsoft Transaction Server** (MTS). MTS is a sophisticated application that is designed to assist in working with objects.

MTS helps to manage objects. For our purposes, when a web page requires a component that is under the control of MTS, the web server realizes this and asks MTS to supply an instance of that object. That is the basic story but, like so much else, there is a lot more to it.

MTS does a lot of things to make the task of developing and using objects easier and more efficient. It plays a strong part in the future of Microsoft's plans for development, and offers many advantages, of which we are only going to use two.

The bits that we are interested in are:

❑ DLLs in MTS are no longer in process to the web server.

❑ It is possible to make a web server on computer A use components running in MTS on computer B.

These features do not do justice to the full capabilities of MTS, but by themselves they are still significant advantages for our web application. To learn about the other capabilities that MTS offers web developers, Wrox Press have some excellent books that cover the subject in detail, for example *Professional Visual Basic 6 MTS Programming*, (ISBN 1-86100-24-4). We are going to look at how to use our subset of features to improve our web application.

Using MTS to Improve Your Application

The first big advantage that using MTS offers us is that all of a sudden the DLLs are no longer in process to the web server. This offers a huge advantage in terms of robustness and scalability.

Application robustness is enhanced because:

❑ It is no longer necessary to shut down the web server in order to upgrade or repair the component.

❑ If the component is corrupt, the web server continues happily serving out pages to its users, minus the output of the component, of course. Meanwhile, MTS is very robust at handling such errors so the effect is minimized. MTS also records any fatal errors in the event log for you if you are using Windows NT.

❑ Because of the other advantage (scalability), there are less timeouts, making for a more robust application. A timeout can occur when it takes too long for a web server to send details to the client browser – if one web server is serving hundreds of users with in process DLLs, chances are it's going to be busier than a server where a different computer handles the DLLs, resulting in more timeouts.

Scalability refers to how well the application handles increasing numbers of users. Scalability is enhanced because:

❑ The web server application no longer processes all of the object work.

❑ It is possible to split the load out over multiple computers, by actually having the web server talk to an object sitting in MTS on a different computer. This greatly reduces the processor overload when dealing with thousands of customers.

Now that we know the advantages that MTS will give us, we need to know how to make use of it.

Installing Components into MTS

MTS is installed as part of the NT4 Option pack, or with Personal Web Server (PWS). The interface under Windows 98 and Windows NT4 is fairly similar, although in NT4 it has been integrated into the **Microsoft Management Console** (MMC). We will look at using MTS in Windows 98 as supplied with Personal Web Server. The main interface is called the **Transaction Server Explorer**, which enables you to explore the structure of objects within MTS in a similar manner to exploring files on your computer.

MTS refers to objects as **components**, and groups them in **packages**. The picture opposite shows some packages in the Transaction Server Explorer:

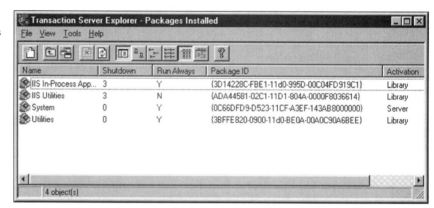

It is possible to create your own packages, which work in a similar manner to directories. Within each package, you can add one or more objects (components), which can be drilled down into using Transaction Server Explorer:

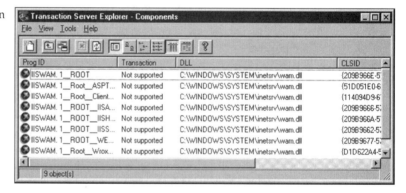

Once a component has been installed into MTS then the manner in which it is referenced by Windows is permanently changed. From then on, if our web page uses a `Server.Createobject` statement, then that object will be provided by MTS.

Let's have a look at the process of creating a package and installing a component:

Try it Out – Installing a Component into MTS

We are going to install our `WroxCamerasCatalogue` component into MTS.

1. Start Transaction Server Explorer. If using PWS, it will be in your Start menu under the Microsoft Transaction Server sub menu of the PWS directory. If you can't find it here then try using Find for mtxexp.exe.

2. The Transaction Server Explorer works in a similar manner to Windows Explorer. Double click on My Computer to drill down into the packages installed on your computer.

3. Double click on Packages installed to bring up a list of installed packages.

4. Click on File | New to create a new package:

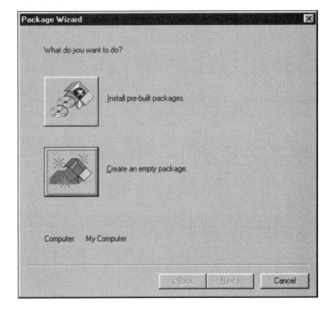

5. We want to create an empty package. It is also possible to export packages to other machines and then install them there, which would be done using the Install pre-built packages option. Click on Create an empty package.

6. In the next dialog, type the name of the package as Wrox Cameras and press Finish. The Transaction Explorer window should now display your package:

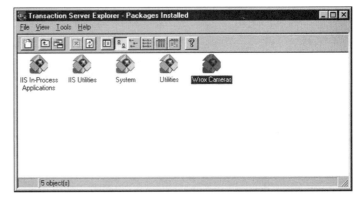

7. Now that we have created a package, we need to add our component to it. Double click on the Wrox Cameras package.

8. Double click on the Components icon to display the components that are in the package – currently none.

9. Select File | New to create a new component.

10. Seeing as how we have already registered our component, select Import component(s) that are already registered.

11. A list of all in process servers (i.e. DLLs that have not been configured to run with MTS) will appear. Select WroxCamerasCatalogue.Catalogue and press Finish.

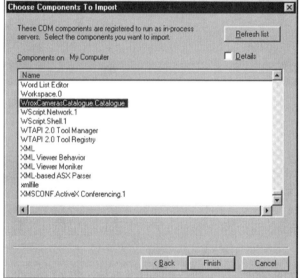

12. The Components window should now show your component. The last thing we should do is to enter a description for our component. Right mouse click on the component and select Properties.

13. In the description box, type in Displays Catalogue in HTML form, or specific Product Details, for Wrox Cameras Site. And press OK.

That's it. Now, whenever a program references the `WroxCamerasCatalogue` component, it will be managed by MTS.

If you now switch back to the **WroxCameras** web project in Visual InterDev, then view the `products.asp` page in your browser, you will see that everything still works as before. Under the surface, however, MTS is doing a lot of the work that the web server was previously doing.

As a little tip – if you leave the Transaction Server Explorer open and display your component, and then display the `products.asp` page, you will see that the icon for the component begins to animate and spin around when you access the page. This is a little nicety that can help you to ensure that your components are in fact working in MTS.

Defining the User Account in Windows NT

If you are installing your component into MTS running on Windows NT, there is an important step, which is to define an NT account under which the component will run.

Each component can access resources on an NT computer as if it were a user. When a component is first registered on a computer, it defaults to using the interactive user account – i.e. whoever happens to be logged in. This has two disadvantages: you require somebody to be logged in, and that person has to have the necessary rights to get at the resources (such as drives, files, databases, and so on) that the component requires.

The recommended solution for this is to specify a valid NT User account that the service will run under. To do this:

1. You need to first off create an account, or specify an existing one such as the local administrator, that has the necessary security permissions.

2. During the creation of a new package with MTS under NT you will get an additional dialogue, **Set Package Identity**, where you can specify the name of the user that will be used for this component.

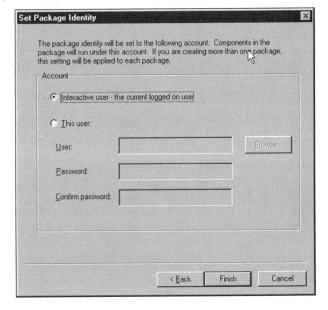

If you choose Interactive user - the current logged on user at this point, you can specify the name of the user after installation of the component by right clicking on the installed package icon and selecting Properties. Then in the Identity tab you can specify the name of the user.

Once this has been done, the component will access all resources as if they were in fact the specified user. This means the component can even work when nobody has logged in. You still need the computer to be switched on however!

Spreading the Workload Using MTS

We have mentioned that MTS can be used to spread the workload across multiple computers. This is done by placing components on a different machine that is also running Microsoft Transaction Server. The advantage of doing this is to free up the resources of the web server to doing what it does best – serving web pages to client computers. On a large site, this distributed processing capability is necessary to ensure that the web server doesn't grind to a halt.

Another great advantage of all this is that the code in our web pages does not need to worry itself about where the object actually resides – it might be on the same PC or even in a different building. The code to talk to the object remains the same, and MTS takes care of the rest.

This sort of capability also brings to the forefront the issue of *design*. The first thing to realize is that there is a slight cost in performance involved in talking to components on a remote machine – but in normal cases this is still a marked improvement over overloading the web server. In a well organized environment, you might find one or more PCs acting as a web server, one or more PCs acting as object servers, and one or more PCs acting as database servers. Depending on your costs, there are significant options for doubling up.

In our WroxCamerasCatalogue example, it might actually be a good idea if the component ran on the same PC as the database, seeing as it actually only returns a string of text. This would save MTS having to copy across the whole result set to perform its calculations.

Once you have decided to spread the workload in this manner, the actual mechanics are quite simple:

1. Open the Transaction Server Explorer.

2. Initially, you will just see an icon for My Computer, representing your local computer. We need to add a new computer to this window. To do this, click on File | New.

3. In the dialog that appears, type the name of the computer to add, or Browse to locate one on the network:

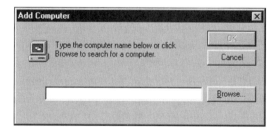

4. An icon for the new computer will now appear beside the My Computer icon. This enables you to browse and manage the packages on the remote computer in the same way as on the local computer.

5. Browse the local machine represented by the My Computer icon until you find the package that you want to export.

6. Right mouse click on the package. In the dialog that appears, enter a name for the export file (.pak extension) that MTS will create for exporting:

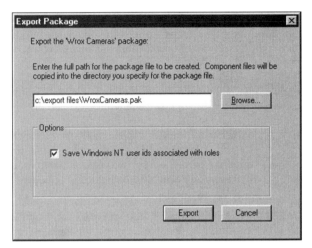

7. The package can then be installed in the same manner as detailed in our example above, except that you will select Install pre-built packages.

This process exports all of the necessary information for MTS on one machine to use the objects on another.

> This process does not actually copy the files that make up the components – just the information.

So, if we wanted to put the WroxCamerasCatalogue component on the database server, we would have to perform the following steps:

1. If it was registered on our local machine, we would first need to delete its package from MTS, then un-register the DLL by using something like regsvr32 /u WroxCamerasCatalogue.DLL at an MS-DOS command prompt.

2. Register the DLL on the remote computer by running a setup program or regsvr32, as described in a previous example.

3. Create a package and install the component on the remote machine.

4. On the remote machine, export a package containing the component details using the steps outlined earlier.

5. On the local machine, install the package exported in step 4 above.

Once this process had been completed, the remote computer would handle the workload for the WroxCamerasCatalogue component, freeing up our web server to serve pages.

Application Architecture

As you might have realized, what we've been touching on here are ways of improving the architecture of our application. In fact, we've been looking at the building blocks of one of those big IT buzzwords – an **n-tier architecture**. A web application, like any program, has an architecture that defines how it is built and works.

A program can be said to consist of three elements, and the architecture of an application is determined by where the processing of those elements is carried out. The three elements are:

❏ **Presentation services**. These services are concerned with the presentation of information to the user. This includes aspects such as functionality, navigation, interface consistency and integrity, and so on. In the Wrox Cameras example, these services would include the pages that the client downloads, including the client side script, as well as the navigation controls that Visual InterDev provides.

❏ **Application logic**. These services exist to implement the rules and processes of the business. This includes logic to carry out business policies, generation of information from data that the business can make sense of, and so on. An example of this within our Wrox Cameras site would be the calculation of payment based on the user's selected payment method.

❏ **Data services**. This is concerned with the data requirements of the application, i.e. the storage and retrieval of persistent data. It also covers such things as data integrity, definition of the data, and so on. An example of this in our Wrox Cameras site would be SQL Server and the Wrox Cameras database.

As has been said, by specifying where the processing and work behind these services occurs, you are in fact defining the architecture of an application. There are many sorts of architectures available, not all of which can accommodate a web application. Here are the common types of application architecture.

Single-Tier Model

This is the simplest structure of an application, where all of the processing is performed in one place. In other words, the presentation, application logic, and data services all are carried out in the same place.

In the dark ages of computing, this work would have all been carried out on the server, which would have been a mainframe. Nowadays, examples of single-tier applications are prevalent in many desktop programs, such as an Access application. By its very nature, a web application cannot be a single-tier application, but for the sake of completeness, it is included here.

Two-Tier Model – Client/Server

The two-tier model is often referred to as client/server applications. In this model, the client computer groups the presentation and application logic into one program, then communicates to a database server for the data services. This model is typical of many corporate applications, such as a traditional Visual Basic application that talks to a SQL Server database server for information. These applications work well in applications with modest numbers of users, typically under 100, and a fast network environment.

Multi-Tier Model (n-Tier)

Your average web application will probably use a 3-tier solution. In this case, the client's web browser supplies the user services, the web server provides the business logic in the form of ASP script, and a separate SQL Server machine provides the data store for the data services.

What we have covered in this chapter is using MTS to break out of a 3-tier environment into a larger, n-tier environment. This was achieved in the examples in this chapter by breaking the business logic services onto different machines. Using our new understanding, we used MTS to build an architecture like this:

Element	Processed By
User Services	Client's web browser (this includes client side script, Design Time Controls, and DHTML).
Business Logic	Internet Information Server web server on Server A. MTS and COM components on Server B.
Data Services	SQL Server on Server C.

We also mentioned other possibilities, such as putting MTS onto the SQL Server machine, which would draw a stronger link between the business logic and data services elements.

The advantages of following an n-tier approach are best summarized in one word: scalability. An application designed to spread the workload over multiple servers is much more capable of servicing multiple users than one where all the work is processed on a single machine. Other advantages include a greater clarity in the business logic layer that promotes enhanced reusability, maintenance, and performance.

Summary

In this chapter, we have looked at how to use components and MTS to create a more robust and scalable web site. We learned how to develop components, in Visual Basic 6, that can replace large blocks of ASP script with concise objects, and then we learned how to put them into action. At the end of all this, we saw that what we were in fact doing was building an n-tier architecture that creates a very scalable application.

This is a large topic, one which we have only lightly touched on, but mastering the use of objects is a very important step towards creating web applications that do more than just 'hold together'. Object technology enables the creation of a web application that is more dynamic and flexible than a purely script based site, and including MTS can also free up valuable computer resources into the bargain.

In summary, we learned that:

❑ Components add value to all stages of web development and the life of your application.

❑ COM components can be created in many programming languages, including Visual Basic.

❑ Once created, a component can be easily used in ASP script to replace unwieldy code.

❑ MTS can be used to improve the reliability and performance of your objects.

❑ MTS can be used to spread object workloads across multiple computers, freeing up your web server's resources. This creates an n-tier application that is inherently more scalable than the standard 3-tier model of an Internet application.

This chapter touched on measures that can be used to improve the reliability and scalability of your site. In the next chapter, we will introduce other technologies and techniques for improving your site, as well as looking at ways of making it easy to maintain.

Deployment and Designing for the Bigger Picture

In the previous chapter we learned how to improve our web application through the use of components and MTS. This introduced us to some ideas and methods for optimizing a site for real-life use.

In this, the penultimate chapter, we are going to look at how to deploy a solution and various ways in which your site can be designed to cope with large demand, have better performance, and be easily maintained. We will cover areas such as optimizing code use, use of components, maintenance, and so on. We will look at various manners of achieving goals that are important for any successful web application, namely:

- ❑ Hitting a balance between features and reach, in other words ensuring that you have the best features available that are applicable to the majority of your target audience.

- ❑ Improving performance - ensuring that the application runs quickly and smoothly, without big download times.

- ❑ Building scalability into your web application, by ensuring that the application continues to perform well as its user base grows.

- ❑ Building a maintainable solution - making an application that is easy to amend and keep in good working order.

- ❑ Using Visual SourceSafe for source control when developing in teams.

- ❑ Using the Visual Component Manager to keep track of any items which you want to use.

This chapter will draw on the knowledge that you have gained throughout this book, and will in some cases cover suggestions that have already been made. The goal here is to promote in one place the necessary advice to enable you to build a strong solution that can meet the requirements demanded of it.

Deploying Your Solution

The last step in creating your application (or maybe not – web applications are reiterative beasts after all!) is to **deploy** it to a server where your readers can get at it. If you are working in a team, it is probably a good idea to assign one person the responsibility of managing deployment, to save bits and pieces being deployed by everyone individually. Visual InterDev offers two easy ways of deploying your application to a target server: you can either copy it using a Copy Web Project option, or you can use Visual InterDev's deployment features. We'll look at both methods here.

Copy Web Project Option

This is the easiest method of deploying your application, but it does require that the target server has FrontPage Server Extensions installed, and that you have write access on the web server. Given these requirements, it is then an easy task to deploy your project using Visual InterDev:

1. In the Project Explorer window, select the project that you want to deploy.

2. In the main menu, select Project | Web Project | Copy Web Application.

3. In the Copy Project dialog box that appears, choose the copy of the application that you want to deploy. You would normally deploy the master version as opposed to your local version, since in a team environment this is going to contain the latest versions of files from everyone.

4. In the Server Name box, type in the name of the target web server.

5. In the Web project box, type in the name that users will enter for the URL of the project.

6. Remove the check from the Copy changed files only checkbox. This ensures that all files are copied – not just those that have changed since the last deployment. The final dialog should look something like this:

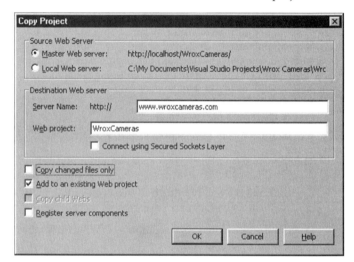

7. Press OK. The project will be deployed to the destination server.

Using Visual InterDev's Deployment Features

Visual InterDev includes a fairly comprehensive utility that enables you to deploy a project, and the various components that it includes, onto a remote server that does not use FrontPage Extensions. The utility is useful for deploying projects to a single target server, multiple servers, and also to deploy any COM components that your application might use.

Before using the utility, there are a few requirements that must be met:

❑ To deploy COM components, you must have Microsoft Internet Information Server installed, with the Visual InterDev RAD Remote Deployment Support option selected at the time of installation.

❑ You need to have write access on the destination server, which will be granted by whoever manages that server.

❑ Either the destination web should have been created, or you must have write access to the root web, so that the deployment utility can create it for you.

❑ Microsoft Posting Acceptor 2 needs to have been installed on the server. This is a component located on the web server that enables the posting of content to it.

So, let's have a look at how to use the deployment features in Visual InterDev.

Deployment Targets

The first step in using the deployment feature is to specify where the target server is. This is done by creating **deployment targets** that contain the URL of the target server. Here is how to do this:

1. Select Project | New Deployment Target.

2. Enter the URL of the target in the Deploy to (URL) box in the dialog that appears, then press OK:

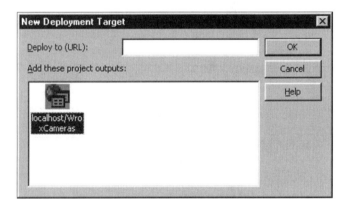

This process can be repeated to create multiple deployment targets. The project has not been deployed by creating the targets - you have just told it possible destinations where it might be deployed to.

If you then select Project | Deploy, you will see that the new deployment target(s) appear as sub menu options.

The Deployment Explorer Window

Creating deployment targets causes a new window, the **Deployment Explorer** window, to appear as a tab of the Project Explorer window:

The Deployment Explorer displays where the project will be deployed to, with the default target in bold. It is a good idea to leave this set to Deploy to My Computer, which effectively does nothing. There is a very good reason for this – every time you select Debug | Start Project, or Project | Deploy Solution, the project is deployed to this target. If you do not leave it set to your computer, then every time you start a debugging session, your project will be deployed!

When you do want to deploy a project, however, this is the easiest place to tell it where to be deployed to. Simply right click on a target and select Deploy to deploy to that target.

Apart from being an easy place to kick-start the deployment process, this window has one other big use: it is where you add files that will be deployed that are outside of the project. Initially, as is shown in the picture above, there are no outside files that will be deployed. By default, all files within the project will be deployed automatically. To add an external file, right mouse click on the line Web Content, Controls, and Applets and select Add Files. Repeat this process to add all of the necessary files.

Deploying Components

It is also possible, as long as Visual InterDev RAD Remote Deployment Support has been installed on the remote web server, to automatically have components, such as COM DLLs and MTS packages, deployed and registered on a server using the Deployment Explorer window. This feature is not always enabled because it can let developers happily throw all sorts of DLLs up to the server. However, assuming it is enabled, then it becomes possible to deploy components using either of the 'copy web project' or 'deployment' methods described above.

To Specify a Server Component

If the component is an object that will run on the web server, i.e. it is an in-process server object that has not been set up to run in MTS, then follow these steps to specify the component for deployment:

1.   In the Project Explorer window add the component to your web project.

2.   Right mouse click on the component in the Project Explorer window and select Properties.

3. In the Component Installation tab, place a check in the Register on server checkbox, then press OK:

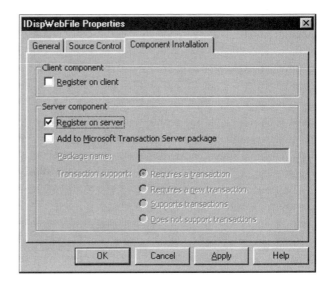

To Specify a Component to be Packaged for MTS

If the component is a server component designed to be run within MTS, then it is possible for the component to be configured such that Visual InterDev will automatically create a package for it within MTS on the target server.

1. In the Project Explorer window add the component to your web project.

2. Right mouse click on the component in the Project Explorer window and select Properties.

3. In the Component Installation tab place a check in the Register on server checkbox.

4. Place a check in the Add to Microsoft Transaction Server package checkbox.

5. In the Package name textbox, type the name of the package to which the component is to be added.

6. If your component supports transactions (the ones we created do not), set the appropriate Transaction supports option. For the objects we created in Chapter 12, you would select Does not support transactions. Transactions are used by MTS to ensure that an action only occurs if every step in that action is successfully completed – if any one step is not, the whole action (or transaction) is rolled back, i.e. everything involved in the transaction reverts back to its state at the beginning of the transaction. More information about this can be found in the Wrox Press book *Professional MTS & MSMQ Programming with VB and ASP* (ISBN 1-861001-4-60).

7. Press OK.

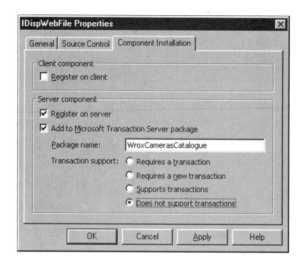

Once configured, the next time that you deploy your web application to a target server using either the 'copy web project' method or the 'deployment' method, a server component will automatically be registered on the server. Note that if you use the deployment method, you still have to add the file to the list of files to be deployed.

Having now covered deployment of your web solution, we're going to take a look at some issues relating to designing your web applications for a larger audience. So, let's begin with our old favorite, features versus reach.

Features Versus Reach

Perhaps the biggest issue facing any web developer is achieving a balance between the features required of a web application, and the technology used by its intended clients. We looked at this in our coverage of client side script and server side script, where we discussed how the features offered by each browser differ from one to the other. This is only one of the issues that a web developer must face.

The problem arises from high expectations. You will often be asked to develop features into a web application that are easy in a traditional programming language such as Visual Basic, or C++. In these environments, it is simple to develop programs with all sorts of rich features and interface possibilities. The finished application is compiled to run in a specific operating system, such as Windows, and contains all of the information necessary within itself to work as intended.

When such an application is under consideration for porting to the web, the designers often want to keep the existing functionality and expand its reach through the marvelous medium of the Internet. For the reasons we have covered, this sadly does not always turn out to be an easy task.

In managing the issue of features versus reach, the following are some of the points that you will need to consider.

Browser Type

If the application is intended for an intranet, is there a standard browser that is in use? If so, you should target your application at this browser – assuming that there is no vision of expanding the application beyond the immediate intranet.

If you are lucky enough to be using Internet Explorer 4.0 and above, you have a lot of capabilities offered by DHTML and VBScript. Netscape Navigator 4 will also offer you a good range of features, albeit to a slightly different tune to Internet Explorer 4. Whichever the case, developing for an intranet using version 4 or higher browsers is the 'holy grail' of web design – an enviable position to be in!

If your environment is the Internet, you will often find yourself having to design for multiple browser types. Your options in this situation are many:

❑ Don't use any client side script at all – this option is often not a valid one, but the use of server side script can give a lot of functionality all by itself.

❑ Code using script that will work for all of your target audience – this will normally result in you using a low subset of JavaScript without any advanced DHTML capabilities. It is still possible to do *basic* mouse rollover effects, calculations, and so on.

❑ Specify a minimum browser type, i.e. Internet Explorer 4, and also provide a slightly less optimal version for other browser types. This is quite a common approach, often seen in instances where the main site uses frames and advanced features, but offers an alternative for those who don't have the specific browser. This can be a high maintenance option, though alleviated to some degree by ASP. It is often a good idea to provide a link to the supplier of the specific browser so that readers can upgrade their browser if they want to.

❑ Use browser-sniffing capabilities, such as the Browser Capabilities component that we covered in Chapter 7, and ASP, to write code compatible with the specific browser that a client is using. This option takes a lot of work, but ultimately can produce the best site if you really need to cater for everyone.

Aside from scripting issues, another big issue in targeting multiple browsers is the use of Java Applets or ActiveX components that run on the client side. If your application makes heavy use of one of these, sometimes you will be limited by the component as to what browsers you can target. For example, if you use ActiveX controls on the client side, expect them only to work on Windows systems running Internet Explorer. Java Applets have a slightly larger reach but, as we have discussed before, there is no guarantee that your reader hasn't disabled Java Applet support for security or speed reasons. This can be a deciding factor when designing a site, and should be looked at early on.

In some cases it may be possible to work around a problem by creating a server side version of a client object, as covered in the last chapter. Another solution might be to create a client script only page that offers similar functionality.

Browser compatibility issues all add to the challenge of web design. Getting the correct flavor of client side script, server side script, and objects, can be one of the most important factors for determining the success of your application.

Bandwidth Limitations

Another factor that needs to be taken into account when designing your site is not just what browser the client will be using, but how they will be *connecting* to your site. Depending on the connection method, there could be issues of limited **bandwidth**.

Bandwidth is the measurement of how much data a particular communications media can carry, and is normally measured in bps (bits per second), Kbps (thousands of bits per second), or Mbps (millions of bits per second).

Across the Internet, your users might typically be using a modem operating at 28.8 Kbps, 33.6 Kbps, or 56.6 Kbps. They might also use an ISDN (Integrated Services Digital Network) line, which works at 128 Kbps and therefore gives a much faster browsing experience than a normal modem. New and expanding technologies such as cable modems and ADSL also offer fast connections, but the use of these solutions is, for now, still limited. Users on an intranet, such as that found in an office environment, will typically have connection speeds of from 1 Mbps up to 100 Mbps in a modern environment – at which stage you don't really have to worry quite so much about bandwidth!

Once you have determined the average speed of your users' connections, you might come up with a problem. If most access will be via an intranet or ISDN, then the problem is minimal. In most cases however, an Internet application should expect to attract a fair number of users with 28.8 Kbps modems. In this case, if you want to keep as many users as possible, you should design for the weakest link, which means that the graphical content you include in your pages should be kept to a minimum.

A page takes time to download – and large graphics, audio, and especially video, can take forever on a slower modem. In general, where bandwidth is an issue you should use graphics that have a small file size (achieved, for example, by dropping the resolution and limiting the color palette), absolutely minimal audio, if any, and you shouldn't even consider adding video content. Also, you might want to reconsider using larger components that run on the client side, as these might also be guilty of increasing the traffic to an unacceptable level for the user. With a component, the actual downloading of the component for the first time is where the main speed issue arises, but after that it is normally faster. However, this download time can put people off, and depending on how the component gets its information from the server, continuing speed issues can sometimes exist. The best way to measure these speeds is by looking at performance reports from the web server and ensuring that the speed is acceptable. If adding a large component causes a downgrading of performance, then consider removing it.

Improving Performance

When a user visits a site they expect to get a fairly snappy response. If they end up waiting for extended periods of time while your application chugs away in the background, they will either leave or repeatedly click on links to try and make things go faster. An important consideration in designing a site, therefore, is to write it to perform well.

Here are a number of tips and methods for getting the best performance out of your application:

❑   Get a powerful server. It should come as no surprise that the more powerful your server is, the faster the application will perform. Always get the maximum you can afford, in terms of RAM, processor speed, and hard disk access time. This should not be just your web server that is beefed up, but also your database server and any other server in the link.

In today's rapidly changing hardware environment, it is hard to give an exact specification of what should be used for a web server. Suggestions for a minimum configuration, serving maybe hundreds of users, would be:

Server	Processor	RAM
IIS web server, with database and MTS on different server.	Pentium 266	128
IIS web server with MTS and a few objects, database on different server.	Pentium 2 266	128-196
IIS web server with MTS and SQL Server on the same machine (this is not a great idea because all of these packages individually demand a lot of resources. Putting it all together on one machine can rapidly cause it to grind to a stand still.)	Pentium 2 366	196-256+

It is very difficult to say exactly what is required, as there are so many variables. Definitely, it is best to not overload the server. A good way to get a handle on the performance is to use the **NT Performance Monitor** found under the Administrative Tools of the Start menu. This can be used to determine the bottlenecks on your server and how it reacts to heavy user loads.

❑ Use the best data access technology. Many developers are familiar with ODBC, for example, and happily write objects and code to use it. As a method of accessing databases it works, but it is by no means the fastest. With the advent of ADO and OLE DB, as discussed in Chapter 9, developers can use a much faster means of retrieving data. Make sure that, where possible, you use an OLE DB provider for your database, not the OLE DB for ODBC driver which is just ODBC with an added extra layer of complexity. By speeding up your database access, you will significantly reduce wait time.

❑ Do not use data bound DTCs. The data bound DTCs covered in Chapter 5 are great for quickly prototyping Internet sites or pages, and for use in high bandwidth environments such as an intranet. As soon as you get into an Internet environment with lots of users, however, the advantages they offer in ease of development are massively outweighed by their poor performance and lack of scalability. DTCs scale poorly and do not perform wonderfully because they are based on script, meaning that the processor has to do a lot of work to make them perform their magic. In high demand environments, use either ASP script with ADO and OLE DB as covered in Chapter 9, or even better, use COM components that handle the database access using ADO and OLE DB, as covered in Chapter 12.

❑ Limit data returned by your queries. If your application makes heavy use of databases, try and limit the amount of data returned by your queries. Use stored procedures on the database server to not only retrieve information but to process it as much as possible. The best way to use stored procedures is to get them to calculate and return just the minimum data necessary – this is much more efficient than retrieving whole tables of data and then using script to remove the unnecessary records. By reducing the amount of data passed you can significantly cut down on processing time – especially if it's being handled by ASP script on a web server.

❑ Use client side script. Once you overcome compatibility issues, work processed on the client is work that the server doesn't have to do. As long as the script itself isn't thousands of line long, this can be a good time saver – especially if it cuts back on round trips to the server.

397

❑ Validate input on the client side. If you are able to use client side script, one very useful thing that it can do is to validate the contents of a form's fields prior to submitting them. By trapping invalid entries and prompting the user to correct them before submitting the form to the server, you can make large cuts in the volume of traffic that the server needs to handle. It also cuts down on the validation that needs to be done on the server.

❑ Write blocks of script. Try not to write little snippets of script interspersed amongst HTML code. Write big blocks of script so that the web server can process them all at once – it's faster. Also, when writing ASP script, use the <%...%> script blocks as opposed to the <SCRIPT RUNAT=Server> tags. This not only helps to make things visually different for the programmer, but the server gets a marginal performance gain by knowing immediately that it is dealing with server side script.

❑ Disable session state if you are not using it. If your application does not use session variables, as covered in Chapter 7, disable the session state on the web server – it demands a lot of server resources to maintain a session state, and you can speed up your application if it's not used. The default for a web application is to provide a session, so if you do not want to use this, you need to disable it. To disable session state, you simply need to write the following server side script statement:

```
<%@ EnableSessionState=False %>
```

Alternative methods to achieve the same result are to view the properties for the page in Visual InterDev and set EnableSessions to False. You can also select the Sessionless ASP Page option in the Properties Page dialog.

❑ Use application variables for static data. If your site normally gets information from various sources such as databases, files, and so on, and normally gets them either once per session or at other times, it might be useful to store them in application variables. Assuming that the data remains static, write some code in the global.asa (as shown in Chapter 7) to load the information once per application instead of once per user, or once per user per page. This can significantly cut back on the work that the server has to do. There is one disadvantage that you should be aware of if you do follow this suggestion – the web site needs to be restarted if you want any changes in this underlying data to take effect.

❑ Use Response.Write infrequently. If you are using ASP script to write information to the page, make one big block of script wherever possible, that only writes once to the page. This is achieved by using a local variable to contain a string, then building the string in your script before writing it to the page once using Response.Write. This cuts back on the amount of jumping back and forth that the server needs to do, and results in faster pages.

❑ Use local variables. Always use the Dim or var statement to create variables before using them, and wherever possible use local variables inside a sub procedure or function. They use a lot less resource than global variables. Refer to the section on scope in Chapter 6 for information about how to do this. A good way to enforce declaring variables in VBScript is to add the following line of code at the top of your page, in a script block:

```
Option Explicit
```

This forces you to declare any variable using a `Dim` statement before using it. If you try to use a variable that has not been declared, an error will occur.

❑ Copy collection values to local variables. While we are discussing the advantages of local variables, another good tip is to copy frequently used collection values to local variables. If, for example, your code makes frequent reference to a `Request.Querystring` variable, add some code such as:

```
Dim ItemId

ItemID = Request.Querystring("ItemId")
```

From there on in, referring to the local variable involves a lot less work than asking the server to look through the object model every time the value needs to be retrieved.

Improving the performance of your application can involve a lot of different activities, but the end result is definitely worth it. Some of the suggestions above might not at first glance look significant, but a well designed page with precise code can run circles around a poorly designed one any day.

Scalability

Scalability refers to how well your application deals with an increased number of users. It is very similar to performance, but is subtly different. A site can perform well with ten or twenty users, but perform terribly with hundreds or thousands of users. Such a site would have bad scalability.

In the Internet world, designing a site is normally about attracting customers. If you do your job well, and the site is well marketed, there is the potential for a huge number of people to visit your site. If you are not well prepared, what initially looked like a robust and well performing application with a handful of users will fall over in the most embarrassing fashion when subjected to heavy demand.

When a site has been designed in a manner that does not scale well, often the only way to fix it when scalability issues arise is by shutting it down and doing an intensive redesign. Not only is this costly in terms of resources, but you will potentially lose customers in the meantime. For this reason, designing your sites in a scalable manner can be one of the most important parts of any web project. Let's take a look at how you can make your site scale well.

Making a Scalable Application

If you've already applied the tips above to achieve good performance, then you have taken the first step towards designing a scalable solution – you have got it working well for a few users, and have got it working in the most efficient manner by removing unnecessary clutter. Building a scalable application then involves working with its *architecture*.

A web application, by its very nature, is a **distributed** application; it distributes work between the web server and various clients. Designing a scalable web application involves extending that architecture so that the load is spread even further, as we discussed in the previous chapter.

Let's take a look at some of the ways that you can make your application scale well:

❑ Place ASP code into COM components. Chapter 12 discussed removing code from the web page to components. This process is perhaps the easiest way to make a big difference to the scalability of your application. Using a COM component reduces the amount of work that the web server needs to do in order to send results.

❑ Use MTS to implement server objects. By using MTS it is easy to distribute the workload across multiple servers. This capability removes work from the web server's processor onto other machines that can be optimized for the work they need to do. If you have components that need to get information from a database, for example, it might be a good idea to run them on the database server. If you have other objects that calculate complex logic but return simple answers, placing them on a separate machine can readily reduce the load on your web server.

❑ Do not over use include files. Now that you know how to use COM components, try to limit the use of include files in your application. Include files, as mentioned in Chapter 7, enable developers to quickly insert reusable code into ASP pages. The problem with using include files is that, quite often, developers create large include files containing many functions, when they only need to use one of those functions in a particular page. By inserting the include file, the server has to load the whole file to get at the one function – a process that becomes processor-intensive with large numbers of users.

❑ Do not create application and session variables for objects. By using application and session variables it is very easy to store information for use across your site. One trap to avoid, however, is creating *objects* that have session or application scopes. This would be done using code such as:

```
Set session("AnObject") = Server.CreateObject("AnObject.Class")
```

There are many developers who do this, because once coded like this they have easy access to the object throughout the life of the session. This is a huge waste of resources, especially since in most cases the object is used in only a few pages. It is normally a better idea to simply create the object when needed, or load it once and then create session variables that store the property values of the object and use them instead.

Maintainability

Designing a site that works well, scales well, and looks good can be a difficult and time-consuming task. This being the case, it makes sense to be able to support, upgrade, and repair the site without having to reinvent the wheel every time.

A web application can quickly include client side script, HTML code, ASP code, components, include files, DTCs, and so on, making the interactions between these various pieces very complex. The best way to save yourself, or others, a lot of heartache is to design your application from the outset with maintenance in mind. Here are some ways to make life easier:

❑ Use site diagrams. Even if you do not use the navigation controls that are provided with Visual InterDev, site diagrams, as covered in Chapter 4, provide a good overview of your site that can help new developers to quickly determine the layout. The site diagram can also be used to easily and rapidly change the navigation structure of a site that has made use of the navigation DTCs. The links view feature also enables you to quickly look at the links on a page and determine what is broken. To use the links view, simply select a page in the Project Explorer window and select View | View Links from the main menu. The selected page will appear in the center, with links *into* it on the left, and links *from* the page on the right.

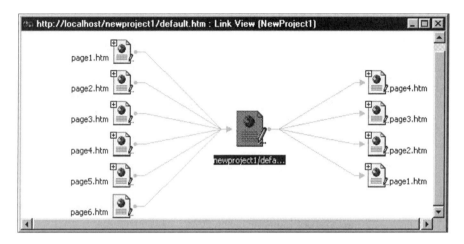

❑ Comment your code. Adding comments to your code can vastly improve its readability, making all the difference if you come back to a difficult bit six months down the track. As long as your web server is Internet Information Server 4.0 or above, server side script comments make no difference to the speed of your application, as they are automatically ignored when the script is processed. However, if you add comments to your client side script, then they are still sent to the client's browser, resulting in more information being sent. Also, if you are using Internet Information Server 3.0, then server side script comments will slow your code down. Therefore, if you are using IIS 3.0 or want to use comments about your client side script, make a copy of the file with comments in and save it in a comments directory separate from the main site.

❑ Use a coding standard. If your code is all written to the same standard, it becomes significantly easier to maintain. A standard can be as simple as the following:

```
<%@ Language=VBScript %>
<%Option Explicit 'ensure all variables explicitly declared with DIM %>

<HTML>
<HEAD>
<META NAME="GENERATOR" Content="Microsoft Visual Studio 6.0">
</HEAD>
<BODY>
<%

'variables must be declared using Dim, and Hungarian notation
Dim strAnyString
```

401

```
sub AnySub()
        'PURPOSE: always include the purpose of a procedure at the top
        'Also include lots of white space to improve readability

        'l prefixes a local variable within a sub procedure
        Dim lstrLocalString

        lstrLocalString = "Hi there"
        lstrLocalString = lstrLocalString & "<BR>How are you?"

        'use Response.Write only once where possible
        Response.Write lstrLocalString

End Sub

call AnySub()

%>


</BODY>
</HTML>
```

❑ Use COM components where possible. Using COM components, as covered in the previous chapter, is great for maintainability – not only is the ASP script shorter, but the component can be upgraded without needing to stop the web server.

❑ Use PageObject DTCs where COM components are not possible. If your site is being hosted on another ISP, sometimes they will not let you place COM components on their server, or it might be difficult to do so. PageObject design time controls, as covered in Chapter 8, can give similar functionality to COM objects as far as reusability is concerned, and they are considerably easier to implement in supported environments. The trade off of using these is scalability – they do not compare at all well with COM components and MTS. Still, when maintainability is an issue, the PageObject DTC can be a suitable solution.

If you include these features in the applications that you create, maintaining them can be greatly simplified. A large application that does not use these features can often be difficult and expensive to maintain – and doubly more expensive if a critical upgrade needs to occur within a certain time frame!

Using Visual SourceSafe

An inescapable fact when building a large web application is that you're going to end up with a lot of files. At the beginning of this book we looked at how Visual InterDev uses local and master mode to control master copies and local development copies of the files in an application. This works fine, and is a great solution for quick and dirty applications, but as soon as you have a large application with lots of developers, more is needed. This is where **Visual SourceSafe 6.0** (VSS) enters the scene.

VSS is a database that controls the use of files in an application, and keeps track of the various versions, changes, and history of those files. Using VSS it is possible to roll back to an earlier version at any time if an error occurs – a potential lifesaver if a big mistake is made. VSS is also a great help when working in a team, as it allows you to lock other developers out of a file while you are working on it. Let's take a look at the components that make VSS work.

Visual SourceSafe Components

VSS requires a few components in order to work:

- ❑ **Visual SourceSafe Server**. This is the master database and control program for VSS that needs to be installed on your master web server. When installing it, you need to ensure that the integrations options are selected.

- ❑ **FrontPage Extensions**. As discussed in Chapter 2 of this book, the FrontPage Extensions need to be installed on your web server for many features of Visual InterDev and VSS to work.

- ❑ **Visual InterDev**. Once the VSS server is installed on a web server that has the FrontPage Extensions, Visual InterDev has all of the necessary menu and interface options to communicate with VSS. There is also a separate **VSS Client**, which is an Explorer-like utility that can be installed separately. This is not necessary with Visual InterDev, since it handles communications with VSS for you. If, however, you require complete control of VSS, it is best to install the VSS Client, which can be launched from within Visual InterDev by selecting Project | Source Control | SourceSafe. This gives you access to detailed versioning information, history, and other capabilities that are not easily achieved in the Visual InterDev environment.

How to Use Visual SourceSafe

Once VSS is set up and installed correctly, it is a simple matter to use it from within Visual InterDev. The use of VSS is best described as a series of tasks that you need to perform from time to time. These tasks involve configuring and maintaining your source code. They can include adding a web application to Source Control, after which it is in the VSS database, and checking files in and out of VSS when you need to work on them.

Let's take a look at how these tasks are performed.

Adding a Web Application to Source Control

To add your application to source control, follow these steps:

1. Open the web application.

2. Select the project that you wish to add in the Project Explorer window.

3. From the main menu, select Project | Source Control | Add to Source Control.

4. In the dialog that appears, select to either add the selected project - (Selection), if you want to add just the selected one, or the whole Solution of projects, if you want to add all of the projects within the open solution:

5. The next step is to login to VSS. If you are the only developer, chances are that the user name will be admin, and the password will be blank. This can all be changed using the Visual SourceSafe Administration program on the master server, where it is also possible to create individual logins and passwords. Enter the Username and Password if required and press OK:

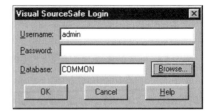

6. In the next dialog, enter the name that the project will be saved as, which becomes the name of the folder in which it will appear within VSS. You can specify where the folder will be using the Explorer-like pane:

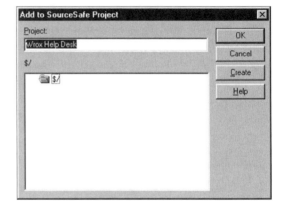

7. You will be prompted to create the directory, seeing as it does not already exist. Accept this.

8. In the next dialog, select the specific solutions that will be added to Source Control, as well as entering any comments you might want for the solution, such as the purpose of the project:

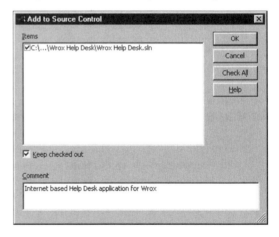

9. The last dialog box asks you to confirm that you want to enable Source Control for the project. Press OK. Your computer will chug away for a while, copying the files up to the master VSS server and enabling Source Control.

Checking Files In and Out of Source Control

Once your application is under Source Control, you can easily check in and check out files, from within Visual InterDev. This is done in exactly the same way as you have already been doing while using Get Working Copy and Release Working Copy.

A file that is under VSS control will have its context menu (i.e. the menu that appears when you right mouse click on the file in the Project Explorer window) changed, so that instead of saying Get Working Copy and Release Working Copy, you are instead given options to:

- ❑ Check Out a file - this retrieves an editable version of the file from VSS into your local web application.

- ❑ Check In a file – this updates the VSS copy of the file with the copy in your local web application – it also updates the copy on the master web application. The version that is left in your local and master web applications is normally then set to be read only, promoting the need to check a file out again later in the correct manner.

- ❑ Get Latest Version of a file – this gets the latest version (read only) of the file from Source Control and replaces your copy with it. This option is slightly different from the option of the same name when you do not use VSS – without VSS this does a similar thing, but gets the latest version from the master copy of the web.

Basically, when you right mouse click on a file, the options are very similar to what you have been using, and are easy to use and understand. One thing to be aware of is that when you save a file as normal, it does not update the file into VSS. This is only done by the use of the Check In command.

One last option that you have in Visual InterDev is to compare versions, which is achieved by selecting Project | Source Control | Compare Versions. This gives you the option of comparing two versions of a file, and viewing the differences. This can be very useful in tracking the history of a file and understanding what changes have been made. This option is also available within the VSS Explorer if you have installed it, where it is much easier to use and more comprehensive.

Simultaneous Checkout and Merging

An option that can be configured within the Visual SourceSafe server is to allow simultaneous checkouts. This basically enables multiple developers to check out and work on the same file at once – a situation that can potentially be confusing. Where possible avoid this, but if you must use this feature, then read on…

If this option is set within the VSS server, and somebody else has made changes to a file while you had it checked out, VSS will warn you of this. You are then given the option to review the differences between the two files and either merge them, accept specific changes, or disregard changes from either version.

This capability gives you the option to control what goes into SourceSafe – and it works best if you each agree to work on a different part of a file. In a team environment, this can often be a good way to ensure that work is finished for a tight deadline. Just be careful and take time to understand the changes that you check into VSS. At worst, you can always rollback to an earlier version of the page.

Using Visual Component Manager

The **Visual Component Manager** (VCM) is used as a storage place for components, reusable project files, and so on. It is accessible in the Visual InterDev Enterprise edition only, by selecting View | Other Windows | Visual Component Manager, and is used to store and share work between team members. This work can include components created in other development environments, such as Visual Basic, Visual C++, and so on. An example of the Visual Component Manager is shown:

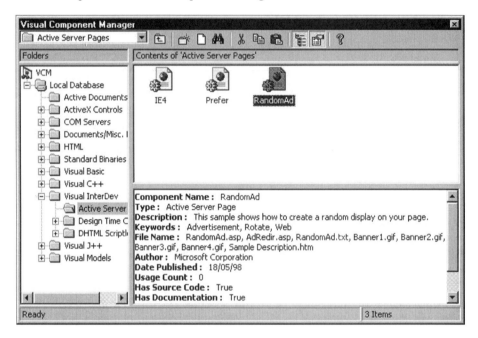

The Visual Component Manager has a comprehensive commenting and indexing facility to enable developers to retrieve their components, by performing searches on the contents of the Visual Component Manager. To search for a component, simply click on the binoculars icon in the toolbar, and enter in your search details.

On top of this search facility, the Visual Component Manager is organized in the familiar Windows Explorer method of folders and files, meaning that you can store your components in a logical place and quickly browse to them later. Once located, a component can easily be added to the current Visual InterDev project.

What is a Component in VCM?

A component within the Visual Component manager can consist of many separate files, such as images, web pages, ASP pages, COM components, Visual Basic source files, and so on. Components are stored in folders that detail their purpose, for example Visual InterDev Active Server Page components are kept in the folder Visual InterDev\Active Server Pages.

Creating a New Folder

If you cannot find a folder that suits your purpose, it is easy to create your own. This can often be advantageous if you work in a project-oriented environment, where you might want one folder per project. You might instead group your components based on purpose, such as database access, financial calculations, payment information, and so on.

To create a new folder:

1. Open the Visual Component Manager by selecting View | Other Windows | Visual Component Manager.

2. In the left hand pane, open the database and folder that will be the parent of the new folder.

3. Right mouse click on the parent folder and select New | Folder.

4. The new folder will appear under the parent folder with the name New Folder highlighted. Simply type in the name of the new folder and press *Return*.

The new folder is then ready for use!

Adding Components to the Visual Component Manager

Once you have created a component that is suitable for reuse, you can easily add it to the VCM to share it between your projects and with other team members. Along with the component, you can store various support files such as help files, sample code, and so on. You can also index it for later reuse.

To add a component to the VCM:

1. Open the Visual Component Manager by selecting View | Other Windows | Visual Component Manager.

2. Open a folder in the left hand pane where you want to store the component, or create a new folder by right clicking on the Visual InterDev folder and selecting New | folder.

3. Right mouse click in the pane and select New | Component from the menu, or click on the 'publish a new component' icon in the toolbar (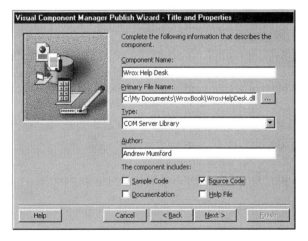). This starts the Component Publishing wizard. If you see an Introduction screen, skip it by pressing Next to get to step 1 of the wizard:

4. Enter a name for the component that will be useful for retrieving it later. If we were creating a component for the `WroxCameras` COM object that we created in Chapter 12, the name might be WroxCameras Component.

5. Enter or select the file name of the primary file. This might be the `.dll` of a COM component, or else an `.asp` page or `.htm` page.

6. From the drop down Type box, select the best description for the component's type.

7. Enter your name as the Author.

8. Place check marks next to any optional information you will include in the package, then press Next.

9. Enter a description for the component that will help you retrieve it.

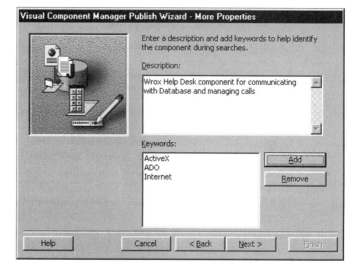

10. Next, add some keywords that will help you retrieve the component. Press Add to bring up the Item Keywords dialog:

11. The arrow keys move words from the Available list to the Selected list on the right. If the keyword is not available, press the "+" button to add a new keyword. Pressing OK takes you back to the Component Publishing wizard.

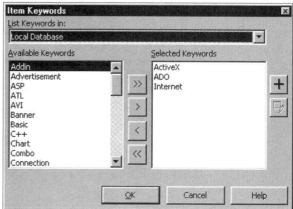

12. Press Next to go on to the next step. This is where you add any files that you wish to include with the project. These should ideally match what you specified in the first step of this wizard. Use the Add Files button to add files, or Remove Files button to remove incorrectly added files.

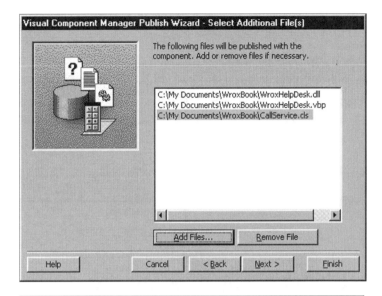

13. Press Next to move on to the next step of the wizard. This is where you specify which (if any) files require registering as a COM object when installed on a new computer. This will automatically register the object as a COM server object and make it ready for use in any script that you might have in your web pages. Place a check next to the files that should be registered:

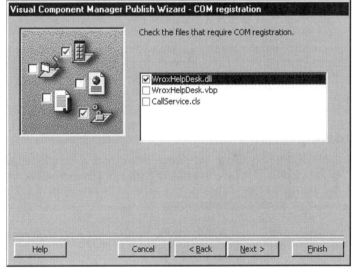

14. Press the Next button to go on to the confirmation page. This asks you to press Finish to create the component in VCM. Press Finish, and the component will be created!

You should now see an icon created in the top right hand pane for your new component. The bottom pane will display a lot of information that you added in the publishing process:

How VCM Stores Components

Components are stored in a database that is called a **repository**. The repository can either be based on a SQL Server or Access database. When installed, each user will automatically have their own local repository, which appears as Local VCM Database in the folders pane.

The local VCM database is visible only by yourself. Any components that you add here are not available on other PCs. To share your components with other team members, you need to create a new repository on a shared network drive that all team members have access to.

Creating a New Repository

It is possible to create new repositories for sharing work between team members – to do this, simply right mouse click in the folders pane and choose Repository | New. You will be prompted to select the type and location of the new database, which should be in a location visible by all members of the team – in other words on a shared network drive.

After a new database is made, team members can save their components to this shared repository and thereafter use each other's components.

Adding a Component to Your Project

After a component has been added, anyone with access to the VCM database to which it was added can find the component, then easily add it and all of its files to their current project.

In order to assist in retrieving a component, the VCM has an extensive search facility that enables a user to search for components based on any of the keywords added in the publishing process, or by matching text in the component name or description.

The search facility is accessed by pressing the binoculars (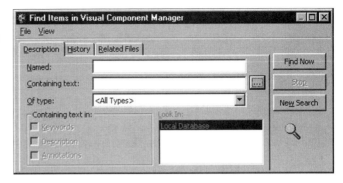) button on the main toolbar of the VCM:

Once you have found the component, it is easy to use it in your project by right mouse clicking on the component and selecting one of the following:

- ❑ **Add to Project** if it is a web page, file, or standard executable program. This adds the relevant files to the web project.

- ❑ **Add to Toolbox** if it is a COM server object or ActiveX control. This adds the component to the Visual InterDev Toolbox, from where it can then be easily added to any web pages in your project.

You do not need to remember which of the above methods to choose, as you will only be given one option depending on the type of component that you have selected.

Summary

We started this chapter by showing how to deploy web applications, which you should now be able to create, having worked through almost the entire book. Deployment enables you to put the applications that you've just developed into use in a production environment.

We also saw that designing a web application is a task that incorporates a lot of skill and effort. Visual InterDev offers many tools to assist throughout the whole process, and coupled with a good design that takes into account the topics covered in this chapter, robust and dynamic sites can be created.

A web application brings together many diverse technologies into a medium with more reach than most other programs. A complex web site consists of many pages, objects and stores of data that interact with each other to provide a hopefully seamless whole. Throughout this book, we have looked at how to create such applications using Visual InterDev, and we have seen how the powerful features and tools it offers can make developing them an easier task. In this chapter, we have seen a lot of tips and methods that will make the sites we create durable and successful.

We have also discussed two useful features for making life as a web developer a little easier. We saw how Visual SourceSafe can give a degree of recoverability to our projects, at the same time as enhancing the ability of a team of developers to work together. We also looked at using the Visual Component Manager to easily manage any items that you want to use, share and reuse in your web projects.

In the next chapter, we will tie up the book by creating a new application that uses some of the techniques covered in this and earlier chapters. The application will also make use of Microsoft Access 2000 as a back end in place of SQL Server 7, to give you a look at how to use another database system with your web projects.

Case Study: Intranet Help Desk

To wrap up this book and conclude the topics that we've introduced in the preceding chapters, we are going to look at creating one more web site. This site will be a new one, leaving behind our familiar Wrox Cameras store, and will be the beginnings of a simple *intranet-based help desk system*. To demonstrate again how the various technologies work together, we will be incorporating a database, ASP server side script, a Visual Basic COM component, and of course web pages, to make the finished product.

The application that we will make is a simple one – it is a system for logging support calls, and providing supervisors with the ability to review and close those calls. To add a little bit of difference, we will be using Microsoft Access 2000 as the database solution in place of Microsoft SQL Server 7, which we've used so far. (We'll also mention how to convert a database from Access to SQL Server). Access is the 'little brother' of SQL Server, and while it is not up to enterprise level applications, it is adequately capable for smaller applications, and worth learning how to use. More on that soon, but for now let's look at a list of the features that the solution is to provide:

- ❑ Any user should be able to log a call.

- ❑ The user will fill in an HTML form whose contents will be submitted into the Access database.

- ❑ The Access database will maintain a list of supervisors who can read the list of calls.

- ❑ Supervisors must login to be recognized – their user name and password will be compared to the database.

- ❑ Supervisors will be able to view a list of calls filtered by status: all calls, open calls, and closed calls.

- ❑ Supervisors should be able to change the status of calls from open to closed, and also enter their own calls.

- ❑ There will be a page where supervisors can view statistics on calls logged.

We will assume that the supervisors deal with the calls outside of this system. This is a fairly simple features list that nonetheless gives us the capability to include some of the technologies that we have covered in this book.

The COM component that we create will provide services for submitting calls to the database, reviewing the calls, reviewing call statistics, and updating the status of a call. The login functionality of the login page will retrieve its information from the database directly by using server side script. The completed system that we'll create can be represented by the following diagram:

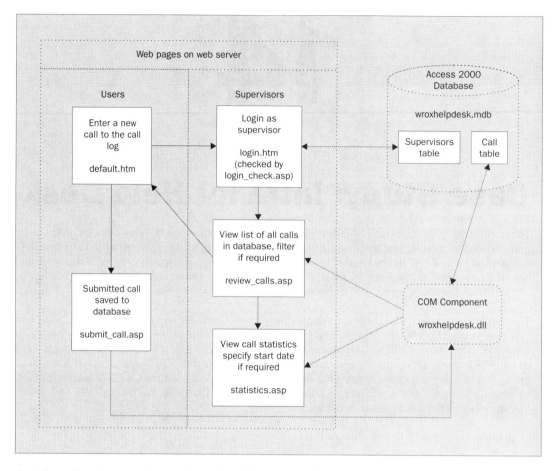

Let's begin by designing the database that will store the calls.

Designing the Database

As mentioned, this help desk system will be designed to use a Microsoft Access 2000 database as the back end data solution. This has been chosen for the simple reason that Access is a very pervasive database that is in use in many offices, it is cheap and, by including it here, you can learn how to use it with your web applications. Access should not be considered as a replacement for SQL Server in high use environments, as it is nowhere near as scaleable as SQL Server. However, Access is a good solution for quick prototypes or low use scenarios without hundreds of users.

In designing our database, the first thing that we need to do is to look at the requirements. The features list above details the two tables that will be required – a table to support the *calls*, and a table containing the names and passwords of the *supervisors*. Here is a summary of the design of these tables:

Call table:

Field	Data Type	Size	Default	Description
call_id	Autonumber	Long integer	-	Unique ID of the call, automatically generated.
name	Text	100	-	User name of person who placed call.
title	Text	100	-	Job title.
emailaddress	Text	100	-	Email address.
extension	Text	20	-	Telephone extension number.
product	Text	100	-	Name of product that user is having problem with.
priority	Number	Integer	-	Priority from 1 (low) to 5 (high).
subject	Text	100	-	Short subject line of problem.
description	Memo	-	-	Detailed description of problem.
timesubmitted	Date/Time	-	=now()	Time the call was submitted, automatically generated by the database.
status	Text	100	Open	Status of call: Open or Closed (finished) – database defaults all new calls as Open.

The call_id field is of a special datatype – **autonumber**. An autonumber field is a numeric field that offers a few benefits:

❑   It is a long integer field that is automatically incremented by the database every time a new record is added. (However, this does have the downside of meaning that you cannot update an autonumber field yourself.)

❑   It is guaranteed to be unique, making it ideal for primary keys. This is the use to which we have put it here.

415

Supervisor table:

Field	Data Type	Size	Default	Description
user_name	Text	50	-	User name of the supervisor for login purposes.
password	Text	50	-	Password of the user.

By maintaining the records in the supervisor table, it will be possible to control exactly who has access to the call list features of the application. This means that users who are not supervisors will not be able to close calls, view other people's calls, and so on. In this way, we are designing some basic security into the site.

*In a larger environment there would probably also be a separate users table, that would store details of all of the users who can access the system. There would then need to be a **security_level** field to define whether the user is a normal user, a supervisor, or whatever. Having a users table would allow us to avoid repetition of users' details in the calls table when a user enters more than one call. However, for our small system, the tables that we've designed will do the job just fine.*

Let's now look at how to create this database.

Try it Out – Creating a Database in Access 2000

This process is similar in older versions of Access, and can be adapted to suit. If you are using an older version, the screens shown will be slightly different, but the functionality and steps you take will be pretty much the same.

1. Start Access 2000. In the dialog that appears, select Blank Access database and press OK:

2. Type in the name of the database file to be created and select a location. The database we will be creating should be named **wroxhelpdesk.mdb**. (The **mdb** extension is automatically added for Microsoft Access Databases.) The location of the database is quite important, because when our web application component connects to the database, it will need to know the location, and have all the necessary security rights to open the database file. It is also a good idea to place the database in a location where it will be backed up regularly, in case of errors. You will want this path to be mirrored in the production environment also, because the location details are hard-coded into the web pages and components that we create. A simple solution is to put the database in a very simple directory, for example c:\databases\wroxhelpdesk.mdb, and then ensure that it exists like this on the production server as well.

3. Press *Return* or click **Create**, and in the window that opens, you are given a list of options for creating tables - double click on **Create table in Design view**:

4. Type in the **Field Names**, **Data Types**, **Sizes**, and **Default Values** specified earlier to create the call table. Note that data types can be quickly entered by selecting them from a drop down list in the **Data Type** field. Right mouse click on the call_id field and make it the **Primary Key** for the table. When finished, close the table and save it as **call**:

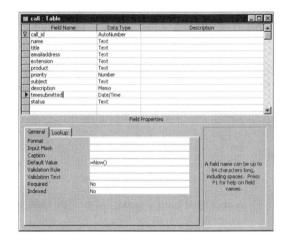

5. Create a new blank table in design view.

6. Type in the **Field Names**, **Data Types**, **Sizes**, and **Default Values** specified earlier to create the supervisor table. When finished, close the table and save it as **supervisor**:

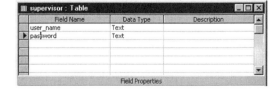

417

7. When prompted to define a primary key, select No.

8. Double click on the supervisor table to open it in data entry mode. Enter some user names and passwords, as shown opposite:

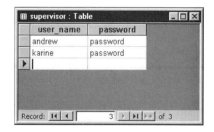

9. Close the table (this automatically saves it), and then quit Access – the database is completed.

With the database finished, whenever you want to add new supervisors to the application, it is a simple matter of opening the database, double clicking on the supervisor table, and adding new records.

If you want to switch to using SQL Server, it is a straightforward task to 'upsize' the Access database into SQL Server. To do this, within Access select Tools | Database Utilities | Upsizing Wizard, and follow the steps of the wizard. This process will create your database structure and copy all of the data in your tables across to SQL Server, making it a better option than simply recreating the database from scratch in SQL Server. If you don't have Access, then you have no option but to create the database *manually* in SQL Server.

Creating the VB COM Component

This application will involve a lot of database access, which can make for large ASP files, with all of the disadvantages discussed in Chapter 13. The database access falls into two main categories – *logging in*, and *talking to the call table*. For enhanced coverage of our options, we are going to use ASP script in our web application to control logging in, but we are going to create a Visual Basic COM component to manage communications with the call table.

The COM component will run on the server and talk to the Access database using ADO and OLE DB. It will be called `WroxHelpDesk`, and will have a class called `CallService`. The class object will expose five methods, as follows:

❑ `NewCall`: this method will be used to enter a new call, and will accept as parameters the details of the call.

❑ `ShowAllCalls`: this method will return a string that is an HTML table of calls, filtered by status. The filter will be a parameter, containing either 'ALL', 'OPEN', or 'CLOSED'.

❑ `ShowOneCall`: this method will return a string containing HTML to display the full details of a single call. It will accept as a parameter the call id.

❑ `ShowStatistics`: this method will return a string that is an HTML table displaying basic statistics of all calls, in date order. It will accept a start date as a parameter, and will show all calls from the start date until the current date.

❑   `UpdateStatus`: this method will change the status of a call and it will accept two parameters - the id of the call to be changed, and the new status for that call.

In order to connect to the database, we will be storing our connection string in the registry, which we will explain shortly. To retrieve the connection string from the database, we will have one private function that will be used internally by our COM component:

❑   `GetConnectionString`: private function to retrieve connection information from the registry. The fact that this is private means that it is not visible or usable by any controlling programs.

The component will only return the information necessary to meet the request. It will also not actually return database queries to the web page, but will instead return a string. This is a much better method than passing complete recordsets to the client, and then using script to carry out the filtering. The method used here performs and scales in a much better manner.

With this simple design in mind, let's look at making our component. The first part we will look at is the private function for retrieving the database connection string.

GetConnectionString (Private Function)

This function is private, meaning that it cannot be seen or used by any controlling applications – it is only usable by code within the component. The purpose of this function is to return a string that contains the connection string necessary to access the database.

In the COM component that we created previously for our Wrox Cameras application, we wrote the database connection string directly into our code. This is far from ideal for maintenance purposes, because every time the connection information changes, we have to change the COM component and recompile it. With an Access database, the connection string includes the path to the location of the database file – if you had to recompile the whole COM component every time you moved this file, you would not have created the best of components.

The solution is to store the connection string inside the **registry**. The registry is the descendant of old `.ini` files, which store information important for the configuration of Windows and various applications. With Visual Basic, it is possible to use some built-in functions to save settings into the registry and later retrieve them. By using the registry to store the connection string, we need to first off set the value in the registry of the computer where the component will run. Every computer that uses the component will need this information set, or else the component will report an error.

Try it Out - Manually Setting a Value in the Registry

1.   In the Windows Start menu, select Run.

2.   In the dialog that appears, type in regedit and press OK:

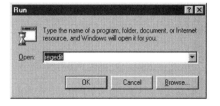

3. The Registry Editor will open. The built-in Visual Basic functions that we will be using automatically save information to the following location: HKEY_CURRENT_USER\Software\VB and VBA Program Settings. Locate this in the Registry Editor, which works in a similar manner to Windows Explorer.

4. Click on the VB and VBA Program Settings node. From the main menu, choose Edit | New | Key. A new key will appear entitled New Key #1. Change its name by overtyping it with WroxHelpDesk, which is the name of our component.

5. Create a new key by selecting the WroxHelpDesk key that we just created, and selecting Edit | New | Key again. Change the name of this key to read Settings.

6. We are now going to create a string value to store the connection string. Select the Settings key that we just created, then select Edit | New | String Value from the main menu. This time, a new value will appear in the right hand pane, which you can overwrite as before. Overwrite it with ConnectionString.

7. We now need to enter the value of the connection string. Select ConnectionString in the right hand pane and then choose Edit | Modify from the main menu. In the dialog that appears, enter the value:

Provider=Microsoft.Jet.OLEDB.4.0;Data Source=C:\databases\wroxhelpdesk.mdb;User ID=Admin;Password=""

8. In this string, replace the value after Data Source with the path to the Access database that we created earlier. Also, this example specifies a user name of Admin and a blank password. This is the default for any Access database that has not been secured. If you secure your Access database (by selecting Tools | Security within Access itself), then you will need to specify a value User ID and Password here.

9. Once the string is correct, press OK to save the value. The Registry Editor should now look like this:

10. Close the Registry Editor.

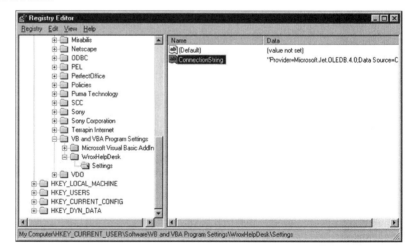

We have just created the connection string for our component in the registry. It can now be used by our COM component and, every time the connection string needs to be changed, we simply change it in the registry and our component will automatically use the new value.

Now that we have stored the value in the registry, we need to write the GetConnectionString function into our COM component, to retrieve it.

Try it Out – Creating the COM Component

1. When starting Visual Basic 6, select to create a new **ActiveX DLL**. Once the DLL has been opened, choose **Project | Project1 Properties** to bring up the **Project Properties** dialog, where you can set the various configurations for an ActiveX DLL. The settings should be as shown:

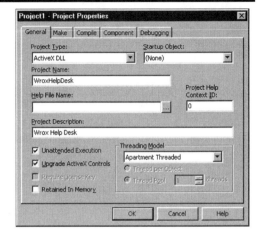

2. Click **OK**, then in the **Properties** window change the **Name** of the class module that has been created to **CallService**. This will result in access to the class, by creating an object of `WroxHelpDesk.CallService`.

3. It is also necessary to add a project reference to the ADO type library so that our component knows how to communicate with the database. To do this, select **Project | References**, and in the dialog list that appears, place a check mark in the box before **Microsoft ActiveX Data Object Library 2.1** (or whichever is the highest number that will be available on the server), then press **OK**. After this has been done, we get down to creating the methods of the class.

4. To create the function, type in **Private Function GetConnectionString() as String** into the general declarations section of the Visual Basic class module. Pressing *Return* will add the corresponding `End Function` line and position your cursor for typing. Don't forget, if you want to use the IntelliSense feature to help you, press *Ctrl + Space* after typing a few characters. Here is the listing for this function:

```
Private Function GetConnectionString() As String

    'purpose: retrieve the connection string from the registry
    'putting the path in the registry improves the portability
    'of the application

    On Error GoTo err_GetConnectionString

    Dim strConnectionString
    strConnectionString = GetSetting("WroxHelpDesk", "Settings", _
                "ConnectionString", "EMPTY")
    If strConnectionString = "EMPTY" Then
      Err.Raise 9999, "GetConnectionString", "Unable to find a _
                connection string for WroxHelpDesk within the registry."
```

```
  Else
    GetConnectionString = strConnectionString
  End If

  exit_GetConnectionString:
    Exit Function

  err_GetConnectionString:
    Err.Raise Err.Number, "GetConnectionString", Err.Description
    Resume exit_GetConnectionString

End Function
```

This function simply uses the `GetSetting` statement of Visual Basic to retrieve the value that we have stored within the registry. If there is no value, then the `GetSetting` statement returns a value of `EMPTY`, as specified in the last parameter. The `If` statement then checks to ensure that the value is not empty - if it is, an error is returned - if it is not, then the `ConnectionString` value is returned as the result of the function.

The function can then be called from anywhere within the component, using the following code:

```
Dim strConnectionString As String

StrConnectionString = GetConnectionString()
```

This is exactly what we do in all the other methods of this component. Because it is private, the function will not work from outside the COM component.

We have also included here an error handling routine that will cause any errors to be passed to the controlling application of our COM component – in this case the ASP page. This is achieved by using the `Err.Raise` method, as in:

```
    Err.Raise 9999, "GetConnectionString", "Unable to find a _
              connection string for WroxHelpDesk within the registry."
```

This raises an error that the ASP page can then handle in the normal manner. The `Err.Raise` method has the following parameters:

- ❑ `Number`   The error number of the generated error.
- ❑ `Source`   A string specifying where the error occurred.
- ❑ `Description`   A string specifying the error description.
- ❑ `HelpFile`   An optional string specifying a help file in which further details can be found.
- ❑ `HelpContext`   An optional number to identify the Context ID in the help file for the error.

The ASP page can then retrieve these properties from the `Err` object whenever this error occurs in our COM component.

NewCall Method

The `NewCall` method is used to create a new call in the database. As this does not return any values, we use a sub routine rather than a function. This routine should be typed in below the `GetConnectionString` function. The listing for this method is shown below:

```
Public Sub NewCall(strName As String, strTitle As String, _
            strEmailAddress As String, strExtension As String, _
            strProduct As String, strPriority As String, _
            strSubject As String, strDescription As String)


  On Error GoTo err_NewCall


  'retrieve all calls from DB and write to table
  Dim adoConn As New ADODB.Connection
  Dim adoCmd As New ADODB.Command
  Dim strConnectionString As String
  Dim strCommand As String


  'retrieve connection string
  strConnectionString = GetConnectionString()


  'build command string by concatenation
  strCommand = "INSERT INTO call (name,title,emailaddress,extension, _
            product,priority,subject,description) VALUES ("
  strCommand = strCommand & Chr(34) & strName & Chr(34) & ","
  strCommand = strCommand & Chr(34) & strTitle & Chr(34) & ","
  strCommand = strCommand & Chr(34) & strEmailAddress & Chr(34) & ","
  strCommand = strCommand & Chr(34) & strExtension & Chr(34) & ","
  strCommand = strCommand & Chr(34) & strProduct & Chr(34) & ","
  strCommand = strCommand & strPriority & ","
  strCommand = strCommand & Chr(34) & strSubject & Chr(34) & ","
  strCommand = strCommand & Chr(34) & strDescription & Chr(34) & ")"


  'set ADO Command Properties
  adoCmd.CommandType = 1        '1 signifies a type of adCmdText
  adoCmd.CommandText = strCommand


  'open the Connection
  adoConn.Open strConnectionString


  'associate the Command with the Open Connection
  adoCmd.ActiveConnection = adoConn
```

```
    'execute the command
    adoCmd.Execute


exit_NewCall:
    'close connection and set ADO objects to nothing
    adoConn.Close
    Set adoConn = Nothing
    Set adoCmd = Nothing
    Exit Sub


err_NewCall:
    Err.Raise Err.Number, "NewCall", Err.Description
    Resume exit_NewCall


End Sub
```

This method accepts as parameters the values of each of the fields in the call table. The component will be passed these parameters from an ASP page that receives input from the user. The code then simply inserts the values into the database using an INSERT SQL statement, with the two remaining values of timesubmitted and status defaulting to the default values set in the database.

Any errors in this, and other procedures within the component, are handled by the Err.Raise statement, which passes the error details back to the controlling application – meaning in this case that the ASP page will handle the error.

ShowAllCalls Method

The ShowAllCalls method returns a string that is the HTML contents of a table. It does this without returning the beginning or ending <TABLE> tags. The soon to be covered ShowOneCall method does include the <TABLE> tags. These two methods are written differently to show you some of the flexibility that you can code into your components. By excluding the beginning table tags, it is possible to change the appearance of the table in the HTML page. By including the table tags, you do not need to write as much script into your web page.

The ShowAllCalls method accepts a parameter of strStatus. This is a string to which our ASP page will pass the values ALL, OPEN, or CLOSED. Using this parameter, the method returns a filtered list of calls retrieved from the database. Type the following listing after that for the previous method:

```
Public Function ShowAllCalls(strStatus As String) As String


  On Error GoTo err_ShowAllCalls


  'retrieve all calls from DB and write to table
  Dim adoConn As New ADODB.Connection
  Dim adoCmd As New ADODB.Command
  Dim adoRS As New ADODB.Recordset
```

```
Dim strConnectionString As String
Dim strCalls As String        'string to hold the call list's HTML
Dim strCommand As String       'string to build SQL query


'retrieve connection string
strConnectionString = GetConnectionString()


'define command string
If strStatus = "ALL" Then
  strCommand = "SELECT * FROM call ORDER BY timesubmitted"
Else          'filter based on strStatus
  strCommand = "SELECT * FROM call WHERE status=" & Chr(34) & _
            strStatus & Chr(34) & " ORDER BY timesubmitted"
End If


'set ADO Command Properties
adoCmd.CommandType = 1
adoCmd.CommandText = strCommand


'open the Connection
adoConn.Open strConnectionString


'associate the Command with the Open Connection
adoCmd.ActiveConnection = adoConn


'retrieve recordset
Set adoRS = adoCmd.Execute
If adoRS.EOF Then
  strCalls = ""          'write nothing -no results
Else
  Do While Not adoRS.EOF
    'process results to create table
    strCalls = strCalls & "<TR>" & vbCrLf
    strCalls = strCalls & "<TD><A HREF=" & Chr(34) & _
            "review_calls.asp?showcall=" & adoRS("call_id").Value _
            & Chr(34) & ">" & adoRS("subject").Value & "</A></TD>" & vbCrLf
    strCalls = strCalls & "<TD>" & adoRS("name").Value & "</TD>" & vbCrLf
    strCalls = strCalls & "<TD>" & adoRS("timesubmitted").Value & "</TD>" & vbCrLf
    strCalls = strCalls & "<TD>" & adoRS("status").Value & "</TD></TR>" & vbCrLf
    adoRS.MoveNext
  Loop
End If


'return contents of strCalls to user
ShowAllCalls = strCalls
```

```
exit_ShowAllCalls:
  'close connection and set ADO objects to nothing
  adoConn.Close
  Set adoConn = Nothing
  Set adoCmd = Nothing
  Set adoRS = Nothing
  Exit Function


err_ShowAllCalls:
  Err.Raise Err.Number, "ShowAllCalls", Err.Description
  Resume exit_ShowAllCalls


End Function
```

ShowOneCall Method

The ShowOneCall method returns a string containing the HTML for a table displaying the full details of one call. It accepts as a parameter the call id of the call to be displayed. Here is the listing, which you should add to the code that you've already typed:

```
Public Function ShowOneCall(strCallID As String) As String


  On Error GoTo err_ShowOneCall


  'retrieve all calls from DB and write to table
  Dim adoConn As New ADODB.Connection
  Dim adoCmd As New ADODB.Command
  Dim adoRS As New ADODB.Recordset
  Dim strConnectionString As String
  Dim strCall As String  'string to hold the call list's HTML


  'retrieve connection string
  strConnectionString = GetConnectionString()


  'set ADO Command Properties
  adoCmd.CommandType = 1
  adoCmd.CommandText = "SELECT * FROM call WHERE call_ID=" & strCallID


  'open the Connection
  adoConn.Open strConnectionString


  'associate the Command with the Open Connection
  adoCmd.ActiveConnection = adoConn
```

```
  'retrieve recordset
  Set adoRS = adoCmd.Execute
  If adoRS.EOF Then
    strCall = "" 'write nothing -no results
  Else
    'return information about call
    strCall = "<TABLE BORDER=0 CELLPADDING=1 CELLSPACING=1 WIDTH='80%'>"
    strCall = strCall & "<TR> <TD>Full Name: </TD><TD>" & _
               adoRS("name").Value & "</TD></TR>"
    strCall = strCall & "<TR> <TD>Title: </TD><TD>" & _
               adoRS("title").Value & "</TD></TR>"
    strCall = strCall & "<TR> <TD>Email Address: </TD><TD>" & _
               adoRS("emailaddress").Value & "</TD></TR>"
    strCall = strCall & "<TR> <TD>Extension: </TD><TD>" & _
               adoRS("extension").Value & "</TD></TR>"
    strCall = strCall & "<TR> <TD>Product: </TD><TD>" & _
               adoRS("product").Value & "</TD></TR>"
    strCall = strCall & "<TR> <TD>Priority: </TD><TD>" & _
               adoRS("priority").Value & "</TD></TR>"
    strCall = strCall & "<TR> <TD>Subject: </TD><TD>" & _
               adoRS("subject").Value & "</TD></TR>"
    strCall = strCall & "<TR> <TD>Description: </TD><TD>" & _
               adoRS("description").Value & "</TD></TR>"
    strCall = strCall & "<TR> <TD>Time Submitted: </TD><TD>" & _
               adoRS("timesubmitted").Value & "</TD></TR>"
    strCall = strCall & "<TR> <TD>STATUS: </TD><TD>" & _
               adoRS("status").Value & "</TD></TR>"
    strCall = strCall & "</TABLE>"
  End If


  'return contents of strCall to user
  ShowOneCall = strCall


exit_ShowOneCall:
  'close connection and set ADO objects to nothing
  adoConn.Close
  Set adoConn = Nothing
  Set adoCmd = Nothing
  Set adoRS = Nothing
  Exit Function


err_ShowOneCall:
  Err.Raise Err.Number, "ShowOneCall", Err.Description
  Resume exit_ShowOneCall


End Function
```

ShowStatistics Method

The `ShowStatistics` method will return a string that is an HTML table displaying basic statistics of all calls, in date order. It will accept as a parameter a start date, and will show all calls logged from the start date until the current date. The start date parameter can either accept the value `ALL`, in which case all calls irrelevant of date are included, or else a valid date string to act as the start date. Here is the listing for this method – again, add it to your existing code:

```
Public Function ShowStatistics(strStartDate As String) As String


 On Error GoTo err_ShowStatistics


 'retrieve all calls from DB and write to table
 Dim adoConn As New ADODB.Connection
 Dim adoCmd As New ADODB.Command
 Dim adoRS As New ADODB.Recordset
 Dim strConnectionString As String
 Dim strCallStatistics As String          'string to hold HTML for call statistics
 Dim strCommand As String        'string to build SQL query


 'retrieve connection string
 strConnectionString = GetConnectionString()


 'define command string
 If strStartDate = "ALL" Then
   strCommand = "SELECT name, count(call_id) AS CallCount, status _
             FROM call GROUP BY name, status ORDER BY name"
 Else        'filter based on strStatus
   'first off, ensure that strStartDate is valid date
   If IsDate(strStartDate) Then
     strStartDate = FormatDateTime(strStartDate, vbShortDate)     'short date format
     strCommand = "SELECT name, count(call_id) AS CallCount, status _
             FROM call GROUP BY name, status, timesubmitted _
             HAVING timesubmitted >= #" & strStartDate & "# ORDER BY name"
   Else
     Err.Raise 9999, "ShowStatistics", "You must enter a valid date format"
   End If
 End If


 'set ADO Command Properties
 adoCmd.CommandType = 1
 adoCmd.CommandText = strCommand


 'Open the Connection
 adoConn.Open strConnectionString
```

```
'associate the Command with the Open Connection
adoCmd.ActiveConnection = adoConn


'retrieve recordset
Set adoRS = adoCmd.Execute
If adoRS.EOF Then
   strCallStatistics = ""          'write nothing -no results
Else
   Do While Not adoRS.EOF
      'process results to create table
      strCallStatistics = strCallStatistics & "<TR>" & vbCrLf
      strCallStatistics = strCallStatistics & "<TD>" & adoRS("name").Value & _
            "</TD>" & vbCrLf
      strCallStatistics = strCallStatistics & "<TD>" & adoRS("status").Value & _
            "</TD>" & vbCrLf
      strCallStatistics = strCallStatistics & "<TD>" & adoRS("CallCount").Value & _
            "</TD></TR>" & vbCrLf
      adoRS.MoveNext
   Loop
End If


'return contents of strCallStatistics to user
ShowStatistics = strCallStatistics


exit_ShowStatistics:
   'close connection and set ADO objects to nothing
   adoConn.Close
   Set adoConn = Nothing
   Set adoCmd = Nothing
   Set adoRS = Nothing
   Exit Function


err_ShowStatistics:
   Err.Raise Err.Number, "ShowStatistics", Err.Description
   Resume exit_ShowStatistics

End Function
```

UpdateStatus Method

The UpdateStatus method is a simple one – it accepts as parameters a call id and a new status, then executes a query to update the status of the call to the new value. Here is the listing, to be added to your current code:

```
Public Sub UpdateStatus(strCallID As String, strStatus As String)
```

```
On Error GoTo err_UpdateStatus


'updates status of specified call
Dim adoConn As New ADODB.Connection
Dim adoCmd As New ADODB.Command
Dim strConnectionString As String


'retrieve connection string
strConnectionString = GetConnectionString()


'set ADO Command Properties
adoCmd.CommandType = 1
adoCmd.CommandText = "UPDATE call SET status=" & Chr(34) & strStatus & _
             Chr(34) & " WHERE call_ID=" & strCallID


'open the connection
adoConn.Open strConnectionString


'associate the command with the open connection
adoCmd.ActiveConnection = adoConn


'execute the command
adoCmd.Execute

exit_UpdateStatus:
  'close connection and set ADO objects to nothing
  adoConn.Close
  Set adoConn = Nothing
  Set adoCmd = Nothing
  Exit Sub


err_UpdateStatus:
  Err.Raise Err.Number, "UpdateStatus", Err.Description
  Resume exit_UpdateStatus


End Sub
```

These five methods represent the completed component. Once you have entered the code, all that is then required is to compile the component into a DLL, by selecting File | Make WroxHelpDesk.dll. When prompted, save the project and then close Visual Basic.

As discussed in Chapter 12, once the DLL is made, it is a completed object, which can be used in a web page by simply writing `Server.CreateObject`. *If desired, it is very easy to run it within MTS. To do this, create a package for it, as covered in Chapter 12. Whichever way you choose, it makes no difference to this application from a code perspective – it all remains the same. Normally you would see strong scalability gains by using MTS, especially if you spread the workload across multiple computers. This scalability increase offered by MTS is not going to be a major factor in this application because we are using Access 2000 as our database platform. Access, by its very nature, is not a flagship of scalability. If, however, we were using SQL Server, then excellent scalability would be achieved by running our component in MTS.*

Creating the Web Application

Now that we have created the database and COM component, we are ready to use Visual InterDev to create the web pages. This is not going to be a guided tour, but instead a listing of each page, along with an explanation of what the code does. If you become stuck at any point, refer back to the relevant chapter of the book for a recap.

This example purposely does not use client side script, themes, layouts, or design time controls. These subjects have been covered in depth throughout the book and are not part of the case study – by excluding them we can focus on the code that is important for getting the application to work. You can experiment with these aspects on your own afterwards!

This example uses the `WroxHelpDesk` component that we have just created. Sometimes when you are using a component with many properties and methods, or if you are using many components, it can be a tough job to memorize just exactly how to use the component. Before jumping in and developing our web pages, let's take a quick look at a tool that Visual InterDev offers, called the **Object Browser window**, and see how it can help us in this situation.

Using the Object Browser Window

The Object Browser window is a tool for viewing the properties, methods, events, and collections of any objects referenced in the project. It also displays the parameters of each object method and provides links to any help files that might be associated with it.

The Object Browser window is a useful tool when you are working with objects because it saves you having to remember everything that an object is capable of. It uses a familiar browsing method where you can drill down into the collections and properties, quickly giving an overview of how to use a particular object.

The Object Browser window is opened by selecting View | Other Windows | Object Browser. Initially, it does not display any classes unless you add them to the window. To add an object to the window, perform the following steps.

Try it Out – Adding an Object to the Object Browser Window

1. Create a new project, WroxHelpDesk, that we will use for the rest of this chapter. Do not use any themes or layouts.

2. Open the Object Browser window by selecting View | Other Windows | Object Browser.

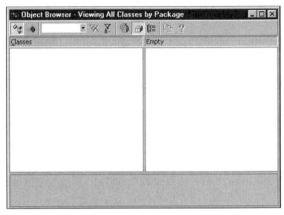

3. Right mouse click in the left hand pane and choose Select Current Packages/Libraries.

4. Select the Add button to add a new package/library. In the component list that appears, find the WroxHelpDesk component that we created earlier in this chapter. Press OK to add the component. If you extend the nodes below Other Packages and Libraries you should now see the following entries in the Select Packages/Libraries list:

5. Press OK. You should now see the details of the WroxHelpDesk component in the Object Browser window, as shown:

6. Once you have added an object to the **Object Browser** window in this manner, you can click on the properties and methods displayed to view their details. Selecting a class or collection, such as **CallService** above, displays the members of that object in the right hand pane.

Once you have selected a line, you can right mouse click on it and select **Copy** to copy the property name to the clipboard. If you then switch to a web page you can paste the correct spelling into your page. Used in conjunction with the IntelliSense drop down menus that you have previously used in your coding, the **Object Browser** window makes working with objects easy!

Now that we know how to use the **Object Browser** window to help us to use our `WroxHelpDesk` component, it is time to develop the web pages for the project. There are six altogether - each one is presented and explained in the following pages. Work through and add each page to your project, using the techniques that you have learned throughout the rest of the book.

default.htm

The default page of the application is where users can enter a call, and where supervisors can select to view the list of calls. The page contains an HTML form where users can submit call details, which then get sent to `submit_call.asp`.

Here is an example of what the page looks like:

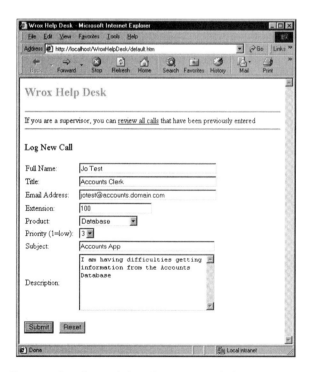

The listing of the page is shown below. You will notice that this and the other pages include many HTML controls, which can be lengthy to type in by hand. Use the features of Visual InterDev to help you when writing these pages – for example, use the editor and drag controls from the Toolbox to save you typing them in by hand. This is especially advantageous for the list boxes, which can be quite time-consuming to code manually.

433

```
<HTML>

<HEAD>
<META NAME="GENERATOR" Content="Microsoft Visual Studio 6.0">
<TITLE>Wrox Help Desk</TITLE>
</HEAD>

<BODY>
<FONT SIZE=5 COLOR="orange"><STRONG>Wrox Help Desk</STRONG></FONT>
<P></P><HR>
If you are a supervisor, you can <A HREF="review_calls.asp?showcall=ALL">review all
calls</A> that have been previously entered
<BR>
<HR>
<P></P>

<FORM ID=frmSubmitCall NAME="frmSubmitCall" ACTION="submit_call.asp" METHOD="post">
<P><FONT SIZE=4>Log New Call</FONT></P>

<TABLE BORDER=0 CELLPADDING=1 CELLSPACING=1 WIDTH="80%">

  <TR>
    <TD>Full Name: </TD>
    <TD><INPUT ID=txtName NAME=txtName STYLE="HEIGHT: 22px; WIDTH: 290px"
            MAXLENGTH=100></TD></TR>
  <TR>
    <TD>Title: </TD>
    <TD><INPUT ID=txtTitle NAME=txtTitle STYLE="HEIGHT: 22px; WIDTH: 290px"
            MAXLENGTH=100></TD></TR>
  <TR>
    <TD>Email Address: </TD>
    <TD><INPUT ID=txtEmailAddress NAME=txtEmailAddress STYLE="HEIGHT: 22px; WIDTH:
            290px" MAXLENGTH=100></TD></TR>
  <TR>
    <TD>Extension: </TD>
    <TD><INPUT ID=txtExtension NAME=txtExtension MAXLENGTH=20></TD></TR>
  <TR>
    <TD>Product: </TD>
    <TD>
    <SELECT ID=selProduct NAME=selProduct>
    <OPTION SELECTED>Other</OPTION>
    <OPTION>Word processor</OPTION>
    <OPTION>Spreadsheet</OPTION>
    <OPTION>Database</OPTION>
    <OPTION>Mail</OPTION>
    <OPTION>Internet</OPTION>
    </SELECT>
    </TD></TR>
  <TR>
    <TD>Priority (1=low): </TD>
    <TD>
    <SELECT ID=selPriority NAME=selPriority>
    <OPTION>1</OPTION>
```

```
      <OPTION>2</OPTION>
      <OPTION SELECTED>3</OPTION>
      <OPTION>4</OPTION>
      <OPTION>5</OPTION>
      </SELECT>
      </TD></TR>
  <TR>
      <TD>Subject: </TD>
      <TD><INPUT ID=txtSubject NAME=txtSubject STYLE="HEIGHT: 22px; WIDTH: 287px"
              MAXLENGTH=100></TD></TR>
  <TR>
      <TD>Description: </TD>
      <TD><TEXTAREA ID=txtDescription NAME=txtDescription STYLE="HEIGHT: 115px; WIDTH:
              287px"></TEXTAREA></TD></TR>
</TABLE>
<BR>

<INPUT ID=btnSubmit NAME=btnSubmit TYPE=submit VALUE=Submit>  
<INPUT ID=btnReset NAME=btnReset TYPE=reset VALUE=Reset>

<BR>

</FORM>

</BODY>
</HTML>
```

As you can see, there are no surprises on this page. For supervisors, it contains a link to
review_calls.asp and passes a parameter in the query string that will be discussed shortly. For users
submitting a call there is a simple form, which submits details to a page called submit_call.asp.

submit_call.asp

submit_call.asp is a page to which the default.htm form is submitted. The purpose of this page is
to put the information contained on the form directly into the database as a new call. To do this, the page
uses the COM component that we created earlier.

Here is what the page looks
like after the information is
submitted:

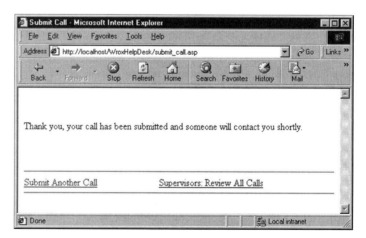

Here is the script for the page:

```
<%@ Language=VBScript %>
<%
  Option Explicit
%>
<HTML>
<HEAD>
<META NAME="GENERATOR" Content="Microsoft Visual Studio 6.0">
<TITLE>Submit Call</TITLE>
</HEAD>
<BODY>

<%
  Dim objWroxHelpDesk
  Dim strWrite

  On Error Resume Next

  Set objWroxHelpDesk = Server.CreateObject("WroxHelpDesk.CallService")

  objWroxHelpDesk.NewCall Request.Form("txtName"),Request.Form("txtTitle"), _
              Request.Form("txtEmailAddress"),Request.Form("txtExtension"), _
              Request.Form("selProduct"),Request.Form("selPriority"), _
              Request.Form("txtSubject"),Request.Form("txtDescription")

  If Err<>0 then         'an error occurred
    strWrite "An error occurred. The error was: <BR>" & Err.Number & " " & _
              Err.Description
  Else         'no error, tell user that it was a success
    strWrite = "<P> </P>"
    strWrite = strWrite & "<P>Thank you, your call has been submitted and _
              someone will contact you shortly.</P>"
  End if

  Response.Write strWrite

%>
<P> </P>

<HR>
<A HREF="default.htm">Submit Another Call</A>
             
            
<A HREF=review_calls.asp?showcall=ALL>Supervisors: Review All Calls</A>
<HR>
</BODY>
</HTML>
```

As you can see, the server side script simply creates our COM component, then it calls the newcall method, passing the values of the submitted form. As long as no error occurs, the user will see a message saying "Thank you....". If an error occurred, then the details are displayed to the user.

After submitting, plain HTML writes out the page that the user sees, giving the option to write a new call by going back to default.htm, or to view the supervisor list by jumping to review_calls.asp.

review_calls.asp

review_calls.asp is supervisor territory. To ensure that users are supervisors, at the beginning of the page there is some script that looks at some server variables to ensure that the user is logged in as a supervisor. If they are not, the user is redirected to login.htm.

Here is an example of how the page looks when it is first opened, depending on what information has been submitted:

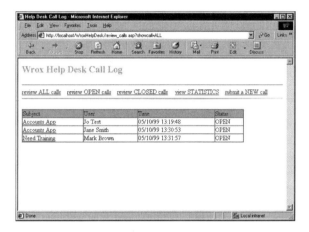

If the user clicks on a subject line, they are taken to a detailed view of that call. This is in fact the same page, but called with a call id in the showcall parameter, which will be explained shortly:

There are several other options available on this page:

❑ Along the top of the view are three links for filtering the view, which simply recall the page with a different parameter (ALL, OPEN, or CLOSED) in the showcall querystring.

❑ Also at the top of the page is another option, view STATISTICS, which is a link to the page statistics.asp. This link has a querystring of startdate=ALL, which specifies to initially show all calls. This page is explained shortly.

❑ The final link at the top of the page takes the user back to the form page for submitting a new call.

437

❑ At the bottom of the detail view are links to change the status of the call (OPEN or CLOSED). These simply recall the page with the same id as before, but with the querystring parameter of newstatus set to the new status to be changed to.

This is quite a busy page! Let's take a look at the script that makes it work:

```asp
<%@ Language=VBScript %>

<%
  Option Explicit
  Response.Buffer=true
%>

<HTML>
<HEAD>
<META NAME="GENERATOR" Content="Microsoft Visual Studio 6.0">
<TITLE>Help Desk Call Log</TITLE>

<%
  'ensure user has logged in
  If session("ValidUser") = False then
    'redirect to login page
    Response.Redirect "login.htm"
  End if
%>

</HEAD>
<BODY>
<FONT SIZE=5 COLOR="orange"><STRONG>Wrox Help Desk Call Log</STRONG></FONT>
<P></P><HR>
<A HREF="review_calls.asp?showcall=ALL">review ALL calls</A>    
<A HREF="review_calls.asp?showcall=OPEN">review OPEN calls</A>    
<A HREF="review_calls.asp?showcall=CLOSED">review CLOSED calls</A>
    <A HREF="statistics.asp?startdate=ALL">view STATISTICS</A>
    <A HREF="default.htm">submit a NEW call</A>
<BR>
<HR>
<BR>

<%
  Dim objWroxHelpDesk
  Dim strWrite

  Set objWroxHelpDesk=Server.CreateObject("WroxHelpDesk.CallService")


  On Error Resume Next        'enable error handling


  'determine if a request to change status has been submitted, if so, do it
  If Request.QueryString("newstatus") <> "" then
```

```
      objWroxHelpDesk.UpdateStatus Request.QueryString("showcall"), _
               Request.QueryString("newstatus")
  End if

  If not isnumeric(Request.QueryString("showcall")) then
    'means it is either ALL, OPEN, or CLOSED
    strWrite = "<TABLE BORDER=1 BORDERCOLOR=gray CELLPADDING=0 CELLSPACING=0
               WIDTH='85%'>
               <TR BGCOLOR=orange><TD>Subject</TD><TD>User</TD><TD>Time</TD>
               <TD>Status</TD></TR>"
    strWrite = strWrite & _
               objWroxHelpDesk.ShowAllCalls(Request.QueryString("showcall")) _
               & "<TABLE>"
  Else
    strWrite = objWroxHelpDesk.ShowOneCall(Request.QueryString("showcall"))
    'write a line of links to change the call status
    strWrite = strWrite & "<P> </P><HR>Change Call status to: _
               <BR><BR><A HREF='review_calls.asp?showcall=" & _
               Request.QueryString("showcall") & _
               "&newstatus=OPEN'>OPEN</A>    "
    strWrite = strWrite & "<A HREF='review_calls.asp?showcall=" & _
               Request.QueryString("showcall") & "&newstatus=CLOSED'>CLOSED</A><HR>"
  End if

  If Err<>0 then         'an error occurred
    strWrite = "An error occurred. The error was: <BR>" & Err.Number & _
               " " & Err.Description
  End if

  Response.Write strWrite
%>

</BODY>
</HTML>
```

Not much to it at all! Let's examine the code:

❑   This is the first block of code:

```
<%
  'ensure user has logged in
  If session("ValidUser") = False then
    'redirect to login page
    Response.Redirect "login.htm"
  End if
%>
```

This simply checks if the `ValidUser` session value is `false` – if it is, the user is redirected to the `login.htm` page without even seeing the `review_calls.asp` page.

❑   The second block of code is the main logic for the page. Essentially it is just a glorified `If...Else` block. This would be a verbal description of what it is doing:

```
If there is a newstatus value in the querystring then
  Call the newstatus method of the component to update the status
End if
If the showcall parameter contains words then
  It is requesting a filtered list, so call the showallcalls method of the
component and show the table
Else it must be a number, so
  It is requesting details of one call, so call the showonecall method of
the component
End if
```

Using the COM component has made this page in essence very simple, yet at the same time it produces quite diverse results. This is a good example of one of the strong advantages that using a COM component offers.

login.htm

The login.htm page is essentially the same as that detailed in Chapter 7. In this application, it is reached when a user tries to browse to review_calls.asp. If the user has not logged in, they are automatically redirected here.

This is what the page looks like in a browser:

Here is the script for the page, which simply redirects to login_check.asp. This page is very easily created using the Visual InterDev editor and dragging the controls from the Toolbox:

```
<HTML>

<HEAD>
<META NAME="GENERATOR" Content="Microsoft Visual Studio 6.0">
<TITLE></TITLE>
</HEAD>

<BODY>
```

```
<FORM ID=frmLogin ACTION="login_check.asp" METHOD="post">
<P>Please Enter your Login Details below:</P>
<P>User Name: <INPUT ID=txtUsername NAME=txtUserName></P>
<P>Password: <INPUT ID=txtPassword NAME=txtPassword TYPE=password></P>
<P><INPUT ID=btnLogin NAME=btnLogin TYPE=submit VALUE=Login></P>

</FORM>

</BODY>
</HTML>
```

login_check.asp

The next of our pages is `login_check.asp`. This page checks the login details submitted in `login.htm` against the supervisor table in the database. If the details match, then the session variables are set to a valid login, otherwise the user is simply redirected to the `login.htm` page again.

This could be expanded upon by giving feedback to the user explaining the reason that their login failed, or it could keep track of the number of failed logins in a session or application variable and limit it to three attempts, or the ASP script could be replaced with a COM login component. For our purposes, what we have suffices. Here is the script that makes it happen, which needs to be typed in. Remember to enter the correct pathname to the database in the `strConnectionString` definition:

```
<%@ Language=VBScript %>


<%
  Option Explicit
  Response.Buffer=true
%>


<HTML>
<HEAD>
<META NAME="GENERATOR" Content="Microsoft Visual Studio 6.0">


<%
  Dim LoginOK
  Dim adoConn
  Dim adoCmd
  Dim adoRS
  Dim strConnectionString

  Set adoConn= Server.CreateObject("ADODB.Connection")
  Set adoCmd= Server.CreateObject("ADODB.Command")
  Set adoRS= Server.CreateObject("ADODB.Recordset")


  'define connection string
  strConnectionString = "Provider=Microsoft.Jet.OLEDB.4.0;Data Source= _
          C:\databases\wroxhelpdesk.mdb;User ID=Admin;Password=" & Chr(34) & Chr(34)
```

```
'set ADO Command Properties
adoCmd.CommandType = 1
adoCmd.CommandText = "select password from supervisor where user_NAME=" & _
            chr(34) & Request.Form("txtUserName") & chr(34)


'Open the connection
adoConn.Open strConnectionString


'associate the command with the open connection
adoCmd.ActiveConnection = adoConn


'retrieve recordset
Set adoRS = adoCmd.Execute

If adoRS.EOF Then
  'no user matches
  Session("ValidUser") = false
  Session("UserName") = "Not Logged In"
Else
  If Request.Form("txtPassword")=adoRS("password").value then
    Session("ValidUser") = true
    Session("UserName") = Request.Form("txtUserName")
  Else
    Session("ValidUser") = false
    Session("UserName") = "Not Logged In"
  End if
End if

If session("ValidUser") then
  Response.Redirect "review_calls.asp?showcall=ALL"
Else
  Response.Redirect "login.htm"
End if
%>

</HEAD>
<BODY>
</BODY>
</HTML>
```

statistics.asp

Our last page details some basic call statistics. This page uses the ShowStatistics method of our component to retrieve information from the database and present it to the user. When first opened, the page defaults to showing statistics for *all* calls that have been entered. The user can then specify to view less information by entering a start date to view later calls.

Here is what the page looks like when first opened, depending on what is within the database:

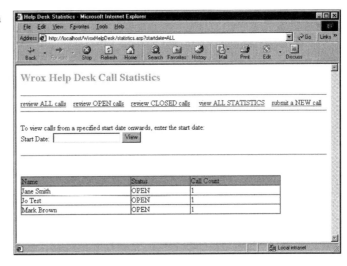

Here is the content of the file:

```asp
<%@ Language=VBScript %>


<%
 Option Explicit
 Response.Buffer=true
%>


<HTML>
<HEAD>
<META NAME="GENERATOR" Content="Microsoft Visual Studio 6.0">
<TITLE>Help Desk Statistics</TITLE>


<%
  'ensure user has logged in
  If session("ValidUser") = False then
    'redirect to login page
    Response.Redirect "login.htm"
  End if
%>


</HEAD>
<BODY>
<FONT SIZE=5 COLOR="orange"><STRONG>Wrox Help Desk Call Statistics</STRONG></FONT>
<P></P><HR>
<A HREF="review_calls.asp?showcall=ALL">review ALL calls</A>    
<A HREF="review_calls.asp?showcall=OPEN">review OPEN calls</A>    
<A HREF="review_calls.asp?showcall=CLOSED">review CLOSED calls</A>
    <A HREF="statistics.asp?startdate=ALL">view ALL STATISTICS</A>
    <A HREF="default.htm">submit a NEW call</A>
```

```
<BR>
<HR>
<FORM ID=frmChangeStartDate NAME=frmChangeStartDate
ACTION="statistics.asp?startdate=SPECIFIED" METHOD="post">
To view calls from a specified start date onwards, enter the start date:<BR>
Start Date:  <INPUT ID=txtStartDate NAME=txtStartDate >
<INPUT ID=submit1 NAME=submit1 TYPE=submit VALUE=View>
<BR><BR><HR>
</FORM>
<BR>


<%
  Dim objWroxHelpDesk
  Dim strWrite

  Set objWroxHelpDesk=Server.CreateObject("WroxHelpDesk.CallService")

  strWrite = "<TABLE BORDER=1 BORDERCOLOR=gray CELLPADDING=0 CELLSPACING=0
              WIDTH='85%'>
                <TR BGCOLOR=orange><TD>Name</TD><TD>Status</TD><TD>Call
              Count</TD></TR>"


  On Error Resume Next


  'if startdate parameter in querystring is ALL, show statistics for ALL
  If Request.QueryString("startdate") = "ALL" then
    strWrite = strWrite & objWroxHelpDesk.ShowStatistics("ALL")& "</TABLE>"
  Else        'otherwise, show based on value in txtStartDate box
    strWrite = strWrite &
     objWroxHelpDesk.ShowStatistics(Request.Form("txtStartDate"))& "</TABLE>"
  End if

  If Err<>0 then
    strWrite = "An error occurred. The error was: <BR>" & Err.Number & _
              " " & Err.Description
  End if

  Response.Write strWrite
%>

</BODY>
</HTML>
```

This page is fairly simple in its operation, and is very similar to the review_calls.asp page to which it is linked. The user can specify a new start date by entering a date into the textbox in the form at the top of the page. This form is then re-submitted with a startdate querystring of SPECIFIED, as you can see from the declaration of the form:

```
<FORM ID=frmChangeStartDate NAME=frmChangeStartDate
ACTION="statistics.asp?startdate=SPECIFIED" METHOD="post">
```

The default value of the `startdate` querystring is ALL - this is the same querystring that is passed if the user clicks on the view ALL STATISTICS link at the top of the page.

To determine what to display, the ASP code then simply reads the value of this querystring. If it is SPECIFIED, then it reads the value of the date the user entered and passes that to the component. If it is ALL, then it passes ALL to the component. The component then replies with the requested information.

In order to handle the possibility that the user enters the wrong date, the ASP code monitors any errors that the component reports. The component specifically checks the date parameter and throws back an error if the date is bad. If you enter a bad date, or no date at all, then the following screen is displayed:

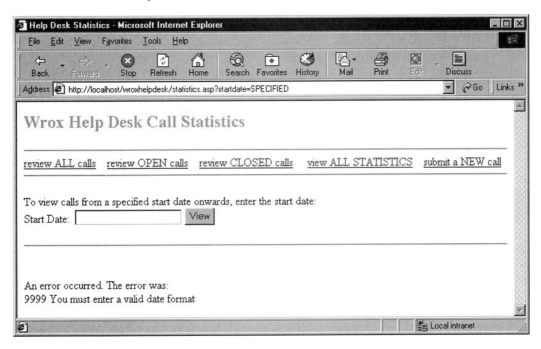

Within our ASP page, the following code monitors the error:

```
If Err<>0 then
  strWrite = "An error occurred. The error was: <BR>" & Err.Number & " " & _
             Err.Description
End if
```

If an error occurs, the `strWrite` variable, which contains the information to be written to the client, is changed to display the error details. This could also have been achieved by writing some client script to validate the contents of the start date textbox prior to submitting the form.

Make sure that you save all of your work – you now have a complete application which you can test out by running it in your web browser, starting with `default.htm`.

Summary

This chapter has shown an example of a complete working web application, albeit a small one. The application included some of the technologies that we have covered in recent chapters, as well as demonstrating how to use Access as an alternative database to SQL Server.

The application leaves great scope for improvement, including possibilities such as:

❑ Enhanced filtering/sorting based on call priority/time submitted.

❑ Ability to record a response when closing a call.

❑ Record which supervisor closed a call.

❑ Have the response automatically sent by email to the caller.

❑ Enhanced reporting options on call statistics.

❑ Improved user interface by using a theme, layout, and JavaScript.

❑ Retrieve the data for the product list drop down box from the database, as opposed to hard coding it into the web page.

This serves to show that there is always room for improvement, and that a web application can offer the same functionality as a traditional program.

We've now come to the end of the book, but in the process we have learned how to use Visual InterDev to develop web applications. You're now armed with plenty of useful knowledge and samples, which you can use to create and develop your own real life applications. If you want to learn more about Visual InterDev, or any of the other topics we have touched on in our explorations, such as JavaScript, VBScript, XML, Microsoft Transaction Server, and so on, visit the Wrox Press books site at http://www.wrox.com for a comprehensive and up to date list of the best books on offer.

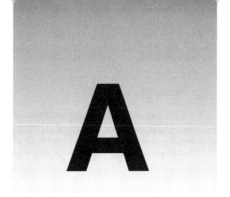

Visual InterDev 6 Menu Reference

This Appendix lists the options available in the various menus that Visual InterDev 6 includes. Many of these menu options have **shortcut keys** (such as *Ctrl + S* to save), or appear in **toolboxes**. The toolboxes are also customizable, using the Tools | Customize Toolbox menu option. Placing the cursor over an icon in a toolbox reveals which menu option it represents.

Many of these menu items will already be familiar to you, as they are often seen in other Windows applications. Options which are specific to Visual InterDev are explained elsewhere in this book, but are included here as a handy reference.

File Menu

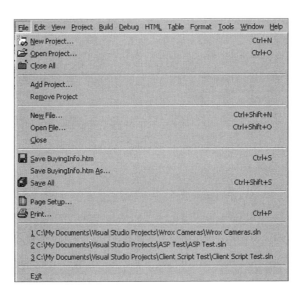

Menu Option	Description
New Project...	Creates a new Visual InterDev project. The dialog gives options to open web projects, databases projects, and so on.
Open Project...	Opens a saved project, giving the option to either close the existing one, or add the new one to the existing project.
Close All	Closes all currently opened projects.
Add Project...	Opens and adds a new or existing project to the currently opened one.
Remove Project	Removes a project from the current solution. This does not delete the project, just removes it from the solution.
New File...	Creates a new file in the existing project.
Open File...	Opens an existing file.
Close	Closes the currently open file.
Save *ProjectName*	Saves the project and all files within it.
Save *ProjectName* **As**...	Saves the project under another filename.
Save All	Saves all open files and projects.
Page Setup...	Controls the paper source, layout, margins, and so on, for printing.
Print...	Prints the currently opened file.
Recently opened files list	Contains a list of the most recently opened files (projects).
Exit	Exits Visual InterDev, after prompting to close any unsaved work.

Edit Menu

Menu Option	Description
Undo	Undoes the last user action.
Redo	Redoes the last undone user action.
Cut	Cuts the current selection to the clipboard.
Copy	Copies the current selection to the clipboard.
Paste	Pastes the contents of the clipboard to the cursor position.
Paste As HTML	Pastes the contents of the clipboard as HTML formatted text, to the cursor position.
Delete	Deletes the current selection.
Select All	Selects all text in the current window.
Find and Replace...	Performs a find and replace across the current selection, window, or project.
Go To...	Moves the cursor to the position specified.

Table Continued on Following Page

Menu Option	Description
List Members	Opens the IntelliSense window, showing all of the methods and properties of the current object.
Parameter Info	Displays information about the parameters of the current method.
Complete Word	Opens the IntelliSense window for the current word, giving the option to select a word to complete your typing.
Insert File as Text...	Inserts the contents of a file as text, into the current document at the cursor position.
Advanced | Format Selection	Formats the currently selected text.
Advanced | Tabify Selection	Applies equal tabs to the current selection.
Advanced | Untabify Selection	Removes tabs from the current selection.
Advanced | Make Uppercase	Makes the current selection uppercase.
Advanced | Make Lowercase	Makes the current selection lowercase.
Advanced | View White Space	Toggles between viewing formatting marks and viewing white space.
Bookmarks | Toggle Bookmark	Adds a bookmark at the current location.
Bookmarks | Next Bookmark	Jumps to the next bookmark.
Bookmarks | Previous Bookmark	Jumps to the previous bookmark.
Bookmarks | Clear All Bookmarks	Clears all bookmarks from the current document.
Apply Theme and Layout	Applies a theme and layout to the current page.

View Menu

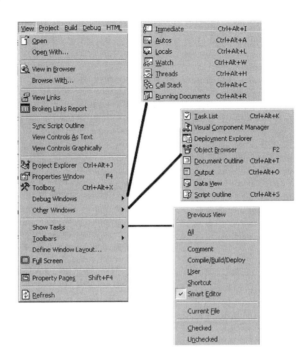

Menu Option	Description
Open	Opens the page selected in the Project Explorer window, in the editor.
Open With...	Same as Open, but gives a choice of editors to open with.
View in Browser	Views the page selected in the Project Explorer window, in the default browser, initially set to Internet Explorer.
Browse With...	Same as View in Browser, but gives an option of which browser to view with, plus offers the ability to set a browser as the default.
View Links	Opens a links view centred on the selected page, showing all links into and out of that page.
Broken Links Report	Shows any broken links to and from the selected page, in a report.
Sync Script Outline	Synchronizes the Script Outline window so that you can see where you are in the context of the whole page.

Table Continued on Following Page

Menu Option	Description
View Controls as Text	When selected, all DTC controls are displayed as text, with their properties and values.
View Controls Graphically	When selected, all DTC controls are displayed graphically.
Project Explorer	Opens the Project Explorer window.
Properties Window	Opens the Properties window.
Toolbox	Opens the Toolbox.
Debug Windows	Opens various Debug windows for use in debugging.
Other Windows	Opens various other windows for editing your project, such as the Object Browser window, Script Outline, Task List window, and so on.
Show Tasks	Contains menu options for filtering the Task List window, and selecting which tasks to show.
Toolbars	Window controlling which of the many built in toolbars are visible. Also contains a customize option to edit the toolbars.
Define Window Layout...	Saves the current window layout with a name, enabling it to be quickly reloaded if changes are made.
Full Screen	Maximises the viewable area of the file by removing all open windows, toolbars, etc, other than the open file.
Property Pages	Views the property pages for the selected object.
Refresh	Refreshes the current page view.

Project Menu

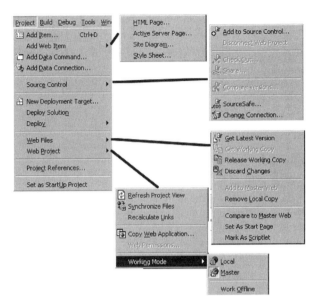

Menu Option	Description
Add Item...	Adds an ASP page, HTML page, site diagram, or style sheet to the project.
Add Web Item	Same as Add Item, but allows selection of type through a sub menu.
Add Data Command...	Adds a new Data Command object to the project.
Add Data Connection...	Adds a new Data Connection object to the project.
Source Control	Sub menu for controlling the interaction between Visual InterDev and Visual SourceSafe, for source control of the project.
New Deployment Target...	Sets a URL to deploy the project to once it is finished.
Deploy Solution	Deploys the solution to a specific URL.
Deploy	Same as Deploy Solution, but any deployment targets are accessed through a sub menu.

Table Continued on Following Page

Menu Option	Description
Web Files	Sub menu for controlling files between master server and local copy, contains options for managing the working copies.
Web Project	Sub menu for refreshing and synchronising the project view, copying the complete project to another location, and changing the working mode between master and local.
Project References...	Controls the various type libraries that are referenced in the project, such as the ADO type library.
Set as StartUp Project	Sets the project as the startup project, i.e. the one that will be started when *F5* or the Run option is selected.

Build Menu

Menu Option	Description
Build *host/projectname*	Builds the specified project.
Build Solution	Builds the complete solution – i.e. all projects in the solution group.
Rebuild Solution	Rebuilds the complete solution, using the solution in its current state, which might be different from before.
Build Configuration	Specifies the build configuration to use: either debug or release. Debug build is used to assist in debugging your web application, where the release option builds a candidate for deployment.

Debug Menu

Menu Option	Description
Continue	Causes execution to continue until the next breakpoint or error condition.
Start Without Debugging	Starts the page that has been set as the startup page, without debugging.
Break	Pauses execution.
End	Ends code execution, closing the debugging session.
Detach all Processes	Stops monitoring any processes that have been attached using the processes menu option.
Restart	Restarts execution from the beginning.
Run to Cursor	Executes code up to the line that the cursor is on.
Step Into	Steps into the next line, causing it to execute.
Step Over	Steps over the next line, causing the line after it to execute.
Step Out	Steps out of the current procedure.
Add Watch	Adds a watch to a variable, which can be monitored in the watch window.
Remove Breakpoint	Removes the breakpoint from the current line.

Table Continued on Following Page

Menu Option	Description
Disable Breakpoint	Temporarily disables the breakpoint at the current line.
Clear All Breakpoints	Removes all breakpoints.
Breakpoints	Opens a window for adding, deleting, and managing breakpoints.
Set Next Statement	Sets the line that the cursor is at to be the next executed line.
Show Next Statement	Displays which line is the next statement to be executed.
Processes	Enables the debugger to attach to a running application, such as Internet Explorer 4 (a process), and monitor any errors in the pages being processed. An error or breakpoint in a monitored process will then cause the Visual InterDev debugging environment to be launched, to debug the application.

HTML Menu

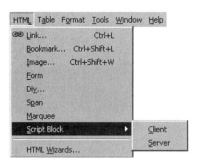

Menu Option	Description
Link	Inserts a hyperlink anchor.
Bookmark	Inserts a bookmark anchor.
Image	Inserts an image.
Form	Inserts a form.
Div	Inserts a div tag.
Span	Inserts a span tag.
Marquee	Inserts a marquee of scrolling text.
Script Block	Inserts script tags, either for a client side script block or a server side script block.
HTML Wizards	Runs any HTML wizards installed on your system, for automatically generating HTML.

Table Menu

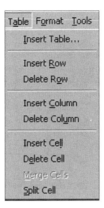

Menu Option	Description
Insert Table	Creates a table, giving you the option of specifying columns, rows, border width, and so on.
Insert Row	Inserts a row at the selection point.
Delete Row	Deletes the selected row.
Insert Column	Inserts a column at the selection point.
Delete Column	Deletes the selected column.
Insert Cell	Inserts a cell at the selection point.
Delete Cell	Deletes the current cell.
Merge Cells	Merges the selected cells into one cell.
Split Cell	Splits the selected cell into one or more columns or rows of cells.

Format Menu

Menu Option	Description
Bold	Makes the selection **bold**.
Italic	Makes the selection *italic*.
Underline	Makes the selection <u>underlined</u>.
Superscript	Makes the selection superscript.
Subscript	Makes the selection subscript.
Decrease Indent	Decreases the indent of the current selection.
Increase Indent	Increases the indent of the current selection.
Absolute Positioning	Enables you to specify exactly where an item will appear on the page – this feature only works in Internet Explorer 4 and later versions.
Lock	Locks the position of items to prevent accidental changes.
Z Order	Changes the order of an object in the z axis (for example front/back/behind text).

Tools Menu

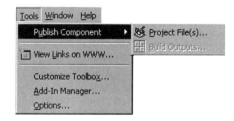

Menu Option	Description
Publish Component	Publishes the project to a URL.
View Links on WWW	Views links for a specified page on the WWW.
Customise Toolbox	Enables you to customise the items that appear in the toolbox.
Add-In Manager	Manages add-ins, which can expand the capabilities of Visual InterDev.
Options	Enables you to modify various settings for Visual InterDev.

Window Menu

Menu Option	Description
Split	Enables the editor window to be split into two separately scrollable views of one file.
Dockable	Specifies whether a window is dockable or not, i.e. whether it can "dock" onto the side of Visual InterDev, as is the default for windows such as the Project Explorer window, Properties window, and so on.
Hide	Hides the current window.
Cascade	Causes all windows to cascade.
Tile Horizontally	Causes all windows to tile horizontally.
Tile Vertically	Causes all windows to tile vertically.
Close All Documents	Closes all open documents.
Open Windows List	Switches to the selected open window.
Windows	Brings up a list of all open windows that you can switch to.

Help Menu

Menu Option	Description
Contents	Opens the MSDN Library (or Visual Studio library) at the contents tab.
Index	Opens the MSDN Library (or Visual Studio library) at the index tab.
Search	Opens the MSDN Library (or Visual Studio library) at the search tab.
Technical Support	Opens the MSDN Library (or Visual Studio library) at the technical support page.
Microsoft on the Web	Offers various locations at the Microsoft web site for getting help with Visual InterDev.
About	Displays the "about Visual InterDev" dialog box.

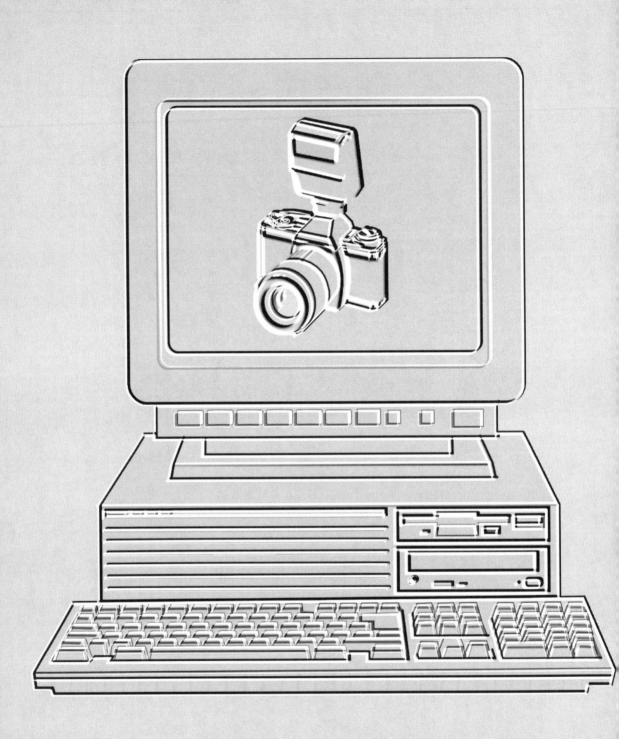

Internet Explorer 5 Object Model

This Appendix offers a handy reference to the Internet Explorer 5 Object Model, and can be of great assistance when coding client side script, as discussed in Chapter 6. The model includes all of the objects, along with their methods, properties, events, and collections.

The Window Object

The Window object represents an open window in the browser. It can be used to control the appearance and properties of that window, as well as providing certain methods for giving feedback to the user, such as Window.Alert.

Window Object Properties	Description
clientInformation	Returns the Navigator object. Used to retrieve information about the version and name of the browser, including which features are enabled.
closed	Returns true if the referenced window is closed, else returns false if it is open.
defaultStatus	Reflects the default message displayed in the status bar at the bottom of the window.
dialogArguments	Returns the variable, or array of variables, that have passed into a window that has been created using the ShowModalDialog method.
dialogHeight	Returns the height of a window that has been created using the ShowModalDialog method.
dialogLeft	Returns the left coordinate of a window that has been created using the ShowModalDialog method.
dialogTop	Returns the top coordinate of a window that has been created using the ShowModalDialog method.

Table Continued on Following Page

Window Object Properties	Description
dialogWidth	Returns the width of a window that has been created using the ShowModalDialog method.
document	Represents the HTML document in a browser window.
event	Represents the state of an event that has occurred for an element in the window. It is only available during an event.
history	Contains information about the URLs that the client has visited previously.
length	Returns the number of frames contained in a window. Not available for modal dialogs.
location	Contains information on the current URL.
name	Specifies the name of a window or the frame, enabling it to be targeted from links in other documents, for example Window.Name="Window Name".
navigator	Contains information about the web browser.
offscreenBuffering	Specifies whether to use off-screen buffering. Defaults to a string "auto", which enables IE 4.0 to decide when offscreen buffering is used. After that, it can be set to a Boolean true/false value.
opener	Returns a reference to the window that created the current window.
parent	Returns the parent object in the object hierarchy. Not available for a modal dialog window.
returnValue	Specifies the return value of a modal dialog window opened using the ShowModalDialog method.
screen	Contains information about the client's screen.
self	Refers to the current window or frame.
status	Sets or reads the message in the status bar at the bottom of the window.
top	Returns the topmost ancestor window, which is its own parent. This is not available for a window opened using the ShowModalDialog method.

Window Object Methods	Syntax	Description
Alert	Window.Alert ([message])	Displays an alert dialog box that contains a message and an OK button.
Blur		Causes the window to lose focus, and fires the onblur event.
ClearInterval	Window.ClearInterval (IntervalID)	Cancels an interval that has been previously started using the SetInterval method.
ClearTimeout	Window.ClearTimeout (TimeoutID)	Clears/cancels a timeout that was previously set using the SetTimeout method.
Close		Closes the current window.
Confirm	Window.Confirm ([message])	Displays a confirm dialog box that contains a message, and OK and Cancel buttons. Returns true if OK is chosen, else returns false if Cancel is chosen.
ExecScript	Window.ExecScript (expression, language)	Executes the script, passed in the expression parameter, in the language defined by the language parameter, which defaults to JScript.
Focus		Causes the window to retrieve the focus, and fires the onfocus event.
MoveBy	Window.MoveBy (x,y)	Moves the screen position of the window by the offsets specified in x and y, in pixels, from its current position.
MoveTo	Window.MoveTo (x,y)	Moves the screen position of the window to the offsets specified in x and y, in pixels, from the top left corner of the screen.
Navigate	Window.Navigate (URL)	This is the same as the Window.location.href property.

Table Continued on Following Page

Window Object Methods	Syntax	Description
Open	Window = Object.Open ([URL [,name [,features [,replace]]]])	Opens a new window and loads the document specified by the URL property. If no URL is supplied it opens a blank document. Features specify values for the window, such as "Height=200, Width=200". Replace specifies whether the URL should create a new entry in the browsing history for the window, or just replace the current entry.
Prompt	Window.Prompt ([message [,inputDefault]])	Displays a prompt dialog box with a message and an input box. Similar to inputbox in Visual Basic. Returns the value that the user types into the input box.
ResizeBy	Window.ResizeBy (x,y)	Changes the size of the window's outer dimensions by the amount specified in the x and y offsets, relative to the current size of the window.
ResizeTo	Window.ResizeTo (x,y)	Changes the size of the window's outer dimensions to be as specified in the x and y parameters.
Scroll	Window.Scroll (x,y)	Causes the window to scroll to the specified x and y offset, relative to the top left corner of the window.
ScrollBy	Window.ScrollBy (x,y)	Causes the window to scroll the specified x and y offset in pixels, from the current scrolled position.
ScrollTo	Window.ScrollTo (x,y)	Same as Scroll - ScrollTo is the preferred method, with Scroll being provided for backwards compatibility only.
SetInterval	IntervalID = Window.SetInterval (expression, msec [,language])	Sets an interval after which code contained in the expression parameter is evaluated. Interval then restarts and evaluates again repeatedly. The language parameter specifies the language that the expression is written in, and defaults to JScript.

Window Object Methods	Syntax	Description
SetTimeOut	TimeoutID = Window.SetTimeOut (expression, msec [,language])	Same as SetInterval, but only evaluates once, then stops.
ShowHelp	Window.ShowHelp (URL [,contextID])	Displays a WinHelp or HTMLHelp file specified by URL. The contextID is an optional argument for passing the context ID to the help file.
ShowModalDialog	variant = Object.ShowModalDialog (URL [,arguments [,Features]])	Opens a window as a modal dialog box, displaying the document specified by the URL parameter. The window retains the focus until it is closed. The arguments parameter passes a variety of arguments that the dialog can retrieve in code using Window.DialogArguments. The features parameter specifies the appearance of the dialog, for example "dialogWidth:200, dialogHeight:200, center:yes".

Window Object Events	Description
onbeforeunload	Fires just prior to a window being unloaded.
onblur	Fires when the window loses the focus.
onerror	Fires when a scripting error occurs.
onfocus	Fires when the window receives the focus.
onhelp	Fires when the user presses *F1* or the browser Help key.
onload	Fires immediately after the browser loads the window.
onresize	Fires at the beginning of a window resize operation.
onscroll	Fires when the scroll box is repositioned.
onunload	Fires immediately prior to the window being unloaded.

The Document Object

The Document object represents an HTML document in the browser window. This object is primarily used to examine and control the elements within the document, and to control events that occur within the object. It is often used to modify the text or attributes of HTML elements within the document.

Document Object Properties	Description
`activeElement`	Refers to the element that has the focus.
`alinkColor`	Sets the color for the active link.
`bgColor`	Sets the background color for the page.
`body`	Specifies the beginning and end of the document body.
`charset`	Sets or returns the character set of the document.
`cookie`	Specifies the string value of a cookie. Cookies are made of value pairs including: name=value; expires=date; domain=domainname; path=path. Can be accessed using string methods in the scripting language in use.
`defaultCharset`	Sets or returns the default character set of the document.
`domain`	Sets or returns the domain of the document, for security.
`expando`	Specifies whether it is possible to create arbitrary variables within an object. The default is true. When true, you can create your own variables simply by setting them and retrieving them, e.g. Object.myvariable="a value". You can then retrieve it with Object.myvariable. The variable will not otherwise affect the object.
`fgColor`	Sets or retrieves the foreground color of the document – in other words the text color.
`lastModified`	If the page contains a last-modified date, it is contained in this property.
`linkColor`	Returns the color of document links within the document.
`location`	Returns information on the current URL, including the following properties - `hash`, `host`, `hostname`, `href`, `pathname`, `port`, `protocol`, `search`.
`parentWindow`	Returns the `Window` object for the document.
`readyState`	Specifies the current state of the document being downloaded - can be `uninitialized`, `loading`, `interactive`, or `complete`.

Document Object Properties	Description
referrer	Specifies the previous URL, but only contains a value if the current page has been reached through a link on the previous page.
selection	Represents the active selection, which is a highlighted block of text and elements on the document for which script can carry out an action.
title	Identifies the contents of the document within the <TITLE> tag.
URL	Indicates the URL of the current document.
vlinkColor	Sets or returns the color of visited links in the document.

Document Object Methods	Syntax	Description
Clear		Clears the document.
Close		Closes the output stream and forces all data in the document to be displayed.
CreateElement	element = Document.CreateElement (tag)	Creates a new element object for the specified tag, which can be only an <IMG> or <OPTION> tag.
CreateStyleSheet	Document.CreateStyleSheet ([URL [, index]])	Creates a style sheet for the document. If URL contains a page, the style information will be added as a link object, if the URL contains style information, then this information will be added to the style object. The index represents where the style sheet is inserted in the style sheets collection, defaulting to the end.
ElementFromPoint	element = Document.ElementFromPoint (x,y)	Returns the element for the specified x and y coordinates from the top left corner.

Table Continued on Following Page

Document Object Methods	Syntax	Description
ExecCommand	boolean = Document.ExecCommand (strCommand [,blnUserInterface [,vntValue4]])	Executes a command over the given document. The optional blnUserInterface parameter specifies whether to display a user interface if the command is able to. The vntValue represents a value to assign, based on the command.
Open	Document.Open (mimeType,replace)	Opens a stream for collecting the output of WriteIn or Write methods. The mimeType currently only works with "text/html". Type "replace" in the replace parameter if you want the document you are writing to replace the current document in the browser's history list.
QueryCommandEnabled	boolean = Document.QueryCommandEnabled (Command)	Returns true if the specified command can be executed based on the current state of the document.
QueryCommandIndeterm	boolean = Document.QueryCommandIndeterm (Command)	Returns true if the specified command is in the indeterminate state, else it returns false.
QueryCommandState	boolean = Document.QueryCommandState (command)	Returns the current state of the specified command - true if it has been finished, false if it has not, and NULL if it can't be determined.
QueryCommandSupported	boolean = Document.QueryCommandSupported (command)	Returns whether the current command is supported on the current document.
QueryCommandText	string = Document.QueryCommandText (command)	Returns the text associated with the current command.
QueryCommandValue	string = Document.QueryCommandValue (command)	Returns the value of the specified command.

Document Object Methods	Syntax	Description
ShowHelp	Document.ShowHelp (URL [,contextID])	Displays a WinHelp or HTMLHelp file specified by URL. The contextID is an optional argument for passing the context ID to the help file.
Write	Document.Write (string)	Writes the value contained in string to the specified document.
WriteIn	Document.WriteIn (string)	Same as Write, but adds a carriage return after the string.

Document Object Events	Description
onafterupdate	Fires immediately after the transfer of data from the element to the data provider, assuming that onbeforeupdate was successful.
onbeforeupdate	Fires before data is transferred from the element to the data provider, or when an element loses the focus, or the document is attempting to unload when the value of the element has changed from what it was when it received the focus.
onclick	Fires when the user clicks on the document with the left mouse button or when they press keys such as *Enter* and *Esc* in a form.
ondblclick	Fires when the user double clicks on the document.
ondragstart	Fires when the user starts to drag a selection or a selected element.
onerrorupdate	Fires when the document's onbeforeupdate event handler has canceled the data transfer. This event is then fired in place of the onafterupdate event.
onhelp	Fires when the user presses *F1* or the browser Help key.
onkeydown	Fires when the user presses a key, and returns a number specifying the keycode of the key that they pressed.
onkeypress	Fires when the user presses a key, and returns a number specifying the unicode of the key that they pressed.
onkeyup	Fires when the user releases a key, and returns a number specifying the keycode of the key that they released.
onmousedown	Fires when the user presses the mouse button.
onmousemove	Fires when the user moves their mouse.

Table Continued on Following Page

Document Object Events	Description
onmouseout	Fires when the user moves their mouse out of an element.
onmouseover	Fires when the user moves their mouse over an element.
onmouseup	Fires when the user releases the button on their mouse over the element.
onreadystatechanged	Fires when the ready state for the document has changed.
onrowenter	Fires to indicate that the row has changed on a databound document element.
onrowexit	Fires just prior to the data source control of a databound document element changing the current row.
onselectstart	Fires at the beginning of a user selecting an element on the document.

Document Object Collections

The Document object has many collections, as shown below. In general, they all work in the same way, which has been expanded upon here for the sake of completeness. The collections available are:

- ❑ all
- ❑ anchors
- ❑ applets
- ❑ children
- ❑ embeds
- ❑ forms
- ❑ frames
- ❑ images
- ❑ links
- ❑ plugins
- ❑ scripts
- ❑ stylesheets

Collection: All	Syntax	Description
all	object.all(index)	Returns an object reference to the collection of all elements contained by the object.
length (property)	object.length	The number of elements in the collection.

Collection: All	Syntax	Description
item (method)	element = object.item (index [,subindex])	Retrieves an element or a collection from the specified collection. The index is a number or string which specifies which element to retrieve. If it is a string, the optional subindex can also specify the number in the collection.
tags (method)	elements = object.tags(tag)	Retrieves a collection of all the elements in the specified collection that match the specified HTML tag name.

Collection: Anchors	Syntax	Description
anchors	object.anchors (index)	Retrieves a collection of all the anchor (A) elements that have a name and/or an ID attribute. The order is based on the order in which they appear in the HTML.
length (property)	object.length	The number of elements in the collection.
item (method)	element = object.item(index [,subindex])	Retrieves an element or a collection from the specified collection. The index is a number or string which specifies which element to retrieve. If it is a string, the optional subindex can also specify the number in the collection.
tags (method)	elements = object.tags(tag)	Retrieves a collection of all the elements in the specified collection that match the specified HTML tag name.

Collection: Applets	Syntax	Description
applets	object.applets (index)	Retrieves a collection of all the Applet objects contained in the document.
length (property)	object.length	The number of elements in the collection.
item (method)	element = object.item (index [,subindex])	Retrieves an element or a collection from the specified collection. The index is a number or string which specifies which element to retrieve. If it is a string, the optional subindex can also specify the number in the collection.
tags (method)	elements = object.tags(tag)	Retrieves a collection of all the elements in the specified collection that match the specified HTML tag name.

Collection: Children	Syntax	Description
children	object.children (index)	Retrieves just the direct descendants of the specified elements. These elements are undefined if the child elements are overlapping tags.

Collection: Embed	Syntax	Description
embeds	object.embeds (index)	Retrieves a collection of all the Embed objects contained in the document. Embed elements are embedded documents.
length (property)	object.length	The number of elements in the collection.
item (method)	element = object.item(index [,subindex])	Retrieves an element or a collection from the specified collection. The index is a number or string which specifies which element to retrieve. If it is a string, the optional subindex can also specify the number in the collection.
tags (method)	elements = object.tags(tag)	Retrieves a collection of all the elements in the specified collection that match the specified HTML tag name.

Collection: Forms	Syntax	Description
forms	object.forms (index)	Returns an object reference to the collection of all form elements contained by the document.
length (property)	object.length	The number of elements in the collection.
item (method)	element = object.item(index [,subindex])	Retrieves an element or a collection from the specified collection. The index is a number or string which specifies which element to retrieve. If it is a string, the optional subindex can also specify the number in the collection.
tags (method)	elements = object.tags(tag)	Retrieves a collection of all the elements in the specified collection that match the specified HTML tag name.

Collection: Frames	Syntax	Description
frames	object.frames (index)	Retrieves a collection of all Window objects defined by the specified document, or defined by the document associated by the specified window, depending on whether the object is a window or a document.
length (property)	object.length	The number of elements in the collection.
item (method)	element = object.item(index [,subindex])	Retrieves an element or a collection from the specified collection. The index is a number or string which specifies which element to retrieve. If it is a string, the optional subindex can also specify the number in the collection.
tags (method)	elements = object.tags(tag)	Retrieves a collection of all the elements in the specified collection that match the specified HTML tag name.

Collection: Images	Syntax	Description
Images	object.images (index)	Retrieves a collection of all the IMG elements in the document. The order is the order in which they appear in the HTML source for the document.
length (property)	object.length	The number of elements in the collection.
item (method)	element = object.item(index [,subindex])	Retrieves an element or a collection from the specified collection. The index is a number or string which specifies which element to retrieve. If it is a string, the optional subindex can also specify the number in the collection.
tags (method)	elements = object.tags(tag)	Retrieves a collection of all the elements in the specified collection that match the specified HTML tag name.

477

Collection: Links	Syntax	Description
links	object.links (index)	Retrieves a collection of all anchor (A) elements that specify an href= attribute, and all area elements in the document.
length (property)	object.length	The number of elements in the collection.
item (method)	element = object.item(index [,subindex])	Retrieves an element or a collection from the specified collection. The index is a number or string which specifies which element to retrieve. If it is a string, the optional subindex can also specify the number in the collection.
tags (method)	elements = object.tags(tag)	Retrieves a collection of all the elements in the specified collection that match the specified HTML tag name.

Collection: Plugins	Syntax	Description
plugins	object.plugins (index)	The plugins collection is an alias for the document's embeds collection described above.
length (property)	object.length	The number of elements in the collection.
item (method)	element = object.item(index [,subindex])	Retrieves an element or a collection from the specified collection. The index is a number or string which specifies which element to retrieve. If it is a string, the optional subindex can also specify the number in the collection.
tags (method)	elements = object.tags(tag)	Retrieves a collection of all the elements in the specified collection that match the specified HTML tag name.

Collection: Scripts	Syntax	Description
scripts	object.scripts (index)	This retrieves a collection of all the script elements in the document in source order.
length (property)	object.length	The number of elements in the collection.

Collection: Scripts	Syntax	Description
item (method)	element = object.item (index [, subindex])	Retrieves an element or a collection from the specified collection. The index is a number or string which specifies which element to retrieve. If it is a string, the optional subindex can also specify the number in the collection.
tags (method)	elements = object.tags(tag)	Retrieves a collection of all the elements in the specified collection that match the specified HTML tag name.

Collection: StyleSheets	Syntax	Description
styleSheets	object.styleSheets (index)	This retrieves a collection of StyleSheets objects that represent the style sheets referred to by the link or style elements of the document. If the style sheet was imported, it is contained within a style element.
length (property)	object.length	The number of elements in the collection.
item (method)	element = object.item (index [, subindex])	Retrieves an element or a collection from the specified collection. The index is a number or string which specifies which element to retrieve. If it is a string, the optional subindex can also specify the number in the collection.
tags (method)	elements = object.tags(tag)	Retrieves a collection of all the elements in the specified collection that match the specified HTML tag name.

The History Object

The History object maintains information about the pages that the user has visited. It is often used to programmatically provide the same functionality as the back and forward buttons on the browser.

History Object Properties	Syntax	Description
length	history.length	Returns the number of elements in the History object collection.

History Object Methods	Syntax	Description
back	history.back()	Loads the previous URL in the history list, exactly as if the user had pressed the **Back** button on their browser.
forward	history.forward()	Loads the next URL in the history list, exactly as if the user had pressed the **Forward** button on their browser.
go	history.go (delta | location)	Loads a URL from the history list. The delta is an integer representing a relative position from the history list, while location is a string that represents all or part of a URL from the history list.

The Navigator Object

The Navigator object contains information about the web browser, which is commonly used to determine what features are available.

Navigator Object Properties	Description
appCodeName	Returns a string that returns the code name of the browser.
appMinorVersion	Returns the application's minor version value.
appName	Returns a string that contains the name of the browser.
appVersion	Returns a string that is the version of the browser.
browserLanguage	Returns a string that indicates the current browser language (as in national language, not computer language).
connectionSpeed	Returns the preferred connection speed of the browser.
cookieEnabled	Returns true if the browser is able to use client side cookies, else returns false.
cpuClass	Returns a string containing the CPU class, i.e. x86, other.
onLine	Returns true if the system is in global online mode, else returns false. Global offline mode is set by selecting **Work Offline** in the Internet Explorer menu.
platform	Returns a string that indicates the platform that the browser is running on, i.e. Win32, Win16, and so on.

Navigator Object Properties	Description
systemLanguage	Indicates the default language that the system is running.
userAgent	Returns the string that represents the user-agent header sent in the HTTP protocol from the client to the server.
userLanguage	Returns a string that indicates the current user language.
userProfile	Contains methods that enable script to request read access to the user's profile information and perform read actions. Methods are addReadRequest, clearRequest, doReadRequest, getAttribute.

Navigator Object Model	Syntax	Description
javaEnabled	boolean=object. javaEnabled()	Returns true if Java is enabled, else false.
taintEnabled	boolean=object. taintEnabled()	Returns true if data tainting is enabled, else returns false. In Internet Explorer 4.0 it always returns false because data tainting is not supported.

Navigator Object Collections	Syntax	Description
mimeTypes	object.mimTypes	In Internet Explorer this always returns an empty collection - it is only included for compatibility with other browsers.
plugins	object.plugins	In Internet Explorer this always returns an empty collection - it is only included for compatibility with other browsers.

The Location Object

Location Object Properties	Description
hash	Sets or returns the subsection of the href property that follows the # symbol, as used in book marking. If there is no hash, the property returns an empty string.

Table Continued on Following Page

Location Object Properties	Description
host	Sets or returns the hostname:port part of the location or URL. This is the concatenation of the hostname and port properties, delimited by a colon. If the port property is null then the host property will be the same as the hostname property.
hostname	Specifies the host name part of the location or URL - if no host name is available then it returns an empty string.
href	Returns the entire URL as a string.
pathname	Returns the file or object path.
port	Returns the port number of the URL.
protocol	Returns the URL's access method, which is the initial substring up to and including the first colon.
search	Returns the substring of the href property that follows the ? symbol. This is the query string or form data as used by Request.Querystring in ASP script.

Location Object Methods	Syntax	Description
assign	object.assign (url)	Sets the current location to that specified in the URL parameter.
reload	object.reload (blnReloadSource)	Reloads the current page. If the blnReloadSource property is true, this will requery the server, else if it is false it will requery the cache. By default, this is false.
replace	object.replace (url)	This replaces the current document by loading the document specified in url. This also removes the current document from the browser's history list.

Event Object

Event Object Properties	Description
altKey	Specifies the state of the *Alt* key - true if the key is down.
button	Specifies which mouse button is pressed. Returns 0 if no button, 1 for left, 2 for right, and 4 for middle button.
cancelBubble	Specifies whether the current event should bubble up the hierarchy of event handlers - if true, the event will not bubble, if false, it will bubble up the event handler hierarchy until it is handled.

Event Object Properties	Description
clientX	Returns the x position where the mouse was clicked relative to the size of the client area of the window, excluding scroll bars and other decorations.
clientY	Returns the y position where the mouse was clicked relative to the size of the client area of the window, excluding scroll bars and other decorations.
ctrlKey	Specifies the state of the *Ctrl* key - true if the key is down.
fromElement	Specifies the element being moved from for the onmouseover and onmouseout events.
keyCode	Returns the unicode key code associated with the key that caused the event.
offsetX	Returns the x position that matches the offsetLeft and offsetTop properties of the element that caused the event.
offsetY	Returns the y position that matches the offsetLeft and offsetTop properties of the element that caused the event.
reason	Returns information about how a data transfer finished for a Datasource object. Returns 0 if it was successful, 1 if it was aborted, and 2 if there was a transfer error.
returnValue	Specifies the return value of the event. Setting this to true cancels the default action of the source element of the event.
screenX	Returns the x coordinate relative to the physical screen size.
screenY	Returns the y coordinate relative to the physical screen size.
shiftKey	Specifies the state of the *Shift* key - true if the key is down.
srcElement	Specifies the element that fired the event.
srcFilter	Specifies the filter object that caused an onfilterchange event to be fired.
toElement	Specifies the element being moved to for the onmouseover and onmouseout events.
type	Returns the name of the event or scripting language as a string. Events returned do not include the "on" prefix, so "onmouseover" becomes "mouseover".
x	Returns the x position of the mouse relative to the element, in the hierarchy that has been positioned using CSS positioning. If nothing has been positioned using this, then the BODY element is returned as the default.
y	Returns the y position of the mouse relative to the element, in the hierarchy that has been positioned using CSS positioning. If nothing has been positioned using this, then the BODY element is returned as the default.

The Screen Object

Screen Object Properties	Description
availHeight	Returns the height of the system's screen in pixels. This is the working area, excluding the toolbar.
availWidth	Returns the width of the system's screen in pixels. This is the working area, excluding the toolbar.
bufferDepth	Specifies an offscreen bitmap buffer which can affect colorDepth.
colorDepth	Returns the bits per pixel value used for colors on the screen.
height	Returns the height of the screen in pixels.
updateInterval	Sets or returns the update interval for the screen.
width	Returns the width of the screen in pixels.

Active Server Pages Object Model

This Appendix details the Active Server Pages Object Model, as discussed in Chapter 7. For each object, there is a description of its properties, methods, and collections.

Request Object

The Request object is used to get information that is sent from the user along with an HTTP request. This object, along with the Response object, is one of the core objects in the ASP Object Model, and is used extensively when a developer needs to work out what a user wants.

Collections	Description
ClientCertificate	Details the values of client certificates sent from the browser. This is read only.
Cookies	Details the values of any cookies sent in the request from the browser. This is read only.
Form	Used to get data from a submitted form. Values of any elements are read only, and can be accessed by Request.Form("ValueName").value.
QueryString	Contains the value of any variables contained in the HTTP string. This is used for sending a request for specific information in a page. Read only.
ServerVariables	Contains values of various HTTP and environment variables on the server. Can provide information such as the server name. Read only.

Property	Description
TotalBytes	This is the number of bytes that the client is sending in the body of the request.

Method	Description
BinaryRead	Used to retrieve data sent to the server from the client as part of the POST request.

Response Object

The Response object is used to control the output from the server to the client. It is used to *send* content, and to control *when* it is sent. You can think of the Response object as the flip side of the Request object. As in English, you make a *request*, for which you receive a *response*. This object is the one that makes that response happen.

Collections	Description
Cookies	This collection is used to specify values of cookies and to send the cookies to the browser.

Properties	Description
Buffer	This indicates whether page output is buffered – meaning it will wait until it is complete before sending it.
CacheControl	Determines whether proxy servers can cache the output generated by ASP.
Charset	Appends the name of the character set to the content-type header.
ContentType	Specifies the HTTP content-type of the response – i.e. "Text/HTML".
Expires	Specifies the length of time until a page cached on a browser will expire.
ExpiresAbsolute	Specifies the date and time when a page cached on a browser will expire.
IsClientConnected	Indicates whether the client has disconnected from the server (False), or is still connected (True).

Methods	Description
PICS	This sets the value of the PICS label field in the response header.
Status	Contains the value of the HTTP status line returned by the server.
AddHeader	Adds or changes a value in the HTML header.
AppendToLog	Adds a string to the end of the web server log entry for this request.
BinaryWrite	Sends a string to the browser without character set conversion.
Clear	Erases any buffered HTML output.
End	Stops processing the page and immediately returns the current result.
Flush	Sends all buffered output immediately.
Redirect	Sends a redirect message to the browser, instructing it to connect to a different URL.
Write	Writes a variable to the current HTTP output as a string.

Application Object

The Application object is used to share information amongst all users of the application. The object stores variables and objects that have an application scope, and information about all currently active sessions within the application.

Collections	Description
Contents	This collection contains all of the items added to the application through script commands.
StaticObjects	This collection contains all of the objects that have been added to the application with the <OBJECT> tag.

Methods	Description
Lock	Locking the application object prevents all other clients from modifying application properties until the Unlock method is called.
UnLock	Allows other clients to modify application properties.
Contents.Remove	Removes a content item from the Contents collection.
Contents.RemoveAll	Removes all contents from the Contents collection.

Events	Description
OnStart	Fires when the first page in the application is referenced.
OnEnd	Fires when the application ends, i.e. when the web server is stopped.

Session Object

The Session object is used to keep track of an individual browser throughout its navigation of your web site. Each browser is given one session, which lasts until the session is terminated, the session times out, or the browser stops navigating the application. The object is used to store information that lasts for the duration of the session.

Collections	Description
Contents	This collection contains all of the items added to the session through script commands.
StaticObjects	This collection contains all of the objects that have been added to the session with the <OBJECT> tag.

Methods	Description
Abandon	This destroys a Session object and releases its resources on the server.
Contents.Remove	Removes a content item from the Contents collection.
Contents.RemoveAll	Removes all contents from the Contents collection.

Properties	Description
CodePage	Sets the code page that will be used for symbol mapping. A code page is a character set that can include numbers, punctuation marks, and so on.
LCID	Sets the locale identifier, which is a standard international abbreviation that uniquely identifies one of the system-defined locales.
SessionID	Returns the session identification unique to this user.
Timeout	Sets the timeout period, in minutes, for the session state for this application.

Events	Description
OnStart	Fires when the server creates a new session.
OnEnd	Fires when the session is abandoned or times out.

Server Object

The Server object is primarily used to create components that run on the server.

Property	Description
ScriptTimeOut	The length of time that a script can run before an error occurs.

Methods	Description
CreateObject	Creates an instance of an object or server component.
Execute	Executes an .asp file.
GetLastError	Returns an ASPError object that describes the error condition.
HTMLEncode	Applies HTML encoding to the specified string, which replaces certain characters with HTML codes, i.e. < is replaced with <.
MapPath	Converts a virtual path into a physical path.
Transfer	Sends all of the current state information to another .asp file for processing.
URLEncode	Applies URL encoding, including escape characters, to a string.

ASPError Object

The ASPError object can be used to get information about an error condition that has occurred in an ASP script. The ASPError object is returned by the Server.GetLastError method outlined above. All properties are read only.

Property	Description
ASPCode	This returns an error code as generated by Internet Information Server.
Number	Returns the standard COM error code that has occurred.
Source	Indicates where the error occurred – internal to ASP, in a component, or in a scripting language.
FileName	Indicates the name of the ASP file being processed when the error occurred.
LineNumber	Indicates the line number within the file where the error occurred.
Description	Returns a short description of the error.
ASPDescription	If the error is ASP related, this returns a more detailed description than the Description property.

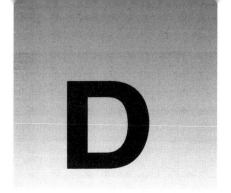

HTML Reference

This Appendix lists all of the HTML element tags in alphabetical order. After the description of what each tag does, you can see which versions of HTML and which browsers support that tag. For each element, the available attributes for use with it are listed. Again, we show which versions of HTML and which browsers support each attribute (those marked with D are deprecated, or in other words supported for backwards compatibility only). The purpose of this reference is to show you the tags available, enabling you to look up help files for further information on how to use them.

A

Defines a hypertext link. The HREF or the NAME attribute must be specified. **ALL**.

Attributes	2.0	3.2	4.0	N2	N3	N4	IE2	IE3	IE4/5
`<event_name>=script_code`	✗	✗	✓	✗	✗	✓	✗	✓	✓
`ACCESSKEY=key_character`	✗	✗	✓	✗	✗	✗	✗	✗	✓
CHARSET=*string*	✗	✗	✓	✗	✗	✗	✗	✗	✗
CLASS=*classname*	✗	✗	✗	✗	✗	✓	✗	✓	✓
COORDS=*string*	✗	✗	✓	✗	✗	✓	✗	✗	✗
`DATAFLD=column_name`	✗	✗	✗	✗	✗	✗	✗	✗	✓
`DATASRC=id`	✗	✗	✗	✗	✗	✗	✗	✗	✓
`DIR=LTR	RTL`	✗	✗	✓	✗	✗	✗	✗	✗	✗
`HREF=url`	✓	✓	✓	✓	✓	✓	✓	✓	✓
`HREFLANG=langcode`	✗	✗	✓	✗	✗	✗	✗	✗	✗
`ID`=*string*	✗	✗	✓	✗	✗	✓	✗	✓	✓
`LANG=language_type`	✗	✗	✓	✗	✗	✗	✗	✗	✓
`LANGUAGE=JAVASCRIPT	JSCRIPT	VBSCRIPT	VBS`	✗	✗	✗	✗	✗	✗	✗	✗	✓
METHODS=*string*	✓	✗	✗	✗	✗	✗	✗	✗	✓
NAME=*string*	✓	✓	✓	✓	✓	✓	✓	✓	✓
`REL=SAME	NEXT	PARENT	PREVIOUS` *string*	✓	✓	✓	✗	✗	✗	✗	✓	✓
REV=*string*	✓	✓	✓	✗	✗	✗	✗	✓	✓

Attributes	2.0	3.2	4.0	N2	N3	N4	IE2	IE3	IE4/5
SHAPE=CIRC | CIRCLE | POLY | POLYGON | RECT | RECTANGLE	✗	✗	✓	✗	✗	✗	✗	✗	✗
STYLE=*string*	✗	✗	✓	✗	✗	✓	✗	✓	✓
TABINDEX=*number*	✗	✗	✓	✗	✗	✗	✗	✗	✓
TARGET=<window_name> | _parent | _blank | _top | _self	✗	✗	✓	✓	✓	✓	✗	✓	✓
TITLE=*string*	✓	✓	✓	✗	✗	✗	✗	✓	✓
TYPE=BUTTON | RESET | SUBMIT	✗	✗	✓	✗	✗	✗	✗	✗	✓
URN=*string*	✓	✗	✗	✗	✗	✗	✗	✗	✓

ABBR

Indicates a sequence of characters that compose an acronym (e.g., "WWW"). **HTML 4.0, IE4, IE5**.

Attributes	2.0	3.2	4.0	N2	N3	N4	IE2	IE3	IE4/5
<event_name>=script_code	✗	✗	✓	✗	✗	✗	✗	✗	✓
CLASS=classname	✗	✗	✓	✗	✗	✗	✗	✗	✓
DIR=LTR | RTL	✗	✗	✓	✗	✗	✗	✗	✗	✗
ID=*string*	✗	✗	✓	✗	✗	✗	✗	✗	✓
LANG=language_type	✗	✗	✓	✗	✗	✗	✗	✗	✓
LANGUAGE=JAVASCRIPT | JSCRIPT | VBSCRIPT | VBS	✗	✗	✗	✗	✗	✗	✗	✗	✓
STYLE=*string*	✗	✗	✓	✗	✗	✗	✗	✗	✓
TITLE=*string*	✗	✗	✓	✗	✗	✗	✗	✗	✓

ADDRESS

Specifies information such as address, signature and authorship. **ALL**.

Attributes	2.0	3.2	4.0	N2	N3	N4	IE2	IE3	IE4/5
<event_name>=script_code	✗	✗	✓	✗	✗	✗	✗	✗	✓
CLASS=classname	✗	✗	✓	✗	✗	✓	✗	✗	✓
DIR=LTR | RTL	✗	✗	✓	✗	✗	✗	✗	✗	✗
ID=*string*	✗	✗	✓	✗	✗	✓	✗	✗	✓
LANG=language_type	✗	✗	✓	✗	✗	✗	✗	✗	✓
LANGUAGE=JAVASCRIPT | JSCRIPT | VBSCRIPT | VBS	✗	✗	✗	✗	✗	✗	✗	✗	✓
STYLE=STRING	✗	✗	✓	✗	✗	✓	✗	✗	✓
TITLE=STRING	✗	✗	✓	✗	✗	✗	✗	✗	✓

APPLET

Places a Java Applet or other executable content in the page. **HTML 3.2, N2, N3, N4, IE3, IE4, IE5, deprecated in HTML 4.0.**

Attributes	2.0	3.2	4.0	N2	N3	N4	IE2	IE3	IE4/5
`<event_name>=script_code`	✗	✗	D	✗	✗	✗	✗	✗	✗
`ALIGN=TOP|MIDDLE|BOTTOM|LEFT|RIGHT|ABSMI` `DDLE|BASELINE|ABSBOTTOM|TEXTTOP`	✗	✓	D	✓	✓	✓	✗	✓	✓
`ALT=text`	✗	✓	D	✓	✓	✓	✗	✓	✓
`ARCHIVE=url`	✗	✗	D	✗	✓	✓	✗	✗	✗
`BORDER=number`	✗	✗	D	✗	✗	✗	✗	✗	✗
`CLASS=classname`	✗	✗	D	✗	✗	✓	✗	✗	✓
`CODE=filename`	✗	✓	D	✓	✓	✓	✗	✓	✓
`CODEBASE=Path|url`	✗	✓	D	✓	✓	✓	✗	✓	✓
`DATAFLD=column_name`	✗	✗	✗	✗	✗	✗	✗	✗	✓
`DATASRC=id`	✗	✗	✗	✗	✗	✗	✗	✗	✓
`DOWNLOAD=number`	✗	✗	✗	✗	✗	✗	✗	✓	✗
`HEIGHT=number`	✗	✓	D	✓	✓	✓	✗	✓	✗
`HSPACE=number`	✗	✓	D	✗	✗	✓	✗	✓	✓
`ID=string`	✗	✗	D	✗	✗	✓	✗	✗	✓
`MAYSCRIPT=YES|NO`	✗	✗	✗	✗	✗	✓	✗	✗	✗
`NAME=string`	✗	✓	D	✗	✗	✗	✗	✓	✓
`OBJECT=string`	✗	✗	D	✗	✗	✗	✗	✗	✗
`SRC=url`	✗	✗	✗	✗	✗	✗	✗	✗	✓
`STYLE=string`	✗	✗	D	✗	✗	✓	✗	✗	✓
`TITLE=string`	✗	✗	D	✗	✗	✗	✗	✓	✓
`VSPACE=number`	✗	✓	D	✗	✗	✓	✗	✓	✓
`WIDTH=number`	✗	✓	D	✓	✓	✓	✗	✓	✓

AREA

Specifies the shape of a "hot spot" in a client-side image map. **ALL except HTML 2.0**.

Attributes	2.0	3.2	4.0	N2	N3	N4	IE2	IE3	IE4/5
`<event_name>=script_code`	✗	✗	✗	✗	✗	✓	✗	✗	✓
`ALT=text`	✗	✓	✓	✓	✓	✓	✗	✓	✓
`CLASS=classname`	✗	✗	D	✗	✗	✓	✗	✓	✓
`COORDS=string`	✗	✓	✓	✓	✓	✓	✓	✓	✓
`DIR=LTR|RTL`	✗	✗	✓	✗	✗	✗	✗	✗	✗
`HREF=url`	✗	✓	✓	✓	✓	✓	✓	✓	✓
`ID=string`	✗	✗	D	✗	✗	✓	✗	✓	✓
`LANG=language_type`	✗	✗	D	✗	✗	✗	✗	✗	✓
`LANGUAGE=JAVASCRIPT|JSCRIPT|VBSCRIPT|VBS`	✗	✗	✗	✗	✗	✗	✗	✗	✓
`NAME=string`	✗	✗	✗	✗	✗	✓	✗	✗	✗
`NOHREF`	✗	✓	✓	✓	✓	✓	✓	✓	✓
`NOTAB`	✗	✗	✗	✗	✗	✗	✗	✓	✗
`SHAPE=CIRC|CIRCLE|POLY|POLYGON|RECT|RECTANGLE`	✗	✓	✓	✓	✓	✓	✓	✓	✓
`STYLE=string`	✗	✗	D	✗	✗	✓	✗	✗	✓
`TABINDEX=number`	✗	✗	✓	✗	✗	✗	✗	✓	✓
`TARGET=<window_name>|_parent|_blank|_top|_self`	✗	✗	✓	✓	✓	✓	✗	✓	✓
`TITLE=string`	✗	✗	D	✗	✗	✗	✗	✓	✓

B

Renders text in boldface where available. **ALL**.

Attributes	2.0	3.2	4.0	N2	N3	N4	IE2	IE3	IE4/5
`<event_name>=script_code`	✗	✗	✓	✗	✗	✗	✗	✗	✓
`CLASS=classname`	✗	✗	✓	✗	✗	✓	✗	✗	✓
`DIR=LTR|RTL`	✗	✗	✓	✗	✗	✗	✗	✗	✗
`ID=string`	✗	✗	✓	✗	✗	✓	✗	✗	✓
`LANG=language_type`	✗	✗	✓	✗	✗	✗	✗	✗	✓
`LANGUAGE=JAVASCRIPT|JSCRIPT|VBSCRIPT|VBS`	✗	✗	✗	✗	✗	✗	✗	✗	✓
`STYLE=string`	✗	✗	✓	✗	✗	✓	✗	✗	✓
`TITLE=string`	✗	✗	✓	✗	✗	✗	✗	✗	✓

BASE

Specifies the document's base URL. **ALL**.

Attributes	2.0	3.2	4.0	N2	N3	N4	IE2	IE3	IE4/5
HREF=url	✓	✓	✓	✓	✓	✓	✓	✓	✓
TARGET=<window_name>|_parent|_blank|_top|_self	✗	✗	✓	✓	✓	✓	✗	✓	✓

BASEFONT

Sets the base font values to be used as the default font when rendering text. **HTML 3.2, N2, N3, N4, IE2, IE3, IE4, IE5 deprecated in HTML 4.0.**

Attributes	2.0	3.2	4.0	N2	N3	N4	IE2	IE3	IE4/5
CLASS=classname	✗	✗	✗	✗	✗	✓	✗	✗	✓
COLOR=color	✗	✗	D	✗	✗	✗	✗	✓	✓
FACE=font_family_name	✗	✗	D	✗	✗	✗	✗	✓	✓
ID=string	✗	✗	D	✗	✗	✓	✗	✗	✓
LANG=language_type	✗	✗	✗	✗	✗	✗	✗	✗	✓
LANGUAGE=JAVASCRIPT|JSCRIPT|VBSCRIPT|VBS	✗	✗	✗	✗	✗	✗	✗	✗	✓
SIZE=1|2|3|4|5|6|7	✗	✓	D	✓	✓	✓	✓	✓	✓

BDO

Turns off the bidirectional rendering algorithm for selected fragments of text. **HTML 4.0**.

Attributes	2.0	3.2	4.0	N2	N3	N4	IE2	IE3	IE4/5
CLASS=classname	✗	✗	✓	✗	✗	✗	✗	✗	✗
DIR=LTR|RTL	✗	✗	✓	✗	✗	✗	✗	✗	✗
ID=string	✗	✗	✓	✗	✗	✗	✗	✗	✗
LANG=language_type	✗	✗	✓	✗	✗	✗	✗	✗	✗
STYLE=string	✗	✗	✓	✗	✗	✗	✗	✗	✗
TITLE=string	✗	✗	✓	✗	✗	✗	✗	✗	✗

BGSOUND

Specifies a background sound to be played while the page is loaded. **IE2, IE3, IE4, IE5**.

Attributes	2.0	3.0	4.0	N2	N3	N4	IE2	IE3	IE4/5
BALANCE=number	✗	✗	✗	✗	✗	✗	✗	✗	✓
CLASS=classname	✗	✗	✗	✗	✗	✗	✗	✗	✓
ID=*string*	✗	✗	✗	✗	✗	✗	✗	✗	✓
LANG=language_type	✗	✗	✗	✗	✗	✗	✗	✗	✓
LOOP=number	✗	✗	✗	✗	✗	✗	✓	✓	✓
SRC=url	✗	✗	✗	✗	✗	✗	✓	✓	✓
TITLE=*string*	✗	✗	✗	✗	✗	✗	✗	✗	✓
VOLUME=number	✗	✗	✗	✗	✗	✗	✗	✗	✓

BIG

Renders text in a relatively larger font than the current font. **HTML 3.2, 4.0, N2, N3, N4, IE3, IE4, IE5**.

Attributes	2.0	3.2	4.0	N2	N3	N4	IE2	IE3	IE4/5
<event_name>=script_code	✗	✗	✓	✗	✗	✗	✗	✗	✓
CLASS=classname	✗	✗	✓	✗	✗	✓	✗	✗	✓
DIR=LTR|RTL	✗	✗	✓	✗	✗	✗	✗	✗	✗
ID=*string*	✗	✗	✓	✗	✗	✓	✗	✗	✓
LANG=language_type	✗	✗	✓	✗	✗	✗	✗	✗	✓
LANGUAGE=JAVASCRIPT|JSCRIPT|VBSCRIPT|VBS	✗	✗	✗	✗	✗	✗	✗	✗	✓
STYLE=*string*	✗	✗	✓	✗	✗	✓	✗	✗	✓
TITLE=*string*	✗	✗	✓	✗	✗	✗	✗	✗	✓

BLINK

Causes the text to flash on and off within the page. **N2, N3, N4**.

Attributes	2.0	3.2	4.0	N2	N3	N4	IE2	IE3	IE4/5
CLASS=classname	✗	✗	✗	✗	✗	✓	✗	✗	✗
ID=*string*	✗	✗	✗	✗	✗	✓	✗	✗	✗
STYLE=*string*	✗	✗	✗	✗	✗	✓	✗	✗	✗

BLOCKQUOTE

Denotes a quotation in text, usually a paragraph or more. **ALL**.

Attributes	2.0	3.2	4.0	N2	N3	N4	IE2	IE3	IE4/5
`<event_name>=script_code`	✗	✗	✓	✗	✗	✗	✗	✗	✓
`CITE=url`	✗	✗	✓	✗	✗	✗	✗	✗	✗
`CLASS=classname`	✗	✗	✓	✗	✗	✓	✗	✗	✓
`DIR=LTR` | `RTL`	✗	✗	✓	✗	✗	✗	✗	✗	✗
`ID=`*string*	✗	✗	✓	✗	✗	✓	✗	✗	✓
`LANG=language_type`	✗	✗	✓	✗	✗	✗	✗	✗	✓
`LANGUAGE=JAVASCRIPT` | `JSCRIPT` | `VBSCRIPT` | `VBS`	✗	✗	✗	✗	✗	✗	✗	✗	✓
`STYLE=`*string*	✗	✗	✓	✗	✗	✓	✗	✗	✓
`TITLE=`*string*	✗	✗	✓	✗	✗	✗	✗	✗	✓

BODY

Defines the beginning and end of the body section of the page. **ALL**.

Attributes	2.0	3.2	4.0	N2	N3	N4	IE2	IE3	IE4/5
`<event_name>=script_code`	✗	✗	✓	✗	✗	✓	✗	✗	✓
`ALINK=color`	✗	✓	D	✓	✓	✓	✗	✓	✓
`BACKGROUND=`*string*	✗	✓	D	✓	✓	✓	✓	✓	✓
`BGCOLOR=color`	✗	✓	D	✓	✓	✓	✓	✓	✓
`BGPROPERTIES=FIXED`	✗	✗	✗	✗	✗	✗	✓	✓	✓
`BOTTOMMARGIN=number`	✗	✗	✗	✗	✗	✗	✗	✗	✓
`CLASS=classname`	✗	✗	✓	✗	✗	✓	✗	✓	✓
`DIR=LTR` | `RTL`	✗	✗	✓	✗	✗	✗	✗	✗	✗
`ID=`*string*	✗	✗	✓	✗	✗	✓	✗	✓	✓
`LANG=language_type`	✗	✗	✓	✗	✗	✗	✗	✗	✓
`LANGUAGE=JAVASCRIPT` | `JSCRIPT` | `VBSCRIPT` | `VBS`	✗	✗	✗	✗	✗	✗	✗	✗	✓
`LEFTMARGIN=number`	✗	✗	✗	✗	✗	✗	✓	✓	✓
`LINK=color`	✗	✓	D	✓	✓	✓	✓	✓	✓
`RIGHTMARGIN=number`	✗	✗	✗	✗	✗	✗	✗	✗	✓
`SCROLL=YES` | `NO`	✗	✗	✗	✗	✗	✗	✗	✗	✓

Attributes	2.0	3.2	4.0	N2	N3	N4	IE2	IE3	IE4/5
STYLE=*string*	✗	✗	✓	✗	✗	✓	✗	✓	✓
TEXT=color	✗	✓	D	✓	✓	✓	✓	✓	✓
TITLE=*string*	✗	✗	✓	✗	✗	✗	✗	✗	✓
TOPMARGIN=number	✗	✗	✗	✗	✗	✗	✓	✓	✓
VLINK=color	✗	✓	D	✓	✓	✓	✓	✓	✓

BR

Inserts a line break. **ALL**.

Attributes	2.0	3.2	4.0	N2	N3	N4	IE2	IE3	IE4/5
CLASS=classname	✗	✗	✓	✗	✗	✓	✗	✓	✓
CLEAR=ALL|LEFT|RIGHT|NONE	✗	✓	D	✓	✓	✓	✓	✓	✓
ID=*string*	✗	✗	✓	✗	✗	✓	✗	✗	✓
LANGUAGE=JAVSCRIPT|JSCRIPT|VBSCRIPT|VBS	✗	✗	✗	✗	✗	✗	✗	✗	✓
STYLE=*string*	✗	✗	✗	✗	✗	✓	✗	✗	✓
TITLE=*string*	✗	✗	✓	✗	✗	✗	✗	✗	✓

BUTTON

Renders an HTML button, the enclosed text used as the button's caption. **HTML 4.0, IE4, IE5**.

Attributes	2.0	3.2	4.0	N2	N3	N4	IE2	IE3	IE4/5
<event_name>=script_code	✗	✗	✓	✗	✗	✗	✗	✗	✓
ACCESSKEY=ley_character	✗	✗	✓	✗	✗	✗	✗	✗	✓
CLASS=classname	✗	✗	✓	✗	✗	✗	✗	✗	✓
DATAFLD=column_name	✗	✗	✗	✗	✗	✗	✗	✗	✓
DATAFORMATAS=HTML|TEXT	✗	✗	✗	✗	✗	✗	✗	✗	✓
DATASRC=id	✗	✗	✗	✗	✗	✗	✗	✗	✓
DIR=LTR|RTL	✗	✗	✓	✗	✗	✗	✗	✗	✗
DISABLED	✗	✗	✓	✗	✗	✗	✗	✗	✓
ID=*string*	✗	✗	✓	✗	✗	✗	✗	✗	✓
LANG=language_type	✗	✗	✓	✗	✗	✗	✗	✗	✓
LANGUAGE=JAVASCRIPT|JSCRIPT|VBSCRIPT|VBS	✗	✗	✗	✗	✗	✗	✗	✗	✓

Attributes	2.0	3.2	4.0	N2	N3	N4	IE2	IE3	IE4/5
NAME=*string*	✗	✗	✓	✗	✗	✗	✗	✗	✗
STYLE=*string*	✗	✗	✓	✗	✗	✗	✗	✗	✓
TABINDEX=number	✗	✗	✓	✗	✗	✗	✗	✗	✗
TITLE=*string*	✗	✗	✓	✗	✗	✗	✗	✗	✓
TYPE=BUTTON|RESET|SUBMIT	✗	✗	✓	✗	✗	✗	✗	✗	✓
VALUE=*string*	✗	✗	✓	✗	✗	✗	✗	✗	✗

CAPTION

Specifies a caption to be placed next to a table. **ALL except HTML 2.0.**

Attributes	2.0	3.2	4.0	N2	N3	N4	IE2	IE3	IE4/5
<event_name>=script_code	✗	✗	✓	✗	✗	✗	✗	✗	✓
ALIGN=TOP|BOTTOM|LEFT|RIGHT	✗	✓	D	✓	✓	✓	✓	✓	✓
CLASS=classname	✗	✗	✓	✗	✗	✓	✗	✗	✓
DIR=LTR|RTL	✗	✗	✓	✗	✗	✗	✗	✗	✗
ID=*string*	✗	✗	✓	✗	✗	✓	✗	✗	✓
LANG=language_type	✗	✗	✓	✗	✗	✗	✗	✗	✓
LANGUAGE=JAVASCRIPT|JSCRIPT|VBSCRIPT|VBS	✗	✗	✗	✗	✗	✗	✗	✗	✓
STYLE=*string*	✗	✗	✓	✗	✗	✓	✗	✗	✓
TITLE=*string*	✗	✗	✓	✗	✗	✗	✗	✗	✓
VALIGN=BOTTOM|TOP	✗	✗	✗	✗	✗	✓	✓	✓	✓

CENTER

Causes enclosed text and other elements to be centered on the page. **HTML 3.2, N2, N3, N4, IE2, IE3, IE4, IE5, deprecated in HTML 4.0.**

Attributes	2.0	3.2	4.0	N2	N3	N4	IE2	IE3	IE4/5
<event_name>=script_code	✗	✗	✗	✗	✗	✗	✗	✗	✓
CLASS=classname	✗	✗	✗	✗	✗	✓	✗	✗	✓
ID=*string*	✗	✗	✗	✗	✗	✓	✗	✗	✓
LANG=language_type	✗	✗	✗	✗	✗	✗	✗	✗	✓
LANGUAGE=JAVASCRIPT|JSCRIPT|VBSCRIPT|VBS	✗	✗	✗	✗	✗	✗	✗	✗	✓

Attributes	2.0	3.2	4.0	N2	N3	N4	IE2	IE3	IE4/5
STYLE=*string*	✗	✗	✗	✗	✗	✓	✗	✗	✓
TITLE=*string*	✗	✗	✗	✗	✗	✗	✗	✗	✓

CITE

Renders text in italics. **ALL**.

Attributes	2.0	3.2	4.0	N2	N3	N4	IE2	IE3	IE4/5
<event_name>=script_code	✗	✗	✓	✗	✗	✗	✗	✗	✓
CLASS=classname	✗	✗	✓	✗	✗	✓	✗	✗	✓
DIR=LTR|RTL	✗	✗	✓	✗	✗	✗	✗	✗	✗
ID=*string*	✗	✗	✓	✗	✗	✓	✗	✗	✓
LANG=language_type	✗	✗	✓	✗	✗	✗	✗	✗	✓
LANGUAGE=JAVASCRIPT|JSCRIPT|VBSCRIPT|VBS	✗	✗	✗	✗	✗	✗	✗	✗	✓
STYLE=*string*	✗	✗	✓	✗	✗	✓	✗	✗	✓
TITLE=*string*	✗	✗	✓	✗	✗	✗	✗	✗	✓

CODE

Renders text as a code sample in a fixed width font. **ALL**.

Attributes	2.0	3.2	4.0	N2	N3	N4	IE2	IE3	IE4/5
<event_name>=script_code	✗	✗	✓	✗	✗	✗	✗	✗	✓
CLASS=classname	✗	✗	✓	✗	✗	✓	✗	✗	✓
DIR=LTR|RTL	✗	✗	✓	✗	✗	✗	✗	✗	✗
ID=*string*	✗	✗	✓	✗	✗	✓	✗	✗	✓
LANG=language_type	✗	✗	✓	✗	✗	✗	✗	✗	✓
LANGUAGE=JAVASCRIPT|JSCRIPT|VBSCRIPT|VBS	✗	✗	✗	✗	✗	✗	✗	✗	✓
STYLE=*string*	✗	✗	✓	✗	✗	✓	✗	✗	✓
TITLE=*string*	✗	✗	✓	✗	✗	✗	✗	✗	✓

COL

Used to specify column based defaults for a table. **HTML 4.0, IE3, IE4, IE5**.

Attributes	2.0	3.2	4.0	N2	N3	N4	IE2	IE3	IE4/5
`<event_name>=script_code`	✗	✗	✓	✗	✗	✗	✗	✓	✗
`ALIGN=CENTER│LEFT│RIGHT│JUSTIFY│CHAR`	✗	✗	✓	✗	✗	✗	✗	✓	✓
`CHAR=`*string*	✗	✗	✓	✗	✗	✗	✗	✗	✗
`CHAROFF=`*string*	✗	✗	✓	✗	✗	✗	✗	✗	✗
`CLASS=classname`	✗	✗	✓	✗	✗	✗	✗	✗	✓
`DIR=LTR│RTL`	✗	✗	✓	✗	✗	✗	✗	✗	✗
`ID=`*string*	✗	✗	✓	✗	✗	✗	✗	✗	✓
`SPAN=number`	✗	✗	✓	✗	✗	✗	✗	✓	✓
`STYLE=`*string*	✗	✗	✓	✗	✗	✗	✗	✗	✓
`TITLE=`*string*	✗	✗	✓	✗	✗	✗	✗	✗	✓
`VALIGN=BOTTOM│MIDDLE│TOP│BASELINE`	✗	✗	✓	✗	✗	✗	✗	✗	✓
`WIDTH=number`	✗	✗	✓	✗	✗	✗	✗	✗	✓

COLGROUP

Used as a container for a group of columns. **HTML 4.0, IE3, IE4, IE5**.

Attributes	2.0	3.2	4.0	N2	N3	N4	IE2	IE3	IE4/5
`<event_name>=script_code`	✗	✗	✓	✗	✗	✗	✗	✗	✗
`ALIGN=CENTER│LEFT│RIGHT│JUSTIFY│CHAR`	✗	✗	✓	✗	✗	✗	✗	✓	✓
`CHAR=`*string*	✗	✗	✓	✗	✗	✗	✗	✗	✗
`CHAROFF=`*string*	✗	✗	✓	✗	✗	✗	✗	✗	✗
`CLASS=classname`	✗	✗	✓	✗	✗	✗	✗	✗	✓
`DIR=LTR│RTL`	✗	✗	✓	✗	✗	✗	✗	✗	✗
`ID=`*string*	✗	✗	✓	✗	✗	✗	✗	✗	✓
`SPAN=number`	✗	✗	✓	✗	✗	✗	✗	✓	✓
`STYLE=`*string*	✗	✗	✓	✗	✗	✗	✗	✗	✓
`TITLE=`*string*	✗	✗	✓	✗	✗	✗	✗	✗	✓
`VALIGN=BOTTOM│MIDDLE│TOP│BASELINE`	✗	✗	✓	✗	✗	✗	✗	✓	✓
`WIDTH=number`	✗	✗	✓	✗	✗	✗	✗	✓	✓

COMMENT

Denotes a comment that will not be displayed. **HTML 4.0, IE2, IE3, deprecated in IE4/5**.

Attributes	2.0	3.2	4.0	N2	N3	N4	IE2	IE3	IE4/5
ID=*string*	✗	✗	✗	✗	✗	✗	✗	✗	✓
LANG=language_type	✗	✗	✗	✗	✗	✗	✗	✗	✓
TITLE=*string*	✗	✗	✗	✗	✗	✗	✗	✗	✓

DD

The definition of an item in a definition list, usually indented from other text. **ALL**.

Attributes	2.0	3.2	4.0	N2	N3	N4	IE2	IE3	IE4/5
<event_name>=script_code	✗	✗	✓	✗	✗	✗	✗	✗	✓
CLASS=classname	✗	✗	✓	✗	✗	✓	✗	✓	✓
DIR=LTR|RTLR	✗	✗	✓	✗	✗	✗	✗	✗	✗
ID=*string*	✗	✗	✓	✗	✗	✓	✗	✓	✓
LANG=language_type	✗	✗	✓	✗	✗	✗	✗	✗	✓
LANGUAGE=JAVASCRIPT|JSCRIPT|VBSCRIPT|VBS	✗	✗	✗	✗	✗	✗	✗	✗	✓
STYLE=*string*	✗	✗	✓	✗	✗	✓	✗	✓	✓
TITLE=*string*	✗	✗	✓	✗	✗	✗	✗	✗	✓

DEL

Indicates a section of the document that has been deleted since a previous version. **HTML 4.0, IE4, IE5**.

Attributes	2.0	3.2	4.0	N2	N3	N4	IE2	IE3	IE4/5
<event_name>=script_code	✗	✗	✓	✗	✗	✗	✗	✗	✓
CITE=url	✗	✗	✓	✗	✗	✗	✗	✗	✗
CLASS=classname	✗	✗	✓	✗	✗	✗	✗	✗	✓
DATETIME=date	✗	✗	✓	✗	✗	✗	✗	✗	✗
DIR=LTR|RTL	✗	✗	✓	✗	✗	✗	✗	✗	✗
ID=*string*	✗	✗	✓	✗	✗	✗	✗	✗	✓
LANG=language_type	✗	✗	✓	✗	✗	✗	✗	✗	✓
LANGUAGE=JAVASCRIPT|JSCRIPT|VBSCRIPT|VBS	✗	✗	✗	✗	✗	✗	✗	✗	✓
STYLE=*string*	✗	✗	✓	✗	✗	✗	✗	✗	✓
TITLE=*string*	✗	✗	✓	✗	✗	✗	✗	✗	✓

DFN

The defining instance of a term. **ALL except HTML 2.0**.

Attributes	2.0	3.2	4.0	N2	N3	N4	IE2	IE3	IE4/5
`<event_name>=script_code`	✗	✗	✓	✗	✗	✗	✗	✗	✓
`CLASS=classname`	✗	✗	✓	✗	✗	✓	✗	✗	✓
`DIR=LTR｜RTL`	✗	✗	✓	✗	✗	✗	✗	✗	✗
`ID=`*string*	✗	✗	✓	✗	✗	✓	✗	✗	✓
`LANG=language_type`	✗	✗	✓	✗	✗	✗	✗	✗	✓
`LANGUAGE=JAVASCRIPT｜JSCRIPT｜VBSCRIPT｜VBS`	✗	✗	✗	✗	✗	✗	✗	✗	✓
`STYLE=`*string*	✗	✗	✓	✗	✗	✓	✗	✗	✓
`TITLE=`*string*	✗	✗	✓	✗	✗	✗	✗	✗	✓

DIR

Renders text so that it appears like a directory-style file listing. **ALL, except deprecated in HTML 4.0**.

Attributes	2.0	3.2	4.0	N2	N3	N4	IE2	IE3	IE4/5
`<event_name>=script_code`	✗	✗	D	✗	✗	✗	✗	✗	✓
`CLASS=classname`	✗	✗	D	✗	✗	✓	✗	✗	✓
`COMPACT`	✓	✓	D	✗	✗	✓	✗	✓	✗
`DIR=LTR｜RTL`	✗	✗	D	✗	✗	✗	✗	✗	✗
`ID=`*string*	✗	✗	D	✗	✗	✓	✗	✗	✓
`LANG=language_type`	✗	✗	D	✗	✗	✗	✗	✗	✓
`LANGUAGE=JAVASCRIPT｜JSCRIPT｜VBSCRIPT｜VBS`	✗	✗	✗	✗	✗	✗	✗	✗	✓
`STYLE=`*string*	✗	✗	D	✗	✗	✓	✗	✗	✓
`TITLE=`*string*	✗	✗	✗	✗	✗	✓	✗	✗	✗
`TYPE=CIRCLE｜DISC｜SQUARE`	✗	✗	✗	✗	✗	✓	✗	✗	✗

DIV

Defines a container section within the page, and can hold other elements. **ALL except HTML 2.0**.

Attributes	2.0	3.2	4.0	N2	N3	N4	IE2	IE3	IE4/5
`<event_name>=script_code`	✗	✗	✓	✗	✗	✗	✗	✗	✓
`ALIGN=CENTER｜LEFT｜RIGHT`	✗	✓	D	✓	✓	✓	✗	✓	✓

Attributes	2.0	3.2	4.0	N2	N3	N4	IE2	IE3	IE4/5
CHARSET=*string*	✗	✗	✓	✗	✗	✗	✗	✗	✗
CLASS=classname	✗	✗	✓	✗	✗	✓	✗	✓	✓
DATAFLD=column_name	✗	✗	✗	✗	✗	✗	✗	✗	✓
DATAFORMATAS=HTML | TEXT	✗	✗	✗	✗	✗	✗	✗	✗	✓
DATASRC=id	✗	✗	✗	✗	✗	✗	✗	✗	✓
DIR=LTR | RTL	✗	✗	✓	✗	✗	✗	✗	✗	✗
HREF=url	✗	✗	✓	✗	✗	✗	✗	✗	✗
HREFLANG=langcode	✗	✗	✓	✗	✗	✗	✗	✗	✗
ID=*string*	✗	✗	✓	✗	✗	✓	✗	✓	✓
LANG=language_type	✗	✗	✓	✗	✗	✗	✗	✗	✓
LANGUAGE=JAVASCRIPT | JSCRIPT | VBSCRIPT | VBS	✗	✗	✗	✗	✗	✗	✗	✗	✓
MEDIA	✗	✗	✓	✗	✗	✗	✗	✗	✗
NOWRAP	✗	✗	✗	✗	✗	✓	✗	✓	✗
REL=relationship	✗	✗	✓	✗	✗	✗	✗	✗	✗
REV=relationship	✗	✗	✓	✗	✗	✗	✗	✗	✗
STYLE=*string*	✗	✗	✓	✗	✗	✓	✗	✗	✓
TARGET	✗	✗	✓	✗	✗	✗	✗	✗	✗
TITLE=*string*	✗	✗	✓	✗	✗	✗	✗	✗	✓
TYPE	✗	✗	✓	✗	✗	✗	✗	✗	✗

DL

Denotes a definition list. **ALL**.

Attributes	2.0	3.2	4.0	N2	N3	N4	IE2	IE3	IE4/5
<event_name>=script_code	✗	✗	✓	✗	✗	✗	✗	✗	✓
CLASS=classname	✗	✗	✓	✗	✗	✓	✗	✓	✓
COMPACT	✓	✓	D	✗	✗	✓	✗	✓	✗
DIR=LTR | RTL	✗	✗	✓	✗	✗	✗	✗	✗	✗
ID=*string*	✗	✗	✓	✗	✗	✓	✗	✓	✓
LANG=language_type	✗	✗	✓	✗	✗	✗	✗	✗	✓
LANGUAGE=JAVASCRIPT | JSCRIPT | VBSCRIPT | VBS	✗	✗	✗	✗	✗	✗	✗	✗	✓
STYLE=*string*	✗	✗	✓	✗	✗	✓	✗	✓	✓
TITLE=*string*	✗	✗	✓	✗	✗	✗	✗	✗	✓

DT

Denotes a definition term within a definition list. **ALL**.

Attributes	2.0	3.2	4.0	N2	N3	N4	IE2	IE3	IE4/5
`<event_name>=script_code`	✗	✗	✓	✗	✗	✗	✗	✗	✓
`CLASS=classname`	✗	✗	✓	✗	✗	✓	✗	✗	✓
`DIR=LTR|RTL`	✗	✗	✓	✗	✗	✗	✗	✗	✗
`ID=string`	✗	✗	✓	✗	✗	✓	✗	✗	✓
`LANG=language_type`	✗	✗	✓	✗	✗	✗	✗	✗	✓
`LANGUAGE=JAVASCRIPT|JSCRIPT|VBSCRIPT|VBS`	✗	✗	✗	✗	✗	✗	✗	✗	✓
`STYLE=string`	✗	✗	✓	✗	✗	✓	✗	✗	✓
`TITLE=string`	✗	✗	✓	✗	✗	✗	✗	✗	✓

EM

Renders text as emphasized, usually in italics. **ALL**.

Attributes	2.0	3.2	4.0	N2	N3	N4	IE2	IE3	IE4/5
`<event_name>=script_code`	✗	✗	✓	✗	✗	✗	✗	✗	✓
`CLASS=classname`	✗	✗	✓	✗	✗	✓	✗	✗	✓
`DIR=LTR|RTL`	✗	✗	✓	✗	✗	✗	✗	✗	✗
`ID=string`	✗	✗	✓	✗	✗	✓	✗	✗	✓
`LANG=language_type`	✗	✗	✓	✗	✗	✗	✗	✗	✓
`LANGUAGE=JAVASCRIPT|JSCRIPT|VBSCRIPT|VBS`	✗	✗	✗	✗	✗	✗	✗	✗	✓
`STYLE=string`	✗	✗	✓	✗	✗	✓	✗	✗	✓
`TITLE=string`	✗	✗	✓	✗	✗	✗	✗	✗	✓

EMBED

Embeds documents of any type in the page, to be viewed in another suitable application. **N2, N3, N4, IE3, IE4, IE5**.

Attributes	2.0	3.2	4.0	N2	N3	N4	IE2	IE3	IE4/5
`ALIGN=ABSBOTTOM|ABSMIDDLE|BASELINE|` `BOTTOM|LEFT|MIDDLE|RIGHT|TEXTTOP|TOP`	✗	✗	✗	✗	✗	✓	✗	✗	✓
`ALT=text`	✗	✗	✗	✗	✗	✗	✗	✗	✓
`BORDER=number`	✗	✗	D	✗	✗	✓	✗	✗	✗

Attributes	2.0	3.2	4.0	N2	N3	N4	IE2	IE3	IE4/5
CLASS=classname	✗	✗	✗	✗	✗	✓	✗	✗	✓
CODE=filename	✗	✗	✗	✗	✗	✗	✗	✗	✓
CODEBASE=url	✗	✗	✗	✗	✗	✗	✗	✗	✓
HEIGHT=number	✗	✗	✗	✓	✓	✓	✗	✓	✓
HIDDEN=string	✗	✗	✗	✗	✗	✓	✗	✗	✗
HSPACE=number	✗	✗	✗	✗	✗	✓	✗	✗	✓
ID=string	✗	✗	✗	✗	✗	✓	✗	✗	✓
NAME=string	✗	✗	✗	✓	✓	✓	✗	✓	✓
PALETTE=FOREGROUND | BACKGROUND	✗	✗	✗	✗	✗	✓	✗	✓	✗
PLUGINSPAGE=string	✗	✗	✗	✗	✗	✓	✗	✗	✗
SRC=url	✗	✗	✗	✓	✓	✓	✗	✓	✓
STYLE=string	✗	✗	✗	✗	✗	✓	✗	✗	✓
TITLE=string	✗	✗	✗	✗	✗	✗	✗	✗	✓
TYPE=mime-type	✗	✗	✗	✗	✗	✓	✗	✗	✗
UNITS=EN | EMS | PIXELS	✗	✗	✗	✗	✗	✓	✗	✓	✓
VSPACE=number	✗	✗	✗	✗	✗	✓	✗	✗	✓
WIDTH=number	✗	✗	✗	✓	✓	✓	✗	✓	✓

FIELDSET

Draws a box around the contained elements to indicate related items. **HTML 4.0, IE4, IE5**.

Attributes	2.0	3.2	4.0	N2	N3	N4	IE2	IE3	IE4/5
<event_name>=script_code	✗	✗	✓	✗	✗	✗	✗	✗	✓
ALIGN=CENTER | LEFT | RIGHT	✗	✗	✗	✗	✗	✗	✗	✗	✓
CLASS=classname	✗	✗	✓	✗	✗	✗	✗	✗	✓
DIR=LTR | RTL	✗	✗	✓	✗	✗	✗	✗	✗	✗
ID=string	✗	✗	✓	✗	✗	✗	✗	✗	✓
LANG=language_type	✗	✗	✓	✗	✗	✗	✗	✗	✓
LANGUAGE=JAVASCRIPT | JSCRIPT | VBSCRIPT | VBS	✗	✗	✗	✗	✗	✗	✗	✗	✓
STYLE=string	✗	✗	✓	✗	✗	✗	✗	✗	✓
TITLE=string	✗	✗	✓	✗	✗	✗	✗	✗	✓

FONT

Specifies the font face, size, and color for rendering the text. **HTML 3.2, N2, N3, N4, IE2, IE3, IE4, IE5, deprecated in HTML 4.0.**

Attributes	2.0	3.2	4.0	N2	N3	N4	IE2	IE3	IE4/5
`<event_name>=script_code`	✗	✗	✗	✗	✗	✗	✗	✗	✓
`CLASS=classname`	✗	✗	D	✗	✗	✓	✗	✗	✓
`COLOR=color`	✗	✓	D	✓	✓	✓	✓	✓	✓
`DIR=LTR|RTL`	✗	✗	D	✗	✗	✗	✗	✗	✗
`FACE=font_family_name`	✗	✗	D	✗	✓	✓	✓	✓	✓
`ID=`*string*	✗	✗	D	✗	✗	✓	✗	✗	✓
`LANG=language_type`	✗	✗	D	✗	✗	✗	✗	✗	✓
`LANGUAGE=JAVASCRIPT|JSCRIPT|VBSCRIPT|VBS`	✗	✗	✗	✗	✗	✗	✗	✗	✓
`POINT-SIZE=`*string*`|number`	✗	✗	✗	✗	✗	✓	✗	✗	✗
`SIZE=number`	✗	✓	D	✓	✓	✓	✓	✓	✓
`STYLE=`*string*	✗	✗	D	✗	✗	✓	✗	✗	✓
`TITLE=`*string*	✗	✗	D	✗	✗	✗	✗	✗	✓
`WEIGHT=`*string*`|number`	✗	✗	✗	✗	✗	✓	✗	✗	✗

FORM

Denotes a form containing controls and elements, whose values are sent to a server. **ALL.**

Attributes	2.0	3.2	4.0	N2	N3	N4	IE2	IE3	IE4/5
`<event_name>=script_code`	✗	✗	✓	✗	✗	✓	✗	✓	✓
`ACCEPT-CHARSET=`*string*	✗	✗	✓	✗	✗	✗	✗	✗	✗
`ACTION=`*string*	✓	✓	✓	✓	✓	✓	✓	✓	✓
`CLASS=classname`	✗	✗	✓	✗	✗	✓	✗	✗	✓
`DIR=LTR|RTL`	✗	✗	✓	✗	✗	✗	✗	✗	✗
`ENCTYPE=`*string*	✓	✓	✓	✓	✓	✓	✗	✗	✓
`ID=`*string*	✗	✗	✓	✗	✗	✓	✗	✗	✓
`LANG=language_type`	✗	✗	✓	✗	✗	✗	✗	✗	✓
`LANGUAGE=JAVASCRIPT|JSCRIPT|VBSCRIPT|VBS`	✗	✗	✗	✗	✗	✗	✗	✗	✓
`METHOD=GET|POST`	✓	✓	✓	✓	✓	✓	✓	✓	✓
`NAME=`*string*	✗	✗	✗	✗	✗	✓	✗	✗	✓

Attributes	2.0	3.2	4.0	N2	N3	N4	IE2	IE3	IE4/5
STYLE=*string*	✗	✗	✓	✗	✗	✓	✗	✗	✓
TARGET=<window_name>|_parent|_blank|_top|_self	✗	✗	✓	✓	✓	✓	✗	✓	✓
TITLE=*string*	✗	✗	✓	✗	✗	✗	✗	✗	✓

FRAME

Specifies an individual frame within a frameset. **HTML 4.0, N2, N3, N4, IE3, IE4, IE5**.

Attributes	2.0	3.2	4.0	N2	N3	N4	IE2	IE3	IE4/5
<event_name>=script_code	✗	✗	✗	✗	✗	✓	✗	✗	✓
ALIGN=CENTER|LEFT|RIGHT	✗	✗	✗	✗	✗	✓	✗	✓	✗
BORDERCOLOR=color	✗	✗	✗	✗	✓	✓	✗	✗	✓
CLASS=classname	✗	✗	✓	✗	✗	✓	✗	✗	✓
DATAFLD=column_name	✗	✗	✗	✗	✗	✗	✗	✗	✓
DATASRC=id	✗	✗	✗	✗	✗	✗	✗	✗	✓
FRAMEBORDER=NO|YES|0|1	✗	✗	✓	✗	✓	✓	✗	✓	✓
ID=*string*	✗	✗	✓	✗	✗	✓	✗	✗	✓
LANG=language_type	✗	✗	✗	✗	✗	✗	✗	✗	✓
LANGUAGE=JAVASCRIPT|JSCRIPT|VBSCRIPT|VBS	✗	✗	✗	✗	✗	✗	✗	✗	✓
LONGDESC=url	✗	✗	✓	✗	✗	✗	✗	✗	✗
MARGINHEIGHT=number	✗	✗	✓	✓	✓	✓	✗	✓	✓
MARGINWIDTH=number	✗	✗	✓	✓	✓	✓	✗	✓	✓
NAME=*string*	✗	✗	✓	✓	✓	✓	✗	✓	✓
NORESIZE=NORESIZE|RESIZE	✗	✗	✓	✓	✓	✓	✗	✓	✓
SCROLLING=AUTO|YES|NO	✗	✗	✓	✓	✓	✓	✗	✓	✓
SRC=url	✗	✗	✓	✓	✓	✓	✗	✓	✓
STYLE=*string*	✗	✗	✓	✗	✗	✗	✗	✗	✓
TITLE=*string*	✗	✗	✓	✗	✗	✓	✗	✗	✓

FRAMESET

Specifies a frameset containing multiple frames and other nested framesets. **HTML 4.0, N2, N3, N4, IE3, IE4, IE5.**

Attributes	2.0	3.2	4.0	N2	N3	N4	IE2	IE3	IE4/5
`<event_name>=script_code`	✗	✗	✓	✗	✗	✗	✗	✗	✗
`BORDER=number`	✗	✗	D	✗	✓	✓	✗	✗	✓
`BORDERCOLOR=color`	✗	✗	✗	✗	✓	✓	✗	✗	✓
`CLASS=classname`	✗	✗	✓	✗	✗	✓	✗	✗	✓
`COLS=number`	✗	✗	✓	✓	✓	✓	✗	✓	✓
`FRAMEBORDER=NO|YES|0|1`	✗	✗	✗	✗	✓	✓	✗	✓	✓
`FRAMESPACING=number`	✗	✗	✗	✗	✗	✗	✗	✓	✓
`ID=`*string*	✗	✗	✓	✗	✗	✓	✗	✗	✓
`LANG=language_type`	✗	✗	✗	✗	✗	✗	✗	✗	✓
`LANGUAGE=JAVASCRIPT|JSCRIPT|VBSCRIPT|VBS`	✗	✗	✗	✗	✗	✗	✗	✗	✓
`ROWS=number`	✗	✗	✓	✓	✓	✓	✗	✓	✓
`STYLE=`*string*	✗	✗	✓	✗	✗	✗	✗	✗	✓
`TITLE=`*string*	✗	✗	✓	✗	✗	✗	✗	✗	✓

HEAD

Contains tags holding unviewed information about the document. **ALL**.

Attributes	2.0	3.2	4.0	N2	N3	N4	IE2	IE3	IE4/5
`CLASS=classname`	✗	✗	✗	✗	✗	✓	✗	✗	✓
`DIR=LTR|RTL`	✗	✗	✓	✗	✗	✗	✗	✗	✗
`ID=`*string*	✗	✗	✗	✗	✗	✓	✗	✗	✓
`LANG=language_type`	✗	✗	✓	✗	✗	✗	✗	✗	✗
`PROFILE=url`	✗	✗	✓	✗	✗	✗	✗	✗	✗
`TITLE=`*string*	✗	✗	✗	✗	✗	✗	✗	✗	✓

Hn

The six elements (H1 to H6) render text as a range of heading styles. **ALL**.

Attributes	2.0	3.2	4.0	N2	N3	N4	IE2	IE3	IE4/5
<event_name>=script_code	✗	✗	✓	✗	✗	✗	✗	✗	✓
ALIGN=CENTER|LEFT|RIGHT	✗	✓	D	✓	✓	✗	✓	✓	✓
CLASS=classname	✗	✗	✓	✗	✗	✓	✗	✗	✓
DIR=LTR|RTL	✗	✗	✓	✗	✗	✗	✗	✗	✗
ID=string	✗	✗	✓	✗	✗	✓	✗	✗	✓
LANG=language_type	✗	✗	✓	✗	✗	✗	✗	✗	✓
LANGUAGE=JAVASCRIPT|JSCRIPT|VBSCRIPT|VBS	✗	✗	✗	✗	✗	✗	✗	✗	✓
STYLE=string	✗	✗	✓	✗	✗	✓	✗	✗	✓
TITLE=string	✗	✗	✓	✗	✗	✗	✗	✗	✓

HR

Places a horizontal rule in the page. **ALL**.

Attributes	2.0	3.2	4.0	N2	N3	N4	IE2	IE3	IE4/5
<event_name>=script_code	✗	✗	✓	✗	✗	✗	✗	✗	✓
ALIGN=CENTER|LEFT|RIGHT	✗	✓	D	✓	✓	✓	✓	✓	✓
CLASS=classname	✗	✗	✓	✗	✗	✓	✗	✓	✓
COLOR=color	✗	✗	✗	✗	✗	✗	✓	✓	✓
DIR=LTR|RTL	✗	✗	✓	✗	✗	✗	✗	✗	✗
ID=string	✗	✗	✓	✗	✗	✓	✗	✓	✓
LANG=language_type	✗	✗	✓	✗	✗	✗	✗	✗	✓
LANGUAGE=JAVASCRIPT|JSCRIPT|VBSCRIPT|VBS	✗	✗	✗	✗	✗	✗	✗	✗	✓
NOSHADE	✗	✓	D	✓	✓	✓	✓	✓	✓
SIZE=number	✗	✓	D	✓	✓	✓	✓	✓	✓
SRC=url	✗	✗	✗	✗	✗	✗	✗	✗	✓
STYLE=string	✗	✗	✓	✗	✗	✓	✗	✓	✓
TITLE=string	✗	✗	✓	✗	✗	✗	✗	✗	✓
WIDTH=number	✗	✓	D	✓	✓	✓	✓	✓	✓

HTML

The outer tag for the page, which identifies the document as containing HTML elements. **ALL**.

Attributes	2.0	3.2	4.0	N2	N3	N4	IE2	IE3	IE4/5
DIR=LTR | RTL	✗	✗	✓	✗	✗	✗	✗	✗	✗
LANG=language_type	✗	✗	✓	✗	✗	✗	✗	✗	✗
TITLE=*string*	✗	✗	✗	✗	✗	✗	✗	✗	✓
VERSION=url	✗	✗	✓	✗	✗	✗	✗	✗	✗

I

Renders text in an italic font where available. **ALL**.

Attributes	2.0	3.2	4.0	N2	N3	N4	IE2	IE3	IE4/5
<event_name>=script_code	✗	✗	✓	✗	✗	✗	✗	✗	✓
CLASS=classname	✗	✗	✓	✗	✗	✓	✗	✗	✓
DIR=LTR | RTL	✗	✗	✓	✗	✗	✗	✗	✗	✗
ID=*string*	✗	✗	✓	✗	✗	✓	✗	✗	✓
LANG=language_type	✗	✗	✓	✗	✗	✗	✗	✗	✓
LANGUAGE=JAVASCRIPT | JSCRIPT | VBSCRIPT | VBS	✗	✗	✗	✗	✗	✗	✗	✗	✓
STYLE=*string*	✗	✗	✓	✗	✗	✓	✗	✗	✓
TITLE=*string*	✗	✗	✓	✗	✗	✗	✗	✗	✓

IFRAME

Used to create in-line floating frames within the page. **HTML 4.0, IE3, IE4, IE5**.

Attributes	2.0	3.2	4.0	N2	N3	N4	IE2	IE3	IE4/5
ALIGN=ABSBOTTOM | ABSMIDDLE | BASELINE | BOTTOM | LEFT | MIDDLE | RIGHT | TEXTTOP | TOP	✗	✗	D	✗	✗	✗	✗	✗	✓
BORDER=number	✗	✗	D	✗	✗	✗	✗	✗	✓
BORDERCOLOR=color	✗	✗	✗	✗	✗	✗	✗	✗	✓
CLASS=classname	✗	✗	✓	✗	✗	✗	✗	✗	✓
DATAFLD=column_name	✗	✗	✗	✗	✗	✗	✗	✗	✓
DATASRC=id	✗	✗	✗	✗	✗	✗	✗	✗	✓
FRAMEBORDER=NO | YES | 0 | 1	✗	✗	✓	✗	✗	✗	✗	✗	✓
FRAMESPACING=number	✗	✗	✗	✗	✗	✗	✗	✗	✓

Attributes	2.0	3.2	4.0	N2	N3	N4	IE2	IE3	IE4/5
HEIGHT=number	✗	✗	✓	✗	✗	✗	✗	✗	✓
HSPACE=number	✗	✗	✗	✗	✗	✗	✗	✗	✓
ID=*string*	✗	✗	✓	✗	✗	✗	✗	✗	✓
LANG=language_type	✗	✗	✗	✗	✗	✗	✗	✗	✓
LANGUAGE=JAVASCRIPT|JSCRIPT|VBSCRIPT|VBS	✗	✗	✗	✗	✗	✗	✗	✗	✓
LONGDESC=url	✗	✗	✓	✗	✗	✗	✗	✗	✗
MARGINHEIGHT=number	✗	✗	✓	✗	✗	✗	✗	✗	✓
MARGINWIDTH=number	✗	✗	✓	✗	✗	✗	✗	✗	✓
NAME=*string*	✗	✗	✓	✗	✗	✗	✗	✗	✓
NORESIZE=NORESIZE|RESIZE	✗	✗	✗	✗	✗	✗	✗	✗	✓
SCROLLING=AUTO|YES|NO	✗	✗	✓	✗	✗	✗	✗	✗	✓
SRC=url	✗	✗	✓	✗	✗	✗	✗	✗	✓
STYLE=*string*	✗	✗	✓	✗	✗	✗	✗	✗	✓
TITLE=*string*	✗	✗	✓	✗	✗	✗	✗	✗	✓
VSPACE=number	✗	✗	✗	✗	✗	✗	✗	✗	✓
WIDTH=number	✗	✗	✓	✗	✗	✗	✗	✗	✓

ILAYER

Defines a separate area of the page as an inline layer that can hold a different page. **N4 only**.

Attributes	2.0	3.2	4.0	N2	N3	N4	IE2	IE3	IE4/5
<event_name>=script_code	✗	✗	✗	✗	✗	✓	✗	✗	✗
ABOVE=object_id	✗	✗	✗	✗	✗	✓	✗	✗	✗
BACKGROUND=*string*	✗	✗	✗	✗	✗	✓	✗	✗	✗
BELOW=object_id	✗	✗	✗	✗	✗	✓	✗	✗	✗
BGCOLOR=color	✗	✗	D	✗	✗	✓	✗	✗	✗
CLASS=classname	✗	✗	✗	✗	✗	✓	✗	✗	✗
CLIP=number[,number,number,number]	✗	✗	✗	✗	✗	✓	✗	✗	✗
ID=*string*	✗	✗	✗	✗	✗	✓	✗	✗	✗
LEFT=number	✗	✗	✗	✗	✗	✓	✗	✗	✗
NAME=*string*	✗	✗	✗	✗	✗	✓	✗	✗	✗
PAGEX=number	✗	✗	✗	✗	✗	✓	✗	✗	✗
PAGEY=number	✗	✗	✗	✗	✗	✓	✗	✗	✗

Attributes	2.0	3.2	4.0	N2	N3	N4	IE2	IE3	IE4/5
SRC=url	✗	✗	✗	✗	✗	✓	✗	✗	✗
STYLE=*string*	✗	✗	✗	✗	✗	✓	✗	✗	✗
TOP=number	✗	✗	✗	✗	✗	✓	✗	✗	✗
VISIBILITY=SHOW|HIDE|INHERIT	✗	✗	✗	✗	✗	✓	✗	✗	✗
WIDTH=number	✗	✗	✗	✗	✗	✓	✗	✗	✗
Z-INDEX=number	✗	✗	✗	✗	✗	✓	✗	✗	✗

IMG

Embeds an image or a video clip in the document. **ALL**.

Attributes	2.0	3.2	4.0	N2	N3	N4	IE2	IE3	IE4/5
<event_name>=script_code	✗	✗	✓	✗	✗	✓	✗	✗	✓
ALIGN=BASBOTTOM|ABSMIDDLE|BASELINE|BOTTOM|LEFT|MIDDLE|RIGHT|TEXTTOP|TOP	✓	✓	D	✓	✓	✓	✓	✓	✓
ALT=text	✓	✓	✓	✓	✓	✓	✓	✓	✓
BORDER=number	✗	✓	D	✓	✓	✓	✓	✓	✓
CLASS=classname	✗	✗	✓	✗	✗	✓	✗	✓	✓
CONTROLS	✗	✗	✗	✗	✗	✗	✓	✓	✗
DATAFLD=column_name	✗	✗	✗	✗	✗	✗	✗	✗	✓
DATASRC=id	✗	✗	✗	✗	✗	✗	✗	✗	✓
DIR=LTR|RTL	✗	✗	✓	✗	✗	✗	✗	✗	✗
DYNSRC=*string*	✗	✗	✗	✗	✗	✗	✓	✓	✓
HEIGHT=number	✗	✓	✓	✓	✓	✓	✓	✓	✓
HSPACE=number	✗	✓	✓	✓	✓	✓	✓	✓	✓
ID=*string*	✗	✗	✓	✗	✗	✓	✗	✓	✓
ISMAP	✓	✓	✓	✓	✓	✓	✓	✓	✓
LANG=language_type	✗	✗	✓	✗	✗	✗	✗	✗	✓
LANGUAGE=JAVASCRIPT|JSCRIPT|VBSCRIPT|VBS	✗	✗	✗	✗	✗	✗	✗	✗	✓
LONGDESC=url	✗	✗	✓	✗	✗	✗	✗	✗	✗
LOOP=number	✗	✗	✗	✗	✗	✗	✓	✓	✓
LOWSRC=url	✗	✗	✗	✓	✓	✓	✗	✗	✓
NAME=*string*	✗	✗	✗	✗	✗	✓	✗	✗	✓
SRC=url	✓	✓	✓	✓	✓	✓	✓	✓	✓

Attributes	2.0	3.2	4.0	N2	N3	N4	IE2	IE3	IE4/5
START=number | *string*	✗	✗	✗	✗	✗	✗	✓	✓	✗
STYLE=*string*	✗	✗	✓	✗	✗	✓	✗	✓	✓
TITLE=*string*	✗	✗	✓	✗	✗	✗	✗	✓	✓
USEMAP=url	✗	✓	✓	✓	✓	✓	✓	✓	✓
VSPACE=number	✗	✓	✓	✓	✓	✓	✓	✓	✓
WIDTH=number	✗	✓	✓	✓	✓	✓	✓	✓	✓

INPUT

Specifies a form input control, such as a button, text or check box. **ALL**.

Attributes	2.0	3.2	4.0	N2	N3	N4	IE2	IE3	IE4/5
<event_name>=script_code	✗	✗	✓	✗	✗	✓	✗	✓	✓
ACCEPT=*string*	✗	✗	✓	✗	✗	✗	✗	✗	✗
ACCESSKEY=key_character	✗	✗	✓	✗	✗	✗	✗	✗	✓
ALIGN=CENTER | LEFT | RIGHT	✓	✓	D	✓	✓	✓	✓	✓	✓
ALT=text	✗	✗	✓	✗	✗	✗	✗	✗	✗
CHECKED=FALSE | TRUE	✓	✓	✓	✓	✓	✓	✓	✓	✓
CLASS=classname	✗	✗	✓	✗	✗	✓	✗	✓	✓
DATAFLD=column_name	✗	✗	✗	✗	✗	✗	✗	✗	✓
DATAFORMATAS=HTML | TEXT	✗	✗	✗	✗	✗	✗	✗	✗	✓
DATASRC=id	✗	✗	✗	✗	✗	✗	✗	✗	✓
DIR=LTR | RTL	✗	✗	✓	✗	✗	✗	✗	✗	✗
DISABLED	✗	✗	✓	✗	✗	✗	✗	✗	✓
ID=*string*	✗	✗	✓	✗	✗	✓	✗	✓	✓
LANG=language_type	✗	✗	✓	✗	✗	✗	✗	✗	✓
LANGUAGE=JAVASCRIPT | JSCRIPT | VBSCRIPT | VBS	✗	✗	✗	✗	✗	✗	✗	✗	✓
MAXLENGTH=number	✓	✓	✓	✓	✓	✓	✓	✓	✓
NAME=*string*	✓	✓	✓	✓	✓	✓	✓	✓	✓
NOTAB	✗	✗	✗	✗	✗	✗	✗	✓	✗
READONLY	✗	✗	✓	✗	✗	✗	✗	✗	✓
SIZE=number	✓	✓	✓	✓	✓	✓	✓	✓	✓
SRC=url	✓	✓	✓	✓	✓	✗	✓	✓	✓
STYLE=*string*	✗	✗	✓	✗	✗	✓	✗	✓	✓

Attributes	2.0	3.2	4.0	N2	N3	N4	IE2	IE3	IE4/5
TABINDEX=number	✗	✗	✓	✗	✗	✗	✗	✓	✓
TITLE=string	✗	✗	✓	✗	✗	✗	✗	✓	✓
TYPE=BUTTON|CHECKBOX|FILE|HIDDEN|IMAGE|PASSWORD|RADIO|RESET|SUBMIT|TEXT	✓	✓	✓	✓	✓	✓	✓	✓	✓
USEMAP=url	✗	✗	✓	✗	✗	✗	✗	✗	✗
VALUE=string	✓	✓	✓	✓	✓	✓	✓	✓	✓

INS

Indicates a section of the document that has been inserted since a previous version. **HTML 4.0, IE4, IE5**.

Attributes	2.0	3.2	4.0	N2	N3	N4	IE2	IE3	IE4/5
<event_name>=script_code	✗	✗	✓	✗	✗	✗	✗	✗	✓
CITE=url	✗	✗	✓	✗	✗	✗	✗	✗	✗
CLASS=classname	✗	✗	✓	✗	✗	✗	✗	✗	✓
DATETIME=date	✗	✗	✓	✗	✗	✗	✗	✗	✗
DIR=LTR|RTL	✗	✗	✓	✗	✗	✗	✗	✗	✗
ID=string	✗	✗	✓	✗	✗	✗	✗	✗	✓
LANG=language_type	✗	✗	✓	✗	✗	✗	✗	✗	✓
LANGUAGE=JAVASCRIPT|JSCRIPT|VBSCRIPT|VBS	✗	✗	✗	✗	✗	✗	✗	✗	✓
STYLE=string	✗	✗	✓	✗	✗	✗	✗	✗	✓
TITLE=string	✗	✗	✓	✗	✗	✗	✗	✗	✓

ISINDEX

Indicates the presence of a searchable index. **ALL. Deprecated in HTML 4.0**.

Attributes	2.0	3.2	4.0	N2	N3	N4	IE2	IE3	IE4/5
ACTION=string	✗	✗	✗	✓	✓	✓	✓	✓	✗
CLASS=classname	✗	✗	D	✗	✗	✓	✗	✗	✓
DIR=LTR|RTL	✗	✗	D	✗	✗	✗	✗	✗	✗
ID=string	✗	✗	D	✗	✗	✓	✗	✗	✓
LANG=language_type	✗	✗	D	✗	✗	✗	✗	✗	✓
LANGUAGE=JAVASCRIPT|JSCRIPT|VBSCRIPT|VBS	✗	✗	✗	✗	✗	✗	✗	✗	✓
PROMPT=string	✗	✓	D	✓	✓	✓	✓	✓	✓

Attributes	2.0	3.2	4.0	N2	N3	N4	IE2	IE3	IE4/5
STYLE=*string*	✗	✗	D	✗	✗	✓	✗	✗	✓
TITLE=*string*	✗	✗	D	✗	✗	✗	✗	✗	✗

KBD

Renders text in fixed-width font, as though entered on a keyboard. **ALL**.

Attributes	2.0	3.2	4.0	N2	N3	N4	IE2	IE3	IE4/5
<event_name>=script_code	✗	✗	✓	✗	✗	✗	✗	✗	✓
CLASS=classname	✗	✗	✓	✗	✗	✓	✗	✗	✓
DIR=LTR|RTL	✗	✗	✓	✗	✗	✗	✗	✗	✗
ID=*string*	✗	✗	✓	✗	✗	✓	✗	✗	✓
LANG=language_type	✗	✗	✓	✗	✗	✗	✗	✗	✓
LANGUAGE=JAVASCRIPT|JSCRIPT|VBSCRIPT|VBS	✗	✗	✗	✗	✗	✗	✗	✗	✓
STYLE=*string*	✗	✗	✓	✗	✗	✓	✗	✗	✓
TITLE=*string*	✗	✗	✓	✗	✗	✗	✗	✗	✓

KEYGEN

Used to generate key material in the page. **N2, N3, N4**.

Attributes	2.0	3.2	4.0	N2	N3	N4	IE2	IE3	IE4/5
CHALLENGE=*string*	✗	✗	✗	✗	✗	✓	✗	✗	✗
CLASS=classname	✗	✗	✗	✗	✗	✓	✗	✗	✗
ID=*string*	✗	✗	✗	✗	✗	✓	✗	✗	✗
NAME=*string*	✗	✗	✗	✗	✗	✓	✗	✗	✗

LABEL

Defines the text of a label for a control-like element. **HTML 4.0, IE4, IE5**.

Attributes	2.0	3.2	4.0	N2	N3	N4	IE2	IE3	IE4/5
<event_name>=script_code	✗	✗	✓	✗	✗	✗	✗	✗	✓
ACCESSKEY=key_character	✗	✗	✓	✗	✗	✗	✗	✗	✓
CLASS=classname	✗	✗	✓	✗	✗	✗	✗	✗	✓
DATAFLD=column_name	✗	✗	✗	✗	✗	✗	✗	✗	✓
DATAFORMATAS=HTML|TEXT	✗	✗	✗	✗	✗	✗	✗	✗	✓

Attributes	2.0	3.2	4.0	N2	N3	N4	IE2	IE3	IE4/5
DATASRC=id	✗	✗	✗	✗	✗	✗	✗	✗	✓
DIR=LTR|RTL	✗	✗	✓	✗	✗	✗	✗	✗	✗
FOR=element_name	✗	✗	✓	✗	✗	✗	✗	✗	✓
ID=string	✗	✗	✓	✗	✗	✗	✗	✗	✓
LANG=language_type	✗	✗	✓	✗	✗	✗	✗	✗	✓
LANGUAGE=JAVASCRIPT|JSCRIPT|VBSCRIPT|VBS	✗	✗	✗	✗	✗	✗	✗	✗	✓
STYLE=*string*	✗	✗	✓	✗	✗	✗	✗	✗	✓
TITLE=*string*	✗	✗	✓	✗	✗	✗	✗	✗	✓

LAYER

Defines a separate area of the page as a layer that can hold a different page. **N4 only**.

Attributes	2.0	3.2	4.0	N2	N3	N4	IE2	IE3	IE4/5
<event_name>=script_code	✗	✗	✗	✗	✗	✓	✗	✗	✗
ABOVE=object_id	✗	✗	✗	✗	✗	✓	✗	✗	✗
BACKGROUND=*string*	✗	✗	✗	✗	✗	✓	✗	✗	✗
BELOW=object_id	✗	✗	✗	✗	✗	✓	✗	✗	✗
BGCOLOR=color	✗	✗	D	✗	✗	✓	✗	✗	✗
CLASS=classname	✗	✗	✗	✗	✗	✓	✗	✗	✗
CLIP=number[,number,number,number]	✗	✗	✗	✗	✗	✓	✗	✗	✗
ID=*string*	✗	✗	✗	✗	✗	✓	✗	✗	✗
LEFT=number	✗	✗	✗	✗	✗	✓	✗	✗	✗
NAME=string	✗	✗	✗	✗	✗	✓	✗	✗	✗
PAGEX=number	✗	✗	✗	✗	✗	✓	✗	✗	✗
PAGEY=number	✗	✗	✗	✗	✗	✓	✗	✗	✗
SRC=url	✗	✗	✗	✗	✗	✓	✗	✗	✗
STYLE=*string*	✗	✗	✗	✗	✗	✓	✗	✗	✗
TOP=number	✗	✗	✗	✗	✗	✓	✗	✗	✗
VISIBILITY=SHOW|HIDE|INHERIT	✗	✗	✗	✗	✗	✓	✗	✗	✗
WIDTH=number	✗	✗	✗	✗	✗	✓	✗	✗	✗
Z-INDEX=number	✗	✗	✗	✗	✗	✓	✗	✗	✗

LEGEND

Defines the title text to place in the 'box' created by a `FIELDSET` tag. **HTML 4.0, IE4, IE5**.

Attributes	2.0	3.2	4.0	N2	N3	N4	IE2	IE3	IE4/5
`<event_name>=script_code`	✗	✗	✓	✗	✗	✗	✗	✗	✓
`ACCESSKEY=key_character`	✗	✗	✓	✗	✗	✗	✗	✗	✗
`ALIGN=BOTTOM|CENTER|LEFT|RIGHT|TOP`	✗	✗	D	✗	✗	✗	✗	✗	✓
`CLASS=classname`	✗	✗	✓	✗	✗	✗	✗	✗	✓
`DIR=LTR|RTL`	✗	✗	✓	✗	✗	✗	✗	✗	✗
`ID=string`	✗	✗	✓	✗	✗	✗	✗	✗	✓
`LANG=language_type`	✗	✗	✓	✗	✗	✗	✗	✗	✓
`LANGUAGE=JAVASCRIPT|JSCRIPT|VBSCRIPT|VBS`	✗	✗	✗	✗	✗	✗	✗	✗	✓
`STYLE=string`	✗	✗	✓	✗	✗	✗	✗	✗	✓
`TITLE=string`	✗	✗	✓	✗	✗	✗	✗	✗	✓
`VALIGN=BOTTOM|TOP`	✗	✗	✗	✗	✗	✗	✗	✗	✓

LI

Denotes one item within an ordered or unordered list. **ALL**.

Attributes	2.0	3.2	4.0	N2	N3	N4	IE2	IE3	IE4/5
`<event_name>=script_code`	✗	✗	✓	✗	✗	✗	✗	✗	✓
`CLASS=classname`	✗	✗	✓	✗	✗	✓	✗	✓	✓
`DIR=LTR|RTL`	✗	✗	✓	✗	✗	✗	✗	✗	✗
`ID=string`	✗	✗	✓	✗	✗	✓	✗	✓	✓
`LANG=language_type`	✗	✗	✓	✗	✗	✗	✗	✗	✓
`LANGUAGE=JAVASCRIPT|JSCRIPT|VBSCRIPT|VBS`	✗	✗	✗	✗	✗	✗	✗	✗	✓
`STYLE=string`	✗	✗	✓	✗	✗	✓	✗	✓	✓
`TITLE=string`	✗	✗	✓	✗	✗	✗	✗	✗	✓
`TYPE=1|a|A|I|I|DISC|CIRCLE|SQUARE`	✗	✓	D	✓	✓	✓	✓	✓	✓
`VALUE=string`	✗	✓	D	✓	✓	✓	✓	✓	✓

LINK

Defines a hyperlink between the document and some other resource. **HTML 2.0, 3.2 & 4.0, IE3, IE4, IE5**.

Attributes	2.0	3.2	4.0	N2	N3	N4	IE2	IE3	IE4/5
<event_name>=script_code	✗	✗	✓	✗	✗	✗	✗	✗	✗
CHARSET=charset	✗	✗	✓	✗	✗	✗	✗	✗	✗
CLASS=classname	✗	✗	✓	✗	✗	✗	✗	✗	✗
DIR=LTR|RTL	✗	✗	✓	✗	✗	✗	✗	✗	✗
DISABLED	✗	✗	✗	✗	✗	✗	✗	✗	✓
HREF=url	✓	✓	✓	✓	✓	✓	✗	✓	✓
HREFLANG=langcode	✗	✗	✓	✗	✗	✗	✗	✗	✗
ID=*string*	✗	✗	✓	✗	✗	✓	✗	✗	✓
LANG=language_type	✗	✗	✓	✗	✗	✗	✗	✗	✓
MEDIA=SCREEN|PRINT|PROJECTION|BRAILLE|SPEECH|ALL	✗	✗	✓	✗	✗	✗	✗	✗	✓
METHODS=*string*	✓	✗	✗	✗	✗	✗	✗	✗	✗
REL=relationship	✓	✓	✓	✓	✓	✓	✗	✓	✓
REV=relationship	✓	✓	✓	✓	✓	✓	✗	✓	✗
STYLE=*string*	✗	✗	✓	✗	✗	✓	✗	✗	✗
TARGET=<window_name>|_parent|_blank|_tope|_self	✗	✗	✓	✗	✗	✗	✗	✗	✗
TITLE=*string*	✓	✓	✓	✓	✓	✓	✗	✓	✓
TYPE=MIME-type	✗	✗	✓	✗	✗	✓	✗	✓	✓
URN=*string*	✓	✗	✗	✗	✗	✗	✗	✗	✗

LISTING

Renders text in fixed-width type. Use `PRE` instead. **HTML 2.0, deprecated 3.2, supported IE2, IE3, IE4, IE5**.

Attributes	2.0	3.2	4.0	N2	N3	N4	IE2	IE3	IE4/5
<event_name>=script_code	✗	✗	✗	✗	✗	✗	✗	✗	✓
CLASS=classname	✗	✗	✗	✗	✗	✗	✗	✗	✓
ID=*string*	✗	✗	✗	✗	✗	✗	✗	✗	✓
LANG=language_type	✗	✗	✗	✗	✗	✗	✗	✗	✓
LANGUAGE=JAVASCRIPT|JSCRIPT|VBSCRIPT|VBS	✗	✗	✗	✗	✗	✗	✗	✗	✓
STYLE=*string*	✗	✗	✗	✗	✗	✗	✗	✗	✓

Attributes	2.0	3.2	4.0	N2	N3	N4	IE2	IE3	IE4/5
TITLE=*string*	✗	✗	✗	✗	✗	✗	✗	✗	✓

MAP

Specifies a collection of hot spots for a client-side image map. **ALL except HTML 2.0**.

Attributes	2.0	3.2	4.0	N2	N3	N4	IE2	IE3	IE4/5
<event_name>=script_code	✗	✗	✗	✗	✗	✗	✗	✗	✓
CLASS=classname	✗	✗	✓	✗	✗	✓	✗	✗	✓
ID=*string*	✗	✗	✓	✗	✗	✓	✗	✗	✓
LANG=language_type	✗	✗	✗	✗	✗	✗	✗	✗	✓
NAME=*string*	✗	✓	✓	✓	✓	✓	✓	✓	✓
STYLE=*string*	✗	✗	✓	✗	✗	✓	✗	✗	✓
TITLE=*string*	✗	✗	✓	✗	✗	✗	✗	✗	✓

MARQUEE

Creates a scrolling text marquee in the page. **IE2, IE3, IE4, IE5**.

Attributes	2.0	3.2	4.0	N2	N3	N4	IE2	IE3	IE4/5
<event_name>=script_code	✗	✗	✗	✗	✗	✗	✗	✗	✓
ALIGN=TOP|MIDDLE|BOTTOM	✗	✗	✗	✗	✗	✗	✓	✓	✗
BEHAVIOR=ALTERNATE|SCROLL|SLIDE	✗	✗	✗	✗	✗	✗	✓	✓	✓
BGCOLOR=color	✗	✗	D	✗	✗	✗	✓	✓	✓
CLASS=classname	✗	✗	✗	✗	✗	✗	✗	✗	✓
DATAFLD=column_name	✗	✗	✗	✗	✗	✗	✗	✗	✓
DATAFORMATAS=HTML|TEXT	✗	✗	✗	✗	✗	✗	✗	✗	✓
DATASRC=id	✗	✗	✗	✗	✗	✗	✗	✗	✓
DIRECTION=DOWN|LEFT|RIGHT|UP	✗	✗	✗	✗	✗	✗	✓	✓	✓
HEIGHT=number	✗	✗	✗	✗	✗	✗	✓	✓	✓
HSPACE=number	✗	✗	✗	✗	✗	✗	✓	✓	✓
ID=*string*	✗	✗	✗	✗	✗	✗	✗	✗	✓
LANG=language_type	✗	✗	✗	✗	✗	✗	✗	✗	✓
LANGUAGE=JAVASCRIPT|JSCRIPT|VBSCRIPT|VBS	✗	✗	✗	✗	✗	✗	✗	✗	✓
LOOP=number	✗	✗	✗	✗	✗	✗	✓	✓	✓

Attributes	2.0	3.2	4.0	N2	N3	N4	IE2	IE3	IE4/5
SCROLLAMOUNT=number	✗	✗	✗	✗	✗	✗	✓	✓	✓
SCROLLDELAY=number	✗	✗	✗	✗	✗	✗	✓	✓	✓
STYLE=*string*	✗	✗	✗	✗	✗	✗	✗	✗	✓
TITLE=*string*	✗	✗	✗	✗	✗	✗	✗	✗	✓
TRUESPEED	✗	✗	✗	✗	✗	✗	✗	✗	✓
VSPACE=number	✗	✗	✗	✗	✗	✗	✓	✓	✓
WIDTH=number	✗	✗	✗	✗	✗	✗	✓	✓	✓

MENU

Renders the following block of text as individual items. Use lists instead. **ALL, deprecated in HTML 4.0**.

Attributes	2.0	3.2	4.0	N2	N3	N4	IE2	IE3	IE4/5
<event_name>=script_code	✗	✗	D	✗	✗	✗	✗	✗	✓
CLASS=classname	✗	✗	D	✗	✗	✓	✗	✗	✓
COMPACT	✓	✓	D	✗	✗	✓	✗	✓	✗
ID=*string*	✗	✗	D	✗	✗	✓	✗	✗	✓
LANG=language_type	✗	✗	D	✗	✗	✗	✗	✗	✓
LANGUAGE=JAVASCRIPT|JSCRIPT|VBSCRIPT|VBS	✗	✗	✗	✗	✗	✗	✗	✗	✓
STYLE=*string*	✗	✗	D	✗	✗	✓	✗	✗	✓
TITLE=*string*	✗	✗	D	✗	✗	✗	✗	✗	✓
TYPE=CIRCLE|DISC|SQUARE	✗	✗	✗	✗	✗	✓	✗	✗	✗

META

Provides various types of unviewed information or instructions to the browser. **ALL**.

Attributes	2.0	3.2	4.0	N2	N3	N4	IE2	IE3	IE4/5
CHARSET=*string*	✗	✗	✗	✗	✗	✗	✗	✓	✗
CONTENT=metacontent	✓	✓	✓	✓	✓	✓	✓	✓	✓
DIR=LTR|RTL	✗	✗	✓	✗	✗	✗	✗	✗	✗
HTTP-EQUIV=*string*	✓	✓	✓	✓	✓	✓	✓	✓	✓
LANG=language_type	✗	✗	✓	✗	✗	✗	✗	✗	✗
NAME=metaname	✓	✓	✓	✓	✓	✓	✗	✓	✓
SCHEME=*string*	✗	✗	✓	✗	✗	✗	✗	✗	✗

Attributes	2.0	3.2	4.0	N2	N3	N4	IE2	IE3	IE4/5
TITLE=*string*	✗	✗	✗	✗	✗	✗	✗	✗	✓
URL=url	✗	✗	✗	✗	✗	✗	✗	✓	✓

MULTICOL

Used to define multiple column formatting. **N2, N3, N4**.

Attributes	2.0	3.2	4.0	N2	N3	N4	IE2	IE3	IE4/5
CLASS=classname	✗	✗	✗	✗	✗	✓	✗	✗	✗
COLS=number	✗	✗	✗	✗	✓	✓	✗	✗	✗
GUTTER=number	✗	✗	✗	✗	✓	✓	✗	✗	✗
ID=*string*	✗	✗	✗	✗	✗	✓	✗	✗	✗
STYLE=*string*	✗	✗	✗	✗	✗	✓	✗	✗	✗
WIDTH=number	✗	✗	✗	✗	✓	✓	✗	✗	✗

NEXTID

Defines values used by text editing software when parsing or creating the document. **HTML 2.0 only**.

Attributes	2.0	3.2	4.0	N2	N3	N4	IE2	IE3	IE4/5
N=*string*	✓	✗	✗	✗	✗	✗	✗	✗	✗

NOBR

Renders text without any text wrapping in the page. **N2, N3, N4, IE2, IE3, IE4, IE5**.

Attributes	2.0	3.2	4.0	N2	N3	N4	IE2	IE3	IE4/5
ID=*string*	✗	✗	✗	✗	✗	✗	✗	✗	✓
STYLE=*string*	✗	✗	✗	✗	✗	✗	✗	✗	✓
TITLE=*string*	✗	✗	✗	✗	✗	✗	✗	✗	✓

NOEMBED

Defines the HTML to be displayed by browsers that do not support embeds. **N2, N3, N4**.

NOFRAMES

Defines the HTML to be displayed in browsers that do not support frames.**HTML 4.0, N2, N3, N3, IE3, IE4, IE5.**

Attributes	2.0	3.2	4.0	N2	N3	N4	IE2	IE3	IE4/5
ID=*string*	✗	✗	✗	✗	✗	✗	✗	✗	✓
STYLE=*string*	✗	✗	✗	✗	✗	✗	✗	✗	✓
TITLE=*string*	✗	✗	✗	✗	✗	✗	✗	✗	✓

NOLAYER

Defines the part of a document that will be displayed in browsers that don't support layers. **N4**.

NOSCRIPT

Defines the HTML to be displayed in browsers that do not support scripting. **HTML 4.0, N3, N4, IE3, IE4, IE5**.

OBJECT

Inserts an object or other non-intrinsic HTML control into the page. **HTML 4.0, IE3, IE4, IE5.**

Attributes	2.0	3.2	4.0	N2	N3	N4	IE2	IE3	IE4/5
<event_name>=script_code	✗	✗	✓	✗	✗	✗	✗	✗	✓
ACCESSKEY=key_character	✗	✗	✗	✗	✗	✗	✗	✗	✓
ALIGN=ABSBOTTOM | ABSMIDDLE | BASELINE | BOTTOM | LEFT | MIDDLE | RIGHT | TEXTTOP | TOP	✓	✓	D	✗	✗	✗	✗	✓	✓
ARCHIVE=urllist	✗	✗	✓	✗	✗	✗	✗	✗	✗
BORDER=number	✗	✗	D	✗	✗	✗	✗	✓	✗
CLASS=classname	✗	✗	✓	✗	✗	✗	✗	✗	✓
CLASSID=*string*	✗	✗	✓	✗	✗	✗	✗	✓	✓
CODE=filename	✗	✗	✗	✗	✗	✗	✗	✗	✓
CODEBASE=url	✗	✗	✓	✗	✗	✗	✗	✓	✓
CODETYPE=url	✗	✗	✓	✗	✗	✗	✗	✓	✓
DATA=*string*	✗	✗	✓	✗	✗	✗	✗	✓	✓
DATAFLD=column_name	✗	✗	✗	✗	✗	✗	✗	✗	✓
DATASRC=id	✗	✗	✗	✗	✗	✗	✗	✗	✓
DECLARE	✗	✗	✓	✗	✗	✗	✗	✓	✗
DIR=LTR | RTL	✗	✗	✓	✗	✗	✗	✗	✗	✗

Attributes	2.0	3.2	4.0	N2	N3	N4	IE2	IE3	IE4/5
EXPORT	✗	✗	✓	✗	✗	✗	✗	✗	✗
HEIGHT=number	✗	✗	✓	✗	✗	✗	✗	✓	✓
HSPACE=number	✗	✗	✓	✗	✗	✗	✗	✓	✗
ID=*string*	✗	✗	✓	✗	✗	✗	✗	✗	✓
LANG=language_type	✗	✗	✓	✗	✗	✗	✗	✗	✓
LANGUAGE=JAVASCRIPT|JSCRIPT|VBSCRIPT|VBS	✗	✗	✗	✗	✗	✗	✗	✗	✓
NAME=*string*	✗	✗	✓	✗	✗	✗	✗	✓	✓
NOTAB	✗	✗	✗	✗	✗	✗	✗	✓	✗
SHAPES	✗	✗	✓	✗	✗	✗	✗	✓	✗
STANDBY=*string*	✗	✗	✓	✗	✗	✗	✗	✓	✗
STYLE=*string*	✗	✗	✓	✗	✗	✗	✗	✗	✓
TABINDEX=number	✗	✗	✓	✗	✗	✗	✗	✓	✓
TITLE=*string*	✗	✗	✓	✗	✗	✗	✗	✓	✓
TYPE=MIME-type	✗	✗	✓	✗	✗	✗	✗	✗	✗
USEMAP=url	✗	✗	✓	✗	✗	✗	✗	✓	✗
VSPACE=number	✗	✗	✓	✗	✗	✗	✗	✓	✗
WIDTH=number	✗	✗	✓	✗	✗	✗	✗	✓	✓

OL

Renders lines of text that have `<LI>` tags as an ordered list. **ALL**.

Attributes	2.0	3.2	4.0	N2	N3	N4	IE2	IE3	IE4/5
<event_name>=script_code	✗	✗	✓	✗	✗	✗	✗	✗	✓
CLASS=classname	✗	✗	✓	✗	✗	✓	✗	✗	✓
COMPACT	✓	✓	D	✓	✓	✓	✗	✓	✗
DIR=LTR|RTL	✗	✗	✓	✗	✗	✗	✗	✗	✗
ID=*string*	✗	✗	✓	✗	✗	✓	✗	✓	✓
LANG=language_type	✗	✗	✓	✗	✗	✗	✗	✗	✓
LANGUAGE=JAVASCRIPT|JSCRIPT|VBSCRIPT|VBS	✗	✗	✗	✗	✗	✗	✗	✗	✓
START=number	✗	✓	D	✓	✓	✓	✓	✓	✓
STYLE=*string*	✗	✗	✓	✗	✗	✓	✗	✓	✓
TITLE=*string*	✗	✗	✓	✗	✗	✗	✗	✗	✓
TYPE=1|a|A|I|I	✗	✓	D	✓	✓	✓	✓	✓	✓

OPTGROUP

Creates a collapsible and hierarchical list of options.

Attributes	2.0	3.2	4.0	N2	N3	N4	IE2	IE3	IE4/5
<event_name>=script_code	✗	✗	✓	✗	✗	✗	✗	✗	✗
CLASS=classname	✗	✗	✓	✗	✗	✗	✗	✗	✗
DISABLED	✗	✗	✓	✗	✗	✗	✗	✗	✗
DIR=LTR|RTL	✗	✗	✓	✗	✗	✗	✗	✗	✗
ID=string	✗	✗	✓	✗	✗	✗	✗	✗	✗
LABEL=string	✗	✗	✓	✗	✗	✗	✗	✗	✗
LANG=language_type	✗	✗	✓	✗	✗	✗	✗	✗	✗
STYLE=string	✗	✗	✓	✗	✗	✗	✗	✗	✗
TITLE=string	✗	✗	✓	✗	✗	✗	✗	✗	✗

OPTION

Denotes one choice in a SELECT drop-down or list element. **ALL**.

Attributes	2.0	3.2	4.0	N2	N3	N4	IE2	IE3	IE4/5
<event_name>=script_code	✗	✗	✓	✗	✗	✗	✗	✗	✓
CLASS=classname	✗	✗	✓	✗	✗	✓	✗	✗	✓
DIR=LTR|RTL	✗	✗	✓	✗	✗	✗	✗	✗	✗
DISABLED	✗	✗	✓	✓	✓	✗	✗	✗	✗
ID=string	✗	✗	✓	✗	✗	✓	✗	✗	✓
LABEL=string	✗	✗	✓	✗	✗	✗	✗	✗	✗
LANG=language_type	✗	✗	✓	✗	✗	✗	✗	✗	✗
LANGUAGE=JAVASCRIPT|JSCRIPT|VBSCRIPT|VBS	✗	✗	✗	✗	✗	✗	✗	✗	✓
PLAIN	✗	✗	✗	✓	✓	✓	✗	✗	✗
SELECTED	✓	✓	✓	✓	✓	✓	✓	✓	✓
STYLE=string	✗	✗	✓	✗	✗	✓	✗	✗	✗
TITLE=string	✗	✗	✓	✗	✗	✗	✗	✗	✗
VALUE=string	✓	✓	✓	✓	✓	✓	✓	✓	✓

P

Denotes a paragraph. The end tag is optional. **ALL**.

Attributes	2.0	3.2	4.0	N2	N3	N4	IE2	IE3	IE4/5
`<event_name>=script_code`	✗	✗	✓	✗	✗	✗	✗	✗	✓
`ALIGN=CENTER｜LEFT｜RIGHT`	✗	✓	D	✓	✓	✓	✓	✓	✓
`CLASS=classname`	✗	✗	✓	✗	✗	✓	✗	✓	✓
`DIR=LTR｜RTL`	✗	✗	✓	✗	✗	✗	✗	✗	✗
`ID=string`	✗	✗	✓	✗	✗	✓	✗	✓	✓
`LANG=language_type`	✗	✗	✓	✗	✗	✗	✗	✗	✓
`LANGUAGE=JAVASCRIPT｜JSCRIPT｜VBSCRIPT｜VBS`	✗	✗	✗	✗	✗	✗	✗	✗	✓
`STYLE=string`	✗	✗	✓	✗	✗	✓	✗	✓	✓
`TITLE=string`	✗	✗	✓	✗	✗	✗	✗	✗	✓

PARAM

Used in an `OBJECT` or `APPLET` tag to set the object's properties. **ALL except HTML 2.0**.

Attributes	2.0	3.2	4.0	N2	N3	N4	IE2	IE3	IE4/5
`DATAFLD=column_name`	✗	✗	✗	✗	✗	✗	✗	✗	✓
`DATAFORMATAS=HTML｜TEXT`	✗	✗	✗	✗	✗	✗	✗	✗	✓
`DATASRC=id`	✗	✗	✗	✗	✗	✗	✗	✗	✓
`ID`	✗	✗	✓	✗	✗	✗	✗	✗	✗
`NAME=string`	✗	✓	✓	✓	✓	✓	✗	✓	✓
`TYPE=string`	✗	✗	✓	✗	✗	✗	✗	✓	✗
`VALUE=string`	✗	✓	✓	✓	✓	✓	✗	✓	✓
`VALUETYPE=DATA｜REF｜OBJECT`	✗	✗	✓	✗	✗	✗	✗	✓	✗

PLAINTEXT

Renders text in fixed-width type without processing any tags it may contain. **Deprecated in HTML 2.0, 3.0, N2, N3 and N4, supported in IE2, IE3, IE4, IE5**.

Attributes	2.0	3.2	4.0	N2	N3	N4	IE2	IE3	IE4/5
`<event_name>=script_code`	✗	✗	✗	✗	✗	✗	✗	✗	✓
`CLASS=classname`	✗	✗	✗	✗	✗	✗	✗	✗	✓
`ID=string`	✗	✗	✗	✗	✗	✗	✗	✗	✓

Attributes	2.0	3.2	4.0	N2	N3	N4	IE2	IE3	IE4/5
LANG=language_type	✗	✗	✗	✗	✗	✗	✗	✗	✓
LANGUAGE=JAVASCRIPT|JSCRIPT|VBSCRIPT|VBS	✗	✗	✗	✗	✗	✗	✗	✗	✓
STYLE=string	✗	✗	✗	✗	✗	✗	✗	✗	✓
TITLE=string	✗	✗	✗	✗	✗	✗	✗	✗	✓

PRE

Renders text in fixed-width type. **ALL**.

Attributes	2.0	3.2	4.0	N2	N3	N4	IE2	IE3	IE4/5
<event_name>=script_code	✗	✗	✓	✗	✗	✗	✗	✗	✓
CLASS=classname	✗	✗	✓	✗	✗	✓	✗	✗	✓
DIR=LTR|RTL	✗	✗	✓	✗	✗	✗	✗	✗	✗
ID=string	✗	✗	✓	✗	✗	✓	✗	✗	✓
LANG=language_type	✗	✗	✓	✗	✗	✗	✗	✗	✓
LANGUAGE=JAVASCRIPT|JSCRIPT|VBSCRIPT|VBS	✗	✗	✗	✗	✗	✗	✗	✗	✓
STYLE=string	✗	✗	✓	✗	✗	✓	✗	✗	✓
TITLE=string	✗	✗	✓	✗	✗	✗	✗	✗	✓
WIDTH=number	✓	✓	✓	✓	✓	✓	✗	✗	✗

Q

A short quotation, such as the URL of the source document or a message. **HTML 4.0, IE4, IE5**.

Attributes	2.0	3.2	4.0	N2	N3	N4	IE2	IE3	IE4/5
<event_name>=script_code	✗	✗	✓	✗	✗	✗	✗	✗	✓
CITE=url	✗	✗	✓	✗	✗	✗	✗	✗	✗
CLASS=classname	✗	✗	✓	✗	✗	✗	✗	✗	✓
DIR=LTR|RTL	✗	✗	✓	✗	✗	✗	✗	✗	✗
ID=string	✗	✗	✓	✗	✗	✗	✗	✗	✓
LANG=language_type	✗	✗	✓	✗	✗	✗	✗	✗	✓
STYLE=string	✗	✗	✓	✗	✗	✗	✗	✗	✓
TITLE=string	✗	✗	✓	✗	✗	✗	✗	✗	✓

S

Renders text in strikethrough type. **Supported in HTML 3.2, N3, N4, IE2, IE3, IE4, IE5 deprecated in HTML 4.0**.

Attributes	2.0	3.2	4.0	N2	N3	N4	IE2	IE3	IE4/5
`<event_name>=script_code`	✗	✗	D	✗	✗	✗	✗	✗	✓
`CLASS=classname`	✗	✗	D	✗	✗	✓	✗	✗	✓
`DIR=LTR|RTL`	✗	✗	D	✗	✗	✗	✗	✗	✗
`ID=`*string*	✗	✗	D	✗	✗	✓	✗	✗	✓
`LANG=language_type`	✗	✗	D	✗	✗	✗	✗	✗	✓
`LANGUAGE=JAVASCRIPT|JSCRIPT|VBSCRIPT|VBS`	✗	✗	✗	✗	✗	✗	✗	✗	✓
`STYLE=`*string*	✗	✗	D	✗	✗	✓	✗	✗	✓
`TITLE=`*string*	✗	✗	D	✗	✗	✗	✗	✗	✓

SAMP

Renders text as a code sample listing, usually in a smaller font. **ALL**.

Attributes	2.0	3.2	4.0	N2	N3	N4	IE2	IE3	IE4/5
`<event_name>=script_code`	✗	✗	✓	✗	✗	✗	✗	✗	✓
`CLASS=classname`	✗	✗	✓	✗	✗	✓	✗	✗	✓
`DIR=LTR|RTL`	✗	✗	✓	✗	✗	✗	✗	✗	✗
`ID=`*string*	✗	✗	✓	✗	✗	✓	✗	✗	✓
`LANG=language_type`	✗	✗	✓	✗	✗	✗	✗	✗	✓
`LANGUAGE=JAVASCRIPT|JSCRIPT|VBSCRIPT|VBS`	✗	✗	✗	✗	✗	✗	✗	✗	✓
`STYLE=`*string*	✗	✗	✓	✗	✗	✓	✗	✗	✓
`TITLE=`*string*	✗	✗	✓	✗	✗	✗	✗	✗	✓

SCRIPT

Specifies a script for the page that will be interpreted by a script engine. **HTML 3.2, 4.0, N2, N3, N4, IE3, IE4**.

Attributes	2.0	3.2	4.0	N2	N3	N4	IE2	IE3	IE4/5
`ARCHIVE=url`	✗	✗	✗	✗	✗	✓	✗	✗	✗
`CHARSET=charset`	✗	✗	✓	✗	✗	✗	✗	✗	✗
`CLASS=classname`	✗	✗	✗	✗	✗	✓	✗	✗	✓
`DEFER`	✗	✗	✓	✗	✗	✗	✗	✗	✗
`EVENT=<event_name>`	✗	✗	✗	✗	✗	✗	✗	✗	✓
`FOR=element_name`	✗	✗	✗	✗	✗	✗	✗	✗	✓
`ID=`*string*	✗	✗	✗	✗	✗	✓	✗	✗	✓
`LANGUAGE=JAVASCRIPT`|`JSCRIPT`|`VBSCRIPT`|`VBS`	✗	✗	D	✓	✓	✓	✗	✓	✓
`SRC=url`	✗	✗	✓	✗	✓	✓	✗	✓	✓
`STYLE=`*string*	✗	✗	✗	✗	✗	✓	✗	✗	✓
`TITLE=`*string*	✗	✗	✗	✗	✗	✗	✗	✗	✓
`TYPE=`*string*	✗	✗	✓	✗	✗	✗	✗	✓	✓

SELECT

Defines a list box or drop-down list. **ALL**.

Attributes	2.0	3.2	4.0	N2	N3	N4	IE2	IE3	IE4/5
`<event_name>=script_code`	✗	✗	✓	✗	✗	✓	✗	✗	✓
`ACCESSKEY=key_character`	✗	✗	✗	✗	✗	✗	✗	✗	✓
`ALIGN=ABSBOTTOM`|`ABSMIDDLE`|`BASELINE`|`BOTTOM`|`LEFT`|`MIDDLE`|`RIGHT`|`TEXTTOP`|`TOP`	✗	✗	✗	✗	✗	✗	✗	✗	✓
`CLASS=classname`	✗	✗	✓	✗	✗	✓	✗	✗	✓
`DATAFLD=column_name`	✗	✗	✗	✗	✗	✗	✗	✗	✓
`DATASRC=id`	✗	✗	✗	✗	✗	✗	✗	✗	✓
`DIR=LTR`|`RTL`	✗	✗	✓	✗	✗	✗	✗	✗	✗
`DISABLED`	✗	✗	✓	✗	✗	✗	✗	✗	✓
`ID=`*string*	✗	✗	✓	✗	✗	✓	✗	✗	✓
`LANG=language_type`	✗	✗	✓	✗	✗	✗	✗	✗	✓
`LANGUAGE=JAVASCRIPT`|`JSCRIPT`|`VBSCRIPT`|`VBS`	✗	✗	✗	✗	✗	✗	✗	✗	✓
`MULTIPLE`	✓	✓	✓	✓	✓	✓	✓	✓	✓

Attributes	2.0	3.2	4.0	N2	N3	N4	IE2	IE3	IE4/5
NAME=string	✓	✓	✓	✓	✓	✓	✓	✓	✓
SIZE=number	✓	✓	✓	✓	✓	✓	✓	✓	✓
STYLE=string	✗	✗	✓	✗	✗	✓	✗	✗	✓
TABINDEX=number	✗	✗	✓	✗	✗	✗	✗	✗	✓
TITLE=string	✗	✗	✓	✗	✗	✗	✗	✗	✓

SERVER

Used to run a Netscape LiveWire script. **N2, N3, N4**.

Attributes	2.0	3.2	4.0	N2	N3	N4	IE2	IE3	IE4/5
CLASS=classname	✗	✗	✗	✗	✗	✓	✗	✗	✗
ID=string	✗	✗	✗	✗	✗	✓	✗	✗	✗

SMALL

Specifies that text should be displayed with a smaller font than the current font. **HTML 3.2, 4.0, N2, N3, N4, IE3, IE4, IE5**.

Attributes	2.0	3.2	4.0	N2	N3	N4	IE2	IE3	IE4/5
<event_name>=script_code	✗	✗	✓	✗	✗	✗	✗	✗	✓
CLASS=classname	✗	✗	✓	✗	✗	✓	✗	✗	✓
DIR=LTR|RTL	✗	✗	✓	✗	✗	✗	✗	✗	✗
ID=string	✗	✗	✓	✗	✗	✓	✗	✗	✓
LANG=language_type	✗	✗	✓	✗	✗	✗	✗	✗	✓
LANGUAGE=JAVASCRIPT|JSCRIPT|VBSCRIPT|VBS	✗	✗	✗	✗	✗	✗	✗	✗	✓
STYLE=string	✗	✗	✓	✗	✗	✓	✗	✗	✓
TITLE=string	✗	✗	✓	✗	✗	✗	✗	✗	✓

SPACER

Used to specify vertical and horizontal spacing of elements. **HTML 3.2, 4.0, N2, N3, N4, IE3, IE4, IE5**.

Attributes	2.0	3.2	4.0	N2	N3	N4	IE2	IE3	IE4/5
ALIGN=ABSBOTTOM|ABSMIDDLE|BASELINE|BOTTOM|LEFT|MIDDLE|RIGHT|TEXTTOP|TOP	✗	✗	✗	✗	✓	✓	✗	✗	✗
CLASS=classname	✗	✗	✗	✗	✗	✓	✗	✗	✗

Attributes	2.0	3.2	4.0	N2	N3	N4	IE2	IE3	IE4/5
HEIGHT=number	✗	✗	✗	✗	✓	✓	✗	✗	✗
ID=string	✗	✗	✗	✗	✗	✓	✗	✗	✗
SIZE=number	✗	✗	✗	✗	✓	✓	✗	✗	✗
STYLE=string	✗	✗	✗	✗	✗	✓	✗	✗	✗
TYPE=BLOCK|HORIZONTAL|VERTICAL	✗	✗	✗	✗	✓	✓	✗	✗	✗
WIDTH=number	✗	✗	✗	✗	✓	✓	✗	✗	✗

SPAN

Used (with a style sheet) to define non-standard attributes for text on the page. **HTML 4.0, IE4, IE5**.

Attributes	2.0	3.2	4.0	N2	N3	N4	IE2	IE3	IE4/5
<event_name>=script_code	✗	✗	✓	✗	✗	✗	✗	✗	✓
CLASS=classname	✗	✗	✓	✗	✗	✓	✗	✗	✓
CHARSET=string	✗	✗	✓	✗	✗	✗	✗	✗	✗
DATAFLD=column_name	✗	✗	✗	✗	✗	✗	✗	✗	✓
DATAFORMATAS=HTML|TEXT	✗	✗	✗	✗	✗	✗	✗	✗	✓
DATASRC=id	✗	✗	✗	✗	✗	✗	✗	✗	✓
DIR=LTR|RTL	✗	✗	✓	✗	✗	✗	✗	✗	✗
HREF=url	✗	✗	✓	✗	✗	✗	✗	✗	✗
HREFLANG=langcode	✗	✗	✓	✗	✗	✗	✗	✗	✗
ID=string	✗	✗	✓	✗	✗	✓	✗	✗	✓
LANG=language_type	✗	✗	✓	✗	✗	✗	✗	✗	✓
LANGUAGE=JAVASCRIPT|JSCRIPT|VBSCRIPT|VBS	✗	✗	✗	✗	✗	✗	✗	✗	✓
MEDIA	✗	✗	✓	✗	✗	✗	✗	✗	✗
REL=relationship	✗	✗	✓	✗	✗	✗	✗	✗	✗
REV=relationship	✗	✗	✓	✗	✗	✗	✗	✗	✗
STYLE=string	✗	✗	✓	✗	✗	✓	✗	✓	✓
TARGET	✗	✗	✓	✗	✗	✗	✗	✗	✗
TITLE=string	✗	✗	✓	✗	✗	✗	✗	✗	✓
TYPE	✗	✗	✓	✗	✗	✗	✗	✗	✗

STRIKE

Renders text in strikethrough type. **HTML 3.2, N3, N4, IE3, IE4, IE5, deprecated in HTML 4.0.**

Attributes	2.0	3.2	4.0	N2	N3	N4	IE2	IE3	IE4/5
`<event_name>=script_code`	✗	✗	D	✗	✗	✗	✗	✗	✓
`CLASS=classname`	✗	✗	D	✗	✗	✓	✗	✗	✓
`DIR=LTR`|`RTL`	✗	✗	D	✗	✗	✗	✗	✗	✗
`ID=`*string*	✗	✗	D	✗	✗	✓	✗	✗	✓
`LANG=language_type`	✗	✗	D	✗	✗	✗	✗	✗	✓
`LANGUAGE=JAVASCRIPT`|`JSCRIPT`|`VBSCRIPT`|`VBS`	✗	✗	✗	✗	✗	✗	✗	✗	✓
`STYLE=`*string*	✗	✗	D	✗	✗	✓	✗	✗	✓
`TITLE=`*string*	✗	✗	D	✗	✗	✗	✗	✗	✓

STRONG

Renders text in bold face. **ALL.**

Attributes	2.0	3.2	4.0	N2	N3	N4	IE2	IE3	IE4/5
`<event_name>=script_code`	✗	✗	✓	✗	✗	✗	✗	✗	✓
`CLASS=classname`	✗	✗	✓	✗	✗	✓	✗	✗	✓
`DIR=LTR`|`RTL`	✗	✗	✓	✗	✗	✗	✗	✗	✗
`ID=`*string*	✗	✗	✓	✗	✗	✓	✗	✗	✓
`LANG=language_type`	✗	✗	✓	✗	✗	✗	✗	✗	✓
`LANGUAGE=JAVASCRIPT`|`JSCRIPT`|`VBSCRIPT`|`VBS`	✗	✗	✗	✗	✗	✗	✗	✗	✓
`STYLE=`*string*	✗	✗	✓	✗	✗	✓	✗	✗	✓
`TITLE=`*string*	✗	✗	✓	✗	✗	✗	✗	✗	✓

STYLE

Specifies the style properties (i.e. the style sheet) for the page. **HTML 3.2, 4.0, N4, IE3, IE4, IE5.**

Attributes	2.0	3.2	4.0	N2	N3	N4	IE2	IE3	IE4/5
`DIR=LTR`|`RTL`	✗	✗	✓	✗	✗	✗	✗	✗	✗
`DISABLED`	✗	✗	✗	✗	✗	✗	✗	✗	✓
`ID=`*string*	✗	✗	✗	✗	✗	✓	✗	✗	✗
`LANG=language_type`	✗	✗	✓	✗	✗	✗	✗	✗	✗

Attributes	2.0	3.2	4.0	N2	N3	N4	IE2	IE3	IE4/5
MEDIA=SCREEN|PRINT|PROJECTION|BRAILLE|SPEECH|ALL	✗	✗	✓	✗	✗	✗	✗	✗	✓
SRC=url	✗	✗	✗	✗	✗	✓	✗	✗	✗
TITLE=*string*	✗	✗	✓	✗	✗	✗	✗	✓	✓
TYPE=*string*	✗	✗	✓	✗	✗	✓	✗	✓	✓

SUB

Renders text as a subscript using a smaller font than the current font. **HTML 3.2, 4.0, N2, N3, N4, IE3, IE4.**

Attributes	2.0	3.2	4.0	N2	N3	N4	IE2	IE3	IE4/5
<event_name>=script_code	✗	✗	✓	✗	✗	✗	✗	✗	✓
CLASS=classname	✗	✗	✓	✗	✗	✓	✗	✗	✓
DIR=LTR|RTL	✗	✗	✓	✗	✗	✗	✗	✗	✗
ID=*string*	✗	✗	✓	✗	✗	✓	✗	✗	✓
LANG=language_type	✗	✗	✓	✗	✗	✗	✗	✗	✓
LANGUAGE=JAVASCRIPT|JSCRIPT|VBSCRIPT|VBS	✗	✗	✗	✗	✗	✗	✗	✗	✓
STYLE=*string*	✗	✗	✓	✗	✗	✓	✗	✗	✓
TITLE=*string*	✗	✗	✓	✗	✗	✗	✗	✗	✓

SUP

Renders text as a superscript using a smaller font than the current font. **HTML 3.2, 4.0, N2, N3, N4, IE3, IE4, IE5.**

Attributes	2.0	3.2	4.0	N2	N3	N4	IE2	IE3	IE4/5
<event_name>=script_code	✗	✗	✓	✗	✗	✗	✗	✗	✓
CLASS=classname	✗	✗	✓	✗	✗	✓	✗	✗	✓
DIR=LTR|RTL	✗	✗	✓	✗	✗	✗	✗	✗	✗
ID=*string*	✗	✗	✓	✗	✗	✓	✗	✗	✓
LANG=language_type	✗	✗	✓	✗	✗	✗	✗	✗	✓
LANGUAGE=JAVASCRIPT|JSCRIPT|VBSCRIPT|VBS	✗	✗	✗	✗	✗	✗	✗	✗	✓
STYLE=*string*	✗	✗	✓	✗	✗	✓	✗	✗	✓
TITLE=*string*	✗	✗	✓	✗	✗	✗	✗	✗	✓

TABLE

Denotes a section of <TR> <TD> and <TH> tags organized into rows and columns. **ALL except HTML 2.0.**

Attributes	2.0	3.2	4.0	N2	N3	N4	IE2	IE3	IE4/5
<event_name>=script_code	✗	✗	✓	✗	✗	✗	✗	✗	✓
ALIGN=CENTER|LEFT|RIGHT	✗	✓	D	✗	✗	✓	✓	✓	✓
BACKGROUND=string	✗	✗	✗	✗	✗	✗	✓	✓	✓
BGCOLOR=color	✗	✗	D	✗	✓	✓	✓	✓	✓
BORDER=number	✗	✓	D	✓	✓	✓	✗	✓	✓
BORDERCOLOR=color	✗	✗	✗	✗	✗	✗	✓	✓	✓
BORDERCOLORDARK=color	✗	✗	✗	✗	✗	✗	✓	✓	✓
BORDERCOLORLIGHT=color	✗	✗	✗	✗	✗	✗	✓	✓	✓
CELLPADDING=number	✗	✓	✓	✓	✓	✓	✗	✓	✓
CELLSPACING=number	✗	✓	✓	✓	✓	✓	✗	✓	✓
CLASS=classname	✗	✗	✓	✗	✗	✓	✗	✓	✓
CLEAR=ALL|LEFT|RIGHT|NONE	✗	✗	✗	✗	✗	✗	✗	✓	✗
DATAPAGESIZE=number	✗	✗	✗	✗	✗	✗	✗	✗	✓
DATASRC=id	✗	✗	✗	✗	✗	✗	✗	✗	✓
DIR=LTR|RTL	✗	✗	✓	✗	✗	✗	✗	✗	✗
FRAME=ABOVE|BELOW|BORDER|BOX|HSIDES|LHS|RHS|VOID|VSIDES	✗	✗	✓	✗	✗	✗	✗	✓	✓
HEIGHT=number	✗	✗	✗	✓	✓	✓	✗	✗	✓
HSPACE=number	✗	✗	✗	✗	✗	✓	✗	✗	✗
ID=string	✗	✗	✓	✗	✗	✓	✗	✓	✓
LANG=language_type	✗	✗	✓	✗	✗	✗	✗	✗	✓
LANGUAGE=JAVASCRIPT|JSCRIPT|VBSCRIPT|VBS	✗	✗	✗	✗	✗	✗	✗	✗	✓
NOWRAP	✗	✗	✗	✗	✗	✗	✗	✓	✗
RULES=ALL|COLS|GROUPS|NONE|ROWS	✗	✗	✓	✗	✗	✗	✗	✓	✓
SUMMARY	✗	✗	✓	✗	✗	✗	✗	✗	✗
STYLE=string	✗	✗	✓	✗	✗	✓	✗	✓	✓
TITLE=string	✗	✗	✓	✗	✗	✗	✗	✗	✓
VALIGN=BOTTOM|TOP	✗	✗	✗	✗	✗	✗	✓	✓	✗
VSPACE=number	✗	✗	✗	✗	✗	✓	✗	✗	✗
WIDTH=number	✗	✓	✓	✓	✓	✓	✗	✓	✓

TBODY

Denotes a section of `<TR>` and `<TD>` tags forming the body of the table. **HTML 4.0, IE3, IE4, IE5**.

Attributes	2.0	3.2	4.0	N2	N3	N4	IE 2	IE3	IE4/5
`<event_name>=script_code`	✗	✗	✓	✗	✗	✗	✗	✗	✓
`ALIGN=CENTER｜LEFT｜RIGHT｜JUSTIFY｜CHAR`	✗	✗	✓	✗	✗	✗	✗	✗	✓
`BGCOLOR=color`	✗	✗	D	✗	✗	✗	✗	✗	✓
`CHAR=`*string*	✗	✗	✓	✗	✗	✗	✗	✗	✗
`CHAROFF=`*string*	✗	✗	✓	✗	✗	✗	✗	✗	✗
`CLASS=classname`	✗	✗	✓	✗	✗	✗	✗	✓	✓
`DIR=LTR｜RTL`	✗	✗	✓	✗	✗	✗	✗	✗	✗
`ID=`*string*	✗	✗	✓	✗	✗	✗	✗	✓	✓
`LANG=language_type`	✗	✗	✓	✗	✗	✗	✗	✗	✓
`LANGUAGE=JAVASCRIPT｜JSCRIPT｜VBSCRIPT｜VBS`	✗	✗	✗	✗	✗	✗	✗	✗	✓
`STYLE=`*string*	✗	✗	✓	✗	✗	✗	✗	✓	✓
`TITLE=`*string*	✗	✗	✓	✗	✗	✗	✗	✗	✓
`VALIGN=BASELINE｜BOTTOM｜CENTER｜TOP`	✗	✗	✓	✗	✗	✗	✗	✗	✓

TD

Specifies a cell in a table. **HTML 3.2, 4.0, N2, N3, N4, IE3, IE4, IE5.**

Attributes	2.0	3.2	4.0	N2	N3	N4	IE2	IE3	IE4/5
`<event_name>=script_code`	✗	✗	✓	✗	✗	✗	✗	✗	✓
`ABBR=`*string*	✗	✗	✓	✗	✗	✗	✗	✗	✗
`ALIGN=CENTER｜LEFT｜RIGHT｜JUSTIFY｜CHAR`	✗	✓	✓	✓	✓	✓	✓	✓	✓
`AXIS=cellname`	✗	✗	✓	✗	✗	✗	✗	✗	✗
`BACKGROUND=`*string*	✗	✗	✗	✗	✗	✗	✓	✓	✓
`BGCOLOR=color`	✗	✗	D	✗	✓	✓	✓	✓	✓
`BORDERCOLOR=color`	✗	✗	✗	✗	✗	✗	✓	✓	✓
`BORDERCOLORDARK=color`	✗	✗	✗	✗	✗	✗	✓	✓	✓
`BORDERCOLORLIGHT=color`	✗	✗	✗	✗	✗	✗	✓	✓	✓
`CHAR=`*string*	✗	✗	✓	✗	✗	✗	✗	✗	✗
`CHAROFF=`*string*	✗	✗	✓	✗	✗	✗	✗	✗	✗
`CLASS=classname`	✗	✗	✓	✗	✗	✓	✗	✓	✓

Attributes	2.0	3.2	4.0	N2	N3	N4	IE2	IE3	IE4/5
COLSPAN=number	✗	✓	✓	✓	✓	✓	✗	✓	✓
DIR=LTR|RTL	✗	✗	✓	✗	✗	✗	✗	✗	✗
HEADERS= *string*	✗	✗	✓	✗	✗	✗	✗	✗	✗
HEIGHT=number	✗	✓	D	✗	✗	✓	✗	✓	✗
ID=*string*	✗	✗	✓	✗	✗	✓	✗	✓	✓
LANG=language_type	✗	✗	✓	✗	✗	✗	✗	✗	✓
LANGUAGE=JAVASCRIPT|JSCRIPT|VBSCRIPT|VBS	✗	✗	✗	✗	✗	✗	✗	✗	✓
NOWRAP	✗	✓	D	✓	✓	✓	✗	✓	✓
ROWSPAN=number	✗	✓	✓	✓	✓	✓	✗	✓	✓
SCOPE=ROW|COL|ROWGROUP|COLGROUP	✗	✗	✓	✗	✗	✗	✗	✗	✗
STYLE=*string*	✗	✗	✓	✗	✗	✓	✗	✓	✓
TITLE=*string*	✗	✗	✓	✗	✗	✗	✗	✗	✓
VALIGN=BASELINE|BOTTOM|CENTER|TOP	✗	✓	✓	✓	✓	✓	✗	✓	✓
WIDTH=number	✗	✓	D	✓	✓	✓	✗	✓	✗

TEXTAREA

Specifies a multi-line text input control. **ALL**.

Attributes	2.0	3.2	4.0	N2	N3	N4	IE2	IE3	IE4/5
<event_name>=script_code	✗	✗	✓	✗	✗	✓	✗	✗	✓
ACCESSKEY=key_character	✗	✗	✗	✗	✗	✗	✗	✗	✓
ALIGN=BASBOTTOM|ABSMIDDLE|BASELINE|BOTTOM|LEFT|MIDDLE|RIGHT|TEXTTOP|TOP	✗	✗	✗	✗	✗	✗	✗	✗	✓
CLASS=classname	✗	✗	✓	✗	✗	✓	✗	✗	✓
COLS=number	✓	✓	✓	✓	✓	✓	✓	✓	✓
DATAFLD=column_name	✗	✗	✗	✗	✗	✗	✗	✗	✓
DATASRC=id	✗	✗	✗	✗	✗	✗	✗	✗	✓
DIR=LTR|RTL	✗	✗	✓	✗	✗	✗	✗	✗	✗
DISABLED	✗	✗	✓	✗	✗	✗	✗	✗	✓
ID=*string*	✗	✗	✓	✗	✗	✓	✗	✗	✓
LANG=language_type	✗	✗	✓	✗	✗	✗	✗	✗	✓
LANGUAGE=JAVASCRIPT|JSCRIPT|VBSCRIPT|VBS	✗	✗	✗	✗	✗	✗	✗	✗	✓
NAME=*string*	✓	✓	✓	✓	✓	✓	✗	✓	✓

Attributes	2.0	3.2	4.0	N2	N3	N4	IE2	IE3	IE4/5
READONLY	✗	✗	✓	✗	✗	✗	✗	✗	✓
ROWS=number	✓	✓	✓	✓	✓	✓	✓	✓	✓
STYLE=*string*	✗	✗	✓	✗	✗	✓	✗	✗	✓
TABINDEX=number	✗	✗	✓	✗	✗	✗	✗	✗	✓
TITLE=*string*	✗	✗	✓	✗	✗	✗	✗	✗	✓
WRAP=PHYSICAL|VERTICAL|OFF	✗	✗	✗	✓	✓	✓	✗	✗	✓

TFOOT

Denotes a set of rows to be used as the footer of a table. **HTML 4.0, IE3, IE4, IE5**.

Attributes	2.0	3.2	4.0	N2	N3	N4	IE2	IE3	IE4/5
<event_name>=script_code	✗	✗	✓	✗	✗	✗	✗	✗	✓
ALIGN=CENTER|LEFT|RIGHT|JUSTIFY|CHAR	✗	✗	✓	✗	✗	✗	✗	✗	✓
BGCOLOR=color	✗	✗	D	✗	✗	✗	✗	✗	✓
CHAR=*string*	✗	✗	✓	✗	✗	✗	✗	✗	✗
CHAROFF=*string*	✗	✗	✓	✗	✗	✗	✗	✗	✗
CLASS=classname	✗	✗	✓	✗	✗	✗	✗	✓	✓
DIR=LTR|RTL	✗	✗	✓	✗	✗	✗	✗	✗	✗
ID=*string*	✗	✗	✓	✗	✗	✗	✗	✓	✓
LANG=language_type	✗	✗	✓	✗	✗	✗	✗	✗	✓
LANGUAGE=JAVASCRIPT|JSCRIPT|VBSCRIPT|VBS	✗	✗	✗	✗	✗	✗	✗	✗	✓
STYLE=*string*	✗	✗	✓	✗	✗	✗	✗	✓	✓
TITLE=*string*	✗	✗	✓	✗	✗	✗	✗	✗	✓
VALIGN=BASELINE|BOTTOM|CENTER|TOP	✗	✗	✓	✗	✗	✗	✗	✗	✓

TH

Denotes a header row in a table. Contents are usually bold and centered within each cell. **HTML 3.2, 4.0, N2, N3, N4, IE2, IE3, IE4, IE5**.

Attributes	2.0	3.2	4.0	N2	N3	N4	IE2	IE3	IE4/5
<event_name>=script_code	✗	✗	✓	✗	✗	✗	✗	✗	✓
ABBR=*string*	✗	✗	✓	✗	✗	✗	✗	✗	✗
ALIGN=CENTER|LEFT|RIGHT|JUSTIFY|CHAR	✗	✓	✓	✓	✓	✓	✓	✓	✓

Attributes	2.0	3.2	4.0	N2	N3	N4	IE2	IE3	IE4/5
AXIS=cellname	✗	✗	✓	✗	✗	✗	✗	✗	✗
BACKGROUND=*string*	✗	✗	✗	✗	✗	✗	✓	✓	✓
BGCOLOR=color	✗	✗	D	✗	✓	✓	✓	✓	✓
BORDERCOLOR=color	✗	✗	✗	✗	✗	✗	✓	✓	✓
BORDERCOLORDARK=color	✗	✗	✗	✗	✗	✗	✓	✓	✓
BORDERCOLORLIGHT=color	✗	✗	✗	✗	✗	✗	✓	✓	✓
CHAR=*string*	✗	✗	✓	✗	✗	✗	✗	✗	✗
CHAROFF=*string*	✗	✗	✓	✗	✗	✗	✗	✗	✗
CLASS=classname	✗	✗	✓	✗	✗	✓	✗	✓	✓
COLSPAN=number	✗	✓	✓	✓	✓	✓	✗	✓	✓
DIR=LTR|RTL	✗	✗	✓	✗	✗	✗	✗	✗	✗
HEADERS= *string*	✗	✗	✓	✗	✗	✗	✗	✗	✗
HEIGHT=number	✗	✓	D	✗	✗	✓	✗	✗	✗
ID=*string*	✗	✗	✓	✗	✗	✓	✗	✓	✓
LANG=language_type	✗	✗	✓	✗	✗	✗	✗	✗	✓
LANGUAGE=JAVASCRIPT|JSCRIPT|VBSCRIPT|VBS	✗	✗	✗	✗	✗	✗	✗	✗	✓
NOWRAP	✗	✓	D	✓	✓	✓	✗	✓	✓
ROWSPAN=number	✗	✓	✓	✓	✓	✓	✗	✓	✓
SCOPE=ROW|COL|ROWGROUP|COLGROUP	✗	✗	✓	✗	✗	✗	✗	✗	✗
STYLE=*string*	✗	✗	✓	✗	✗	✓	✗	✓	✓
TITLE=*string*	✗	✗	✓	✗	✗	✗	✗	✗	✓
VALIGN=BASELINE|BOTTOM|CENTER|TOP	✗	✓	✓	✓	✓	✓	✓	✓	✓
WIDTH=number	✗	✓	D	✓	✓	✓	✗	✓	✗

THEAD

Denotes a set of rows to be used as the header of a table. **HTML 4.0, IE3, IE4, IE5**.

Attributes	2.0	3.2	4.0	N2	N3	N4	IE2	IE3	IE4/5
<event_name>=script_code	✗	✗	✓	✗	✗	✗	✗	✗	✓
ALIGN=CENTER|LEFT|RIGHT|JUSTIFY|CHAR	✗	✗	✓	✗	✗	✗	✗	✓	✓
BGCOLOR=color	✗	✗	D	✗	✗	✗	✗	✗	✓
CHAR=*string*	✗	✗	✓	✗	✗	✗	✗	✗	✗

Attributes	2.0	3.2	4.0	N2	N3	N4	IE2	IE3	IE4/5
CHAROFF=*string*	✗	✗	✓	✗	✗	✗	✗	✗	✗
CLASS=classname	✗	✗	✓	✗	✗	✗	✗	✓	✓
DIR=LTR|RTL	✗	✗	✓	✗	✗	✗	✗	✗	✗
ID=string	✗	✗	✓	✗	✗	✗	✗	✓	✓
LANG=language_type	✗	✗	✓	✗	✗	✗	✗	✗	✓
LANGUAGE=JAVASCRIPT|JSCRIPT|VBSCRIPT|VBS	✗	✗	✗	✗	✗	✗	✗	✗	✓
STYLE=*string*	✗	✗	✓	✗	✗	✗	✗	✓	✓
TITLE=*string*	✗	✗	✓	✗	✗	✗	✗	✗	✓
VALIGN=BASELINE|BOTTOM|CENTER|TOP	✗	✗	✓	✗	✗	✗	✗	✓	✓

TITLE

Denotes the title of the document and used in the browser's window title bar. **ALL**.

Attributes	2.0	3.2	4.0	N2	N3	N4	IE2	IE3	IE4/5
DIR=LTR|RTL	✗	✗	✓	✗	✗	✗	✗	✗	✗
ID=*string*	✗	✗	✗	✗	✗	✓	✗	✗	✓
LANG=language.type	✗	✗	✓	✗	✗	✗	✗	✗	✗
TITLE=*string*	✗	✗	✗	✗	✗	✗	✗	✗	✓

TR

Specifies a row in a table. **HTML 3.2, 4.0, N2, N3, N4, IE3, IE4, IE5.**

Attributes	2.0	3.2	4.0	N2	N3	N4	IE2	IE3	IE4/5
<event_name>=script_code	✗	✗	✓	✗	✗	✗	✗	✗	✓
ALIGN=CENTER|LEFT|RIGHT|JUSTIFY|CHAR	✗	✓	✓	✓	✓	✓	✓	✓	✓
BACKGROUND=*string*	✗	✗	✗	✗	✗	✗	✓	✗	✗
BGCOLOR=color	✗	✗	D	✗	✓	✓	✓	✓	✓
BORDERCOLOR=color	✗	✗	✗	✗	✗	✗	✓	✓	✓
BORDERCOLORDARK	✗	✗	✗	✗	✗	✗	✓	✓	✓
BORDERCOLORLIGHT=color	✗	✗	✗	✗	✗	✗	✓	✓	✓
CHAR=*string*	✗	✗	✓	✗	✗	✗	✗	✗	✗
CHAROFF=*string*	✗	✗	✓	✗	✗	✗	✗	✗	✗
CLASS=classname	✗	✗	✓	✗	✗	✓	✗	✓	✓

Attributes	2.0	3.2	4.0	N2	N3	N4	IE2	IE3	IE4/5
DIR=LTR | RTL	✗	✗	✓	✗	✗	✗	✗	✗	✗
ID=*string*	✗	✗	✓	✗	✗	✓	✗	✓	✓
LANG=language_type	✗	✗	✓	✗	✗	✗	✗	✗	✓
LANGUAGE=JAVASCRIPT | JSCRIPT | VBSCRIPT | VBS	✗	✗	✗	✗	✗	✗	✗	✗	✓
NOWRAP	✗	✗	✗	✗	✗	✗	✗	✓	✗
STYLE=*string*	✗	✗	✓	✗	✗	✓	✗	✓	✓
TITLE=*string*	✗	✗	✓	✗	✗	✗	✗	✗	✓
VALIGN=BASELINE | BOTTOM | CENTER | TOP	✗	✓	✓	✓	✓	✓	✓	✓	✓

TT

Renders text in fixed-width type. **ALL**.

Attributes	2.0	3.2	4.0	N2	N3	N4	IE2	IE3	IE4/5
<event_name>=script_code	✗	✗	✓	✗	✗	✗	✗	✗	✓
CLASS=classname	✗	✗	✓	✗	✗	✓	✗	✗	✓
DIR=LTR | RTL	✗	✗	✓	✗	✗	✗	✗	✗	✗
ID=*string*	✗	✗	✓	✗	✗	✓	✗	✗	✓
LANG=language_type	✗	✗	✓	✗	✗	✗	✗	✗	✓
LANGUAGE=JAVASCRIPT | JSCRIPT | VBSCRIPT | VBS	✗	✗	✗	✗	✗	✗	✗	✗	✓
STYLE=*string*	✗	✗	✓	✗	✗	✓	✗	✗	✓
TITLE=*string*	✗	✗	✓	✗	✗	✗	✗	✗	✓

U

Renders text underlined. **HTML 3.2, N3, N4, IE2, IE3, IE4, IE5, deprecated in HTML 4.0.**

Attributes	2.0	3.2	4.0	N2	N3	N4	IE2	IE3	IE4/5
<event_name>=script_code	✗	✗	D	✗	✗	✗	✗	✗	✓
CLASS=classname	✗	✗	D	✗	✗	✓	✗	✗	✓
DIR=LTR | RTL	✗	✗	D	✗	✗	✗	✗	✗	✗
ID=*string*	✗	✗	D	✗	✗	✓	✗	✗	✓
LANG=language_type	✗	✗	D	✗	✗	✗	✗	✗	✓
LANGUAGE=JAVASCRIPT | JSCRIPT | VBSCRIPT | VBS	✗	✗	✗	✗	✗	✗	✗	✗	✓
STYLE=*string*	✗	✗	D	✗	✗	✓	✗	✗	✓
TITLE=*string*	✗	✗	D	✗	✗	✗	✗	✗	✓

UL

Renders lines of text which have `<LI>` tags as a bulleted list. **ALL**.

Attributes	2.0	3.2	4.0	N2	N3	N4	IE2	IE3	IE4/5
`<event_name>=script_code`	✗	✗	✓	✗	✗	✗	✗	✗	✓
`CLASS=classname`	✗	✗	✓	✗	✗	✓	✗	✓	✓
`COMPACT`	✓	✓	D	✓	✓	✓	✗	✓	✗
`DIR=LTR|RTL`	✗	✗	✓	✗	✗	✗	✗	✗	✗
`ID=`*string*	✗	✗	✓	✗	✗	✓	✗	✓	✓
`LANG=language_type`	✗	✗	✓	✗	✗	✗	✗	✗	✓
`LANGUAGE=JAVASCRIPT|JSCRIPT|VBSCRIPT|VBS`	✗	✗	✗	✗	✗	✗	✗	✗	✓
`STYLE=`*string*	✗	✗	✓	✗	✗	✓	✗	✓	✓
`TITLE=`*string*	✗	✗	✓	✗	✗	✗	✗	✗	✓
`TYPE=CIRCLE|DISC|SQUARE`	✗	✓	✓	✓	✓	✓	✗	✗	✓

VAR

Renders text as a small fixed-width font. **HTML 2.0, 3.2, 4.0, IE2, IE3, IE4, IE5**.

Attributes	2.0	3.2	4.0	N2	N3	N4	IE2	IE3	IE4/5
`<event_name>=script_code`	✗	✗	✓	✗	✗	✗	✗	✗	✓
`CLASS=classname`	✗	✗	✓	✗	✗	✗	✗	✗	✓
`DIR=LTR|RTL`	✗	✗	✓	✗	✗	✗	✗	✗	✗
`ID=`*string*	✗	✗	✓	✗	✗	✗	✗	✗	✓
`LANG=language_type`	✗	✗	✓	✗	✗	✗	✗	✗	✓
`LANGUAGE=JAVASCRIPT|JSCRIPT|VBSCRIPT|VBS`	✗	✗	✗	✗	✗	✗	✗	✗	✓
`STYLE=`*string*	✗	✗	✓	✗	✗	✗	✗	✗	✓
`TITLE=`*string*	✗	✗	✓	✗	✗	✗	✗	✗	✓

WBR

Inserts a soft line break in a block of `NOBR` text. **N2, N3, N4, IE3, IE4, IE5**.

Attributes	2.0	3.2	4.0	N2	N3	N4	IE2	IE3	IE4/5
`CLASS=classname`	✗	✗	✗	✗	✗	✓	✗	✗	✓
`ID=`*string*	✗	✗	✗	✗	✗	✓	✗	✗	✓

Attributes	2.0	3.2	4.0	N2	N3	N4	IE2	IE3	IE4/5
LANGUAGE=JAVASCRIPT | JSCRIPT | VBSCRIPT | VBS	✗	✗	✗	✗	✗	✗	✗	✗	✓
STYLE=*string*	✗	✗	✗	✗	✗	✓	✗	✗	✓
TITLE=*string*	✗	✗	✗	✗	✗	✗	✗	✗	✓

XMP

Renders text in fixed-width typeface, as used for example code. Use PRE or SAMP instead. **HTML 2.0, N2, N3, N4, IE3, IE4, IE5, deprecated in HTML 3.2.**

Attributes	2.0	3.2	4.0	N2	N3	N4	IE2	IE3	IE4/5
<event_name>=script_code	✗	✗	✗	✗	✗	✗	✗	✗	✓
CLASS=classname	✗	✗	✗	✗	✗	✓	✗	✗	✓
ID=*string*	✗	✗	✗	✗	✗	✓	✗	✗	✓
LANG=language_type	✗	✗	✗	✗	✗	✗	✗	✗	✓
LANGUAGE=JAVASCRIPT | JSCRIPT | VBSCRIPT | VBS	✗	✗	✗	✗	✗	✗	✗	✗	✓
STYLE=*string*	✗	✗	✗	✗	✗	✓	✗	✗	✓
TITLE=*string*	✗	✗	✗	✗	✗	✗	✗	✗	✓

!– –

Denotes a comment that is ignored by the HTML parser.

!DOCTYPE

Declares the type and content format of the document.

HTTP 1.1 Error Codes

This part of the Appendix lists the client and server error codes that you might encounter, with default explanations provided by Microsoft Internet Information Server; they are included in case you run into errors as you experiment with ASP.

Code	Short Text	Explanation
400	Bad Request	Due to malformed syntax, the request could not be understood by the server. The client should not repeat the request without modifications.
401.1	Unauthorized: Logon Failed due to server configuration	This error indicates that the credentials passed to the server do not match the credentials required to log on to the server. Please contact the web server's administrator to verify that you have permission to access the requested resource.
401.2	Unauthorized: Logon Failed due to server configuration	This error indicates that the credentials passed to the server do not match the credentials required to log on to the server. This is usually caused by not sending the proper WWW-Authenticate header field. Please contact the web server's administrator to verify that you have permission to access to requested resource.
401.3	Unauthorized: Unauthorized due to ACL on resource	This error indicates that the credentials passed by the client do not have access to the particular resource on the server. This resource could be either the page or file listed in the address line of the client, or it could be another file on the server that is needed to process the file listed on the address line of the client. Please make a note of the entire address you were trying to access and then contact the web server's administrator to verify that you have permission to access the requested resource.
401.4	Unauthorized: Authorization failed by filter	This error indicates that the web server has a filter program installed to verify users connecting to the server. The authentication used to connect to the server was denied access by this filter program. Please make a note of the entire address you were trying to access and then contact the web server's administrator to verify that you have permission to access the requested resource.
401.5	Unauthorized: Authorization failed by ISAPI/CGI app	This error indicates that the address on the web server you attempted to use has an ISAPI or CGI program installed that verifies user credentials before proceeding. The authentication used to connect to the server was denied access by this program. Please make a note of the entire address you were trying to access and then contact the web server's administrator to verify that you have permission to access the requested resource.
403.1	Forbidden: Execute Access Forbidden	This error can be caused if you try to execute a CGI, ISAPI, or other executable program from a directory that does not allow programs to be executed. Please contact the web server's administrator if the problem persists.

Code	Short Text	Explanation
403.2	Forbidden: Read Access Forbidden	This error can be caused if there is no default page available and directory browsing has not been enabled for the directory, or if you are trying to display an HTML page that resides in a directory marked for Execute or Script permissions only. Please contact the web server's administrator if the problem persists.
403.3	Forbidden: Write Access Forbidden	This error can be caused if you attempt to upload to, or modify a file in, a directory that does not allow Write access. Please contact the web server's administrator if the problem persists.
403.4	Forbidden: SSL required	This error indicates that the page you are trying to access is secured with Secure Sockets Layer (SSL). In order to view it, you need to enable SSL by typing "https://" at the beginning of the address you are attempting to reach. Please contact the web server's administrator if the problem persists.
403.5	Forbidden: SSL 128 required	This error message indicates that the resource you are trying to access is secured with a 128-bit version of Secure Sockets Layer (SSL). In order to view this resource, you need a browser that supports this level of SSL. Please confirm that your browser supports 128-bit SSL security. If it does, then contact the web server's administrator and report the problem.
403.6	Forbidden: IP address rejected	This error is caused when the server has a list of IP addresses that are not allowed to access the site, and the IP address you are using is in this list. Please contact the web server's administrator if the problem persists.
403.7	Forbidden: Client certificate required	This error occurs when the resource you are attempting to access requires your browser to have a client Secure Sockets Layer (SSL) certificate that the server recognizes. This is used for authenticating you as a valid user of the resource. Please contact the web server's administrator to obtain a valid client certificate.
403.8	Forbidden: Site access denied	This error can be caused if the web server is not servicing requests, or if you do not have permission to connect to the site. Please contact the web server's administrator.
403.9	Access Forbidden: Too many users are connected	This error can be caused if the web server is busy and cannot process your request due to heavy traffic. Please try to connect again later. Please contact the web server's administrator if the problem persists.

Code	Short Text	Explanation
403.10	Access Forbidden: Invalid Configuration	There is a configuration problem on the web server at this time. Please contact the web server's administrator if the problem persists.
403.11	Access Forbidden: Password Change	This error can be caused if the user has entered the wrong password during authentication. Please refresh the page and try again. Please contact the web server's administrator if the problem persists.
403.12	Access Forbidden: Mapper Denied Access	Your client certificate map has been denied access to this web site. Please contact the site administrator to establish client certificate permissions. You can also change your client certificate and retry, if appropriate.
404	Not Found	The web server cannot find the file or script you asked for. Please check the URL to ensure that the path is correct. Please contact the server's administrator if this problem persists.
405	Method Not Allowed	The method specified in the Request Line is not allowed for the resource identified by the request. Please ensure that you have the proper MIME type set up for the resource you are requesting. Please contact the server's administrator if this problem persists.
406	Not Acceptable	The resource identified by the request can only generate response entities that have content characteristics that are "not acceptable" according to the Accept headers sent in the request. Please contact the server's administrator if this problem persists.
407	Proxy Authentication Required	You must authenticate with a proxy server before this request can be serviced. Please log on to your proxy server, and then try again. Please contact the web server's administrator if this problem persists.
412	Precondition Failed	The precondition given in one or more of the Request-header fields evaluated to FALSE when it was tested on the server. The client placed preconditions on the current resource meta-information (header field data) to prevent the requested method from being applied to a resource other than the one intended. Please contact the web server's administrator if the problem persists.
414	Request-URI Too Long	The server is refusing to service the request because the Request-URI is too long. This rare condition is likely to occur only in the following situations:

A client has improperly converted a POST request to a GET request with long query information.

A client has encountered a redirection problem (for example, a redirected URL prefix that points to a suffix of itself).

The server is under attack by a client attempting to exploit security holes present in some servers using fixed-length buffers for reading or manipulating the Request-URI.

Please contact the web server's administrator if this problem persists. |

Code	Short Text	Explanation
500	Internal Server Error	The web server is incapable of performing the request. Please try your request again later. Please contact the web server's administrator if this problem persists.
501	Not Implemented	The web server does not support the functionality required to fulfill the request. Please check your URL for errors, and contact the web server's administrator if the problem persists.
502	Bad Gateway	The server, while acting as a gateway or proxy, received an invalid response from the upstream server it accessed in attempting to fulfill the request. Please contact the web server's administrator if the problem persists.

> **Please note that server error message files are placed in the `HELP\COMMON` folder of Windows or Windows NT.**

VBScript Reference

In this Appendix you will find a handy reference to using VBScript. We have covered some of the features included here as we have worked through the examples in this book. You may find this Appendix particularly useful as you begin to develop your own web applications.

Array Handling

Dim – declares a variable. An array variable can be static, with a defined number of elements, or dynamic, and can have up to 60 dimensions.

ReDim – used to change the size of an array variable that has been declared as dynamic.

Preserve – keyword used to preserve the contents of an array being resized (otherwise data is lost when ReDim is used). If you need to use this then you can only re-dimension the rightmost index of the array.

Erase – reinitializes the elements of a fixed-size array or empties the contents of a dynamic array:

```
Dim arEmployees ()
ReDim arEmployees (9,1)

arEmployees (9,1) = "Phil"

ReDim arEmployees (9,2)             'loses the contents of element (9,1)
arEmployees (9,2) = "Paul"

ReDim Preserve arEmployees (9,3)    'preserves the contents of (9,2)
arEmployees (9,3) = "Smith"

Erase arEmployees                   'now we are back to where we started - empty array
```

LBound – returns the smallest subscript for the dimension of an array. Note that arrays always start from the subscript zero so this function will always return the value zero.

UBound – used to determine the size of an array:

```
Dim strCustomers (10, 5)
intSizeFirst = UBound (strCustomers, 1)       'returns SizeFirst = 10
intSizeSecond = UBound (strCustomers, 2)      'returns SizeSecond = 5
```

> The actual number of elements is always one greater than the value returned by UBound **because the array starts from zero.**

Assignments

Let – used to assign values to variables (optional).
Set – used to assign an object reference to a variable.

```
Let intNumberOfDays = 365

Set txtMyTextBox = txtcontrol
txtMyTextBox.Value = "Hello World"
```

Constants

Empty – an empty variable is one that has been created, but has not yet been assigned a value.
Nothing – used to remove an object reference:

```
Set txtMyTextBox = txtATextBox      'assigns object reference
Set txtMyTextBox = Nothing          'removes object reference
```

Null – indicates that a variable is not valid. Note that this isn't the same as Empty.
True – indicates that an expression is true. Has numerical value –1.
False – indicates that an expression is false. Has numerical value 0.

Error Constant

Constant	Value
vbObjectError	&h80040000

System Color Constants

Constant	Value	Description
vbBlack	&h000000	Black
vbRed	&hFF0000	Red
vbGreen	&h00FF00	Green
vbYellow	&hFFFF00	Yellow
vbBlue	&h0000FF	Blue
vbMagenta	&hFF00FF	Magenta
vbCyan	&h00FFFF	Cyan
vbWhite	&hFFFFFF	White

Comparison Constants

Constant	Value	Description
vbBinaryCompare	0	Perform a binary comparison.
vbTextCompare	1	Perform a textual comparison.

Date and Time Constants

Constant	Value	Description
vbSunday	1	Sunday
vbMonday	2	Monday
vbTuesday	3	Tuesday
vbWednesday	4	Wednesday
vbThursday	5	Thursday
vbFriday	6	Friday
vbSaturday	7	Saturday
vbFirstJan1	1	Use the week in which January 1 occurs (default).
vbFirstFourDays	2	Use the first week that has at least four days in the new year.
vbFirstFullWeek	3	Use the first full week of the year.
vbUseSystem	0	Use the format in the regional settings for the computer.
vbUseSystemDayOfWeek	0	Use the day in the system settings for the first weekday.

Date Format Constants

Constant	Value	Description
vbGeneralDate	0	Display a date and/or time in the format set in the system settings. For real numbers display a date and time. For integer numbers display only a date. For numbers less than 1, display time only.
vbLongDate	1	Display a date using the long date format specified in the computer's regional settings.

Table Continued on Following Page

Constant	Value	Description
vbShortDate	2	Display a date using the short date format specified in the computer's regional settings.
vbLongTime	3	Display a time using the long time format specified in the computer's regional settings.
vbShortTime	4	Display a time using the short time format specified in the computer's regional settings.

Message Box Constants

Constant	Value	Description
vbOKOnly	0	Display OK button only.
vbOKCancel	1	Display OK and Cancel buttons.
vbAbortRetryIgnore	2	Display Abort, Retry, and Ignore buttons.
vbYesNoCancel	3	Display Yes, No, and Cancel buttons.
vbYesNo	4	Display Yes and No buttons.
vbRetryCancel	5	Display Retry and Cancel buttons.
vbCritical	16	Display Critical Message icon.
vbQuestion	32	Display Warning Query icon.
vbExclamation	48	Display Warning Message icon.
vbInformation	64	Display Information Message icon.
vbDefaultButton1	0	First button is the default.
vbDefaultButton2	256	Second button is the default.
vbDefaultButton3	512	Third button is the default.
vbDefaultButton4	768	Fourth button is the default.
vbApplicationModal	0	Application modal.
vbSystemModal	4096	System modal.

String Constants

Constant	Value	Description
vbCr	Chr(13)	Carriage return only.
vbCrLf	Chr(13) & Chr(10)	Carriage return and linefeed (Newline).
vbFormFeed	Chr(12)	Form feed only.
vbLf	Chr(10)	Line feed only.
vbNewLine	-	Newline character as appropriate to a specific platform.
vbNullChar	Chr(0)	Character having the value 0.
vbNullString	-	String having the value zero (not just an empty string).
vbTab	Chr(9)	Horizontal tab.
vbVerticalTab	Chr(11)	Vertical tab.

Tristate Constants

Constant	Value	Description
TristateUseDefault	-2	Use default setting.
TristateTrue	-1	True.
TristateFalse	0	False.

VarType Constants

Constant	Value	Description
vbEmpty	0	Uninitialized (default).
vbNull	1	Contains no valid data.
vbInteger	2	Integer subtype.
vbLong	3	Long subtype.
vbSingle	4	Single subtype.
vbDouble	5	Double subtype.
vbCurrency	6	Currency subtype.

Table Continued on Following Page

Constant	Value	Description
vbDate	7	Date subtype.
vbString	8	String subtype.
vbObject	9	Object.
vbError	10	Error subtype.
vbBoolean	11	Boolean subtype.
vbVariant	12	Variant (used only for arrays of variants).
vbDataObject	13	Data access object.
vbDecimal	14	Decimal subtype.
vbByte	17	Byte subtype.
vbArray	8192	Array.

Control Flow

For...Next – executes a block of code a specified number of times:

```
Dim intSalary (10)
For intCounter = 0 to 10
   intSalary (intCounter) = 20000
Next
```

For Each...Next – repeats a block of code for each element in an array or collection:

```
For Each Item In Request.QueryString("MyControl")
  Response.Write Item & "<BR>"
Next
```

Do...Loop – executes a block of code while a condition is true or until a condition becomes true. Note that the condition can be checked either at the beginning or the end of the loop: the difference is that the code will be executed at least once if the condition is checked at the end.

```
Do While strDayOfWeek <> "Saturday" And strDayOfWeek <> "Sunday"
   MsgBox ("Get Up! Time for work")
   ...
Loop
```

```
Do
   MsgBox ("Get Up! Time for work")
   ...
Loop Until strDayOfWeek = "Saturday" Or strDayOfWeek = "Sunday"
```

We can also exit from a `Do...Loop` using `Exit Do`:

```
Do
    MsgBox ("Get Up! Time for work")
    ...
    If strDayOfWeek = "Sunday" Then
        Exit Do
    End If
Loop Until strDayOfWeek = "Saturday"
```

`If...Then...Else` – used to run various blocks of code depending on conditions:

```
If intAge < 20 Then
    MsgBox ("You're just a slip of a thing!")
ElseIf intAge < 40 Then
    MsgBox ("You're in your prime!")
Else
    MsgBox ("You're older and wiser")
End If
```

`Select Case` – used to replace `If...Then...Else` statements where there are many conditions:

```
Select Case intAge
Case 21,22,23,24,25,26
    MsgBox ("You're in your prime")
Case 40
    MsgBox ("You're fulfilling your dreams")
Case Else
    MsgBox ("Time for a new challenge")
End Select
```

`While...Wend` – executes a block of code while a condition is true:

```
While strDayOfWeek <> "Saturday" AND strDayOfWeek <> "Sunday"
    MsgBox ("Get Up! Time for work")
    ...
Wend
```

`With` – executes a series of statements for a single object:

```
With myDiv.style
    .posLeft = 200
    .posTop = 300
    .color = Red
End With
```

Functions

VBScript contains several in-built functions that can be used to manipulate and examine variables. These have been subdivided into these general categories:

❑ Conversion functions

❑ Date/time functions

❑ Math functions

❑ Object management functions

❑ Script engine identification functions

❑ String functions

❑ Variable testing functions

For a full description of each function and the parameters it requires, see the Microsoft web site at `http://msdn.microsoft.com/scripting/`.

Conversion Functions

These functions are used to convert values in variables between different types:

Function	Description
Abs	Returns the absolute value of a number.
Asc	Returns the numeric ANSI (or ASCII) code number of the first character in a string.
AscB	As above, but provided for use with byte data contained in a string. Returns result from the first byte only.
AscW	As above, but provided for Unicode characters. Returns the Wide character code, avoiding the conversion from Unicode to ANSI.
Chr	Returns a string made up of the ANSI character matching the number supplied.
ChrB	As above, but provided for use with byte data contained in a string. Always returns a single byte.
ChrW	As above, but provided for Unicode characters. Its argument is a Wide character code, thereby avoiding the conversion from ANSI to Unicode.
CBool	Returns the argument value converted to a Variant of subtype Boolean.
CByte	Returns the argument value converted to a Variant of subtype Byte.
CCur	Returns the argument value converted to a Variant of subtype Currency
CDate	Returns the argument value converted to a Variant of subtype Date.

Function	Description
CDbl	Returns the argument value converted to a `Variant` of subtype `Double`.
CInt	Returns the argument value converted to a `Variant` of subtype `Integer`.
CLng	Returns the argument value converted to a `Variant` of subtype `Long`
CSng	Returns the argument value converted to a `Variant` of subtype `Single`
CStr	Returns the argument value converted to a `Variant` of subtype `String`.
Fix	Returns the integer (whole) part of a number. If the number is negative, `Fix` returns the first negative integer greater than or equal to the number
Hex	Returns a string representing the hexadecimal value of a number.
Int	Returns the integer (whole) portion of a number. If the number is negative, `Int` returns the first negative integer less than or equal to the number.
Oct	Returns a string representing the octal value of a number.
Round	Returns a number rounded to a specified number of decimal places.
Sgn	Returns an integer indicating the sign of a number.

Date/Time Functions

These functions return date or time values from the computer's system clock, or manipulate existing values:

Function	Description
Date	Returns the current system date.
DateAdd	Returns a date to which a specified time interval has been added.
DateDiff	Returns the number of days, weeks, or years between two dates.
DatePart	Returns just the day, month or year of a given date.
DateSerial	Returns a `Variant` of subtype `Date` for a specified year, month and day.
DateValue	Returns a `Variant` of subtype `Date`.
Day	Returns a number between `1` and `31` representing the day of the month.
Hour	Returns a number between `0` and `23` representing the hour of the day.
Minute	Returns a number between `0` and `59` representing the minute of the hour.
Month	Returns a number between `1` and `12` representing the month of the year.
MonthName	Returns the name of the specified month as a string.

Table Continued on Following Page

Function	Description
Now	Returns the current date and time.
Second	Returns a number between 0 and 59 representing the second of the minute.
Time	Returns a Variant of subtype Date indicating the current system time.
TimeSerial	Returns a Variant of subtype Date for a specific hour, minute, and second.
TimeValue	Returns a Variant of subtype Date containing the time.
Weekday	Returns a number representing the day of the week.
WeekdayName	Returns the name of the specified day of the week as a string.
Year	Returns a number representing the year.

Math Functions

These functions perform mathematical operations on variables containing numerical values:

Function	Description
Atn	Returns the arctangent of a number.
Cos	Returns the cosine of an angle.
Exp	Returns e (the base of natural logarithms) raised to a power.
Log	Returns the natural logarithm of a number.
Randomize	Initializes the random-number generator.
Rnd	Returns a random number.
Sin	Returns the sine of an angle.
Sqr	Returns the square root of a number.
Tan	Returns the tangent of an angle.

Miscellaneous Functions

Function	Description
Eval	Evaluates an expression and returns a boolean result (e.g. treats x=y as an *expression* which is either true or false).
Execute	Executes one or more statements (e.g. treats x=y as a *statement* which assigns the value of y to x).
RGB	Returns a number representing an RGB color value.

Object Management Functions

These functions are used to manipulate objects, where applicable:

Function	Description
CreateObject	Creates and returns a reference to an ActiveX or OLE Automation object.
GetObject	Returns a reference to an ActiveX or OLE Automation object.
LoadPicture	Returns a picture object.

Script Engine Identification

These functions return the version of the scripting engine:

Function	Description
ScriptEngine	A string containing the major, minor, and build version numbers of the scripting engine.
ScriptEngineMajorVersion	The major version of the scripting engine, as a number.
ScriptEngineMinorVersion	The minor version of the scripting engine, as a number.
ScriptEngineBuildVersion	The build version of the scripting engine, as a number.

String Functions

These functions are used to manipulate string values in variables:

Function	Description
Filter	Returns an array from a string array, based on specified filter criteria.
FormatCurrency	Returns a string formatted as currency value.
FormatDateTime	Returns a string formatted as a date or time.
FormatNumber	Returns a string formatted as a number.
FormatPercent	Returns a string formatted as a percentage.
InStr	Returns the position of the first occurrence of one string within another.

Table Continued on Following Page

Function	Description
InStrB	As above, but provided for use with byte data contained in a string. Returns the byte position instead of the character position.
InstrRev	As InStr, but starts from the end of the string.
Join	Returns a string created by joining the strings contained in an array.
LCase	Returns a string that has been converted to lowercase.
Left	Returns a specified number of characters from the left end of a string.
LeftB	As above, but provided for use with byte data contained in a string. Uses that number of bytes instead of that number of characters.
Len	Returns the length of a string or the number of bytes needed for a variable.
LenB	As above, but is provided for use with byte data contained in a string. Returns the number of bytes in the string instead of characters.
LTrim	Returns a copy of a string without leading spaces.
Mid	Returns a specified number of characters from a string.
MidB	As above, but provided for use with byte data contained in a string. Uses that numbers of bytes instead of that number of characters.
Replace	Returns a string in which a specified substring has been replaced with another substring a specified number of times.
Right	Returns a specified number of characters from the right end of a string.
RightB	As above, but provided for use with byte data contained in a string. Uses that number of bytes instead of that number of characters.
RTrim	Returns a copy of a string without trailing spaces.
Space	Returns a string consisting of the specified number of spaces.
Split	Returns a one-dimensional array of a specified number of substrings.
StrComp	Returns a value indicating the result of a string comparison.
String	Returns a string of the length specified made up of a repeating character.
StrReverse	Returns a string in which the character order of a string is reversed.
Trim	Returns a copy of a string without leading or trailing spaces.
UCase	Returns a string that has been converted to uppercase.

Variable Testing Functions

These functions are used to determine the type of information stored in a variable:

Function	Description
IsArray	Returns a Boolean value indicating whether a variable is an array.
IsDate	Returns a Boolean value indicating whether an expression can be converted to a date.
IsEmpty	Returns a Boolean value indicating whether a variable has been initialized.
IsNull	Returns a Boolean value indicating whether an expression contains no valid data.
IsNumeric	Returns a Boolean value indicating whether an expression can be evaluated as a number.
IsObject	Returns a Boolean value indicating whether an expression references a valid ActiveX or OLE Automation object.
TypeName	Returns a string that provides Variant subtype information about a variable.
VarType	Returns a number indicating the subtype of a variable.

Variable Declarations

Class – declares the name of a class, as well as the variables, properties, and methods that comprise the class.
Const – declares a constant to be used in place of literal values.
Dim – declares a variable.

Error Handling

On Error Resume Next – indicates that if an error occurs, control should continue at the next statement.
Err – this is the error object that provides information about run-time errors.

Error handling is very limited in VBScript and the Err object must be tested explicitly to determine if an error has occurred.

Input/Output

This consists of Msgbox for output and InputBox for input:

MsgBox

This displays a message, and can return a value indicating which button was clicked.

```
MsgBox "Hello There",20,"Hello Message"
```

The parameters are:

"Hello There" – this contains the text of the message (the only obligatory parameter).

20 – this determines which icon and buttons appear on the message box.

"Hello Message" – this contains the text that will appear as the title of the message box.

The value of the icon and buttons parameter is determined using the following tables:

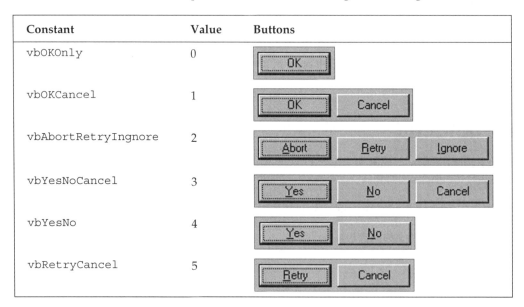

Constant	Value	Buttons
vbOKOnly	0	OK
vbOKCancel	1	OK Cancel
vbAbortRetryIngnore	2	Abort Retry Ignore
vbYesNoCancel	3	Yes No Cancel
vbYesNo	4	Yes No
vbRetryCancel	5	Retry Cancel

Constant	Value	Buttons
vbDefaultButton1	0	The first button from the left is the default.
vbDefaultButton2	256	The second button from the left is the default.
vbDefaultButton3	512	The third button from the left is the default.
vbDefaultButton4	768	The fourth button from the left is the default.

Constant	Value	Description	Icon
vbCritical	16	Critical Message	
vbQuestion	32	Questioning Message	
vbExclamation	48	Warning Message	
vbInformation	64	Informational Message	

Constant	Value	Description
vbApplicationModal	0	Just the application stops until user clicks a button.
vbSystemModal	4096	On Win16 systems the whole system stops until user clicks a button. On Win32 systems the message box remains on top of any other programs.

To specify which buttons and icon are displayed you simply add the relevant values. So, in our example we add together 4 + 0+ 16 to display the Yes and No buttons, with Yes as the default, and the Critical icon. If we used 4 + 256 + 16 we could display the same buttons and icon, but have No as the default.

You can determine which button the user clicked by assigning the return code of the MsgBox function to a variable:

```
intButtonClicked = MsgBox ("Hello There",35,"Hello Message")
```

Notice that brackets enclose the MsgBox parameters when used in this format. The following table determines the value assigned to the variable intButtonClicked:

Constant	Value	Button Clicked
vbOK	1	OK
vbCancel	2	Cancel
vbAbort	3	Abort
vbRetry	4	Retry
vbIgnore	5	Ignore
vbYes	6	Yes
vbNo	7	No

InputBox

This accepts text entry from the user and returns it as a string.

```
strName = InputBox ("Please enter your name","Login","John Smith",500,500)
```

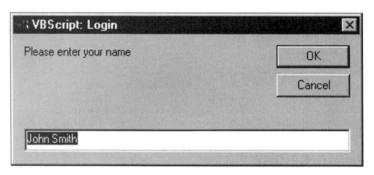

The parameters are:

"Please enter your name" – this is the prompt displayed in the input box.
"Login" – this is the text displayed as the title of the input box.
"John Smith" – this is the default value displayed in the input box.
500 – specifies the x position of the input box in relation to the screen.
500 – specifies the y position of the input box in relation to the screen.

As with the MsgBox function, you can also specify a help file and topic to add a Help button to the input box.

Procedures

`Call` – optional method of calling a subroutine.
`Function` – used to declare a function.
`Sub` – used to declare a subroutine.

Other Keywords

`Rem` – old style method of adding comments to code (it's now more usual to use an apostrophe (').)
`Option Explicit` – forces you to declare a variable before it can be used (if used, it must appear before any other statements in a script).

Visual Basic Run-time Error Codes

The following error codes also apply to VBA code and many will not be appropriate to an application built completely around VBScript. However, if you have built your own components then these error codes may well be brought up when such components are used.

Code	Description
3	`Return` without `GoSub`.
5	Invalid procedure call.
6	Overflow.
7	Out of memory.
9	Subscript out of range.
10	This array is fixed or temporarily locked.
11	Division by zero.
13	Type mismatch.
14	Out of string space.
16	Expression too complex.
17	Can't perform requested operation.
18	User interrupt occurred.
20	`Resume` without error.
28	Out of stack space.
35	`Sub` or `Function` not defined.

Table Continued on Following Page

Code	Description
47	Too many DLL application clients.
48	Error in loading DLL.
49	Bad DLL calling convention.
51	Internal error.
52	Bad file name or number.
53	File not found.
54	Bad file mode.
55	File already open.
57	Device I/O error.
58	File already exists.
59	Bad record length.
61	Disk full.
62	Input past end of file.
63	Bad record number.
67	Too many files.
68	Device unavailable.
70	Permission denied.
71	Disk not ready.
74	Can't rename with different drive.
75	Path/File access error.
76	Path not found.
91	Object variable not set.
92	For loop not initialized.
93	Invalid pattern string.
94	Invalid use of Null.
322	Can't create necessary temporary file.
325	Invalid format in resource file.
380	Invalid property value.
423	Property or method not found.

Code	Description
424	Object required.
429	OLE Automation server can't create object.
430	Class doesn't support OLE Automation.
432	File name or class name not found during OLE Automation operation.
438	Object doesn't support this property or method.
440	OLE Automation error.
442	Connection to type library or object library for remote process has been lost. Press OK for dialog to remove reference.
443	OLE Automation object does not have a default value.
445	Object doesn't support this action.
446	Object doesn't support named arguments.
447	Object doesn't support current locale setting.
448	Named argument not found.
449	Argument not optional.
450	Wrong number of arguments or invalid property assignment.
451	Object not a collection.
452	Invalid ordinal.
453	Specified DLL function not found.
454	Code resource not found.
455	Code resource lock error.
457	This key is already associated with an element of this collection.
458	Variable uses an OLE Automation type not supported in Visual Basic.
462	The remote server machine does not exist or is unavailable.
481	Invalid picture.
500	Variable is undefined.
501	Cannot assign to variable.
502	Object not safe for scripting.
503	Object not safe for initializing.
504	Object not safe for creating.

Table Continued on Following Page

Code	Description
505	Invalid or unqualified reference.
506	Class not defined.
1001	Out of memory.
1002	Syntax error.
1003	Expected ':'.
1004	Expected ';'.
1005	Expected '('.
1006	Expected ')'.
1007	Expected ']'.
1008	Expected '{'.
1009	Expected '}'.
1010	Expected identifier.
1011	Expected '='.
1012	Expected 'If'.
1013	Expected 'To'.
1014	Expected 'End'.
1015	Expected 'Function'.
1016	Expected 'Sub'.
1017	Expected 'Then'.
1018	Expected 'Wend'.
1019	Expected 'Loop'.
1020	Expected 'Next'.
1021	Expected 'Case'.
1022	Expected 'Select'.
1023	Expected expression.
1024	Expected statement.
1025	Expected end of statement.
1026	Expected integer constant.
1027	Expected 'While' or 'Until'.

Code	Description
1028	Expected 'While', 'Until' or end of statement.
1029	Too many locals or arguments.
1030	Identifier too long.
1031	Invalid number.
1032	Invalid character.
1033	Un-terminated string constant.
1034	Un-terminated comment.
1035	Nested comment.
1036	'Me' cannot be used outside of a procedure.
1037	Invalid use of 'Me' keyword.
1038	'Loop' without 'Do'.
1039	Invalid 'Exit' statement.
1040	Invalid 'For' loop control variable.
1041	Variable redefinition.
1042	Must be first statement on the line.
1043	Cannot assign to non-ByVal argument.
1044	Cannot use parentheses when calling a Sub.
1045	Expected literal constant.
1046	Expected 'In'.
1047	Expected 'Class'.
1048	Must be defined inside a Class.
1049	Expected Let or Set or Get in property declaration.
1050	Expected 'Property'.
1051	Number of arguments must be consistent across properties specification.
1052	Cannot have multiple default property/method in a Class.
1053	Class initialize or terminate do not have arguments.
1054	Property set or let must have at least one argument.
1055	Unexpected 'Next'.
1056	'Default' can be specified only on 'Property' or 'Function' or 'Sub'.

Table Continued on Following Page

Code	Description
1057	'Default' specification must also specify 'Public'.
1058	'Default' specification can only be on Property Get.
5016	Regular Expression object expected.
5017	Syntax error in regular expression.
5018	Unexpected quantifier.
5019	Expected ']' in regular expression.
5020	Expected ')' in regular expression.
5021	Invalid range in character set.
32811	Element not found.

For more information about VBScript, visit Microsoft's VBScript site, at
http://msdn.microsoft.com/scripting.

JScript Reference

JScript is the Microsoft implementation of the scripting language, which is specified by ECMA (European Computer Manufacturers Association) as the standard scripting language (see **ECMA-262** specification). While the reference presented in this Appendix is for JScript, if you're interested in the wider compatibility issues surrounding JavaScript and JScript, try referring to *Instant JavaScript*, ISBN 1861001274, also by Wrox Press.

> You should always bear in mind that JScript is case sensitive.

Values

JScript recognizes the following data types:

- **strings** – e.g. "Good Morning"
- **numbers** – both integers (86) and decimal values (86.235)
- **boolean** – `true` or `false` (case sensitive)

A null (*no value*) value is assigned with the keyword `null`.

JScript also makes use of 'special characters' in a similar way to the C++ programming language:

Character	Function
\n	newline
\t	tab
\f	form feed
\b	backspace
\r	carriage return

You may 'escape' other characters by preceding them with a backslash (\), to prevent the browser from trying to interpret them. This is most commonly used for quotes and backslashes, or to include a character by using its octal (base 8) value:

```
document.write("This shows a \"quote\" in a string.");
document.write("This is a backslash: \\");
document.write("This is a space character: \040.");
```

Variables

JScript is a **loosely typed** language. This means that variables do not have an explicitly defined variable type. Instead, every variable can hold values of various types. Conversions between types are done automatically when needed, as this example demonstrates:

```
x = 55;       // x is assigned to be the integer 55
y = "55";     // y is assigned to be the string "55"
y = '55';     // an alternative using single quotes

z = 1 + y;

/* because y is a string, x will be automatically
 converted to a string value, so the result is z = 155. */

document.write(x);
/* the number 55 will be written to the screen. Even
 though x is an integer and not a string, JScript will
 make the necessary conversion for you. */

n = 3.14159;  // assigning a real (fractional) number
n = 0546;     // numbers starting 0 assumed to be octal
n = 0xFFEC;   // numbers starting 0x assumed to be hex
n = 2.145E-5; // using exponential notation
```

The parseInt() and parseFloat() functions (discussed later in this Appendix) can be used to convert strings for numeric addition.

Variable names must start with either a letter or an underscore. Beyond the first letter, variables may contain any combination of letters, underscores, and digits. JScript is case sensitive, so this_variable is not the same as This_Variable.

Variables do not need to be declared before they are used. However, you may use the var keyword to explicitly define a variable. This is especially useful when there is the possibility of conflicting variable names. When in doubt, use var.

```
var x = "55";
```

Assignment Operators

The following operators are used to make assignments in JScript:

Operator	Example	Result
=	x = y	x equals y
+=	x += y	x equals x plus y
-=	x -= y	x equals x minus y
*=	x *= y	x equals x multiplied by y
/=	x /= y	x equals x divided by y
%=	x %= y	x equals x modulus y

Each operator assigns the value on the right to the variable on the left.

```
x = 100;
y = 10;
x += y;  // x now is equal to 110
```

Equality Operators

Operator	Meaning
==	is equal to
!=	is not equal to
>	is greater than
>=	is greater than or equal to
<	is less than
<=	is less than or equal to

Other Operators

Operator	Meaning
+	Addition
-	Subtraction
*	Multiplication
/	Division
%	Modulus
++	Increment
--	Decrement
-	Unary Negation
&	Bitwise AND
|	Bitwise OR
^	Bitwise XOR
<<	Bitwise left shift
>>	Bitwise right shift
>>>	Zero-fill right shift
&&	Logical AND
||	Logical OR
!	Not

String Operators

Operator	Meaning
+	Concatenates strings, so `"abc"` + `"def"` is `"abcdef"`
== != > >= < <=	Compare strings in a case-sensitive way. A string is 'greater' than another based on the Latin ASCII code values of the characters, starting from the left of the string. So `"DEF"` is greater than `"ABC"` and `"DEE"`, but less than `"abc"` (uppercase letters are before lowercase ones in the ASCII character set).

Comments

Operator	Meaning
`// a comment`	A single line comment
`/* this text is a` `multi-line comment */`	A multi-line comment

Input/Output

In JScript, there are three different methods of providing information to the user and getting a response back. (Note that these are methods of the `window` object, and not JScript function calls.)

Alert

This displays a message with an OK button:

```
alert("Hello World!");
```

Confirm

Displays a message with both an OK and a Cancel button. `True` is returned if the OK button is pressed, and `false` is returned if the Cancel button is pressed:

```
confirm("Are you sure you want to quit?");
```

Prompt

Displays a message and a textbox for user input. The first string argument forms the text that is to be displayed above the textbox. The second argument is a string, integer, or property of an existing object, which represents the default value to display inside the box. If the second argument is not specified, "<undefined>" is displayed inside the textbox.

The string typed into the box is returned if the OK button is pressed. `False` is returned if the Cancel button is pressed:

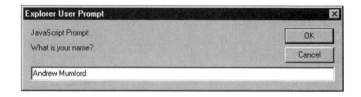

```
prompt("What is your name?", "");
```

Control Flow

There are two ways of controlling the flow of a program in JScript. The first involves **conditional** statements, which follow either one branch of the program or another. The second way is to use a **repeated iteration** of a set of statements.

Conditional Statements

JScript has two conditional statements:

`if..else` – used to run various blocks of code, depending on conditions. These statements have the following general form in JScript:

```
if (condition)
{
  code to be executed if condition is true
}
else
{
  code to be executed if condition is false
};
```

In addition:

❑   The `else` portion is optional.

❑   `if` statements may be nested.

❑   Multiple statements must be enclosed by braces.

Here is an example:

```
person_type = prompt("What are you ?", "");
if (person_type == "cat")
  alert("Here, have some cat food.");
else
{
  if (person_type == "dog")
    alert("Here, have some dog food.");
```

```
  else
  {
    if (person_type == "human")
      alert("Here have some, er, human food!");
  }
};
```

Notice that the curly brackets are only actually required where there is more than one statement within the block. Like many other constructs, they can be omitted where single statements are used. (Although not necessary, it can sometimes be a good idea to include all of the semi-colons and brackets that could be used, as this makes the code easier to modify.)

All statements in JScript are supposed to have a semi-colon line terminator, because a statement can span more than one line without special continuation markers. However, JScript lets you leave it out in quite a few areas, as long as it can tell where a statement is supposed to end. The final semicolon is therefore not mandatory.

switch – used to run various blocks of code, depending on conditions. These statements have the following general form in JScript:

```
switch (expression) {
  case label1 :
    code to be executed if expression is equal to label1
    break;
  case label2 :
    code to be executed if expression is equal to label2
  ...
  default :
    code to be executed if expression is not equal to any of the
    case labels.
}
```

break; can be inserted following the code for a case, to prevent execution of the code running into the next case automatically.

Loop Statements

for – executes a block of code a specified number of times:

```
for (initialization; condition; increment)
{
  statements to execute…
}
```

In the following example, i is initially set to zero, and is incremented by 1 at the end of each iteration. The loop terminates when the condition i < 10 is false:

```
for (i = 0; i < 10; i++)
{
  document.write(i);
}
```

while – executes a block of code while a condition is true:

```
while (condition)
{
  statements to execute ...
}
```

do...while – executes a statement block once, and then repeats execution of the loop while a condition is true:

```
do
{
  statements to execute ...
}
while (condition);
```

break – will cause an exit from a loop regardless of the condition statement:

```
x = 0;
while (x != 10)
{
  n = prompt("Enter a number or 'q' to quit", "");
  if (n == "q")
  {
    alert("See ya");
    break;
  }
}
```

break can also be used in switch, for and do...while loops.

continue – will cause the loop to jump immediately back to the condition statement:

```
x = 0;
while (x != 1)
{
  if (!(confirm("Should I add 1 to n ?")))
  {
    continue;
    // the following x++ is never executed
    x++;
  }
  x++;
}
alert("Bye");
```

with – Establishes a default object for a set of statements. The code:

```
x = Math.cos(3 * Math.PI) + Math.sin(Math.LN10)
y = Math.tan(14 * Math.E)
```

can be rewritten as:

```
with (Math)
{
  x = cos(3 * PI) + sin (LN10)
  y = tan(14 * E)
}
```

When you use the `with` statement, the object passed as the parameter is the default object. Notice how this shortens each statement.

Error Handling Statements

JScript 5 now includes built-in error handling. This is done using the `try...catch` statement. It allows the developer to anticipate certain error messages, and provide a different code path to follow if that error occurs.

```
function ErrorHandler(x)
{
  try {
    try {
      if (x == 'OK')            // Evalute argument
        throw "Value OK";       // Throw an error
      else
        throw "Value not OK";   // Throw a different error
    }
    catch(e) {                  // Handle "x = OK" errors here
      if (e == "Value OK")      // Check for an error handled here
        return(e + " successfully handled.");
                                // Return error message
      else                      // Can't handle error here
        throw e;                // Rethrow the error for next
    }                           // error handler
  }
  catch(e) {                    // Handle other errors here
    return(e + " handled elsewhere.");
                                // Return error message
  }
}
document.write(ErrorHandler('OK'));
document.write(ErrorHandler('BAD'));
```

The `throw` statement is used to generate error conditions that can then be handled by a `try...catch` block. The value that you throw can be any expression, including a string, Boolean or number.

Built-in Functions

JScript provides a number of built-in functions that can be accessed within code.

Function	Description
escape(char)	Returns a new string with all spaces, punctuation, accented characters and any non–ASCII characters encoded into the format %XX, where XX is their hexadecimal value.
eval(expression)	Returns the result of evaluating the JScript expression.
isFinite(value)	Returns a Boolean value of true if value is any value other than NaN (not a number), negative infinity, or positive infinity.
isNaN(value)	Returns a Boolean value of true if value is not a legal number.
parseFloat(string)	Converts string to a floating-point number.
parseInt(string, base)	Converts string to an integer number with the base of base.
typeOf(object)	Returns the data type of object as a string, such as "boolean", "function", etc.
unescape(char)	Returns a string where all characters encoded with the %XX hexadecimal form are replaced by their ASCII character set equivalents.

Built-in Objects

JScript provides a set of built-in data-type objects, which have their own set of properties, and methods – and which can be accessed with JScript code.

ActiveXObject Object

The ActiveXObject object creates and returns a reference to an automation object. To create a new ActiveXObject object, use:

```
ExcelSheet = new ActiveXObject("Excel.Sheet");
   // create an automation object referring to an Excel Spreadsheet
```

Once you have created the object reference, you can interact with the object using it's methods and properties.

Array Object

The `Array` object specifies a method of creating arrays and working with them. To create a new array, use:

```
cats = new Array();      // create an empty array
cats = new Array(10);    // create an array of 10 items

// or create and fill an array with values in one go:
cats = new Array("Boo Boo", "Purrcila", "Sam", "Lucky");
```

Properties	Description
`length`	A read/write integer value specifying the number of elements in the array.

Methods	Description
`array1.concat (array2)`	Returns a new array consisting of the contents of two arrays.
`join ( [string] )`	Returns a string containing each element of the array, optionally separated with string.
`reverse ()`	Reverses the order of the array, without creating a new object.
`slice (start, [end] )`	Returns a section of an array, starting at position start and going up to and including position end.
`sort ( [function] )`	Sorts the array, optionally based upon the results of a function specified by function.
`toString ()`	Returns the elements of an array converted to strings and concatenated, separated by commas.
`valueOf ()`	Returns the elements of an array converted to strings and concatenated, separated by commas. Like `toString`.

Early versions of JScript had no explicit array structure. However, JScript's object mechanisms allow for easy creation of arrays:

```
function MakeArray(n)
{
  this.length = n;
  for (var i = 1; i <= n; i++)
    this[i] = 0;
  return this
}
```

With this function included in your script, you can create arrays with:

```
cats = new MakeArray(20);
```

You can then populate the array like this:

```
cats[0] = "Boo Boo";
cats[1] = "Purrcila";
cats[2] = "Sam";
cats[3] = "Lucky";
```

Boolean Object

The Boolean object is used to store simple yes/no, true/false values. To create a new Boolean object, use the syntax:

```
MyAnswer = new Boolean([value])
```

If value is 0, null, omitted, or an empty string the new Boolean object will have the value false. All other values, *including the string* "false", create an object with the value true.

Methods	Description
toString()	Returns the value of the Boolean as the string true or false.
valueOf()	Returns the primitive numeric value of the object for conversion in calculations.

Date Object

The Date object provides a method for working with dates and times inside of JScript. New instances of the Date object are invoked with:

```
newDateObject = new Date([dateInfo])
```

dateInfo is an optional specification for the date to set in the new object. If it is not specified, the current date and time are used. dateInfo can use any of the following formats:

milliseconds (since midnight GMT on January 1, 1970)
year, month, day (e.g. 1997, 0, 27 is January 27, 1997)
year, month, day, hours, minutes, seconds
    (e.g. 1997, 8, 23, 08, 25, 30 is September 23 1997 at 08:25:30)

Times and dates are generally in **local time**, but the user can also specify Universal Coordinated Time (**UTC**, previously GMT).

Methods	Description
`getDate()` `getUTCDate`	Returns the day of the month as an Integer between 1 and 31, using local time or UTC.
`getDay()` `getUTCDay()`	Returns the day of the week as an Integer between 0 (Sunday) and 6 (Saturday), using local time or UTC.
`getFullYear()` `getUTCFullYear()`	Returns the year as an Integer, using local time or UTC.
`getHours()` `getUTCHours()`	Returns the hours as an Integer between 0 and 23, using local time or UTC.
`getMilliseconds()` `getUTCMilliseconds()`	Returns the milliseconds as an integer between 0 and 999, using local time or UTC.
`getMinutes()` `getUTCMinutes()`	Returns the minutes as an Integer between 0 and 59, using local time or UTC.
`getMonth()` `getUTCMonth()`	Returns the month as an Integer between 0 (January) and 11 (December), using local time or UTC.
`getSeconds()` `getUTCSeconds()`	Returns the seconds as an Integer between 0 and 59, using local time or UTC.
`getTime()`	Returns the number of milliseconds between January 1, 1970 at 00:00:00 UTC and the current `Date` object as an Integer.
`getTimeZoneOffset()`	Returns the number of minutes difference between local time and UTC as an Integer.
`getVarDate()`	Returns the date in `VT_DATE` format, which is used to interact with ActiveX objects.
`getYear()`	Returns the year minus 1900 – (i.e. only two digits) as an Integer.
`parse(dateString)`	Returns the number of milliseconds in a date string, since January 1, 1970 00:00:00 UTC.
`setDate(dayValue)` `setUTCDate(dayValue)`	Sets the day of the month where *dayValue* is an Integer between 1 and 31, using local time or UTC.
`setFullYear(yearValue)` `setUTCFullYear(yearValue)`	Sets the year where *yearValue* indicates the 4 digit year, using local time or UTC.
`setHours(hoursValue)` `setUTCHours(hoursValue)`	Sets the hours where *hoursValue* is an Integer between 0 and 59, using local time or UTC.

Table Continued on Following Page

Methods	Description
setMilliSeconds (msValue) setUTCMilliSeconds (msValue)	Sets the milliseconds where *msValue* is an Integer between 0 and 999, using local time or UTC.
setMinutes (minutesValue) setUTCMinutes (minutesValue)	Sets the minutes where *minutesValue* is an integer between 0 and 59, using local time or UTC.
setMonth (monthValue) setUTCMonth (monthValue)	Sets the month where *monthValue* is an integer between 0 and 11, using local time or UTC.
setSeconds (secondsValue) setUTCSeconds (secondsValue)	Sets the seconds where *secondsValue* is an integer between 0 and 59, using local time or UTC.
setTime (timeValue)	Sets the value of a Date object where *timeValue* is and integer representing the number of milliseconds in a date string, since January 1, 1970 00:00:00 GMT.
setYear (yearValue)	Sets the year where *yearValue* is an integer (generally) greater than 1900.
toGMTString ()	Converts a date to a string using GMT. Equivalent to toUTCString, and included only for backwards compatibility.
toLocaleString ()	Converts a date to a string using local time.
toUTCString ()	Converts a date to a string using UTC.
UTC (year, month, day [,hrs] [,min] [,sec])	Returns the number of milliseconds in a date object, since January 1, 1970 00:00:00 UTC.

Enumerator Object

The Enumerator object is used to enumerate, or step through, the items in a collection. The Enumerator object provides a way to access any member of a collection, and behaves similarly to the For...Each statement in VBScript.

```
newEnumeratorObj = new Enumerator(collection)
```

Methods	Description
atEnd ()	Returns a boolean value indicating if the enumerator is at the end of the collection.
item ()	Returns the current item in the collection.
moveFirst ()	Resets the current item to the first item in the collection.
moveNext ()	Changes the current item to the next item in the collection.

Error Object

The `Error` object contains information about run-time errors generated in JScript code. The scripting engine automatically generates this object. You can also create it yourself if you want to generate your own custom error states.

```
newErrorObj = new Error(number)
```

Properties	Description
description	The descriptive string associated with a particular error.
number	The number associated with a particular error.

Function Object

The `Function` object provides a mechanism for compiling JScript code as a function. A new function is invoked with the syntax:

```
functionName = new Function(arg1, arg2, ..., functionCode)
```

where `arg1`, `arg2`, etc. are the argument names for the function object being created, and `functionCode` is a string containing the body of the function. This can be a series of JScript statements separated by semi-colons.

Properties	Description
arguments[]	A reference to the `arguments` array that holds the arguments that were provided when the function was called.
caller	Returns a reference to the function that invoked the current function.
prototype	Provides a way for adding properties to a `Function` object.

Methods	Description
toString()	Returns a string value representation of the function.
valueOf()	Returns the function.

Arguments Object

The `Arguments` object is a list (array) of arguments in a function.

Properties	Description
length	An integer specifying the number of arguments provided to the function when it was called.

Math Object

Provides a set of properties and methods for working with mathematical constants and functions. Simply reference the `Math` object, then the method or property required:

```
MyArea = Math.PI * MyRadius * MyRadius;
MyResult = Math.floor(MyNumber);
```

Properties	Description
E	Euler's Constant e (the base of natural logarithms).
LN10	The value of the natural logarithm of 10.
LN2	The value of the natural logarithm of 2.
LOG10E	The value of the base 10 logarithm of E.
LOG2E	The value of the base 2 logarithm of E.
PI	The value of the constant π (pi).
SQRT1_2	The value of the square root of a half.
SQRT	The value of the square root of two.

Methods	Description
abs(number)	Returns the absolute value of number.
acos(number)	Returns the arc cosine of number.
asin(number)	Returns the arc sine of number.
atan(number)	Returns the arc tangent of number.
atan2(x, y)	Returns the angle of the polar coordinate of a point x, y from the x-axis.
ceil(number)	Returns the next largest integer greater than number, i.e. rounds up.
cos(number)	Returns the cosine of number.
exp(number)	Returns the value of number as the exponent of e, as in e^{number}.
floor(number)	Returns the next smallest integer less than number, i.e. rounds down.
log(number)	Returns the natural logarithm of number.
max(num1, num2)	Returns the greater of the two values num1 and num2.
min(num1, num2)	Returns the smaller of the two values num1 and num2.
pow(num1, num2)	Returns the value of num1 to the power of num2.

Methods	Description
random()	Returns a random number between 0 and 1.
round(number)	Returns the closest Integer to number i.e. rounds up or down to the nearest whole number.
sin(number)	Returns the sin of number.
sqrt(number)	Returns the square root of number.
tan(number)	Returns the tangent of number.

Number Object

The Number object provides a set of properties that are useful when working with numbers:

```
newNumberObj = new Number(value)
```

Properties	Description
MAX_VALUE	The maximum numeric value represented in JScript (~1.79E+308).
MIN_VALUE	The minimum numeric value represented in JScript (~2.22E-308).
NaN	A value meaning 'Not A Number'.
NEGATIVE_INFINITY	A special value for negative infinity ("-Infinity").
POSITIVE_INFINITY	A special value for infinity ("Infinity").

Methods	Description
toString([radix_base])	Returns the value of the number as a string to a radix (base) of 10, unless specified otherwise in radix_base.
valueOf()	Returns the primitive numeric value of the object.

RegularExpression Object

The RegularExpression object contains a regular expression. A regular expression is used to search strings for character patterns.

```
function RegExpDemo()
{
  var s = "AaBbCcDdEeFfGgHhIiJjKkLlMmNnOoPp"
  var r = new RegExp("g", "i");
  var a = r.exec(s);
  document.write(a);
  r.compile("g");
  var a = r.exec(s);
  document.write(a);
}
```

Properties	Description
lastIndex	Character position at which to start the next match.
source	Text of the regular expression.

Methods	Description
compile()	Converts the regular expression into an internal format for faster execution.
exec()	Executes the search for a match in a particular string.
test()	Returns a boolean value indicating whether or not a pattern exists within a string.

RegExp Object

The RegExp object stores information about regular expression pattern searches. It works in conjunction with the RegularExpression object. In the example below, even though the new method was called with the RegExp object as a parameter, a RegularExpression object was actually created:

```
function regExpDemo()
{
  var s;
  var re = new RegExp("d(b+)(d)","ig");
  var str = "cdbBdbsbdbdz";
  var arr = re.exec(str);
  s = "$1 contains: " + RegExp.$1 + "<BR>";
  s += "$2 contains: " + RegExp.$2 + "<BR>";
  s += "$3 contains: " + RegExp.$3;
  return(s);
}
```

Notice that when checking the properties for the RegExp object, we don't refer to an instance of that object. Rather the reference is made directly to the static RegExp object.

Properties	Description
$1...$9	The 9 most recently found portions during pattern matching.
index	Character position where the first successful match begins.
input	String against which the regular expression is searched.
lastIndex	Character position where the last successful match begins.

String Object

The `String` object provides a set of methods for text manipulation. To create a new `String` object, the syntax is:

```
MyString = new String([value])
```

where *value* is the optional text to place in the string when it is created. If this is a number, it is converted into a string first.

Properties	Description
`length`	An integer representing the number of characters in the string.

Methods	Description
`anchor(nameAttribute)`	Returns the original string surrounded by `<A>` and `</A>` anchor tags, with the `NAME` attribute set to nameAttribute.
`big()`	Returns the original string enclosed in `<BIG>` and `</BIG>` tags.
`blink()`	Returns the original string enclosed in `<BLINK>` and `</BLINK>` tags.
`bold()`	Returns the original string enclosed in `<B>` and `</B>` tags.
`charAt(index)`	Returns the single character at position index within the `String` object.
`charCodeAt(index)`	Returns the Unicode encoding of the character at position index.
`concat(string2)`	Returns a string containing string2 added to the end of the original string.
`fixed()`	Returns the original string enclosed in `<TT>` and `</TT>` tags.
`fontcolor("color")`	Returns the original string surrounded by `<FONT>` and `</FONT>` tags, with the `COLOR` attribute set to `"color"`.
`fontsize("size")`	Returns the original string surrounded by `<FONT>` and `</FONT>` anchor tags, with the `SIZE` attribute set to `"size"`.
`fromCharCode(code1, ...coden)`	Returns the string from a number of Unicode character values.
`indexOf(searchValue [,fromIndex])`	Returns first occurrence of the string searchValue starting at index fromIndex.
`italics()`	Returns the original string enclosed in `<I>` and `</I>` tags.

Table Continued on Following Page

Methods	Description
`lastIndexOf(searchValue [, fromIndex])`	Returns the index of the last occurrence of the string searchValue, searching backwards from index fromIndex.
`link(hrefAttribute)`	Returns the original string surrounded by `<A>` and `</A>` link tags, with the `HREF` attribute set to hrefAttribute.
`match(regExp)`	Returns an array containing the results of a search using the regExp `RegularExpression` object.
`replace(regExp, replaceText)`	Returns a string with text replaced using a regular expression.
`search(regExp)`	Returns the position of the first substring match in a regular expression search.
`slice(start, [end])`	Returns a section of a string starting at position start and ending at position end.
`small()`	Returns the original string enclosed in `<SMALL>` and `</SMALL>` tags.
`split(separator)`	Returns an array of strings created by separating the `String` object at every occurrence of separator.
`strike()`	Returns the original string enclosed in `<STRIKE>` and `</STRIKE>` tags.
`sub()`	Returns the original string enclosed in `<SUB>` and `</SUB>` tags.
`substr(start, [length])`	Returns a substring starting at position start and having a length of length characters.
`substring(indexA, indexB)`	Returns the sub-string of the original `String` object from the character at indexA up to and including the one before the character at indexB.
`sup()`	Returns the original string enclosed in `<SUP>` and `</SUP>` tags.
`toLowerCase()`	Returns the original string with all the characters converted to lowercase.
`toUpperCase()`	Returns the original string with all the characters converted to uppercase.
`toString()`	Returns the value of the `String` object.
`valueOf()`	Returns the string.

VBArray Object

Provides access to an array created in VBScript. Since these arrays use a different memory structure than JScript arrays, it is necessary to use this object to access them. This object only provides read-only access.

```
<SCRIPT LANGUAGE="VBScript">
<!--
dim arVBArray
' populate this VBScript array…
-->
</SCRIPT>
<SCRIPT LANGUAGE="JScript">
<!--
function useVBArray()
{
  var arJSArray = new VBArray(arVBArray);
  var arArray = arJSArray.toArray();
// now arArray can be used like a JScript array
}
-->
</SCRIPT>
```

Methods	Description
dimensions()	Returns the number of dimensions in the VBArray.
getItem(dim1, dim2,… dimn)	Returns the item at the specified location.
lbound(dimension)	Returns the lowest index value used at the dimension specified by dimension.
toArray()	Returns a standard JScript array converted from the VBArray object.
ubound(dimension)	Returns the highest index value used at the dimension specified by dimension.

Reserved Words

The following are reserved words that can't be used for function, method, variable, or object names. Note that while some words in this list are not currently used as JScript keywords, they have been reserved for future use.

abstract	else	int	super
boolean	extends	interface	switch
break	false	long	synchronized
byte	final	native	this
case	finally	new	throw
catch	float	null	throws
char	for	package	transient
class	function	private	true
const	goto	protected	try
continue	if	public	typeof
default	implements	reset	var
delete	import	return	void
do	in	short	while
double	instanceof	static	with

More information on JScript can be found at http://msdn.microsoft.com/scripting.

Useful Resources

This Appendix lists resources that may be useful to you when developing your web applications, many of which are mentioned throughout this book.

On-line Resources

Wrox Support

To download the code for the examples in this book and for support and errata, visit our web site at: www.wrox.com

WWW General

The first place to check out for all issues dealing with the Internet is the World Wide Web Consortium. Here you will find the latest specifications for all web technologies:
http://www.w3.org/

Visual InterDev

The Microsoft Development Network (MSDN) is a great place to look for information concerning all of Microsoft's technologies, including Visual InterDev. Here you will find documentation, articles, and help:
http://msdn.microsoft.com/vinterdev/

Browser Information and Downloads

For updates, downloads and information on Internet Explorer try the following site:
http://www.microsoft.com/windows/ie/default.htm

And for Netscape Navigator try:
http://home.netscape.com/browsers/index.html
http://www.mozilla.org

For the latest version of the Browscap.ini file go to:
http://www.cyscape.com/asp/browscap/

Scripting

The first place to look for information on scripting is Microsoft's site:
`http://msdn.microsoft.com/scripting/`

Additionally, have a look at Sun's site for JavaScript, which contains a forum for Java and JavaScript developers:
`http://developer.java.sun.com/developer/`

HTML and DHTML

HTML and DHTML are covered in the following sites:
`http://msdn.microsoft.com/workshop/author/default.asp`
`http://members.tripod.com/~dynamicboy/`

XML

There are many sites relating to this new and exciting technology. Here are some sites that will get you looking in the right direction:
`http://www.w3.org/xml/`
`http://www.xml.com/`
`http://webdev.wrox.co.uk/reference/xml/doingxml.asp`
`http://www.oasis-open.org/cover`
`http://www.xmlinfo.com`
`http://www.xmlsoftware.com/parsers/`

Active Server Pages

ASP is covered by:
`http://www.asptoday.com`
`http://15seconds.com`
`http://www.learnasp.com/`

Cascading Style Sheets

The WWW Consortium site will provide you with the latest specifications for CSSs:
`http://www.w3.org/Style/css/`

ActiveX Control Verification

To find out more on Active X control verification try:
`www.verisign.com`

Document Object Model

This is the page of the WWW Consortium that contains the latest specification for the DOM:
`http://www.w3.org/tr/rec-dom-level1/`

Internationalization

Need information on non-Western character sets and languages? Try:
`http://www.w3.org/International`

MDAC

For information on the Microsoft Data Access Components, and for the service pack, go to:
`http://www.microsoft.com/data`

ADO

For a complete list of ADO error codes use:
`http://msdn.microsoft.com/library/psdk/dasdk/mdae4dv1.htm`

Books

Wrox Press publish a very comprehensive range of books on many aspects of programming and web related technologies covered in this book:

HTML

Instant HTML Programmer's Reference, HTML 4.0 Edition by Alex Homer *et al.* (ISBN 1-86100-56-8)

DHTML

IE5 Dynamic HTML Programmer's Reference by Brian Francis *et al.* (ISBN 1-861001-74-6)

XML

Professional XML by Stephen Mohr *et al* (ISBN 1-861003-11-0)
XML in IE5 Programmer's Reference by Alex Homer (ISBN 1-8610015-7-6)

Scripting

Instant JavaScript by Nigel McFarlane (ISBN 1-861001-27-4)
VBScript Programmers Reference by Susanne Clark *et al.* (ISBN 1-861002-71-8)

SQL Server

Professional SQL Server 7 Programming by Rob Vieira (ISBN 1-861002-31-9)

Active Server Pages

Beginning Active Server Pages 3.0 by Chris Ullman *et al.* (ISBN 1-861003-38-2)
Professional Active Server Pages 3.0 by Richard Anderson *et al.* (ISBN 1-861002-61-0)

MTS

Professional Visual Basic 6 MTS Programming by Matthew Bortniker and James M Conard (ISBN 1-86100-24-4)
Professional MTS & MSMQ Programming with VB and ASP by Alex Homer and David Sussman (ISBN 1-861001-4-60)

Style Sheets

Professional Style Sheets for HTML and XML by Frank Boumphrey (ISBN 1-861001-65-7)

ADO

ADO 2.1 Programmer's Reference by David Sussman (ISBN 1-861002-68-8)

Index

W